CHANGING FRONTIERS in the science of PSYCHOTHERAPY

Modern Applications of Psychology
under the editorship of
Joseph D. Matarazzo

Allen E. Bergin
TEACHERS COLLEGE,
COLUMBIA UNIVERSITY

Hans H. Strupp
VANDERBILT UNIVERSITY

CHANGING FRONTIERS in the science of PSYCHOTHERAPY

ALDINE · ATHERTON
CHICAGO & NEW YORK

This work is dedicated to the National Institute of Mental Health and its staff. Viewing psychotherapy as a vital area of research, they have sustained this investigation with unfailing interest, encouragement, and support.

About the Authors

ALLEN E. BERGIN, Professor of Clinical Psychology at Teachers College, Columbia University, received his Ph.D. from Stanford University in 1960 and has done postdoctoral work at the Wisconsin Psychiatric Institute, University of Wisconsin. He has taught at a number of universities and serves as a consultant to various institutions and journals. Professor Bergin's contributions to the literature number more than thirty articles, many of which have been widely reprinted. He is coeditor of *Handbook of Psychotherapy and Behavior Change.*

HANS H. STRUPP is Professor of Psychology at Vanderbilt University. Educated at George Washington University, where he received his Ph.D. in 1954, Professor Strupp has published extensively in the field of psychotherapy. He previously taught at the University of North Carolina. He is a member of various executive and editorial boards. His books include *Psychotherapists in Action: Explorations of the Therapist's Contribution to the Treatment Process, Patients View Their Psycho-Therapy,* and *Psychotherapy and the Modification of Abnormal Behavior.*

First published 1972 by
Aldine • Atherton, Inc.
529 South Wabash Avenue
Chicago, Illinois 60605

Library of Congress Catalog Number 75-140004
ISBN *0-202-26031-3*

Designed by Christine Valentine

Printed in the United States of America

Foreword

This book is an extraordinary one, both in its own discipline and as a contribution to the history of ideas. To the best of my knowledge a comparable document has never been published in any of the mental health disciplines, and it probably has few predecessors in the history and sociology of science.

As the reader will learn from the first few pages, a small informal committee was formed in Chicago in the summer of 1966, immediately following the Third APA Conference on Research in Psychotherapy. Its charge was to try to generate *collaborative* research among independent psychotherapy investigators. Since the members of this committee were seasoned researchers in this field, they raised two critical questions at their first meeting in January 1967: Will independently working psychotherapy researchers collaborate with each other? If they will, is the field sufficiently developed that such collaborative research will be productive at this time?

Each committee member had his own answer to these questions. The answers divided the committee into two subgroups—the optimistic members, who answered both questions in the affirmative, and the pessimistic, who answered both in the negative. After two days of unsuccessful attempts to persuade one another, the five members of the committee agreed that more reasoned answers to these questions would come only from a more extensive effort. Furthermore, such an effort would require a nearly full-time commitment, and there was serious doubt that anyone could be persuaded to make it. In addition, it was believed that no single investigator or scholar would have sufficient knowledge of the disparate literature of psychotherapy to do equal justice to the traditional psychodynamic and the newly emerging behavioral schools of thought. Accordingly, the committee decided to invite two individuals, one knowledgeable in each approach, to attempt the Herculean task of reviewing the literature of psychotherapy to discern whether the field was ready for a high-cost, broad-scale, collaborative project, and testing the willingness of potential collaborators to engage in such a cooperative venture. The committee could offer these two individuals only its name as an informal umbrella under which to submit to NIMH a proposal for funds to support the first of these two projects, and the commitment of its members to serve as a continuing group of advisers, if invited.

Fortunately, the two men the committee invited to undertake this project —Hans H. Strupp (Vanderbilt University) and Allen E. Bergin (Columbia University)—accepted the charge in January 1967. Within a few weeks, they prepared and submitted to NIMH an application for their full-time collaborative review of the psychotherapy literature during the forthcoming summer of 1967, and a grant was awarded to fund the first phase of their proposal.

As they make clear in the material that follows, they were so impressed by what they found in the literature that they subsequently (successfully) submitted an application for a grant to fund the second phase of their work. This grant enabled them to visit a number of this country's most active psychotherapy researchers (and several others) to assess the feasibility of cooperation among them. Their review of the literature (project 1) and the interviews with psychotherapy researchers (project 2) constitute the bulk of the present book.

These two parts would, by themselves, constitute a significant contribution to the literature. However, my description of this as an extraordinary book arises from the *extras* that Professors Bergin and Strupp have included —those extras that are the real ingredients of research and scholarship but are rarely published in our aseptic journal article format. The extras are simply the thoughts, hopes, aspirations, convictions, biases, frustrations, changes of heart and viewpoint, the excitement and the despair experienced by every writer and scientist as he pursues his work. It is the interspersing of their more polished final product with this highly personal material that gives this book its unique quality. Furthermore, the authors' remarkable openness in this regard was contagious, and seems to have made their (phase 2) interviewees willing to talk with equally refreshing candor and openness. Thus, this book contains in ample supply those rich personal elements that so many books—especially publications of symposia—promise, but never seem to deliver.

A third ingredient in this book makes it a rich document in the history of ideas—an ingredient that the authors may not see so clearly as the reader, because the authors probably are too close to the material, too involved as the actors on the stage to perceive the nuances that it will be the reader's pleasure to discern and experience. I am referring to the reader's extraordinary glimpse of the step-by-step process through which, over a three-year period, Strupp and Bergin each abandoned some early views and arrived, on some issues, at an intellectual conclusion fully opposite to the one he strongly held at the beginning of this remarkable joint venture (for example, Strupp's warmly open, gradually changing views toward psychoanalysis). Historians and biographers may report such changes in the individual they study, but few can document their material as clearly and meaningfully as do the two authors in the memos, personal letters, and working papers here. A particularly moving example is Bergin's paper, "Vexations of the Spirit."

I have been privileged to read the following material twice: first, as the various letters, memos, formal papers, interviews, dialogues, and so on, were exchanged over the three-year period; second, as they appeared neatly packaged in the final manuscript. Both times I have felt that Strupp and Bergin embarked on and successfully completed a remarkable personal and intellectual odyssey. I believe that in the authors' reports of their successive visits to various psychotherapy laboratories, and in the remarkable insights that successively unfold, the reader will see rich products of the naturalistic study method similar to those of Darwin and Flexner. The decades of the 1950's and 1960's produced thousands of isolated studies on psychotherapy, including its alleged function, process, and potential. Bergin and Strupp have accomplished the remarkable feat of analyzing and distilling these studies. By then traveling from one major laboratory to another, they have reached conclusions about the present status of psychotherapy that could have been expected to emerge only at some distant future date had such information been published piecemeal by individual writers and researchers.

This, then, may be the most valuable contribution of their book: an acceleration, by as much as a decade, of the normal process of information exchange (through journals) among researchers and scholars working in the field of psychotherapy. They achieve this while being very generous in their praise of the work and worth of the individuals whose contributions they reviewed and whose opinions they sought.

Both the beginning student and the more experienced worker in this field will find this book worth reading from cover to cover and will find in it much to interest and challenge him. I found it a most absorbing document.

Joseph D. Matarazzo

Contents

ONE

Introduction

Three national conferences on research in psychotherapy, held in Washington, D.C. in 1957, Chapel Hill in 1961, and Chicago in 1966, pointed up the need for investigators to pool their resources and to consider the design of research projects which might be executed on a collaborative basis. Precedents for such ventures were of course available in biomedical research, but had been conspicuously absent in psychotherapy. Informal suggestions at the first two conferences evidently were not followed by any action; the situation, however, was different at the Chicago conference. For one thing, a small group of investigators was more articulate about the problem; for another, the Clinical Research Branch of the National Institute of Mental Health—all three conferences had been supported by grants from the Na-

Reproduced in part from the *Journal of Abnormal Psychology*, 1970, 76:13–26, by permission of the American Psychological Association.

This report is the last in a series of documents analyzing the current status of psychotherapy research, the promise of large-scale collaborative investigations, and possible future directions of the field. The work has been supported by the National Institute of Mental Health through contracts No. PH-43-67-1386, Hans H. Strupp, Principal Investigator, and No. PH-43-67-1459, Allen E. Bergin, Principal Investigator; and Grant No. MH16250, Hans H. Strupp, Principal Investigator, and Grant No. MH16244, Allen E. Bergin, Principal Investigator. We are most grateful for this support and for the devoted interest and help provided in all phases of our work by Drs. A. Hussain Tuma of NIMH and Joseph D. Matarazzo of the University of Oregon Medical School. We are also grateful to Drs. Jerome D. Frank and John M. Shlien who served as advisors, and to the nearly three dozen consultants and colleagues who gave unreservedly of their talents in response to our requests. They have significantly stimulated our thought and enriched our lives.

tional Institute of Mental Health—was taking an active interest in the possibilities of collaborative research in this area.[1]

As a first step, John M. Shlien, the conference chairman, appointed an informal committee of conference participants to explore the feasibility of a collaborative study of psychotherapy. The following individuals were asked to explore the feasibility issue: Kenneth Mark Colby, Jerome D. Frank, Howard F. Hunt, Joseph D. Matarazzo (Chairman), John M. Shlien, and A. Hussain Tuma.

Although the committee was informal and did not have standing with any official group or organization, it consisted of researchers who believed that examination of the feasibility of coordinated or collaborative research was long overdue and that concerted action should be taken toward this end.

The committee met several times during the 18 months following the conference. At the initial meeting, it was concluded that an answer to the feasibility question required as a first step a critical review of the psychotherapy research literature. It seemed essential that a hard look at what the field had produced to date was necessary in order to determine whether studying other aspects of the feasibility issue would be fruitful.

We were asked by the committee to undertake this critical review of the literature and agreed to do so. We devoted the period from June through December 1967 to this undertaking, carried out under contracts from the National Institute of Mental Health. The results of our analysis were published as the February and March 1969 issues of the *International Journal of Psychiatry* (reprinted in this volume as Chapter 2 and Chapter 3). A bibliography of research in psychotherapy was completed as a by-product (Strupp & Bergin, 1969).

In our review, we reached the conclusion that the field might possibly be ready for one or more major collaborative studies, pending further feasibility testing and pilot work. Concomitantly, we outlined several studies which might prove fruitful.

We subsequently met with the originating committee in January 1968, by invitation of the Clinical Research Branch of the National Institute of Mental Health, and discussed future plans. Donald Kiesler, Nathaniel Raskin, and Charles Truax were also present. As a group, we discerned two possible next steps: (1) Independent investigators might pursue on their own one of the Strupp-Bergin recommendations for promising lines of inquiry; or (2) further investigation of the feasibility issue might be undertaken in greater depth. The latter would involve consideration of such problems as kinds of variables to be studied, by whom, under what conditions, and in which set-

1. Reflecting this programmatic interest, A. Hussain Tuma attended the conference as an official observer, and subsequently both he and Donald Oken, then Chief, Clinical Research Branch of the National Institute of Mental Health, worked with us closely throughout this effort.

tings; research designs which might most profitably be explored; consultants who might be approached for help on such matters as research design, statistical analysis, and professional and practical issues in collaboration; whether independent investigators could be persuaded and motivated to participate in a coordinated or collaborative study; and whether such an undertaking would be economically feasible. Clearly, such an inquiry might also lead to the equally important conclusion that collaborative research, while perhaps desirable, is either premature or not feasible.

At this point, stimulated by our previous work and the undeniable importance of the problem as reflected by the interest of the originating committee and the National Institute of Mental Health, we decided to embark on an examination of the questions outlined above. Accordingly, we submitted an application for a research grant to the National Institute of Mental Health. This application received favorable consideration and we began work on the project in the fall of 1968.

The Feasibility Study

To answer the questions that we and the originating committee posed, we planned the following approach:

1. We would explore in depth the relative merit and priority of several major psychotherapy research questions and relevant experimental designs in consultation with experts on substantive and methodological issues, to scrutinize the designs which we had identified as promising (in our review),[2] and to determine the relative merits, power, feasibility, and potential contribution of the specific studies to the furtherance of knowledge in psychotherapy. This step would involve the possible combination, amalgamation, modification, and specification of projects in an effort to arrive at optimal designs. This phase of the planning would begin from the vantage point of a considerable body of past research and it would reflect the thinking of many investigators who have seriously concerned themselves with general problems of research strategy; we would assess the respective merits of individual and collective or coordinated efforts; we would examine problems of experimental design, choice of variables, and measurement; and we would review strategies of collaborative research in psychotherapy and other areas of comparable complexity. It was of course clear to us that we were dealing with a refractory area of research: administratively, studies have been ex-

2. These designs followed classical experimental models involving therapy, control, and other technique comparison groups along with rigorous selection procedures and preoutcome and postoutcome measures. They were heavily influenced by the tradition of outcome experimentation associated with H. J. Eysenck, C. R. Rogers, R. I. Watson, M. Scriven, D. J. Kiesler, and others.

tremely difficult to implement, and technically, variables have been hard to define, measure, control, or manipulate.

2. We would inventory resources available at various centers in the nation for undertaking major responsibility for collaborative work. We would not begin by organizing a large national network of collaborating centers nor elicit specific commitments from them; rather, we planned to test, through visits and interviews with key personnel at differing levels in each center, the depth of interest and motivation for undertaking coordinated research and to survey the clinical and research resources available. Through intensive work in conjunction with consultants and research centers, we would hope to arrive at progressive approximations representing a reasonable balance between such factors as precision of measurement, acequacy of controls, potential contribution to the advancement of basic knowledge, and investment of manpower, facilities, and financial resources.

3. In our meetings with consultants and our visits to clinical centers, we would keep a record of information and evaluations, which would eventually form the basis of a detailed report on the feasibility of specified collaborative research projects. We would give special attention to the following considerations: (*a*) several models or designs for collaboration may prove feasible, and they may or may not be like those implemented in other fields; (*b*) the planning should aim for ends which cannot be accomplished by individual investigators or agencies; (*c*) master plans may include core variables and standardized measurements but will not preclude measures preferred by or unique to any cooperating therapist or treatment center; (*d*) it is important to be cognizant of the potential value of a variety of therapeutic techniques, influences, and innovations which have not yet been studied extensively but which might profitably be included in future research; and (*e*) a central coordinating mechanism for collaboration will have to evolve from our efforts and report if one or more projects are actually implemented.

4. We planned to devote the first year primarily to the testing of feasibility, development of a research plan (or several alternate plans), including identification of potential participants, investigators, clinical settings, and patient populations. Should a collaborative study of major consequence appear not feasible, then the planning phase terminates and a final substantive report will be submitted. However, should the indications be positive, the planning moves into the second year. We would then devote more of our energies to actually working out specific details needed for mounting a study. This would involve obtaining specific commitments from potential collaborators and then deciding on a specific plan of study with appropriate design and specific measuring instruments, control variables, screening and selection procedures, procedures of selecting and training of raters, and the actual implementation of pilot work.

Consultants were carefully selected in terms of their known expertise and their potential contribution to the objectives outlined in the foregoing. Prior to our visits, we sent each person a copy of our review, the grant proposal, and a set of 18 questions which we had formulated as stimuli for discussion.[3] Between October 1968 and July 1969 we spent from half a day to a full day with the following consultants: Arnold A. Lazarus, Lester Luborsky, Arthur H. Auerbach, Lyle D. Schmidt, Stanley R. Strong, Paul E. Meehl, Bernard F. Riess, Howard F. Hunt, Arnold P. Goldstein, Thomas S. Szasz, Gerald C. Davison, Bernard Weitzman, J. B. Chassan, Kenneth Mark Colby, Albert Bandura, Robert S. Wallerstein, Harold Sampson, Louis Breger, Howard Levene, Ralph R. Greenson, Milton Wexler, Carl R. Rogers, Joseph D. Matarazzo, Charles B. Truax, Neal E. Miller, Henry B. Linford, Peter H. Knapp (with Martin A. Jacobs, Louis Vachon, and Douglas M. McNair), John M. Shlien, David Bakan, Jerome D. Frank, Peter J. Lang, and Marvin A. Smith.

Following each visit, we independently prepared critical résumés based on notes taken during the meeting. In addition to exchanging these documents, we prepared various working papers, met at regular intervals for the purpose of assessing the progress of our endeavor, read extensively (often following up on suggestions made by the consultants), and shared our impressions with selected colleagues.[4]

This book presents chronologically and in detail each phase of the work described in this introduction. We have attempted to provide for the reader a look into the workshop of therapeutic science as it appeared to us during three years of evaluating literature, interviewing scientists and therapists, and exchanging and formulating viewpoints. A number of critical reactions to our positions and viewpoints are included. We have also attempted to weave into the material our personal reflections and experiences and those of others whom we have interviewed. In Chapter 4, we have included working papers, correspondence, and personal material which gives life to the ongoing processes of science and, we think, provides much insight into the realities behind the scenes.

This scientific odyssey begins in Chapters 2 and 3 with our review of the literature and the subsequent reactions of critics.

Reference

Strupp, H. H., & Bergin, A. E. 1969 *Research in individual psychotherapy: A bibliography*. Washington, D.C.: National Institute of Mental Health.

3. These questions are reproduced at the beginning of Chapter 4.
4. A full account of these interviews and related materials is presented in Chapter 4.

TWO

Some empirical and conceptual bases for coordinated research in psychotherapy

Research in psychotherapy[1] has failed to make a deep impact on practice and technique, presumably, because the results of most investigations have

Reprinted from *International Journal of Psychiatry*, 1969, 7, 18–90. By permission of the Editor.

The development and execution of this project resulted from the efforts of an informal committee which came into existence following the Third Conference on Research in Psychotherapy held in Chicago in June of 1966. Grateful acknowledgment for invaluable help, encouragement, and critical advice is made to Dr. Joseph D. Matarazzo, committee chairman, whose foresight and unstinting efforts brought the idea of the project to fruition. We are similarly grateful to Drs. Jerome D. Frank and John M. Shlien, who served on the committee, for their generous contribution in launching the study. In addition, we benefited from and are grateful for critical reviews of the manuscript by Drs. Kenneth Mark Colby, Sol L. Garfield, Donald J. Kiesler, Jum C. Nunnally, Donald Oken, and David F. Ricks.

We are also most appreciative of the important services performed by Lawrence Jasper and Jerry Cunningham who assisted in the literature search, and by Ellen Solomon, Roberta Plybon, and Joan Reese who typed numerous drafts of the manuscript, and by Anne Bloxom, who assisted with bibliographic and editorial matters.

We also wish to acknowledge with deep appreciation the cooperative attitudes of hundreds of persons who sent us reprints and commentaries which were most helpful in making the survey. Particularly for their benefit, we wish to note here that while our writing of the present document was influenced by reading many hundreds of papers, we cannot refer to more than a few of them and thus cannot do full justice to the broad and diverse activities taking place in this field. NIMH has published our comprehensive bibliography of psychotherapy research in the near future which will more explicitly recognize the many papers which have contributed to this field.

1. In using the terms "psychotherapy," "psychotherapist," and "patient" we are simply following convention. The terms as such do not imply theoretical predilections,

not had substantial practical significance. Reasons for this lack include the relatively short period of time systematic research has been focused on the problems of psychotherapy, deficiences in techniques available to the researcher, and practical difficulties in designing and carrying out adequately controlled studies.

Most researchers have been faced with serious limitations in collecting and analyzing data from representative samples of patients and therapists. Follow-up studies have been difficult to carry out; the crucial requirement of enlisting the full cooperation of therapists, patients, and institutions has been a continual stumbling block; and in general, rigorous designs have been difficult to impose upon the therapeutic phenomena themselves. Researchers who have attacked problems in the area through experimental analogues and similar techniques frequently have been unable to relate their findings to actual therapy situations.[2] These issues have been amply discussed by numerous writers (Bordin, 1965; Edwards & Cronbach, 1952; Ford & Urban, 1967; Frank, 1959; Glover, 1952; Goldstein, Heller, & Sechrest, 1966; Hunt, 1952; Kiesler, 1966; Sargent, 1960, 1961).

Two additional problems have limited the practical value of previous studies in psychotherapy, despite the fact that a number of them are of high scientific quality. One is the extreme complexity of the phenomena under study. Because of this factor, individual researchers have by necessity been forced to restrict their efforts to relatively narrow aspects of the larger problem. The other serious problem has been the lack of adequate communication and cooperation among researchers. Consequently, we are faced with a serious lack of comparability in conceptual tools, hypotheses, methods, procedures, subjects, measuring instruments, etc. (Sargent, 1961). To some extent this situation has been due to differences in theoretical viewpoints among researchers, basic convictions about the nature of psychotherapy, and similar factors, which in turn have led to very different and noncomparable data. There has been a lack of agreement on specific aims and objectives of therapy research as well as criteria of outcome (Bergin, 1963). Furthermore, most researchers have been working in relative isolation, and

---

acceptance of a "disease model," notions about the qualifications of therapists, etc. The terms are merely a convenient way to refer to an interpersonal process whose objective is personality or behavior change and the persons participating in it.

2. Kenneth Mark Colby comments: "A practitioner needs a 'causal relation' or variable he can manipulate *with this particular patient.* Research thus far has not given him a reliable guide in this direction because it has mainly been in the tradition of an extensive design. Extensive designs yield only weak group averages, not specific causal mechanisms (cf. Chassan, 1967). There are two lacks we must face: (1) New concepts—it is too early for an all-embracing theory: before one has a theory (a combination of concepts) one must have some good concepts; (2) a reliable taxonomy. Few admit their concepts are inadequate and few want to face the classification problem because it is considered 'undynamic.' But we won't get far with unreliable categories and heterogeneous samples."

they have had little opportunity to examine critically similarities and differences in their research efforts.

It has become increasingly clear that psychotherapy as currently practiced is not a unitary process and is not applied to a unitary problem. Consequently, the traditional question, "Is psychotherapy effective?," is no longer fruitful or appropriate.

In light of these considerations, we feel that the problem of psychotherapy research in its most general terms, should be reformulated as a standard scientific question: What specific therapeutic interventions produce specific changes in specific patients under specific conditions? In order to answer this ultimate question it is essential to achieve greater clarification of the nature of the therapeutic influence and its effects by implementation of empirical inquiries based upon a full recognition of the implications of the following statements:

1. Therapists cannot be regarded as interchangeable units; therefore, different therapists, depending on variables in their personality, training, experience, etc. exert different effects under different conditions.
2. Patients, depending upon variables in their personality, education, intelligence, the nature of their emotional problems, motivation, and other factors, are differentially receptive to different forms of therapeutic influence.
3. Technique variables cannot be dealt with in isolation, but must be viewed in the context of patient and therapist variables enumerated above.
4. Outcome measures are frequently restricted to dimensions derived from specific theoretical positions and thus evidence based upon such measures is difficult to generalize. Other measures are factorially too complex to yield useful empirical or practical meaning, and still others, though factorially pure, are but minimally correlated with other outcome criterion measures.

It is incumbent upon those who are involved in research, practice, and training to devote considerable effort to discovering which therapists and techniques are the best facilitators of change, which clients benefit most readily, and which combinations of these optimize positive results (Luborsky & Strupp, 1962). It is becoming increasingly clear that one of the major challenges for research in this area is to achieve greater precision by treating selected individuals having specified qualities by means of specified kinds of interventions employed by therapists possessing specified skills and personality characteristics.

We also contend that many controversies surrounding the problem of therapeutic effectiveness can be resolved by the application of more complex and theoretically diversified designs which employ a more representative sample of valid criterion measures cutting across theoretical dispositions and the habitual instrumentation biases of given experimenters. (Detailed discussion of these problems are found in recent papers by Bergin (1967a, 1967b), Kiesler (1966), Truax & Carkhuff (1964a, 1964b), Andrews (1966), and Strupp (1968). Such inquiries are likely to be distinctly atheoretical, and we think wisely so.

Many of the issues thus far described have been fruitfully confronted by three national conferences on research in psychotherapy (1958, 1961, and 1966. See: Rubinstein & Parloff, 1959; Strupp & Luborsky, 1962; Shlien, Hunt, Matarazzo, & Savage, 1968) which succeeded in bring together researchers working on related problems. These conferences have served to facilitate exchanges of information and the most recent one sparked interest in positive, cooperative work, which may be expected to meet more directly the major needs of the field.

The purpose of this review is, therefore, to establish a scientific base and lay the necessary conceptual groundwork on which coordinated research can be built. It is our hope that it will serve to facilitate a variety of new researches by investigators who may wish to carry out formal collaborative research, by others who may cooperate in developing parallel research designs for separate projects, and by still others who may conduct independent investigations.

It is expected that specific proposals resulting from this effort will be of value not only to the group of researchers who might agree to carry out one or more of the proposed investigations on a collabrative basis but to the larger community of researchers. It is our hope that by delineating specific variables, measures, designs, and methods, we may succeed in stimulating researchers working in different institutions and centers to study systematically various segments of the proposed research. In this way, we may gradually succeed in overcoming the traditional lack of cooperation which in our judgments has hampered significant progress in this field.

We propose then to (*a*) identify significant and promising trends, problems and issues evident in the burgeoning literature in psychotherapy research; (*b*) summarize evidence and ideas pertaining to the relative value of variables, measures, and procedures that might be utilized in implementing future research studies; and (*c*) suggest hypotheses, designs and domains of investigation meriting major, possibly collaborative, efforts at further inquiry.

The present analysis is largely restricted to objective research relevant to individual psychotherapy with neurotic adult patients. Excluded are other forms of psychotherapy, research focused on other target populations, and studies involving pharmacological agents.

Such a narrow focus might be questioned in light of the current general trend away from individual therapy as the treatment of choice. We cannot offer here a complete justification of our position, but in brief it is based upon the following considerations: (*a*) There is much more favorable evidence regarding the efficacy of individual therapy today, particularly with the development of behavioral therapies, than there was ten years ago; (*b*) this area of the field continues to be lively, controversial and marked by both productivity and heavy investments of professional talent, as witnessed particularly by the fact that approximately 2500 references were collected for this survey, a high proportion of which have appeared since 1964 when Strupp's bibliography comprising about 1,000 items was published; (*c*) even community consultation frequently reduces, in the last analysis, to a one-to-one relationship (between consultant and consultee or between consultee and "client"), and the principles of change-induction governing those contacts are unlikely to be significantly different from those which prevail in individual therapies.

While we have striven to be as objective as possible, our personal convictions and biases will nevertheless be apparent. In many respects this is a personal document, which is presented under no mantle of authority other than our own. It is our view of the field and it conveys throughout our jointly held conviction that the practice of psychotherapy must become based upon a verifiable scientific substrate.

Emerging Trends

We wish to acknowledge, first of all, the overwhelming impact this project has had upon us personally. Although we presumed a fair knowledge of psychotherapy research prior to initiating the review, we came to realize over a brief period of a few months that we had been unaware of an enormous amount of exciting work. After sending out a few hundred form letters requesting reprints, unpublished material, and commentaries, our offices were literally flooded with letters, documents, and books. Given this unusual opportunity to look in on the activities of a great number of persons in the field, we were amazed by the amount of activity, the innovations, the new findings, and the general optimism and excitement which characterize the area. We were enormously encouraged by evidences of scope, vitality, and sophistication which mark the field as definitely a maturing and significant one. This is perhaps the most important trend we detected. The others follow, roughly in order of significance as measured by the substance which backs them up and the generality of their implications.

Keynotes: Empiricism, Innovation, Evaluation. Another stimulating and important trend in the recent literature is represented by an emphasis on empiricism, innovation and evaluation.

New techniques of therapy and research are mushrooming but there is a keen insistence on evaluating the therapeutic utility of these innovations. *The role of clinician and experimenter are merging, and the clinician proposing a new technique is becoming aware of the necessity to demonstrate its utility to the scientific community by means of hard-core data.* The field is accepting—and indeed embracing—empiricism. There is a marked impatience with armchair theorizing and clinical observations unsupported by empirical data. The significance of this trend is hard to overestimate and shows that the field is coming of age. By the same token, some innovations undoubtedly will vanish as fads.

Among the recent innovative trends in psychotherapy, one of the most prominent is a strong reaction against individual one-to-one psychotherapy and a parallel devotion to various multiple methods such as group, family, and milieu therapies and community consultation. It has been persuasively argued that the mental health manpower shortage is so great, the social crises so critical, and the effectiveness of traditional psychotherapy so limited that these multiple techniques will inevitably become dominant in the near future (Albee, 1967). Why then devote much more talent and energy to analyses of an obsolete technique?

First of all, it seems evident to us that many of these innovations consist of little more than old wine in new bottles, and their positive impact is yet to be demonstrated.

Secondly, in the final analysis, the purpose of group techniques is to produce an impact upon individuals. Hence, principles of individual change emerging from systematic psychotherapy research may well provide the foundation upon which effective group techniques will be built. This has already been demonstrated in the case of behavioral therapies by significant application to therapy groups (Lazarus, 1961) and to school classes (Becker, Madsen, Arnold, & Thomas, 1967).

We, therefore, see the analyses presented in this paper, not as irrelevant to the current mainstream, but as generic to processes of change whatever specific technical form they may eventually take.

Learning theory in the ascendancy. The focus on behavioral therapies and upon learning theory interpretations of traditional therapy processes has increased dramatically over the last five years. The number of papers on these subjects in 1966 and 1967 is staggering and will undoubtedly continue. The evidence supporting the value of these approaches and the innovations continuously emerging from them is increasingly impressive, and the thought and practice of many professionals are being greatly affected by them (Cautela, 1967; Emery & Krumboltz, 1967; Franks, 1969; Hain, Butcher, & Stevenson, 1966; Hawkins, Peterson, Schweid, & Bijou,

1966; Krumboltz, Varenhorst, & Thoresen, 1967; Lang, 1968; Lazarus, 1966; Lazarus, Davison, & Polefka, 1965; Lovaas, 1968; MacCulloch & Feldman, 1967; Paul, 1967, 1969a, 1969b; Wolpe & Lazarus, 1966).

While the growing adoption of this approach has resulted in new techniques, it must be recognized that it has barely begun to illuminate many complex learning tasks with which psychotherapy of necessity has to be concerned. Treating a specific phobia is an undertaking different from treating a character disorder, although it may be found that very similar principles apply. The contributions of learning theory to complex problems are as yet less impressive (Breger & McGaugh, 1965), though even here they provide a serious and convincing challenge to traditional methods. Researchers in the area, as demonstrated by their labors, reject Colby's (1962) view that psychotherapy is an applied art and that by its very nature it cannot become a science, although his assertion has not really been refuted.

The wide applicability, rapid cure, and high percentages of improved cases have all been called into question by recent commentators; but no critic who has made empirical studies has seriously questioned the value of behavioral techniques as part of the therapeutic repertoire. Rather, most of them seem to favor its inclusion, despite previous theoretical predilections to the contrary.

The debate over behavioral techniques thus seems to have entered a phase of careful empirical evaluation plus attempts at theoretical rapprochement rather than the simple-minded polemics that characterized the initial, more acrimonious, confrontations of views (Andrews, 1966; Cautela, 1965; Feldman, 1966; Gelder, 1967; Heller & Marlatt, 1969; Lazarus, 1967; Leventhal, 1968; Truax & Carkhuff, 1967; Weitzman, 1967; Wolpin & Raines, 1966).

A further implication is the view that neurotic patterns are learned behavior which, within limits, is modifiable (Dollard & Miller, 1950; Ullmann & Krasner, 1965). Concomitantly, there is deemphasis on historical antecedents, causes, "disease" concepts, intrapsychic factors, and the like. Continuing interest in these factors is important for prevention but perhaps academic as far as the operations of psychotherapy are concerned.

Similar considerations have led many workers to abandon the term "psychotherapy" in favor of behavior modification, social learning, and similar terms. Intrapsychic changes are being relegated, somewhat unjustifiably, to the background in favor of behavioral changes, and fewer therapists continue to grapple with the task of reconstructing the "total personality," which tends to be seen as an extravagent if not impossible endeavor. In keeping with the *Zeitgeist,* a little, but significant, change for a lot of people is seen as preferable to protracted efforts to produce large-scale changes in a few members of the upper social classes. By implication, beneficial changes in target complaints are expected to create a benign cycle whose effects radiate to the patient's total functioning. Despite these changing cultural values, however, we cannot ignore the fact that certain neurotic patterns of behavior are deeply ingrained and often exceedingly difficult to modify. Thus, learning to recognize intractability, developing techniques for dealing with it or defining the limits of therapeutic techniques seems an entirely legitimate research task, which at present is not receiving very sustained attention.

Mechanisms of the Influencing Process. It is becoming increasingly clear that psychotherapy is not a unitary process but "a heterogeneous collection of ingredients or psychological conditions that produce varying degrees of both positive and deteriorative personality change in patients" (Truax & Carkhuff, 1967, p. 21). Therefore, the term "psychotherapy," as traditionally used, encompasses a wide variety of techniques and procedures whose dimensions must be isolated and their relative contributions to the therapeutic process made explicit.

All major systems of psychotherapy employ a number—but a finite number—of specifiable mechanisms or psychological processes, including prominently: (1) counterconditioning; (2) extinction; (3) cognitive learning; (4) reward and punishment; (5) transfer and generalization; (6) social learning, including imitation and identification; (7) persuasion; (8) empathy; (9) warmth; and (10) interpretation. To determine the relative contributions of each process and the extent to which it can be optimally employed, singly or in combination, is a major research task for the future. A crucial prerequisite for determining the extent to which the foregoing mechanisms can become operative is the patient's *amenability* or *receptivity* to the therapist's influence, which varies from patient to patient, from hour to hour, and within each therapeutic dyad.

Even in those instances in which psychotherapy is focused upon a specific symptom, it is highly questionable that a *single* technique is being employed. The therapeutic influence (encompassing the person of the therapist in conjunction with particular techniques) is broad-gauged and always appears to proceed on a wide front. For example, the therapist's influence in psychoanalytic therapy is not stringently or even approximately defined by the techniques of free association and interpretation; similarly, there is more to client-centered therapy than the therapist's empathy, congruence, and unconditional positive regard (Truax, 1966), and behavior therapy employs techniques besides those usually described as characterizing it (Lazarus, 1967).

Toward a Nonschool Approach. The barriers separating the major "schools" of psychotherapy are gradually being eroded, and the predominant direction of research is toward a nonschool approach.

The foregoing judgment is made despite appearances to the contrary. On the surface, acrimonious debates continue between the representatives of different theoretical orientations, and the stridency of the voices appears to be correlated with the particular school's research productivity. With regard to the latter, behavior therapy is clearly the leading contender; client-centered therapy a decided second; and research contributions from the psychoanalytic area are rather inconspicuous. This hierarchical ordering, however, does not fully reflect the pervasive influence of the various schools upon practices, some of which may have become obsolescent.

Signs of an approaching rapprochement—at least in the research area—are shown by the following: (*a*) Lazarus (1966, 1967), a close collaborator of the exponent of behavior therapy, Wolpe, has strongly argued for the abolishment of the simplistic doctrinal substrate upon which behavior therapists have relied; (*b*) Truax & Carkhuff (1967), writing from the vantage point of a large-scale client-centered research program, applaud the value of behavior therapy techniques and suggest their selective inclusion in the client-centered therapist's repertoire; (*c*) Mowrer (1966) has relented and now perceives a few mild virtues in that dastardly Freudian, Wolpe; he also recognizes merit in operant techniques and even more in modeling procedures; (*d*) a psychoanalytic theorist (Weitzman, 1967) has proposed a thoughtful and thorough engagement of desensitization with psychoanalysis; (*e*) Alexander (1963), in one of his last publications, pointed toward a reformulation of psychoanalytic theory in terms of learning theory principles; and (*f*) Rogers (Rogers, Gendlin, Kiesler, & Truax, 1967) is now willing to discuss the possibility that communication training and positive reinforcement exist in client-centered therapy.

This trend, viewed by us as progress, is fraught with positive implications for practice but highlights the difficulties for research designed to compare ostensibly different therapeutic approaches. The practices of most therapists, contrary to their theoretical writings, always have been a mélange of eclecticism. The diversity of operations by a given therapist with a given patient now openly acknowledges the innovative freedom which ingenious clinicians have always exercised. However, it also magnifies the spectre of almost intractable complexity confronting the researcher embarking upon the task of studying the effect of a *single* technique under rigidly defined conditions.

In this connection, it is undeniable that diverse theoretical formulations have significantly contributed to a better understanding of the problems surrounding therapeutic change. Concepts, principles, and techniques stressed by particular schools have done much to direct researchers to more thorough exploration of these facets. For example, research focused on such variables as depth of interpretation, empathy, desensitization, etc. was clearly inspired by the conceptualizations of competing theories, which were usually expounded with considerable conviction.

These developments embody an important lesson for the researcher: *The isolation and manipulation of single variables is essential for advancing knowledge concerning the process of therapeutic change.*[3] *Moreover, it is becoming increasingly feasible to carry out such investigations without dependence on doctrinaire allegiances.* Most research contributions of the past have emerged from, and have been anchored to, a particular theoretical position. Comparative studies across theoretical boundaries are still rare (despite some promising exceptions, e.g., Paul 1966) and beset with great methodological difficulties; however, they hold significant promise for the future. Indeed, we are convinced that they represent one of the most important keys for investigative advance in this field.

Toward Specificity of Techniques. Consistent with the preceding trends is another of equal significance, namely a growing tendency to employ different techniques to suit different problems (Kiesler, 1966; Strupp, 1968). Psychoanalysis has frequently been criticized for selecting patients to fit the method rather than to adapt the method to the characteristics of the patient and his problem. The "classical" technique certainly was restricted to a very narrow band of the population who met stringent criteria of education, intelligence, psychological-mindedness, motivation and the like. To be sure, there have been technical modifications to meet the special needs of different target populations (e.g., in child therapy, therapy with psychotics, etc.) and the possibilities are probably far from exhausted. However, greater flexibility has been shown by behavior therapists who have taken a leading role in applying different therapeutic techniques to persons hitherto considered unreachable.

The trend is toward specificity and toward comparisons of the relative merits of specific techniques. Definition of variables and their experimental evaluation through systematic comparisons is of course part and parcel of the scientific method. While numerous authors have recommended comparative studies for some years (e.g., Rogers, 1958; Strupp, 1957; Wolpe, 1964), the feasibility of such ventures seems vastly greater today. If carefully defined homogeneous techniques are to be studied in relation to specified problems and specified outcomes, a massive research design is clearly called for. (For examples, see Goldstein et al., 1966; Andrews, 1966.)

This emphasis on technology, exemplified by optimum matching of therapist, patient, problem, and technique, is not necessarily opposed to the position of those therapists who extol respect for, and involvement with, the "whole" person; but it would discard the notion that concern for the whole person is relevant in *all* instances of distress. Even when it is applicable, the provision of therapeutic relationships by nonprofessionals with "therapeutic

3. How to isolate and manipulate single or narrowly defined variables in a complex system is of course a central problem in this area as in others dealing with complex processes.

personalities" may well meet the needs of such clients, and at the same time provide one solution to the manpower shortage (Bergin, 1967b). The expert could then concentrate the exercise of his skills upon those situations requiring more elaborate technical procedures. He could also play a significant part in planning appropriate therapeutic interventions, determining promising patient-therapist pairings, programming desensitization, setting up tasks in discrimination learning, and in general contribute to the goal of making psychotherapy a more planful and focused undertaking. Writing in a different context, Anna Freud (1954) may have overstated the situation only slightly when she wrote over a decade ago:

> If all the skill, knowledge and pioneering effort which was spent on widening the scope of application of psychoanalysis had been employed instead on intensifying and improving our technique in the original field [hysteric, phobic, and compulsive disorders], I cannot help but feel that, by now, we would find the treatment of the common neuroses child's play, instead of struggling with their technical problems as we have continued to do (p. 610).

Manipulation vs. Self-Actualization. A persisting issue pertains to the old controversy of manipulation and control vs. permissiveness and freedom (Bugental, 1967; Shostrom, 1967).

Setting aside the pregnant philosophical issues, we view the status of the problem as follows: On the one hand, the use of manipulative techniques may cause further manipulation via imitative learning and may have deleterious effects on the patient's independence, autonomy, and self-determination. On the other hand, techniques which stress permissiveness, self-actualization, and finding one's own solutions may bolster the patient's self-respect, but they may often be ineffective, besides being manipulative in their own right. This issue has changed little since the debate between Rogers & Skinner (1956), and regardless of the merits of these respective viewpoints, there can be little doubt that research in the field as a whole has been veering in the direction espoused by Skinner.

The phenomenological-existentialist position assumes that the patient has the "correct" or therapeutically desirable responses within his repertoire, and that he can find his own solutions when freed of self-defeating neurotic maneuvers. This, of course, was also Freud's position, which may be well suited to inhibited upper middle-class neurotic patients, who are reasonably well functioning and whose problems present relatively modest hindrances to productive living. As experience with the large number of personality and character problems has abundantly shown, however, this ideal situation is rarely if ever present in psychotherapy. More typical are those patients whose personality development has left them with pronounced deficits in adequate prosocial responses and behaviors. The situation is analogous to that of a student who, having missed introductory courses, suddenly finds himself in a class with advanced students; usually he cannot make up the gaps in background and knowledge without going through the same process his classmates have gone through. Herein, parenthetically, lies one of the limitations of behavior therapy when the therapeutic effort is addressed to a specific symptom, such as a phobia. These therapists often seem to proceed on the same (in our view, incorrect) assumption as the phenomenologist, namely that the patient's behavioral repertoire is largely intact except for a specific neurotic symptom. Exceptions include many Skinnerians and A. Lazarus, who uses shaping techniques, behavioral rehearsal, etc.

Our reading of the accumulating evidence strongly suggests that *all forms of psychotherapy exert planful psychological influence,* and they are therefore manipulative in the sense of utilizing principles of social control. This appears to be universally true irrespective of the school's degree of inclination to conceptualize its operation in such terms. Behavior therapists are unequivocal on this point; client-centered therapy, as shown by Truax (1966), employs conditioning procedures; and psychoanalytic therapy demonstrably uses a variety of manipulative principles and techniques.

A patient usually enters therapy because his self-control is defective; and one of the therapist's tasks is to provide him with more adequate techniques of self-direction and control. He can only do this if he somehow succeeds in gaining ascendancy, that is, exerting control, over those impulses, fantasies, feelings, and responses which lead to an autonomous existence. The issue, therefore seems to be largely a pseudo problem, and psychotherapy, almost by definition, influences and indoctrinates the patient, in much the same way as is done by any educational procedure (Frank, 1961).

The basic values transmitted by a therapist (or teacher) are those of the culture. In our culture, prominent values include independence, self-direction, autonomy, self-discipline, careful channeling of aggressive and competitive impulses, and the like. Psychotherapy, to an important degree, is training in socialization (Lennard & Bernstein, 1960), and it may be considered an elaborate and sophisticated educational or teaching process.

Therapist's Personality vs. Techniques. During the past ten years there has been a deepening emphasis on the nature of the therapist's influence. The problem has frequently been approached by postulating a dichotomy between therapist's personality and techniques. Behavior therapy and psychoanalysis, for example, are primarily technique-oriented; client-centered theory, by contrast, has focused on the therapist's personality and attitudes. Our critical look at the field suggests, however, that regardless of the therapeutic objectives and the technical procedures, the therapist must succeed in the following:

1. He must create conditions which make the patient amenable to his influence. Usually this is spoken of in terms of a therapeutic relationship in

which the patient experiences respect, trust, and acceptance, which render him receptive to the therapist's suggestions, interpretations, and the like.

2. While these conditions are being created, the therapist employs a variety of technical procedures (desensitization, interpretations, etc.) to influence the patient in directions considered therapeutically desirable and ultimately intended to increase the patient's independence, self-direction, and autonomy.

These two sets of operations may be—and often are—intertwined, but it is becoming increasingly clear that both are necessary conditions for producing optimal therapeutic change. Client-centered therapy has considered conditions (1) as "necessary and sufficient" (Rogers, 1957), whereas behavior therapy largely emphasizes (2). Psychoanalytic therapy recognizes the importance of both conditions, and (correctly, we believe) sees (1) as an end to (2). As far as the therapeutic enterprise is concerned the therapist's personality is of interest only to the extent that its communicated manifestations exert an influence upon the patient's feelings and behavior. In all instances this influence (despite such intermediate steps in psychoanalysis as fostering the development and resolution of the transference neurosis) operates in the direction of increasing the patient's executive (ego) control and adaptational mastery.

Converging research evidence (Truax & Carkhuff, 1967) strongly suggests that the therapeutic climate produced by the therapist's personality (including prominently such variables as his empathy, warmth, respect, etc.) is indeed a potent therapeutic agent, and that it is created and sustained by the therapist, relatively independent of patient attitudes and characteristics. This holds true despite the fact that in some instances (Strupp, 1960; Strupp & Wallach, 1965) certain patient characteristics (such as hostility, anti-social attitudes, etc.) adversely affect the therapist's liking for and commitment to the patient.

In addition to the climate established through the therapist's warmth, empathy, etc., his basic personality dispositions, his interest and cultural background, and his areas of conflict and anxiety demonstrably influence the therapeutic interaction and perhaps its outcomes. The therapist's technical behavior is seen in these studies as being significantly influenced by his personal qualities and, as a consequence, he is viewed more as a *person* exerting *personal* influence rather than simply an *expert* applying techniques. On the basis of this evidence, too, psychotherapy is seen increasingly as a particular instance of a human relationship. (Truax & Carkhuff, 1967; Betz, 1967; Bergin & Solomon, 1970; Bandura, Lipsher, & Miller, 1960; Winder, Ahmad, Bandura, & Rau, 1962; Matarazzo, Wiens, & Saslow, 1965; Caracena, 1965; McNair, Callahan, & Lorr, 1962; Bergin, 1967b). Lest this conclusion seem confusing in light of previous statements regarding the relative independence of some techniques (such as desensitization) from therapist qualities, we believe that these factors influence the course of therapy in proportion to the extent that the relationship is a prime mediator of the therapeutic influence. Thus, the relevance of therapist dispositions is a matter of degree, though we would assert that such factors are present in all therapeutic transactions regardless of how "technical" some may appear.

The Perennial Criterion and Outcome Problems. The problem of patient selection for particular forms of psychotherapy deserves far greater attention from researchers than it has received in the past. Improved selection is bound to result in greater predictability of outcomes, long a controversial issue in psychotherapy research. In some measure, the disappointment with outcome studies is attributable to the haphazard assignment of patients. There is by now little doubt that *some* patients benefit substantially from psychotherapy whereas many others are poor prognostic risks. Research must play a more important role in specifying those patient variables which should be considered in the selection of individuals for particular methods of therapy.

As Bergin (1963, 1966) has shown, the generally unimpressive results of studies aimed at assessing the effectiveness of psychotherapy *in general* may be partly due to indiscriminate groupings of patients and therapists. For some therapy seems to produce beneficial effects, for some no effects, and for still others deleterious effects. Thus, broad groupings of patients are likely to obscure, if not to vitiate, results that may be clearly demonstrated if more homogeneous groups were being studied. As in other phases of psychotherapy research, a plea for greater specificity must be entered, in this case for the study of homogeneous groups of both therapists and patients.

Failure to observe this caveat has resulted in protracted polemics about the effectiveness of psychotherapy, in which the proponents are challenged to exceed a "spontaneous recovery" criterion (no treatment control) of 70 percent. When therapists are thus proved incapable of "jumping over the moon," and the null hypothesis is invoked, the "ineffectiveness" of psychotherapy is proclaimed. It appears, however, that the spontaneous recovery rate varies markedly across patient types and thus it is difficult to know from past research precisely what base line given therapists should have exceeded in order to demonstrate their effectiveness. Differential spontaneous recovery rates and differential treatment effects with diverse patient groups will have to be demonstrated before this issue is fully resolved.

It has long been recognized that therapy outcomes are multidimensional, hence not directly comparable in different studies, particularly across theoretical orientations. The full implications of this position, however, remain to be taken seriously. Among these, we list the following:

1. It must be demonstrated whether different orientations produce

unique changes, especially those stressed by the particular theory, or whether supposedly unique changes are outweighed by general changes produced by all forms of therapy.

2. If different interventions yielded similar outcomes, a further reduction in provincialism would result since adherents of different schools would be directly confronted with the commonality of therapy outcomes. They might thus become more amenable to employing techniques propounded by their opponents.

3. If some patients showed improvements on some criteria but not on others, we would gain valuable information about techniques most appropriate for those patients. As already suggested, different kinds of expertise may be called for in treating circumscribed symptoms and character disorders.

4. In addition to providing information about theoretical orientations and techniques, such outcome measures would yield important data about divergent criteria and their respective usefulness. For example, are some criteria useful only for patients undergoing a certain type of therapy?

5. In order to explore more adequately than has been done in the past the relative contributions of patient, therapist, and technique variables to therapeutic outcomes, the design of a study must be sufficiently comprehensive.

Additional Specific Trends. 1. The training of therapists is becoming increasingly pragmatic and decreasingly theoretical. Therapists are expected to produce results, and students are being trained accordingly. With few exceptions (Truax & Carkhuff, 1967), however, techniques of training are still very crude, often ineffectual, and inadequately studied. Thorough assessments of training procedures are sorely needed and may lend themselves to collaborative research.

2. Nonprofessional, indigenous modes of therapy continue to develop and thrive. We now have AA, Neurotics Anonymous, Psychotics Anonymous, Recovery, Inc., Synanon, Weight Watchers, etc. Many of these influences may well be worth studying as a context of discovery for naturalistic therapeutic agents. In this regard, the researcher who expects to find a disturbed control group which is not getting some kind of help should beware lest his control subjects receive massive doses of "anonymous" therapy.

3. In contrast to the increasing development of therapeutic techniques derived from general psychology, experimental analogues derived from therapy processes seem to be on the decline, perhaps because previous attempts have been too distant from the practical situation to have had much impact. Studies like those of Colby (1960), Gordon (1957), Grossman (1950, 1952), Keet (1948), Martin (1956), and Quay (1959) have never been vigorously pursued and made relevant to practice. It may be that this approach has more potential than is apparent. If more attention were paid to bridging experiment and practice and if more sustained energy were devoted

to the pursuit of a given hypothesis, good results might yet be forthcoming. Truax & Carkhuff's experiment in vivo (1965a) is one example of adequate bridging, though in this case the analogue was simply used to confirm clinical evidence rather than to discover something new. This is certainly useful and legitimate.

4. A fascinating and awesome trend toward a therapeutic technology is occurring. While only in an emergent phase, it promises to have broad and significant consequences. This is taking several forms: Some investigators have begun to program and computerize therapeutic procedures in both traditional (Colby) and behavioral (Lang) orientations. Therapy machines are almost an inevitability in the future, but they are likely to have advantages and disadvantages similar to those of teaching machines. Another researcher is analyzing the complexities of process content via computer (Harway & Iker, 1966). Conceivably, new vistas may be opened up by these emerging methods for grasping the seeming inscrutability of many therapeutic phenomena.

5. Another emerging trend is the intensive, empirical study of single cases. The potential of this approach is much greater than is commonly realized, provided rigorous methods are applied in the case study. Recent reports by Cartwright (1968), Dinsmoor (1966), Shapiro (1966), Subotnik (1966), and Dukes (1965) as well as imaginative suggestions for design and statistical analysis of single case studies (Chassan, 1967; Shontz, 1965) strongly support this view.

In this connection, more vigorous demands are being made for analysis of small, homogeneous subgroups, which comprise and often confound studies utilizing large group comparisons (Butler, 1966; Kiesler, 1966). It is not uncommon to find that a small minority of subjects in studies using mean comparisons or correlation coefficients account for the statistical significance of the overall results. The psychological significance of such studies is dubious.

6. Concomitant with the reduction in schoolism is an increasing disaffection from psychoanalysis. A number of writers sense a growing skepticism about analytically oriented therapy as it has been traditionally practiced (Matarazzo, 1965; Ricks, 1966; Brill, 1966; Gordon & Gordon, 1966). It appears that younger professionals are less willing to identify themselves with the viewpoints, techniques, and institutions of the analytical establishment, which has held sway for the past few decades. The virtues of this approach are being absorbed into a more empirically oriented therapeutic pragmatism; and at the same time there appears to be a repudiating attitude toward institutionalized psychoanalysis. The very fact that psychoanalysis is an institution as well as a mélange of theory and technique contributes to the negative reaction.

7. There is a strong trend, consistent with many of the others, toward

brief, time-limited therapy. There is some evidence that this procedure is just as effective as unlimited therapy, although some data suggest that only superficial criteria reveal significant change with this technique. Since the vast majority of cases are seen for only a few sessions anyway, it seems very worthwhile to further explore the values of this approach. The works of Gordon & Gordon (1966), Shlien (1962, 1966), Phillips & Weiner (1966), and Bellak & Small (1965) provide positive leads in this area. Diversity of criteria, patients, techniques, and therapists are relevant here just as they are in comparative studies of techniques.

8. An upsurge of techniques for dealing with lower-class and other patients usually considered refractory to verbal-emotive therapy is occurring and is well documented by Cartwright (1968). In some instances this involves modifications of technique and role-induction procedures in others. This trend should have salutary effects on therapy with members of this population and produce a rise of esteem for psychotherapy in the eyes of society. These new procedures are eminently worthy of further development and evaluation.

Lines of Advance in Psychotherapy Research. Since a major objective of this paper is to chart directions for further research, we must address ourselves to three interrelated issues: (1) To what sources are developments in the field of psychotherapy attributable? (2) What contributions has research in psychotherapy made thus far, both with respect to practice as well as scientific understanding of the phenomena? and (3) What role can systematic research play in the future in advancing knowledge in this area? Let us critically examine these questions in turn.

1. Even a cursory look at developments in psychotherapy makes it abundantly clear that significant advances have been closely associated with, and indeed crucially dependent upon, the introduction of new techniques by inventive and sensitive clinicians. Techniques have emerged directly from the crucible of intensive clinical work through the efforts of individuals who have been dissatisfied with the status quo and have empirically searched for new solutions. Most innovators, beginning with Freud, have been clinicians, and their method of investigation has consisted of critical observations in the clinical situation combined with clinical trials. Their theoretical formulations have followed their clinical experience rather than dictated their therapeutic procedures and techniques.

It is apparent that the contributions of the pioneers have followed the general model of exploratory scientific work. These contributions have often been independent of, and at times at sharp variance with, developments in "scientific" psychology and cognate fields. There is, however, a modern trend toward a fuller integration of clinical experimentation and scientific rigor as exemplified by Rogers' efforts to relate his theoretical propositions to self-theory and Wolpe's attempts to derive his formulations from learning research.

2. What part, then, has *research* in psychotherapy played in advancing the field, and what does the future hold in this respect? Although systematic research in this area is barely a quarter of a century old, during this period there has been a monumental growth in the quantity as well as the quality of the investigative effort. The researcher of today is vastly more sophisticated than his colleague circa 1950. He has fashioned tools for measuring, however crudely, such variables as empathy, warmth, depth of interpretation, therapist's attitudes toward patients, patients' verbalizations and motivations for change; he has made beginnings in isolating the components of therapeutic techniques and dimensions of personality and behavior change; and he has become keenly sensitive to the complex methodological issues in comparing different forms of therapy and their outcomes, *although he has yet to carry out truly meaningful comparisons of different methods.*

While psychotherapy research has exerted little demonstrable effect on the therapeutic activities of the average practitioner, it has succeeded in producing important attitudinal changes which now pervade the field. These changes are to be found in a general sharpening of thinking, insistence on empirical verification, and skepticism toward anecdotal clinical accounts of conclusive evidence for assertions made *ex cathedra.*

Of equal, if not greater, importance is a growing rapprochement between research in psychotherapy and the fields of learning, social psychology, perception, motivation, personality development, and education. Thus, psychotherapy is abandoning the status of an esoteric art following principles and techniques peculiarly its own; but it is gradually being seen as an activity which employs common psychological principles. The behaviorally oriented therapists are already liberally and effectively tapping this resource, and Goldstein et al. (1966) have pointed to many additional points of convergence from a social psychological frame of reference. According to this trend, psychotherapy is viewed simply as a special case of the more general area of interpersonal behavior; therefore, the principles governing psychotherapy are intrinsically no different from those operating in other human relationships (Cartwright, 1968; Rogers et al., 1967; Truax & Carkhuff, 1967; Matarazzo et al., 1965; Alexander, 1963).

Research in psychotherapy has often played a confirmatory function in the sense of documenting clinical assertions and practices (exemplified by Rogers & Dymond, 1954); it has brought the field within the framework of scientific investigation and infused it with the credo of science; and it has begun, in a preliminary way, to test in the laboratory processes which some day may have therapeutic applications. However, it has yet to provide the clinician with new tools, insights, and recommendations he can put to practical use; and thus far it has proved unequal to the challenge of answering crucial questions, such as those dealing with the relative effectiveness of different techniques, their range and limits of applications, kinds of changes conceivably produced by different techniques, and the like.

3. The last question has in part been answered by the preceding discussion. Colby (1962) views the scientist's job as one of elucidating "acute difficulties in the art." He states:

> [The clinician] wants help with failures, with troubles, with lapses from the expected. . . . Guided by the artisan, a scientist must select a certain crucial problem in the art and judge whether the problem is ready and accessible to a systematic inquiry using currently available procedures. A scientist hopes to reduce the degree of (blind) empiricism in the art by finding that some acute problem in it can be solved through understanding an underlying explanatory principle (p. 95).

What acute problems can future psychotherapy research profitably elucidate? Colby (personal communication), in keeping with his views expressed elsewhere (see Footnote 2), sees considerable promise in individualized measures for each patient, which in turn are an aspect of intensive designs:

> We are not trying to solve the problem of justified inductive generalization. Physics, chemistry and medicine (e.g., heart transplants in single patients) progressed without representativeness of samples. They relied on repeatability of observations by independent observers and the development of a series of cases one by one. The population of observations we should be interested in at this time is a series of single case populations. It is hopeless to seek to generalize about 'all' patients. No 'all' exists about anything.

Thus, there is considerable controversy concerning optimum procedures for advancing knowledge in this exceedingly complex area of investigation. At the same time it is clear that a very considerable amount of research effort has been invested in this field which of necessity will influence and guide subsequent work. In the following sections we shall therefore attempt to present a broad overview of major variables, measures, and research techniques which have been brought to bear on the problems in this domain.

Variables, Measures, and Procedures

Therapist's Personality. With the advent of more sophisticated conceptions of psychotherapy it has become almost axiomatic that the relationship between patient and therapist is interactive. Thus, techniques, regardless of the underlying theory, cannot be regarded as operating in a vacuum but they are almost inextricably intertwined with the therapist's personality. Thus, in defining the nature of the therapeutic influence, it is incumbent upon the researcher to assess the contribution of the therapist's personality to the therapeutic relationship and its outcome.[4] During the past two decades a sizable number of studies bearing upon this problem have been carried out (for more extensive reviews see Bergin, 1967a; Bordin, 1968; Gardner, 1964; Strupp, 1962); however, with the rise of behavior therapy and its relative deemphasis on therapist variables, this body of work has not kept apace with contributions in other areas of psychotherapy research. Furthermore, it has become clear that, while the therapist's personality is a potent force, it seems to account for only a small portion of the variance in therapy outcomes, as currently defined and measured.

Personality Characteristics. Holt and Luborsky (1958) isolate three sets of variables considered desirable in the psychotherapist: (1) genuineness vs. facade; (2) social adjustment with co-workers; and (3) freedom from status-mindedness. In addition, self-objectivity (akin to self-insight), mature heterosexual adjustment and adequate emotional control were mentioned as promising variables. Krasner (1963) listed several dozen laudatory characteristics which the "ideal" therapist, according to various authors, is supposed to possess. No human being obviously can be such a paragon of virtues. Therefore, it is questionable whether the concept of the "ideal therapist" has much practical meaning (Goldstein et al., 1966, p. 190). Nor do general personality variables seem to have much bearing on the quality of the therapeutic relationship, a conclusion drawn by Gardner (1964) from several studies in which a large number of personality variables were correlated with the quality of the therapeutic relationship. Studies in which therapist personality characteristics were measured in the context of the therapeutic interaction, as will be seen, have shown greater promise.

Warmth, Acceptance, Empathy. Deriving from Rogers' formulations, warmth, acceptance, empathy, effort to understand, spontaneity, and related variables have been studied extensively (Raush & Bordin, 1957; Truax & Carkhuff, 1967). Truax's Accurate Empathy Scale has emerged as one of the popular measures. He defines accurate empathy as ". . . sensitivity to current feelings and the verbal facility to communicate this understanding in a language attuned to the client's current being." Empathy is judged directly from tape recordings by two or more raters. This and other measures of empathy have been utilized in studies which all demonstrate a positive correlation between therapist empathy, patient self-exploration, and independent criteria of patient change.

Another important finding (Truax & Carkhuff, 1967) is that empathy, warmth, etc. are created by the therapist and largely independent of patient

4. It must be considered that therapy is a transaction in which the patient may also affect and change the therapist. No one seems to have studied this problem in a systematic way.

characteristics, a result supporting the earlier research of Fiedler (1950a, 1950b, 1951), which has never been adequately replicated. Truax & Carkhuff also conclude that therapist variables, besides those investigated by them, may contribute equally to therapeutic outcomes. In the light of this evidence, empathy, acceptance, and warmth are best viewed as necessary but not sufficient conditions, a position at variance with that of Rogers (1957). Similarly, Wallerstein (1966), commenting on Frank's (1961) important stress on the therapist's ability to instill faith, confidence, and hope in his patients, stated that there is no evidence that these variables are the only, or even the most important ones. The evidence, however, strongly suggests that some therapists are more effective than others—they seem to have greater "penetrance"—and one essential difference may lie along one of the foregoing dimensions.

Therapist Types, Styles, and Values. The notion of therapist "types" (called *A* and *B*) dates from the studies of Whitehorn & Betz (1954; 1960). Therapists who were successful with schizophrenic patients *(A)* apparently placed technical considerations in the service of a truly colloborative relationship with the patient, which in turn produced favorable therapeutic results. Missing, unfortunately, were concrete data on the implementation of the relationship as well as the patient's perceptions of the therapist and the therapeutic experience. Moreover, the criterion of improvement was relatively gross, and the statistical analyses were carried out on secondary data. Subsequent work with this typology became anchored to a scale derived from the Strong Vocational Interest Blank. McNair et al. (1962) found *B* therapists to be more effective with neurotic patients. Carson (1967) in a critical review of this literature appraises the *A-B* dimension as "a very useful organizing framework for exploring important process-outcome relationships in the psychological treatment of behavior disorders" (p. 53). Of special interest is the apparent relationship of the *A-B* dimension to cognitive styles (psychological differentiation), as defined by Witkin and his group (Pollack & Kiev, 1963; Shows & Carson, 1966).

The problems of therapeutic styles, as reflected in preferred practices, approaches to specific problems in therapy, and the like have been studied by numerous authors (McNair & Lorr, 1964; Sundland & Barker, 1962; Wallach & Strupp, 1964). Factor analysis of a series of statements expressing therapists' views on a given therapeutic issue was the preferred technique in this work. Despite some apparent differences, the factor structures emerging from these studies have shown notable resemblence. A major dimension was represented by the degree to which therapy was viewed as a technical procedure over which the therapist exercises control ("analytic" in a broad sense) versus a conception of therapy as an experiential process whose unfolding the therapist facilitates. *The available evidence suggests that a small number of dimensions is adequate to characterize the therapist's approach to the treatment process.* Another promising line of investigation has been pursued by Rice (1965) who approached the problem of therapist style in terms of such variables as voice quality, freshness of words and word combinations, vocal modulation, and the like. Isolating three types of therapists, she found that fresh connotative language and expressive voice quality tended to be associated with more favorable treatment outcomes.

Therapists' values, a problem related to the work on therapist types, have been the subject of several investigations (Buhler, 1962; Mayfield, 1962; Seward, 1962; Welkowitz, Cohen, & Ortmeyer, 1967), some of which have employed Morris' Ways to Live Scale as a measure. (For a recent review of this area, see Kessel & McBrearty, 1967). Rosenthal (1955) showed that patients who improved in therapy tended to revise certain of their moral values in the direction of the therapist's values. The research of Bandura and his group (Bandura, 1965) clearly suggests that part of the therapeutic influence involves modeling and imitation. However, much work needs to be done to explore the potentialities and limits of this process (Goldstein et al., 1966).

Therapist–Patient Similarity. Bergin (1967a) concludes from a review of a number of studies bearing on this topic that there is as yet much speculation and little hard evidence. Bordin (1968), in a similar vein, comments on the related question of patient-therapist compatibility: "Presumably, a patient is not functioning successfully either interpersonally or intrapersonally. If we say that he and his therapist are compatible because they now function similarly, are we saying either that the patient is already a very successful person or that his therapist is really a patient? If the former, then there seems little room for improvement. If the latter, can we expect the blind to lead the blind?" This problem area is obviously in need of better conceptualization.

Perhaps a concept of therapist-patient *pairing* would be more appropriate. Research might then focus on which specific therapist characteristics are more often related to positive outcome with regard to specific client characteristics. Thus, for example, it might be found that clients who score low on a dominance scale, show the highest probability of improvement with a therapist who scores at a moderate level on the same scale but a lower probability of improvement with therapists who score high and low. Complex contingencies might then be developed for stating given probabilities of improvement by including in the matrix a larger number of personality dimensions. This would avoid the pitfalls of global measures of personality and would also resolve the dilemmas that arise when the concept of similarity is invoked.

Interest and Liking. The hypothesis that the therapist's interest and liking may be a therapeutic factor has produced contradictory evidence (McNair, Lorr, & Callahan, 1963; Stoler, 1963; Waskow, 1963). Very likely, neither variable bears a straight-line relationship to therapeutic outcomes. On the other hand, it seems safe to predict that therapists who actively dislike certain patients will not work well with them (Strupp, 1960; Strupp & Williams, 1960).

Countertransference. While sketchy and suffering from severe methodological difficulties, evidence in this area (Bandura, 1956; Bandura et al., 1960; Cutler, 1958; Fiedler, 1951; Heller, Myers, & Kline, 1963; Murray, 1956; Winder et al., 1962) generally suggests that therapist conflicts in relation to hostility, dependency, warmth, and intimacy, etc. have an inhibiting effect upon the patient's performance in therapy. Other studies (Strupp, 1958; Strupp & Wallach, 1965) have shown that therapists respond differentially to a particular patient (presented by means of a sound film analogue), and that their attitudes toward the patient are intertwined with their diagnostic and prognostic formulations as well as the degree of empathy shown in their communications. The extent to which such therapist reactions influence outcome is still an open question, although the dependent variables (client process measures) assessed in these studies are quite similar to some that have been shown to correlate with independent outcome indices.

Therapist Experience Level. Experience is not strictly a personality variable, nor has it been possible so far to study systematically effects of the therapist's experience on outcome. Apart from the fact that experience is a global term (including training, maturation, personal therapy, etc.), sizable samples of experienced therapists have not been available to researchers. Indeed, many findings in the entire area are based on the performance of neophytes who often fail to merit the appellation "psychotherapist." Investigations bearing on this variable not unexpectedly favor experienced therapists (Ashby, Ford, Guerney, & Guerney, 1957; Bohn, 1965; Cartwright & Vogel, 1960; Fiedler, 1950a, 1950b; Rice, 1965; Strupp, 1955b), but it remains to be demonstrated how experience and its dimensions heighten therapeutic competence.

Theoretical Orientation. Relationships between the therapist's theoretical orientation and practices have been demonstrated in a number of studies (Strupp, 1962), but there is little evidence on the association of either variable to independently assessed personality dimensions. We may speculate that predilection for a given theoretical orientation is partly a function of important personality variables (see the earlier discussion on the "analytic" vs. "experiential" dimension), and it may be possible to undergird the more or less haphazard self-selection process in therapy training by encouraging candidates exhibiting particular personality trends to seek therapeutic training along specific dimensions.

Conclusions and Recommendations. 1. Evidence documented by research as well as clinical observation leaves no doubt that the person of the therapist, in both a positive and negative sense, represents an important force in the therapeutic encounter. Client-centered therapists have placed personal qualities of the therapist on a pedestal, whereas psychoanalysts and behavior therapists have accorded them relatively scant attention. The route by which therapist personality factors enter and influence technical operations, however, needs to be mapped out much more thoroughly. At present it is not at all clear how therapist personality and technical operations are to be differentiated, yet separation of these strands is an important research task which might be greatly aided by collaborative endeavors.

2. Prominently researched personality dispositions of the therapist include such variables as empathy, warmth, and genuineness. Measurement of these variables has met with fair success. Contrary to earlier contentions, however, they can not be regarded as the sole, or even the major, factor determining therapeutic outcome. It seems more reasonable to conclude that once the therapist has achieved a fair level of therapeutic skills and is successful in providing a modicum of warmth, empathy, etc., outcome is more importantly a function of technical competence and patient characteristics. The therapeutic effects of empathy and warmth *per se* appear to be circumscribed, except in the possible event that a specifiable subset of clinic clients are significantly helped by a warm and emphatic relationship as such. If such is the case, it is possible that for them therapist relationship variables can account for most of the variance in outcome—a speculative but real possibility.

3. Effects of personality conflicts, needs, and attitudes of the therapist toward the patient have been investigated in a variety of studies, and while some evidence exists that these variables have significant effects, sweeping generalizations are decidedly premature. Patient personality characteristics also demonstrably influence the therapist's effectiveness, which provides support for the conclusion that patients must be selected more carefully to match the therapist's capabilities. Therapists appear to be differentially effective with particular patient groups; however, thus far it has not been possible to isolate salient dimensions. Work along these lines has been hampered by the general unavailability of adequate samples of experienced therapists, who clearly are the ones to study, not beginners, on whose performance many of the findings reported in the literature are unfortunately based. Progress will be limited until this situation is remedied.

4. From problems and variables in this area the following growing edges may be identified:

(*a.*) Since therapists appear to be differentially successful in their ability to influence patients, the personality characteristics potentiating this influence are urgently in need of more exhaustive study. The ability to instill trust, confidence, and faith has frequently been mentioned, but has eluded quantification.

(*b.*) The extent to which the therapist's values, attitudes, and behaviors can serve as models to be emulated by the patient, and the process by which the patient modifies himself in accordance with these variables should be studied more closely. Laboratory and analogue studies appear more fruitful in this connection than research involving naturalistic observation.

(*c.*) Further research to identify therapist's cognitive styles (along the lines of the *A-B* dimension) appears promising.

(*d.*) Since therapist types appear to be reducible to a few salient dimensions, refinement of these typologies seems indicated.

(*e.*) Scales measuring warmth, empathy, and genuineness are now available, and assessment of these variables in experimental studies is considered essential. Specific assessments of selected therapist dimensions in general appear to be a more promising approach than global personality evaluations.

Techniques

Research dealing with the problem of techniques is basic to the area of psychotherapy research since it deals with the crucial question of how one person, through planful interventions, influences the behavior of another. Techniques clearly are not applied in a vacuum but must take into account (*a*) individual differences among the persons to be influenced (patients); (*b*) individual differences among the persons transmitting the influence through a set of technical operations (the therapist in conjunction with his techniques); and (*c*) social, interpersonal, and situational variables, including for example the way in which the therapeutic situation is structured by the therapist, the patient's amenability to psychological influence at a given point in time, the quality of the relationship between the two participants, and the like (Sarason, 1965, p. 233). Techniques in psychotherapy, therefore, represent only one class of independent variables, though a significant one.

Research on techniques may be divided into two broad areas: (*a*) investigations which focus on the naturally occurring events in psychotherapy (a form of guided naturalistic observation); and (*b*) investigations in which technique variables are manipulated experimentally. The former area, historically the older, has been advanced through the development of systems of content-analysis.

Content-analysis. As an indication of the growing significance of content-analysis, the first major review of this area (Auld & Murray, 1955) covered about 100 references, the second (Marsden, 1965) approximately twice that number. Additional reviews have been contributed, among others, by Dittes, 1959; Matarazzo, 1962; Pool, 1959; and Strupp, 1962. Within the confines of this discussion it is possible to provide only the most cursory summary of the complex issues, methodological problems, and substantive yields.

The so-called classical model of content-analysis was defined by Berelson (1952) as "a research technique for the objective, systematic, and quantitative description of the manifest content of communication." This approach assumes that the frequency of occurrence of a given communication content is highly correlated with intensity, hence an important index of its importance. The assumption is clearly open to challenge on numerous grounds. The "classical" model, which places a premium on objectivity, has been contrasted with the "pragmatic" model which attempts to achieve psychological meaningfulness through direct quantification of complex clinical constructs. A third variant, the nonquantitative technique is exemplified by linguistic analysis, in which notable advances, though not bearing directly on psychotherapy research, have been made (Marsden, 1965).

Among the older systems, several of which originated within the client-centered framework, the following achieved prominence: Porter (1943a, 1943b) and Snyder (1945) developed systems for classifying therapist as well as client communications, which were employed in a number of studies. Haigh (1949) developed a measure of defensiveness. A general system of interaction process analysis, one of whose virtues is theoretical neutrality, is the system of Bales (1950). Derived from Hull's learning theory were the Discomfort-Relief Quotient (DRQ) (Dollard & Mowrer, 1953) and the Positive-Negative-Ambivalent Quotient (PNAvQ) developed by Raimy (1948). Of more recent vintage are the systems of Matarazzo (1962), Strupp (1957), Leary & Gill (1959), and Gendlin, Beebe, Cassens, Klein, & Oberlander (1968). The majority of the systems fall within the "classical" model.

Research problems to which these systems have been addressed have included the description of patient behavior, therapist behavior, patient-therapist interaction, as well as inferences concerning internal, psychodynamic states, notably within patients.

With respect to patient behavior, researchers have been interested in demonstrating therapeutic movement toward "psychological health," as shown by changes in the patient's self-concept (Dollard & Mowrer, 1953; Raimy, 1948), greater openness to experiencing (Rogers et al., 1967), depth and meaningfulness of self-exploration (Truax, 1961), and the like. In general, these studies have yielded quantitative confirmation of the theoretical position from which they originated. Researchers have also succeeded in differentiating successful from less successful cases (Rogers, 1959, 1961) and to predict outcome on the basis of the patient's manner of verbalization in early interviews (Rice, 1965). Unclarities about outcome criteria have generally hampered these efforts.

Research focusing on patient behavior unrelated to treatment outcomes, mediated by a system of content-analysis focused on certain formal, nonlexical dimensions, has been carried out by Matarazzo, Saslow and their associates (Matarazzo, 1962; Matarazzo, Hess, & Saslow, 1962). Matarazzo's work is based upon the use of the interaction chronograph, developed by Chapple, and the latter's theoretical notion that time relationships in human interactions provide useful clues to the nature of the relationship between the participants. Since in this research program the behavior of the interviewer was varied systematically and treated as an independent variable, these investigations are equally germane to the experimental studies discussed below. In their early studies these workers found marked stability of interviewee behavior, but significant changes were observed as a function of planned variations in the behavior of the interviewer. More recently this group (Matarazzo, Wiens, Matarazzo, & Saslow, 1968) has tested their earlier measures in seven cases of freely occurring psychotherapy. Hypotheses deriving from this work are currently being tested under controlled experimental conditions (Matarazzo, personal communication).

Another prominent research effort involving nonlexical measures is exemplified by the work of Mahl (1960, 1968) which has dealt with the quantification of speech disturbances. Mahl believes that nonlexical content-analysis systems may be more fruitful in studying emotional states than systems based on lexical content alone.

A potentially fruitful line of investigation, which apparently has not been pursued vigorously, was initiated by Lorenz & Cobb (1954) and Lorenz (1955). Using word-count procedures, these investigators succeeded in differentiating major diagnostic groups. The importance of this work lies in the effort to provide operational definitions of diagnostic groupings which, at least in principle, seem to be of greater value than the traditional labels for designating them.

Turning to therapist characteristics, objective differences in theoretical orientation, experience level, and related attributes have been studied by Strupp in a series of investigations (1955a, 1955b, 1955c). This work was initially based on Bales' systems of interaction process analysis and subsequently on a newly developed system (Strupp, 1957). In addition to a number of substantive findings, this approach demonstrated the feasibility of comparing techniques of therapists adhering to different theoretical orientations.

Such differentiations of therapist behaviors deriving from diverse theories is crucial for specifying (*a*) the extent to which techniques actually differ, and (*b*) the ultimate effects of such differences on outcome. While it has been possible to demonstrate differences between some techniques both in analogue studies and actual therapy interviews, this area of inquiry remains primitive by comparison with what is needed in order to specify particular techniques for particular problems. Nevertheless this work has contributed empirical evidence of differences between therapists varying in level of experience, theoretical orientation, professional affiliation, personal analysis, empathy, and the like. Further references and suggestions will be found in our discussion of trends, patient variables, outcome, and research designs.

The concept of "depth of interpretation" has been the locus of interest in the work of the Michigan research group (Bordin, Cutler, Dittmann, Harway, Raush, & Rigler, 1954; Bordin, 1955; Cutler, Bordin, Williams, & Rigler, 1958; Harway, Dittmann, Raush, Bordin, & Rigler, 1955). This research, in the course of which a number of process correlates of "depth" have been explored, is clearly one of the promising departures for measuring therapeutic operations and their effects upon client behavior and ultimate change.

Significant contributions to the measurement of therapist activity were also made by Lennard & Bernstein (1960), who developed a "specificity" scale consisting of 8 categories designed to measure the extent to which the therapist "tends to place limits upon the array of verbal responses from which the patient may choose," and Howe & Pope (1961a, 1961b), whose work was concerned with the investigation of therapist activity level and its dimensionality.

Noteworthy among research dealing with interactional systems are numerous investigations based on Bales' 12 categories (see Marsden, 1965, for references). The system, despite its utility in quantifying verbal interaction, particularly in small groups, seems too general for most purposes of psychotherapy research. Small group theory also was the point of departure for a major research effort by Lennard & Bernstein (1960), who analyzed in detail patient-therapist interactions. The usefulness of the Type-Token Ratio, employed in a series of investigations by Jaffe (1957, 1961) and its heuristic value for understanding patient-therapist interactions must still be considered an open question. (See also Jaffe, 1966, for a discussion of linguistic analysis.)

Extensive research involving complex constructs, exemplifying the "pragmatic model," based on the psychoanalytic theory of defense mechanisms, affects, and primary and secondary process has been carried out by Gottschalk and his associates (Gottschalk, Gleser, & Springer, 1963). Prominent in this work has been the development of scales designed to measure anxiety, hostility, and intrapersonal conflict. Coding reliability, based on grammatical clauses as the unit of analysis, has proven quite satisfactory (in the .80's); validity data have also been reported.

Similarly, a complex system for scoring dynamic motives has been developed by Dollard & Auld (1959), of which the work by Murray (1956) was a precursor. Salient findings resulting from this work include the demonstration that analytically oriented therapists are more likely to intervene following resistances than at other times and that interpretations were not followed by increased resistance.

Another pragmatic model system emerged from the research of Haggard and his research group (Sklansky, Isaacs, & Haggard, 1960; Sklansky, Isaacs, Levitov, & Haggard, 1966). These workers also started from analytic concepts and developed an interactional system which proved useful for studying the manifest and latent meaning of patient communications in relation to certain aspects of therapists' communications.

Indirectly related to research involving content-analysis are recent efforts to differentiate on the basis of quantitative measures "productive" from "nonproductive" therapy hours (Orlinsky & Howard, 1967; Auerbach, in progress; Strupp, Chassan, & Ewing, 1966). While the long-range utility of this research is difficult to assess, it may form a link between relatively global process measures and therapeutic outcomes.

Research dealing with the analysis of linguistic, paralinguistic, kinesic, and other modes of communication has been contributed by Pittenger, Hockett, & Danehy (1960), whose analysis of the first five minutes of an initial interview filled a fair-sized book; McQuown (1957); Dittmann & Wynne (1961); Scheflen (1963); Birdwhistell (1960); and Dittmann (1962). Despite noteworthy advances in this area, progress has been slow, partly because of the tremendous amount of tedious effort required in dealing with microscopic interview segments; it exceeds considerably the time needed for analyzing communication content by the classical and pragmatic models, which in itself is far from inconsequential. It would be premature to venture a prediction whether the potential yield, particularly in linguistic analysis, justifies the investment; however, it is reasonably clear that spectacular breakthroughs are not immediately in the offing.

Interactional systems are in general preferable to those in which only therapist or patient characteristics are assessed, because they begin to specify effects of particular therapeutic interventions upon patient behavior. Examples of promising systems are: Matarazzo et al. (1965); Lennard & Bernstein (1960); Bordin et al. (1954); Gottschalk, Winget, Gleser, & Springer (1966); Dollard & Auld (1959); Haggard & Isaacs (1966). The advantages of these systems are seen in the fact that (*a*) they are based on careful development over a period of years; (*b*) their reliability and to some extent their validity has been studied extensively; (*c*) their focus is upon salient aspects of the therapeutic interaction (including lexical content, internal states, noncontent variables, and other system components). Hence the combination of different systems in research designed to compare different forms of psychotherapy may broaden and enrich considerably the quantitative analyses. Thus far, very few studies have applied different systems to identical interview materials, nor have extensive comparisons of different forms of therapy been made (see, however, Gottschalk, 1961; Gottschalk & Auerbach, 1966, for a beginning in this direction). *We believe the heuristic value of different systems can be effectively explored through research in which the systems mentioned above* (and possibly others) *are systematically applied to the same interview material and their respective yield is scrutinized.*

Even under propitious circumstances, however, progress along these lines will be circumscribed because of numerous methodological difficulties. The problem of agreeing on appropriate units of analyses is only one obvious impediment. If the researcher focuses on microscopic units (e.g., a grammatical clause or a phrase), the immediate reaction of the patient to a given therapist intervention cannot be accepted as a valid index of the effect produced by that intervention. When larger segments (e.g., a single hour) are chosen as the unit, it becomes virtually impossible to make inferences about the effects of specific interventions.

Another serious technical problem concerns the assessment of latent motives and meanings (Dollard & Auld, 1959). Just as a dream cannot be accepted at face value, so the patient's verbal communications in therapy are merely a starting point for grasping the nature of the difficulties with which he is struggling. Quantifications which are restricted to surface meanings of communications may be superficial and perhaps even grossly misleading. "Depth" interpretations, on the other hand, must necessarily go beyond the atomistic units of single communications and take into account context, nonverbal cues, etc. Thus, objectivity is exceedingly hard to achieve.

The general problem is one of delineating a growth process by making cross sectional measurements. However, by taking repeated measures it may gradually be possible to pinpoint the process through procedures analogous to slow-motion techniques. No investigator working in this area has illusions about the formidable amount of effort required to push the frontiers ahead, and it is probably this realization that has extinguished the efforts of many but the most intrepid workers.

A word should be said about the contributions of psychophysiological studies to the psychotherapeutic process and outcome. The steadily growing literature and the methodological intricacies in this area of research have been incisively discussed by Lacey (1959). In numerous studies, measures of autonomic and skeletal-motor functions (e.g., heart rate, skin temperature, muscle potentials, and skin resistance) have been used as indicators of arousal or affect in therapeutic or quasi-therapy situations. Akin in some respects to lie-detection procedures, these measures have been employed as allegedly objective indicators of focal conflict areas, the influence of the therapist's communications on the patient's affective state, qualitative changes in the patient-therapist relationship, etc. While autonomic and skeletal-motor responses are indeed sensitive indicators, they are highly variable and do not have simple meanings that can readily serve as bases for making inferences concerning the psychological aspects of the therapeutic transaction. Nor can somatic changes occurring in therapy be used as criteria for the effectiveness of therapy, either in the therapeutic situation or outside. Lacey argues convincingly that reliance cannot be placed on single physiological variables, and that at present we have only a very inadequate understanding of the principles underlying the patterning of somatic responses. Discounting the heuristic value of such traditional concepts as homeostasis, arousal, sympathetic vs. parasympathetic function, Lacey believes that researchers desiring to forge a link between psychotherapy and psychophysiology should search for new concepts, such as visceral afferent feedback, to guide their investigations. Evidence of significant breakthroughs from this quarter are as yet not discernible. Working along somewhat different lines, however, Knapp, Mushatt, & Nemetz (1966) have done important pioneer work in establishing relationships between psychological observations in psychoanalytic interviews, biochemical data (adrenal steroids and catecholamines), and physiological observations of patients suffering from bronchial asthma.

Experimental manipulations of technique. Whereas the considerable body of research involving systems of content-analysis has been heavily influenced by client-centered and psychoanalytic theory, the impetus for experimental manipulations of specified technique variables has come from researchers favoring behavioral approaches. The former kind of research has almost exclusively been performed *in situ,* whereas the latter not infrequently has employed therapeutic analogues, which tend to shade into other areas of psychology (for example, problems of attitude change, and the like).

The work by Matarazzo and his collaborators is an outstanding illustration of the manipulation of selected formal characteristics of the interview situation. In essence, these investigators programmed certain noncontent aspects of the verbal behavior of the interviewer. In addition to a number of studies involving laboratory-type situations, quantitative analyses have also been conducted on actual therapy interviews. Matarazzo et al. (1965) conclude that "noncontent measures, either alone or, more likely, in combination with content-derived psychotherapy measures, appear to have a higher than average probability of furthering our understanding of 'process' and related psychotherapy phenomena" (p. 209).

The burgeoning literature on verbal conditioning is supported by the following claims advanced by its proponents (Krasner, 1965): "Verbal conditioning is a major part of traditional psychotherapy; verbal conditioning is a 'treatment' procedure in its own right" (p. 226). Originally, this work had as its aim the reinforcement of all emotional words through minimal social approval, such as head-nodding, smiling, "mm-hmm," and "good." Subsequently, research became concerned with verbal conditioning as a direct form of psychotherapy. Among the topics investigated, Krasner (1965) lists: effects of examiner differences, effects of instructional sets, generalization effects, atmosphere effects, relationships to other behavior influence situations such as hypnosis, and others. In the same paper Krasner emphasizes the similarities between verbal conditioning and psychotherapy as opposed to differences that had been stressed by Luborsky & Strupp (1962). Apart from a large number of substantive contributions, this form of research has systematically focused on the effects of a variety of technical operations. There is still considerable doubt about the extent to which verbal conditioning plays a *major* role in effecting personality and behavior change in psychotherapy.

In the context of social reinforcement procedures, a broad cross section of which is reported in a collection of papers edited by Krasner & Ullmann (1965), the work by Bandura and his group (Bandura, 1965) demonstrates convincingly the heuristic (and within limits, the therapeutic) value of modeling procedures and vicarious learning in behavior modification. This work is rich in implications for psychotherapy research, and the finding that film-mediated human models can be as effective as real-life models in modifying responses may lead to greater utilization of this medium in psychotherapy research. There can be little question that the therapist, as part of this repertoire, models attitudes and behaviors which are learned by the patient. Further systematic research designed to explore the limits as well as the permanence of changes effected by these techniques is clearly called for, and may be facilitated by coordinated efforts.

The recent work on computer simulation by Colby (1967) and Bellman, Friend, & Kurland (1966) represents a unique effort to bring relevant variables in the patient-therapist interaction under the control of the researcher. These investigators are keenly aware of the early state of this art, whose ultimate promise cannot possibly be assessed.

Research involving the experimental manipulation of techniques subtly shades into principles governing behavior change. In a recent annual review of the literature, Ford & Urban (1967) differentiate and document such processes as insight, desensitization, extinction, avoidance conditioning, social modeling, and various situational manipulations. They favor the hypothesis that "different kinds of responses may be governed by different principles and may require different procedures for their modification" (p. 345). In addition to the more systematically explored techniques and methods for specifying them, there is of course the welter of poorly differentiated technical operations which traditionally have characterized the craft of psychotherapy. The foregoing review indicates that research thus far has failed to assess the differential effects and utility of different techniques under stated conditions. Paul's (1966) work, aimed at comparing different techniques in treating fear of public speaking, is an important, though hardly conclusive, beginning in this direction.

Conclusions and Recommendations. 1. It is amply apparent that the traditional appellations ("client-centered," "psychoanalytic," etc.) provide only the grossest information about a technique. Furthermore, assertions that all forms of psychotherapy include large "nonspecific" components or that they are a function of "placebo effects" add little to our knowledge about the nature of the therapeutic influence mediated by the therapist, unless they can be more precisely measured and separated from other influences. In the same manner, the concept of a "good" or "ideal" therapeutic relationship must be dissected into its operative components before the term acquires heuristic value. There is by now general agreement, well documented by the studies to which reference has been made, that the therapeutic procedures and effects in all therapeutic systems are broad-gauged rather than specific. Ford & Urban (1963) state: "When one examines the descriptions of how free association, inquiry, or relationship are implemented, one finds these conceptual labels refer to fairly elaborate sets of procedures. Each is not an operation, but a whole set of interrelated events. . . . Thus, speaking about technique in such general terms tends to obscure the heterogeneity of procedures actually used and reduces the precision with which therapeutic operations can be communicated to others" (pp. 675–77).

It appears that the mainstream of contemporary research on therapeutic techniques is designed to remedy this situation by insisting on greater specificity. It is also increasingly recognized that specific techniques do not operate under all conditions; rather, they are situationally determined, and their range of applicability, particularly with reference to specific patient states, must be made explicit.

2. A vast amount of research has been focused on the analysis of both verbal and nonverbal interview content. This work has proceeded on the reasonable assumption that psychotherapy must be understood in terms of the ongoing interaction between the two participants, and that it is possible to isolate salient elements of the therapeutic influence from the communication content. The second approach, favored by behavior therapists and others sympathetic to this viewpoint, has involved the construction of laboratory or quasi-therapy situations in which one mechanism has been manipulated systematically. A major difficulty in this second approach is that its relevance to psychotherapy has not always been clear, nor is the translation of laboratory-based research to the complexities of the therapeutic situation as simple and straightforward as has sometimes been assumed.

3. *On balance we lean toward the conclusion that controlled experimen-*

tation with specifiable methods of influence (Goldstein et al., 1966) *has a brighter future than the "therapy-centered" approach, which takes the uncontrolled events in therapy as the starting point. This conclusion is broadly supported by the conceptualization of psychotherapy as a learning process, and a growing conviction that the full implications of this view are best implemented through experimentation designed to make explicit the instrumentalities and conditions of therapeutic learning.*

If psychotherapy is viewed as a learning process, then principles of learning at all levels apply, and research dealing with problems of learning in the various areas of psychology must be used to illuminate the processes involved. Conversely, psychotherapy may enrich these areas since the psychotherapy situation represents a unique laboratory situation for studying personality and behavior change. Because many problems with which psychotherapy is concerned are considerably more complex than those in other areas of learning, great care must be taken to design experiments which are maximally relevant to the therapeutic enterprise. In practice, this has been quite difficult.

The above recommendation, however, should not be construed as a facile dismissal of the very substantial contributions made by content-analysis and related approaches. These studies represent a refined form of naturalistic observation guided by techniques that over the past two decades have become increasingly sophisticated. The contributions of the ethologists should serve as a warning that experimentation in contemporary psychology continually runs the danger of oversimplification. This danger is inherent in all laboratory research in which one principle may erroneously become elevated as the sole explanatory construct. It is likely that the patient-therapist interaction in psychotherapy is much too complex to yield to such approaches. Hence, it is considered advisable to complement controlled experimentation, salient examples of which have been cited, by continued naturalistic observation. Such studies should employ one of the more promising content-analysis schemes as a tool for exploring systematic relationships in the communications of the two participants, even if the resulting indices can not immediately be related to therapeutic outcomes.

4. To a large extent the future of psychotherapy hinges upon the refinement of existing techniques and the development of new ones. New techniques emerge from the context of discovery and have typically been evolved by clinicians working intensively with patients. The repertoire of the contemporary psychotherapist, however, includes an impressive list of techniques, which often are employed in combination but more or less intuitively and unsystematically. Reward and punishment, warmth, empathy, delay of gratification, modeling, desensitization, assertive training, interpre-

tation of unrecognized impulses and strivings, etc. are typical examples of widely employed and promising techniques. No form of psychotherapy can lay claim to using one technique exclusively, although schools of therapy differ in their relative emphases upon particular techniques. It is precisely in this area that research should play a significant part—through the execution of systematic and increasingly refined comparisons between different techniques in specified situations and the assessment of differential effects. For this reason, the comparative study of techniques and the application of methods for mediating such comparisons is given high priority by these reviewers. We also believe that collaborative efforts can make a signal contribution toward this goal.

Patient

The study of patient characteristics in relation to therapeutic change has, for the most part, focused around one basic issue: How do patient variables influence and predict the immediate reaction to and ultimate course of psychotherapy? We feel that this is not the most appropriate issue. The more significant question is: Which patient characteristics and problems are most amenable to which techniques conducted by which type of therapist in what type of setting? Thus, rather than the more common approach of trying to determine the type of patient or initial status which will respond best to a nebulous and heterogeneous definition of psychotherapy, it is more important to devise specific therapies that will change particular kinds of patients or problems. While it may seem totally obvious that differential initial status should be paired with differential treatment, there is hardly a program of research in existence which deals systematically with this problem.

It is true, as noted in our "trends" statement, that increasing numbers of therapists are experimenting with different techniques for different patients, and while these attempts are noteworthy and commendable, their intuitive and uncontrolled nature makes it impossible to draw conclusions regarding this most essential of questions. The best that can be done here is to: (1) briefly describe and evaulate the few exceptions where a differential approach is being attempted, (2) summarize the promising data on patient suitability and amenability for that undefinable influence process known as "traditional" psychotherapy, including evidence on patient-therapist pairing as a means of differentially applying therapist influence to diverse conditions in patients, and (3) briefly comment upon attempts to modify "traditional" therapy in order to adapt it to the needs and qualities of divergent patients.

DIFFERENTIAL EFFECTS OF DIFFERENT TECHNIQUES

Studies of the differential effects of different treatments are small in number. Where they do exist, they have nearly always been tested on a single type of patient or on one heterogeneous sample which has been randomly divided into two or more groups; and, even in these cases, the findings are nearly always ambiguous because of defects in design and control. The most that can be concluded at the present time from these inquiries is that:

1. There is currently no evidence that different types of patients or symptoms are differentially responsive to psychoanalytic, client-centered, or other common types of traditional therapy. This does not mean that such differences do not exist. If homogeneous versions of these methods were compared across different sets of patients, such differences might appear; but at present both the patient groups and the techniques used are too overlapping and heterogeneous to permit any conclusions whatsoever.

2. There is substantial evidence that patients suffering from conditioned avoidance responses respond more favorably to desensitization than to other techniques (e.g., Paul, 1966).

3. Other behavioral techniques, such as conditioned aversion, behavorial rehearsal, operant conditioning, etc. also appear to be significantly more effective than traditional procedures in modifying specific behaviors or focal symptoms; though the evidence favoring their superiority is less substantial than in the case of desensitization.

4. Behavioral techniques appear to vary in their effect on different problems, thus (*a*) desensitization may be more relevant to conditioned avoidance responses, (*b*) operant conditioning may be more relevant to instrumental responses at the level of motoric and simple symbolic behavior, (*c*) modeling may be more relevant to acquisition of complex responses, though not excluded from the other domains, and (*d*) aversion techniques may be more relevant to impulse control problems.

5. Criteria which measure the more subtle and complex affective and cognitive types of change presently reveal no significant differences between behavioral and other procedures.

One of the most promising lines of inquiry in this domain has been developed by Paul (1966, 1967), and by Marks and Gelder (Gelder, Marks, & Wolff, 1967). In their studies, psychoanalytically oriented therapy and desensitization have been compared. Marks and Gelder studied patients whose presenting symptoms included a main phobia, subsidiary phobias, anxiety and depression. Thus far, they find that desensitization is more effective in decreasing phobic responses of a specific or focal type, much as Paul found in his study; but that the differences between treatments wash out when patients with more complex symptoms or more severe anxiety are studied, or when criteria measuring anxiety and depression are used as outcome indices. While their studies lack elegance of measurement, are based upon work by inexperienced psychiatric residents, and have been severely criticized by behavior therapists, they are, along with Paul's work, illustrative of the very direction of movement in research and treatment which we consider to be of greatest significance.

PATIENT STABILITY AND AMENABILITY FOR TRADITIONAL THERAPIES

Since traditional therapies embrace diverse, and often contradictory, conditions, generalizations concerning which kinds of patients or symptoms respond best to them must necessarily be limited to findings that are sizeable and repeatedly confirmed. Such findings are most likely to be tapping common elements of the therapies that have potency in relation to the processes of change. Areas of investigation which reveal contradictory or tenuous information in relation to specific variables may still be tapping important phenomena, but they are probably specific to given procedures or therapists which are as yet unidentified. No conclusions or recommendations can, therefore, be made about them. The following discussion, thus focuses on patient variables which can presently be considered the most valid ones to use in setting up controls for research designs, in selecting patients for treatment experiments, and in measuring correlates of the change process.

Openness to Therapeutic Influence. It is often recognized that some patients are more "open" to therapeutic influence than others. Several lines of investigation converge in suggesting the importance of the patient's willingness to relate to his problems and to express himself with some depth of feeling as a predictor of positive movement in psychotherapy. The best measures of this characteristic have been derived from patient verbal behavior during initial interviews. They include: A complex scoring scheme for initial interviews devised by White, Fichtenbaum, & Dollard (1964), a similar but simpler and less well-substantiated system by Kirtner & Cartwright (1958), a Depth of Self Exploration Scale developed by Truax (Truax, 1962; Truax & Carkhuff, 1967), and a measure of client experiencing level (Rogers et al., 1967). These measures include reference to client characteristics or behaviors such as: willingness to express feelings vs. resistance, liking for the therapist and the therapy process, having and experiencing strong dependency needs, experiencing guilt and anxiety, sensing personal responsibility for problems, wanting help, avoiding a physiological focus on problems (White, Fichtenbaum, Cooper, & Dollard, 1966), attending to internal events, etc. It seems clear that these measures gain their value in part from being samples of *in vivo* behavior. It may therefore be desirable, for the purpose of obtaining such assessments, to accept patients for therapy on a trial basis, or to conduct initial intake interviews in a manner consistent with the needs for measurement.

Patient Attractiveness. While the therapist's technical expertise is important, it is equally clear that his personal reactions to the patient influence the course and outcome of therapy. It is apparent that a number of the variables noted above obtain their significance not only by their relationship to the effects of particular techniques but also by the fact that they determine how the therapist responds to them personally. In order to examine this question specifically, a global, dichotomous rating of attractiveness was devised by Nash, Hoehn-Saric, Battle, Stone, Imber, & Frank (1965), which yielded significantly different outcomes favoring the more attractive patients. Heller and Goldstein (1961) also report positive results using this variable. These measures are similar to rating scales that evaluate patient likability, a variable which has yielded contradictory results, but which generally indicates a more favorable prognosis for the more likable patients. No studies have separated the qualities and effects of such attractiveness measures from the motivational and behavioral qualities described under "openness to therapeutic influence," so it is presently unclear how interdependent these sets of measures are. This question is obviously a good one for further research.

Patient Relatability. In addition to facilitating engagement in the process of self evaluation and change, the preceding variables probably determine the extent to which a relationship is formed between therapist and patient. To the extent that the relationship itself is a therapeutic agent, this factor becomes crucial. Isaacs & Haggard (1966), using a TAT-derived measure of "relatability," found striking differences in outcome of patients rated high and low in this quality. Presumably, the differentiating power of this variable as well as the preceding ones could be enhanced by more carefully *pairing* patients and therapist in order to heighten the openness, attractiveness, and relatability of the patient (and possibly vice versa).

Patient-Therapist Similarity and Pairing: Personality. Cutler (1958) found that therapist responses to patient statements which were relevant to his conflict areas were judged less adequate than therapist responses to patient statements that were not relevant to the therapist's conflict areas. While no measure of patient conflicts was taken, it seems clear from these findings that a therapist paired with a patient whose conflicts were similar to his own would perform much less adequately than a therapist paired with a patient who had conflicts dissimilar to his own.

Bandura et al. (1960) found that therapists who were rated as having conflicts in the area of hostility tended to evade or avoid their clients expressions of hostility to a greater degree than therapists who were rated as having fewer hostility conflicts. Conversely, the therapists with fewer conflicts in the area of hostility tended to approach client verbalizations of hostility more frequently. Similar findings were obtained by Winder et al. (1962) in relation to dependency conflict. No attempts were made to measure patient conflict areas in these studies, but the findings have clear implications for patient-therapist matching. Conflict similarity has not yet been studied in relation to therapy outcome, and patient conflicts have not been measured in the same way as therapist conflicts. This variable is generally of sufficient apparent importance to warrant more vigorous study.

Dominance-submission has also been studied in relation to process and outcome (Swensen, 1967; Snyder, 1961; Plummer, 1966; Tuma & Gustad, 1957). The results have tended to indicate that there must be a complementarity of client and therapist (therapist dominant) on this dimension in order for the most favorable therapy relationship to develop; although there are enough questions about the data in these studies to make any conclusion tentative.

Although not a personality variable but rather a test, Schutz's Fundamental Interpersonal Relationships Orientation Inventory (FIRO-B), which deals with how one treats others and likes to be treated by others, appears to have a great deal of promise in matching patients and therapists. Since this instrument has been used successfully for pairing subjects so as to yield maximum conditioned response levels in an operant verbal conditioning procedure (Sapolsky, 1960, 1965) and since compatibility, as measured by this instrument, correlates positively with therapy outcome ratings of hospitalized psychiatric patients in individual therapy, this instrument will probably see continued profitable use.

Congruence in Patients' and Therapists' Expectations. This variable has been shown to be consistently related to the psychotherapy process (Lennard & Bernstein, 1960). Heine & Trosman (1960) and Overall & Aronson (1963) have found that congruence in what the patient expects of psychotherapy and what the therapist expects of it is positively related to continuation in therapy. Clemes & D'Andrea (1965) reported that patients who received an interview from a psychiatric resident compatible with their expectations were significantly less anxious than those who had an interview that conflicted with their expectations. Also, therapists indicated that the non-expected interviews were more difficult to conduct, and those patients having expectations congruent with those of other therapists remained longer in therapy. Two main types of patient expectation have been noted in this area of research. They have been characterized by Heine & Trosman as guidance expectation, or the expectancy of receiving advice and being told what to do, and participation expectation, which is the expectancy of taking an active role in the attempt to arrive at a solution to one's problems.

The type of findings obtained in this area of research have led at least two authors to propose that the patient is helped more when he receives therapy which is consistent with his expectations (Goin, Yamamoto, & Silverman, 1965; Levitt, 1966).

Despite findings that show consistently that congruence of patient and therapist expectations has a favorable effect upon the process and duration of therapy, it would be of value to know how congruence or discrepancy in expectation influences outcome measures. Also, these studies have more or less uniformly assumed that therapists are homogeneous with respect to the expectations they have of the therapy relationship and that it is the patients who have varying expectations. However, future designs should also measure how the therapist expects the patient and himself to behave towards each other. This should be done because many studies necessarily use beginning therapists whose expectations of the therapy relationship could possibly be as diverse as their own unique interpersonal experiences have been.

Socio-economic Class. Although this is generally not considered to be a similarity variable because there are no or very few lower-class therapists, and it is the difficulties in working with lower-class patients that have raised this issue, there is some justification for viewing this as a similarity variable. Many writers have noted the difficulty when patient and therapist are of a different socio-economic class (Hollingshead & Redlich, 1958; Strupp & Williams, 1960; Auld & Myers, 1954, etc.).

The variable of similarity in socio-economic class may come to have relevance to practice in view of the trend towards utilizing more lay therapists who could be of lower socio-economic class. Several studies have indicated that therapists of lower socio-economic class or educational level are as effective or more effective with lower-class patients than professionals (Poser, 1966; Deane & Ansbacher, 1962; Lohrenz, Hunter, & Schwartzman, 1966; Carkhuff & Truax, 1965). The results of one study (Keith-Spiegel & Spiegel, 1967) is especially interesting in this regard. They found that the higher the educational level of the patient, the more psychiatrists and psychologists were viewed as most helpful and the lower the educational level of the patient the more help was seen as having been given by aides and fellow patients. One male patient with a reported I.Q. of 83 is quoted as saying:

> My doctor was a nice enough guy but I never knew what the hell he was talking about. He didn't make no sense at all. Only time I felt better was when me and the boys would knock around our problems while playing pool (Cartwright, 1968, p. 397).

Studies of *A* and *B* therapists (Carson, 1967) also suggest that these therapists do better with patients that have interests and perhaps socio-economic backgrounds like their own. The study which could tell us whether similarity on the *A–B* variable is really related to outcome and to social class is yet to be done, so no definitive conclusions can yet be reached.

Similarity of Values. So far no consistent relationship of values similarity and process and outcome in psychotherapy has been observed. One of the difficulties in conducting research in this area appears to be that similarity in values may really have a great deal to do with similarity in mental health. Thus the two variables of values and mental health are too easily confounded.

A refinement that could be added at small cost in any future designs investigating patient-therapist matching for similarity would be to measure the patient's perception of the similarity or compatibility of himself and the therapist in addition to using objective test measures. The reason for including this additional measure would be that the patient's perception or experience of the conditions in the therapy relationship many times seems more highly correlated with outcome measures than do "objective" ratings by an outside observer. For example, in the work by Sapolsky (1960), much higher correlations between patient perception of similarity to his therapist and ultimate outcome were obtained than between therapist perception of similarity and outcome. Overall & Aronson found that the degree of discrepancy between expectations of the initial interview and patient description of the interview was a better predictor of continuance in therapy than the discrepancy between patient expectations and therapist description of the interview. In the same vein, a third study by Feitel (1968) showed that a patient's rating of feeling understood correlated more highly with outcome than did objective measures of empathy.

It is important to point out here that all of the preceding are ways of measuring in a *general* way the client's receptiveness to therapeutic influence. It may be equally important to develop ways of measuring specifically *when* each patient is most open to change, for such states are far from omnipresent during the course of therapy. It appears that characteristics of the therapeutic relationship, as they may be determined by patient variables we have been discussing, markedly influence the quality and timing of susceptibility to influence and change. Relationship factors, therefore, may be seen as a prerequisite for therapeutic influence, rather than an end in itself. It may be regarded as the matrix within which planful interventions can occur. Therefore, therapist personality characteristics in conjunction with patient characteristics under optimal conditions interact to produce a state of influenceability in the patient, and part of the therapist's skill is demonstrated by (1) creating this condition and (2) recognizing its existence, at which times (3) he can employ technical maneuvers to therapeutic ends. It is the *manner* in which the therapist uses and perhaps exploits this condition, whenever it exists at varying times in therapy, that constitutes his effectiveness as a "professional influencer," "reinforcer," "desensitizer," "model" or whatever term one chooses.

Additional Specific Variables. Additional personal, demographic, and nonpsychological variables have been shown to correlate with patient "stayability," engagement in the therapeutic process and eventual personality change. They have been measured chiefly by tests, questionnaires and rating scales. Those we consider to be most promising are listed below:

Terminator-remainer battery (McNair et al., 1963)

Psychiatric types (based on the Interpersonal Behavior Inventory, Lorr, Bishop, & McNair, 1965)

Need to change (Cartwright & Lerner, 1963)

Geographic and financial variables (distance from clinic, cost, etc.) (Garfield, 1963; Dworin, Green, & Young, 1964; Kadushin, 1968)

Social group influence (friends and associates who stimulate and reinforce therapy-oriented attitudes and behavior) (Kadushin, 1968)

Fluency, verbal ability, sophistication, education (Kamin & Coughlan, 1963; Kadushin, 1968; Raskin, 1961)

"Readiness" (a global measure apparently related to adjustment) (Lipkin, 1954)

Motivation, need for change (Raskin, 1961; Strupp, 1960; Wallach & Strupp, 1960; Cartwright & Lerner, 1963)

"Relatability" (Isaacs & Haggard, 1966; Lohrenz et al., 1966)
- capacity for empathy
- ability to be objective about oneself
- capacity for interpersonal and object relations
- sense of individuality of self and others

Agreement on aims or methods of help (Heine & Trosman, 1960)

Psychological-mindedness (ability for self-scrutiny) (Rayner & Hahn, 1964)

Felt disturbance, anxiety, inner pressure (Siegal & Rosen, 1962; Truax & Carkhuff, 1967, p. 169; Strupp, Wallach, & Wogan, 1964; Stone, Frank, Nash, & Imber, 1961; Hiler, 1959)

Low overt disturbance (Stephens & Astrup, 1965; Strupp, Fox, & Lessler, 1969)

Hope (perhaps related to motivation) (Frank, 1968)

Being married, being employed (Strupp et al., 1969; Kamin & Coughlan, 1963)

Relatively recent onset of disturbance (lack of chronicity) (Strupp et al., 1969; Lohrenz et al., 1966)

Dependency (Andrews, 1966; Heller et al., 1963)

Need for approval (Strickland & Crowne, 1963)

Suggestibility and placebo responsiveness (Stone, Imber, & Frank, 1966; Imber, Frank, Gliedman, Nash, & Stone, 1956)

Therapist unresponsiveness to client dependency may have deleterious effects (Roth, Rhudick, Shaskan, Slobin, Winkinson, & Young, 1964)

Capacity for friendliness (Heller et al., 1963; Snyder, 1961)

Ethical values (Snyder, 1961), responsibility and persistence (Rayner & Hahn, 1964)
Social class (Hollingshead & Redlich, 1958; Yamamoto & Goin, 1966)
Expectation regarding therapy and the therapist (Apfelbaum, 1958; Goldstein, 1962, 1966; Garfield & Wolpin, 1963; Stone, Frank, Hoehn-Saric, Imber, & Nash, 1965)

Several studies suggest that patients who are relatively better adjusted show the greatest improvement, while the more severely disturbed patients show the least improvement (Gelder et al., 1967; Stone et al., 1961; Stephens & Astrup, 1965). This is consonant with Luborsky's (1959) wry summary:

> Those who stay in treatment improve; those who improve are better off to begin with than those who do not; and one can predict response to treatment by how well they are to begin with (p. 324).

Nevertheless, other studies tend to contradict this notion (Wood, Rakusin, & Morse, 1962; Truax & Carkhuff, 1964a, 1967, p. 169) and still others suggest a curvilinear relationship (Luborsky, 1962). The dilemma created by the inconsistent results of these rigorous studies has possibly been resolved by Truax & Carkhuff (1967) who state: "*the greater the initial psychological disturbance* (measured by self-report psychological test, etc.) but *the lesser the initial behavioral disturbance* (measured by prior length of institutionalization, etc.) the greater the predicted improvement" (p. 170–72). This summary statement is of considerable interest because it may indicate that those patients who, while struggling with severe psychological conflicts, still manage to meet life's responsibilities are the better therapeutic risks. Further implications of this statement may be that the better risk patients are more anxious (yet still coping), have greater ego strength (as demonstrated by their continuing struggle against inner conflicts), and for these reasons are more highly motivated to enter therapy, stay in therapy once they are accepted and see it through (Strupp et al., 1969).

General comments. 1. It is important to define the entire complexity of initial patient status so that one can determine whether a given technique is modifying only part or all of the patient's symptomatology. Thus, while it may be important to know that phobias are responsive to desensitization, it is equally important to know what is happening to the rest of the patient's experience and life. An associated issue has to do with the complexity vs. simplicity of presenting symptoms. Marks and Gelder's work clearly demonstrates differential responsiveness to treatment based on such a dichotomy.

2. It is important to realize that patients sometimes terminate therapy or do not do well in therapy because the quality of the practice is poor. It may be that the most adaptive thing that some patients can do is to leave a bad therapy situation. This seems highly appropriate in light of the notion

that traditional therapy is actually appropriate for only a small minority of disturbed people.

3. It is important for therapists to realize that their views of living and experiencing and their emphasis on self-knowledge and introspection are greatly determined by their own particular values and styles of living. There is therefore nothing sacred about the kinds of demands and criteria that they tend to impose upon patients. It may well be that the patients are quite right, at least many of them, in expecting or demanding advice or technical treatment. One study indeed showed that patients who wanted advice and got it improved more than those who wanted it and did not get it (Goin et al., 1965). In this regard it may well become the case that behavioral therapies will be much more widely accepted than the traditional variety.

4. It is also important to take into account the point at which the patient enters thereapy in relation to the initial time of onset of his disturbance. It has been cogently argued by Lesse (1964) that there may be natural cycles of disturbance ("spontaneous rhythms"); and outcomes may vary directly as a function of the point in this cycle when the client enters treatment.

Modifications of Traditional Therapies to Meet Specific Client Needs. The preceding lists and commentaries crudely describe the patients who respond best to traditional therapies as they are currently practiced. While it cannot be said that these therapies or this idealized description define homogeneous entities, the information does highlight variables useful for further inquiry. It also permits us to focus on the notion that any diagnostic assessment of a prospective patient should lead to recommendations concerning (1) the degree and quality of changes that may be expected as a result of therapeutic intervention; (2) the kind of therapy from which the patient is likely to benefit (as well as methods that may be less suitable for him); and (3) the kind of therapist characteristics to which the patient may be expected to respond most favorably.

With respect to (1), there may be large groups of patients who are unsuitable for almost all forms of treatment because of such variables as poor intelligence, lack of motivation for the *active* participation required in traditional forms of psychotherapy, severity and chronicity of disturbance, deeply ingrained characterological deficits, poor ability to introspect and verbalize feelings, and the like. Psychotherapy or behavior therapy may not be the treatment of choice for all applicants, and it is no more than realistic to face this likely possibility. In exceptional cases it may still be desirable to accept for therapy a patient whose prognosis is poor, but in that event the chances for improvement must be weighed against the expenditure of time, effort, expense, and the like. Such judgments, of course, have long been made informally by clinicians, but there exists a great need to empirically formalize them and to isolate those factors which singly or in combination lead to the foregoing evaluations.

Since any evaluation of potential patients based on measuring methods described under (1) and (2) reveals that a minority of disturbed persons are suitable for and amenable to ordinary insight therapies, increasing attention is being paid to modifying traditional techniques to meet the needs of these various subclasses of patients.

Behavioral therapies have, to some extent, met this need, although there are significant indications that they, too, are chiefly effective with the kinds of patients described by our idealized list of variables. This is not, however, in any way to underestimate either their significant contributions to the treatment of autism, schizophrenic withdrawal, sexual perversions, etc. or their potential for further development in such directions. These developments are all very promising.

Attempts to directly modify traditional approaches have focussed first upon the use of information, instruction, and modeling as techniques for overcoming inability or resistance to using therapy in an efficient way. Hoehn-Saric, Frank, Imber, Nash, Stone, & Battle (1964) used a role induction technique that involved all three of these procedures and which significantly enhanced therapy-oriented behavior. Truax & Carkhuff (1965b) successfully utilized a tape recording of "good therapy behavior" as a vicarious therapy experience. Goldstein et al. (1966) suggest the use of films for similar purposes.

Other workers have found that: high anxious subjects respond best to focussed interviews whereas low anxious subjects respond best to free association interviews (Kaplan, 1966; Sifneos, 1967); lower-class subjects who are given concrete advice improve more than those who do not receive it (Goin et al., 1965); blue collar workers respond better when the therapist is more informal, flexible, directive, physically active, concrete, and willing to meet outside of the consulting room (Gould, 1967); more open, and mature, accepting and flexible therapists are able to modify their approaches to meet the needs of less "appropriate" clients and thus are more successful and keep more of them in treatment (84%) (Baum, Felzer, D'Zmura, & Shumaker, 1966); a job-oriented, concrete, flexible, individually tailored program incorporating intensiveness of contact and remedial education is successful in helping delinquent boys (Massimo & Shore, 1963, 1966). These studies are cited chiefly from Cartwright (1968).

Evidently, increasing energy and system are being put into the development of a diverse repertoire of techniques that should eventually permit a precise application of different methods to different symptoms and patient types. These innovations are encouraging and they also set useful guidelines for further research on patient variables as they may manifest differential responsiveness to these methods.

Outcome

In our opinion, it is not possible at the present time to draw strong conclusions concerning the relative value of outcome criteria. The summaries provided below are, however, based upon a good deal of empirical substance and should be regarded as more than tentative. The conclusions take into account the more common issues such as (*a*) the low intercorrelations of many criteria, and (*b*) the importance of values and theoretical predilections in the choice and weighting of measures.

CONCLUSION 1

The most obvious thing to be concluded from the various intercorrelations of therapy outcome criteria (Forsyth & Fairweather, 1961; Cartwright, Kirtner, & Fiske, 1963, etc.) and from the divergent results obtained by using different criteria with the *same* client group (Rogers & Dymond, 1954; Malan, Bacal, Heath, & Balfour, 1967, etc.) is that the process of therapeutic change in patients is multifactorial. As simple and obvious as this sounds, it has profound implications for both research and practice. It means that divergent processes are occurring in therapeutic change, that people themselves embody divergent dimensions or phenomena, and that divergent methods of criterion measurement must be used to match the divergency in human beings and in the change processes that occur within them. This confirms the notion that any assumptions of uniformity in client characteristics or in changes thereof are simply mythical (Kiesler, 1966, 1968).

Factor analyses of multiple change criteria used in complex psychotherapy outcome studies yield generally similar findings. The main factors derived from such data tend to be closely associated with the measurement method or type of observation used rather than being identified by some conceptual variable which would be expected to cut across techniques of measurement. The most typical factors are (*a*) client self-evaluation, (*b*) therapist evaluation, (*c*) TAT or other fantasy evaluation, (*d*) indices of concrete overt behaviors, and (*e*) a miscellany of factors associated with specific instruments such as interest inventories, sentence completions, personality inventories (e.g., subsets of MMPI and CPI scales), etc. (Cartwright et al., 1963; Gibson, Snyder & Ray, 1955; Forsyth & Fairweather, 1961; Nichols & Beck, 1960; Shore, Massimo, & Mack, 1964; Shore, Massimo, & Ricks, 1965).

In addition to evidence of this type, factor-analytically derived measures of particular dimensions have been used as therapy criteria, but they tend to be confined to self-report techniques (Cattell, 1966) and are therefore limited in scope. One related technique, the Psychiatric Status Schedule, is, however, broader in scope and shows considerable promise (Spitzer, Endicott, & Cohen, 1967). It will be discussed further.

Numerous other studies report intercorrelations among two or more outcome measures; and while the results appear to sometimes confirm the factor-analytic findings, they are highly variable and difficult to interpret cogently at the present time (Ends & Page, 1957; Parloff, Kelman, & Frank, 1954; Dietze, 1966, 1967; Paul, 1966; Shore, Massimo, & Mack, 1965; Shostrom & Knapp, 1966; Knapp, 1965; etc.). A puzzling aspect of these studies is that significant correlations between different criteria occur, in contradiction to the factor-analytic evidence, but they do not occur consistently across studies. Whether this is due to chance fluctuations in the diverse data or to some more substantial factors we are as yet unable to determine.

RECOMMENDATION 1

(*a*) Major research effort should be expended in more carefully delineating the *divergent* processes of change which take place as a result of the extant therapies. This may best be done by studying more extensively the relationships among client characteristics, change techniques, and the specific *kinds* of change that occur. We feel quite strongly that researchers and therapists should begin to think more precisely in terms of *kinds of change* rather than in terms of a general multiform change; (*b*) A correlated activity would be the more rigorous and extensive development of *measures* for tapping different *kinds* of change. Some attempts in this direction will be discussed in conclusions 2 and 3; (*c*) Another fruitful inquiry, based directly upon the factor analytic work, would involve: (1) More rigorous specification of the variables underlying client's and therapist's ratings of outcome so that it can be determined whether differences between their ratings are spurious, responsive to different dimensions of the change process, or a function of differing values; and (2) careful comparison of the other outcome factors, fantasy responses, overt behavior, and inventory responses with the *process* of change, in order to detect and describe what is happening in these three domains as a result of therapy. This kind of inquiry would complement and overlap the suggestions listed under conclusions 2 and 3.

CONCLUSION 2

The clearest issue in criterion development and selection at the present time is whether evaluation should be based chiefly upon external behavior or internal states of experience. This issue emerges directly from the theoretical and technical controversies surrounding the confrontation between behavioral and more traditional therapies.

While behavioral indices more often correlate with follow-up measures, it is also true that follow-up measures are usually of a behavioral nature. Overt behavioral criteria are, therefore, currently more impressive, though not necessarily more important. The problem of measuring experiential phenomena with adequacy and precision remains a crucial one for future research in criterion development.

The distinction between dynamic vs. symptomatic or experiential vs. behavioral has proven valuable in the interpretation of change data. Truax & Carkhuff (1967) review a number of studies of patient characteristics and patient change in which they find that certain contradictions of outcome can be accounted for on the basis that these two types of criteria tend to be mixed together indiscriminately, or outcomes are compared between studies based on these two dimensions when they may not be actually comparable. They point out, for example, that initial level of inner disturbance is positively correlated with outcome whereas initial level of behavioral disturbance is negatively related to outcome. Malan et al. (1967) have taken this concept one step further and devised what they call an assessment of internal or dynamic change as opposed to external change. They demonstrate that the percentage of remission in an experimental or therapy group fluctuates markedly depending on which of these two criteria are used. They point out that the spontaneous remission rate in a control group tends to be only 33 to 50 percent on dynamic criteria as opposed to 60 to 70 percent in external criteria. Cattell (1966) argues in favor of two major sets of factors, source traits and surface traits. Source traits refer to the underlying source of behavior or symptoms and are rated by his 16 personality factor questionnaire; surface traits refer to constellations or syndromes of symptoms such as are measured by the MMPI. Factor-analytic studies also reflect this dichotomy when they derive factors representing self-evaluation or TAT factors, and behavioral and other concrete factors based on post-therapy achievement or life functioning. For some years this dichotomy has been recognized implicitly in the work of Frank and his associates (Stone et al., 1961) in their focus on an overt social ineffectiveness scale and an internal discomfort scale.

RECOMMENDATION 2

(*a*) Since "internal" and "external" criteria measure different human characteristics, since these characteristics are significant, since changes occur in both domains during therapy, and since important decisions regarding the value of different techniques continue to be based on the extent of change induced by them, we recommend that future studies include representative measures derived from this dichotomy. Recommendations for specific measures are discussed later in this document. (*b*) We suggest further that specific therapist technique indices, such as those characteristic of divergent therapists, be correlated with each of these kinds of criteria in order to determine more precisely how differing types of change are effected and whether single techniques have multiple effects. (*c*) We encourage the refinement of work such as that being done by Malan, in which parallel systems of change measures are being developed based on notions concerning these two domains of change. (*d*) We feel that energy might also be more vigorously devoted to specifying which type of client change is more crucial in a given case, thus laying the groundwork for eventually providing the kind of therapy most appropriate to the change desired.

CONCLUSION 3

The possibility of tailoring change criteria to each individual in therapy is being mentioned with increasing frequency, and the idea offers intriguing alternatives for resolving several recalcitrant dilemmas in measuring change.

This notion strongly supports the development of a general trend toward *specific* rather than global improvement indices. Thus, if a person seeks help for severe depression, we would tend to measure change in depression rather than his global psychological status. Taken together, the trend to specify and the trend to individually tailor criteria offer a strong antidote to the vague and unimpressive conclusions so often reported in the outcome literature.

This implication takes several forms. First, all clients might be measured on the same criteria, but improvement could be indicated by changes in opposite directions for different clients. For example, Jewell, 1958 (reported by Volsky, Magoon, Norman, & Hoyt, 1965) asked judges to evaluate client diagnostic material to determine which direction of change should be considered positive on each of three scales for each client. On the "defensiveness scale," the judges agreed that *no change* was required for 60 per cent of the cases. On the "anxiety scale," it was judged that anxiety level should not be altered for 53 per cent of the cases and in 10 per cent it should be increased! In relation to problem solving, it was agreed that all clients needed to increase their skill. In a correlated study by Vosbeck, reported by the same authors, it was found that in using grade-getting and degree-getting as criteria for effectiveness of college counseling, counselors were often working "against" themselves by encouraging some individuals to seek alternative goals not requiring a college degree. Volsky et al. (1965); Rogers (1963); and Mintz (1965) have also all similarly suggested that some clients *appear* equally bad off or worse as a result of therapy because they have become more open about their inadequacies, more fluid and flexible in their styles of responding, and thus *appear* less well-regulated.

Second, different standardized measures might be used for different cases, depending upon the type of change sought. Thus, for one case we might be primarily interested in measures of anxiety and depression, while for others our concern might variously focus upon compulsive defensiveness, somatic complaints, impulsivity, passivity, etc.

Third, unique criteria could be devised for each client. This might entail the use of self-descriptive items in an idiographic Q sort which would still permit the calculation of self-ideal correlations and other computations (Shlien, 1962, 1965; Weiss & Schaie, 1964), or it could depend upon brief self-descriptions which were unitized and rated (Allport, 1958). In order to make comparisons across uniquely defined client measures, standard scores could be used or judges could use a standard scale for crudely evaluating amount of change on each criterion.

RECOMMENDATION 3

(*a*) We suggest that both old and new outcome studies might well be analyzed using one or more of these techniques. The thought impresses us that the meager yields of many studies may have resulted from misapplications of the same criteria to different patients. It is entirely conceivable that significant therapeutic effects have been obscured by these blanket applications and that startling new findings await the creative researcher who refines criterion estimation so as to account for the divergent processes simultaneously occurring in groups of therapy cases.

(*b*) We feel that the evidence presented under conclusion 3, along with that presented in the first two conclusions, affirms the value of the trend noted earlier toward the utilization of criteria specific to the change-induction technique and to the specific target symptoms. We assume that this kind of precision can be applied in even the most complex cases by the use of multiple, but specifically applied, criteria; and that the processes of change will thus be illuminated and the actual effects of psychotherapy more accurately assessed.

CONCLUSION AND RECOMMENDATION 4

It is obvious that adequate outcome measurement in psychotherapy is dependent upon the scientific status of personality measurement in general. Given the primitive and controversial nature of this field of inquiry, it is not surprising that difficulties arise when research in this area is *applied* to clinical phenomena.

We can only applaud and encourage the present variety of efforts underway to dimensionalize human behavior in meaningful ways. We would suggest, however, two things: (*a*) that the dimensions of the clinical distress erupting all about us today require both a sense of urgency in this matter and the need for more programmatic efforts; and (*b*) that the processes of therapeutic change might themselves be a fruitful set of phenomena for measurement specialists to attend to in their research, for during personality change we might assume that the more powerful variables in human experience become salient and more readily observable.

CONCLUSION AND RECOMMENDATION 5

The following material consists of brief commentaries on outcome criteria that have proved useful or appear promising. In light of the fact that our card file lists several hundred outcome studies, we hope the reader will charitably accept the fact that our intuition has played a dominant role in the selection of the particular measuring techniques listed here. We also hope that no one whose creative work has gone unmentioned, either in this section or elsewhere in the paper, will feel that his contributions have been slighted or inaccurately evaluated. It should also be noted that many valuable measures have been developed and tested chiefly on psychotic populations (Lorr, Wittenborn, etc.) and they will not be reviewed here.

Assessment Interviews. Several procedures have reached useful levels of development in standardizing interview evaluation of client status before, during and after therapy. The work of Spitzer, Fleiss, Burdock, & Hardesty (1964); Spitzer et al. (1967), Rogers et al. (1967), and Landfield, O'Donovan, & Narvas (1962) all converge upon the notion that rigorous standardization of the interviewer as a diagnostic stimulus is a valuable method of clinical assessment. Thus far their views seem to be borne out.

This approach has been carried to rigorous dimensions particularly by the Spitzer group who have developed five procedures, the most prominent of which is the *Psychiatric Status Schedule*. This standardized interview covers factor-analytically derived dimensions of mental status in addition to a broad spectrum of behavioral manifestations of psychopathology. Interjudge reliabilities of the scores it yields are excellent. While much of the content is oriented toward inpatients and initial experiments have revealed modest validity data, the procedure appears to be among the most promising of all evaluation measures.

The Rogers group introduced the important innovation of obtaining this type of standard interview sampling at intervals throughout the course of therapy, much as samples might be drawn from tape recordings.

A further question to be answered in this area is whether the samplings are not systematically biased by the use of *one* interviewer who may evoke only particular kinds of information and behavior in the patient. This is similar to the patient-therapist pairing problem in therapy itself. Sampling interviews must be affected by similar variables.

MMPI. Among the traditional measures that have been used, certain *MMPI scales* repeatedly yield evidence that they are able to detect client change. Among those scales which appear to provide consistent validity as change indices are *D, Pt,* and *Sc.* Scales that correlate with these, such as *Si, K,* and *Es,* also frequently manifest change. Anxiety scales derived from the MMPI such as the Taylor scale or the Welsh scale also seem to be reasonable change indices, though they correlate highly with *D* and *Pt.* The sum of clinical scales has also been widely used and is of similar value (Dahlstrom & Welsh, 1960; Fulkerson & Barry, 1961). While MMPI scales thus provide some merit for future work, strong statements are being made to the effect that it is an essentially outmoded instrument. This is in part for theoretical reasons having to do with the lack of clear meaning of the scales and the items comprising them, in part because of the strongly nosological orientation of the scales, and partly because the scales are not factorially pure and are not intentionally designed with specific types of therapeutic change in mind. Despite such defects, no other paper-pencil measure of psychopathology based on self-report offers anything better to the researcher.

Behavioral Assessment. A new philosophy and methodology of diagnosis is developing within the behavioral school. It is being complemented by the work of an increasing number of eclectically oriented psychiatrists who tend to focus upon pragmatic, behavioral criteria such as being in or out of school, maintaining marriage or becoming divorced, frequency of arrest, being in or out of the hospital, etc. While still in its infancy, this approach is having an increasing impact upon clinical assessment and upon the specification of outcome criteria for research purposes (Kanfer, 1967; Goldfried, 1967). These techniques focus upon concrete, behavioral aspects of the patient's life. They include inventories of specific symptoms such as the *Fear Survey Schedule* (Lang & Lazovik, 1963) and the "Target Complaints" technique (Battle, Imber, Hoehn-Saric, Stone, Nash, & Frank, 1966) developed at Johns Hopkins. Other procedures involve rating schemes or frequency counts applied to the patient's behavior by observers. These include the "Timed Behavioral Checklist for Performance Anxiety" (Paul, 1966), the "behavior rating category system" used by Becker et al. (1967), the *Finney Therapy Scale* (Finney, 1954; Forsyth & Fairweather, 1961), and various ratings of work proficiency, interpersonal behavior, and achievement (Massimo & Shore, 1963). In addition, several ratings of social behavior based on interviews by assessors with either the patient or an informant continue to prove valuable [Social Ineffectiveness (Stone et al., 1961); Social Adjustment (Miles, Barabee, & Finesinger, 1951; Gelder et al., 1967); Psychiatric Status Schedule (Spitzer et al., 1967)]. Measures of these types have consistently yielded high reliabilities and have sensitively reflected therapeutic change.

Self-concept Measures. Scales measuring self-esteem or self-acceptance continue to have strong influence in psychotherapy outcome research as described particularly by Butler (1966) and by Truax and Carkhuff in reporting their series of studies (1967). In addition to the original *Q* sort devised by Butler & Haigh (1954), several instruments have been devised which are reliable and valid. They include Dymond's *Q* Adjustment Score (1954), Van der Veen's *Family Concept Q Sort* (1965), Gergen & Morse's new Self-Consistency Score (1967), Endler's adaptation of the *Semantic Differential* for self-descriptions (1961), and various adaptations of Kelly's *Role Construct Repertory Test.* The intercorrelations of these measures is probably high and it is difficult to select from them on bases other than personal predilection or popularity. The factor-analytic studies reported earlier suggest that measures of this type add practically nothing to what is obtained from the MMPI or similar instruments, and vice versa. They are all basically ways of reporting subjective distress.

Thematic Stories. In general, the TAT and derivatives thereof continue to have modest, but durable, value as outcome indices. Reviews of the research evidence by Murstein (1963) and by Zubin, Eron, & Schumer (1965) confirm this conclusion as do the factor-analytic studies, which usually yield a separate TAT factor. Various scoring systems and new cards continue to be added to this venerable approach and some have yielded rather useful criterion measures (Massimo & Shore, 1963). It is clear that the best validities are obtained when specific variables are examined via a number of cards that sample responses on that dimension, e.g., aggression, dependency, etc. We strongly endorse the approach advocated by Zubin et al. to this type of instrument. They suggest "purifying" the dimensions or component parts of the TAT, broadening the range or sampling of stimuli, and rigorously accumulating normative data on responses in connection with assessments of experimenter, subject, "apparatus" (test), task, and situational characteristics. We also agree with their conclusion that the TAT, used in the classical way, cannot be considered a valid instrument; but that specific scores and sets of cards (old and new) have validity under specified conditions for given purposes, such as criterion measurement of a given dimension of experience.

Patient Checklists and Self-Ratings. Patient self-ratings of outcome are too numerous and unstandardized to list here. They are mostly simple, homemade instruments and there is no obvious evidence that one is superior to another. There is also little evidence that they add significantly to what is measured by standardized self-report instruments such as the MMPI or *Q* sorts.

A factor-analyzed instrument based on Gough's adjective checklist has been produced by Parker & Megargee (1967). They find that the adjective checklist in its current revised form by Gough & Heilbrun can be reduced to four primary factors. The first factor was a bipolar one labeled "positive vs. negative" and is apparently very similar to the self-evaluation factors found in therapy outcome studies. The second factor is more or less an ascendance-submission factor, the third an emotionality vs. stolidity and the fourth factor represented the total number of adjectives checked. This type of factor structure on checklists has been found a number of times across different samples and seems to be a fairly reliable finding. Adjective checklists are easy to administer and appear to have value in assessing change and in other types of evaluation.

Therapist Rating Scales. These scales have the same virtues and deficiencies that patient self-ratings do. They seem to measure an independent factor in change, or perhaps it is simply point-of-view that is being measured. A venerable global outcome measure is the nine-point rating scale developed for the Rogers & Dymond project (1954). It is still in considerable use and correlates so highly with other more complex and sophisticated therapist ratings (Cartwright, Robertson, Fiske, & Kirtner, 1961) that it may well be the measure of choice for this purpose. More specific and behavioral ratings are becoming more widely used, however. (See Gelder et al., 1967; and Spitzer's *Psychiatric Status Schedule,* 1967.)

Several standardized checklists have been developed, which appear to be very efficient and valuable evaluation measures. One of these, which has already demonstrated its value in therapy research, is that by Lorr & McNair (1963, 1965), based on the Leary Interpersonal Checklist (1957). The authors describe the instrument as follows:

> The inventory items were correlated, factored, and assembled into thirteen scales. Nine of the scales could be arranged into a circular order. Supporting evidence was found in data reported by Stern, by Campbell, and in new data on the Leary Checklist. Three similar overlapping higher order factors, *dominance, affiliativeness vs. detachment,* and *compliant abasement,* accounted for the correlations in each matrix.

They suggest that this measure may be particularly useful in studies designed to clarify hypotheses concerning defense mechanisms.

Factor-Analytic Batteries. General studies of personality assessment continue to yield therapy criteria. The most prominent and frequently used continue to be the *Eysenck Personality Inventory* and various measures from Cattell's *Objective-Analytic Personality Factor Battery* (experimental instrument) and *Sixteen Personality Factor Questionnaire.* The "neuroticism" and "anxiety" scores from these batteries tend to be of greatest interest to psychotherapy researchers, and it appears that they are rather well-developed measures which are sensitive to therapeutic change, though they are limited in being based solely on self-report.

Mood Scales. Another intriguing type of measurement—which has not been explored very much in therapy research except by the Frank group in their role-induction inverviews, placebo studies, and long-term follow-ups—is the analysis of moods. There is increasing evidence of a fairly substantial nature that moods can be reliably studied while retaining the experiential validity of the phenomena. This is evidenced in the work of Wessman & Ricks (1966), Clyde, Nowlis, Dittmann, and McNair & Lorr. The Wessman & Ricks volume in particular contains a variety of new scales and also reveals a fact quite relevant to therapy research, namely that people can be reliably characterized by their mood levels and by their degree of stability or variability, and that there tend to be quite different mood patterns across individuals. It has been noted by Frank et al. that moods can be dramatically effected by brief encounters with diagnostic evaluators and initial interviewers. It may be that mood scales will eventually be a good way to evaluate what might be considered the superficial effects of attention-expectancy and other placebo-related effects. If these measures then can be shown to be relatively independent of other outcome measures we will have a way of reasonably differentiating between this type of effect and another, namely the superficial and the more substantial. On the other hand, it may also be that moods tap something much more deep and profound than is currently thought, in light of Balkin's finding (1968) that the Wessman-Ricks measures significantly differentitate groups beginning and ending therapy and that the level scores for those ending therapy are not different from scores for normals.

Personal Orientation Inventory. We are impressed with the potentialities of the *Personal Orientation Inventory* (Shostrom, 1963; Shostrom, & Knapp, 1966; Knapp, 1965) which measures life-orientation, self-actualizing tendency, inner direction, and similar dimensions usually considered to be in the domain of values and health-oriented qualities. A series of studies relating it to the MMPI, the Eysenck scales, therapeutic change, and differences between diagnostic groups reveals both its validity and its ability to measure important dimensions not tapped by traditional scales. A good measure of values is sorely needed in psychotherapy research, and perhaps this is it.

Self-Regulation Measures. A trend correlated with the preceding program of research concerns the dimensions of self-control and self-regulation. A few measures have been developed which tap this area of common difficulty among modern clinic populations. This domain has been inadequately tapped in the past and is one that is relevant to several of the newer therapies such as Reality Therapy (Glasser, 1965) and Integrity Therapy (Mowrer, 1968). Studies by Ricks, Umbarger, & Mack (1964) of temporal perspective in successfully treated deliquents are relevant here as are studies of delay of gratification (Mischel, 1966), long-range planning (Spivack & Levine, 1964), and general goal-orientation. This dimension of patient change seems important, and measures of it are arising which have substance, partly because they derive from an area of general experimentation in psychology.

Peer Ratings. Peer ratings were once touted as potentially very valuable measures and new evidence is coming from several quarters that they may still be of more value than is suggested by the frequency with which they are used. There is some evidence from Peace Corps studies that peer ratings are among the better if not the best predictor of overseas performance, and there is evidence from one study where the peer ratings were confined to an anxiety dimension that they are of considerable value (Dildy & Liberty, 1967).

Duncan's reputation test of personality integration (1966) seems to have value similar to the peer anxiety ratings. This test, however, requires a setting in which peers have regular opportunities to observe one another's behavior. It was derived on a college campus and may be especially relevant to college students.

Miscellany. There are numerous additional measures which have possible value for psychotherapy research and we do not demean their potentialities, but Buros' *Handbook* cannot be reproduced here. Suffice it to say that nearly any scale developed by measurement specialists has potential value as a diagnostic and therapy change evaluator. We hope that more bridge-building between these two domains will occur and on a programmatic basis.

In addition, numerous other measures have been used in therapy research such as the Rorschach, Knight's criteria, percentage of improvement, etc. On the basis of evidence to date, we have little faith in them as change measures.

Control Groups. It now seems clear that a true no-therapy control group is essentially impossible to set up and implement except in a carefully restricted institutional setting. This is due to the fact that clients in control groups are almost always involved in a variety of help-seeking behaviors which yield encounters with therapeutic agents existing in the community. The best control for this problem is probably to institute a procedure for obtaining samples of the help-receiving events which are occurring among control group cases. This can be done during both therapy and follow-up periods. Counts of the frequency and duration of these events would be most helpful not only in the life experience of controls but also for experimental cases.

An attention-placebo control is probably also necessary in any future outcome or comparative study in light of the fact that a number of investigators have discovered significant effects of such variables (Frank, 1961; Paul, 1966; Shapiro, 1971). Many people argue that variables such as expectancy, attention, etc. are quite powerful and are the essence of what effects change in the therapeutic transaction. Another view, and the one we are more convinced of, is that these influences are a necessary and real part of most human relationships, particularly those that focus upon helping. We view them as being facilitative but far from the essence of therapy. It appears likely that some of the more dramatic consequences of these influences are really somewhat misleading. They appear to effect more superficial changes (moods, ratings of well-being), although they are sometimes so obvious and overt that they seem more significant than they really are. One of the defects of most previous research on outcome is that these factors have not been taken into account, and it has not been demonstrated which criteria they do and do not relate to; therefore it has been impossible to tell exactly which therapeutic ingredients, placebo or otherwise, are doing most of the work in creating change.

Follow-up. There have been some consistent deficiencies in follow-up procedures of therapy outcome studies. These should be easily remediable. One is that follow-up does not usually include intensive observation procedures such as those that occur during the therapy period. One, therefore, never really knows what the long-range effect of the therapeutic procedure is, for there is no precise determination of the intervening influences which may effect the client's status in one direction or another. There is currently enough evidence that patients, after they leave therapy, experience both strong deteriorative and therapeutic influences, such that a procedure for obtaining examples of their experiences at regular intervals seems essential in any further follow-up studies.

A second deficiency in previous follow-up studies has been the lack of long-term follow-up. This defect is relevant to both experimental and control groups. If long-term follow-up were the rule, it would be much more evident whether or not there are cycles in the neurotic process which follow a regular periodic interval. It would be of great interest and value in the study of therapy itself to conduct a long-range naturalistic inquiry into the fluctuations of pathology and distress of both neurotic control groups and experimental follow-up groups. Periodic fluctuations could then be noted and plotted, and environmental events and interpersonal encounters could be correlated with these fluctuations. The potential contribution of such an inquiry or series of inquiries would be to cast more light on the natural history of the conditions treated by psychotherapy and, thus, to reveal more precisely which changes can validly be attributed to the influence of therapy.

Deterioration Effects. Our review of outcome studies goes back to the 1920's. The more we examine this material, the more evidence we find of deterioration effects among patients as a result of inept psychotherapy of the type reported in recent articles (Truax, 1963; Truax & Carkhuff, 1967; Bergin, 1963, 1966, 1967a, 1967b). In contrast with previous data, however, it now appears that deterioration effects do occur in some, though a small number, of control patients. Whether this is due to deleterious environmental events or to some natural cyclical process is quite unclear, but it does make it evident that deterioration might be occurring among some patients who are in therapy but for reasons that have nothing to do with the therapy. Another observation of interest is the fact that, in general, the proportion of patients who seem to be deteriorating among a therapy group is not large. While there is definite variability across studies in the proportion of cases that seem to be deteriorating, the problem is not as pervasive as it might be, though its mere existence has serious implications for the field.

There is additional evidence of therapist variability as far as effecting therapeutic change is concerned. Sources of this variability remain somewhat unclear but it is certainly an item of high priority to investigate therapist correlates of this particular phenomenon. It is also an intriguing and related fact that great variability occurs across clinics which seem to treat reasonably similar client populations. The reasons for this variability are equally important and deserve rigorous empirical attention.

In this connection we have done a careful review of reports of percentages of improvement in the papers by Eysenck and also by Levitt. They each report a large number of studies in which the percentages of improvement varied dramatically: In Eysenck's (1965) report, for example, from 39 to 77 percent, and in Levitt's (1966) study from 43 to 86 percent. A careful rereading of the original documents on which the Eysenck and Levitt reports were based revealed some most interesting findings. First of all, it is apparent that these reviews could be carefully redone in such a way as to yield more favorable evidence regarding the effect to therapy. As Strupp (1963) has stated, it is evident that these reviewers have taken severest possible accounting of the effects of therapy in the studies which they reviewed. The second, even more remarkable, fact evident in these studies is that in many cases those which reveal the highest percentages of improvement are also those in which the more sophisticated and intensive type of treatment was given, whereas those yielding low percentages of improvement seem to receive more superficial, brief, and less meaningful treatment (to the patient).

Comparative Studies. Comparative studies seem to be coming into their own recently, particularly comparative studies of outcome in behavior therapy as opposed to other more traditional treatment techniques. While many of these studies favor behavioral therapy, they also almost invariably utilize criteria that derive from behavioral theory. Other deficiencies in comparative studies have been noted. Many of these deficiencies are functions of the complexity and cost of doing a comparative study adequately. Previous deficiencies concern the use of criteria unique to a particular theoretical orientation, the use of criteria specific to a single aspect of personality, the study of patient types particularly amenable to only one of the two or more approaches being examined, extremely limited therapy durations, the use of more than one technique by a single therapist with the inevitable biases involved, the lack of relating different processes that are discovered and documented to actual outcome, lack of careful definition of the actual processes occurring in the different therapies and precisely how they differ, not avoiding large overlap in the procedures used, studying outcomes without reference to process differences, etc. All of these deficiencies could presumably be overcome in a complex design. This type of design is especially amenable to collaborative work and might well be one of the most significant contributions of such a large type program of research.

Gordon Paul's (1966) comparative study of behavioral and insight techniques meets many of these deficiencies but also suffers from several of them.

It is of interest to note that the behavioral technique excelled in relation to behaviorally oriented criteria, but that it did not with regard to other criteria. Unfortunately, the therapy was limited to six sessions, and therefore an adequate test of insight therapy in relation to behavior therapy on other criteria was not possible. The basic design which Paul used, however, might well form the basic rudiments of a future adequate study.

The renewed interest in comparative studies of outcome seems quite realistic in light of the obvious need to test the differential effects of particular procedures on particular patients and particular symptoms. It is also of interest to note that in the literature references to comparative studies are very frequent. The small number of studies of this type are very frequently referred to and much interest is shown in them. This is further evidence of the strong potential that such studies have for influencing progress in the field.

Designs and Domains of Inquiry

In the following we are presenting brief sketches of a few illustrative projects which, on the basis of our review of the research literature, appear to follow promising leads. It will be seen that some projects represent more ambitious and large-scale attempts to further the psychotherapy research enterprise; others address themselves to somewhat more circumscribed problems in the area.

Keeping in mind the fact that we are ultimately interested in knowing how technique and therapist variables interact to influence client behavior under specifiable conditions, we are inclined to reiterate here that coordinated or collaborative research offers a significant new potential for resolving dilemmas in this field, and we feel that programmatic inquiry of this sort should be given a vigorous try. We cannot help but be increasingly impressed by this notion as we have immersed ourselves in the current literature.

An obvious question to be asked is whether the field is ready for such an adventure. We feel that the answer is in the affirmative. Despite the relatively primitive nature of many of our variables and measures, we feel that there is considerably more substance to the field than there was even five years ago. It seems to us that a number of significant variables have been identified and that crude but usable measures are available for estimating some of them. These variables are likely to be studied and refined regardless of what we may assert here; but we do think that their relative value and specific applicability can expeditiously be determined through coordinated work. At the same time, we are keenly conscious of the motivational, interpersonal and administrative problems inherent in collabortive research programs; we have no illusions that such projects are easily implemented, but we think the potential payoff is worth an energetic trial.

As an introduction to our proposed research studies, we list here, in brief, the variables, response classes, measures, and techniques we feel show the greatest promise for unraveling the processes of personality and behavior change. Some important ones are bound to be missed either by accident or unwitting bias. We hope for tolerant reactions to such human errors and subsequent corrective research efforts by others.

The problems, variables, or techniques below appear to have considerable potency and are subject to reasonably adequate measurement. We believe that they could well be the subject of a series of inquiries, including comparative studies which use factorial designs:

Therapist Characteristics:

- empathy
- warmth
- congruence
- position on A-B continuum
- orientation or style

Techniques:

- desensitization
- reinforcement
- modeling

extinction
role-induction
time-limited and extended dosage

Client Prognosis:

motivation for change
severity of disturbance
symptom complexity
degree of internal and environmental resources
cultural, eductional, and economic status

Client Dependent Variables:

self-esteem
inner-experiential vs. external-behavioral indices
fearful, phobic, avoidant behavior

Before going on to describe ways in which the above might be examined, we list below additional promising variables that appear to have value but which lack as yet the strong empirical foundations of the preceding ones:

Therapist Characteristics:

therapist conflict or anxiety
therapist experience level

Techniques:

depth of interpretation
behavior rehearsal or role playing

Client Variables:

client likability
client repressiveness vs. subjective discomfort
client deviation, such as anti-social behavior, sexual perversions, etc.
client mood
client-therapist similarity, e.g., on SES background
appropriate client role expectations
client dependency

Additional variables may have promise, but they have been chiefly described rather than measured. Some examples include:

cognitive reorienting

repentance

therapist confidence and prestige: so-called placebo inducers

therapist persuasive ability or ability to influence attitude change

client self-insight

The secondary, but promising, set of variables listed above lend themselves readily to the types of research that are already well-developed. For example, straightforward outcome studies could test the value of the "depth of interpretation" variables more fully, as would be true of the techniques of inducing guilt-acceptance, responsibility, or cognitive reorienting which Mowrer (1968), Glasser (1965), and Ellis (1962) respectively advocate. Small-scale, but rigorous, studies could further evaulate the usefulness of mood indices in assessing readiness for change and amount of change, etc. It is the first set of more refined and apparently potent variables which we feel justify more elaborate studies.

PROJECT 1: TOWARD A COMPARATIVE ANALYSIS OF THE MAJOR THERAPIES

Several of the major technique and therapist variables, which can be measured and which have been shown to effect positive change, have been isolated as a result of efforts by schools of therapy. The client-centered and behavioral approaches have yielded most of the promising variables; but for several reasons we feel that the psychoanalytic approach should be included in the designs we propose. First, it dominates the thinking and practices of most clinicians. Second, several variables derived from the tradition appear promising even though they have never been rigorously tested. Third, the effects, or alleged deficiencies of psychoanalytic therapy, have not been documented with adequate precision; it is obvious that this task should be performed.

There are two primary ways in which the comparative effects of these therapies should be evaluated. One consists of studying them more or less naturalistically as they are practiced, with appropriate pre- and post-testing and controls. A second involves selecting specific techniques from these approaches and testing them as homogeneous influences with at least two types of homogeneously defined presenting symptoms. Researchers are likely to differ in terms of the potential value they assign to these two approaches at the present stage of progress. We prefer the latter because we have become convinced that the therapy of the future will consist of a set of specific techniques that can be differentially applied under specifiable conditions to specific problems, symptoms, or cases. Such an approach would be necessarily a non-school approach.

While the three major therapies currently in vogue appear to have their greatest effects in those cases commonly considered neurotic and well-motivated, there is at least crude evidence that behavior therapy is superior in dealing with specific symptoms and that the success of the other therapies rests with broader and more diffuse problems. It would seem simple but significant enough to extract variables from each of these therapies, which could be pitted against each other and also tested for differential effects across symptom types. The warmth-empathy dimension from client-centered therapy and the desensitization technique from behavioral therapy are explicitly enough defined so that it should be possible to either select therapists who are quite homogeneous and highly effective in their respective use of these techniques, or who would be willing and able to adhere to them more or less strictly for the purposes of the study. Although no adequate process measure of the quality of desensitization is currently available, the evidence suggests that one could be developed. In either case, the therapy input must be defined in terms of performance rather than verbal espousal of a technique. It would be essential for two experts or trained raters in each of the respective schools to evaluate the performance of the experimental therapists prior to the study (e.g., on the Truax Empathy Scale, etc.) in order to insure that their performance equaled the requirement of a homogeneous set of technique inputs.

The question of whether quality, accuracy or depth of interpretation could be adequately enough measured for the purposes of a study of this type is open to question and would have to be the subject of pilot work. An alternative would be to leave the psychoanalytic technique in somewhat grosser form by requiring it to only meet the criterion of homogeneity defined by a crude rating scale, which experts could use in establishing that therapists selected for the project were following a relatively uniform psychoanalytic method. Obviously, this would have to be a method that overlapped minimally with a client-centered approach. Again, pilot work would be essential to refine the procedure to be followed if an analytic approach were to be included in the study.

As for the types of patients that might be included in the design, it seems apparent to us that two or more subsamples should be included, viz., a sample with specific target symptoms such as a dominant phobia, a sample with a standard mixture of anxiety, depression and existential indecision, and possibly a sample of persons whose chief complaint is some form of interpersonal conflict. Presumably these patient types would roughly approximate the types for which each of these therapies has been considered optimal. While such descriptions give a general idea of relevant client variables, it is clear that more precise definitions would be required for the study itself.

The specific nature of the design seems best left to those who implement these suggestions. We note, however, our doubt that it would be wise to vary therapist characteristics in a study of the foregoing complexity; therefore, it would be of great importance to equate them on experience level, personal adjustment, sex-pairings, SES, A-B continuum, etc. The important point is to involve enough experts and resources in the design so that some of the crucial questions of what works best with whom could be determined.

The exact design of this study could benefit from findings and paradigms suggested by Paul (1966), Kiesler (1968), Campbell & Stanley (1963) and Scriven (1959), and from a series of results obtained by Gelder & Marks (1966) and Gelder et al. (1967) which go far toward suggesting the specific applicability and limits of behavior therapy and which outline a paradigm for similarly testing any therapy.

PROJECT 2: THE EFFECTIVENESS OF PSYCHOTHERAPY AS PRACTICED BY EXPERTS

This project is focused upon the effectiveness of psychotherapy as practiced by highly experienced and competent therapists. It could be conducted as a study of one type of therapy, of a heterogeneous sample of therapies, or as a comparison of several homogeneous therapies. This design, with some modifications, is based on suggestions advanced by Goldstein et al. (1966). They state the issue as follows:

> No matter how poor the outcome of psychotherapy under current conditions or in the hands of current practitioners, it still remains entirely possible that experts operating under good or even ideal conditions might achieve rather remarkable effects. If experts operating under ideal conditions do *not* achieve fairly impressive results, we may as well abandon the field as it is now conceived and begin again. Therefore what is needed is an approximation of what we choose to call the optimal experiment. The requirements for the optimal experiment are well established by the criticisms frequently made of "real" experiments. First and foremost, a sample of really expert psychotherapists should be identified. How they might be identified is probably not a critical issue, but the clinical community must acknowledge their superior competence. Second, these therapists must be allowed to select the patient with whom they will work. There is no reason to suppose that psychotherapy will work with every patient, and different therapists may have special areas of competence. All that would be necessary would be the identification of *pairs* of carefully matched patients, one of whom, randomly chosen, would be examined in some way and either accepted or rejected for treatment by the therapist. Whenever a patient is selected, his matched pair goes into a control group. The control group might be of the delayed treatment variety, or an invited or enlisted treatment design could be used. Third, the conditions for treatment should be established by the therapist to conform to his best judgment about such matters as the decor of his office, the schedule of visits, and the length of treatment. Finally, each therapist should be permitted to state the results he intended to produce by his ministrations and appropriate measures should be chosen or developed. In addition, it would

> probably be desirable to have an independent panel state for each patient just what outcomes would be considered evidence of successful therapy. After such efforts in design and planning, we would demand a clear-cut difference between the psychotherapeutically treated patients and their controls (pp. 60–61).

As the above authors suggest, if the results were negative, this experiment would provide relatively conclusive evidence regarding "the practice of psychotherapy *as it is currently conceived.*" On the other hand, positive results would imply what is possible, though not necessarily what is probable for the general run of practice. Positive results would also stimulate further inquiry into the precise nature of the successful therapists' influence. Perhaps this last type of inquiry should have been the prime topic of outcome research all along in light of the fact that we now know that enormous energy has been wasted testing the effects of "average", minimal-impact therapy (Eysenck, 1965) while significant variability in therapist effectiveness exists (Truax & Carkhuff, 1967; Bergin, 1966).

This project was proposed by Goldstein et al. in somewhat rudimentary form; consequently, it would be necessary to refine the study by including specific controls such as those proposed in our analysis of outcome research. For example, it would seem important to include an attention-placebo condition as well as a carefully designed procedure for studying the "life-events" of a no therapy, waiting-list control group.

The matching of clients who are to be assigned to each of these three groups could be done according to principles discussed in other sections of our material. As for selecting the expert therapists to be involved in a study of this type, it would seem essential that some procedure such as the one proposed in our comparative study be used. It could make a substantial difference to select therapists on the basis of in-therapy behavior as rated by two independent experts who are using a check list or rating sheet, rather than on the basis of reputation alone. Reputation tends to be influenced by extraneous factors such as the personality of the therapist, his writing ability, the number of publications he has in print, etc. We feel that, in general, the project proposed by Goldstein et al. could provide very useful information given some of the refinements suggested.

In addition, a related design might be implemented which could have even clearer implications by defining each therapist's input in terms of measured level of performance with a pilot subsample of his previous patients. This would be a study of variability in the effects of psychotherapists who perform at widely varying levels in the pilot testing.

Presumably, it would not be too difficult to obtain the cooperation of a diverse sample of therapists who would permit researchers to test outcomes with their patients. The patients selected for outcome evaluation would have to be roughly homogeneous across therapists, or, if they were not so selected, careful measurements of client characteristics would be needed so that differences in client populations could be taken into account statistically when comparisons within and between therapist effects are made.

Once the preliminary task of establishing a range of therapeutic effectiveness with, say, a restricted subgroup of clients had been accomplished, then a primary focus could be aimed at determining what the characteristics and techniques are that seem to correlate with degree of effectiveness or which clearly differentiate specified levels of therapist effectiveness.

This would probably require a second full-fledged study, one in which the full gamut of measures would be applied to the therapist as a person and to his behavior during the therapy process. Therapist differences would then be directly related to differential outcome, and the potent characteristics of one of the dominant variables in therapy would begin to be specified, namely the qualities of the therapist which are therapeutic and those which are not, or which may even be harmful.

This focus on variability derives directly from increasingly significant evidence of enormous differences in therapist effectiveness in the research literature (Bergin, 1966, 1967a, 1967b; Truax & Carkhuff, 1967).

PROJECT 3: STUDY OF MENTAL OPERATIONS OF THERAPISTS

This project might well be pursued as a corollary of the study on "psychotherapy as practiced by experts." If that study were to produce significantly positive results, then the one described here could be a useful follow-up in describing the nature of the process which effects such results. Once again, this study could be implemented in several ways: as an examination of one therapy, as a comparative study of several types, or as an unselected mixture.

The objective of this project is to specify the kinds of observations the therapist makes on the patient's communications, the inferences he draws from verbal and nonverbal content, the manner in which he decides on a course of action, and the way he implements it. As Ford & Urban (1963) state the problem:

> 'Successful therapy' is likely to occur when the therapist is explicitly aware of the changes he wants to effect, and skillfully applies specific procedures to effect them. *Each time a therapist responds to his patient, he is implicitly or explicitly making a judgment that his responses may produce certain results at that point in time.* Dozens of such judgments probably go on in every therapy interview. For example, each time a Rogerian conveys

his "understanding" to the patient, he is selective in what he says, and this represents an implied judgment that he will try to modify certain responses with certain statements (p. 681).

Colby (1962) provides an additional rationale:

> Psychotherapy is . . . a practical art, a craft like agriculture or medicine or wine-making in which an artisan relies on an incomplete, fragmentary body of knowledge and empirically established rules traditionally passed on from master to apprentice. The artisan . . . looks to science for help, not to make him an applied scientist—which cannot be done anyway—but *to elucidate acute difficulties in the art.* He wants help with failures, with troubles, with lapses from the expected. When called upon for help, a scientist in turn realizes *he* cannot (since life is short and art is long) develop a tested explanatory theory accounting for every event in a practical art, nor is it even necessary. His repertoire of scientific procedures is highly limited relative to the number of questions which can be asked about any subject matter. If a scientist is to contribute to a problem he must be able to formulate a *decidable* question about it. By "decidable" I mean a question which is worded in such a way that there are only two possible and incompatible answers, yes and no. Guided by the artisan, a scientist must select a certain crucial problem in the art and judge whether the problem is ready for and accessible to a systematic inquiry using currently available procedures. A scientist hopes to reduce the degree of empiricism in the art by finding that some acute problem in it can be solved through understanding the underlying explanatory principle. Other problems in the art will continue to be managed by the artisan using judgment, intuition, and personal skills (p. 95).

And further:

> If we consider a therapist to be an artisan . . . why don't we methodically study the on-going mental operations of that artisan, his flow of associations, *while performing his task?* . . . . The design would involve a therapist describing out loud the moment-to moment sequences of his mental states as he listens to the sequential descriptions of a patient's self-observation. It should be an intensive design [see Chassan's (1967) recent book on this subject] running through stretches of time long enough to capture the stochastic properties of both therapist and patient state-sequences. In this manner we can study not only the interactional but transactional nature of psychotherapy in which a patient has a reciprocal influence on a therapist . . . (pp. 97–98).

It is clear that in most forms of therapy the therapist is proceeding on a broad front, except in some instances of behavior therapy where the focus is on a highly explicit and restricted procedure. It is also being realized that for the most part the operations of the therapist are relatively nonspecific. The effectiveness of therapy would be enhanced if the therapist's influence were less diluted and more systematically articulated to the goals to be achieved. Hence this project appears to have considerable theoretical and practical implications.

It would appear important and pragmatically useful to make this study a comparative one in which therapists of differing orientations reported their thoughts, feelings and experiences during the processes of on-going therapy. It would be necessary in such a study to outline some rough guidelines or stimuli for the therapist to follow, such as how or why he conceptualizes the processes as he does, how he makes particular on-the-spot decisions, and why he chooses to communicate as he does. It would also be of great importance to receive communications from him regarding his subjective experiences during the course of the interaction. It would be ideal if these reports of subjective experience, decision making, and conceptualizing of the process of therapy could be received in such a manner that a researcher could tell at what moment during therapy the therapist was experiencing these particular items. Methodologically, this creates some difficulties but pilot work has indicated the possibility of developing a technology for the therapist's reporting his subjective experience during the course of the therapy hour itself by manipulating hand-operated signal systems which can be hooked up to a polygraph and located comfortably and operationally close to him. Other technologies include giving immediate reports at the end of the session, or playing back the tape and receiving from the therapist free associations or other information regarding the moment by moment process (Kagan, Krathwohl, & Miller, 1963).

PROJECT 4: EFFECTIVENESS OF DIFFERENT THERAPEUTIC METHODS WITH PHOBIC PATIENTS

This proposal is focused on the investigation of different therapeutic methods as applied to phobic patients, a widely studied group. The recommendations are based on a recent review and suggestions for research by Andrews (1966):

1. Andrews' review suggests that phobics show a high degree of overt dependence and a generalized avoidant life pattern; therefore it is important to include in any therapy research design following from his review, a breakdown of therapeutic procedures into those which respond specifically to the avoidant life pattern (for example, desensitization) and a procedure that responds directly to the problem of dependency (analytic or client-centered techniques, for example).

2. Related to the foregoing, the parents of phobics might be studied to determine whether they show patterns complementary to the phobic's avoid-

ant-dependent role, that is, "overprotectiveness" and the like. It may be that parents of phobics are themselves phobic and hypersensitive to problems of separation. This phase of the research, involving longitudinal studies, may shed light on the relationship between phobic problems, parental attitudes, modeling and reinforcement effects and the like.

3. The hypothesis that both dependency gratification and encouragement to face fears are necessary conditions for effective therapy with phobics should be tested. While some existing studies (e.g., Lazarus, 1961; Weinberg & Zaslove, 1963) approximate this design, it is necessary to randomize personality and attitudes of the therapist. Alternately, it may prove valuable to compare the effectiveness of therapists whose personalities do and do not approximate the supportive pattern which, according to Andrews, is most fruitful for the therapist to adopt with phobics.

4. As an expansion of the foregoing, research might involve testing the hypothesis that the support-encouragement strategy is equally or less effective with other patient groups, and specifically with different types of phobics. It is evident from the reports of Wolpe (1964), Lazarus (1967), Gelder & Marks (1966), and Gelder et al. (1967) that phobic symptoms vary considerably in complexity, in relative salience in the client's symptom syndrome, in their historical precursors and current maintaining influences, and in their responsiveness to desensitization. We, therefore, feel that it is essential in a study or studies of the type Andrews describes to clearly define and differentiate subgroups of phobics to be treated. Thus, to carry out the real intention of this research may require a factorial design.

5. Contrary to most available research, close attention must be paid to the kinds of outcome criteria by which the treatment results are evaluated.

6. Andrews states a final objective which has wider applicability to research in psychotherapy. The hypothesis states: In order to change a maladaptive pattern, the therapist must first establish a relationship with the patient on the basis of that pattern, which is initially the patient's major mode of interaction. Subsequently, the therapist can begin to introduce new elements into the original relationship pattern, elements which have the effect of breaking up the form of the original relationship and of teaching the patient to interact in new, more adaptive ways. In terms of the phobic patient, this means that the therapist first allows the patient to become dependent (often the patient may have built up complex defenses against his dependent needs, e.g., negativism), in order to eventually make him independent. Transfer of this hypothesis to other disorders involves establishing the dominant pattern in each instance and then defining the types of therapist behaviors which are necessary to the alignment of that pattern. A corollary of this hypothesis is that psychotherapy will be ineffective where the patient lacks the capacity to form such a relationship, or where the therapist is unable to create such a relationship.

This series of interrelated studies would serve to (1) determine the relative effectiveness of different methods of therapy for specified subgroups of phobic patients; (2) define the characteristics of specific patient groups and their amenability to different therapeutic procedures; (3) explore the *range* of applicability for different methods of psychotherapy; (4) increase understanding of the kinds of personality and behavior changes that can be achieved by different forms of therapy.

PROJECT 5: STUDY OF TIME-LIMITED THERAPY

There are numerous reasons for proposing a comprehensive and intensive study of time-limited therapy. An obvious reason is that if this type of therapy can be shown to have equal or greater effects than unlimited therapy, at least with some sub-samples of clients, then it would be an enormously important addition to the therapeutic repertoire. The great economic and practical clinical implications are obvious and numerous. A second reason for undertaking such a study would be to determine more clearly which processes in therapy are doing the work of changing personality. If time-limited therapy were highly successful, this would suggest that variables such as expectancy, frequency of treatment, etc. were of prime importance. On the other hand, if unlimited therapy were more highly successful, then it would appear that the more significant variables in therapy have to do with distributed learning, relationship factors, and all the usual notions attributed to therapeutic change. Another reason for such an inquiry would be to carefully test the limits and specific areas of applicability of time-limited therapy. It may well be that variations of this approach will be highly effective with some clients and not with others. To have such information would be invaluable to the clinician. Obviously, no single study can answer all questions in this area; but a significant beginning could be made by means of a large collaborative or coordinated project in which time limits were studied rigorously and systematically.

Any design of a time-limited therapy study would obviously refer in part to the studies by Shlien, Mosak, & Dreikurs (1962), and Shlien (1966). Their comparison of Adlerian and client-centered therapy under conditions of limits and no limits was a significant contribution to this domain of inquiry. Their evidence suggests the wisdom of continuing to include in any time-limited design, therapies of different varieties in addition to patients of different types. It would be important, however, to include criteria that cut across the different theoretical orientations and methodological biases of different groups.

This study could simply vary limits by dividing cases into groups receiving possibly ten, twenty, thirty, and an unlimited number of sessions. In addition it would seem useful to examine the effectiveness of the type of time limits used by Gordon & Gordon (1966). They use what they call "extensive time-limited therapy" in which the patient is first seen for ten sessions, then returns monthly, bi-monthly, quarterly, and semi-annually on a progressive basis. Their comparisons of this procedure with unlimited therapy and with time limits confined strictly to ten sessions reveal that the extensive time-limited procedure is as effective, in general, as unlimited therapy and is more effective than ten-session therapy.

A study of this type could be conducted within the context of a comparative design or as an examination of a single type of therapy. The case samples should be divided into homogeneous sub-groups based on type of problem and severity of problem. Diverse criteria representing the major dimensions discussed in our material on criteria should be used, especially those that already show promise in yielding differences between time-limited and unlimited treatment. (For example, mood scales and other "superficial" criteria fluctuate more markedly in time-limited therapy.) Therapists would have to be standardized or matched on pertinent variables relevant to outcome. We would suggest that, based on our review of the literature, this type of study should have relatively high priority in the near future.

PROJECT 6: COMPARATIVE PROCESS ANALYSIS OF TRADITIONAL AND BEHAVIORAL THERAPIES

As stated in our review of emerging trends, it is becoming increasingly clear that a good deal of reinforcement, extinction, counterconditioning, etc. occurs in traditional therapy and that relationship variables operate in behavior therapy. We would argue that this evidence suggests the necessity for more clearly isolating the effects of divergent influences which take place in any given case. We therefore suggest a multi-staged program of research for clarifying this problem.

First, it is essential that new process measures be developed which adequately embrace behavioristic techniques. This seems at first to be a simple matter; but it must be kept in mind that if variables are to be isolated in a manner approximating scientific requirements for definition, then the behavorial process indices must be restricted to behavioral techniques and must not significantly sample relationship behaviors. While it is true that relationship and behavioral measures may correlate regardless of such attempts, they should be made. Of course, if it should prove impossible to construct behavioral process measures that did not embrace relationship qualities, this would be an instructive lead to be followed in and of itself.

Second, divergent process measures representing differing variables and viewpoints should be applied across the *same* samples of traditional and behavioral therapies, *as they are regularly practiced.* Intercorrelations of measures could then be computed and the *extent* of behavioral processes in traditional therapy and vice versa could be determined.

Third, the various process indices could be factor-analyzed or otherwise "purified" in order to determine the salient elements of the therapies as they are practiced.

Fourth, the factors or measures representing them could be estimated on the same or a new sample and then correlated with client behaviors or with outcome indices, thus further clarifying which variables are really doing the work in producing outcome.

It should be noted that behavorial process measures might require some adaptation before applying them to traditional interview sessions. Thus, for example, a good process measure of straight desensitization would be inapplicable to a typical psychoanalytic interview. Such a measure would have to be modified somewhat by carefully defining what is meant by desensitization in the course of a conversation. This would necessarily be a part of the first stage in this project, and a very important one.

The process measures applied in this study could, of course, be multiplied to include those not specifically deriving from one of the major theoretical orientations. Such a procedure has much to recommend it, and we refer the reader to our analysis of process measures for further discussion of the possibilities in this regard.

PROJECTS DERIVING FROM NONPSYCHOTHERAPY RESEARCH

In addition to studies that examine the "live" therapeutic process or restricted aspects thereof, there is an increasingly widespread inclination to derive techniques from other fields of psychological research or to apply such research directly to modifying the usual approaches. Learning and behavior modification research offers a good illustration of this, and additional fruitful applications are likely to come from many other areas of psychological inquiry. Some of the most promising possibilities in this domain have been explicated by Goldstein et al. (1966).

The following suggestions for research derive from their work and are presented only in the barest outline. In our judgment, they call for a large-scale program to be carried out over an extended period of time. We consider the systematic investigations of these problems of the utmost significance for research in psychotherapy and view them as steps in the direction of a highly desirable rapproachement among the fields of social psychology, social learning, and clinical application. Serious thought should be given to bringing such a concerted research program into being.

Enhancing the Therapeutic Relationship. The formation of a workable therapist-patient relationship is one of the most important steps in maximizing the therapist's influence. Research must be undertaken (*a*) to determine which patients are capable of forming such a relationship and (other things being equal) thus become good risks for psychotherapy; (*b*) to explore techniques by which a satisfactory therapeutic relationship can best be formed and thus the therapist's influence increased; and (*c*) to study systematically the extent to which other technical operations interact with and potentiate the therapist's influence. To increase interpersonal attraction between patient and therapist is a prerequisite for effective therapy rather than an end in itself.

Goldstein et al. (1966) propose the following hypothesis:

> Patient attraction to the therapist may be increased by cognitive dissonance induced by patient participation in overt behaviors discrepant with resistive behavior (p. 97).

They regard role playing as the first class of dissonance-arousing manipulations discrepant with resistive behavior. In developing this hypothesis they state:

> For maximal attitude change in the form of heightened attraction to occur, it seems important that this procedure [patient role playing] include high levels of (1) patient *choice* regarding participation in the role playing, (2) patient *commitment,* in the sense that undoing, disowning or uncommitting himself from the discrepant behavior is made difficult, (3) patient *improvisation* (the role-play structuring should be in outline form, requiring that the role player fill in the specifics himself), and (4) post role playing patient *reward,* that is, approval, reinforcement or other means of stabilizing the patient's new perspective toward his psychotherapist (pp. 108–109).

A related hypothesis states:

> Patient attraction to the psychotherapist may be increased by cognitive dissonance induced by patient exposure to information discrepant with resistive behavior (p. 112).

Goldstein, Heller, & Sechrest outline a number of conditions and procedures that may be used to increase the likelihood to effect a reorientation of resistive patients following exposure to communications which place the therapist and therapeutic participation in a favorable light. One approach would consist of procedures to make the therapeutic relationship *temporarily* more attractive. This practice, in effect, has long been followed by analytic therapists, based on a suggestion of Ferenczi's to the effect that the relationship must first achieve stability before technical operations (interpretations) can be undertaken. Goldstein, Heller, & Sechrest review a large body of research literature which, while for the most part not done in the therapeutic framework, may have considerable relevance for the latter.

Research on Techniques for Overcoming Resistance to Behavior Change. While difficulties in establishing a viable working relationship may be one important source of resistance to behavior change, psychotherapy is continually beset with the problem of overcoming resistances. In fact, analytic therapists see this problem as the principal task of psychotherapy. Goldstein, Heller, & Sechrest outline a number of research projects aimed at elucidating this problem and concomitantly enhancing the therapist's influence. Samples of their hypotheses are quoted:

> Resistance in psychotherapy is reduced by messages which immunize the patient against subsequent counter-argument (p. 183).
>
> Resistance in psychotherapy can be reduced by training the patient to view the therapist as a positive but discriminating reinforcer (p. 192).

They comment:

> The indiscriminate permissiveness often associated with the psychotherapy of the inhibited neurotic has no place in the treatment of most resistant patients, as it provides an invitation to aggression by the habitually hostile and a poor basis for learning by the unmotivated and the chronically asocial (p. 196).

It may be added that the "inhibited neurotic" also is frequently very resistant, and most patients at one time or another resist by hostile, aggressive, and negativistic tactics.

> Resistance in psychotherapy can be reduced by maximizing the opportunities for imitation learning by the patient (p. 197).

This hypothesis makes explicit the well known but often insufficiently recognized fact that most patients must learn *new* ("prosocial") responses, patterns of relating, etc. In this connection, the extensive research by Bandura and his co-workers is highly relevant. The therapist must come to serve as a model which is accepted by the patient. As Goldstein, Heller, & Sechrest point out, *active therapist behaviors* are most promising as a technique for stimulating imitation learning, as shown also by the program of Matarazzo and his group.

Transfer of Therapeutic Learning. This third area identified by Goldstein, Heller, and Sechrest again offers a rich ground for controlled research which is likely to have highly important practical applications. They state:

> It is of more than passing interest that the concept of transfer has long been considered highly relevant to psychotherapy, but in a strikingly different

way; that is, in *negative transfer from real life to psychotherapy.* The habits that an individual has acquired before psychotherapy are transferred to (transference) the psychotherapy situation and keep him from forming a realistic relationship with the therapist (p. 223).

By the same token, these authors recommend, we must study the specific conditions under which in-therapy learning is transferred to extra-therapy situations. Little is as yet known about this problem. They hypothesize:

> Transfer of learning from psychotherapy to extratherapy situations will be greater when the therapy stimuli are representative of extratherapy stimuli (p. 226).
>
> Transfer of learning from spychotherapy to extratherapy situations will be greater if therapy is conducted outside an office in a variety of situations in which the patient will ultimately have to respond (p. 227).
>
> Greater effectiveness of psychotherapy will be achieved if very strong emphasis is placed in therapy on emitting of responses considered desirable in other circumstances (p. 236).
>
> Concentration on positive feelings and responses and exclusion of negative feelings and responses will result in an increase in the effectiveness of psychotherapy (p. 237).
>
> Giving patients prior information about the nature of psychotherapy, the theories underlying it, and the techniques to be used will facilitate progress in psychotherapy (p. 245).

Research focused on a "role induction" interview, explored previously by Hoehn-Saric et al. (1964), and the utilization of training films designed to dispel misapprehensions of many patients concerning psychotherapy seem highly promising avenues to pursue. This thinking is summarized by the following hypothesis:

> Pretherapy vicarious learning opportunities provided to waiting-list patients will lead to a "telescoping" in time of behavior change-inhibiting stages of subsequent psychotherapy (p. 261).

In addition to the foregoing studies, we also wish to note the following possible inquiries that manifest feasibility and promise:

1. Patient-Therapist Pairing in Relation to Process and Outcome. There is increasing evidence that in those cases where the patient-therapist relationship is an important ingredient of the change process, particular pairings of patient and therapist types may enhance or retard positive outcomes. A number of variables relevant to this question have been discussed in this paper, and we suggest that this domain might be ripe for a major study.

2. The Processes of "Spontaneous" Remission. We noted in the review that the term, "spontaneous remission," continues to be used as an explanatory concept, which it is not. We think that a careful examination needs to be made of processes other than psychotherapy which produce personality change in disturbed persons. Detailed suggestions are given in our section on follow-up studies.

3. A Series of Initial Interview Experiments to Study Therapist or Patient Behavior or Both. Many issues, such as those which divide behavioral and traditional therapists, might be fruitfully examined by means of single interviews or brief series of interviews. For example, the question of relationship factors in desensitization or of contingent reinforcement in psychotherapy interviews, might be studied this way. Such an approach is a compromise between naturalistic inquiry and the control possible via experimental analogue studies.

4. A Multifactorial Process Study. Several of the complex studies described could include careful recording of verbal and nonverbal events during the therapy process or a study focusing on process could be conducted. The objective would be to correlate process measures of diverse kinds in an attempt to refine, conceptually and statistically, the meaning and value of measures now extant.

5. A Methodological Study of Outcome Measurement. This study would focus entirely upon outcome measurement techniques, their correlations, their relationships to specific process variables and kinds of change, and their predictive value in relation to follow-up. Such a study would take up where previous factor-analytic studies had left off and would include many more measures, but measures having logical relevance to hypothesized types of change.

We fully recognize that the studies proposed in this section are a small and selected sample of research considered promising by these reviewers. However, they emerged from and are faithful to the dominant themes and empirical trends in the field today. The reader will find many more suggestions for research threaded throughout this document. We hope that these suggestions will provide a stimulus to interested researchers.

THE PROBLEM OF IMPLEMENTATION

The design of any study akin to those presented here will, of course, entail a considerable amount of additional planning, which must remain a task for the future. Planning and pilot work alone will require effort of an order not previously attempted in this field.

It is obvious to us that the designs we have sketched require refinement, possibly merging of some elements, and pilot testing. While we consider them to be responsive to central issues and questions in the field, they are no more than stimuli for research. The task remains of (*a*) testing their feasibility in both substantive and practical terms, and (*b*) refining them, or originating entirely new projects, to a point where one or more of them could be fruitfully implemented.

With these goals in mind, we would give special attention to the following considerations: (*a*) Several models or designs for collaboration may prove feasible and they may or may not be like those implemented in other fields; (*b*) the planning should aim for ends which cannot be accomplished by individual agencies or investigators; (*c*) master plans may include core variables and standardized measurements, but will not preclude measures preferred by or unique to any cooperating therapist or treatment center; (*d*) it is important to be cognizant of the potential value of a variety of therapeutic techniques, influences, and innovations which have not yet been studied extensively but which might be profitably included in future research, such as any of a variety of group techniques, nonprofessional and natural therapeutic influences, personality change under induced emotional arousal, etc.; and (*e*) a central coordinating mechanism for collaboration will have to evolve from any planning effort which includes:

1. The involvement of a few prominent research centers which have the facilities, personnel, resources, and research commitment to ensure continued participation over a period of years.
2. The development of a single office responsible for overall coordination at all stages of the research, which means close contact among participating centers and frequent consultation on problems of design, data collection, data analysis, report writing, etc.
3. Augmentation of the work of the data-collection centers by a somewhat larger cadre of researchers who would apply their respective measures and techniques to the data collected at the main research centers.

If tests of feasibility and correlated pilot work reveal that a design can be agreed upon, that the necessary commitments can be made and an adequate administrative machinery set up, then the launching of collaborative work in psychotherapy research could become a reality. We would judge that if the obstacles to these important preliminary steps can be overcome, then a truly fruitful outcome seems probable. Given the possible prospects in terms of practical knowledge, such an effort seems worth a vigorous trial.

References

Albee, G. W. 1967. Give us a place to stand and we will move the earth. *The Clinical Psychologist* 20: 51–53.

Alexander, F. 1963. The dynamics of psychotherapy in the light of learning theory. *American Journal of Psychiatry* 120: 440–48.

Allport, G. 1958. What units shall we employ? In G. Lindzey ed. *Assessment of human motives*. New York: Grove Press, pp. 239–60.

Andrews, J. D. W. 1966. Psychotherapy of phobias. *Psychological Bulletin* 66: 455–80.

Apfelbaum, B. 1958. *Dimensions of transference in psychotherapy*. Berkeley: University of California Press.

Ashby, J. D., Ford, D. H., Guerney, B. G., Jr., & Guerney, L. F. 1957. Effects on clients of a reflective and a leading type of psychotherapy. *Psychological Monographs* 71: 24 (Whole No. 453).

Auerbach, A. H. Research in progress. Personal communication.

Auld, F., Jr., & Murray, E. J. 1955. Content-analysis studies of psychotherapy. *Psychological Bulletin* 52: 377–95.

Auld, F., Jr., & Myers, J. K. 1954. Contributions to a theory for selecting psychotherapy patients. *Journal of Clinical Psychology* 10: 56–60.

Bales, R. F. 1950. *Interaction process analysis*. Cambridge: Addison-Wesley Press.

Balkin, J. L. 1968. Once more, with feeling: Psychotherapy revisited. Unpublished doctoral dissertation, Teachers College, Columbia University.

Bandura, A. 1956. Psychotherapists' anxiety level, self insight, and psychotherapeutic competence. *Journal of Abnormal and Social Psychology* 52: 333–37.

———. 1965. Behavioral modification through modeling procedures. In L. Krasner and L. P. Ullmann, eds., *Research in behavior modification*. New York: Holt, Rinehart & Winston, pp. 310–40.

Bandura, A., Lipsher, D., & Miller, P. E. 1960. Psychotherapists' approach-avoidance reactions to patients' expressions of hostility. *Journal of Consulting Psychology* 24: 1–8.

Battle, C. C., Imber, S. D., Hoehn-Saric, R., Stone, A. R., Nash, E. H., & Frank, J. D. 1966. Target complaints as criteria of improvement. *American Journal of Psychotherapy* 20: 184–92.

Baum, O. E., Felzer, S. B., D'Zmura, T. L., & Shumaker, E. 1966. Psychotherapy, dropouts and lower socioeconomic patients. *American Journal of Orthopsychiatry* 36: 629–35.

Becker, W. C., Madsen, C. H., Jr., Arnold, C. R., & Thomas, D. R. 1967. The contingent use of teacher attention and praise in reducing classroom behavior problems. *Journal of Special Education* 1: 287–307.

Bellak, L., & Small, L. 1965. *Emergency psychotherapy and brief psychotherapy*. New York: Grune & Stratton.

Bellman, R., Friend, M., & Kurland, L. 1966. Simulation of the initial psychiatric interview. *Behavioral Science* 11: 389–99.

Berelson, B. 1952. *Content analysis in communication research*. Glencoe, Ill.: Free Press.

Bergin, A. E. 1963. The effects of psychotherapy: Negative results revisited. *Journal of Counseling Psychology* 10: 244–50.

———. 1966. Some implications of psychotherapy research for therapeutic practice. *Journal of Abnormal Psychology* 71: 235–46.

———. 1967a. An empirical analysis of therapeutic issues. In D. Arbuckle, ed., *Counseling and psychotherapy: An overview*. New York: McGraw-Hill, pp. 175–208.

———. 1967b. Further comments on psychotherapy research and therapeutic practice. *International Journal of Psychiatry* 3: 317–23.

Bergin, A. E., & Solomon, S. 1970. Personality and performance correlates of empathic understanding in psychotherapy. In J. T. Hart and T. M. Tomlinson, eds., *New directions in client-centered therapy*. Boston: Houghton Mifflin, pp. 223–36.

Betz, B. J. 1967. Studies of the therapist's role in the treatment of the schizophrenic patient. *American Journal of Psychiatry* 123: 963–71.

Birdwhistell, R. L. 1960. Critical moments in the psychiatric interview. Paper presented at the Tenth Anniversary Symposium, Galesburg State Research Hospital, Galesburg, Illinois, October.

Bohn, M. J., Jr. 1965. Counselor behavior as a function of counselor dominance, counselor experience, and client type. *Journal of Counseling Psychology* 12: 246–352.

Bordin, E. S. 1955. Ambiguity as a therapeutic variable. *Journal of Consulting Psychology* 19: 9–15.

———. 1965. Simplification as a strategy for research in psychotherapy. *Journal of Consulting Psychology* 29: 493–503.

———. 1968. The personality of the therapist as an influence in psychotherapy. In M. J. Feldman, ed. *Studies in psychotherapy and behavioral change*. Buffalo: State University of New York, pp. 37–54.

Bordin, E. S., Cutler, R. L., Dittmann, A. T., Harway, N. I., Raush, H. L., & Rigler, D. 1954. Measurement problems in process research on psychotherapy. *Journal of Consulting Psychology* 18: 79–82.

Breger, L., & McGaugh, J. L. 1965. Critique and reformulation of "learning-theory" approaches to psychotherapy and neurosis. *Psychological Bulletin* 63: 338–58.

Brill, N. Q. 1966. Results of psychotherapy. *California Medicine* 104: 249–53.

Bugental, J. F. T., ed., 1967. *Challenges of humanistic psychology*. New York: McGraw-Hill.

Buhler, C. 1962. *Values in psychotherapy*. New York: Free Press.

Butler, J. M. 1966. Self-acceptance as a measure of outcome of psychotherapy. *British Journal of Social Psychiatry* 1: 51–62.

Butler, J. M., & Haigh, G. 1954. Changes in the relation between self-concepts and ideal concepts consequent upon client-centered counseling. In C. Rogers and R. Dymond, eds., *Psychotherapy and personality change*. Chicago: University of Chicago Press, pp. 55–75.

Campbell, D. T., & Stanley, J. 1963. *Experimental and quasi-experimental designs for research*. Chicago: Rand McNally.

Caracena, P. F. 1965. Elicitation of dependency expressions in the initial stage of psychotherapy. *Journal of Counseling Psychology* 12: 268–74.

Carkhuff, R. R., & Truax, C. B. 1965. Lay mental health counseling. *Journal of Consulting Psychology* 29: 426–31.

Carson, R. C. 1967. A and B therapist "types": A possible critical variable in psychotherapy. *Journal of Nervous and Mental Disease* 144: 47–54.

Cartwright, D. S., Kirtner, W. L., & Fiske, D. W. 1963. Method factors in changes associated with psychotherapy. *Journal of Abnormal and Social Psychology* 66: 164–75.

Cartwright, D. S., Robertson, R. J., Fiske, D. W., & Kirtner, W. L. 1961. Length of therapy in relation to outcome and change in personal integration. *Journal of Consulting Psychology* 25: 84–99.

Cartwright, R. D. 1968. Psychotherapeutic processes. In P. R. Farnsworth ed. *Annual review of psychology*. Palo Alto: Annual Reviews, pp. 387–416.

Cartwright, R. D., & Lerner, B. 1963. Empathy, need to change, and improvement with psychotherapy. *Journal of Consulting Psychology* 27: 138–44.

Cartwright, R. D., & Vogel, J. L. 1960. A comparison of changes in psychoneurotic patients during matched periods of therapy and no therapy. *Journal of Consulting Psychology* 24: 121–27.

Cattell, R. B. 1966. Evaluating therapy as total personality change: Theory and available instruments. *American Journal of Orthopsychiatry* 20: 69–88.

Cautela, J. R. 1965. Desensitization and insight. *Behaviour Research and Therapy* 3: 59–64.

———. 1967. Covert sensitization. *Psychological Reports* 20: 459–68.

Chassan, J. B. 1967. *Research design in clinical psychology and psychiatry*. New York: Appleton-Century-Crofts.

Clemes, S. R., & D'Andrea, V. J. 1965. Patients' anxiety as a function of expectation and degree of initial interview ambiguity. *Journal of Consulting Psychology* 29: 397–404.

Colby, K. M. 1960. Experiment on the effects of an observer's presence on the imago system during psychoanalytic free-association. *Behavioral Science* 5: 216–32.

———. 1962. Discussion of papers on therapist's contribution. In H. H. Strupp and L. Luborsky, eds., *Research in psychotherapy*. vol. 2. Washington, D.C.: American Psychological Association, pp. 95–101.

———. 1967. Computer simulation of change in personal belief systems. *Behavioral Science* 12: 248–53.

Cutler, R. L. 1958. Countertransference effects in psychotherapy. *Journal of Consulting Psychology* 22: 349–56.

Cutler, R. L., Bordin, E. S., Williams, J., & Rigler, D. 1958. Psychoanalysts as expert observers of the therapy process. *Journal of Consulting Psychology* 22: 335–40.

Dahlstrom, W. G., & Welsh, G. S. 1960. Treatment. In W. Dahlstrom and G. Welsh, eds., *An MMPI handbook*. Minneapolis: University of Minnesota Press, pp. 355–93.

Deane, W. N., & Ansbacher, H. L. 1962. Attendant-patient commonality as a psychotherapeutic factor. *Journal of Individual Psychology* 18: 157–67.

Dietze, D. 1966. Staff and patient criteria for judgments of improvements in mental health. *Psychological Reports* 19: 379–87.

———. 1967. Consistency and change in judgment of criteria for mental health improvement. *Journal of Clinical Psychology* 23: 307–10.

Dildy, L. W., & Liberty, P. G., Jr. 1967. Investigation of peer-rated anxiety. *Proceedings of the 75th Annual Convention of the American Psychological Association*, pp. 371–72.

Dinsmoor, J. 1966. Comments on Wetzel's treatment of a case of compulsive stealing. *Journal of Consulting Psychology* 30: 378–80.

Dittes, J. E. 1959. Previous studies bearing on content analysis of psychotherapy. In J. F. Dollard and F. J. Auld eds. *Scoring human motives*. New Haven, Conn.: Yale University Press, pp. 325–51.

Dittmann, A. T. 1962. The relationship between body movements and moods in interviews. *Journal of Consulting Psychology* 26: 480.

Dittmann, A. T., & Wynne, L. C. 1961. Linguistic techniques and the analysis of emotionality in interviews. *Journal of Abnormal and Social Psychology* 63: 201–204.

Dollard, J., & Auld, F., Jr. 1959. *Scoring human motives: A manual.* New Haven, Conn.: Yale University Press.

Dollard, J., & Miller, N. E. 1950. *Personality and psychotherapy.* New York: McGraw-Hill.

Dollard, J., & Mowrer, O. H. 1953. A method of measuring tension in written documents. In O. H. Mowrer, ed., *Psychotherapy, theory and research.* New York: Ronald Press, pp. 235–56.

Dukes, W. F. 1965. N=1. *Psychological Bulletin* 64: 74–79.

Duncan, C. B. 1966. A reputation test of personality integration. *Journal of Personality and Social Psychology* 3: 516–24.

Dworin, J., Green, J. A., & Young, H. H. 1964. A follow-up study of relationships between distance from the clinic, degree of disability, and requests for psychiatric treatment. *Journal of Clinical Psychology* 20: 393–95.

Dymond, R. F. 1954. Adjustment changes over therapy from self-sorts. In C. R. Rogers and R. F. Dymond, eds., *Psychotherapy and personality change.* Chicago: University of Chicago Press, pp. 76–84.

Edwards, A. L., & Cronbach, L. J. 1952. Experimental design for research in psychotherapy. *Journal of Clinical Psychology* 8: 51–59.

Ellis, A. 1962. *Reason and emotion in psychotherapy.* New York: Lyle Stuart.

Emery, J. R., & Krumboltz, J. D. 1967. Standard versus individualized hierarchies in desensitization to reduce text anxiety. *Journal of Counseling Psychology* 14: 204–209.

Endler, N. S. 1961. Changes in meaning during psychotherapy as measured by the semantic differential. *Journal of Counseling Psychology* 8: 105–11.

Ends, E. J., & Page, C. W. 1957. Functional relationships among measures of anxiety, ego strength, and adjustment. *Journal of Clinical Psychology* 13: 148–50.

Eysenck, H. J. 1965. The effects of psychotherapy. *International Journal of Psychiatry* 1: 97–178.

Feitel, B. 1968. Feeling understood as a function of a variety of therapist behaviors. Unpublished doctoral dissertation, Teachers College, Columbia University.

Feldman, M. P. 1966. Aversion therapy for sexual deviations: A critical review. *Psychological Bulletin* 65: 65–80.

Fieldler, F. E. 1950a. The concept of an ideal therapeutic relationship. *Journal of Consulting Psychology* 14: 239–45.

———. 1950b. A comparison of therapeutic relationships in psychoanalytic, non-directive and Alderian therapy. *Journal of Consulting Psychology* 14: 436–45.

———. 1951. Factor analyses of psychoanalytic, non-directive and Alderian therapeutic relationships. *Journal of Consulting Psychology* 15: 32–38.

Finney, B. C. 1954. A scale to measure interpersonal relationships in group psychotherapy. *International Journal of Group Psychotherapy* 7: 52–66.

Ford, D. H., & Urban, H. B. 1963. *Systems of psychotherapy.* New York: Wiley.

———. 1967. Psychotherapy. In P. R. Farnsworth ed. *Annual Review of Psychology.* Palo Alto: Annual Reviews, pp. 333–72.

Forsyth, R., & Fairweather, G. W. 1961. Psychotherapeutic and other hospital treatment criteria. *Journal of Abnormal and Social Psychology* 62: 598–605.

Frank, J. D. 1959. The dynamics of the psychotherapeutic relationship, determinants and effects of the therapist's influence. *Psychiatry* 22: 17–39.

———. 1961. *Persuasion and healing*. Baltimore: Johns Hopkins Press.

———. 1968. The role of hope in psychotherapy. *International Journal of Psychiatry* 5: 383–95.

Franks, C. M., ed., 1969. *Behavior therapy: Appraisal and status*. New York: McGraw-Hill.

Freud, A. 1954. The widening scope of indications for psychoanalysis. *Journal of American Psychoanalytic Association* 2: 607–20.

Fulkerson, S. C., & Barry, J. R. 1961. Methodology and research on the prognostic use of psychological tests. *Psychological Bulletin* 58: 177–204.

Gardner, G. G. 1964. The psychotherapeutic relationship. *Psychological Bulletin* 61: 426–37.

Garfield, S. L. 1963. A note on patients' reasons for terminating therapy. *Psychological Reports* 13: 38.

Garfield, S. L., & Wolpin, M. 1963. Expectations regarding psychotherapy. *Journal of Nervous and Mental Disease* 137: 353–62.

Gelder, M. G. 1967. Behaviour therapy. *Hospital Medicine* 3: 306–13.

Gelder, M. G., & Marks, I. M. 1966. Severe agoraphobia: A controlled prospective trial of behavior therapy. *British Journal of Psychiatry* 112: 309–19.

Gelder, M. G., Marks, I. M., & Wolff, H. H. 1967. Desensitization and psychotherapy in the treatment of phobic states: A controlled inquiry. *British Journal of Psychiatry* 113: 53–73.

Gendlin, E. T., Beebe, J., Cassens, J., Klein, M., & Oberlander, M. 1968. Focusing ability in psychotherapy, personality, and creativity. In J. M. Shlien, H. F. Hunt, J. D. Matarazzo, & C. Savage, eds., *Research in psychotherapy*. vol. 3. Washington, D.C.: American Psychological Association, pp. 217–41.

Gergen, K. J., & Morse, S. J. 1967. Self-consistency: Measurement and validation. *Proceedings of the 75th Annual Convention of the American Psychological Association* 2: 207–208.

Gibson, R. L., Snyder, W. U., & Ray, W. S. 1955. A factor analysis of measures of change following client-centered psychotherapy. *Journal of Counseling Psychology* 2: 83–90.

Glasser, W. 1965. *Reality therapy*. New York: Harper & Row.

Glover, E. 1952. Research methods in psychoanalysis. *International Journal of Psychoanalysis* 33: 403–409.

Goin, M. K., Yamamoto, J., & Silverman, J. 1965. Therapy congruent with class-linked expectations. *Archives of General Psychiatry* 13: 133–37.

Goldfried, M. 1967. Assessment for behavior therapy. Paper presented at the meeting of the American Psychological Association, Washington, D.C., September.

Goldstein, A. P. 1962. *Therapist-patient expectancies in psychotherapy*. New York: Pergamon Press.

———. 1966. Prognostic and role expectancies in psychotherapy. *American Journal of Psychotherapy* 20: 35–44.

Goldstein, A. P., Heller, K., & Sechrest, L. B. 1966. *Psychotherapy and the psychology of behavior change*. New York: Wiley.

Gordon, J. E. 1957. Leading and following psychotherapeutic techniques with hypnotically induced repression and hostility. *Journal of Abnormal and Social Psychology* 54: 405–10.

Gordon, R. E., & Gordon, K. K. 1966. Is short term psychotherapy enough? *Journal of the Medical Society of New Jersey* 63: 41–44.

Gottschalk, L. A., ed., 1961. *Comparative psycholinguistic analysis of two psychotherapeutic interviews*. New York: International Universities Press.

Gottschalk, L. A., & Auerbach, A. H., eds., 1966. *Methods of research in psychotherapy*. New York: Appleton-Century-Crofts.

Gottschalk, L. A., Gleser, G. C., & Springer, K. J. 1963. Three hostility scales applicable to verbal samples. *Archives of General Psychiatry* 9: 254–79.

Gottschalk, L. A., Winget, C. M., Gleser, G. C., & Springer, K. J. 1966. The measurement of emotional changes during a psychiatric interview: A working model toward quantifying the psychoanalytic concept of affect. In L. A. Gottschalk and A. H. Auerbach, eds., *Methods of research in psychotherapy*. New York: Appleton-Century-Crofts, pp. 93–126.

Gould, R. E. 1967. Dr. Strangeclass: Or how I stopped worrying about the theory and began treating the blue-collar worker. *American Journal of Orthopsychiatry* 37: 78–86.

Grossman, D. 1950. An experimental investigation of the effectiveness, in terms of insight, of reflection of feeling versus interpretation. *American Psychologist* 5: 469–70.

———. 1952. An experimental investigation of a psychotherapeutic technique. *Journal of Consulting Psychology* 16: 325–31.

Haggard, E. A., & Isaacs, K. S. 1966. Micromomentary facial expressions as indicators of ego mechanisms. In L. A. Gottschalk and A. H. Auerbach eds. *Methods of research in psychotherapy*. New York: Appleton-Century-Crofts, pp. 154–65.

Haigh, G. 1949. Defensive behavior in client-centered therapy. *Journal of Consulting Psychology* 13: 181–89.

Hain, J. D., Butcher, R. H. G., & Stevenson, I. 1966. Systematic desensitization therapy: An analysis of results in twenty-seven patients. *British Journal of Psychiatry* 112: 295–307.

Harway, N. I., Dittmann, A. T., Raush, H. L., Bordin, E. S., & Rigler, D. 1955. The measurement of depth of interpretation. *Journal of Consulting Psychology* 19: 247–53.

Harway, N. I., & Iker, H. P. 1966. Computer analysis of content of psychotherapy. In G. E. Stollak, B. G. Guerney, & M. Rothberg, eds. *Psychotherapy research: Selected readings*. Chicago: Rand McNally, pp. 667–69.

Hawkins, R. P., Peterson, R. F., Schweid, E., & Bijou, S. W. 1966. Behavior therapy in the home: Amelioration of problem parent-child relations with the parent in a therapeutic role. *Journal of Experimental Child Psychology* 4: 99–107.

Heine, R. W., & Trosman, H. 1960. Initial expectations of the doctor-patient interaction as a factor in continuance in psychotherapy. *Psychiatry* 23: 275–78.

Heller, K., & Goldstein, A. P. 1961. Client dependency and therapist expectancy as relationship maintaining variables in psychotherapy. *Journal of Consulting Psychology* 25: 371–75.

Heller, K., & Marlatt, G. A. 1969. Verbal conditioning, behavior therapy, and behavior change: Some problems in extrapolation. In C. M. Franks, ed., *Behavior therapy: Appraisal and status.* New York: McGraw-Hill.

Heller, K., Myers, R. A., & Kline, L. V. 1963. Interviewer behavior as a function of standardized client roles. *Journal of Consulting Psychology* 27: 117–21.

Hiler, E. W. 1959. Initial complaints as predictors of continuation in psychotherapy. *Journal of Clinical Psychology* 15: 344–45.

Hoehn-Saric, R., Frank, J. D., Imber, S. D., Nash, E. H., Stone, A. R., & Battle, C. C. 1964. Systematic preparation of patients for psychotherapy. I. Effects on therapy behavior and outcome. *Journal of Psychiatric Research* 2: 267–81.

Hollingshead, A. B., & Redlich, F. C. 1958. *Social class and mental illness.* New York: Wiley.

Holt, R. R., & Luborsky, L. 1958. *Personality patterns of psychiatrists.* 2 vols. New York: Basic Books.

Howe, E. S., & Pope, B. 1961a. The dimensionality of ratings of therapist verbal responses. *Journal of Consulting Psychology* 25: 296–303.

———. 1961b. An empirical scale of therapist verbal activity level in the initial interview. *Journal of Consulting Psychology* 25: 510–20.

Hunt, J. McV. 1952. Toward an integrated program of research on psychotherapy. *Journal of Consulting Psychology* 16: 237–46.

Imber, S. D., Frank, J. D., Gliedman, L. H., Nash, E. H., & Stone, A. R. 1956. Suggestibility, social class and the acceptance of psychotherapy. *Journal of Clinical Psychology* 12: 341–44.

Isaacs, K. S., & Haggard, E. A. 1966. Some methods used in the study of affect in psychotherapy. In L. A Gottschalk and A. H. Auerbach, eds., *Methods of research in psychotherapy.* New York: Appleton-Century-Crofts, pp. 226–39.

Jaffe, J. 1957. An objective study of communication in psychiatric interviews. *Journal of the Hillside Hospital* 6: 207–15.

———. 1961. Dyadic analysis of two psychotherapeutic interviews. In L. A. Gottschalk, ed., *Comparative psycholinguistic analysis of two psychotherapeutic interviews.* New York: International University Press, pp. 73–90.

———. 1966. Psycholinguistics and computational linguistics. In S. Arieti ed. *American handbook of psychiatry.* vol. 3. New York: Basic Books, pp. 689–704.

Jewell, W. O. 1958. Differential judgments of manifest anxiety, defensiveness, and effective problem solving in counseling. Unpublished doctoral dissertation, University of Minnesota.

Kadushin, C. 1968. *Why people go to psychiatrists.* New York: Atherton.

Kagan, N., Krathwohl, D. R., & Miller, R. 1963. Stimulated recall in therapy using video tape: A case study. *Journal of Counseling Psychology,* 10: 237–43.

Kamin, I., & Coughlan, J. 1963. Patients report the subjective experience of outpatient psychotherapy: A follow-up study. *American Journal of Psychotherapy* 17: 660–68.

Kanfer, F. 1967. Discussion. Symposium on behavioral assessment at the meeting of the American Psychological Association, Washington, D.C., September.

Kaplan, F. 1966. Effects of anxiety and defense in a therapy like situation. *Journal of Abnormal Psychology* 71: 449–58.

Keith-Spiegel, P., & Spiegel, D. 1967. Perceived helpfulness of others as a function of compatible intelligence levels. *Journal of Counseling Psychology* 14: 61–62.

Keet, C. D. 1948. Two verbal techniques in a miniature counseling situation. *Psychological Monographs* vol. 62 (7, Whole No. 294).

Kessel, P., & McBrearty,J. F. 1967. Values and psychotherapy: A review of the literature. *Perceptual and Motor Skills* 25: 669–90.

Kiesler, D. J. 1966. Some myths of psychotherapy research and the search for a paradigm. *Psychological Bulletin* 65: 110–36.

———. 1968. A grid model for theory and research in the psychotherapies. In L. D. Eron ed. *The relationship of theory and technique in psychotherapy*. Chicago: Aldine • Atherton.

Kirtner, W. L., & Cartwright, D. S. 1958. Success and failure in client-centered therapy as a function of initial in-therapy behavior. *Journal of Consulting Psychology* 22: 329–33.

Knapp, P. H., Mushatt, C., & Nemetz, S. J. 1966. Collection and utilization of data in a psychoanalytic psychosomatic study. In L. A. Gottschalk and A. H. Auerbach, eds. *Research methods in psychotherapy*. New York: Appleton-Century-Crofts, pp. 401–21.

Knapp, R. R. 1965. Relationship of a measure of self-actualization to neuroticism and extraversion. *Journal of Consulting Psychology* 29: 168–72.

Krasner, L. 1963. The therapist as a social reinforcer: Man or machine. Paper presented at the meeting of the American Psychological Association, Philadelphia.

———. 1965. Psychotherapy as a laboratory. *Psychotherapy* 2: 104–107.

Krasner, L., & Ullmann, L. P. 1965. *Research in behavior modification*. New York: Holt, Rinehart & Winston.

Krumboltz, J. D., Varenhorst, B. B., & Thoresen, C. E. 1967. Non-verbal factors in the effectiveness of models in counseling. *Journal of Counseling Psychology* 14: 412–18.

Lacey, J. I. 1959. Psychophysiological approaches to the evaluation of psychotherapeutic process and outcome. In E. A. Rubenstein and M. B. Parloff, eds., *Research in psychotherapy*. vol. 1. Washington, D.C.: American Psychological Association, pp. 160–208.

Landfield, A. W., O'Donovan, D., & Narvas, M. M. 1962. Improvement ratings by external judges and psychotherapist. *Psychological Reports* 11: 747–48.

Lang, P. J. 1968. Fear reduction and fear behavior: Problems in treating a construct. In J. M. Shlien, H. F. Hunt, J. D. Matarazzo, & C. Savage, eds., *Research in psychotherapy*. vol. 3. Washington, D. C.: American Psychological Association, pp. 90–102.

Lang, P. J., & Lazovik, A. D. 1963. Experimental desensitization of a phobia. *Journal of Abnormal and Social Psychology* 66: 519–25.

Lazarus, A. A. 1961. Group therapy of phobic disorders by systematic desensitization. *Journal of Abnormal and Social Psychology* 63: 504–10.

———. 1966. Broad-spectrum behavior therapy and the treatment of agoraphobia. *Behaviour Research and Therapy* 4: 95–97.

———. 1967. In support of technical eclecticism. *Psychological Reports* 21: 415–16.

Lazarus, A. A., Davison, G. C., & Polefka, D. A. 1965. Classical and operant factors in the treatment of a school phobia. *Journal of Abnormal Psychology* 70: 225–29.

Leary, T. F. 1957. *Interpersonal diagnosis of personality*. New York: Ronald Press.

Leary, T., & Gill, M. 1959. The dimensions and a measure of the process of psychotherapy: A system for the analysis of the content of clinical evaluations and patient-therapist verbalizations. In E. A. Rubenstein and M. B. Parloff, eds., *Research in psychotherapy*. vol. 1. Washington, D. C.: American Psychological Association, pp. 62–95.

Lennard, H. L., & Bernstein, A. 1960. *The anatomy of psychotherapy*. New York: Columbia University Press.

Lesse, S. 1964. Placebo reactions and spontaneous rhythms; their effects on the results of psychotherapy. *American Journal of Psychotherapy* 18: 99–115.

Leventhal, A. M. 1968. The use of a behavioral approach within a traditional psychotherapeutic context: A case study. *Journal of Abnormal Psychology* 73: 178–82.

Levitt, E. 1966. Psychotherapy research and the expectation-reality discrepancy. *Psychotherapy* 3: 163–66.

Lipkin, S. 1954. Clients' feelings and attitudes in relation to outcome of client-centered therapy. *Psychological Monographs* vol. 68 (1, Whole No. 372).

Lohrenz, J. G., Hunter, R. C., & Schwartzman, A. E. 1966. Factors relevant to positive psychotherapeutic responses in university students. *Canadian Psychiatric Association Journal* 11: 38–42.

Lorenz, M. 1955. Expressive behavior and language patterns. *Psychiatry* 18: 353–66.

Lorenz, M., & Cobb, S. 1954. Language patterns in psychotic and psychoneurotic subjects. *Archives of Neurology and Psychiatry* 72: 665–73.

Lorr, M., Bishop, P. F., & McNair, D. M. 1965. Interpersonal types among psychiatric patients. *Journal of Abnormal Psychology* 70: 468–72.

Lorr, M., & McNair, D. M. 1963. An interpersonal behavior circle. *Journal of Abnormal and Social Psychology* 67: 68–75.

———. 1965. Expansion of the interpersonal behavior circle. *Journal of Personality and Social Psychology* 2: 823–30.

Lovaas, O. I. 1968. A behavior therapy approach to the treatment of childhood schizophrenia. In J. Hill, ed., *Minnesota symposium on child psychology*. Minneapolis: University of Minnesota Press.

Luborsky, L. 1959. Psychotherapy. In P. R. Farnsworth and Q. McNemar eds. *Annual review of psychology*. Palo Alto: Annual Reviews, pp. 317–44.

———. 1962. The patient's personality and psychotherapeutic change. In H. H. Strupp and L. Luborsky, eds., *Research in psychotherapy*. vol. 2. Washington, D.C.: American Psychological Association, pp. 115–33.

Luborsky, L., & Strupp, H. H. 1962. Research problems in psychotherapy: A three-year follow-up. In H. H. Strupp and L. Luborsky, eds., *Research in psychotherapy*. vol. 2. Washington, D.C.: American Psychological Association, pp. 308–29.

MacCulloch, M. J., & Feldman, M. P. 1967. Personality and the treatment of homosexuality. *Acta Psychiatrica Scandinavica* 43: 300–17.

Mahl, G. F. 1960. The expression of emotions on the lexical and linguistic levels. Paper read at American Association for the Advancement of Science Symposium, New York, December.

———. 1968. Gestures and body movements in interviews. In J. M. Schlien, H. F. Hunt, J. D. Matarazzo, & C. Savage, eds., *Research in psychotherapy*. vol. 3. Washington, D.C.: American Psychological Association, pp. 295–346.

Malan, D. H., Bacal, H. A., Heath, E. S., & Balfour, F. H. G. 1967. Psychodynamic study of changes in "untreated" neurotic patients. Unpublished manuscript, Tavistock Clinic, London, W. 1, England.

Marsden, G. 1965. Content analysis studies of therapeutic interviews: 1954–1964. *Psychological Bulletin* 63: 298–321.

Martin, B. 1956. Galvanic skin conductance as a function of successive interviews. *Journal of Clinical Psychology* 12: 91–94.

Massimo, J. L., & Shore, M. F. 1963. The effectiveness of a comprehensive, vocationally oriented psychotherapeutic program for adolescent delinquent boys. *American Journal of Orthopsychiatry* 33: 634–42.

———. 1966. A comprehensive vocationally oriented psychotherapeutic program for delinquent boys: A follow-up study. *American Journal of Orthopsychiatry* 36: 609–15.

Matarazzo, J. D. 1962. Prescribed behavior therapy: Suggestions from interview research. In A. J. Bachrach, ed., *Experimental foundations of clinical psychology*. New York: Basic Books, Ch. 14.

———. 1965. Psychotherapeutic processes. In P. R. Farnsworth, ed., *Annual Review of Psychology*. Palo Alto: Annual Reviews, pp. 181–224.

Matarazzo, J. D., Hess, H. F., & Saslow, G. 1962. Frequency and duration characteristics of speech and silence behavior during interviews. *Journal of Clinical Psychology* 18: 416–26.

Matarazzo, J. D., Wiens, A. N., Matarazzo, R. G., & Saslow, G. 1968. Speech and silence behavior in clinical psychotherapy and its laboratory correlates. In J. M. Shlien, H. F. Hunt, J. D. Matarazzo, & C. Savage, eds., *Research in psychotherapy*. vol. 3. Washington, D.C.: American Psychological Association, pp. 347–94.

Matarazzo, J. D., Wiens, A. N., & Saslow, G. 1965. Studies in interview speech behavior. In L. Krasner & L. P. Ullmann, eds., *Research in behavior modification: New developments and their clinical implications*. New York: Holt, Rinehart, & Winston, pp. 179–210.

Mayfield, P. N. 1962. The Weltanschauung of psychotherapists and selected correlates in a quasi-therapy situation. Unpublished doctoral dissertation, University of North Carolina.

McNair, D. M., Callahan, D. M., & Lorr, M. 1962. Therapist "type" and patient response to psychotherapy. *Journal of Consulting Psychology* 26: 425–29.

McNair, D. M., & Lorr, M. 1964. An analysis of professed psychotherapeutic techniques. *Journal of Consulting Psychology* 28: 265–71.

McNair, D. M., Lorr, M., & Callahan, D. M. 1963. Patient and therapist influences on quitting psychotherapy. *Journal of Consulting Psychology* 27: 10–17.

McQuown, N. A. 1957. Linguistic transcription and specification of psychiatric interview materials. *Psychiatry* 20: 79–86.

Miles, H. H. W., Barabee, E. L., & Finesinger, J. E. 1951. The problem of evaluation of psychotherapy: With a follow-up study of 62 cases of anxiety neurosis. *Journal of Nervous and Mental Disease* 114: 359–65.

Mintz, E. 1965. Evaluation of psychotherapy: A three-year study. Paper presented at the meeting of the Third Scientific Conference on Psychoanalysis, New York.

Mischel, W. 1966. Research and theory on delay of gratification. In B. A. Maher ed. *Progress in experimental personality research.* vol. 3. New York: Academic Press, pp. 85–132.

Mowrer, O. H. 1966. Behavior therapies with special reference to modeling and imitation. *American Journal of Psychotherapy* 20: 439–61.

———. 1968. Loss and recovery of community: A guide to the theory and practice of integrity therapy. In G. M. Gazda, ed., *Theories and method of group psychotherapy and counseling.* Springfield, Ill.: Thomas.

Murray, E. J. 1956. A content-analysis method for studying psychotherapy. *Psychological Monographs* vol. 70 (13, Whole No. 420).

Murstein, B. I. 1963. *Theory and research in projective techniques.* New York: Wiley.

Nash, E. H., Hoehn-Saric, R., Battle, C. C., Stone, A. R., Imber, S. D., & Frank, J. D. 1965. Systemic preparation of patients for short-term psychotherapy. II: Relation to characteristics of patient, therapist, and the psychotherapeutic process. *Journal of Nervous and Mental Disease* 140: 374–83.

Nichols, R. C., & Beck, K. W. 1960. Factors in psychotherapy change. *Journal of Consulting Psychology* 24: 388–99.

Orlinsky, D. E., & Howard, K. I. 1967. The good therapy hour. *Archives of General Psychiatry* 16: 621–32.

Overall, B., & Aronson, H. 1963. Expectations of psychotherapy in patients of lower socioeconomic class. *American Journal of Orthopsychiatry* 33: 421–30.

Parker, G. V. C., & Megargee, E. I. 1967. Factor analytic studies of the adjective check list. *Proceedings of the 75th Annual Convention of the American Psychological Association,* pp. 211–12.

Parloff, M. B., Kelman, H. C., & Frank, J. D. 1954. Comfort, effectiveness, and self-awareness as criteria of improvement in psychotherapy. *American Journal of Psychiatry* 3: 343–51.

Paul, G. L. 1966. *Insight vs. desensitization in psychotherapy.* Stanford, California: Stanford University Press.

———. 1967. Strategy of outcome research in psychotherapy. *Journal of Consulting Psychology* 31: 104–18.

———. 1969a. Outcome of systematic desensitization. I: Background, procedures and uncontrolled reports of individual treatment. In C. M. Franks ed. *Behavior therapy: Appraisal and status.* New York: McGraw-Hill.

———. 1969b. Outcome of systematic desensitization. II: Controlled investigations of individual treatment, technique variations, and current status. In C. M. Franks, ed., *Behavior therapy: Appraisal and status.* New York: McGraw-Hill.

Phillips, E. L., & Weiner, D. N. 1966. *Short-term psychotherapy and structured behavior change.* New York: McGraw-Hill.

Pittenger, R. E., Hockett, C. F., & Danehy, J. J. 1960. *The first five minutes: A sample of microscopic interview analysis.* Ithaca, New York: Paul Martineau.

Plummer, N. A. 1966. Patient-therapist need compatibility and expectation of psychotherapeutic outcome. *Dissertation Abstracts* 27B: 1628–29.

Pollack, I. W., & Kiev, A. 1963. Spatial orientation and psychotherapy: An experimental study of perception. *Journal of Nervous and Mental Disease* 137: 93–97.

Pool, I. 1959. Trends in content analysis today: A summary. In I. Pool ed. *Trends in content analysis*. Urbana: University of Illinois Press, Ch. 7.

Porter, E. H., Jr. 1943a. The development and evaluation of a measure of counseling interview procedures. I. The development. *Educational and Psychological Measurement* 3: 105–26.

———. 1943b. The development and evaluation of a measure of counseling interview procedures. II. The evaluation. *Educational and Psychological Measurement* 3: 215–38.

Poser, E. 1966. The effect of therapists' training on group therapeutic outcome. *Journal of Consulting Psychology* 30: 283–89.

Quay, H. 1959. The effect of verbal reinforcement on the recall of early memories. *Journal of Abnormal and Social Psychology* 59: 254–57.

Raimy, V. C. 1948. Self reference in counseling interviews. *Journal of Consulting Psychology* 12: 153–63.

Raskin, A. 1961. Factors therapists associate with motivation to enter therapy. *Journal of Clinical Psychology* 17: 62–65.

Raush, H. L., & Bordin, E. S. 1957. Warmth in personality development and in psychotherapy. *Psychiatry* 20: 351–63.

Rayner, E. H., & Hahn, H. 1964. Assessment for psychotherapy: A pilot study of psychological test indications of success and failure in treatment. *British Journal of Medical Psychology* 27: 331–42.

Rice, L. N. 1965. Therapist's style of participation and case outcome. *Journal of Consulting Psychology* 29: 155–60.

Ricks, D. F. 1966. Looking ahead for therapy and counseling. In D. A. Hansen ed. *Counseling and therapy in contemporary society*. Boston: Houghton Mifflin.

Ricks, D., Umbarger, C., & Mack, R. A. 1964. A measure of increased temporal perspective in successfully treated adolescent delinquent boys. *Journal of Abnormal and Social Psychology* 69: 685–89.

Rogers, C. R. 1957. Training individuals to engage in the therapeutic process. In C. R. Strother, ed., *Psychology and mental health*. Washington, D.C.: American Psychological Association, pp. 76–92.

———. 1958. A process conception of psychotherapy. *American Psychologist* 13: 142–49.

———. 1959. A tentative scale for the measurement of process in psychotherapy. In E. A. Rubinstein & M. B. Parloff, eds., *Research in psychotherapy*. vol. 1. Washington, D.C.: American Psychological Association, pp. 96–107.

———. 1961. The process equation of psychotherapy. *American Journal of Psychotherapy* 15: 27–45.

———. 1963. The concept of the fully functioning person. *Psychotherapy* 1: 17–26.

Rogers, C. R., & Dymond, R. F. 1954. *Psychotherapy and personality change*. Chicago: University of Chicago Press.

Rogers, C. R., Gendlin, E. T., Kiesler, D., & Truax, C. B. 1967. *The therapeutic relationship and its impact: A study of psychotherapy with schizophrenics*. Madison: University of Wisconsin Press.

Rogers, C. R., & Skinner, B. F. 1956. Some issues concerning the control of human behavior: A symposium. *Science* 124: 1057–66.

Rosenthal, D. 1955. Changes in some moral values following psychotherapy. *Journal of Consulting Psychology* 19: 431–36.

Roth, I., Rhudick, P. J., Shaskan, D. A., Slobin, M. S., Winkinson, A. E., & Young, H. H. 1964. Long-term effects on psychotherapy of initial treatment conditions. *Journal of Psychiatric Research* 2: 283–97.

Rubinstein, E. A., & Parloff, M. B. 1959. Research problems in psychotherapy. In E. A. Rubinstein and M. B. Parloff, eds., *Research in psychotherapy*. vol. 1. Washington, D.C.: American Psychological Association, pp. 276–93.

Sapolsky, A. 1960. Effect of interpersonal relationships upon verbal conditioning. *Journal of Abnormal and Social Psychology* 60: 241–46.

———. 1965. Relationship between patient-doctor compatibility and mutual perception of outcome and treatment. *Journal of Abnormal and Social Psychology* 70: 70–76.

Sarason, I. G. 1965. The human reinforcer in verbal behavior research. In L. Krasner and L. P. Ullmann, eds., *Research in behavior modification*. New York: Holt, Rinehart, & Winston, pp. 229–43.

Sargent, H. D. 1960. Methodological problems of follow-up studies in psychotherapy research. *American Journal of Orthopsychiatry* 30: 495–506.

———. 1961. Intrapsychic change: Methodological problems in psychotherapy research. *Psychiatry* 24: 93–108.

Scheflen, A. E. 1963. Communication and regulation in psychotherapy. *Psychiatry* 26: 126–36.

Scriven, M. 1959. The experimental investigation of psychoanalysis. In S. Hook, ed., *Psychoanalysis, scientific method, and philosophy*. New York: New York University Press, pp. 252–68.

Seward, G. H. 1962. The relation between psychoanalytic school and value problems in therapy. *American Journal of Psychoanalysis* 22: 1–15.

Shapiro, A. K. 1971. Placebo effects in medicine, psychotherapy, and psychoanalysis. In A. E. Bergin and S. L. Garfield, eds., *Handbook of psychotherapy and behavior change: An empirical analysis*. New York: Wiley, pp. 439–73.

Shapiro, M. 1966. The single case in clinical-psychological research. *Journal of General Psychology* 74: 3–23.

Shlien, J. M. 1962. Toward what level of abstraction in criteria? In H. H. Strupp and L. Luborsky, eds., *Research in psychotherapy*. vol. 2. Washington, D.C.: American Psychological Association, pp. 142–54.

———. 1965. Cross-theoretical criteria in time-limited therapy. In *The Sixth International Congress of Psychotherapy, London, 1964, Selected Lectures*. New York: S. Karger.

———. 1966. Cross-theoretical criteria for the evaluation of psychotherapy. *American Journal of Psychotherapy* 20: 125–34.

Shlien, J. M., Hunt, H. F., Matarazzo, J. D., & Savage, C. 1968. *Research in psychotherapy*. vol. 3. Washington, D.C.: American Psychological Association.

Shlien, J. M., Mosak, H. H., & Dreikurs, R. 1962. Effect of time limits: A comparison of two psychotherapies. *Journal of Counseling Psychology* 9, 31–34.

Shontz, F. C. 1965. *Research methods in personality*. New York: Appleton-Century-Crofts.

Shore, M. F., Massimo, J. L., & Mack, R. 1964. The relationship between levels of guilt in thematic stories and unsocialized behavior. *The Journal of Projective Techniques and Personality Assessment* 28: 346–49.

———. 1965. Changes in the perception of interpersonal relationships in successfully treated adolescent delinquent boys. *Journal of Consulting Psychology* 29: 213–17.

Shore, M. F., Massimo, J. L., & Ricks, D. F. 1965. A factor analytic study of psychotherapeutic change in delinquent boys. *Journal of Clinical Psychology* 21: 208–12.

Shostrom, E. L. 1963. *Personal Orientation Inventory*. San Diego: Educational and Industrial Testing Service.

———. 1967. *Man, the manipulator*. New York: Abingdon Press.

Shostrom, E. L., & Knapp, R. R. 1966. The relationship of a measure of self-actualization (POI) to a measure of pathology (MMPI) and to therapeutic growth. *American Journal of Psychotherapy* 20: 193–202.

Shows, W. D., & Carson, R. C. 1966. The A-B therapist "type" distinction and spatial orientation: Replication and extension. *Journal of Nervous and Mental Disease* 141: 456–62.

Siegal, R. S., & Rosen, I. C. 1962. Character style and anxiety tolerance: A study in intrapsychic change. In H. H. Strupp and L. Luborsky, eds., *Research in psychotherapy*. vol. 2. Washington, D.C.: American Psychological Association, pp. 206–17.

Sifneos, P. E. 1967. Two different kinds of psychotherapy of short duration. *American Journal of Psychiatry* 123: 1069–74.

Sklansky, M. A., Isaacs, K. S., & Haggard, E. A. 1960. A method for the study of verbal interaction and levels of meaning in psychotherapy. In J. S. Gottlieb and G. Tourney, eds., *Scientific papers and discussion*. Washington, D.C.: American Psychiatric Association, pp. 133–48.

Sklansky, M. A., Isaacs, K. S., Levitov, E. S., & Haggard, E. A. 1966. Verbal interaction and levels of meaning in psychotherapy. *Archives of General Psychiatry* 14: 158–70.

Snyder, W. U. 1945. An investigation of the nature of nondirective psychotherapy. *Journal of General Psychology* 33: 193–223.

———. 1961. *The psychotherapy relationship*. New York: MacMillan.

Spitzer, R. L., Endicott, J., & Cohen, G. 1967. The Psychiatric Status Schedule: Technique for evaluating social and role functioning and mental status. New York State Psychiatric Institute and Biometrics Research, 722 W. 168th Street, New York.

Spitzer, R. L., Fleiss, J. L., Burdock, E. I., & Hardesty, A. S. 1964. The Mental Status Schedule: Rationale, reliability and validity. *Comprehensive Psychiatry* 5: 384.

Spivack, G., Levine, M. 1964. *Self-regulation in acting out and normal adolescents*. Devon, Pa.: The Devereux Foundation.

Stephens, J. H., & Astrup, C. 1965. Treatment outcome in "process" and "non-process" schizophrenics treated by "A" and "B" types of therapist. *Journal of Nervous and Mental Disease* 140: 449–56.

Stoler, N. 1963. Client likability: A variable in the study of psychotherapy. *Journal of Consulting Psychology* 27: 175–78.

Stone, A. R., Frank, J. D., Hoehn-Saric, R., Imber, S. D., & Nash, E. H. 1965. Some situational factors associated with response to psychotherapy. *American Journal of Orthopsychiatry* 35: 682–87.

Stone, A. R., Frank, J. D., Nash, E. H., & Imber, S. D. 1961. An intensive five-year follow-up study of treated psychiatric outpatients. *Journal of Nervous and Mental Disease* 133: 410–22.

Stone, A. R., Imber, S. D., & Frank, J. D. 1966. The role of non-specific factors in short-term psychotherapy. *Australian Journal of Psychology* 18: 210–17.

Strickland, B. R., & Crowne, D. P. 1963. Need for approval and the premature termination of psychotherapy. *Journal of Consulting Psychology* 27: 95–101.

Strupp, H. H. 1955a. An objective comparison of Rogerian and psychoanalytic techniques. *Journal of Consulting Psychology* 19: 1–7.

———. 1955b. Psychotherapeutic technique, professional affiliation and experience level. *Journal of Consulting Psychology* 19: 97–102.

———. 1955c. The effect of the psychotherapist's personal analysis upon his techniques. *Journal of Consulting Psychology* 19: 197–204.

———. 1957. A multidimensional system for analyzing psychotherapeutic techniques. *Psychiatry* 20: 293–306.

———. 1958. The psychotherapist's contribution to the treatment process: An experimental investigation. *Behavioral Science* 3: 34–67.

———. 1960. *Psychotherapists in action: Explorations of the therapist's contribution to the treatment process.* New York: Grune & Stratton.

———. 1962. Patient-doctor relationships: Psychotherapist in the therapeutic process. In A. H. Brachrach, ed., *Experimental foundations of clinical psychology.* New York: Basic Books, pp. 576–615.

———. 1963. The outcome problem in psychotherapy revisited. *Psychotherapy* 1: 1–13.

———. ed. 1964. *A bibliography of research in psychotherapy.* Private circulation.

———. 1968. Overview and developments in psychoanalytic therapy: Individual treatment. In J. Marmor, ed., *Modern psychoanalysis and perspectives.* New York: Basic Books.

Strupp, H. H., Chassan, J. B., & Ewing, J. A. 1966. Toward the longitudinal study of the psychotherapeutic process. In L. A. Gottschalk and A. H. Auerbach, eds., *Methods of research in psychotherapy.* New York: Appleton-Century-Crofts, pp. 361–400.

Strupp, H. H., Fox, R. E., & Lessler, K. 1969. *Patients view their psychotherapy.* Baltimore: Johns Hopkins Press.

Strupp, H. H., & Luborsky, L., eds., 1962. *Research in psychotherapy.* vol. 2. Washington, D.C.: American Psychological Association.

Strupp, H. H., & Wallach, M. S. 1965. A further study of psychiatrists' responses in quasi-therapy situations. *Behavioral Science* 10: 113–34.

Strupp, H. H., Wallach, M. S., & Wogan, M. 1964. Psychotherapy experience in retrospect: Questionnaire survey of former patients and their therapists. *Psychological Monographs* vol. 78 (11, Whole No. 588).

Strupp, H. H., & Williams, J. V. 1960. Some determinants of clinical evaluations of different psychiatrists. *Archives of General Psychiatry* 2: 434–40.

Subotnik, L. 1966. Transference in child therapy: A third replication. *Psychological Record* 16: 265–77.

Sundland, D. M., & Barker, E. N. 1962. The orientations of psychotherapists. *Journal of Consulting Psychology* 26: 201–12.

Swensen, C. H. 1967. Psychotherapy as a special case of dyadic interaction: Some suggestions for theory and research. *Psychotherapy* 4: 7–13.

Truax, C. B. 1961. A scale for the measurement of accurate empathy. *Psychiatric Institute Bulletin,* Wisconsin Psychiatric Institute, University of Wisconsin 1: 12.

———. 1962. A tentative scale for the measurement of depth of intrapersonal exploration (DX). *Discussion Papers,* Wisconsin Psychiatric Institute, University of Wisconsin.

———. 1963. Effective ingredients in psychotherapy: An approach to unraveling the patient-therapist interaction. *Journal of Counseling Psychology* 10: 256–63.

———. 1966. Reinforcement and non-reinforcement in Rogerian psychotherapy. *Journal of Abnormal and Social Psychology* 71: 1–9.

Truax, C. B., & Carkhuff, R. R. 1964a. For better or for worse: The process of psychotherapeutic personality change. In *Recent advances in the study of behavior change.* Montreal, Canada: McGill University Press, pp. 118–63.

———. 1964b. Significant developments in psychotherapy research. In L. E. Abt and B. F. Reiss, eds., *Progress in clinical psychology.* New York: Grune & Stratton, pp. 124–55.

———. 1965a. The experimental manipulation of therapeutic conditions. *Journal of Consulting Psychology* 29: 119–24.

———. 1965b. Personality change in hospitalized mental patients during group psychotherapy as a function of the use of alternate sessions and vicarious therapy pretraining. *Journal of Clinical Psychology* 21: 225–28.

———. 1967. *Toward effective counseling and psychotherapy: Training and practice.* Chicago: Aldine • Atherton.

Tuma, A. H., & Gustad, J. 1957. The effects of client and counselor personality characteristics on learning in counseling. *Journal of Counseling Psychology* 4: 136–41.

Ullmann, L. P., & Krasner, L., eds., 1965. *Case studies in behavior modification.* New York: Holt, Rinehart, & Winston.

Van der Veen, F. 1965. The parent's concept of the family unit and child adjustment. *Journal of Counseling Psychology* 12: 196–200.

Volsky, T., Jr., Magoon, T. M., Norman, W. T., & Hoyt, D. P. 1965. *The outcomes of counseling and psychotherapy.* Minneapolis: University of Minnesota Press.

Wallach, M. S., & Strupp, H. H. 1960. Psychotherapists' clinical judgments and attitudes toward patients. *Journal of Consulting Psychology* 24: 316–23.

———. 1964. Dimensions of psychotherapists' activity. *Journal of Consulting Psychology* 28: 120–25.

Wallerstein, R. S. 1966. The current state of psychotherapy: Theory, practice, research. *Journal of American Psychoanalytic Association* 14: 183–225.

Waskow, I. E. 1963. Counselor attitude and client behavior. *Journal of Consulting Psychology* 27: 405–12.

Weinberg, N. H., & Zaslove, M. 1963. "Resistance" to systematic desensitization of phobias. *Journal of Clinical Psychology* 19: 179–81.

Weiss, J. M. A., & Schaie, K. W. 1964. The Psychiatric Evaluation Index. *American Journal of Psychotherapy* 18: 3–14.

Weitzman, B. 1967. Behavior therapy and psychotherapy. *Psychological Review* 74: 300–17.

Welkowitz, J., Cohen, J., & Ortmeyer, D. 1967. Value system similarity: Investigation of patient-therapist dyads. *Journal of Consulting Psychology* 31: 48–55.

Wessman, A. E., & Ricks, D. F. 1966. *Mood and personality.* New York: Holt, Rinehart, & Winston.

White, A. M., Fichtenbaum, L., Cooper, L., & Dollard, J. 1966. Physiological focus in psychiatric interviews. *Journal of Consulting Psychology* 4: 363.

White, A. M., Fichtenbaum, L., & Dollard, J. 1964. Measure for predicting dropping out of psychotherapy. *Journal of Consulting Psychology* 28: 326–32.

Whitehorn, J. C., & Betz, B. J. 1954. A study of psychotherapeutic relationships between physicians and schizophrenic patients. *American Journal of Psychiatry* 111: 321–31.

———. 1960. Further studies of the doctor as a crucial variable in the outcome of treatment with schizophrenic patients. *American Journal of Psychiatry* 117: 215–23.

Winder, C. L., Ahmad, F. Z., Bandura, A., & Rau, L. 1962. Dependency of patients, psychotherapists' responses, and aspects of psychotherapy. *Journal of Consulting Psychology* 26: 129–34.

Wolpe, J. 1964. Behavior therapy in complex neurotic states. *British Journal of Psychiatry* 110: 28–34.

Wolpe, J., & Lazarus, A. A. 1966. *Behavior therapy techniques.* New York: Pergamon Press.

Wolpin, M., & Raines, J. 1966. Visual imagery, expected roles and extinction as possible factors in reducing fear and avoidance behavior. *Behavioral Research and Therapy* 4: 25–37.

Wood, E. C., Rakusin, J. M., & Morse, E. 1962. Interpersonal aspects of psychiatric hospitalization: II. Some correlations between admission circumstances and the treatment experience. *Archives of General Psychiatry* 6: 39–45.

Yamamoto, J., & Goin, M. K. 1966. Social class factors relevant for psychiatric treatment. *Journal of Nervous and Mental Disease* 142: 332–39.

Zubin, J., Eron, L. D., & Schumer, F. 1965. *An experimental approach to projective techniques.* New York: Wiley.

THREE

Critiques, replies, and correspondence

Researchers Are Weeded Out

KENNETH MARK COLBY, M. D.*

Who reads these discussions? I start this way because it is the "who" of psychotherapy research I wish to emphasize.

My experience has been in the fields of biological sciences, medicine, psychiatry, psychoanalysis, psychology and computer science. For years I have read critiques in journals such as this one, lining up the good guys versus the bad guys, groaning over banal recitals of factional loyalties, hoping to hear a new idea, enjoying a good fight, celebrating a talent like Meehl and shooting down mountebanks like Eysenck. In each of these fields, when it comes time to lament about progress, discussants address themselves to the "what" and "how" of research. In biological and computer sciences this is indeed the main point because, having a steady supply of high-quality people for research, they need not be concerned about the "who." But in clinician-dominated fields there exists a crucial but little noted problem in that, over time, high quality researchers no longer appear, or if they do they get pushed in some other direction. Then the field sits around and discusses at length the

The critiques are reprinted from *International Journal of Psychiatry* 7 (1969) 116–68. By permission of the Editor.

* Dr. Colby is Senior Research Associate, the Computer Science Department, at Stanford University, Stanford, California.

"what" and "how" of research without recognizing a higher priority problem of the "who."

Research is a function of certain types of people. One would think that, at least in the psychiatric and psychological sciences, there would be greater sensitivity to this truism. But there is not. As evidence I would ask you to re-read the most comprehensive and best survey of psychotherapy research ever conducted, Strupp and Bergin's monumental review in this issue.

My claim is that psychology, psychiatry and (if anybody still cares) psychoanalysis as institutions have developed, under the guise of upholding standards, selective mechanisms which exclude or drive out the best people needed to advance a field through research. This is not an entirely idiosyncratic view. I have discussed it many times with leaders in each of these fields. Over a few drinks they agree, but they have no wish, and understandably so, to take on in a public fight entrenched mediocrities who have little else to do but defend status quo institutions.

This state of affairs has arisen in the mental health sciences out of a power struggle that exaggerated traditional contempt-envy conflicts between clinician and researcher. These conflicts exist not only between people but also within individuals. Perhaps no one in our field is free of them.

A clinician wants to help patients and make good money. He is contemptuous of the researcher whom he feels uses patients and exploits clinical situations to get a paper, tenure or national recognition. He is envious of the researcher's free-spirited parasitism and squirms a bit at the suggestion of a "higher" goal such as scientific knowledge.

A researcher wants to find out things. Some of these may be used one day to help patients, but a lot of them will not. He feels a clinician is a bumbler who simply does not know what he is doing with powerful forces he does not understand and who may be harming as many or more patients than he helps. A researcher is contemptuous of the well-off "doctah" full of service-minded proclamations but obviously dollar-minded in his super-plastic acquisitions. The researcher is envious of the clinician's current dominance of the mental health territory.

It is the clinician who has the power, and his dominance is reflected in accreditation procedures. Both in psychiatry and psychology, clinicians control who becomes accredited as a mental health professional. They select those types who, like themselves, are more helpers than finders. Then at conventions they hold meetings with themes like, 'Hey, how come we're not getting very far?'

Graduate education is designed to create a particular kind of neurosis, a monomania, a passionate commitment. The helping commitment directs a clinician to help suffering people with available knowledge. The finding commitment directs a researcher to discover new knowledge. I submit that our present selection and accreditation policies drive away or drive out the best finders. The best finders are intelligent and curious oddballs who do not just go against the grain but who want to be scientific about their goings. That is, they not only pose challenging questions but devise decidable ways of answering them. To attract good researchers we need do nothing, because problems of human behavior, psychopathology and psychotherapy are inherently fascinating to thousands of these types each year. To keep them, we offer room and respectability in the field.

It is difficult to be against cooperation and collaboration such as Strupp and Bergin recommend for psychotherapy research. My doubts about it stem from my feeling that researchers are too highly individualistic to get large-scale consensus except on trivial points. The logistics of a collaborative undertaking are appalling, and after five to ten years I wonder what it would all show. As Strupp and Bergin warn us, it is meaningless to study vague questions such as the effectiveness of psychotherapy. Unless we have bright ideas and explicit testable questions about what it is we are trying to understand, the best methods, using even larger numbers of people, are of no avail. We need a larger input of new minds more than (I'm not saying "rather than") a collective output from those we already have.

In their critique Strupp and Bergin have been fair to everyone and even too nice to some, including myself. My remarks, scolding standard-waving clinicians, have not been nice, but this is the way I see a crucial obstacle to improved psychotherapy research. It won't make much difference anyway. My opening question was, "Who reads these discussions?" It should have been, "who reads?"

Standard Methods Needed

NOBLE A. ENDICOTT, M. D.*

In this very ambitious monograph, Strupp and Bergin present a critical review of the research on individual psychotherapy with adult neurotics. In addition, they propose a number of research projects which follow promising leads derived from their review.

The authors have produced an excellent overview of this area of research, which should be read by everyone interested in the investigation of psychotherapy. It is written in a clear, concise style, and virtually all of the many diverse areas of individual psychotherapy research are discussed.

Those criticisms I do have concern the authors' proposals for future research. At several points in the monograph the authors clearly recognize the importance of collecting relatively standardized psychotherapeutic data, i.e.,

* Dr. Endicott is Attending Psychiatrist at Roosevelt Hospital in New York City.

the use of the same methods of patient categorization and description and, at least in part, the same therapist, process, and outcome measures. Unless standard methods of measurements are extensively employed, psychotherapy research will continue to be carried out on a piecemeal basis and the data collected will suffer from the same lack of comparability as most past and current research. This lack of comparability prevents the evaluation of the effects of various psychotherapeutic techniques across a large number of different patient types.

The main thrust of the authors' solution to this lack of data comparability lies in their proposal for cooperative research involving two or more clinical centers. I heartily agree with the ideal embodied in this suggestion, but feel this in itself is not sufficient to provide the sheer quantity of comparable data needed. In order to accumulate the type of information necessary to have a decided effect on clinical practice and training, many large scale studies and/or a great many smaller investigations will have to be completed, which utilize the same methods of patient categorization and at least some of the same outcome measures.

In addition, while the authors allude to the difficulties that might be encountered in collaborative studies, they are not specific and provide no solutions to the many problems which can be expected. One pitfall, which will almost assuredly be encountered in any long term study, is the loss of key personnel. A precaution, which might be taken to protect those portions of the study not directly affected by the loss, would be to design the entire project so that each investigator's part of the total study constituted a "complete" investigation within itself. This could be accomplished by directing the collaborative effort toward the utilization of comparable methods of data collection and assigning each investigator one or more relatively homogeneous patient groups to study. For example, investigator A might be assigned patient types W and X while Doctor B would be assigned patient types Y and Z. Half of all four patient groups would be treated with type S psychotherapy and half with type T psychotherapy. If the same measures were used, we would probably have comparable data on the treatment of four patient types using S and T type psychotherapy. If investigator A's project were never completed, the study by B would not be affected and would constitute a complete study in itself, comparing two methods of treatment with two patient types.

Strupp and Bergin's research suggestions are most open to criticism because of their lack of specificity regarding the recommended therapist, process, and outcome measures. While they often list several variables to be evaluated in each area, their suggestions tend to be relatively non-specific and they fail to recommend any specific measures for the variables given. For example, the following client-dependent variables are recommended: self esteem; inner-experiential vs. external-behavioral indices; and fearful, phobic, avoidant behavior. This includes only two relatively specific variables and does not suggest how they might best be measured. A list of a few symptomatic variables, (e.g., anxiety, depression, somatic concern, suspiciousness) and personality characteristics, (e.g., dependency, impulse control, assertiveness, anxiety tolerance, cognitive and perceptual distortions, disturbances in interpersonal relationships) with specific rating scales and/or other objective measures would have been more helpful. The authors may have avoided more specific recommendations because there are no well-established, reliable and valid measures for most of these variables. While this is essentially true, the authors are advising that some type of measures be used, and their proposals would have been much more valuable to the future of psychotherapy research if they had included specific therapist, process, and outcome measures. For example, while earlier in the monograph they mention the advantages of the interview schedules and rating scales developed by Spitzer, et al., they do not refer to them again in listing the client-dependent variables. In addition to such ratings made by clinicians, specific measures based on tests could have been suggested. My colleagues and I have developed reasonably reliable and valid measures of depression and suspiciousness using the Holtzman Inkblot Technique, Thematic Apperception Test and the MMPI (Endicott and Jortner, 1966; Endicott, Jortner, & Abramhoff, 1969). Preliminary unpublished data indicate that reliable and valid measures of several other clinically important dimensions (e.g., anxiety, dependency, impulse control, and cognitive disturbances) can be derived from the same three tests. These three tests plus some of the measures developed by Spitzer and his group (Spitzer, Endicott, & Fleiss, 1967; Spitzer & Endicott, 1969) might thus serve as a relatively economical core battery of evaluation criteria to which other measures could be added for each project and/or each individual patient.

In the authors' brief discussion of controls in outcome research they correctly point out that a no-therapy control group is essentially impossible to maintain outside an institutional setting since many of the controls will seek informal psychological help or formal psychological treatment elsewhere. To control for independent help-seeking among the untreated patients Strupp and Bergin propose a sampling in both the treated patients and the controls of those events occurring outside the treatment situation which are presumed to be "therapeutic." Such a procedure has much to recommend it, but would be extremely difficult to implement and interpret.

Alternative to Attention-Placebo Controls. As another approach to the control problem, the authors recommend an attention-placebo control in future outcome or comparative studies. While controls of this type would definitely be indicated in studies attempting to evaluate the effects of different aspects of a given type of psychotherapy, I would not recommend such procedures as a general control method, since there are many methodological and practical objections to attention-placebo control groups. In outcome studies comparing a treatment and a control group, difficulties will quickly arise if the attention-placebo controls are seen for the same amount of time as the treatment cases. What does one do with the patient for 45–50 minutes once or twice a week after the initial history is obtained? Won't the patient's expectancies be disappointed if the "therapist" continues to inquire about the history hour after hour, or if he insists on talking about neutral topics? What if the patient asks for advice or begins to unburden himself emotionally to the "therapist"? Will the "therapist" change the subject? If so how will this be evaluated? If a decision is made not to control for the quantity (i.e., duration) of the attention, and this appears to be the only practical solution, there are still a host of difficulties to be considered. 'Attention" is not a unidimensional variable but may include every type of interaction of which human beings are capable, except various forms of inattention. Decisions would have to be made regarding which aspects of attention would be evaluated. For example, would attention include sympathetic or empathetic responses or would the attention-giver attempt to respond to the patient in a neutral manner? If empathy is allowed, the attention becomes "therapy" according to Rogerian definitions. On the other hand, it could be seriously argued that maintaining a neutral attitude over an extended period with a person seeking help would have an anti-therapeutic effect on many patients.

A more practical solution to the control problem might be found in following the lead of psychotropic drug research, which, in general, no longer uses a placebo control. Rather, the effects of a new drug are compared with a drug of known effectiveness. Since drug treatment is of established value in the symptomatic treatment of a variety of psychological disorders and from many vantage points is relatively the most economical form of treatment for these problems, this type of therapy would have a number of advantages when used as a control in psychotherapy outcome studies. First, combined with standardized instructions regarding the therapist's attitude and behavior, psychotropic medication would provide a relatively inexpensive, widely acceptable, easily replicable form of treatment with which various forms of psychotherapy could be meaningfully compared. If a given variety of psychotherapy with a specific type of patient cannot produce results which are superior in some respect to those obtained with medication, there would be little justification in employing that form of psychotherapy with these patients.

Second, drug treatment should primarily affect symptomatic variables rather than the more permanent personality traits usually associated with adaptive capacity. Since the major advantages of reconstructive or insight psychotherapy are believed to lie in bringing about relatively permanent changes in such variables, studies comparing these two forms of treatment would be of considerable practical significance and, if properly designed, should add to our knowledge of the processes involved in symptom formation, maintenance, and dissolution.

References

Endicott, Noble A., & Jortner, Sidney. 1966. Objective measures of depression. *Archives of General Psychiatry* 15: 249–55.

Endicott, Noble A., Jortner, Sidney, & Abramoff, E. 1969. Objective measures of suspiciousness. *Journal of Abnormal Psychology* 74: 26–32.

Spitzer, Robert L., Endicott, J. & Fleiss, Joseph L. 1967. Instruments and recording forms for evaluating psychiatric status and history: Rationale, method of development and description. *Comparative Psychiatry* 8:321–43.

Spitzer, Robert L., & Endicott, 1969. Diagno II: Further developments in a computer program for psychiatric diagnosis. *American Journal of Psychiatry* 125: 12–21.

Common Features Account for Effectiveness

JEROME D. FRANK, M. D.*

This is a remarkably comprehensive, complete, balanced and constructively critical survey, which should have considerable influence on research in psychotherapy. Rather than dwelling on its many virtues, however, to promote discussion I shall focus on certain of its limitations.

The authors, for clearly stated reasons, limit their purview to individual psychotherapy with adult neurotics, with a view toward delineating what is known, and what needs to be known, about what specific types of intervention will produce what specific changes in specific types of patients under specific circumstances, in the hope that new knowledge in these areas will lead to improved therapeutic efficacy. Any effort to increase understanding of the processes involved in the particular type of dyadic relation known as psychotherapy must investigate these questions, but it is doubtful that new knowledge of this type will greatly affect practice any more in the future than it has to date. The reason for this is not hard to find. It is simply that research has not produced any method of individual psychotherapy that is significantly more effective than those now in current vogue. If such a form of therapy were discovered for any broad category of neurotics, there would be no doubt about the impact of this discovery—consider, for example, the

* Dr. Frank is Professor of Psychiatry at The Johns Hopkins University School of Medicine, Baltimore, Maryland.

effect of the phenothiazines on the treatment of schizophrenia after advocates of different forms of psychotherapy for this condition had been struggling in vain for years to demonstrate that their own method was superior to those of their rivals.

My reason for doubting that a particular form of individual psychotherapy will prove to be significantly superior to all others is my still unshaken conviction that the common features of all forms of individual therapy account for most of their effectiveness with most adult neurotics. If significant breakthroughs in therapy are to come, I believe they will be through methods that mobilize group forces to involve the entire person, or direct approaches to the nervous system through psychological, pharmacological or neurophysiological interventions.

Before defending these rather sweeping assertions, let me digress to raise some issues concerning follow-up studies, which the authors pass by. They rightly stress that observations of the patients at the time of follow-up need to be as careful and objective as those on which improvement immediately after treatment is based and that more information is needed about the natural course of neurotic illnesses so as to be better able to determine whether improvement under treatment reflects fluctuations that would occur in any case. The presentation, however, neglects important methodological difficulties of follow-up studies, which raise questions as to whether in any particular case the time and effort involved are worth the yield. These include, especially, the attrition of any patient sample over time, requiring ever-increasing effort to round up the defectors, and the unreliability of the patient's reports of the events that have transpired since the previous evaluation, which suffer from the general distortions introduced by memory as well as (according to one careful study) deliberate failure to mention psychological help obtained in the interim.

Factors Influencing Long-Term Effectiveness. The main question, however, is whether the authors' assumption is valid that the ultimate criterion of the success of psychotherapy is its long-term effectiveness. It is probable that at least three processes are involved in the production of attitude change, which may vary independently. The first is the production of the change; the second, its duration; and the third, its generalizability. The crucial question about any form of psychotherapy is whether it produces changes in the patient's attitudes and behavior. If not, it is of no interest. If it is an effective agent of change, the conceptually distinct questions then arise as to the factors accounting for the duration of the change and the extent to which it generalizes to new situations. These need not be the same as those causing the change in the first place—indeed we know that often they are not.

Since the forms of misery that psychotherapy aims to ameliorate are interwoven with the patient's life situation, the duration of improvement produced by psychotherapy will always partly depend on the vicissitudes of the patient's subsequent life. If changes produced by therapy lead to reinforcing changes in those about the patient, his improvement will probably persist and increase; if his changes are opposed by others, he may slip back to his previous attitudes and behaviors. Successes in life unrelated to treatment may enhance its effects, and tragic events diminish them.

Failure to maintain the conceptual distinction between the three aspects of behavior and attitude change may lead to underestimation of an effective therapeutic method because the changes it produces do not endure. Judged solely by follow-up results, electroconvulsive therapy for depressions, for example, would have to be considered a failure because it does not lengthen the intervals between recurrences.

As a matter of fact, the evidence from many studies of psychotherapy is quite consistent that a patient's condition immediately after psychotherapy is a good prognosticator of how he will be five years hence, a further reason for carefully weighing the costs of follow-up studies against their potential gains.

Importance of Transient Crises and Constitutional Vulnerabilities. Returning now to the main theme of this discussion, I believe the hope is illusory that further psychological research will lead to significant advances in the ability to fit different forms of individual psychotherapy to different types of neurotic illness. For the hope is based on an overemphasis on neuroses as disorders of learning, and neglect of two of their other features. One is the important part played by transient crises in leading neurotic patients to seek treatment, which makes for a favorable outcome of all forms of psychotherapy. The other is the patient's constitutional vulnerabilities and deficits, which set limits to the effectiveness of all forms. In combination, they limit the extent to which different forms of psychotherapy can be differentially effective.

If neurotic symptoms are conceived primarily as expressions of learned faulty patterns of perceiving and behaving produced by different kinds of reinforcement schedules interacting with different types of personalities, then it is reasonable to hope that more knowledge of these variables and their interaction will make it possible to devise specific therapeutic learning experiences tailored to specific classes of neuroses. The apparently greater effectiveness of desensitization therapy than insight therapy in relieving certain phobias has fanned this hope. Parenthetically, it may be mentioned that these represent no more than five per cent of patients and that some recent work has raised questions about the specificity of desensitization therapy.

In any case, neurotics ordinarily seek psychotherapy for relief of distress related to current life stress, not for a course in adult education. The stress may exceed the patient's adaptive capacities because it is very severe—a so-called crisis—or because the patient's equipment for coping with stress is inadequate. This inadequacy may be the end result of learned faulty habits of perceiving and behaving that cause him to create undue stresses for himself or to resort to self-defeating ways of resolving them. Another source of inadequate responses to stress, however, lies in constitutional vulnerabilities or defects; that is, flaws in a person's adaptive capacities created by prenatal or post-natal life experiences or by congenital defects that set limits to what he can accomplish and that are not reparable by new experiences.

Most neurotics seek treatment while in the throes of some sort of crisis in living. In this connection, it is important to recall that the victims of catastrophes display the entire gamut of neurotic as well as psychotic symptoms. Psychotherapists in the United States see a great many persons whose misery is a response to an immediate problem in living and who in other cultures would not dream of seeking professional help. Americans are mental hypochondriacs, perhaps because, having been raised to believe that the pursuit of happiness is an inalienable right, they are reluctant to reconcile themselves to the miseries of the normal human lot.

Along the same lines, despite the emphasis in the literature on long-term psychotherapy, in actual practice most patients are seen for fewer than 10 sessions; suggesting that the main function of therapy was to help them recover their emotional equilibrium.

If the psychotherapist lifts his gaze from the subtleties of the therapeutic interaction to encompass the patient's life situation, he will find that the improvement he attributes to his maneuvers often coincides with major changes in the patient's pattern of life—divorce, reconciliation, changing homes or jobs, departure from the home of a burdensome relative and the like. These changes coincide too often with psychotherapy for the relationship to be fortuitous. Perhaps they were imminent just as the patient sought therapy and this was his reason for coming, or his entering psychotherapy may have tipped the balance of forces in his environment by causing others to change their view of him, or probably most commonly, the therapeutic encounter gave him the needed courage to make the change. In any case, the specific therapeutic maneuvers would have less to do with the favorable outcome than the morale-boosting aspects of the therapeutic relationship itself. Patients reacting to a crisis would be expected to respond well to any supportive personal contact.

At the other extreme are patients such as those with neurotic character disorders, severe anxiety and obsessional or hysterical symptoms, whose difficulties, as Freud contended, probably reflect a constitutional factor that creates a heightened vulnerability to stress as well as characteristic ways of responding to it. This component could be affected only indirectly by psychotherapy, if at all.

A current persuasive view of the etiology of certain types of schizophrenia may help to clarify this point. For years many psychopathologists maintained that the etiology of so-called functional psychoses lay in destructive experiences encountered by the patient early in life. It is now clear that many have a large neurobiological component, which eluded discovery for so long because the appropriate investigative tools were lacking. According to this view, some forms of schizophrenia are caused primarily by a constitutional deficiency in certain enzymes necessary for the metabolism of bioamines such as adrenalin. Stress leads to the production of more bioamines than the defective enzyme system can handle, resulting in the production of abnormal metabolites, which interfere with the patient's thought processes, making life more stressful for him. Anything that interrupts this vicious circle at either the psychological or physiological level would be therapeutic. Psychotherapy can help by reducing the stress through teaching the patient more effective ways of coping with life's vicissitudes, but the most direct and effective means of helping him would be to correct his biochemical defect. Phenothiazines may do this by cutting down the production of the substrate.

The view that the bulk of adult neurotics are either reacting to crises on the one hand or sagging under the weight of constitutional burdens on the other would account for the findng mentioned earlier that a patient's immediate response to psychotherapy is typically a good prognosticator of his state years later. Disappearance of circumscribed phobias or of symptoms produced by resolution of a non-current crisis obviously would persist since there is nothing in the environment to cause a relapse. On the other hand, patients whose failure to respond to psychotherapy is due primarily to constitutional factors would not be expected to improve subsequent to treatment.

A further corollary of this position is that regardless of the relative contribution of constitutional and situational components in neuroses, the beneficial effects of all forms of psychotherapy for most of these conditions would depends on their ability to strengthen the patient's ability to cope with stress. The therapist helps the patient to modify his inappropriate behavior and redefine his personal problems so that he can manage them better; but it remains doubtful whether any particular form of behavioral training or cognitive map is better than any other for this purpose. Viewed as a healing art rather than a form of re-education, the most effective ingredients of psychotherapy lie in those aspects of the therapeutic relationship which raise the patient's morale and inspire him with courage to try new ways of coping with the stresses that beset him. These healing components lie in the realm of feelings. Arousal of such emotions of hope, faith, reverence, even sometimes fear, characterize all forms of healing in non-industrial societies. Such emotional states seem to increase accessibility to the healer's influence and facilitate attitude change. Starting with Freud's use of abreaction, emotional arousal has received recurrent emphasis in Western psychotherapy, its latest manifestations being marathon groups and techniques of emotional flooding. Why interest in it waxes and wanes is an interesting question that cannot be pursued here—in this it resembles hypnosis—but whether or not psychotherapeutic methods that stir patients emotionally are in fashion at any particular moment, proponents of all schools of psychotherapy have always agreed that purely intellectual insight is of little value.

Promising New Methods in Psychotherapy. Thus, if there were a striking difference in favor of any type of psychotherapy, one would expect it to lie in group and family therapies, psychodrama, sensitivity training and other approaches which utilize insights gained from individual psychotherapy but go beyond them to evoke powerful emotions and to help patients deal directly with the interpersonal stresses underlying their misery.

Like almost all important therapeutic innovations, these have grown up outside the universities and psychological laboratories and are championed by rival enthusiasts, some of whom have dubious credentials and are more interested in helping people than studying how they do it. Moreover, some of these new procedures verge on the disreputable, according to prevailing standards, and present formidable methodological difficulties for research. Such a scene is understandably uninviting to objective scientists such as the authors of this review. So, while acknowledging the possible potentialities of group methods, they quickly pass on to an exclusive concern with individual therapies. Although they are right in maintaining that, in the last analysis, the aim of psychotherapy is improvement of the individual patient, it may well be that groups contain more powerful means of achieving this end than those at the disposal of the therapist in a one-to-one relationship.

Since almost all neuroses involve excessive responses of the autonomic nervous system, methods that train the patient to control his heart rate and other visceral reactions may have great promise. Perhaps because, in the form of Yoga and the like, such methods have been long practiced in the Orient and therefore carry an aura of mysticism, they seem not to have aroused much interest among American psychologists, although they are closely related to such procedures as autogenous training and progressive relaxation. With the recent demonstration that visceral responses are modifiable by operant conditioning procedures, however, this area has become scientifically respectable, and a surge of research in it can be anticipated.

Dramatic improvement in the treatment of those neurotics whose disability involves a large constitutional component (dramatic improvement in the treatment of situational neurotic responses is not possible because psychotherapy is already so effective) probably awaits pharmacological or electrical interventions in the brain that, for example, would heighten the patient's amenability to the therapist's influence, obliterate neurotic "strategies" ingrained in his nervous system, or stimulate brain centers related to elevation of mood. This prospect has alarming ethical implications, but is virtually upon us and must be faced.

In short, this analysis suggests that, although individual psychotherapies effectively relieve those forms of neurotic distress in which constitutional vulnerabilities play little part, there is little reason to hope that different forms of individual treatment will yield strikingly different results, since they differ only in their cognitive formulations and behavioral training methods, which are probably largely interchangeable, but have in common the powerful healing ingredients of all therapeutic relationships. The one group of individual approaches which hold some promise of achieving significant breakthroughs are those which attempt directly to control the patient's over-reactive autonomic responses.

Group methods which mobilize strong group forces to evoke healing emotions and speed interpersonal learning also hold some promise of significant advance, since they intensify the non-specific components of therapy beyond what is possible in the dyadic interview.

In those neurotic patients whose capacity for coping with stress is limited by constitutional deficiencies or vulnerabilities—probably a larger number than most American psychotherapists would care to admit—specific remedies for specific defects must be sought in the biological, not psychological, realms. Insofar as psychological approaches are effective, it would be in helping such patients to live within their limitations while making fuller use of their assets.

In confining itself to individual psychotherapy, therefore, this review excludes many forms of treatment that may prove to be more effective. The authors are well aware of this possibility and offer cogent arguments for their decision, based primarily on the state of development of the field. Judged in terms of their goals, they have been remarkably successful. They have prepared a thorough, constructively critical review of a complex, not to say chaotic, field, coupled with provocative suggestions for further research. As such, their work will be of the greatest help to all researchers in psychotherapy.

Domains and Dilemmas

ARNOLD P. GOLDSTEIN, PH.D.*

Strupp and Bergin have written an article of major importance, an article in which they seek to accomplish several goals. They attempt to identify a

* Dr. Goldstein is Professor of Psychology at Syracuse University, Syracuse, New York.

number of significant issues relevant to the investigation of psychotherapy, to summarize evidence of use in framing further research and to suggest both hypotheses and designs for maximizing investigative progress. They have succeeded admirably in all three domains. Their critical efforts range broadly, and at times deeply, over almost all areas of significant concern in contemporary psychotherapy research. We wish here to comment briefly on certain of these areas, those which we view as particularly salient for the advance of psychotherapy.

Commonalities and Differences. Strupp and Bergin suggest that all major approaches to psychotherapy utilize a finite number of specifiable mechanisms of psychological influence—counterconditioning, extinction, discrimination learning, reward, punishment, imitation, identification, persuasion, empathy, warmth and interpretation. They hold, and we most strongly agree, that "to determine the relative contributions of each process and the extent to which it can be optimally employed . . . is a major research task of the future." We have long viewed psychotherapy, as practiced, as including major, efficiency reducing trappings, that is, procedures and conceptualizations embedded in clinical lore, which are largely or totally irrelevant to patient change. One of the healthiest signposts for the future of psychotherapy is the increasing number of investigators who, in a manner reminiscent of psychopharmacological research, are increasingly seeking to identify the *active* ingredients in psychotherapy. The increasing disaffection from traditional psychoanalysis, and the current movement towards a nonschool approach noted by Strupp and Bergin, are further reflections of this "active ingredients" focus.

The notion of commonalities may be extended beyond psychotherapeutic approaches to other types of influence processes as a further aid in discerning the therapeutic in psychotherapy. Social and experimental psychology have provided vast amounts of information regarding change processes which appear to have immense potential relevance for therapeutic change. We have developed this theme elsewhere (Goldstein, Heller, and Sechrest, 1966) with particular reference to resistive patients, and will not dwell on it at length here, save to note that studies of interpersonal influence, interpersonal attraction, attitude change, cognitive consistency and group dynamics have already been meaningfully used to augment the efficiency of the psychotherapeutic interaction (Goldstein and Simonson, 1971). Frank (1961) has also developed in detail the idea of commonality of active ingredients across change processes in his discerning comparative analysis of psychotherapy, primitive healing, miracle cures, brainwashing and experimental studies of persuasion. His efforts further highlight the likely value of increased research focus on change process commonalities. Thus, we are led to strongly agree with Strupp and Bergin's recommended research strategy of

> selecting specific techniques from these [psychotherapeutic] approaches and testing them as homogeneous influences with at least two types of homogeneously defined presenting symptoms. . . . We prefer [this strategy] because we have become convinced that the therapy of the future will consist of a set of specific techniques that can be differentially applied under specifiable conditions to specific problems, symptoms or cases. Such an approach would be necessarily a non-school approach.

Note in this statement not only recognition of the need to identify the active ingredients leading to patient change, but also awareness that these ingredients in no sense need be the same across all patients—or even within a single patient at different stages in his therapy. In much of contemporary psychotherapeutic practice, one finds operating what might be called the one-true-light assumption, the either-or assumption or, more generally, the assumption that eventually one and only one type of psychotherapy will prove "best" or prove applicable to all patients. Such an assumption, it should be noted, is not only true for those parochially wedded to a psychoanalytic approach, but also for many now adhering in a highly cultish manner to the behavior therapies. Bonded to this one-true-light assumption is the corollary prediction that all other therapies will be proven "wrong," or less adequate, or somehow to be pseudotherapies. Contemporaneously, this assumption finds expression in the implicit or explicit feeling that psychotherapies can be arranged hierarchically on some sort of effectiveness, rightness or goodness dimension for all patients. Clearly there is a viable alternative assumption. It is an assumption, as Heller (1965) has put it, that we need precision rifles and not a shotgun, psychotherapies and not psychotherapy. It is an assumption made explicit by Kiesler's (1966) discussion of the patient uniformity myth and by Strupp and Bergin's marshalling of evidence from outcome studies to demonstrate the multi-factorial nature of therapeutic change in patients. Whether one subscribes to a medical model of psychotherapy or a learning-educative model of behavior modification in treating patients, one can find extremely few medical or learning problems which are universally resolvable for *all* persons experiencing the given problem by a single type of intervention. Psychotherapy, we would propose, should be viewed in a similar multi-outcome, multi-method manner. Maslow (1962), for example, has meaningfully distinguished between deficit needs and being needs. One need not necessarily subscribe to his essentially existential position to propose that the former may be more readily helped by a behavior therapy approach, the latter by therapies more focussed upon actualization, fulfillment and the like.

Strupp and Bergin urge increasing concern that diagnostic assessment of the patient-candidate lead to recommendations regarding the kind of therapy from which the patient is likely to benefit. We strongly concur, and point to correction of the contemporary irrelevance of most diagnostic efforts for the task of selecting therapeutic precision rifles as a primary research necessity. Galbrecht & Klett (1967) have recently published a research report entitled "The right drug for the right patient." Hopefully, it will not be too long before an analogous paper, "The right psychotherapy for the right patient" appears on the scene.

"Nonprofessional" Therapists. Several lines of evidence examined by Strupp and Bergin converge to support the encouragement of greater utilization of nonprofessional psychotherapists. The Truax and Carkhuff (1967) research, for example, heavily underscores the therapeutic potency of therapist personality variables, as opposed to more formalized and institutionalized technique considerations. As Strupp and Bergin note, the therapist ". . . is viewed more as a person exerting personal influence than simply as an expert applying techniques. It is on the basis of this type of evidence that psychotherapy tends to be seen more and more as simply a particular instance of human relationships in general." A number of studies have similarly demonstrated the importance for outcome of therapist-patient similarity on certain demographic and personality dimensions—only one of which is represented by social class similarity. Clearly this, too, is relevant to the use of nonprofessional therapists. The search for active therapeutic ingredients noted earlier is similarly in the spirit of the notion that the diploma on the wall is of ever-decreasing relevance, and the personality of the therapist of ever-increasing relevance to therapeutic outcome. To the present writer, the significance of this movement is sufficiently great to suggest that Strupp and Bergin have not accorded it its due. More and more research reports are appearing which demonstrate the psychotherapeutic potency of nurses (Ayllon & Michael, 1959; Daniels, 1966), aides (Ayllon & Haughton, 1964; Carkhuff & Traux, 1965), patients' parents (Allen & Harris, 1966; Guerney, 1964; Straughan, 1964; Wahler, Winkel, Peterson, & Morrison, 1965), college undergraduates (Poser, 1967; Schwitzgebel & Kolb, 1964), psychological technicians (Cattell & Shotwell, 1954; Poser, 1966), convicts (Benjamin, Freedman, & Lynton, 1966), housewives (Rioch, 1966; Magoon, 1968), auxiliary counselors (Costin, 1966; Harvey, 1964), human service aides (MacLennon, 1966), and foster grandparents (Johnston, 1967). Surely we perform a gross disservice to the large number of unseen but real therapy candidates if we fail to be responsive to these research findings.

In addition to the straightforward recommendation that the use of nonprofessional therapists be encouraged, the increasing focus on therapist personality as therapeutically potent suggests a reorientation in our training emphases—for both professional and nonprofessional psychotherapists. Less concern, it seems apparent, need be given to training in specific psychotherapeutic techniques and greater attention need be paid to the personal and interpersonal qualities of the psychotherapist. The training in empathy, warmth and genuineness which Truax & Carkhuff (1967) have demonstrated is possible, is one worthwhile avenue of approach. The personal analysis requirement of long standing in formal psychoanalytic training, a baby so often thrown out with the psychoanalytic bath, is a second meaningful tack. Sensitivity training, either in T-group (Bradford, Gibb, & Benne, 1964) or individual (Goldstein et al., 1966) form, is yet another way of bringing the therapist in closer touch with the nature of his interpersonal impact upon others. Whatever route one follows in altering training approaches to be responsive to a therapist personality, and not technique emphasis, it is clear that such a focus is a high priority requirement. Bergin and Solomon (1970) report *negative* correlations between empathy ratings of graduate student therapists-in-training and both their grade point averages and grades in therapy practicum courses. With the repeated demonstrations of an association between therapist empathy and patient change in mind, we consider the Bergin and Solomon findings to be immensely important and, in some ways, to represent a striking indictment of many current therapy training programs. Surely we must heed its message.

Researchers versus Practitioners. From the broadest perspective, it is clear that Strupp and Bergin's over-riding intent in integrating such a massive amount of research literature is to encourage large scale, cooperative research—research whose findings hold promise for the advance of psychotherapy. However, a major precondition to cooperative research is *cooperation* and, as simple as this notion first appears, there are indeed very complex and enduring obstacles to cooperative research. Certain of these obstacles are manifest, i.e., problems associated with adequate measurement of variables, availability of research populations of therapists and patients, need for creative hypotheses, appropriate designs and research strategies, and the like. These, of course, are the level of problem with which Strupp and Bergin deal so adequately. However, in actually conducting cooperative research, in experimentally implementing one's creative efforts, certain latent issues exist which appear to serve as obstacles of equal or greater significance. In particular we refer here to researcher-practitioner differences. The report of the Joint Commission on Mental Illness and Health (1961) notes, "Practitioners find that they cannot understand the research reports nor see their relevance to their daily problems. Research workers, on the other hand . . . cannot understand the resistance of the practitioner to such elementary and necessary principles of good research as experimental controls and adequate sampling procedures." Similarly, Strupp (1960) has commented in an earlier paper:

> Psychotherapy is a focal point of the on-going debate between the operationally-empirically minded investigator and the seeker of intuitive understanding. The former often dismisses the insights of the latter as insufficiently validated or even as incapable of unambiguous validation. The latter, if he is a clinician, may fail to see how results statistically validated at the .05 level of confidence can help him deal with unique and complex troubled persons . . . whom he is trying to help.

Observation such as these are common (Chassan, 1953; Reznikoff & Toomey, 1959; Soskin, 1966) and highly relevant to the divergent inter- and intra-professional state of affairs existing today. The extremely slight impact to date of therapy research upon the practice of psychotherapy stands as direct, behavioral evidence of just how unconsummated is the research-practice marriage. Attempts to examine this disharmony have pointed towards several likely responsible agents, involving researchers and practitioners alike. Parloff and Rubinstein (1959) have stressed the degree to which the research community has shown marked unconcern over applied implications and applications of their investigative findings. Mitchell and Mudd (1957) note that the researcher ". . . often does little to resolve the problem of terminology or semantic differences between clinician and researcher. He is frequently hesitant to take time to acquaint the clinician with fundamental principles of his tests, questionnaires and statistical techniques." Hamburg (1961) and Landfield (1954) have commented upon similar breakdowns in communication and, in particular, have underscored the manner in which such faulty communication can decrease the likelihood of subsequent involvement in research by the clinician. Yet another factor contributed by the researcher may be suggested. Much of the psychotherapy research which has been conducted has been high in precision but low in psychological significance. Strupp and Bergin are correct, a great deal of sophisticated research is being conducted. But sheer activity should not deceive us, for activity and relevance are not one and the same. We would hold that the ultimate goal of psychotherapy research is to improve the efficiency of psychotherapeutic practice. A significant proportion of contemporary psychotherapy research is irrelevant to this goal. Astin's (1961) admonitions regarding the functional autonomy of therapeutic practice, and our extension of this notion to therapy research (Goldstein & Dean, 1966) are as germane today as when first written. The flight in the 1950's from global outcome studies to process research was a healthy development for the field at that time. However, as Strupp and Bergin note, our knowledge and research skills have grown and, we would hold, grown sufficiently for much greater attention to be now turned directly upon what we have described elsewhere (Goldstein & Dean, 1966) as outcome-related process variables.

The practitioner's contribution to research-practitioner disharmony is similarly many-sided. Shoben (1953) has commented, for example, "Working on the basis of necessity and with little help from their experimentally inclined colleagues, they (clinicians) have built up a body of 'intuitive' techniques which have been reinforced by a sense of inner certitude and quasi success. . . . Where certainty exists, no matter how tenuously based, there is little motive for investigation." A related antecedent to an anti-research position among clinicians has been pointed to by Luszki (1957). "Regardless of whether the research worker is interfering with the ongoing work of the practitioner, there is the possibility of threat in the very fact that the research may bring new knowledge that will lead to changes in practice." Luszki thus brings us a step closer to the heart of the matter, which seems to us to be very much a psychodynamic issue involving personal threat and values assimilated from one's reference group during training. Brody (1957) has developed this theme most fully. He views the following as the psychodynamic bases for clinician research resistance:

1. Hostility against being forced into a new, unwanted role.
2. Guilt associated with using the patient for research as equivalent to serving the therapist's needs, and not the patient's.
3. Hostility due to new status hierarchy problems in the research-clinical group.
4. Threatened loss of self-esteem following the removal or lowering of accustomed defenses which operate when the therapist works in privacy.

Thus, when viewed as a group, the obstacles to a more productive working relationship between clinicians and researchers are substantial, as is the price paid for this disharmony. Practice suffers from a grossly insufficient number of substantive research findings by which its efficiency might be enhanced. Practice continues to rest primarily on the rather shaky foundation of clinical lore and intuition. Research suffers from insufficient opportunity to examine aspects of psychotherapy of potential use to the practitioner, and particularly from little opportunity to do so with experienced therapists. As for the patient, he suffers too—and this time in a literal sense—on both counts. The practical meaningfulness of our growing research sophistication is, thus, severely attenuated by these latent obstacles to cooperative research. Their broad recognition and active correction thus looms as of the highest priority.

References

Allen, K. E., & Harris, F. R. 1966. Elimination of a child's excessive scratching by training the mother in reinforcement procedures. *Behaviour Research and Therapy* 4:79–84.

Astin, A. W. 1961. The functional autonomy of psychotherapy *American Psychologist* 16:75–78.

Ayllon, T., & Haughton, E. 1964. Modification of symptomatic verbal behavior of mental patients. *Behaviour Research and Therapy* 2:87–98.

Ayllon, T., & Michael, J. 1959. The psychiatric nurse as a behavioral engineer. *Journal for the Experimental Analysis of Behavior* 2:323–34.

Benjamin, J. G., Freedman, M. K., & Lynton, E. F. 1966. *Pros and cons: New roles for nonprofessionals in corrections.* Washington, D.C.: Dept. Health, Education and Welfare.

Bergin, A. E., & Solomon, S. 1970. Personality and performance correlates of emphatic understanding in psychotherapy. In J. T. Hart and T. M. Tomlinson eds. *New directions in client-centered therapy.* Boston: Houghton Mifflin, pp. 223–36.

Bradford, L. P., Gibb, J. R., & Benne, K. D. 1964. *T-group theory and laboratory method.* New York: John Wiley.

Brody, E. B. 1957. Discussion of Mitchell, H. E., and Mudd, Emily H. Anxieties associated with the conduct of research in a clinical setting. *American Journal of Orthopsychiatry* 27:327–30.

Carkhuff, R. R., & Truax, C. B. 1965. Lay mental health counseling. *Journal of Consulting Psychology* 29:426–31.

Cattell, R. B., & Shotwell, A. M. 1954. Personality profiles of more successful and less successful psychiatric technicians. *American Journal of Mental Deficiency* 58:496–99.

Chassan, J. B. 1953. The role of statistics in psychoanalysis. *Psychiatry* 16:153–65.

Costin, S. B. 1966. Training nonprofessionals for a child welfare service. *Children* 13:63–68.

Daniels, A. M. 1966. Training school nurses to work with groups of adolescents. *Children* 13:210–16.

Frank, J. D. 1961. *Persuasion and healing.* Baltimore: Johns Hopkins Press.

Galbrecht, C. R., & Klett, C. J. 1967. *Predicting response to phenothiazines: The right drug for the right patient.* Perry Point, Md.: Central Neuropsychiatric Research Laboratory, Veterans Administration.

Goldstein, A. P., & Dean, S. J. 1966. *The investigation of psychotherapy.* New York: John Wiley.

Goldstein, A. P., Heller, K., & Sechrest, L. B. 1966. *Psychotherapy and the psychology of behavior change.* New York: John Wiley.

Goldstein, A. P., & Simonson, N. R. 1971. Social psychological approaches to psychotherapy research. In A. E. Bergin & S. L. Garfield, eds., *Handbook of psychotherapy and behavior change: An empirical analysis.* New York: Wiley, pp. 154–95.

Guerney, B. 1964. Filial therapy: Description and rationale. *Journal of Consulting Psychology* 28:304–10.

Hamburg, D. A. 1961. Recent trends in psychiatric research training. *Archives of General Psychiatry* 4:215–24.

Harvey, L. V. 1964. The use of non-professional auxiliary counselors in staffing a counseling service. *Journal of Counseling Psychology* 11:348–51.

Heller, K. 1965. *A broader perspective for interview therapy.* Presented at Midwestern Psychological Association, Chicago.

Johnston, R. 1967. Foster grandparents for emotionally disturbed children. *Children* 14:46–52.

Joint Commission on Mental Illness and Health. 1961. *Action for mental health.* New York: Science Editions, Inc.

Kiesler, D. J. 1966. Some myths of psychotherapy research and the search for a paradigm. *Psychological Bulletin* 65:110–36.

Landfield, A. W. 1954. Research avoidance in clinical students. *American Psychologist* 9:240–42.

Luszki, M. B. 1957. *Interdisciplinary team research: Methods and problems.* New York: New York University Press.

MacLennon, B. W. 1966. New careers as human service aides. *Children* 13:190–94.

Magoon, T. M. 1968. *Mental health counselors at work.* New York: Pergamon Press.

Maslow, A. H. 1962. *Toward a psychology of being.* Princeton, N. J.: Van Nostrand.

Mitchell, H. E., & Mudd, E. H. 1957. Anxieties associated with the conduct of research in a clinical setting. *American Journal of Orthopsychiatry* 27:310–23.

Parloff, M. B., & Rubinstein, E. A. 1959. Research problems in psychotherapy. In E. A. Rubinstein and M. B. Parloff, eds., *Research in psychotherapy.* vol. 1. Washington, D. C.: American Psychological Association, pp. 276–93.

Poser, E. G. 1966. The effect of therapists' training on group therapeutic outcome. *Journal of Consulting Psychology* 30: 283–89.

———. 1967. Training behavior therapists. *Behaviour Research and Therapy* 5:37–42.

Reznikoff, M., & Toomey, L. C. 1959. *Evaluation of changes associated with psychiatric treatment.* Springfield, Ill.: Charles C. Thomas.

Rioch, M. J. 1966. Changing concepts in the training of therapists. *Journal of Consulting Psychology* 30:290–91.

Schwitzgebel, R., & Kolb, D. A. 1964. Inducing behavior change in adolescent delinquents. *Behaviour Research and Therapy* 1:297–304.

Shoben, E. J. 1953. Some observations on psychotherapy and the learning process. In O. H. Mowrer ed. *Psychotherapy, theory and research.* New York: Ronald Press, pp. 120–39.

Soskin, W. F. 1966. Research resources in mental health. New York: Basic Books.

Straughan, J. H. 1964. Treatment with child and mother in playroom. *Behaviour Research and Therapy* 2:37–42.

Strupp, H. H. 1960. Some comments on the future of research in psychotherapy. *Behavioral Science* 5:60–71.

Truax, C. B., & Carkhuff, R. R. 1967. *Toward effective counseling and psychotherapy.* Chicago: Aldine • Atherton.

Wahler, R. G., Winkel, G. H., Peterson, R. F., & Morrison, D. C. 1965. Mothers as behavior therapists for their own children. *Behaviour Research and Therapy* 3:113–24.

Research Cannot Yet Influence Clinical Practice

LESTER LUBORSKY, PH. D.*

Strupp and Bergin's opus is essential reading for anyone devoted to psychotherapy research, any one of the hundreds of researchers who are now trying to make progress in this area. Theirs is by far the most authorita-

* Dr. Luborsky is Professor of Psychology in the Department of Psychiatry at the University of Pennsylvania School of Medicine.

I wish to thank my colleagues, Arthur H. Auerbach, Jim Mintz and Martin Orne, for their comments.

tive, comprehensive and judicious of the many attempts to review this body of work. Twenty-five-hundred references were collected! It is written in a simple, direct style, with the main points highlighted by numbers and italics, so that it is remarkably accessible. Neat summaries are offered of the most promising variables for researchers to investigate.

Most reviews summarize the main conclusions and then evaluate the contributions and limitations. In Strupp and Bergin's work the contribution is obvious; there is no need for more explication. As a matter of fact, I share the view of the authors to such an extent that it is almost like reviewing one's own work; I naturally agree and sympathize with most of it. I will therefore list the main areas of contribution, a few limits, some other interpretations of findings they present, and a consideration of the possible impact of their review on the behavior of practitioners of psychotherapy.

The Areas of Contribution. The purview of the survey is phenomenally broad—the authors include not only research about psychotherapy in the usual sense, but also behavior therapies and the research with treatment analogues. From all of this they have extracted the main research issues and listed the promising "growing edges" of the field. Research results are then summarized for the contribution of each of the main sources of influence on psychotherapy: *(a)* the therapist; *(b)* the techniques of treatment; *(c)* the patient variables; *(d)* the patient-therapist similarity variables; *(e)* outcome measures and the problems in each. Finally, they emerged with propositions for six large-scale projects: *(a)* a comparative analysis of the major therapies; *(b)* the effectiveness of psychotherapy as practiced by experts; *(c)* a study of the mental operations of therapists; *(d)* the effectiveness of different therapeutic methods with phobic patients; *(e)* a study of time-limited therapy; *(f)* comparative process analysis of traditional versus behavior therapies.

A Few Limits to the Completeness of the Survey. While the scholarship is generally successful in discerning the main issues of the field and covering a staggeringly huge number of studies, occasional areas appear in which relevant research is missed. These are a few examples:

In summarizing the relationship between the *therapist's level of experience* and the outcome of the patient's treatment, only about half of the available references are included. Furthermore, their implication is that studies of the amount of experience of the therapist show that experience is always significantly related to the outcome of the treatment. In a review by Luborsky, Chandler, Cohen, and Bachrach (1971), 12 studies were found in which the therapist's level of experience was related to the outcome of the treatment. Eight of these studies show a significant relationship to patient's improvement (Barrett-Lennard, 1962; Cartwright & Lerner, 1963; Cartwright & Vogel, 1960; Katz *et al.*, 1958; Knapp *et al.*, 1960; Miles *et al.*, 1951; Myers & Auld, 1955; Rice, 1965). However, four studies were found in which the therapist's level of experience was *not* significantly related to the outcome of the treatment (Fiske *et al.,* 1964; Grigg, 1961; Mindess, 1955; Sullivan *et al.,* 1958). It is amazing that, of the studies mentioned under the relevance of therapist's level of experience to outcome, Strupp and Bergin's seven references have only two in common (Cartwright & Vogel, 1960; Rice, 1965) with the 12 that I have listed in my review, and most of the others that they mention are only *indirectly* related to *outcome* of the patient's treatment (Ashby *et al.,* 1957; Bohn, 1965; Fiedler, 1950a; 1950b; Strupp, 1955b). The same spotty coverage is found, for example, on the topic of *the patient's general adequacy of personality functioning* in relation to the benefit the patient obtains from psychotherapy. Although they covered only a small fraction of the relevant studies, their conclusion seems to be essentially correct (i.e., to correspond to one from a more complete coverage of the literature): The initially better adjusted patients show more improvement. In my review, 26 studies were found in which the initial level of adjustment was related to some measure of the benefit from psychotherapy. Twelve showed the main relationship, that the better adjusted patients improved more. Only one study reported a significant negative relationship. Thirteen found a nonsignificant relationship. Detailed review of all studies enables a conclusion which is more precise than the one in Strupp and Bergin: A significant relationship is obtained in about half the studies, and almost always when there is a significant relationship it is a *positive one.* Their conclusion from the review of studies of *therapist and patient similarity* could also be more specific. They conclude that there is "much speculation and little hard evidence." Actually, my review shows a fair number of studies, and the predominance of these suggest that factors which imply or suggest to the patient and therapist that they have something in common, facilitate gains from psychotherapy. Fourteen studies were located: Nine of them show a significant positive relationship, and one a significant negative relationship with regard to some form of initial similarity between patient and therapist and the eventual benefits from the psychotherapy. These nine positive studies include: Similar interests and values, compatibility of orientation to interpersonal relations, shifts toward similarity with therapist's Rorschach, and social class similarities.

Another Interpretation to the Finding that Patients Get Worse through Psychotherapy. According to earlier findings of Bergin (1966), patients may become better *or worse,* in comparison with untreated controls. This finding may be exactly what it seems to be—if treatment can make a patient better, why can't it also make him worse? But it is also possible that some of the effect is an artifact of the method by which it is established; that is, by a comparison of treated with untreated groups. The two groups have incomparable expectations, and these, in part, account for the finding. Patients who come for treatment start with, and feel they have the basis for, the expectation that they will be helped. When this is not forthcoming, they sometimes become upset by the lack of realization of what they had wished for, and therefore become worse, or *report* they are worse. A disappointed patient may indicate via his self-reports that he is worse, while actually he may be unchanged. Patients in a control (untreated) group set up no such expectation, and, therefore, there are no hopes to be dashed. When they are retested after an interval, they test approximately the same as they did the first time. To make a true comparison, one would have to set up an expectation of being helped in a control group, and then not meet it.

In sum, the reinterpretation is not intended to say that the finding adduced by Bergin is not a real one, but that there may be some contributory factors to it, apart from the immediate effects of the treatment *per se*.

Their Emphasis upon the Promise of Behavior Therapy. Strupp and Bergin may be caught up in over-optimism about behavior therapy. There are, so far, no studies that are even nearly adequate in which behavior therapy is compared with forms of insight-giving psychotherapy. I'm reminded of Parloff's (1968) neat way of putting into perspective the issue of therapeutic effectiveness: "Unfortunately, objective standards and techniques for assessing the outcome of any form of therapy—group or individual—are not yet available. Like beauty, therapeutic effectiveness is in the eye of the beholder. No form of psychotherapy has ever been initiated without a claim that it has unique therapeutic advantages, and no form of psychotherapy has ever been abandoned because of its failure to live up to these claims." A longer time-perspective would be useful in evaluating behavior therapy or any other therapy. The advent of every new drug and every form of psychotherapy is at first greeted with high hopes on the basis of a few promising findings (and the high hopes generated may possibly have been, in part, responsible for some of the promising findings), but after further testing, soberer evaluation takes place. When there has been further research experience with behavior therapy, it will become clearer when it can be used best, and with whom, and what is involved in the transaction beyond the usual, limited behavior therapy theories. Behavior therapy has been adopted mainly by some psychologists who are innovating another brand of psychotherapy, but much of the new treatment is really territory being newly discovered by people who haven't had much experience with the phenomena of psychotherapy. Strupp and Bergin recognize this when they use the expression to describe this rediscovery of "putting old wine in new bottles."

There certainly is a need to wait for comparative studies of behavior therapy with other treatment modes, before jumping to conclusions about their relative suitability. At least two such studies are now in progress—one by John Paul Brady at the University of Pennsylvania, Department of Psychiatry, and the other at Temple University, Department of Psychiatry. A published study by G. L. Paul (1967) is cited by Strupp and Bergin as one of the best of the comparisons between behavior therapy and psychotherapy

(psychotherapy defined in terms of insight-giving therapy). They cite this study, acknowledging that it suffers from several deficiencies but stating that it still might contain the basic rudiments for a future study. Since it is considered to be one of the best comparisons, it is worth looking at. This study illustrates some of the reasons why a comparison between behavior therapy and psychotherapy has yet to be adequately made:

1. In Paul's study (1967), there are no patients—only volunteers from a speech course. They do not have any symptoms for which they would have sought treatment. The population is therefore totally incomparable to that in the literature based upon patients treated by psychotherapy. The motivation of Paul's subjects may have been, in large part, to get a good grade in a speech course.

2. From what is said in the article, nothing is known about the students' attitudes toward behavior therapy vs. insight therapy. It would be good to know which of the two forms of treatment have more magic for them. Is it possible that the students knew of the experimenter's bias?

3. The treatment is extremely short—only five sessions. Such brevity is especially hindering to insight-giving therapy.

4. The comparison is between desensitization procedures, which are focused on getting rid of a speech anxiety, and a form of psychotherapy that has no special focus except on what the patient happens to wish to discuss. The fortunate students assigned to desensitization, therefore, had mass-practice focussed on the speech anxiety; those having insight therapy (and those having attention-placebo therapy) had no such focus. Desensitization, therefore, was especially tailored to the speech anxiety problem, while the insight therapy had no such appropriateness. Imagine another kind of experiment in which a sample of patients suffering from ambiguously formulated personal problems with no discernible focused symptoms were being treated by desensitization versus psychotherapy—the shoe might be on the other foot!

At another point in the review, a statement is made which may also reflect overoptimism about mechanical procedures. "Therapy machines are an inevitability of the future." Shouldn't the sentence have read, instead, "The *attempt* to develop therapy machines will inevitably continue, and if they accomplish anything positive, one would very likely be tempted to apply Dr. Samuel Johnson's reflection about women preachers: 'A woman preacher is like a dog standing on its hind legs; one doesn't marvel that it's well done, but that it's done at all.' "

Some of the optimism about behavior therapy and mechanical procedures extends also to controlled experiments in the area of psychotherapy, which tends to mean setting up experimental analogues and changing certain variables systematically. "On balance we lean toward the conclusion that controlled experimentation with specifiable methods of influence has a brighter future than the 'therapy-centered' approach." This seems like a balanced view, and yet it, too, has not yet been crowned with success. One of the main and serious liabilities of the controlled experiment and analogue approach is the difficulty of being sure that a psychotherapeutic atmosphere exists, and exists in some comparable way to what emerges in the real thing. Even more crucial, the final test of the relevance of such research has to be the demonstration that conclusions reached from analogue settings have meaningful application to actual psychotherapy.

Psychoanalytic psychotherapy comes in for relatively little approval, or even coverage, in comparison with behavior therapy, mechanical procedures and controlled experimentation. The spirit of the Strupp and Bergin review is eclectic, with some wavering effort to weld together the non-dynamic with the dynamic, but the end-product is an uneven meld. Some of the neglect of the psychoanalytic literature may be justified because of its deficiency in quantification, but Strupp and Bergin have left out the few quantitative psychoanalytic studies such as Klein (1960), Knapp *et al.* (1960), and Hamburg *et al.* (1967). Gottschalk's *et al.* (1967) promising contribution of an "object relations" scale might also be included.

Can the Review Achieve Its Aim: To Have an Impact on the Practice of Psychotherapy? The Strupp and Bergin review is the largest scale attempt to influence clinicians with a broad array of quantitative research. Similar attempts in the past have been on the basis of single studies, anthologies of studies, or symposia.

I believe that this review will become better known to the practitioners of psychotherapy than any other, but then it is unlikly to alter their practice very much. Psychotherapists will continue to trust their clinical experience and their clinical mentors. Except for a few therapeutic innovators, the way the psychotherapist practices psychotherapy is determined by where he was trained, and, in turn, the choice of place of training probably reflects the personality of the applicant and chance life-events.

The lack of research-determined revision of therapeutic practice has had a solid basis so far. There is still not enough contributed by quantitative psychotherapeutic research for a clinician to follow. It is obvious that the superiority of one form of therapy over another has not been established by quantitative research. There are some findings about the kind of therapist who performs better with neurotic versus psychotic patients and the kind of therapist who seems to be more effective in general. But even these findings are not sufficiently bolstered for a clinician to be forced to take notice. The largest contributions have been in the area of the kind of patient who will do best in psychotherapy. However, even on this topic, the necessity for exact screening procedures is usually not crucial, since most patients who apply have the opportunity *somewhere* of being accepted for treatment, and most patients get better.

Psychotherapists who are also psychotherapy researchers are apt to be more influenced in their practice than the journeymen psychotherapists. At least the psychotherapists-researchers will try harder to see the application of the Strupp and Bergin review to their own work. However, even here the impact will be limited. I recall that at a conference about ten years ago, one of the most productive psychotherapy researchers remarked to a group of other psychotherapy researchers that his own therapeutic practice had hardly been influenced in any way by his own psychotherapy research. Most of the psychotherapy-researchers present agreed with him.

In sum, then, on the question of how far the review can accomplish its major goal of influencing clinical practice, the answer is that it cannot, at this time, for three main reasons: (*a*) The traditional determiners of therapist's style of practice are not based on quantitative research; (*b*) the relevant research to specific clinical questions has to be even more systematically, critically and completely reviewed with a view to spelling out clinical applications; (*c*) the findings of quantitative psychotherapy research will have to be more compelling. At present, whatever findings have been consistently established and cross-validated have not been enough to force, entice or persuade clinicians into modifying their entrenched patterns of behavior.

Strupp and Bergin are keenly aware of these impediments and are among the psychotherapy researchers who are most actively trying to overcome them. Their understanding of the present state of the field has led to numerous large-scale research suggestions. The worst that can be said about most of them is that they would be cumbersome to carry out, even at times a bit utopian. To pick an example at random, they recommend that the various outcome criteria be related to different therapeutic techniques in order to determine how different types of change are effected. It is a fine idea, but there has been no psychotherapy project so far with sufficient scope to deal with this aim—they recommend a huge collaborative effort. The further implication I draw is the necessity for a broad, multivariate, predictive study of all of the main factors influencing outcome of intensive treatment. I suspect that most of their research suggestions will not be carried out soon, but if even *some* of them are, the field will be in a better state ten years from now.

References

Bergin, A. 1966. Some implications of psychotherapy research for therapeutic practice. *Journal of Abnormal Psychology* 71:235–46.

Gottschalk, L., Mayerson, P., & Gottlieb, A. 1967. Prediction and evaluation of outcome in an emergency brief psychotherapy clinic. *Journal of Nervous and Mental Disease* 144:77–96.

Hamburg, D., Bibring, G. L., Fisher, C., Stanton, A., Wallerstein, R., Weinstock, H., & Haggard, E. 1967. Report of ad hoc committee on central fact-gathering data of the American Psychoanalytic Association. *Journal of the American Psychoanalytic Association* 15:841–61.

Klein, Henriette. 1960. A study of changes occurring in patients during and after psychoanalytic treatment. In P. H. Hoch and J. Zubin, eds., *Current approaches to psychoanalysis: Proceedings of the 48th annual meeting of the American Psychopathological Association.* New York: Grune & Stratton, pp. 151–75.

Knapp, P. H., Levin, S., McCarter, R. H., Wermer, H., & Zetzel, Elizabeth. 1960. Suitability for psychoanalysis: A review of 100 supervised analytic cases. *Psychoanalytic Quarterly* 29:459–77.

Luborsky, L., Auerbach, A. H., Chandler, M., Cohen, J., & Bachrach, H. M. 1971. Factors influencing the outcome of psychotherapy: A review of quantitative research. *Psychological Bulletin* 75:145–85.

Parloff, M. B. 1968. Analytic group psychotherapy. In J. Marmor, ed., *Modern psychoanalysis.* New York: Basic Books, pp. 492–531.

Paul, G. L. 1967. Insight vs. desensitization in psychotherapy two years after termination. *Journal of Consulting Psychology* 3:333–48.

Empiricism Is Accepted

ISAAC M. MARKS, M.D.*

One sign of maturation in a discipline is the development of congruence in viewpoints of its different practitioners. It is heartening to see such convergence described by Strupp and Bergin in their excellent and constructive review. In a field often marked by sterile disputation, they have cut the Gordian knot of polemic by synthesis of the different streams of research in psychotherapy, identified salient problems, and made recommendations for future research which are likely to be fruitful.

Convergence is evident in the way the field of psychotherapy is accepting empiricism, and recognising the need to test out all ideas in the light of repeatable experiments. Accompanying this is a sharpening of concepts and methods, a realization that global ideas of disorder, treatment and improvement are too vague. Increased emphasis is now placed on specificity of the disorder to be treated, the technique to be employed and the criteria to be used in the evaluation of change. It is noted that different techniques may be necessary to alleviate the different kinds of problems which confront the clinician.

In medicine as a whole it has long been accepted that no single method of treatment can be expected to cure all physical disorders. It has taken us

* Isaac M. Marks is Senior Lecturer and Consultant Psychiatrist at the Institute of Psychiatry, Maudsley Hospital, London, England.

much longer to reach the same conclusion for psychological disorders and to realise that every technique has its indications and contraindications, its uses and limitations. The idea could probably only take root when specific and effective techniques became available to demonstrate this truism. As long as one method seemed to be as good as any other in a wide spectrum of pathologies, then one could argue that different psychopathologies were essentially similar for the purposes of treatment. However, once one could sort the sheep who respond to a particular treatment method from the goats who don't, then the different species of disorder become clearer.

We have reached the threshold of this stage in psychotherapy. The early writings about behavior therapy tended to espouse it as a panacea for all forms of disturbance, thus repeating an error which was so conspicuous in early psychoanalytic writings. But recent writings have become more sober and looked for specific applications of each technique.

The Search for Specific Therapies. Strupp and Bergin have rightly stressed how crucial it is to develop specific therapies which will change particular kinds of patients or problems. The techniques used in psychotherapy must be specified in detail. Not only are traditional labels like "client centered therapy" a complex set of interrelated processes, but even simpler techniques like desensitization comprise multiple components each of which may contribute to the patient's improvement. The different active ingredients in each procedure have to be painstakingly isolated before we can understand the nature of the therapeutic process.

Particularly valuable is the clarity with which Strupp and Bergin have analysed the role of the therapeutic relationship in effecting change in the patient. "Once the therapist has achieved a fair level of therapeutic skills and is successful in providing a modicum of warmth, empathy, etc. outcome is more importantly a function of technical competence and patient characteristics. The therapeutic effects of empathy and warmth *per se* appear to be circumscribed. . . . [The relationship] is a prerequisite for therapeutic influence, rather than end in itself. [It is] the matrix within which planful interventions can occur." The logical conclusion from this is that further progress in psychotherapy will come from the refinement of existing techniques and the development of new ones, rather than from the search for extraordinarily gifted therapists. Leitenberg *et al.* (1969) have shown that an important aspect of desensitization is the way the therapist praises the patient as soon as he reports progress during the session. It is not so much the relationship itself that is important, but, rather what is done with that relationship. The patient does not improve simply by basking in a warm empathic glow emitted by the therapist. The therapist transmits his influence through a set of technical operations.

The search for specific techniques immediately implies that a given technique will improve a patient in one area of disfunction but leave another area of disability untouched. One could not agree more with Strupp and Bergin that it is essential to measure many aspects of a patient's disfunction in order to detect the limits of therapeutic outcome in a patient or group of patients. Thus the specific effect of desensitization in phobias can only be shown by demonstrating that phobic symptoms change significantly while other symptoms of depression, obsessions and sexual maladjustment do not. Similarly, in the use of electric aversion one can demonstrate its specific effectiveness by showing how it removes only that deviant behaviour which has been treated, while heterosexual behaviour improves far less, and depression or relationship difficulties improve hardly at all.

At times Strupp and Bergin seem to forget their own message about specificity and lapse into general statements about "improvement" or "disturbance" which are not particularly meaningful. They cite the writer's own work on phobias as general evidence that "severely disturbed patients show the least improvement." This statement has limited meaning unless it is first specified what is indicated by "disturbed." A patient who has a very intense phobia, but no other symptoms, is disturbed if one uses intensity of phobias as the criterion of disturbance, but that patient is not disturbed if one uses the criterion of presence of other symptoms such as free-floating anxiety or obsessions. The intensity of the phobia does *not* set limits on the improvement of the phobia with desensitization, but the presence of other symptoms such as free-floating anxiety or severe obsessions certainly does retard progress. Similarly with use of the term "improved." In a patient with a dog phobia and disturbed personal relations, desensitization will effect improvement in his phobia but not in his personal relationships, while insight psychotherapy can improve his relationships but not his phobias.

Furthermore, what constitutes "disturbance" for one clinical syndrome such as phobic disorder is not necessarily relevant to prognosis in another syndrome such as transvestism. Free-floating anxiety and obsessions are not the chief criteria that predict change in sexual deviations after electric aversion treatment. Most transvestites can lose their deviation with electric aversion, but if they also have strong transsexual feelings, electric aversion has little change of helping them lose their transvestite desires. To take another example, cases with mild writer's cramp who had no free-floating anxiety, obsessions or transsexualism nevertheless did badly with behavioral methods. Their symptom was refractory to existing techniques even though it was mild and one would not label the patients as "disturbed." The symptom was a relatively isolated and simple phenomenon.

Such findings illustrate that it is misleading to suggest without qualification that "simplicity vs. complexity of presenting symptoms" determines differential responsiveness to treatment. This may be true for phobic disorders if one defines "complexity" in terms of number of neurotic symptoms admitted to on a questionnaire, but it is not true for writer's cramp, where even isolated symptoms are not lastingly responsive to behavioral treatments. The relevance to outcome of simplicity vs. complexity depends upon which syndrome, which definition of complexity and which treatment are under consideration at the time. In fact, Strupp and Bergin stress this point elsewhere, even though they ignore their own advice occasionally.

It is clearly important to specify the kind of disorder one is dealing with in any discussion, and Strupp and Bergin do point out the need for natural history studies to delineate different patient states and outcome, since at the moment it is not always clear what the main syndromes are. Traditional nosologies form a useful starting point, which can be refined as time goes on. For example, international and American nomenclature differentiate between phobic and obsessive-compulsive disorders. Results with desensitization support the distinction between obsessive and other phobias, since desensitization has reasonably good results in phobic states, but in obsessive disorders it has either no effect or requires Herculean therapeutic efforts, which preclude its use with more than a handful of patients.

Cost–Effectiveness Considerations. This raises the issue of cost-effectiveness of treatment. One may be able to make significant reductions in obsessive-compulsive behaviour after 200 sessions of desensitization, but a busy clinician has many other patients to attend to who can be effectively helped in a much shorter time, and the clinician can ill afford such strenuous efforts for every obsessive-compulsive patient who asks for treatment. What we need is techniques which can produce change in a reasonably short time, with the technique capable of being learned fairly quickly. Desensitization would be of very limited use if one had to go through five years of training before one could use it. Fortunately, *in the right kind of condition,* it can be used very successfully by the average clinician after only a few hours of instruction. In focal phobias, a clinician can produce excellent improvement in 25 sessions.

Finding the right kind of condition is one of the keynotes to success. Unfortunately, at the present time it is not usually known which conditions, if any, are suited to most techniques. Each technique that holds promise has to be painstakingly tested in repeated controlled clinical trials with homogeneous samples of patients, gradually delimiting those samples that respond and those that don't. One difficulty is in knowing which techniques and which conditions to select for testing. This is a matter for skilled judgment. As Colby is quoted in the review: "Guided by the artisan, a scientist must select a certain crucial problem in the art and judge whether the problem is ready and accessible to a systematic enquiry using currently available procedures." Having selected the technique to be studied, another difficulty arises in assembling a homogeneous sample of patients. In uncommon disorders this is only possible in centers to which large numbers of patients are regularly referred, from these a tiny number are suitable for inclusion in the homogeneous sample one wishes to study. Selection of the sample can be so time consuming that it severely limits research possibilities. Consider the clinician who wishes to assemble a series of obsessive-compulsive patients to be assigned at random into one of two treatment conditions. He will need at least 20 such cases for a start, but obsessive-compulsive neuroses (not personality) make up only 0.5-3 per cent of the psychiatric outpatients in Britain and the USA. This means the clinician will need a starting population of about 2,000 cases to sift from before he can find his sample, and even then this assumes that all his colleagues are referring every suitable patient to him. In practice, at a large center such as the Maudsley Hospital, it would take up to two years to accumulate a series of obsessive-compulsives for study.

The process is slow but essential, and Strupp and Bergin's plea for homogeneity of patient samples is to be thoroughly endorsed. There is little point in testing a mixture of diverse syndromes only one of which can be expected to respond to a given technique, since the non-responding groups could well mask an effect in the one syndrome that is improving. Of course, we often do not know which conditions are valid syndromes and which are rather artificial constructs. But, for a start, we should at least keep chronic paranoid schizophrenics, severe depressives, phobics, obsessive-compulsives, sexual deviants, conversion hysterics and abnormal personalities all as separate groups. Other syndromes will become apparent as time goes on.

This touches one of the few weak points in Strupp and Bergin's otherwise valuable review viz. their lack of sophistication in discussion of clinical syndromes. They suggest that desensitization may be relevant to "conditioned avoidance responses," operant conditioning to "instrumental responses at the level of motoric and simple symbolic behavior," modelling to "acquisition of complex responses," and aversion to "impulse control problems." But this is just the vague kind of formulation they so rightly decry elsewhere in their review. "Conditioned avoidance responses" could be any of many psychiatric symptoms. Virtually all overt behavior can be construed as "instrumental responses at the level of motoric and simple symbolic behavior." And what distinguishes "simple symbolic behavior" from "complex responses"? It is possible to describe much more precisely the different classes of behavior and disorder to which these techniques are potentially applicable. Thus, desensitization is relevant to any condition which is dominated by a focal source of anxiety or autonomic disfunction, such as phobic disorders, inability to micturate in public or psychogenic impotence. Operant conditioning has been helpful in shaping new skills, e.g. in teaching delinquents to read or chronic schizophrenics to be better behaved in the ward; modelling has been helpful in the extinction of mild fears in volunteers, etc.

Lack of precision also marks Strupp and Bergin's uncritical acceptance of the notion of "spontaneous rhythms" of disturbance. This notion is meaningless if used indiscriminately in all conditions. Certainly there are "natural cycles" of disturbance in manic-depressive psychoses, periodic catatonia or agoraphobia, but there are none in conditions such as animal phobias in adults. Indeed, the opposite is true, since animal phobias are distinguished by a constant unremitting course in adult life and have shown no signs of remission without treatment in at least eight studies which employed no-treatment controls. It follows that the importance of "spontaneous rhythms" in assessing results depends upon the condition being treated. Of course, where such cycles are prominent the whole point of a controlled trial of treatment is to eliminate this effect, amongst others, from the results. It bears remembering that the term "spontaneous rhythms" indicates fluctuations due to various causes we know nothing about and cannot identify at present.

Clinical Psychologists versus Hospital Psychiatrists. Disagreement often arises in the field of psychotherapy because clinical psychologists and hospital psychiatrists generally see rather different types of patients. Their divergent views result partly from experience of different clinical problems. Clinical psychologists tend to see more clients with interpersonal difficulties of varying degree, mild anxiety symptoms, career problems, and the like. Hospital psychiatrists see far more schizophrenics, cases of severe depression, varieties of severe neuroses, sexual deviations, character disorders, alcoholism and so on. This may partly account for the greater importance attached to psychiatric diagnosis by hospital psychiatrists. One cannot deny that psychiatric diagnosis is crude and needs to be greatly refined, but that is not the same as eschewing it altogether. Strupp and Bergin's analysis of mood change shows little appreciation of the varying significance of psychiatric symptoms. A depressive mood can be one of the dominant symptoms of a manic-depressive illness, an incidental feature of a chronic schizophrenic disorder, or a response to recurrent interpersonal stress. Only the last can reasonably be regarded as the psychotherapist's domain, and psychotherapeutic efforts with the other two conditions are largely wasted. Similarly, phobias may be the major aspect of a phobic disorder, or they may wax and wane with a severe depressive illness. Desensitization is only fruitful in the first group, while in the latter example appropriate drugs and if necessary EST are more useful and also incidentally less demanding of therapist time.

When Strupp and Bergin suggest that "psychotherapy or behavior therapy may not be the treatment of choice for all applicants," they make quite an understatement. It is dubious whether these techniques are the treatment of choice for more than 20 per cent of routine psychiatric outpatient referrals. This is not to diminish the importance of such techniques. Far from it. Nobody decries the use of digitalis because it is helpful in less than 5 per cent of cases in a general practice. In the right disorder, digitalis is a lifesaver, and in disorders appropriate to them psychotherapeutic techniques have an important place in the therapist's therapeutic armamentarium, along with many other measures including drugs, EST and social rehabilitation. It would be a pity to devalue the psychotherapeutic currency by using it in the wrong area.

Much of this may sound strange to those who deal not with hospital patients but with clients in a private practice, especially that of a clinical psychologist. Such clients frequently have only relationship problems or neurotic symptoms of relatively minor severity. Such a population would include more people who might respond to current psychotherapeutic techniques, but it is well to keep these in proper perspective with the totality of psychological disorder in the community.

As Strupp and Bergin point out, perspective is also necessary in translating results of laboratory experiments to the clinical situation. That handy laboratory animal, the psychology undergraduate, has been as useful as the white rat in testing out new techniques. However, what works with volunteers may not work with patients who have a related problem in more complex form. This became evident when the success of desensitization in numerous experiments with volunteers could be repeated only in a selected group of all phobic patients. Modelling and flooding procedures have also been impressive in controlled experiments with volunteer phobics, but only careful and controlled clinical appraisal will determine how useful these procedures are in the hospital clinic.

Two small errors in the review can conveniently be corrected here. Paul's results (1966) were said to have been with patients, but in fact this study dealt with student volunteers. Secondly, in the discussion on outcome criteria, self-report symptom inventories like the Fear Survey Schedule are described under the heading of "Behavioral assessment" when they would be more accurately classified under "Patient checklist and self-ratings."

The section on control groups might usefully have discussed more fully the question, "Controlling for what?" Since any treatment is multifactorial, only careful selection of appropriate controls ensures that one is isolating precisely that therapeutic ingredient in which one is interested. Which control is appropriate depends obviously upon the clinical question under consideration. The reviewers draw attention to the pervasive importance of controlling the attention received by patients, while arguing that attention and expectancy are "facilitative but far from the essence of therapy." This argument is persuasive.

It was salutary to be reminded by the reviewers that patients sometimes leave treatment not because of "resistance" but because the therapy itself was poor or inappropriate. Another timely point is that patients may be quite right in expecting advice or technical treatment and can improve more when they get it.

The notion of resistance has value, but there is a danger that it can be extended too far. Patients often fail to improve not because they are resistant or uncooperative, but simply because the treatment itself is ineffective for their type of disorder. One project recommended by Strupp and Bergin was research on techniques for overcoming resistance to behavior change. To be useful, such a project would need to define resistance operationally in order to discriminate it from variables such as severity of the disorder being treated. It was an interesting suggestion to increase patient receptivity and diminish resistance by active therapist behavior which stimulates imitation learning. The whole area of modelling procedures in treatment is a promising one for future investigation.

In the search for objectivity, psychophysiological measures have long been tried as a check on clinical and psychological data. Unfortunately, as Strupp and Bergin comment, it is usually only too true that "autonomic and skeletal-motor responses do not have simple meanings which can readily serve as bases for making inferences concerning the psychological aspects of the therapeutic transaction." An exception, which they do not mention, is the measurement of penile erection by a penis transducer. This measure usually has a fairly simple psychological meaning and has proved helpful in monitoring changes during treatment of sexual deviations. The review also does not mention another measure which can be useful, this time with certain phobic patients. This is the galvanic skin resistance. It is true that this measure is notorious for two reasons. On the one hand, it is liable to change equally with many different psychological states, and so have a variable meaning, and on the other hand, it steadily refuses to change in some patients despite gross psychological disturbance. Nevertheless, with those many phobics for whom the GSR does correlate with fear or anxiety, it can be a convincing check on progress, and can also be of prognostic value for response to desensitization. Finally, recent controlled work has elicited electroencephalographic correlates of meditation. If these results are sustained, they could lead the way to systematic investigation of meditation as a psychotherapeutic technique.

A seminal aspect of the review is the way in which ideas are proposed for future research, many of them in sufficient detail to appear immediately practicable propositions. Some of the larger proposals may be more viable if they are carried out in collaboration between two or more major centers which have access to large populations of patients and therapists. A large pool of patients is necessary before one can filter off a homogeneous sample of reasonable size, and having many therapists would ensure that a therapy trial would not take too long. Collaborative studies might be particularly valuable for research into the natural history of neurotic disorders, and for the study of time-consuming treatments such as analytically oriented insight psychotherapy.

Rarely does one see a review of psychotherapy in which Freud's name is hardly mentioned, or read an appraisal of behavioral techniques without Watson's name being raised. Perhaps this is a sign that psychotherapy has moved forward since the days of those pioneers. This review is a forward-looking document that scans a broad canvas concisely, and the authors are to be congratulated on their achievement and sound conclusions. The review is required reading for anybody interested in psychotherapy research.

References

Bancroft, J. H., Jones, H. & Pullan, B. R. 1966. A simple transducer for measuring penile erection, with comments on its use in the treatment of sexual disorders. *Behaviour Research & Therapy* 4:239–41.

Bancroft, J. H., & Marks, I. M. 1968. Electric aversion therapy of sexual deviations. *Procedures of the Royal Society of Medicine* 16:796–99.

Cooper, J. E., Gelder, M. G., & Marks, I. M. 1965. Results of behaviour therapy in 77 psychiatric patients. *British Medical Journal* 1:1222–25.

Fenwick, P., & Hebden, A. 1968. The E. E. G., in meditation and drowsiness: A controlled study. Paper presented to Troisième Institution Internationale D'Etudes Supérieures en electroencephalegraphie Humaine, Marseilles, September.

Gelder, M. G., & Marks, I. M. 1968. Desensitization and phobias: A crossover study. *British Journal of Psychiatry* 114: 323–28.

Gelder, M. G., Marks, I. M., & Wolff, H. H. 1967. Desensitization and psychotherapy in the treatment of phobic states: A controlled enquiry. *British Journal of Psychiatry* 113:53–73.

Hare, E. H. 1965. *Triennial statistical report, 1961–1963*. Bethlem Royal and Maudsley Hospital.

Ingram, I. M. 1961. Obsessional illness in mental hospital patients. *Journal of Mental Science* 107:401.

Lader, M. H., Gelder, M. G., & Marks, I. M. 1967. Palmar skin conductance measures as predictors of response to desensitization. *Journal of Psychosomatic Research* 11: 283–90.

Leitenberg, H., Agras, W. S., Barlow, D. H., & Oliveau, D. C. 1968. Contribution of selective positive reinforcement and therapeutic instructions to systematic desensitization therapy. *Journal of Abnormal Psychology* 74:113–18.

Marks, I. M. 1969. *Fears and phobias*. London: Heinemann.

Marks, I. M., & Gelder, M. G. 1967. Transvestism and fetishism: Clinical and psychological changes during faradic aversion. *British Journal of Psychiatry* 113:711–29.

Marks, I. M., Crowe, M., Drewe, E., Young, J., & Dewhurst, W. G. 1969. Obsessive neuroses in identical twins. *British Journal of Psychiatry* 115:991.

Michaels, J. J., & Porter, R. T. 1949. Psychiatric and social implications of contrast between psychopathic personality and obsessive-compulsive neurosis. *Journal of Nervous and Mental Disease* 109:122.

Paul, G. L. 1966. *Insight versus desensitization in psychotherapy: An experiment in anxiety reduction*. Stanford, Calif.: Stanford University Press.

Politt, J. D. 1960. Natural history studies in mental illness. A discussion based on a pilot study of obsessional states. *Journal of Mental Science* 106:93–113.

Wolpe, J. 1964. Behaviour therapy in complex neurotic states. *British Journal of Psychiatry* 110:28–34.

Effectiveness of Psychotherapy Is Amply Demonstrated

JULIAN MELTZOFF, PH. D.*

In the hope of stimulating and helping to steer the course of future coordinated research, Strupp and Bergin call attention to the limited impact that research has had on practice. They attribute this to the failure of research to provide recommendations, new tools and insights that can be put to practical use. They may be right, but I see no good way of judging the impact that research has had. Theoreticians and clinicians have been the innovators in psychotherapy, and the wellsprings of testable hypotheses. Researchers have generally been the evaluators. Theirs is not a glamorous research of discovery and invention, but laborious, painstaking and time-consuming testing of notions and procedures that have usually been originated by others. Since results of a single research project are not always definitive and incontrovertible, a practitioner is well-advised to wait for findings of several independent studies to solidify a point before uncritically adopting a new technique or abandoning an old one. It takes a long time for the evidence to mount to the point where it can be accepted with confidence and word of it circulated among practitioners. There is considerable time lag between the end of a given project, its merger with other complementary studies, its reconciliation with contradictory ones and its final emergence as accepted knowledge. Only then should it reasonably begin to have a genuine impact upon practice. The whole process takes not a matter of months, but of a professional generation (probably a decade or so). The bulk of the research in psychotherapy has been done within the past decade, and I for one am confident that its effects *are* beginning to be felt and will be of increasing importance. Each generation of clinicians is taught a slightly different gospel from that of the past, and there are clear signs that the teaching has been influenced by research findings.

Research in psychotherapy is now being produced in such quantities that there is an acute need to summarize what *is* known and what is *thought* to be known and to ask what *ought* to be known. Strupp and Bergin have made an important contribution in this direction. The enormity of the task that they carve out for themselves, however, precludes its comprehensive coverage in a single monograph. For the most part their conclusions are warranted, their comments germane, their suggestions cogent and their

* Dr. Meltzoff is Chief of the Psychology Section at the Veterans Administration Outpatient Clinic, Brooklyn, New York.

omissions plentiful. They are to be congratulated for covering as much as they did in the space allotted. Inevitably, however, the result is that of cursory and at times uncritical appraisal of important research areas. In an effort to delimit the scope of their monograph they have restricted themselves to research on individual psychotherapy with adult psychoneurotics, realizing full well that this represents but a small portion of the available research literature. Many of the research findings that were reported, nevertheless, and the conclusions drawn by Strupp and Bergin, were derived from studies that were done on other populations and in other contexts. They repeatedly stress the need for specificity in psychotherapy research, but they themselves generalize findings derived from other groups to individual psychotherapy with adult psychoneurotics.

The Efficacy of Psychotherapy. The central issue that Strupp and Bergin manage to by-pass, but not escape from, is that of the efficacy of psychotherapy. It is not the kind of problem that can be mentioned in passing or lightly dismissed, for if the efficacy of psychotherapy is not established, extensive research on the therapeutic process is largely superfluous. The authors dismiss the outcome research that has been done as "meagre," "unimpressive" and "wasted" without reviewing it. They tell us that untreated control groups are impossible to get, and argue that the question is no longer fruitful or appropriate. Yet they come back at the end and give high priority to recommendations for a study designed to find out if therapy in the hands of masters *can* be effective. It is apparent that they have accepted Eysenck's analysis of the effects of psychotherapy and the contemporary view, as expounded by Truax and Carkhuff, that psychotherapy, as it is practiced, in the hands of the average clinician has not been demonstrated as efficacious.

In preparing a book[1] on psychotherapy research I have reviewed most of the same literature as Strupp and Bergin, as well as the bulk of the outcome and process research that has been done on all patient types and therapeutic methods. When the evidence from controlled experiments is examined and weighed, the conclusion becomes quite clear that the effectiveness of psychotherapy with a wide variety of patient types, as ordinarily performed by journeymen therapists, has already been amply demonstrated. The research evidence to document this statement obviously cannot be presented here, but it has been steadily accumulating over the last 15 years. It now amounts to over 100 controlled outcome studies, most of which have yielded positive results. Admittedly the evidence as regards adult neurotics is not as ample or as clear as it is for other patient groups, probably because of experimental design problems. But efficacy, relative to untreated controls, has been demonstrated with psychosomatic disorders, anti-social behavior problems,

1. J. Meltzoff and M. Kornreich, *Research in psychotherapy* (Chicago: Aldine • Atherton, Inc., 1970).

schizophrenics and other clinical groups considered far more difficult to treat than neurotics. Failure to recognize this conclusion (certainly a controversial one) has influenced much of the thinking and recommendations in Strupp and Bergin's review.

As far as they have gone in reviewing existing research, Strupp and Bergin have briefly but admirably covered most of the important issues concerning therapist, patient and technique variables and criterion problems. They have given a broad and sweeping view of much of the research that has been done, and have presented many of the newer and more interesting areas of contemporary research. Perhaps a minor issue is an understandable tendency on their part to focus upon the more dynamic and eye-catching variables. In their excellent discussion of patient characteristics that may be related to therapeutic change, for example, they overlook a number of obvious background and organismic variables. Research on the effects of such evident patient characteristics as age, sex, marital status, IQ and education needs to be considered before looking at research dealing with less prosaic characteristics such as "relatability" and "attractiveness." Similarly, it is not more elaborate and better personality assessment measures that are needed to resolve the criterion measure problem. Most of the good outcome studies that have been done have used simple, overt, observable behaviors whose meaning was clear and which could be judged with a low level of inference.

Suggested Research Projects. Having laid the groundwork by reviewing research that has been done, Strupp and Bergin go on to suggest a number of coordinated research projects. The first calls for comparative analysis of the three major therapies (client-centered, behavioral and psychoanalytic) despite an avowed de-emphasis of "schoolism" in their paper. There are so many variants of each school that one hardly knows what "psychoanalytic therapy," for example, means any more. It certainly is no longer a fixed and unitary process that can be treated as an entity. This is precisely the argument that is advanced against research evaluating "psychotherapy" in the first place. In that general context I am not impressed with the argument, but it carries great weight in research designed to draw direct comparisons between schools. Further, it is doubtful that these *are* the three major therapies. More therapists are probably eclectics, who draw on techniques from all schools, than anything else. I do not believe that this issue is any longer a matter of central concern in psychotherapy research. Two of the other projects recommended are related to this: the study of the comparative effectiveness of different therapeutic methods with phobias, and the comparative process analysis of traditional and behavioral therapies. Some of this kind of research, particularly that of comparing different ways of treating phobias, has already been done, but of course there is room for more.

The project proposing to evaluate the effectiveness of psychotherapy as practiced by experts to find out if therapy *can* work under optimal conditions is obsolete for the reasons cited earlier. Therapy has already been demonstrated to have a positive effect under less than ideal conditions in the hands of lesser lights. The projected study of the mental operations of therapists, presumably for the purpose of finding out what makes therapists click, is both difficult and interesting, but I have real doubts that it would yield much generalizable information. Studies of time-limited therapy have been done, and have shown promise. I agree that further research on the subject would meet urgent practical needs. Of all the research suggested, it would have the greatest chance of affecting practice.

As a group, these major projects can hardly be expected to develop the new tools and insights that Strupp and Bergin feel past research has failed to provide. I am not suggesting that they are without interest and value, but the number and variety of worthwhile hypotheses about psychotherapy that need testing could keep any number of research institutes busy for years to come. After surveying the research literature one develops a greater appreciation of its magnitude and vast potential for further research, accompanied by an urge to point out the road to the promised land by indicating what ought to be done in large scale coordinated research efforts that rarely take wing. Researchers tend to be an independent breed, and I think that, as in the past, they will continue to follow what they consider to be promising leads, and will seek answers to questions that arouse their special interests. From time to time the bits and pieces will be fitted together by writers such as Strupp and Bergin to give us the broader picture.

Traditional Reductionism Is Unsatisfactory

LEWIS L. ROBBINS, M.D.*

The increase of interest in psychotherapy research and in the development of new psychotherapeutic techniques has been accompanied by a great number of publications which needed condensation, correlation and evaluation. Strupp and Bergin in their scrutiny of some 2,500 articles, most of which have been published in the past four years, have performed a tremendous service to the field. Particularly useful is their assessment of a great range and variety of methodological experiments and their potential value in determining which variables in patients, in therapists and therapeutic techniques might prove to be most rewarding in further investigations.

Because research in psychotherapy is still rather primitive it is inevitable

* Dr. Robbins is Psychiatrist-In-Chief at the Hillside Hospital, Glen Oaks, New York.

and desirable that the authors express their own views with regard to the directions in which future psychotherapy research should go.

Their choice of a limited focus, dealing only with objective research relevant to the individual psychotherapy of adult neurotics, while understandable, may be open to question. At present, there is great confusion regarding the nosology of psychiatric disorders, and concomitantly there is also likely to be considerable disagreement, (perhaps more among clinicians than researchers) regarding the nature of the clinical problem being studied.

Strupp and Bergin, in fact, acknowledge this dilemma when they point out that little is known about the natural history of most psychiatric disorders and that in all the investigations reviewed there has been a notable lack of follow-up studies. In view of these deficiencies in the field, it is somewhat understandable that diagnostic considerations are often limited to one or two presenting symptoms, and both experimental and clinical attention are similarly circumscribed. Although this is not inconsistent with the hypotheses of learning theory and behavior therapy, it is in contradiction to the general experience of clinical psychiatry. Phobias, anxiety and depression, for example, are frequently encountered as symptoms of broader disturbances. In the opinion of this writer, they are often similar to the symptoms of headache and fever, which, although they may respond to the administration of aspirin, nonetheless reflect a variety of possible causes. If a patient is suffering from a self-limited condition such as the common cold, then such symptomatic treatment is sufficient. But if the underlying cause is a brain tumor, for example, viewing the patient as only suffering from a headache is a serious error.

It is perhaps a reflection of this writer's psychoanalytic viewpoint that it seems imperative not only to attempt to determine what a patient is reacting to and how he is reacting, but also to understand what in the life development of the patient makes it necessary for him to react to his situation in his particular way at the particular time he seeks help. This is not to imply that all treatment must attempt to deal with the underlying genetic factors, but it does require an understanding of what they might be. Research that also ignores the personality matrix in which a symptom develops seems likely to be relatively unrewarding from the clinical standpoint. The authors remark how little clinical practice has been influenced, as yet, by research, and perhaps the explanation lies in this area.

Along this same line, it is to be noted that relatively few of the investigations reported deal with the content of the psychotherapy. Most of the studies are concerned with parts of the whole, such as a few personality variables of the therapist and patient and how they may interact, with linguistic styles and non-verbal patterns, or with efforts to scale relatively isolated fragments of the total interaction. Such studies are valuable, even though they do not embrace all the variables that exist in psychotherapy, for they are adding a great deal to our knowledge. What would be desireable would be more evidence of an awareness of the great complexity of the psychotherapeutic dyad rather than what appears to be a tendency to reduce this complexity to a few simple (or even simplistic dimensions). More scientific knowledge of psychotherapeutic processes cannot be adequately developed by relying only on the traditional reduction approach in which the components of a system are broken down into ever smaller pieces, with the conviction that ultimate understanding lies in knowing all there is to know about the parts. Humanistic science requires new concepts different from and complementery to present theories. Human beings, society and man and his total environment are functioning wholes in nature, with unique attributes that cannot be understood by analyses of the parts alone. New approaches are needed to emphasize the holistic nature of man and of the systems—biological, psychological and social—of which he is an integral part.

For many years clinicians have been concerned about the effect of various research approaches and techniques on the course of psychotherapy itself. Considerable attention has been given to the introduction of tape recorders, special testing procedures and the intrusion of research personnel into the treatment situation. While perhaps these are more disturbing to the therapist than to the patient, their effects are not insignificant. Nowhere in this otherwise thorough review is there any discussion of this issue. Perhaps this, too, is an indication of the preponderance of experimental as contrasted to clinical studies which have been published.

The authors correctly call our attention to the fact that the desire to offer help to all who may need it, which characterizes the current community mental health movement, calls for many psychotherapeutic innovations. For many years psychoanalytic concepts have dominated the clinical field and have been incorporated into the general field of psychotherapy. The influence of psychoanalysis has largely been due to the fact that it offers a theory of personality and its disorders along with a rational system of therapy encompassing the complexities and subtleties of the psychotherapeutic situation. This understanding is not, as many seem to believe, limited to psychoanalysis as a particular form of treatment but has potential relevance to all forms of therapy. As the authors have pointed out, psychoanalysis as a method of treatment has certain important limitations, and it cannot be denied that the goals of community psychiatry cannot be realized should we be confined to such a difficult time-consuming one-to-one therapy. However, in the dual pursuit of new and widely applicable methods of treatment and of scientifically exact experiments, caution must be exercised that we do not "throw out the baby with the bath."

Although psychoanalytic experiments and other methodological studies have been few, we cannot overlook, as Strupp has acknowledged elsewhere, that "clinical penetration and scientific rigor have varied inversely. . . . If the advances of psychoanalysis as a therapeutic technique are compared with the experimental research contributions, there can be little argument as to which has more profoundly enriched the theory and practice of psychotherapy." As Gill stated, there is a dilemma between the significant and the exact in psychotherapy research, and our efforts to achieve quantifiable rigor must not ignore the subtleties of the clinical situation. For a more thorough discussion of these issues the reader is referred to Wallerstein's excellent discussion of psychoanalysis and psychotherapy research.

One of the most important points made by the authors is that our investigations should point the way toward greater sophistication with respect to which techniques may be most effective in which conditions, stating, "We have become convinced that the therapy of the future will consist of a set of specific techniques that can be differentially applied under specifiable conditions to specific problems, symptoms or cases. Such an approach would be necessarily a non-school approach."

Those interested in engaging in psychotherapy research would be well advised to study this remarkable review in order to extend the field in the most promising directions, avoiding unnecessary duplications and fruitless repetitions.

The proposals offered for future research projects are logical derivatives of this review and the authors' view of the field. Although it is doubtful that the scientific community is ready for such widespread collaborative efforts, the suggestions have validity. Among the several recommendations, one that is particularly important is the use of experienced psychotherapists as subjects rather than relative neophytes. This along with better follow-up studies, improved methods for measuring change, more precise delineations of the natural history of psychiatric disorders and better comparative studies are all urgent. Finally, the cautions expressed by the authors against too readily generalizing from the laboratory to clinical situations must be constantly kept in mind.

Perhaps the day will come when investigators will be more secular in their approaches and attitudes, showing greater understanding of and respect for many differing points of view. Probably because of the urgency to relieve suffering persons and the intense interpersonal aspects of psychotherapy, the maintenance of objectivity about what takes place and the freedom to experiment in the clinical situation has been hindered. Whether the complex art of psychotherapy can ever be totally understood scientifically, and its effects measured precisely, is certainly questionable. But efforts to ask questions and seek answers with greater precision can only aid in moving the field forward from its present confused and confusing state. In working toward this goal, this review is of inestimable value.

Psychotherapeutic Efficacy and Objective Research

JOSEPH WOLPE, M.D.*

Strupp and Bergin's article has the highly laudable purpose of promoting the principle that "the practice of psychotherapy must become based upon a verifiable scientific substrate." They endeavor "to establish a scientific base and lay the necessary groundwork" for future research, and apply great erudition and admirable dedication to their task.

Unfortunately, they are only partly successful. They do put forward a considerable number of useful rules for the conduct of controlled studies; but while the content of many of the actual studies they propose is unexceptionable, many others are headed towards the futility that has characterized so much past psychotherapy research because of the very persistent influence of some of the same misconceptions about the issues that have beclouded previous work. The force they wield becomes manifest in the four basic statements for whose "full recognition" they plead. The burden of these statements is that psychotherapy is too complex for questions about its efficacy to be simply put and simply answered. This has long been the main premise of those who have argued against the feasibility of rigorous research and who have looked for pretexts for ignoring unwelcome data. Bergin and Strupp are, of course, in favor of research and cannot be accused of ignoring data, but their attitude to some of it is very much influenced by this "complexity" bugbear.

For example, they minimize outcome data reported by behavior therapists on the argument that the particular measures used are "restricted to dimensions derived from a specific theoretical position and thus evidence based upon such measures is difficult to generalize." The authors argue that comparative studies favor behavior therapy because they tend "to utilize criteria which derive from behavioral theory." With specific reference to Gordon Paul's (1966) brilliant comparative study they comment: "It is of interest to note that the behavioral technique excelled in relation to behaviorally oriented criteria, but that it did not with regard to other criteria." If there is one thing that is clear when a patient applies for treatment it is that he is suffering and in some ways disabled. From the sufferer's point of view, whatever technique excells in diminishing the suffering and disability that Paul's behavioral measurements were concerned with has the greatest relevance and the highest merit.

* Dr. Wolpe is Professor of Psychiatry at the Temple University School of Medicine and Eastern Pennsylvania Psychiatric Institute, Philadelphia, Pennsylvania.

And what were the "other criteria" in which, in Paul's study, behavior therapy did not "excel"? Bergin and Strupp do not specify. Perhaps it did not excel at producing "maturation" of personality. Such shortcomings are irrelevant to the objective of overcoming the fear of public speaking of Paul's subjects. I am not objecting to dimensions of personality like "maturation" being assessed, once they are clearly defined. In some patients it may then be an appropriate aim to increase "maturation"; and studies could be devised to compare the potency of different methods in achieving this. I am taking issue with the position that when behavior therapy overcomes fears of public speaking but does not increase "maturation" (or whatever else psychoanalytic theory postulates as desirable), then somehow the value of its accomplishment is in doubt. This is exactly like arguing that we must suspend judgment about the efficacy of a drug that cures syphilis by killing the spirochete, if that drug does not also raise the blood count—because of someone's theory that anemia is part of the cause of syphilis.

Strupp and Bergin are commendably aware that they have biases, and that their objectivity could be affected by them; but they clearly do not realize to what an extent they have actually been influenced. They take for granted, at least in its broad outlines, the psychoanalytic conception of personality—and what this implies for a theory of therapy. They assume that interpersonal factors are the prime agents of therapeutic change. They frequently write as if they believe in what Astin (1961) called the "functional autonomy of psychotherapy," seeing psychotherapy as an "entity" to be studied for its own sake. The question central to their interest turns out to be "What happens in psychotherapy?," rather than the question they themselves initially pose: "What specific therapeutic interventions produce specific changes in specific patients under specific conditions?" The latter question is the practical one. It makes no special commitment to what is called "psychotherapy." It implies interest in the therapist only in so far as he may be an agent of change. (There is, as a matter of fact, good evidence that the therapist *per se* is often not an adequate agent (e.g., Paul, 1966) and at least sometimes not even necessary (e.g., Migler & Wolpe, 1967)).

A minor but very revealing manifestation of the power of the authors' preconceptions is the complaint that in Gordon Paul's study, therapy was limited to six sessions and therefore did not provide an adequate test of insight therapy. The implication is that in 12, 20, or 50 sessions insight therapy might show results as good as achieved by systematic desensitization in six!

Although Strupp and Bergin are favorably disposed towards behavior therapy, their presentation calls for correction at certain points. They allege that I derived my theoretical formulations about behavior therapy from clinical experiences.[2] In fact, the formulations arose from observations of the treatment of experimental neuroses; and the clinical procedures followed the formulations. It is important to point this out because it is this sequence that makes behavior therapy an *applied science* and distinguishes it from other psychotherapeutic systems. Because they do not appreciate this distinction, Strupp and Bergin fail to see that behavior therapy is not a school homologous with the schools of psychoanalysis. Neither its principles nor its practices are sacrosanct. Both are ever vulnerable to the findings of research. This is not true of the schools.

The techniques of behavior therapy are, as far as possible, derived from experimentally established general principles—as would be the case with any applied science. It is, however, entirely acceptable to use methods not suggested by any principle if for their effectiveness there are scientifically acceptable empirical grounds. This is a humane and practical usage of traditional medicine. What is not acceptable is the employment of techniques that are *neither* rooted in experimentally established principle *nor* empirically supported—for example self-disclosure therapy. The adoption of such techniques by my onetime pupil, A. A. Lazarus (1967), however much Strupp and Bergin may applaud it, does not bring the techniques into behavior therapy but projects Lazarus outside it.

The authors are also mistaken in their impression that behavior therapists often proceed on the assumption that the patient's behavioral repertoire is largely intact except for a specific neurotic symptom. That this is not so can easily be ascertained from any standard work on the subject, e.g., Wolpe (1958, 1969). A thorough study is made of each patient to educe and adjudge areas of maladaptive behavior and behavioral deficit; and then therapeutic measures are fitted to the particular problems. It is of some importance to emphasize that habitual behavior—especially emotional behavior —not "symptoms" is the target. "Symptom" merely denotes the patient's awareness of the reactions that go on within him.

A central plea by Strupp and Bergin is for "coordinated research." They point with satisfaction to signs of agreement between proponents of disparate viewpoints. The underlying supposition is that everybody is partly right; and that if all points of view can be brought together a forward movement in concert will result. Perhaps this is a way of resolving political problems; but scientific truth is not established by consensus. That Alexander, Rogers, and Mowrer should have become sufficiently cognizant of the data to entertain the possibility of processes that they previously placed beyond the pale is of sociological interest only. The ideas that guide the actions of psychotherapists must, as in any other field, be *individually* subjected to empirical

2. This criticism refers to an earlier version of the article.

test. In this way alone will the true relationships between phenomena be revealed and the most effective treatments be evolved.

References

Astin, A. W. 1961. The functional autonomy of psychotherapy. *American Psychologist* 16:75.

Lazarus, A. A. 1967. In support of technical eclecticism. *Psychological Reports* 21:415.

Migler, B., & Wolpe, J. 1967. Automated self-desensitization: A case report. *Behaviour Research and Therapy* 5:133.

Paul, G. L. 1966. *Insight versus desensitization in psychotherapy.* Stanford, Calif.: Stanford University Press.

Wolpe, J. 1958. *Psychotherapy by reciprocal inhibition.* Stanford, Calif.: Stanford University Press.

———. 1969. The Practice of Behavior therapy. New York: Pergamon Press.

The "Last Word" on Psychotherapy Research: A Reply

ALLEN E. BERGIN AND HANS H. STRUPP

First and foremost, we wish to express our deep appreciation to all discussants for their thoughtful comments and criticisms of our survey. We are, of course, flattered but also somewhat overwhelmed by the generosity of their praise, which, in all honesty, we feel is not fully deserved. Admittedly, we worked hard and did our best, but our time was sharply limited; therefore, we never aspired to produce an exhaustive review of research in psychotherapy. We intended our survey to be selective and focussed specifically on a sampling of issues and studies most relevant to our task of exploring the feasibility of coordinated or collaborative research. (In this task we are currently immersed, and in this endeavor the comments by the discussants are proving particularly valuable.)

Thus, having unwittingly engendered excessive expectations, we have found ourselves placed on a pedestal by some discussants who have then proceeded to knock us down, at least a bit. A case in point is the criticism of having omitted citations of studies that might have been included in a truly comprehensive review. We anticipated this problem and acknowledged explicitly in our manuscript the selective nature of our analysis. At the same time, we attempted to select representative studies for evaluation, and we take some pride in the observation that no discussant seriously faulted us for

Discussions not commented on in this rejoinder were unavailable to us at the time of writing.

drawing erroneous inferences or conclusions from the available evidence, so that the trends we isolated are evidently sound. If this is true, the survey achieved its stated purpose.

Several discussants raised the question of how our treatise can have an impact upon the practice of psychotherapy. We must simply state that this was not our purpose. We regretted to observe that research has influenced practices only on a modest scale. We tried to assess the reasons and to lay the groundwork for studies that will make a perceptible difference. We labored under no illusion that the survey itself would achieve such a purpose.

Even given a common understanding of the foregoing points, we were cautioned in several of the critiques regarding the enormous obstacles to successful collaborative research. Again, we take these comments seriously. Our first few months of pilot work testing the feasibility of collaboration in psychotherapy research have brought this message home loud and clear. We are presently neither pessimistic nor optimistic about a major effort along these lines; but the potential problems of administration, scientific controls and interpersonal relations have been indelibly impressed upon us.

Before turning to some specific points raised by particular reviewers, it may be opportune to say a word about the authors' biases as perceived by some discussants, most acutely by Luborsky. In general, he notes our (undue) "optimism about behavior therapy and mechanical procedures," upon which he elaborates as follows:

> The spirit of the Strupp and Bergin review is eclectic, with some wavering effort to weld together the nondynamic with the dynamic, but the end product is an uneven meld.

Another discussant (Marks), somewhat in the same vein, feels that we have paid insufficient attention to problems of (dynamic?) psychopathology and overemphasized psychotherapy as a learning (educational) experience. We believe that our failure or inability to achieve a more satisfactory synthesis of divergent viewpoints seems to reflect as much the current status of the field as it highlights our respective convictions. While Bergin confesses to behavioral and client-centered biases and Strupp to psychoanalytic ones, we find ourselves in agreement on many issues. In particular, we believe that psychotherapy of all kinds employs psychological principles which are a proper area of scientific inquiry. To the extent that these principles are made explicit through systematic investigation, to that extent psychotherapy has a future as a scientific discipline. How this investigative effort is to be carried forward is precisely our concern. It is also an issue open to debate and surrounded by a great deal of uncertainty. However, in terms of our basic orientation and goals, we consider ourselves in the scientific tradition which is exemplified as cogently by Freud as it is by Rogers or Wolpe. In our view, neurosis and behavior disorders are not "diseases" nor is psychotherapy analogous to a form of medical treatment. More important, we share a strong distaste for and an impatience with all practices which derive their support solely or preponderantly from untested assertions and which continue to be accepted on faith.

Dr. Marks. We must confess to having found Dr. Marks' critique stimulating reading in itself. It is hard to disagree with his well-reasoned views, particularly when so many of them are consonant with our own. We find many of his specific comments achieving a kind of detail and penetration that was impossible to consistently maintain in the broad sweep of our review.

His analysis of "levels of disturbance," "complexity-simplicity," and "differential diagnosis" in relation to treatment technique and prognosis we can only applaud. They are thoughtful, relevant and probably right.

We take mild exception to a few specifics, however, that are worth mentioning.

While our brief categorizing of methods relevant for different syndromes is somewhat general, we still defend its general outlines and do not believe that Dr. Marks' rephrasing changes our meaning. It is important to point out here, and also in connection with the more general issues of diagnosis which he raises, that we think a new system of dimensionalizing behavior disorders is of high priority. We have hinted at such a reformulation in the paper, and are inclined to argue that diagnostic and prognostic statements of the future are likely to derive from psychological assessments of people who change differentially under specified conditions. Thus, the system of diagnosis is derived from observing responses to given interventions. One begins with therapy and winds up with a diagnostic system rather than vice versa. This follows a behavioral-probability model from psychology rather than the categorical thinking of psychiatry.

Dr. Marks alludes to the differences in experiences of psychologists and psychiatrists with regard to the broad spectrum of pathology. The issue of professional roles is a complex one, and it is clear from Marks' comments that there are marked divergencies in styles of practice and interprofessional relationships in England and the U.S. Thus, his analysis of this point does not seem applicable to conditions in the U.S.

Dr. Colby. As usual, Ken Colby is hard-hitting and blunt—at times embarrasingly so. If we lived in Socrates' day, we would be concerned about his personal safety. As it is, gadflies like Colby are bound to be very irritating to the "Establishment," but we derive encouragement from the fact that they can speak their mind. Perhaps this is a sign of progress, after all. His plea for "a larger input of new minds" highlights the point that scientific advances arise from the works of *creative* people, not from individuals committed to the niceties of methodology and experimental design. His comment that researchers (like many clinicians) are an individualistic lot is well taken and fuels our apprehensions about the prospects of getting a group of researchers to work together in harmony. The problem would be potentiated by expecting researchers and clinicians to collaborate.

While we thus agree with Colby's view that the "who" of research is of great significance, we take issue to a degree with the assertion that creative researchers are being excluded or driven out of this field. This may be true for some programs, but it is less true now than ever before and we think it has rarely been the case in most university departments. While graduate and medical training may indeed dull creativity, they do not do so any more significantly in mental health fields than in others.

We think a very real problem is one of attracting the creative geniuses into therapy research in the first place. This was difficult to do when many leaders in the area were disillusioned and demoralized by their own work. We doubt that these models and their potential emulators were discouraged so much by the challenge of this field or its social dynamics as by the *apparent* weakness of the phenomena being studied.

A radical change has taken place recently, and we believe our review documents the fact that there is a new vibrancy to the field. There is a spirit of optimism, commitment and youthful involvement which makes us more confident than Colby that we can attract some of the best young people, and that their efforts will yield valuable results.

Dr. Frank. Frank advances a rather pessimistic view concerning the future of research in psychotherapy and his main thesis ("the hope is illusory that further psychological research will lead to significant advances in the ability to fit different forms of individual psychotherapy to different types of neurotic illness") is diametrically opposed to the spirit of our review. Frank's argument rests on the basic assumptions that (1) the nonspecific effects of any healing relationship far outweigh any technical psychological interventions that could possibly be devised or refined; and (2) constitutional factors severely limit the effectiveness of these nonspecific psychological influences.

Frank's own work over the years has stressed the common elements in all forms of psychotherapy, and it may well be true that when the totality of the therapist's influence is dissected, his ability to inspire hope, trust and confidence in the patient's strength and ability to cope will overshadow the effects of specific learning experiences he might mediate through interpretations, modeling, desensitization, cognitive restructuring, modification of the patient's expectations, and the like. It seems to us, however, that it is precisely the task of the researcher to study the ingredients of these nonspecific factors. What makes some therapists effective and others relatively ineffective? Why do some therapists succeed with certain patients but not with others?

Frank's position leads to the conclusion that therapists are born, not made, from which it would follow that training is futile. We contend that the "nonspecific factors" are in need of explanation and that the scientist cannot rest content to leave them under this heading, which seems to be as much an umbrella term as "psychotherapy" itself.

Frank buttresses his argument by asserting that most patients seek the help of a psychotherapist when they experience a crisis, that American patients are "mental hypochondriacs" who are averse to reconciling themselves to the "miseries of the normal human lot," and that therapy typically does no more than help them over an immediate stress situation, without lasting effects.

The experience of therapists working in clinics and that of private practitioners simply does not support Frank's view, which cannot be proven by the statement that "in actual practice most patients are seen for fewer than 10 sessions." The reasons for early termination and dropouts are complex and have been carefully researched by Frank's own research group. However, there is strong reason to believe that many patients are suffering from *chronic,* rather than acute, distress, although their difficulties may be exacerbated by a current crisis. Typically,one finds problems of long standing and maladaptive patterns pervading the totality of the patient's life. It may be true that outpatient clinics, because of manpower shortages and other factors, often do little to provide the patient with impressive corrective emotional experiences, but this does not prove that it cannot be done under propitious circumstances. There is evidence to show (e.g., Strupp, Fox, & Lessler, 1969) that a good many patients do achieve lasting changes in outlook; they view reality and their place in life differently following individual therapy; and they report that they are better able to cope with their problems in living. We do not dismiss such changes as trivial nor are we disheartened by the possibility that subsequent life experiences may produce reverses. As Freud pointed out long ago (*"Analysis terminable and interminable"*) psychotherapy cannot be expected to confer life-long "immunity" and the medical man does not abandon his efforts because a disease recurs nor does he despair because constitutional factors have rendered a patient vulnerable to certain diseases. These facts simply have to be faced, allowances have to be made and one's therapeutic zeal has to be tempered by reality. The psychotherapist, like the educator, the physician and other professional helpers, is no magician and he should not be expected to perform miracles. Nor, of course, should he undertake tasks which he is not equipped to do or which are doomed to failure at the outset.

The foregoing statements embody important questions to which research, in our judgment, can make a significant contribution. What can be changed and under what conditions? Who can effectively work toward realistic changes? Why do some patients fail to change although one would assign a reasonable probability to their improvement? Why do some patients succeed when the prognosis is judged poor?

Frank says in effect that where alleged psychotherapeutic changes are observed they would have occurred anyway because of situational factors in the patient's life so that the therapist merely boosted, however slightly, the patient's morale; for the rest the therapist's efforts are rendered ineffective by constitutional factors which he cannot hope to modify by psychological techniques. Apparently disenchanted by the future of individual psychotherapy, Frank pins his hopes on (1) correcting the patient's biochemical defects, and (2) the arousal of powerful emotions in group and family therapies, psychodrama, sensitivity training and the like.

With respect to (1), it is entirely possible that advances in that area may revolutionize the field; however, to the extent that many neurotic problems are the end result of unfortunate learning experiences in early childhood, it is difficult to envisage the possibility that biochemical agents can rectify maladaptive patterns of behavior and help the patient acquire more suitable ones, any more than drugs can provide him with a knowledge of French. Admittedly, if the adverse effects of deeply ingrained behavior patterns could be undone by chemical means, this might greatly facilitate the work of the psychotherapist and in some cases help him succeed where at present he fails. With respect to (2), the principles underlying these—essentially psychological—techniques are the proper concern of the behavioral scientist, and we are obligated to examine them as seriously as anything that transpires in individual psychotherapy. Any approach which, in Frank's words, helps patients "to live within their limitations while making fuller use of their assets" commands the investigator's serious attention. At least in principle the effective ingredients of therapeutic learning can be made explicit, which indeed sums up our faith in the potentialities of research in this area.

Everyone has to decide at some point where he believes the potent variables are, and we would not deny that biological factors are important influencers of behavior. In spite of the fact that he is in good company, we think that Frank has jumped to a premature conclusion. There is too much evidence of the power of behavioral variables to ignore this source of variance. Even the behavior of schizophrenics, the pet monkeys of behavioral geneticists, responds significantly to social variables. We hope that Jerry's thoughtful critique does not anticipate or stimulate a new wave of therapeutic nihilism.

Dr. Goldstein. Goldstein's critique nicely brings into focus a number of significant issues. It is difficult to find exception to his views since they are so consonant with our own. There are two points, however, on which we may differ in emphasis.

1. With regard to the role of personal qualities as therapeutic agents, we agree that there is considerable evidence supporting the notion of their po-

tency. This evidence is of great importance and should not be underestimated. The implications Goldstein draws for therapist selection and training and for utilization of non-professionals with therapeutic personalities are well founded; however, we think it would be erroneous to assume, as some writers in this area do, that these personal dimensions are always the chief requirement for effecting positive change in patients.

On the contrary, we think that the personal impact of the help-giver is considerably less relevant to many symptomatologies. Treatment of phobias, compulsion neuroses, marital discord, impotence, frigidity, sexual disorders, etc., are more a function of technical skill than personal impact. Depression, anxiety, existential malaise, etc., may be more responsive to the therapist's personality. We suspect that the key to efficient practice in the future is more likely to be in making such differentiations, which permit sophisticated differential pairings of problems with techniques and persons. The role of the nonprofessional or of the trained therapist with special interpersonal attributes will surely have an important place in the therapeutic repertoire of the future; but this role will be well-defined and specified in relation to predictable outcomes with given disorders. It will not suffice to simply advocate a broad-gauged relationship therapy for all comers.

Another implication of viewing the personal qualities of the therapist as all-important, is the assumption that psychotherapists are born, not made. While native talent very probably plays an important part in a therapist's effectiveness, few would argue that native talent cannot be significantly enhanced by training, experience and sheer hard work. Outstanding achievements in art, music, science and any other field of human endeavor invariably are characterized by these qualities, and there is no reason to believe that it can be otherwise in as intricate a field as psychotherapy. Indeed, it seems to us that in reports stressing the beneficial effects of nonprofessional workers the foregoing *technical* dimensions are vastly underestimated. Nor can we take seriously the claim that qualities like empathy, understanding and warmth are easily acquired. At its best, psychotherapy is a highly creative activity, which probably requires what amounts to a "talent"; but this must be potentiated by training. Just as musical aptitude alone does not transform a person into a proficient musician, therapeutic aptitude alone does not make one a skilled psychotherapist.

2. While we often find ourselves commiserating along the same lines that Goldstein does regarding the disarticulation of research and practice, we are not fully convinced of his argument as to why research has had an "extremely slight impact" on practice.

First of all, if one looks carefully at the current scene, there is some evidence that therapists are adopting elements of therapeutic technique which have been isolated by client-centered and behavioral researchers.

Secondly, much of the research on traditional therapy has had little impact, not just because the research was poor, but because results on averaged group data tended not to lead in any specific directions. Research findings cannot be expected to change practices very much if the main conclusion of the research is that the therapy lacks potency for effecting change. About all that this does is make therapists either defensive or puzzled about where innovations will come from. Good research should yield new alternatives.

In general, Goldstein's commentary is incisive and helpful. We are grateful to him for providing a stimulus for us to elaborate on critically important current issues.

Dr. Luborsky. We agree that there are as yet no fully satisfactory comparative studies—between behavior therapy and dynamic therapy or any other forms. Our reasons for this assertion are spelled out in the review, and are apparently shared by Luborsky. Paul's (1966) study is indeed a beginning, but it falls short of demonstrating in a conclusive way the superiority of behavior therapy over "insight-giving" therapy except in a circumscribed manner. One of us (Strupp, Fox & Lessler, 1969) has noted some of the same shortcomings cited by Luborsky. The fact is, however, that what limited comparisons have been made are mostly favorable to behavioral methods. When one pieces together the mounting fragments of evidence, their consistency is impressive despite the limitations of single studies.

Luborsky's reinterpretation of the deterioration effect is an ingenious one, but it is difficult to reconcile with the fact that patients show up worse on non-self-report criteria (Bergin, 1967). Differential expectations may very well influence self-reports, but this should not diminish the importance of recognizing and combating the existence of noxious "therapy."

In general, it is difficult to argue with someone who "agrees and sympathizes with most. . ." of the paper. We are naturally grateful to find someone as esteemed as Dr. Luborsky who can support most of our conclusions.

Dr. Meltzoff. In spite of several positive evaluations, which we warmly accept, Meltzoff seems to argue that we should have done a comprehensive review of the entire field of psychotherapy research instead of the focussed analysis which we did.

While we, in fact, read literally thousands of papers, we deliberately selected domains of inquiry and sets of studies that were most likely to accelerate progress in the field. Our purpose was to search for promising leads and fertile programs of inquiry. Thus, we reviewed in a special way—a way which yielded variables and measures which met these criteria. It was our hope that in this way scholars in the field might be spared having to labor through a mountainous review of minutiae. Even though they must thereby depend upon us and our particular personal biases, we doubt that a more elaborate, and more redundant, review would have obviated this problem.

This discussant also addresses himself to the "impact" issue. He agrees with our position that theoreticians and clinicians have generally been the innovators whereas the researchers have been the evaluators. However, in developing his point he seems to subscribe to the view that there is some kind of orderly process in which the clinician follows his intuitions and hunches while waiting eagerly for the researcher to provide definitive answers to some technique problem. Then, when he believes that the evidence is sufficiently convincing, he changes his practices. The history of science amply shows that this is not the way in which basic orientations (or techniques, for that matter) change. Changes occur when someone, on the basis of available knowledge and inventive genius, recasts a theory into an entirely new frame, which is more heuristic or satisfying to the scientific community, whereupon perceptible shifts occur which remain in vogue until another genius comes upon the scene.

Lykken (1968) has recently provided a neat demonstration that the verisimilitude of a theory is in no wise enhanced by statistical findings significant at the .01 level. It is indeed difficult to determine when a particular study can be cited as confirming or disconfirming evidence. When is a generalization from an analogue study to the clinical situation justified? When is a patient sample adequate? What are the applications of results obtained in a group setting to individual psychotherapy? There are no stringent criteria, although at times it is abundantly clear that such translations are not in order. This problem is not unique to psychotherapy research, and the best we can do is to assert that we have been mindful of it.

With regard to some of Meltzoff's specific points, we offer the following:

1. *Citing studies other than individual therapy with adult neurotics.* This we did on occasion, and consciously so. We occasionally came upon material too important to leave out simply because it did not focus on individual therapy with neurotics. Fortunately these studies nearly always served mainly to amplify and clarify points under discussion. Studies of the therapist's personal impact and behavioral studies were especially pertinent here.

2. *Bypassing the efficacy of psychotherapy.* Having written five separate analyses of the psychotherapy outcome literature, and having cited all of them in passing, we were puzzled by Meltzoff's assertion that we had bypassed but not escaped from the outcome issue. We were equally amazed to learn that the whole field has been floundering over this question while Meltzoff knows of 100 controlled outcome studies, most of which yielded positive results! We can only conclude that Meltzoff's criteria for acceptability of evidence are different from our own. We noted in an earlier review (Bergin, 1967) that another reviewer (Dittmann, 1966) had discovered 14 recent outcome studies, 10 of which yielded positive results. Our own analysis of the same 14 studies revealed only two as indicating that therapy, as prac-

ticed on the average, "had any effect, and neither of them would be universally acceptable as evidence."

We are not overly impressed with the therapeutic potency of the "average" clinician and perhaps in that sense we share Eysenck's view. But what does this prove concerning psychotherapy, particularly of the "traditional" (dynamic) variety, of which Eysenck is most critical? The "average" craftsman in any field may not be very competent, but this does not disprove that some achieve a very high and impressive level of skill. We have been fortunate to know a few psychotherapists whom we consider masters of the art, which is precisely our reason for rejecting the more pessimistic side of Eysenck's view. It follows that we must turn to an inquiry of what makes these experts effective, which in part provides the rationale for the "Study of Experts," as a somewhat promising design. We do not mean to suggest that only a small handful of practitioners have effects on patients. All kinds of people can be helpful to their fellows in a variety of ways; what remains to be demonstrated is the extent of such help, how unique it is to psychotherapists, the kinds of changes it effects and the psychological principles which mediate change. We do appreciate Meltzoff's optimism, however, and tend to think that eventually we will have evidence that at least *some* therapists are highly effective with *some* patients.

3. *Criticisms of proposed designs.* Meltzoff begins by critiquing a study we never proposed. Our study of major therapies was to be a comparative analysis of specific homogenized methods extracted from the major therapies, e.g., empathy, desensitization and intepretation. It does not matter that most therapists are eclectics, a point with which we agree. Our intent was to isolate and define the effects of specific interventions with specific problems in keeping with our general advocacy of a multidimensional approach to research and treatment. Even this degree of isolation and homogenization may be difficult if not impossible, a thought we are all too aware of.

The study of effectiveness of experts still seems cogent to us for reasons cited in the paper and in the foregoing section of this critique, however, we are uncertain about its level of priority. It may be of some interest to note, in any case, that among the experts we have recently consulted regarding future collaborative designs, this one is frequently cited as a relevant and important one.

As for the designs in a general sense, we never intended that they provide more than stimuli for thought. Meltzoff's incisive comments on some of them are much to the point, and we share many of his reservations.

References

Bergin, A. E. 1967. An empirical analysis of therapeutic issues. In D. Arbuckle ed. *Counseling and psychotherapy: An overview*. New York: McGraw-Hill, pp. 175–208.

Dittmann, A. T. 1966. Psychotherapeutic processes. In P. R. Farnsworth, Olga McNemar & Q. McNemar, eds., *Annual review of psychology*. Palo Alto: Annual Reviews 16:51–78.

Lykken, D. T. 1968. Statistical significance in psychological research. *Psychological Bulletin* 70:151–59.

Paul, G. 1966. Insight vs. desensitization in psychotherapy. Stanford, Calif: Stanford University Press.

Strupp, H. H., Fox, R. E., & Lessler, K. 1969. *Patients view their psychotherapy*. Baltimore: Johns Hopkins Press.

Further "Last Words" on Psychotherapy Research: Correspondence

The following letter to the Editor was sent by Dr. Frank in response to our reply to him in the foregoing article. It is followed by a letter to the Editor submitted by us.

April 22, 1969

Dr. Jason Aronson, Editor
International Journal of Psychiatry

Dear Dr. Aronson:

As an enthusiastic practitioner, researcher, trainer and teacher of psychotherapy, I am puzzled, not to say alarmed, that Drs. Bergin and Strupp found my comments to be "pessimistic concerning the future of research in psychotherapy" and to imply that "training is futile." Worst of all, they feared the comments might "anticipate or stimulate a new wave of therapeutic nihilism."

Only two conclusions are possible—either I do not realize the implications of my position or I have been misunderstood. Embracing the more palatable alternative, let me attempt very briefly to clarify some possible sources of misunderstanding.

1. To question whether different techniques of individual psychotherapy are differentially effective with neurotics is not the same as to claim that they are ineffective, i.e. to be nihilistic. Every therapist must make use of some technique to maintain a relationship with his patient—they can't just sit and stare at each other—and this technique contributes to his therapeutic success. The issue is only whether he could have obtained equally good results with a different technique.

2. Stress on the importance of non-specific factors does not imply pessimism as to the future of psychotherapy research in general, but only research in techniques. The use of the term "non-specific" may have caused

the misunderstanding. It was intended to refer to all aspects of therapy other than technique. Thus it would include features of patient and therapist and their interaction that affect therapeutic success, mentioned by Bergin and Strupp as a promising research area, as well as others mentioned in my comments.

3. While therapists almost certainly differ in their innate abilities to convey certain therapeutic attitudes, it is unlikely that any therapist can achieve his full potential without training. There is no reason to think, for example, that therapists could not be trained to be more empathic or genuine, even though their natural talents set limits and the specific ways in which they express these qualities may differ in accordance with their individual styles.

4. Finally, even in patients whose distress and disability have a largely constitutional or biological base, raising their morale can markedly improve their happiness and level of functioning. The disability of all chronic illness depends more on loss of morale, discouragement and the like than on organically based limitations. This point has been amply demonstrated by the success of rehabilitation programs for chronic schizophrenics. Perhaps the most dramatic example was a project conducted in a veterans hospital for chronic neurological diseases. A rehabilitation program stressing rekindling of hope, restoration of morale, and re-establishment of links with the outside world enabled 70% of a group of severely handicapped patients, hospitalized three to ten years, to resume community living and 30% became self-supporting.[3]

The ability of one human being to help another through psychological means is often very great. The fact that it may be possible to offer this help equally well in different ways should not lead to underestimation of its effectiveness.

Sincerely,
Jerome D. Frank, M.D.

May 19, 1969

Dear Dr. Aronson:

We are grateful for this clarification of Dr. Frank's position. We had interpreted his original critique to mean that biological factors dominated the domain of psychopathology and personality change. We concur with the view presented in his letter to the effect that: "The ability of one human being to help another through psychological means is often very great." Most of his other points are equally cogent and corresponding to our own.

However, we doubt that nonspecific relationship factors are the only effective change agents in the therapeutic process; but, even if they were, we

3. A. B. Baker and J. R. Brown, *Rehabilitation of the chronic neurologic patient.* V.A Pamphlet 10–29, Washington, D. C.: Veterans Administration, May, 1949.

would consider it essential to make these "nonspecific" factors explicit and thereby identify the precise mechanisms operating in the therapeutic influence process. In other words, the fact that we are forced to call certain aspects of one person's psychological influence on another "nonspecific" points up the existence of significant gaps in our knowledge which future work must seek to close. It is precisely this goal which sets modern psychotherapy apart from other forms of psychological healing which have been practiced over the centuries.

We appreciate opportunities like this to exchange and clarify views, and we hope they will be useful.

Hans H. Strupp
Allen E. Bergin

The following additional correspondence concerning our review was selected for reproduction here because of the cogent and useful remarks contained therein. These letters are illustrative of the spectrum of reactions we received by private correspondence.

August 28, 1967

Dear Hans and Allen:

The fruit of your summer's work has arrived just as I am leaving for a month abroad, so that my comments are based on a very cursory reading. Many may actually be considered in the text. They are offered with the understanding that you don't hold me to any of them except the first.

1. I am immensely impressed with what you have accomplished in a few short months. The evaluative summary is a superb overview, and it is comforting that much of it accords with my own evaluation of the state of the field (plus a lot of points I hadn't thought of).

2. Without being able to be more specific, I feel that you perhaps have not devoted enough thought to the conceptualization of "mental illness" as a series of patterns of maladaptation. This would lead to more emphasis on much of psychotherapy as crisis management. . . . It would also imply that some consideration should be given to methods of group and family therapy, which could well be the patterns for the future. It may be too difficult to design research, especially of a collaborative sort, on them, but this should have some thought.

3. Similarly, I miss any reference to the role of emotional arousal in the process of learning and unlearning. The increasing use of drugs like LSD as adjuncts to psychotherapy should receive some attention. . . .

4. The design for comparative study of psychotherapies suffers from the omissions I have referred to above, especially the lack of inclusion of group therapy. However, it requires so much organization that it is obviously far in the future.

5. The effectiveness of psychotherapy as practiced by experts focusses on an important problem but, I fear, would shatter on the reluctance of most experts to subject themselves to this kind of scrutiny. After all, they would be putting their professional reputations on the line.

6. The projects concerning the study of mental operations of therapists and imitation versus vicarious learning seem to me very premature, whatever their theoretical interest. First we had better prove that the effects of psychotherapy are sufficiently strong to justify this kind of detailed study practically.

7. The one that appeals to me most is the study of time-limited therapy, especially with the inclusion of Gordon's "extensive time-limited therapy" and some sort of role induction interview. This has the advantage of having great practical implications as well as contributing to a better understanding of the therapeutic process.

It should be added that the protocols for the projects are in themselves illuminating and instructive documents.

In short, congratulations on a superb job.

With best regards,

Sincerely,
Jerome D. Frank, M.D.

In a subsequent letter Dr. Frank added the following points.

December 28, 1967

Dear Hans and Allen:

I have . . . only one, rather minor, comment to make, which concerns the page on follow-up. Perhaps it should not be so unmitigatedly favorable. Follow-up studies are desirable, of course, but one has to weigh their cost against the potential gain in information. They probably do not help much in the evaluation of therapy. Several studies show that the state of the patient at the end of psychotherapy correlates very highly with his state years later. Furthermore, as Gordon Paul points out in his follow-up study,[4] patients' reports as to intercurrent treatment may be highly unreliable, and with each passing year the attrition problem becomes more formidable. I suspect that follow-up studies cast more light on the natural history of the conditions treated by psychotherapy than on the relative effectiveness of different forms. . . .

My misgivings as to the practicality of most of the large, collaborative projects outlined in the end remain unassuaged. . . .

Sincerely,
Jerome D. Frank, M.D.

4. G. L. Paul, Insight versus desensitization in psychotherapy two years after termination, *Journal of Consulting Psychology* 31 (1967): 333–48.

The following letter by Dr. Matarazzo includes material relevant to the history of this project.

December 26, 1967

Dear Hans and Allen:

I have spent a very enjoyable pre-Christmas Saturday carefully reading your production. It is a first-rate job, clearly reveals your vast familiarity with an overwhelmingly complex and multifaceted phenomenon, and over and over gives evidence of the many weeks and months you both invested in the work. The several professions and their infant sciences, as well as your colleagues on this committee, owe you a sincere debt of gratitude. . . .

The second part of my critique has more to do with substance and here, as with the suggestions above, I share my remarks so that you can see what, if any of them, you wish to use.

1. Section One, overview and emerging trends, is beautifully done. It is an excellent introduction for the sections which follow. My main criticism is that, for me, the section ended too abruptly. . . .

2. Your section on "Outcome" is for me the best and most original methodological and theoretical treatment of this complex problem since Rogers and Dymond[5] faced it square on in the opening remarks to their book. . . .

Now that we are finished and have something concrete to report, I will communicate this fact to the other participants of the Third Research Conference and to the president of PIAP[6] (Fred Spaner) as well as Nat Raskin (PIAP Research Committee chairman). With the "map" of the problem so brilliantly executed I now can easily and happily report that a *formal* group to plan and execute a collaborative study is feasible. As I indicated in my November 30 memo to you, our major responsibility on January 23-24 will be to identify the principal investigators who will submit (by February 1, 1968) an application for this planning phase, and to actually write this application before we leave Washington. With the Strupp-Bergin review as the major evidence that we know what are about, the rest of the application need be no more complicated, nor longer, than the application John Shlien submitted when applying for the Third Research Conference.

I am more optimistic than ever about the success of this undertaking, and look forward to turning the helm over next month to the principal investigator(s) of the planning grant. He (or they) may ask some of us to serve on a *formal* advisory committee to him and thus take advantage of (*a*) the var-

5. C. R. Rogers and R. F. Dymond, *Psychotherapy and personality change* (Chicago: University of Chicago Press, 1954).

6. Psychologists Interested in the Advancement of Psychotherapy, now the Division of Psychotherapy of the American Psychological Association.

ious selective degrees of expertness existing in our informal committee and (*b*) the work and interest in this whole project of such members during the past two years. Some names have been suggested for the principal investigator(s) of the planning grant and possibly some preliminary work on the grant application can be done before January 23.

To Hans and Allen a final word of thanks and to all of you a warm wish for a Happy New Year.

Sincerely yours,
Joseph D. Matarazzo, Ph.D.

January 9, 1968

Dear Hans:

Thank you for sending me a copy of the fine review by yourself and Bergin. Here are a few nonrandom comments.

A practitioner needs a "causal relation" or variable he can manipulate *with this particular patient*. Research thus far has not given him a reliable guide in this direction because it has mainly been in the tradition of an extensive design. Extensive designs yield only weak group averages, not specific causal mechanisms. Chassan's book on research design[7] is very good on this point. There are two lacks we must face (1) new concepts [it is too early for an all-embracing theory; before one has a theory (a combination of concepts) one must have some good concepts], (2) a reliable taxonomy. Few admit their concepts are inadequate and few want to face the classification problem because it is considered "undynamic." But we won't get far with unreliable categories and heterogenous samples. . . .

I don't see how one can hope to isolate and manipulate single variables in complex systems. This can only be done in some simple physical systems and not at all in living systems. One might be able to do it in an artificial system such as a model, but if one is studying something so simple as a monotonic relation between two variables there is no need to have a model. In therapy research one is studying communicators between two complex systems. It is not the large number of variables which is bothersome but the degree of control one has over them. . . .

There's an old saying that the trouble with psychotherapy is the therapist. Since therapy is an interaction and therapists are human, they also change as a result of the interaction. A therapist is not a chemical catalyst which can accelerate a process without being changed itself. I have been struck by the observation that those patients whom I changed the most changed me

7. J. B. Chassan, *Research design in clinical psychology and psychiatry* (New York: Appleton-Century-Crofts, 1967).

the most. One hope for computer therapy in certain conditions rests on the fact that a computer program would *not* be changed by the interaction.

The best discussion of work in content analysis is in the *General Inquirer* by Stone et al., M.I.T.[8]

One trouble with the Lorenz and Cobb[9] study was again the taxonomy problem. The diagnostic categories in which the patients were placed to begin with were in part a function of their verbal behavior. Also the study was not controlled for educational level. Regarding content and linguistic analysis you might also consult Jaffe's new chapter in Vol. III of the *American Handbook of Psychiatry.*[10]

Other ideas for measures can be found in the Webb, et al. book, *Unobtrusive Measures.*[11]

Therapy researchers would profit greatly from Campbell and Stanley's classic paper "Experimental and Quasi-experimental Designs"[12] which appeared in Gage's *Handbook of Research on Teaching* (1963). Incidentally, if it ever comes to the point of carrying out the Meehl-Scriven-Goldstein, etc. experiment (see below) I would suggest that Campbell be on the designing committee. This "optimal" assignment was initially designed years ago by Meehl and Scriven (see Scriven in the Hook symposium on psychoanalysis).[13] It has several flaws which can be eliminated easily. For example, suppose experienced therapists are good at picking patients who would recover anyway. Let the therapist select 2 cases and then take one away from him for the control group by random slection. There are other points like this about which Campbell would be insightful.

1. Again let me mention something I mentioned in Chicago. Why will no one talk about money? Most psychotherapy is paid for. Yet no one considers money as a relevant variable. I believe it has many non-trivial implications for what happens in therapy. Therapists among themselves talk

8. P. J. Stone, D. C. Dunphy, and D. Ogilvie, *The general inquirer: A computer method of content analysis for the behavioral sciences* (Cambridge: Massachusetts Institute of Technology, 1966).

9. M. Lorenz and S. Cobb, Language patterns in psychotic and psychoneurotic subjects, *Archives of Neurology and Psychiatry* 72 (1954): 665–73.

10. J. Jaffe, The study of language in psychiatry: Psycholinguistics and computational linguistics. In S. Arieti, ed., *American handbook of psychiatry,* vol. III (New York: Basic Books, 1966), pp. 689–704.

11. E. J. Webb, D. T. Campbell, R. D. Schwartz, and L. Sechrest, *Unobtrusive measures: Nonreactive research in the social sciences* (Chicago: Rand McNally, 1966).

12. D. T. Campbell and J. C. Stanley, *Experimental and quasi-experimental designs for research* (Chicago: Rand McNally, 1966).

13. M. Scriven, The experimental investigation of psychoanalysis. In S. Hook, ed., *Psychoanalysis, scientific method and philosophy* (New York: New York University Press, 1959), pp. 252–68.

about sex freely. But when money, fees, incomes of therapists, etc. come up everyone has a good (but uneasy) laugh. The fact that it is *not* dealt with in research means to me there is something there we are not honestly facing.

2. I believe in individualized measures. Scales should be constructed for each patient. This too is an aspect of intensive designs. We are not trying to solve the problem of justified inductive generalization. Physics, chemistry and medicine (e.g., heart transplants in single patients) progressed without worrying about representativeness of samples. They relied on repeatability of observations by independent observers and the development of a series of cases one by one. The population of observations we should be interested in at this point in time is a series of single-case populations. It is hopeless to seek to generalize about "all" patients. No "all" exists about anything.

I hope the above will be of some help. Good luck in your efforts and once again my congratulations to you and Bergin.

Regards,
Kenneth M. Colby

January 18, 1968

Dear Hans:

Sorry for the delay in this reply, but I've been snowed under lately and still am. I hope this reaches you before you leave for Washington.

In the first place you've obviously done a hell of a lot of work in compiling the paper. I hope you publish it someplace. In that vein I would certainly appreciate a copy of the bibliography you describe.

Let me comment primarily on the suggested therapy studies, which I'm sure will be the focus of your Washington meeting. I think I've changed my position since the Washington meeting I attended—in other words, I'm beginning to see the potential value of a major collaborative study at this time, certainly partly as a result of reading your paper. But a corollary of this new position is that it will take a lot of money to do the job right. If you can't get the big bundle, then my feeling is it might be wiser to forget it.

Now, regarding your proposed studies at the end of your report: I think these are excellent suggestions. I'll make a general comment first. The projects that seem most exciting to me are Projects 2 and 4. In fact, I would say you basically have two projects and the others can be logically subsumed.

Project 2 (Study of Experts) grabs me the most. It's in the tradition of: "If you had all the money you could want, any therapists and patients you might want, what kind of study would you design?" I would opt for as much heterogeneity as possible among therapists. I would get the best "experts" around even if I had to match their accustomed annual incomes for a year or so. If that can be done, by the way, why not bring them all together for a year or so in a large metropolitan area where you're sure you can get all of the patients you may want. This might also insure that people cooperate and that data gets collected in the way desired. Re "expertness": Peers should agree they're experts, previous patients should say they're pretty damn good. Re patients: Let the *T*s select, but insist that they specify clearly their criteria for selection. Likewise, not only should the *T*s be permitted to state the results they intended, but they should be required to do so beforehand, specifying what they expect to change in the therapy hour, and what outside the therapy hour; and specify what they intend specifically to do to produce that change. (In your outcome discussion you don't make a clear distinction between "in-therapy" outcome vs. "extra-therapy" outcome. You also do not emphasize measures of "in-therapy" patient change or outcome). Require the *T*s to specify beforehand which of the measures of in- and extra-therapy outcome they would expect to reflect the change they anticipate, as well as the ones they would not expect to reflect change. As another way of handling the control group problem, in addition to your waiting-list controls, why not include a group of defined "nonexperts" (clearly non-expert) who would operate in the design the same way as experts. If you can demonstrate a clear difference between the expert and nonexpert groups, you take much of the burden off the control group comparisons.

I think *Project 3* (Mental Operations of Therapists) logically *should* be included in Project 2. It would take so little extra effort and expense, that it would be extremely uneconomical not to include it. Including it would also make Project 2 a stronger study. I would suggest that to attain the objective —to specify the kinds of observations the therapist makes on the patient's communications, the inferences he draws from verbal and nonverbal content, the manner in which he decides on a course of action, and the way he implements it—it might be more meaningfully approached (either instead of or in addition to your proposed "hand operated signal systems") by *video* tape recordings of all the therapy sessions. (You could give the *T*s some practice in the video procedure beforehand.) Then you might routinely use a method suggested and researched by Norm Kagan et al., at Michigan State,[14] which they call "Interpersonal Process Recall"—and consists of video playbacks independently to both *T* and *P* for associations or anything else you might want to ask (e.g., Where were the significant points of the interview? How were you feeling then?). I think this might very effectively help you get at what you want for the Project.

14. N. Kagan, D. R. Krathwohl, and R. Miller, Stimulated recall in therapy using video tape: A case study, *Journal of Counseling Psychology* 10 (1963): 237–43.

Project 6 (Comparative Process Study) could also easily be incorporated into Project 2 and partly into Project 4 (Effectiveness of Different Methods with Phobias). If you had all the video tapes and other data available, any process researcher in the country could apply his measure to the videotape. By having video as well as audio, you have *all* the data and anyone can slice it any way that may be appropriate to his particular measure (e.g., transcripts could be made, if they were needed). Along this line, why not suggest in your proposal that the data of your projects be placed into a "National Library of Psychotherapy Research Data" (maybe under NIMH auspices). The Library would contain the data of your projects, and could be a central depository for any previous or future large scale or other project data. The data could then be made accessible to any researcher. For example, the Wisconsin study tapes and data are now lying around unused somewhere; also University of Illinois Counseling Service project, University of Chicago Counseling Center projects, and the like. The data you collect in these projects and the other data could be fruitfully used for some time in both training and research.

Project 5 (Time-limited Therapy) could be subsumed also under Project 1 simply by finding "experts" who believe in and are practicing "time-limited" therapy. If you wanted to keep it a separate project, then I suggest you define arbitrarily the time-dimension—i.e., some of your time-limited *T*s would be required to see patients only for 5 interviews, some for 10, some for 15, etc.

To this point, I am basically proposing that you incorporate Projects 3, 5, and 6 under Project 2, and consider all of it one project, with each aspect equally important. If I had to choose one project for your committee to come up with as a proposal, it would be this redefined Project 2.

The next major study, as I see it, would be *Project 4* (Different Methods with Phobias). This bows to behavior therapists, and rightfully so. I think your point about "There are phobias and there are phobias" is an excellent one and should be implemented by clearly explicating the differences. It seems you might want to look for neo-analysts who consider themselves expert in working with phobias, and throw them into the pot. A point that applies here, as well as throughout your paper, is that it's quite important not to talk about "behavior therapy" as a homogeneous entity, but rather to talk about operant BT, implosive BT, deconditioning BT, aversive BT, negative practice BT. The power of Project 4 could very well lie in relatively comparing the different behavior therapies, as well as in contrasting them with neo-analytic treatments.

This leaves *Project 1* (Comparative Analysis of Major Therapies). This is certainly the kind of experimental, manipulative study we direly need, and which probably would yield the most clearcut results. But my feeling is that it's premature (since we can't really agree on essential ingredients yet, even within schools), and would be quite difficult to implement. Most of the problems could come from the "therapists": Where would you get them? Would they be experts? or experienced? If they were experts or experienced, they would likely bias the application of the technique you programmed for them. How would you program sequential aspects of technique (Do A before you do B, and after the patient does C, etc.)? Unlimited interviews? However, if you could practicably implement this kind of study (I seriously doubt it) it would indeed be a contribution. Parenthetically, it would be helpful, I think, to distinguish clearly orthodox analysis from neoanalysis (e.g., Sullivanian and Fromm-Reichmann tradition) in your discussion. Do you think you can get some orthodox analysts to participate in anything?

Your projects listed under the heading "Projects Deriving from Non-psychotherapy Research" are fine ones, but could *best* be implemented, I think, by the authors who originally suggested them, via individual grants of their own. The ideas are their theoretical babies, and if the studies are to be done well they need loving nurturance by their progenitors.

Well, that about does it (Thank God, you say). I think your review was excellent and your research suggestions creative. One final parenthetical comment: When you discuss process measures, I think it is very important to mention the methodological problems (unit size, where to sample, and the like) that have to be worked out for process measures, and so often are not. I'll send along separately a paper of mine which deals with these issues.[15]

Good luck in Washington. I hope I've been helpful and constructive—that was my intent.

Best regards,
Donald J. Kiesler, Ph.D.

April 2, 1968

Dear Allen:

I am sending you the following comments on your joint paper with Hans Strupp, in accordance with the request made on the circular which accompanied it.

(1) You state that "Lazarus, a close collaborator of the exponent of behavior therapy, Wolpe, has strongly argued for the abolishment of the simplistic doctrinal substrate upon which behavior therapists relied." It is true that Lazarus has so argued, but this is by no means to be interpreted as a

15. D. J. Kiesler, Basic methodological issues implicit in psychotherapy process research, *American Journal of Psychotherapy* 20 (1966): 135–55.

sign of "an approaching rapprochement." All that is really implied here is that Lazarus has abandoned the essential principles of behavior therapy and adopted an eclectic position. The same is not true, as far as I know, of any other leading figure in the behavior therapy field; and it can really not be expected to happen with anybody who clearly perceives the behavior position, which is a persistent design to apply experimentally established knowledge of the learning process to bringing about change in what are diagnosed as maladaptive behaviors that owe their existence to learning. In general, the idea of rapprochement appears to me to be misguided; for at all times the role of the scientist is to consider and test propositions that theoreticians (or practical men) put forward. Those propositions that the facts support earn the respect of all. Plainly, it is worth noting that people like Alexander and Rogers are now willing to discuss the possibility of processes that they would previously have excluded; but the behavior therapist has *always* been willing to entertain anything that scientifically acceptable evidence might support.

(2) You allege that behavior therapists often seem to proceed on the same assumption as the phenomenologist—that the patient's behavioral repertoire is largely intact except for a specific neurotic symptom. This is quite incorrect, as you can easily ascertain from a study of many passages in *Psychotherapy by Reciprocal Inhibition* [16] or in *The Practice of Behavior Therapy* [17] Behavior therapists, when properly schooled, always make a thorough study of each patient and direct their efforts to overcoming every detectable kind of maladaptive behavior. Incidentally, it is of some importance to emphasize that behavior is the target, not the symptoms; for symptoms, as understood in medicine, are merely the patient's subjective report of processes that go on within him—and the processes that we are concerned with are the responses to stimuli that produce activity in nerve circuits. Behavior therapists in general use whatever learning principles seem to be applicable to whatever needs to be changed. The distinctive feature of A. Lazarus is that he freely employs procedures which have no relation to experimentally established principles—such as self-disclosure, interpretations, and dyadic interactions—even though there is not even empirical support for the efficacy of particular kinds of things that he does.

(3) I am very much astonished at your allegation that my theoretical formulations have followed my clinical experience. I thought that you were fully aware that my methods arose out of my observations on the treatment of experimental neuroses in cats.

16. J. Wolpe, *Psychotherapy by reciprocal inhibition* (Stanford, California: Stanford University Press, 1958).

17. J. Wolpe, *The practice of behavior therapy* (New York: Pergamon Press, 1969).

(4) The statement that comparative studies favor behavioral therapy because they tend to utilize criteria which derive from behavioral theory is one of the usual alibis that "dynamic" theorists are always resorting to. The one thing that is clear whan a patient applies for treatment is that he is suffering and perhaps disabled; and the removal of such suffering and disablement is an objective which seems to me to be quite indispensable. What point is there in obtaining "maturation of personality" if the individual suffering is as before? I have no objection to other kinds of change—such as maturation —being assessed; but so far I have not come across any kind of concrete suggestion from the psychoanalysts regarding how this should be done or precisely what the criteria are. In this area, also, of course, the excuse is made that the criteria are so enormously complex that it is difficult to formulate them. I regard this as an utterly indefensible position to hold.

(5) The complaint that the therapy in Gordon Paul's study being limited to six sessions does not provide an adequate test of insight therapy is rather amusing. Surely, if insight therapy had been shown to achieve in 12 or 20 or 50 sessions the same results that desensitization achieved in six, it would not be much of a recommendation for insight therapy.

(6) What exactly do you mean by an "adequate process measure of the quality of desensitization"?

With kind regards,

Yours sincerely,
Joseph Wolpe, M.D.

April 10, 1968

Dear Joe:

Thank you for your letter of April 2. I offer the following reactions and also have suggested to Dr. Strupp that he respond as well.

(1) It seems to me that there are two issues here. The first is whether Lazarus is representative of a movement within the behavioral position. From what I have gathered, he is. Also, in both his case and mine, rapprochement does not mean uncritical eclecticism. It means accepting what works, regardless of source. I don't believe that most of what is done in traditional therapy is much good; but I think some of it is, and that I accept.

The second issue is whether behavior therapists and theorists are open to all sources of data or not. You seem to be on both sides of the fence on this point. On the one hand you state that the behavior position applies "experimentally established knowledge of the learning process" and on the other hand that it will entertain "anything that scientifically acceptable evidence might support." Does this mean that the only scientific evidence that exists supports a learning process conception? I seriously doubt this. I think that if you were open to all data, you would have to accept the evidence of the potency of warmth and empathy, for example, and not just as reinforcers. I personally feel that it is a mistake to foster behaviorism or any other special *theory,* when what should be fostered is *empiricism.* It is true that empiricism supports much of behaviorism, but not all. It also supports relationship therapy which is impossible to construe in learning terminology. I think that if behavior theory is ever stretched to convincingly embrace subjective states such as those surrounding empathy and its effects, it will no longer be recognizable as behavior theory.

(2) I fully accept and agree with your statement that behavior therapists "when properly schooled—direct their efforts to overcoming every detectable kind of maladaptive behavior." The problem is that behavior therapy as currently practiced does not meet this norm. We were careful to state that it *often seemed* that behavior therapists proceed on erroneous assumptions regarding the complexities of pathology. I am very conscious of your efforts to explicitly show how complex cases should be dealt with, and perhaps we should add a line at the bottom of this page noting your position.

(3) You are correct that the history of your work is unlike that of Freud, Rogers, Alexander, etc., and that your techniques are more directly based upon experimental work. We were aware of this, but in trying to make the point that most innovations have come from practicing clinicians we obscured the differences that exist between innovators. In making various revisions, this misleading presentation had escaped me. It will be changed in the final version.

(4) I think you have misinterpreted us. We do not accept the alibis and defenses that many traditionalists engage in; but we do feel it is important to use multiple criteria. There are reliable TAT, self-concept, MMPI and other types of criteria that tap phenomena not measured by behavioral criteria. We are only saying that these should be used and that the phenomena which they measure should not be ignored.

(5) We did not intend to criticize the excellent results of behavior therapy with regard to the main behavioral symptom. It was merely to point out that additional processes seemed to be occurring in the realm of self-understanding and self-esteem that are worth studying more fully. Apparently, neither approach had much effect on this domain in 6 sessions. Your other points here are well taken.

(6) There is no system of content analysis for behavior therapy which is well-developed. This would be analogous to Strupp's or Truax's systems, but would be designed to evaluate the quality of desensitization or other techniques, by having judges observe the process or listen to recordings of it. Truax can rate the quality of empathy on a 9-point scale, and I assume that variations in the quality of behavior therapy could also be measured.

I hope you did notice in our paper the many very positive assertions we made about your work and your influence.

With best regards.

Cordially,
Allen E. Bergin

October 11, 1968

Dr. Isaac M. Marks

Dear Isaac:

Thank you for your kindness in sending me a copy of your discussion for the *International Journal of Psychiatry*. I very much appreciated your thoughtful comments, which will prove most helpful to Allen and myself in exploring further the feasibility of collaborative research. . . .

While the name of Freud may be mentioned only rarely in the paper, I for one continue to be one of his staunch admirers. I can see where this did not come across. Likewise we obviously failed to communicate sufficiently on the topic of psychopathology, concerning whose importance I fully share your views.

Thanks again for all your help. With best regards.

Sincerely,
Hans H. Strupp

October 21, 1968

Dear Hans,

. . . I had not meant to slur the name of Freud in my discussion, only to point out how we had moved on and developed further in the field. . . . It was an arrogant assumption that our local view of clinical syndromes is the most appropriate at the present time. I would love to be proved wrong. . . .

With best wishes,

Yours sincerely,
Isaac M. Marks

October 28, 1968

Dear Isaac:

Thank you for your letter of October 21. I am pleased to hear that you are forging ahead, and I hope you will keep Allen and me posted.

I believe there are real differences between the British and American views regarding psychopathology, particularly among American psychologists who are behaviorally oriented. Having worked closely with a British analyst for several years, I think I have a fairly good appreciation of the British position, and, I might add, a good deal of respect for it.

The issue is too broad to discuss in a letter, but I tend to think that the British emphasis represents an exceedingly important dimension in psychotherapy research. In essence, I feel there are different kinds of "knowing," and clinicial knowledge, while typically obtained in an uncontrolled setting, can at least be a source of very fruitful hypotheses. I also feel that in your critique you pointed out a real weakness in our manuscript, and I did not mean to suggest in the slightest that you should modify your remarks. . . .

With best regards,

Cordially,
Hans H. Strupp

FOUR

Testing the feasibility of major collaborative efforts

In the autumn of 1968, after the preceding reviewing and critiquing, we embarked upon a feasibility study exploring the potentialities for large-scale collaborative work. As indicated in Chapter 1, we approached this task by visiting a variety of centers of research and clinical activity and interviewing key individuals. In each instance we sent in advance a copy of our review paper, our grant application and the following questions as stimuli for discussion:

Questions for Consultants

1. Consider what we call the "standard scientific question": "What specific therapeutic interventions produce specific changes in specific patients under specific conditions?" What kinds of studies do you consider most promising in working toward the objective of different methods for different problems? What priorities would you assign? What kinds of studies are likely to result in the greatest "payoff"?
2. What are the relative merits of the following general strategies at this stage of psychotherapy research?
   a. Studies of the live therapy process and outcomes.
   b. Experimental analogue studies—quasi-therapy situations.
   c. Laboratory studies of basic change processes within the context of a general psychology of change.

d. Is now the time to isolate and dimensionalize this process, or do we need more hypothesis-generation?
e. Can we advance best by temporarily ignoring complexity and isolating and manipulating a few variables at a time?

3. Is it possible to advance psychotherapy research significantly without getting embroiled in theoretical differences between "schools"? Is this desirable? Is it folly to launch ahead without some kind of coordinating theoretical framework for our research? Or, have theories impeded progress in the past?
4. Is it possible to focus research on such major variables as patient, therapist, techniques, outcome criteria, process, etc. Where, in your judgment, can the purest "gold" be mined?
5. The kinds of problems psychotherapists typically deal with usually are not single symptoms (e.g., a snake phobia) but complex problems. Yet all therapists ignore certain aspects of the "richness of the phenomena" and reduce complexity to certain "basic problems" on which they operate in therapy. Consider this brief sketch:

> An attractive woman of 28 came for treatment because she was in acute distress as a result of her lovers' casual treatment of her. Every one of her very numerous love affairs had followed a similar pattern—first she would attract the man, then she would offer herself on a platter. He would soon treat her with contempt and after a time leave her. In general she lacked assurance, was very dependent, and was practically never free from feelings of tension and anxiety.[1]

a. Can one design studies which do justice to this complexity? If no, can "simple" analogues serve as adequate substitutes?
b. Different therapists will conceptualize a "problem" very differently on the basis of the patient's description of his symptoms. They will diverge even more sharply as soon as they make inferences from the patient's descriptions. This raises the question of nosology, how to conceptualize a "problem," how to compare changes from initial status, etc. The current status of nosology is still very primitive.
c. Can intensive single case studies, say, by therapists of different persuasions, who treat patients suffering from relatively homogeneous problems (if such exist) contribute something of value? Consider, for example, the "castrating female" syndrome (presumably a character disorder) which comes closer to the therapist's actual work than a monosymptomatic condition.

1. J. Wolpe, Reciprocal inhibition as the main basis of psychotherapeutic effects. In H. J. Eysenck, ed., *Behavior therapy and the neuroses* (New York: Pergamon Press, 1960), p. 108.

   d. Can semi-naturalistic, intensive, single case studies, augmented by repeated measures be counted on to yield fruitful results? Can an optimum middle ground be found between the complexity of the natural phenomena and an impoverished analogue?

6. a. Of the variables listed in the last chapter of our review, which are most worth studying? Have we missed significant variables?
   b. Do any of the complex designs sketched in the survey document excite your imagination?
7. Perhaps what is needed is not collaborative research but more systematic research on a given problem. Can such systematic research on a specific problem be generated "synthetically"?
8. Colby has said that the therapist needs help from the researcher to solve "acute difficulties in the art." What might that kind of help look like?
9. It is becoming increasingly clear that the supposedly divergent therapies are multidimensional processes which overlap with each other. What are good ways to determine what the really potent agents are in these methods? Client-centered therapy is not adequately defined by "reflection of feeling," psychoanalytic therapy is not simply "interpretations," and behavior therapy is more than "counterconditioning."
10. One tends to be overwhelmed with the number of uncontrolled variables operating in psychotherapy and the virtual impossibility of adequately controlling them *in vivo*. What are good ways to make scientific advances on this problem?
11. a. To what extent are expectations of significant breakthroughs in psychotherapy research unrealistic, in light of limited knowledge and measurement techniques in personality and psychopathology?
    b. To what extent is valid and relevant differential diagnosis available for psychotherapy research?
12. How much can we learn from group data on patients and therapists using traditional sampling and statistical procedures? About basic change processes? About practical questions of technique with single cases?
13. Is desensitization basically a cognitive process as suggested by recent experiments and Perry London's analysis in terms of expectancy?[2]
14. If cognitive and relationship variables operate strongly in behavioral methods, can designs be precisely enough formulated to isolate and define their effects relative to conditioning effects?
15. Can a series of designs be formulated which will first demonstrate the range and limits of effectiveness of various change inducers (e.g., modeling) and which will then increasingly add together sets of variables so

2. P. London, *The modes and morals of psychotherapy* (New York: Holt, Rinehart and Winston, 1964).

that complexity can be achieved and interactions precisely observed. In other words, can we take variables that are potent and gradually build them into a system which can match the complexity of a disturbed human being. Or, is this latter folly? Should we take a cue from medicine and rarely even try to treat the "whole" man. A related question: To what extent are the dimensions or systems in psychological phenomena independent vs. correlated? Note that one can treat the nervous system without treating the circulatory system. Does answering this require a lot more basic research prior to designing studies relevant to practice?"

16. Can an interview-analysis technology be designed which will make it possible to test the effects, over time, of given interventions or classes of interventions by therapists? E.g., how do you measure the effect of an interpretation? Is such a technology necessary prior to comparing effects of *in vivo* interventions?
17. Is psychodynamic therapy *passé,* as *The New York Times*[3] suggests it is? Is there anything viable here for future research, or are its contributions in the past?
18. It seems essential to design research which will result in "strong" conclusions, as opposed to "trends." Such strong conclusions should make a real difference in therapy theory and practice. Much previous research in the area has failed to accomplish this end. Lykken,[4] for example, criticizes an empirical study which allegedly provides support for the theory that some psychiatric patients entertain an unconscious belief in the "cloacal theory of birth." Such patients should be inclined to manifest eating disorders. They should also be inclined to see cloacal animals, such as frogs, on the Rorschach. A sample of clinicians presented with the theory responded by saying "I don't believe it." When shown empirical data supporting the theory at the usual level of statistical significance, the consensus remained the same: "I still don't believe it." Empirical data confirming or disconfirming a hypothesis should make a difference in one's confidence that a given theory is true. If this does not occur, something is amiss. How can the impact of psychotherapy research be maximized?

We independently summarized the interviews that followed. These reports were later coalesced into single documents, were reviewed by the people interviewed, and are printed here with their permission.

3. John Leo, Psychoanalysis, after 50 years of strong influence in many fields, reaches crossroads. *The New York Times* (Aug. 4, 1968), p. 58.

4. D. T. Lykken, Statistical significance in psychological research. *Psychological Bulletin* 70 (1968): 151–59.

The Pre-Interview Period

Working papers and correspondence which shed light on the process of scientific inquiry and which focus on issues central to our study are interspersed with the interviews in chronological order. Our account begins with excerpts from some of this correspondence. We have tried in this chapter to make public the inner workings of our project through dialogues between us, personal ruminations, the vivid exchanges of the interviews, and the impact of these experiences upon our perspectives and convictions. We publish selections from this material not out of any assumption that our cerebrations are above those of other men, but in the conviction that herein lie the essential processes of scientific development—in the intuitive reaching of the minds of men. In this sense, we have become convinced that, at root, all science is art. While the quality of our own intuitive searching and formulating waxes and wanes, we wanted readers to *experience* as much as possible what we have experienced. What follows, therefore, embraces our high and low points, our frustration and excitement, and our personal experience in attempting to understand and perhaps to a limited degree influence the future of this domain of inquiry.

September 13, 1968

Dear Hans:

I have been thinking a good deal about our project since discussing it with you at APA and I'd like to get your reactions to the following thoughts:

1. We seem to be agreed on contacting people who have done collaborative work in this and other fields. You mentioned those involved in pharmacology. . . . Len Ullmann and Maurice Lorr have coordinated large VA research studies and Truax apparently has been working hard at this with non VA populations. Rogers, of course, has successfully conducted coordinated studies by many individuals on the same subjects in one setting. This seems to be a topic we can hit at numerous times during our visits with people. I do agree though that we should do as much of this as possible at the earliest time.

2. We need to specify what our goals are, i.e., what we want to know when we make visits. This is outlined in part on pp. 12–16 of our grant application, but I would like to spell it out a bit further. I think we would want to know from our consultants and others we visit:

a. Their reactions to the eleven designs outlined in our paper plus additional designs we have developed since then.

b. Their proposals regarding variables, issues, techniques, and designs for collaborative study.

c. Their suggestions regarding existing valuable measures and new measures which need developing.

d. A "yes" or "no" judgment on the feasibility of one or more collaborative projects along with supporting commentary.

e. If feasible, a judgment of the relative value of such studies.

f. In the case of potential collaborators, an analysis of personal plans, group and institutional commitments, research skills and resources available, etc.

3. As you suggested, we will need some kind of record of our discussions. After considering our ideas on recording meetings, having someone take shorthand notes, etc., I've come to the conclusion that we would never wade through an enormous pile of complete transcripts. I think we'd be better off to take our own notes during such discussions. With both of us present in most meetings, we could alternate responsibility for note-taking, i.e., digesting, selecting the important points, taking down occasional verbatim quotations, etc.

4. Obviously, we also need to formulate an explicit system for making visits which includes a list of people and places we have agreed upon. . . .

With best regards.

Cordially,
Allen E. Bergin

September 19, 1968

Dear Allen:

Thank you for your letter of September 13. Obviously you have done a good deal of additional thinking on the various topics we began to explore in San Francisco. I have weighed these matters myself and turned them over in my mind. I have more questions than answers, and the magnitude of the undertaking impresses me as somewhat staggering. In the following I would like to respond to your various points and make a few additional observations. . . .

For the sake of convenience let me introduce a few short-hand labels to refer to the kinds of experts we need to consult (no value judgment implied):

A. Experts on methodology, design, measurement, philosophy of science, who may or may not be highly experienced in psychotherapy research per se.

B. Individuals who have had experience in conducting collaborative research, not necessarily in the area of psychotherapy, and are familiar with problems of coordination, etc.

C. Key individuals at selected centers which may ultimately participate in a collaborative study and whose commitment is of course a sine qua non.

Obviously there will be overlap and some consultants may be exceedingly helpful in all three areas. In a sense they may be the most valuable ones for our purposes. However, I see some danger in getting prematurely committed to a design (or designs) without adequate prior exploration of our key questions. In the end, no doubt, our recommendations will partly reflect a value judgment; I for one want to be very clear on this point. The issue, it seems to me, has never been squarely confronted in previous efforts, or at least it has not been made very explicit. Unless a projected study can, at least in principle, lead to "strong" conclusions (as opposed to "trends"), it may not be worth the trouble.

As you know, some experts (e.g., Colby) have already arrived at negative conclusions on this matter, or so it seems to me. But in any event, I think we want to listen very carefully to the arguments pro and con.

I am aware that the issue cannot be discussed in the abstract for very long without getting involved in questions of design and practicalities, and one of our problems is that everything we will begin to tackle is necessarily related to everything else. But some conceptual distinctions should still be made, and my own preference would be to start at this point. Thus I suggest we concentrate on Type A consultants first and postpone discussions with B and C experts. . . .

Something else is important here: Because of our respective orientations, biases, and predilections we are bound to be more impressed by people whose thinking we find congenial. Therefore, it seems of the utmost importance that both of us listen to people whose views may differ from our own. If we see such people singly, there is bound to be a factor of "selective inattention." If we do it jointly, this danger will be greatly minimized.

After all is said and done, the decisions, recommendations, etc. will be our responsibility and we cannot let others do our thinking for us. This will be true no matter how many experts we consult, most of whom unquestionably will add something to our knowledge, understanding, and grasp of the problems. There will be a measure of safety in numbers, but we should not overestimate it. While we can learn from many people, I don't believe that anyone has THE insight we are after. . . . Some of this will be a matter of luck or serendipity, and all we can do is to try to maximize our chances. . . .

I have been pondering, as you have, the kinds of questions we want to pose to our consultants, and how we might best approach this task. I think we have rather clear ideas about what we are after, and we know a fair amount about each consultant's area of interest and specialization. So we are not going on a blind fishing expedition. We should certainly ask them for their reactions to our survey document, particularly about the eleven designs, but some undoubtedly will want (and should be encouraged) to go further afield. This is in line with my earlier comments. My experience in matters of this sort has taught me that some consultants will have done their "homework" prior to our meeting them; but others will not. In any event, there is bound to be a "warm-up period," review of past efforts, establishing a common ground, etc. before we can get down to business. From this I conclude that we have to spend the better part of a day with each "major" consultant and perhaps more. It also seems to me that we are bound to have a more profitable interaction if we visit a consultant in his own habitat or have him visit for the specific purpose of our project. I am less optimistic about the value of catching someone who happens to be in town on some other business.

There may be merit in getting a small number of carefully selected consultants (say 2 or 3) for group meetings. I can see advantages and disadvantages in this proposal.

Having given the matter of recording further thought, I am inclined to agree with your conclusion that verbatim transcripts, tape recordings, etc. are cumbersome, and while it will somewhat cramp our style, we probably have to assign the job of taking notes to ourselves. A tape recorder, just for the purpose of preserving possible rare and precious interchanges, may still be helpful. . . .

Part of our effort is concerned with the general problem of psychological change and the principles governing it; thus, we have to decide the most promising settings and circumstances in which to study it. On the whole I am still impressed by the cogency of the arguments we advanced in our review favoring the study of individual psychotherapy. Our objective, as I see it, is not to embark on an odyssey to discover the "best" method of psychotherapy—I am pretty firmly convinced that there are no miracle techniques around—but to shed light on the mechansims and conditions of therapeutic change. I still feel that individual psychotherapy is one of the best (if not the best) setting for this purpose.

Cordially,
Hans H. Strupp

September 23, 1968

Dear Hans:

Your letter of September 19 reminded me once again what a lucky "accident" it was that we were asked to collaborate. We are different enough in viewpoint and style to represent significant diverse influences in the field and yet close enough in basic principles to be able to work together fruitfully.

Your letter reminds me of my tendencies to jump to conclusions, to rush in headlong, to become grandiose, and to be highly specific; but you convey your points with such warmth and wisdom that I always learn from them. I guess this is just a way of saying that I appreciated the letter and that I'm very pleased that it happens to be you I'm working with.

As for the specifics of your letter, I have the following reactions:

1. I agree wholeheartedly that we should begin by meeting with persons on our "basic list" and that the discussions should be long and leisurely enough to permit a full and fruitful development of views. . . .

2. Your recommendation that we focus at first on Type A experts gives me pause. Is it better to have a lot of design ideas in our minds when we go to the therapy researchers, or, would it be better to go to the design people *after* gaining a fuller view of the variables and issues people think are of prime significance? I tend to prefer the latter. I must confess that despite my own personal proclivities toward theories of design and of science, I basically do not trust methodologists, mathematicians, and philosophers of science. Their kind of expertise has a high priestly aura about it which in my opinion too often squelches creative science. I always enjoy talking to them, but, privately, I always have my guard up to keep from being "snowed."

Cheers!

Best regards,
Allen E. Bergin

September 26, 1968

Dear Allen:

Your letter of September 23 considerably brightened my day and I am very happy to repay your compliment. In view of the magnitude and the difficulty of our undertaking, about which I expressed my feelings earlier, I am particularly happy to collaborate with a man of your expertness, dedication and capacity for sheer hard work. I am more than glad not to be involved in this alone or with a lesser man.

Your points are well taken. Since we shall soon have an opportunity to discuss all these matters in detail, I shall forego responding to them at this time.

Best regards,
Hans H. Strupp

October 14, 1968

TO: Hans
FROM: Allen
RE: Notes on our meeting of October 4th and 5th, and further thoughts prior to our meeting of October 16–17.

For my own benefit, I have extracted the following ideas from comments and discussion about our project:

1. We give the appearance of being biased in favor of collaborative research, and perhaps we are, particularly me. The point is that enthusiasm should not obscure or minimize perception of the real difficulties.

2. Our statement of the basic question to be answered in this field is agreed upon by many as the crucial issue: "What specific therapeutic interventions produce what specific changes in which specific patients under what specific conditions?" Surprisingly, many people seem to agree that the therapeutic enterprise *is* multidimensional.

3. Complex research *can* be done by single centers if planning and support are adequate, and this may be more efficient than collaborative efforts *between* centers. As the number of collaborators increases arithmetically, the problems increase geometrically.

4. An imaginative design will not evolve from the work of a committee. It must come from motivated individuals who make their creative hunches explicit.

5. The stages and priorities of our planning can best be summarized as follows:

   a. What are the crucial questions to be answered?
   b. What designs or programs of research will most efficiently answer them?
   c. If appropriate designs include collaborative ones, will given practitioners and researchers participate and how effectively will they carry through?
   d. If a, b, and c lead to a positive plan, then pilot work would be initiated.

6. Although we seem to favor collaborative research, our review did not lead to any unified designs deriving logically from the research evidence we discussed.

7. It is important for us to recognize that although our minds are being fertilized by doing reviews and meeting with brilliant people, in the last analysis it will be our own creative intuitions which will synthesize the conclusions to be drawn from all this. We have to be independent enough to formulate views that are truly our own. This is most crucial during this early phase. . . .

8. We seem to find ourselves already thinking far beyond our review. We are no longer very enthusiastic about many of the designs we proposed there, particularly the mammoth comparative ones.

9. For the moment, we seem more excited by precision and refinement in design and analysis of variables, rather than by global, naturalistic studies. We seem to see value in studying psychotherapy as it now exists, but we seem to be leaning more toward research of the type Bandura has done or which Goldstein, Heller, and Sechrest propose. Thus, we are (I am?) begin-

ning to be persuaded that the best change techniques will most efficiently be derived from a general psychology of change rather than from clinical practice, per se.

Analogue research may be a correlated avenue toward more powerful methods, but we have reservations about its relevance to psychotherapy practice. Maybe we should do as Krasner suggests: forget about relevance to traditional methods and build new ones based upon precision research. This is a true dilemma in light of the fact that the experimental psychologists are finding that they must invoke cognitive, emotional, and social variables to account for individual differences in classical conditioning! Can analogue studies adequately incorporate complexity (i.e., interaction effects) as it occurs in change processes? Are we foolish to try to simplify in the area of psychotherapy when the area of experimental psychology is being forced toward complexity? Is there, on the other hand, value in isolating a few specifiable variables and "manipulating them to death"?

10. I predict that we are likely to eventually recommend that the best solution is to *provide greater continuing support for single centers* which have the capacity to implement a *program* of *systematic,* complex research. This might be something like The Research and Development Centers being funded by the Office of Education. I am becoming increasingly skeptical of the advisability of projects developed by several centers, especially if they exist in more than one city.

TO: Allen
FROM: Hans
RE: Notes from our October 16-17 Meeting

In our discussion reference was made to a recent article by Albert Ellis,[5] who views the major changes in any form of psychotherapy as (1) cognitive-perceptual; (2) emotional (conditioning); and (3) motoric. This distinction seems useful.

Human behavior is exceedingly complex. The psycholinguists have been impressed with this problem and have criticized Skinner on this score. There are no basic units in psychology (unlike physics) and S–R or similar paradigms are bound to be inadequate. The field is beginning to recognize this fact.

Wolman, in a 1964 paper in the *Journal of the American Psychoanalytic Association,*[6] deals with this problem, asserting that we must accept the complexity of the phenomena as a given; in his view, psychoanalytic theory

5. A. Ellis, What really causes psychotherapeutic change? *Voices* 4(1968):90–95.

6. B. B. Wolman, Evidence in psychoanalytic research. *Journal of the American Psychoanalytic Association* 12 (1964): 717–31.

recognizes this complexity. The trouble lies not with the theory but with the complexity of the phenomena.

We cannot pit theories against each other; there are no crucial experiments. In therapy we are always dealing with techniques—we don't disprove theories. We need many micro-theories. In these, many operations (for example, conditioning) can find a place. Also, we can influence an individual in a variety of ways by operating on a given dimension.

Techniques are vastly different from the theories, and most of the latter seem quite inadequate.

It seems that we are most successful in psychotherapy research when we are more specific. This argues for the potential value of (1) analogue research; (2) experimental manipulation of a variable; and (3) study of part processes. It argues against large multifactorial studies of the Menninger variety; the latter seem to result in "weak" answers and confounded measures. Furthermore, they shed no light on cause and effect.

There seems to be a new recognition of the importance of *cognitive* factors in behavior therapy. Davison is working on the problem. Information processing is very powerful.

The typical outcome study provides no definitive answers.

What is operative in behavior therapy: relationship, desensitization, a combination of the two?

The intensive study of individual cases, perhaps combined with some experimental interventions in the treatment, seemed promising. Research can sharpen the therapist's observational powers and thereby make an important contribution. We might study expert therapists at work. This approach involves a naturalistic study with a "built-in" design.

Any therapy study involves compromises—there cannot be a perfectly "clean" one. Some middle ground between complexity and experimental rigor must be found.

Some question was raised about the payoff of *systematic* research using a particular research technique, that is, research focused on part-processes carried out over a long period of time.

We discussed again the relative virtues of analogue versus naturalistic studies.

All therapists ignore complexity to some extent and are reductionistic in their work. This applies to analysis, client-centered therapy, behavior therapy, and others.

We felt it might be useful to put a few therapists of differing orientations to work on a fairly well delineated syndrome and carefully evaluate the results.

Under what conditions does a particular form of therapy work (or fail to work)?

To what extent does the primitive status of our knowledge in the area of psychopathology limit what we can do in therapy?

The manner in which the therapist construes the patient's "problem" determines his technique, and the process of construing involves his theoretical assumptions about his approach to therapy and the patient.

On the basis of our discussion we formulated a set of questions to be presented as an "advance stimulus" to our consultants.

The Interview Period

After the foregoing preliminaries, we began our interviews with experts. This intellectual odyssey became a truly "peak experience" for both of us and one which we will never forget. The reader will see why as he wends his way through the interview material. We began our visits with a trip to Philadelphia where we met first with Arnold Lazarus and then Lester Luborsky and Arthur Auerbach.

INTERVIEW: ARNOLD A. LAZARUS*

Philadelphia, October 24–25, 1968

Perhaps the most striking of Dr. Lazarus' comments concerned his views of behavior therapy. They were surprisingly unguarded and critical, perhaps because of the controversy in which he was then engaged with Joseph Wolpe regarding the (behavioral) "purity" and scientific status of behavioral techniques. In this debate Lazarus has consistently advocated dropping behavioristic theory and adopting a technical eclecticism.

Lazarus felt strongly that one cannot talk about the therapeutic dyad in terms of "external reinforcement," a concept he considers inadequate and often inappropriate. Certain behavior therapists appear to be embarked on a mission to establish S-R as *the* basic unit, and Lazarus believes this mission won't work. He pointed out that reinforcement terminology is inadequate in any work outside of a dyadic situation and noted that Patterson's work (1971) on operant conditioning in the home is a good example of a situation where it is difficult to apply precise reinforcement concepts in accounting for the complexities of family interaction.

*Dr. Lazarus is Visiting Professor and Director of Clinical Training at the Psycho-Educational Clinic of Yale University.

He expressed the belief that only 1% of phobias are situational. These are the true traumatic, monosymptomatic neuroses. All others vary in degrees of complexity and often require more than a simple desensitization process. Even when desensitization is applied, he believes that it represents primarily a cognitive process involving "pleasing the therapist," "demand characteristics" of the therapist, "graded structure" and modification of patient "expectancies." He finds that if a patient gets into an "inner circle" or in other words feels accepted after revealing affect-laden material, a phobia often disappears. This outcome means to him that phobias and other forms of purported emotional conditioning are not maintained necessarily by "conditioning" at all. As a corollary, he states that he seriously doubts that there is much connection between experimental laboratory studies in behavior theory and what is done by behavior therapists. However, he feels that there is a somewhat neglected possibility of incorporating much data from social psychology into therapeutic situations.

With regard to his own techniques Lazarus stressed the importance of *assessment,* which he considers crucial. Faulty or inadequate assessments result in confused outcome criteria. *Multiple outcome criteria* are needed and *independent assessments* are called for. Arnold felt that the family therapist's insistence on evaluating the husband-wife dyad is valuable. He also cited a case of a woman with a water phobia which he felt needed to be understood in *interpersonal* rather than straight physical terms.

He stated that within his broad spectrum approach he is willing to employ virtually any method that appears promising. For example, he has extensively used bibliotherapy in addition to urging patients to work on regular homework assignments between sessions. He even uses a number of Mowrer-like techniques by which the patient is encouraged to make amends for his past misdeeds and which help him to resolve his guilt.

Another important point which emerged was the immensely intuitive nature of the process of therapy even as conducted by this behaviorally oriented expert. He makes extensive use of fantasy and imagery in therapy. The manner in which he picks up cues and determines what manipulation he will use next remains a somewhat subjective process. Yet he believes that these maneuvers can be taught. He indicated that when all is said and done he really does little more in his therapy than exercise compassion toward his patients and apply a good measure of intuitive ingenuity in the service of provoking change. While this procedure often seems to entail a good deal of focus and specificity, it need not be behavioristic at all. What it is in his therapy that effects change he summed up this way: "At this stage, I am uncertain but optimistic in that I have many ideas and impressions which can be crystallized by careful research."

Lazarus asserted that we have too much hypothesis generation and that we don't need new ones. He allowed that laboratory research which would ignore the usual complexities in research might be productive but he seemed to favor research in the clinical situation. "We always deal with techniques —not theories! At this stage, psychotherapy research should focus on the study of techniques. Many widely accepted theories are misleading or irrelevant, but ultimately we need good theories upon which to anchor our methods and we need theories which will generate even more effective techniques. But there is no reason why we should not first develop a really effective technology."

With regard to paradigms for inquiry in the therapy area, Lazarus described a comparative study currently being done by Sloane and Yorkston at Temple University which involves three experienced behavior therapists and three experienced analytically oriented therapists. Therapists are matched for experience level and each participating therapist sees at least 10 patients for approximately 20 sessions. Careful independent assessments are made by means of the SSIAM check list, and other elaborate procedures are followed. He raised some doubts about this study in which he is participating as a behavior therapist, wondering whether it is realistic to compare behavior therapy and eclectic psychotherapy because the two overlap so much. He said: "Everybody has been out to prove the wrong kind of thing." He seemed to mean that comparing therapies was not nearly as important as search for the real change agents in the complexity of the therapeutic transaction. Possibly this view arises in part from his own practice which (like everyone else's) is highly multidimensional and thus lacks the kind of technical purity to which some behavior therapists aspire.

Another strong theme was his conviction that the most fruitful option for research would be to study a series of individual patient-therapist pairs in all their complexity, including the analysis of therapist personal characteristics and techniques. Such a study, he believed, should not be designed to generate hypotheses but rather to approach the complexity of the whole person and to begin specifying what it is that produces what changes under what conditions. The "pure gold" is to be found in in-depth study of therapists and their patients under these conditions. He is dubious about analogue studies which isolate part processes in the laboratory; for example, he considered animal studies "often unproductive" and characterized the cat studies of Masserman and Wolpe as "irrelevant." However, he expressed high regard for the kind of research carried out by Lovaas even though Lazarus himself feels temperamentally unsuited to do "that type of thing." (We characterized the Lovaas research in terms of first experimentally refining and isolating a highly specific, but potent change-inducing technique and then employing it systematically and precisely with individual cases, studying the effects of the techniques across cases—a type of single-case repeated experiment.)

We concluded that there may indeed be some "gold to be mined" from carefully designed single case studies repeated across patients by carefully selected, effective therapists. (Project 2, the study of experts, got another boost.) Such a study would have to be relatively naturalistic, but some manipulation of variables may be possible within this context. For example, each expert might be assigned a carefully selected cross section of patients so that it could be determined whether different things are being done with different patients, under what conditions, and with what effects. Of course, the potent dimensions of change induction might be even better ascertained by including a sample of poor therapists.

Emerging from this discussion were points by Strupp such as: "Expert clinicians have never been studied systematically," and "A lifetime isn't long enough to study the kinds of observations that were done on Franz Alexander at Mt. Sinai," thus favoring Lazarus' emphasis but warning of the danger of being overwhelmed by a mass of data.

Lazarus also advocated a retrospective study to ferret out the ingredients of change. For example, he would establish a prognosis beforehand and attempt to discover why the prognosis was not accurate when the patient's course of therapy deviated from the predictions. For example, why don't some prime therapy cases respond well, and why do some poor prognosis cases change markedly? Retrospective analysis of such low probability events would provide a context for discovery. Also, he suggested the idea of using a number of observers from different points of view in order to search for agreement on the nature of the raw facts, rather than their interpretation. The key here seems to be the prognostic statement. That is, it would be important to have a description of the patient's history, the onset of his problems and the exact therapeutic conditions under which persons with this kind of history and problem seem to respond best and worst.

Another important point was Dr. Lazarus' conviction that it is vital to study the effects of the degree of match or harmony between the therapist and the patient. He feels that this harmony is a main key to effectiveness. He gave an apt illustration of a patient whose aggressiveness clearly annoyed him and he referred her to a therapist who was like her. The "match" worked out beautifully!

Comments by Bergin. I felt that Arnie was very much the clinician and not very much excited by theory or research. I found this refreshing coming from a behavior therapist; but I am a little uncertain about what I learned that was really new. Maybe it amounted mostly to hearing someone I really respected emphasize repeatedly the importance of studying the therapeutic process in its complexity. Another feeling I had was that Arnie genuinely does appreciate and support the idea of experimentally zeroing-in on a specific change methodology, but only if that methodology is then studied on live cases rather than in analogue situations. Another impression I came away with was the feeling that there probably are highly technical procedures that do effectively produce change in some people or some restricted problems and that these should not be ignored or underestimated.

On the other hand, I was deeply impressed once again with the importance for many people of having a therapeutic experience with a person who is able to create a real impact upon him. This process of personal influence impresses me over and over again and I have to admit that I don't think this ability is unique to therapists and I also doubt that much can be done in the way of educating people to acquire it. I really think it requires certain personal characteristics plus a lot of experience with patients. This may be why volunteer therapists do so well as a group. They may include a proportion of these strong personal impact types who may account for the average positive change which occurs, much as it may be that a small proportion of therapists account for the positive change that occurs in professional therapy. The modest amount of change occurring in therapy groups of either type may also be due to the fact that only some patients are responsive to the personal impact kind of experience. Others and their problems may be more responsive to a technique or procedure which is less personal. I think Lazarus hinted at this a few times himself.

References

Patterson, G. R. 1971. Behavioral intervention procedures in the classroom and in the home. In A. E. Bergin & S. L. Garfield eds. *Handbook of psychotherapy and behavior change: An empirical analysis.* New York: Wiley, pp. 751–75.

INTERVIEW: LESTER LUBORSKY AND ARTHUR AUERBACH*

Philadelphia, October 25, 1968

Drs. Luborsky and Auerbach gave us a summary of their recently activated "80 case study," a project designed to explore the "optimal conditions" of psychotherapy. This carefully designed investigation employs a multiple regression approach in an attempt to apportion the variance in therapy outcome to patient, therapist, and patient-therapist interaction. Les strongly subscribes to the view that much more in psychotherapy research must be

* Dr. Luborsky is Professor of Psychology in the Department of Psychiatry of the University of Pennsylvania School of Medicine. Dr. Auerbach is Assistant Professor in the Department of Psychiatry.

tied to outcome, and he follows Astrup (as well as most clinicians) in the belief that the patient variable accounts for the largest segment in the outcome variance (Astrup & Noreik, 1966).

Variables for measurement were selected on the basis of an intensive review of the research literature in this field, a valuable document in its own right (Luborsky et al., 1971). Studies favoring and not favoring particular variables or measure were compiled and the most promising ones were selected from this tabulation. These summaries, in coordination with our own, could help establish the relative value of given variables in the event that major coordinated studies are planned in the future. The multifactorial design under discussion will permit the investigators to correlate the variables with a diverse range of outcome criteria, and a multiple correlation can also be computed in relation to various criteria of outcome. Thus the relative contribution of the three classes of variables to therapeutic change can be determined.

The investigators' conviction that the patient variable is the most powerful with regard to outcome across therapies is manifested in several ways in the study. They have developed a prognostic index based on an intensive 1½ hour assessment interview, which looks promising. On the basis of this interview the patient is evaluated by the interviewer and by a pair of raters using the same outline. This will make it possible to equate patients and to form meaningful subgroups for analysis of differential response to the therapeutic influence. Subgroups of therapists can also be established as well as groups based on particular kinds of therapist-patient pairing. This process, however, will be limited by the relatively small number of therapists.

Les and Art are also using the Klopfer Prognostic Rating Scale which, they assert, did a good job of predicting outcome in 8 out of 10 studies. This scale seems to be a measure of "health-sickness," as measured by the Menninger Health-Sickness Rating Scale, which Les and Art are still using as a key measure. (It could be that a number of studies supported the Klopfer scale, but we will have to be convinced that these studies are really methodologically sound before we can accept their conclusion. One possibility is that the Klopfer Scale picks up something like verbal ability which has little to do with the Rorschach stimuli themselves.)[7]

Les reiterated his view that the greater the patient's subjective distress, the better the outcome (as shown for example in the Phipps Symptom Check List); however, the greater the severity of the illness and disturbance of functioning, the poorer the outcome.

7. Luborsky comments: "I agree; the studies *may* not be methodologically sound. But '8 out of 10' come out in one direction despite differences in samples, etc. Therefore, we felt we had to go to the trouble of trying the Klopfer scale even though it is quite time consuming."

This study is perhaps among the most rigorous to focus on the therapy process performed in a comparatively traditional way. Bergin, however, felt that the products of the study may be limited because (*a*) the amount of change occurring among these patients may be small, due to the fact that whenever a heterogeneous sample of therapists is studied, the results are not powerful and (*b*) the small number of patients and therapists precludes extensive subgrouping for further analyses after the data are gathered. In spite of these drawbacks, the study may be expected to yield important results, such as data on the relationships among the large number of measures of the three classes of predictor variables (patient, therapist, and patient-therapist interaction); or the four classes of variables, if we include outcome criteria. One by-product already seems to be significant. A recently completed factor analysis of ratings of psychotherapy process revealed a large first factor pertaining to characteristics usually associated with the "good therapist" ("Optimal Empathic Relationship") similar to a Carl Rogers' type of dimension, a second which is essentially interpretive, and another which is an active directive mode (Mintz et al., 1971).

We talked at some length about research strategies, how to bring about involvement and commitment of clinicians and researchers of different orientations. Les mentioned the example of the Psychoanalytic Research Group of the Institute of the Pennsylvania Hospital of which he is a member. This group is currently proceeding with the design of a study involving tape recorded analyses by a number of its members. It is evidence of a certain change in the psychoanalytic *Zeitgeist* that such a group exists. It was also apparent that in order to have access to such a group one must contribute as one of its members. If one can do this, there is ground for optimism. Les felt that "farming out" of methods developed in successful projects either to practicing therapists (as was done by Nat Raskin in a recent study involving members of the American Academy of Psychotherapists) or to other potential research groups was preferable to centralized control of collaborating projects. Rudolf Ekstein once commented that true collaboration among researchers (or between clinicians and researchers) was very rare and hard to come by, and Luborsky and Auerbach agreed quite strongly that it is rare for research people (especially those with different orientations) to develop a way of working together harmoniously. This seems like an essential precondition for collaborative work and one has to raise a serious question as to whether it can be established adequately across centers, unless one center is the primary designer of the research and farms out specific parts to others who essentially accepted the "package." For collaboration to succeed, it is essential that everyone has an equal commitment to the basic design, and that each person feels he is getting something out of the project which is important to him personally. It is usually easier to develop one's own research in a center than to match and coordinate efforts across centers.

On the subject of philosophy of design and approach to inquiry in this field, Les and Art expressed a rather strong commitment to the clinical setting. They seemed to feel that the systematic study of the clinical process, quantitative, clinical research of the type they are doing, will permit us to mine the purest gold. Furthermore, they seemed to opt for the idea that we can learn most at this point from a study of therapy in all of its complexity because this permits us to tease out more potent factors than single-variable or analogue studies. Luborsky reiterated a statement he made at the beginning of our discussion: "Let's study what therapists are actually doing." He quoted Morris Parloff: "No new technique was ever invented in the laboratory; and none was ever discarded because of laboratory findings." (Research may result in greater specification but not in breakthroughs. This view argues that it is only clinical phenomena and clear changes in patients as a result of technique which will result in the acceptance of new techniques.)

Les admitted a bias against experimental studies (including "for-purposes-of-research" practicing a technique) and expressed himself in favor of letting therapists do what they usually do. Project 2 (the study of experts) again was considered promising. Les argued that we do not know enough to compare techniques by artifically homogenizing them, and therefore feels it would be a significant contribution to show the amount of overlap occurring in the behaviors of therapists of different persuasions. This would require researchers to let therapists operate "naturally." In this context he also made the point that it is important to evaluate the kinds of changes occurring in people who are undergoing therapy by different therapists of different persuasions. He emphasized that the real issue is to what extent change is a function of technique or orientation and to what extent a function of personal influence. Les and Art hope to learn more about this problem from their own study.

They feel that it may also be valuable to study intensively patients who, on the basis of prognostic ratings, would be expected to improve but don't (and vice versa). This kind of research would help the clinician with what Colby calls "acute difficulties in the art," a point with which Lazarus also agrees.

Both investigators are in the psychoanalytic tradition, and they view the rise of behavior therapy with detached interest. They believe that more controlled studies are needed to establish its therapeutic indications. They favor the continuing exploration of behavior therapy, not only because of possible therapeutic benefits, but for the light it might throw on basic processes such as influence and changes in attitudes. They see as the major contribution of behavior therapy its emphasis on symptoms and specificity. Moreover, the behaviorists have focused on the educational problem, that is, What does a person need to know in order to change a symptom? These are the "learning things" which are an important part of therapy and fully deserving the focus accorded them by the behavior therapists. However, different patients clearly need different things from therapy: Some need "retraining;" others need a "relationship;" and so on. Due to this fact, Les and Art said: "Let's not unduly emphasize the educational aspects of psychotherapy."

Les considered Lovaas' approach interesting. The fact that Lovaas is a behavior therapist who is treating cases and not doing analogue studies was significant to him.

It appears that all therapists focus on specifics to a greater or lesser extent and ignore idiosyncratic variables in the patient's life. That is, all science ultimately must be nomothetic.

Much valuable work in medicine is not curative but meliorative. It would help if psychotherapists got around to this view. In the process they might spare themselves disappointments, but they also would have to give up some grandiosity.

Clinical knowledge, according to Luborsky (and applauded by Strupp), is not to be disparaged, and clinicians "know" a great deal on the basis of their experience with patients even though such knowledge often has not been tested in the laboratory. "There is a gap between what one knows clinically and what one comes to know through other ways of knowing." Bergin considered this a striking statement because it implies that there are many ways of knowing, as Carl Rogers and others have suggested. This could be somewhat bothersome in that it seems that when one knows something it should be explicit enough so that it is scientific and not just "clinical." Perhaps it would be better to make a distinction between "sensing" and "knowing." Clinically we sense many things although we do not have the subjective experience of "knowing." Reference was made to a recent paper on knowledge by Anatol Rapoport (1968).

Toward the end of our discussion we learned of several other studies. Henry Bachrach, a member of the Luborsky-Auerbach project, recently completed a study showing a significant positive correlation between regression "in the service of the ego" (measured by Holt's Rorschach scoring system) and empathy. A comparative study involving behavior therapy and other approaches is currently in progress at the University of Pennsylvania; Paul Brady is the principal investigator. The study involves the treatment of frigidity. Luborsky commented on overlap in techniques and the difficulty of obtaining agreement on criteria. We also learned about an (as yet unpublished) study by Merton Gill and Irving Paul (City University of New York) dealing with the effects of interpretations. There was high agreement among clinicians as to what constitutes a "good interpretation," but the patient's statements did not seem to matter very much!

Comments by Bergin. It seemed to me that these men were sophisticated clinicians and researchers whose work is very likely to improve our ability to set up a refined methodology through their large study of the natural therapy process. However, I doubt that their own study or any similar one of any type of therapy will shed light on the processes of therapeutic change because when the therapists are not pre-selected to include primarily a group who are potent change agents the results are ambiguous. This appears to result from heterogeneous effects flowing from a heterogeneous sample of therapists. While a few of them may obtain powerful effects, the average effect of the group is weak.

I feel that if the therapy process is to be studied naturalistically the design must expressly require a procedure for selecting therapists who make a difference. If there is no significant change occurring, then all the methodological refinements in the world will not matter, for we will obtain only an elegant description of a weak technique.[8]

Another thing impressed me, namely that Luborsky and Lazarus had a similar evaluation of Lovaas' work. This seems very important because it suggests that dedicated clinicians from varying viewpoints can agree substantially that it is possible to isolate a change-inducing technique on the basis of laboratory work and then develop it into a clinical procedure.

Comments by Strupp. As might be expected, I found Les and Art's approach quite congenial and felt that they were embarked on a rather important program of research in which they attempt to take maximal advantage of clinical knowledge and insight. They are fully aware that variables do not come singly and that research designs must defer to clinical complexities rather than be dictated by available measuring instruments. I share Bergin's concerns about the difficulties of isolating the effects of single variables, a problem which is inherent in all correlational studies. Furthermore, since the number of patient-therapist pairs is limited in the major study we learned

8. Luborsky comments: "I think that this is an unjustified downgrading of the therapists in the study. In fact at no point do I recall having described the nature of the therapist's group. Why assume that they're not potent change agents? If *they* are not, who is? There are to be about 40 therapists. About 20 of them will be residents (and possibly residents are relatively not potent change agents though I doubt that), but then we have 20 highly experienced therapists who probably are as potent as any change agents that can be found anywhere. Regardless of the form of treatment or the technical innovation, the potency of a change agent undoubtedly comes from the ability of the therapist to set up a relationship, and that is somewhat independent of the particular technique he uses."

about from Les and Art, the task of disentangling the complex interactions is vastly complicated.

I remain torn between the advantages of clinical research and analogue studies, and see no really satisfactory solution to the problem.

It is apparent that both Les and Art are fully committed to a research career. However, they are also very sophisticated clinicians firmly convinced that psychotherapy in the hands of competent people is worthwhile. They reject fads and gimmicks; and they are unimpressed by claims of rapid, sure-fire cures for people's neurotic ills. Their research may not yield conclusive answers, but there is no doubt in my mind that their work will enrich our knowledge about the psychotherapeutic process.

It is an interesting sidelight on the sociology of research, that there is a virtual absence of communication, not to mention collaboration, among psychotherapy researchers in the Philadelphia area. For example, Luborsky and Auerbach had little contact with the investigators at Temple University and vice versa. I gather that differences in theoretical orientation, therapeutic practices, research philosophy, and personal factors account for this lack. Whatever the reasons, the facts represent a mute commentary on our task of exploring the feasibility of collaborative research.

References

Astrup, C., & Noreik, K. 1966. *Functional psychoses, diagnostic and prognostic models.* Springfield, Illinois: Charles C. Thomas.

Luborsky, L., Chandler, M., Auerbach, A. H., Cohen, J., & Bachrach, H. M. 1971. Factors influencing the outcome of psychotherapy: A review of quantitative research. *Psychological Bulletin* 75:145–85.

Mintz, J., Luborsky, L., & Auerbach, A. H. 1971. Dimensions of psychotherapy: A factor analytic study of ratings of psychotherapy sessions. *Journal of Consulting Psychology* 36:106–20.

Rapoport, A. 1968. Psychoanalysis as science. *Bulletin of the Menninger Clinic* 32:1–20.

INTERVIEW: LYLE D. SCHMIDT AND STANLEY R. STRONG

Minneapolis, October 31, 1968

Drs. Schmidt, Donald H. Blocher and Strong are experimenting with different kinds of training procedures for counselors. They believe that there are

* Dr. Schmidt is Professor of Psychology at Ohio State University; Dr. Strong is Associate Professor of Psychology at the University of Minnesota.

three primary counselor styles: didactic, intuitive, and pragmatic. As I see these styles they are somewhat like those of rational therapy, dynamic therapy, and behavior therapy respectively. They find that if they take a group of students and arbitrarily assign them to one of these training procedures, the students respond in highly individualistic ways. This outcome suggests to them that there are personal predispositions which influence one's therapeutic predilections.

We toyed for a time with a rather elaborate design for testing separate effects of counselor life style and his technique. This discussion assumed that there are three major kinds of life style: the intuitive, didactic, and pragmatic. If these types or styles could be identified, then it would be a simple matter to have therapists of each type work with each of several types of therapy to see which combinations of style and technique produce the best results with given cases. For example, take a group of 60 intuitive people and assign 20 of them to do desensitization, 20 to do an empathic-dynamic kind of therapy and another 20 to do a didactic-rational kind of therapy. In addition, a group of 60 didactic-style therapists and a group of 60 pragmatic-style therapists could be similarly divided. This design eventually became too large to pursue.

Another point we dwelt on for some time concerned a different area of research in which they are involved: the focus on counseling as a setting for persuasion à la Jerry Frank's *Persuasion and Healing* (1961) and the literature on communication, persuasion, and attitude change. They are studying perceived expertness of the therapist in relation to opinion change and change in self ratings of clients. They have culled a set of therapists' statements from tape recordings which they present in written form to college undergraduates who rate them in terms of a scale of expertness or credibility. The idea is to determine which kinds of therapist verbal behavior college students perceived as most persuasive. Therapist's verbal behavior can be rated in a number of other dimensions similarly derived from the persuasion literature. Once these statements have been formed into scales, a number of possibilities become feasible. For example, therapy tapes can be analyzed for content and correlations run between therapist expertness or persuasiveness and various kinds of client change. Another possibility is to standardize the therapist's role by setting up a quasi-therapy situation and systematically studying the differential effects of high and low therapist expertness statements. This line of work derives from such noted people as Goldstein, Heller, Sechrest, and Bergin!

Following this discussion, we devoted considerable time to the issue of laboratory versus clinical research. It was felt that derivations of change techniques from laboratory research would be very fruitful, but that it was necessary to gather a special staff for this purpose and designate a particular service center as a therapy experimentation center. It was pointed out that the work of therapists in such a center would function perhaps in an intuitive way with gifted clinicians developing methodologies based on laboratory research done by others.

Dr. Strong made an interesting comment that it may be wise to stop focusing on diagnosis and study therapies, find out what works differentially with patients, and base a diagnostic system on these findings. Dr. Meehl or Dr. Tuma mentioned later that this type of thing had been done in drug studies.

There was also considerable discussion, in terms of persuasion, of what might be called a "convergence phenomenon" (Pepinsky and Karst, 1964) in therapy in which the therapist's and client's views begin to converge. It could be that therapy is over when the counselor's view of the patient's trouble is transferred to the patient. This is the "world view" conception of therapeutic change and may indeed be a potent force. If it is, this makes the persuasion literature all the more relevant. In this context, one has to begin to consider the question of how a person comes to be reinforcing, that is, how he builds trust and has an influence. This is very much relevant to the reinforcement literature, the persuasion literature, and the therapy process literature.

There was also considerable discussion of the research strategies that might be employed in coordinated efforts. It was noted that Luborsky and Lazarus did not seem fully aware of what the other was doing in research in the same city. Apparently, both are being supported to an extent by NIMH funds. It was noted how helpful the visit was in the sense of informing them of things going on around the country. They felt that something like this might well be formalized more to keep people up to date. This would require financial support and perhaps semi-annual meetings to stimulate and motivate people. Such efforts provide immediate reinforcement for workers in the field. We discussed that there were few centers set up to receive all kinds of patients and it would be important to have collaboration to solve many of the problems and that well-financed investigators are probably less likely to be interested in collaboration. Even within a collaborative study, it would be important to do diverse things with diverse people via diverse strategies, even though we might use standard measures across studies.

The most salient feeling I came away with after this discussion was the concern, the importance, or possible importance, of developing a center for experimentation in clinical methods, particularly as these methods may be derived from laboratory work. Could we conceive, for example, bringing together in a single center a group of researchers and innovative clinicians who would collaborate in building a new personality change technology based on laboratory research? Such a "center for research in psychotherapy and behavior change" might well produce results.[9]

9. Circumstances curtailed the length of this interivew; therefore readers are referred to Dr. Stanley Strong, Student Life Studies, University of Minnesota, for

References

Frank, J. D. 1961. *Persuasion and healing.* Baltimore: The Johns Hopkins Press.

Pepinsky, H. B., & Karst, T. O. 1964. Convergence: A phenomenon in counseling and in psychotherapy. *American Psychologist* 19: 333–38.

INTERVIEW: PAUL E. MEEHL*

Minneapolis, November 1, 1968

Diagnosis, Biology, and Therapeutic Change. Dr. Meehl is convinced that diagnosis is an important key to the mental health problem particularly because the genetic and biochemical factors which influence disordered behavior frequently go undetected. He suggested that our survey had paid insufficient attention to psychopathology and the problem of diagnosis (a point also made by Isaac Marks, but from a different perspective). This led to a discussion of his views concerning schizophrenia, a topic in which he has had a longstanding interest. He believes that schizotypes (individuals with genetic defects that are minimally responsive to psychological intervention) are often treated as if they were neurotics, and over half of the patients applying for help to the typical clinic are probably pseudoneurotic schizophrenics. Whenever shifts in diagnosis occur after therapy gets underway, they are usually in the direction of schizophrenia. Basic to Paul's thinking is the assumption that in doing psychotherapy with schizotypes we are attempting to modify learned behavior, with limitations set by CNS parameters that are genetically aberrated. This change cannot be brought about by psychological techniques; thus, we don't "cure" such patients, but we may succeed (if we are lucky) in keeping them compensated. The tendency toward "cognitive slippage," and the like, is genetically determined. The "right" combination of therapist (Type A, see Whitehorn and Betz, 1954) and drugs may be the best that can be hoped for. However this outcome is not bad: We don't "cure" schizophrenia any more than the physician cures diabetes. Therapists need to set realistic goals which are limited by the patient's genetic make-up.

Paul has considerable faith in possible contributions coming from the field of behavioral genetics and is convinced of the existence of "huge" in-

---

further details of the research program or for reprints of the papers which have issued from several correlated studies. This interview was conducted by Bergin.

* Dr. Meehl is Regent's Professor of Psychology at the University of Minnesota. Also present at this session was Dr. A. Hussain Tuma of the Clinical Research Branch, National Institute of Mental Health.

nate individual differences in personality predispositions that may amount to 15 or 20 major dimensions which "we can't do a damn thing about." He lists some illustrations, such as anxiety level, conditionability, anhedonia (essentially a weakness in the positive reinforcement parameters), and rage potential. He summed up his reference to this material and to differences in energy levels and body types with the statement: "Some people are born with more salt and pepper in the limbic system and some people are born three drinks behind." He made the important point that any focal center in the brain, such as the limbic system, must certainly yield a range of individual differences in behavior. Chemical means are needed to change these predispositions, and reinforcement is "weak medicine" in this respect. He thought there even was something to be said in favor of somatotypes, exemplified by Sheldon's "mesomorphic toughness." In the total variance of behavior, Paul believes, genetic factors account for most: "The pendulum is swinging away from environmentalism."

He gave further illustrations of the very powerful effects of hereditary influences. For example, if you take A-type and B-type rats you find that both types can learn complex behavior as a function of reinforcement, but the parameters of the learning curves which these different types manifest may be due primarily to genetic influences.

In answer to the question of how to cope with people whose genes reduce their behavioral effectiveness, he suggested the importance of drug therapy. Such therapy, effectively developed, might consist of maintenance dosages which would be required for the rest of a person's life. Mild depressions are an example. Genetic contributions to anxiety must also be considered. He used the analogy of thyroid deficiencies which are treated by regular drug intake in order to maintain biochemical equilibrium. He suggested, and we all agreed, that a similar approach may be necessary in some people to maintain a behavioral equilibrium. (This analogy may also apply to "dosages" of psychotherapy.)

Paul saw no fundamental conflict between the foregoing views and learning approaches to psychotherapy. He noted that there are many problems with drug therapy, one of which is that if too large a dosage is given the patient may lose his motivation for psychotherapy. It is therefore important to adjust drug dosages so that the person maintains some kind of equilibrium and yet retains his motivation for psychotherapeutic work aimed at helping him develop a more adaptive repertoire to deal with stress. In this context, it was brought out that our outcome criteria in many cases may be unrealistically high and that we need to establish specific therapeutic goals for each patient, which may often be rather modest ones. Our criterion of success would then be equivalent to meeting this modest goal rather than what Strupp described as "jumping over the moon."

Meehl also called attention to the importance of diagnosis by illustrating the differential responsiveness of patients to drugs. He pointed out that in the course of their Ford Foundation Research Project they had developed a multivariate psychological system comprising three distinct psychological subgroups which might respond differentially to the same drugs. He felt somewhat dubious that this would be possible and felt that the main distinction should be between schizotypes and neurotics. This viewpoint is, of course, close to Eysenck's. He indicated that he has developed a check list and an MMPI key for schizotypes. (It is now available from Meehl, together with item weights and cutting score.)

He went on to point out that existing measurement methods may simply be too primitive for large-scale collaborative studies at the present time. In our own view, it may be possible to develop measures of pertinent variables which can be estimated at least crudely. However, we all agreed on the great need for new instrumentation. Meehl pointed out the importance of being able to measure the genetic bases of behavior, such as a "genetic anxiety base."

Outcome Study. Part of the poor showing of outcome studies in psychotherapy is attributable to (1) frequently low competence of therapists, and (2) poor selection of patients, specifically, patients who are poor prognostic risks (because of genetic factors) are accepted for therapy more or less indiscriminately. In this connection, Paul referred to his earlier (published) assertion that if the probability of a patient being a good prognostic risk is .2, and the percentage of really competent therapists is also .2, then the likelihood of pairing an appropriate patient with a competent therapist reduces itself to .04. The view that many therapists are not very competent (shared fully by us) came up in the course of our discussion. Meehl felt very strongly that, given the right kind of patient and the right kind of therapist, psychotherapy has a great deal to offer. He also believed that a study demonstrating this (thereby refuting Eysenck's assertions) was well worth the effort. Incidentally, he thought that genetic limitations are not in the least an argument against psychotherapy per se, only against grandiose goals. Paul called our attention to a "beautiful statement" by Freud (1912):

> I take this opportunity of defending myself against the mistaken charge of having denied the importance of innate (constitutional) factors because I have stressed that of infantile impressions. A charge such as this arises from the restricted nature of what men look for in the field of causation: in contrast to what ordinarily holds good in the real world, people prefer to be satisfied with a single causative factor. Psychoanalysis has talked a lot about the accidental factors in aetiology and little about the constitutional ones; but that is only because it was able to contribute something fresh to the former, while to begin with, it knew no more than was commonly

known about the latter. We refuse to posit any contrast in principle between the two sets of aetiological factors; on the contrary, we assume that the two sets regularly act jointly in bringing about the observed result.

[Endowment and Chance] determine a man's fate—rarely or never one of these powers alone. The amount of aetiological effectiveness to be attributed to each of them can be arrived at in every individual case separately. These cases may be arranged in a series according to the varying proportion in which the two factors are present, and this series will no doubt have its extreme cases. We shall estimate the share taken by constitution or experience differently in individual cases according to the stage reached by our knowledge; and we shall retain the right to modify our judgment along with changes in our understanding. Incidentaly, one might venture to regard constitution itself as a precipitate from the accidental effects produced on the endlessly long chain of our ancestors (p. 99, fn. 2).

On the other hand, he thought deeply ingrained tendencies and behavior patterns in the patient (whether genetically determined or not) are not likely to yield to therapeutic efforts. He cited the analogy of "unlearning" the multiplication table through conditioning or other therapeutic procedures. Similarly, a patient's firm belief of being unlovable is extremely difficult to change via psychotherapy and it probably cannot be done. A patient may improve, but *basic* change is unlikely.

Meehl was quite concerned about Eysenck's critique of therapeutic effectiveness. He feels that "Clever Hans" has never been adequately answered and this seems to bother Meehl quite a bit. He likes certain aspects of our proposed Design #1 and our Study of Experts as a way of testing the general modal effects of psychotherapy. He suggests a study in which one would treat the therapist pool as an MMPI item pool—pick good items and cross-validate.

Another way of doing this would be to test the effects of specific interventions on certain problems. Thus, experts might be chosen in terms of their expertise with a specific technique. The diagnostic issue is relevant here too. For example, some sub-samples of people respond very well to attention and "love." These are individuals who probably show placebo effects or who evince spontaneous remission. Other cases are probably more difficult to manage therapeutically and it is well to remember this distinction in planning an outcome study.

With further reference to Eysenck's criticisms, Paul thought a study could be conducted to investigate whether internal medicine "does any good." Obviously, such a study would be trivial because the evidence is clear and no demonstrations are called for. For many reasons the situation in psychotherapy is different and a study, along the lines indicated above, could prove very fruitful.

The "spontaneous remission argument" came in for some discussion.

Meehl agreed with Bergin that the tendency for patients to improve for unspecified reasons was a fact. Strupp's view was that patients suffering from *chronic* conditions (neuroses or character problems) basically remain unchanged without therapy. Partly we may be dealing with a semantic problem of what constitutes personality change. Certainly one observes that patients often seek help from a clinic when they are in an acute crisis and rapidly disappear from the clinic rosters when the crisis abates.

Any effort to study therapy with some homogenous patient groups is likely to result in greater precision. In this context Strupp floated an idea for a study with which he had recently become intrigued. This would involve a comparison of treatment approaches to anorexia nervosa. While this condition is relatively rare, he sees numerous advantages to using it in this kind of research: (1) the syndrome is relatively homogeneous so that diagnosis would not present a problem; (2) the syndrome is found predominantly in adolescent girls, thus providing considerable homogeneity in the patient population; (3) the condition has been treated both by dynamic techniques (Thomä 1961) and by operant methods (Bachrach et. al., 1965) and in principle lends itself to both approaches; (4) at least one important outcome criterion (weight gain) can be specified.

Paul agreed that the advantages were undeniable, but the proposal did not generate any visible enthusiasm in the group.

Clinical Process Studies. With respect to the problem of the therapist's personal impact versus the effectiveness of techniques, Paul said that he would "bet" on the former as a more important ingredient in therapy outcomes. A discussion followed about discrepant viewer reactions to films showing Ellis, Rogers, and others, at work. Paul stated that he felt "turned on" by Ellis and would find him quite congenial as a therapist, whereas other viewers had strong negative reactions. It seemed to Strupp that one might learn something from a study in which prospective patients (or others) would be exposed to films showing different therapists and therapeutic approaches; one could then attempt to study the viewer's personality characteristics, problems, and the like, as a function of his positive or negative reaction to the stimulus situation. His hunch was that one could tease out systematic factors among viewers which might be helpful in predicting their response to a given form of therapy and/or a given therapist.

Meehl evinced a good deal of interest in research designed to find out which of Freud's insights, as based on therapy material, can be shown to hold up in systematic research. He allowed that a good many people (including his colleague, MacCorquodale) feel it wasn't worth the trouble. Bergin shared that view.

Paul is also interested in studies of the clinical process in which psychoanalytic inference is studied, including the problem of inexact interpretations and their effects. He is very curious as to how we can test the empirical validity of the therapist's constructs as he develops them in the course of therapy.

As an example, he introduced the observation that whenever a male patient reports a dream dealing with fire (or a related topic), the rest of the hour is devoted to the topic of ambition and shame surrounding it. (Zero exceptions!) He thought it was worthwhile to study such clinical themes systematically as well as the therapist's mental processes in unscrambling them. All of this may have little utility as far as therapeutic operations are concerned, but Paul confessed to a "strong intellectual interest" in these matters, including the therapist's cognitive input (through his inferences and constructions on the basis of the clinical material emerging during the therapeutic hour.) In this connection, he considers psychoanalytic theory, despite its widespread unpopularity in certain quarters, as "by far the most exciting theory around."

Another example: It has been noted that a good (correct) interpretation in analytic therapy tends to induce laughter in the patient, often a very paradoxical response. Of course, one doesn't know whether this is causal, but it would be interesting to find out.

He noted that studies of verbal content too often assume that something important has to be made out of every 50 minutes of verbal material. He feels that this is an impossible task and forces the therapist and the researcher to construe what is impossible. He also feels that in terms of studying clinical training or developing good clinicians, it may be important to divest oneself of empirical data and focus on the clinical lore to the extent that it is required and defensible.

With further reference to therapy techniques, Paul raised a question about the utility of "theoretical translations" of the Dollard-Miller variety, and Strupp argued that they have done little to advance our knowledge. Meehl expressed the view that operant techniques flow directly from Skinner's theory, which cannot be said about the therapeutic techniques of most other theorists. We gathered that this recognition did not imply unconditional endorsement of operant techniques for all purposes.

On a related topic, Paul said: "Once the patient trusts you, you can be 'tough' in terms of 'cognitive corrections.' For example, you can then say to the patient: 'This is screwy thinking.' " He voiced skepticism concerning the value of "traditional" psychotherapy, yet for some people (probably very few) it is *the* method of choice. Of this he was convinced. He spoke favorably of the process of catharsis (which Strupp felt has generally been neglected since Breuer and Freud's early work) and viewed listening, even by untrained "therapists" as a very helpful thing. In a whimsical vein, he proposed a study in which housewives (à la Rioch) might be trained to function as therapists and that they be tutored in a completely "nutty" theory of therapy. He thought that their therapeutic effectiveness would be equally good. Paul believes that because of Freud we have downgraded cognitive (intellective) factors at the expense of emotional ones. With regard to task-setting in the treatment of phobias, we noted the importance of the patient's trying to overcome his phobia by actively opposing his avoidance tendencies, the approach stressed by Freud and since echoed by many others.

Methodology. A number of mini-discussions centered on problems of methodology. First, Paul tended to agree with the idea that we can mine the most gold from the laboratory rather than from the armchair, even though he is impressed by clinical analyses and "believes" in many clinical insights. He is also inclined to believe that large-scale multivariate studies don't answer practical questions of what to do with patients because results are weakened by the large number of interactions. As a result, we are unable to draw specific, strong conclusions. He suspects that the behavior change technology of the future will be based upon laboratory study instead of analyses of the clinical process. Personally, he does not consider himself temperamentally suited to this type of laboratory study or applications of laboratory work to the behavior change process. As already noted, he finds psychoanalytic theory and therapy more intellectually or cognitively exciting. In spite of inclinations to try to choose an optimal research strategy, we all felt that there may be some danger in trying to fix upon a single approach. Strupp pointed out in this context that it is probably unrealistic to expect that one can synthetically produce scientific or clinical illumination. Reference was made here by Meehl to work by philosophers of science such as Feyerabend and Polanyi. He also noted that certain approaches to single case studies have not seemed to fire anyone up very much and gave as an example Luborsky's (1953) article on P-technique.

Bergin cited the preference for clinical research expressed recently (and independently) by Lazarus and Luborsky, and referred to this personal predilection for bringing the basic science tradition to bear upon clinical work, as Lovaas had been doing. Paul stated that naturalistic studies of the therapeutic process have not exactly given us "blinding illuminations" (but perhaps laboratory studies have not done so either). Bergin felt it was important to go "where the powerful variables are," as examplified by Lovaas' work.

Paul cited Feyerabend to the effect that we should get in the habit of actively seeking revolutions in science instead of acquiescing in Kuhn's analysis to the effect that "normal science" proceeds until some difficulty with the prevailing paradigm is encountered. According to Polanyi, Einstein did not set out to disprove existing theories. He said: "I cooked up the relativity theory 'out of whole cloth.' "

Paul discussed a paper on which he was currently working which shows some of the problems involved in matching subjects in experimental or clinical research designs. He noted that this can be a special problem where a third variable is correlated with each of two additional variables of interest. For example, we may find that diagnosis and perceptual speed are both correlated with socio-economic status (SES). We may have, for example, a diagnosis yielding subsamples of manic-depressives and schizophrenics who are differentiable on SES. At the same time some criterion performance measure which we may have on these subjects is also correlated with SES. The following problems may be involved in attempts to match groups on SES:

1. If we match groups on SES, each subject involved is atypical of his own group. For example, manic-depressives tend not to be low in SES and schizophrenics tend not to be high; but if we attempt to match the groups we have to find manic-depressives who are lower and schizophrenics who are higher. Therefore, if we match, we have a strange group of schizophrenics and a strange group of manic-depressives which makes our results not very generalizable. In fact, we must assume that we are somewhat uncertain just what these groups are. The problem is similar to the situation in which one would try to "correct a positive Wasserman for ownership of a Cadillac."

2. Matching thus implies that we are systematically unmatching for some unknown fourth or fifth variable which accounts for the strangeness of these groups when we attempt to match.

3. Another consequence of matching can be causal ambiguity. If it is possible that SES creates diagnostic differences and at the same time diagnostic differences create differences in SES, then we have a circular causality. This means that analysis of variance or partial correlation is irrelevant because both assume one direction of causality. If we match on SES, we overcorrect and if we match on diagnosis we undercorrect for this problem. Yee and Gage's (1968) article on crossover correlational techniques is relevent here.

4. If we match, we may also eliminate the chance of finding something we were not looking for. One remedy may be simply not to match at all and do analysis of co-variance. This answers problems 1 and 2 but not problem 3. Many of our problems are caused by the fact that we have taken over models from the agricultural case, that is, statistical models.

5. Reference was made to an article on causality by Simon and Rescher (1966) and to work by Wilford Dixon of UCLA on a mathematical model for single case studies.

Another important methodological note concerned the general desensitization effect of psychotherapy. This suggestion was based on the interpretations of the type made by Shoben (1949) in his *Psychological Bulletin* article. Meehl feels that this principle of desensitization occurring in many contexts as a result of a positive human relationship is a general principle which must be attended to in any methodological formulations for psychotherapy research or spontaneous personality change.

Theory. We spent some time discussing the relevance of theory and problems surrounding the dimensionalizing of human phenomena in a systematic way. The goal here is to develop appropriate methods for defining and measuring relevant dimensions. This of course will be a prerequisite for a multidimensional therapy in which specific methods are applied to specific problems. We discussed Bergin's theory to some extent that human personality functions in terms of systems much as our bodies function in terms of semi-independent biological systems. Meehl suggested a behavioral genetics dimension, a learning dimension, and a cognitive dimension. We reformulated this somewhat and included an emotional-motivational system as well. We discussed the possibility that people may be deficient in one system and not another, but that other individuals may be deficient in several or all systems. Paul pointed out that in the realm of cognitive functions a person may have a defect typically labeled as "ego weakness." This may involve a poor set of self-corrective cognitive habits, and the therapy of choice may require teaching him cognitive skills with regard to interpersonal relations. He also noted that people with a problem of this type could have "cognitive slippage" due to a chemical imbalance. Some patients may need compensatory training and possible drug treatment to make up for these deficiencies, whereas others may need very different treatment.

The Mental Health Problem. Meehl believes that individual psychotherapy may not be very relevant to the mental health problem since perhaps only 10% of the pathological conditions can be helped by this method. This situation is a real public health issue. He lamented the fact that psychiatric training programs typically turn out practitioners in the traditional mode who don't know how to do anything but psychoanalysis. They charge $30 an hour and treat only a tiny group of people. They don't know anything about task-setting, rational therapy, behavior modification, and the like. (This is an overstatement in my opinion—H.H.S.) In this context Tuma mentioned that people are not properly selected to be therapists in the first place.

Meehl felt that in a way we were asking him to play God. He felt our review was comprehensive and insightful, and that the kinds of questions and conclusions we had advanced were very similar to what we would eventually conclude and propose. In a sense, we were asking him questions we could not answer and he felt rather certain that he could not answer them either.

Comments by Strupp. Obviously it is difficult to summarize a discussion that ranged as far and wide as this one; however, it may be useful to record a few personal impressions.

Contrary to Paul's earlier view that he had nothing of great value to add to our survey, I felt the visit was exceedingly stimulating, largely because of Paul's breadth and depth of knowledge, his originality, and his willingness to consider seriously divergent theoretical views.

Since Paul is basically not a psychotherapy researcher, he approached problems in this domain from a broader perspective, and it is of course this broader perspective that we had in mind when we scheduled our meeting with him. Furthermore, he is less committed to a particular theoretical viewpoint than most people, and is able to understand and critically assess a number of them. For example, he is intellectually and personally interested in psychoanalytic theory and therapy,[10] and at the same time appropriately critical of some of its aspects. While being convinced of the importance of genetic factors, he can see virtues in learning approaches to psychotherapy.

As a corollary of the preceding point, he is less preoccupied with the problem of therapeutic effectiveness as the sole criterion for research in this area. That is, he is quite willing to entertain research ideas which may illuminate a scientific rather than a technological problem. I found this both refreshing and congenial.

I was impressed with his stress on the usefulness of demonstrating that psychotherapy "works," in the sense of refuting Eysenck's position through a careful design in which patients are carefully chosen and assigned to highly competent therapists. On a "gut level" he is convinced that this kind of study will yield positive results. Personally I share this view. Parenthetically it may be worth recording the truism that we all tend to believe what we want to believe and our personal experience with a given form of therapy undoubtedly is a strong determinant of such beliefs. In Meehl's view (and mine), analytic therapy has something valuable to offer because the experience was valuable to him personally; others oppose it because of their own respective experience.

The emphasis on genetic factors and the corresponding limitations of psychotherapy impressed me as highly important. The lesson, as I see it, is that we must work in the direction of setting realistic goals with each patient. Meehl agreed with the analogy that in education, too, we don't aspire to put a student with an I.Q. of 95 through graduate school, nor do we reject formal education because it can't be done.

Finally, I was impressed by the importance he placed on meticulous psychological assessment of prospective patients and the stress upon the therapist's competence. This is of course part of our own emphasis on achieving

10. Commenting on this passage of the interview report, Paul noted: "You willing to help me counter-act the 'Meehl stereotype'? If so, insert here that 'Meehl has a couch in his office, prefers couch cases, but regrets that it is not the treatment of choice for most patients and problems.' "

greater specificity with respect to patient, therapist, and technique variables. Keeping this in mind, it seems to me that we have to look very carefully at the existing literature; contrary to prevailing practice, the findings often cannot be generalized and must remain restricted to the setting in which they were obtained. At this stage, few broad generalizations seem justified.

Comments by A. Hussain Tuma. I enjoyed reading your excellent summary of our discussions with Paul Meehl and have really very little to add to it. The main points which impressed me greatly and which I thought were most relevant to your expectations at this juncture were his clear emphasis on the provision for adequate clinical diagnosis and careful description and use of experienced and competent therapists and on the identification of specific, realistic and measurable goals of treatment. He, too, seemed to put his bets on "therapeutic personality" as a fundamental instrument of change. However, I think that Betz & Whitehorn's A and B dichotomy, though useful in focusing attention on an important research issue, i.e., therapist personality, is not as good a device as the general impression that it seems to have made on the field.

Another part of Paul's discussion which, to me, has the greatest relevance to future outcome research is the relative weight Paul assigns to the role of genetic determinants of psychopathological behavior. It is in the light of this consideration that such aspects of a study as selection of patient samples, choice of comparison groups, target goals, etc., become so clearly crucial. More concretely, I would avoid the choice of a psychotic population such as process schizophrenics for a study, except perhaps as a comparison group.

Finally, I must admit that I am not as motivated as Paul seemed to be regarding the importance of generally demonstrating that psychotherapy at large "works" for purposes of refuting such positions as that of Eysenck's. For me the burning issues relate to the discovery of the specific conditions and factors that account for behavior change or its resistance to change. Answering Eysenck's challenge should remain if at all only a possible side issue, not an important goal.

References

Bachrach, A. J., Erwin, W. J., & Mohr, J. P. 1965. The control of eating behavior in an anorexic by operant conditioning techniques. In L. P. Ullmann & L. Krasner, eds., *Case studies in behavior modification.* New York: Holt, Rinehart & Winston, pp. 153–63.

Freud, S. 1912. The dynamics of transference. In vol. 12 of *The standard edition of the complete psychological works of Sigmund Freud.* London: Hogarth Press.

Luborsky, L. 1953. Intraindividual repetitive measurements (P technique) in understanding psychotherapeutic change. In O. H. Mowrer, ed., *Psychotherapy: Theory and research.* New York: Ronald Press.

Shoben, E. J., Jr. 1949. Psychotherapy as a problem in learning theory. *Psychological Bulletin* 46: 366–92.

Simon, H. A., & Rescher, N. 1966. Cause and counterfactual. *Philosophy of Science* 33: 323–40.

Thomä, H. 1961. *Anorexia nervosa.* Stuttgart, Germany: Huber • Klett.

Whitehorn, J. C., & Betz, B. J. 1954. A study of psychotherapeutic relationships between physicians and schizophrenic patients. *American Journal of Psychiatry* 111: 321–31.

Yee, A. H., & Gage, N. L. 1968. Techniques for estimating the source and direction of causal influence in panel data. *Psychological Bulletin* 70: 115–26.

WORKING PAPER BY STRUPP

November 18, 1968

1. We must make a distinction between the search for more effective techniques and the function of research. With respect to the former, research cannot be relied upon to make a significant contribution—this must come from clinicians; with respect to the latter, research can serve to *confirm* therapeutic claims and clarify various relationships between variables.

2. As far as comparative studies are concerned, we must not forget our own assertion that there are no homogeneous techniques, and we cannot hope to make them so. This means that in any comparative study, there can only be a relative emphasis on certain techniques. While I vacillate, I wonder how much such studies have to teach us.

3. It may well be that large coordinated or collaborative studies are not worth the effort and not likely to yield clear-cut results. This may be true despite our own assertions in the survey paper. Maybe creative research cannot be "prescribed."

4. There still may be considerable merit in studies in which single variables are manipulated even though this is done in an analogue situation. Clearer results are to be expected from such studies although their relevance to therapy may be in question.

5. We never change single symptoms nor do we influence one specifiable aspect of the patient. We are always dealing with a total experience. I doubt that we can ever specify, except in very crude form, what makes a given dyad "click." The problem lies in the complexity of human beings which is perennially underestimated in the various therapy theories. The reductive process followed by any therapist (who has anything resembling a consistent

viewpoint) has merit in a limited way. Yet I am convinced that given interpretations (for example) cannot be credited with curative power. It is interpretations *and a lot of other things in the relationship* that make the difference. In analysis, I believe that becoming a child in relation to the therapist (in a circumscribed way) and becoming re-educated emotionally makes a big difference. In other forms of therapy a similar paradigm may be applicable.

6. I am becoming more convinced of the great hiatus between theories and practice. It follows that it is vastly more important to study what the therapist *does* than *what he says he does* in therapy.

7. Making explicit the *belief systems*[11] by which the patient operates (Ellis' emphasis here is close to analytic theorizing) seems of the utmost importance. This process has to proceed very slowly and emerge from the patient's verbalizations.

8. One of the crucial questions to be answered, it seems to me, is whether psychotherapy of any kind produces changes over and beyond what Frank has called "the non-specific effects." This would have great implications for nonprofessional helpers, as one important example. It should be possible to design a study in which the therapist offers only understanding, respect, nonjudgmental listening, that is, a form of love, which would be compared with other forms in which, additionally, *technical* interventions of some kind are provided. Are there differences? What kinds? With what kinds of patients? (I believe it is impossible to provide only technical interventions without a "relationship.")

9. I like the idea (see Bergin's discussion with Schmidt and Strong) of finding out what techniques work with what patients and then working backwards to see what patient variables were responsible. A new diagnostic system might result. I am sure this could be done in a gross way, and clinicians already implicitly apply various criteria to their selection of patients; however, once such broad selections are made, I am convinced that there is a subtle and complex interaction of factors in patient and therapist which determines success (or failure). This interaction may be highly idiosyncratic to the dyad and not replicable or generalizable. In short, there could be many combinations that work (or don't work).

10. I am ambivalent about Meehl's proposal to answer Eysenck's criticisms by a well designed study. This may be good for some people's morale, and if the methodology were refined we might thus demonstrate that a good

11. This has cognitive as well as emotional implications. For example, if the patient considers himself basically an unlovable (or hostile) person, he will cognitively as well as emotionally react to others as if they were the same. He will also unwittingly stimulate hostility and rejection from others.

study can yield good results and muddy methodology leads to useless ones. On the other hand, is the investment of time, money, and manpower worth it? Critics like Eysenck are not going to be convinced anyway, and the clinicians will say that the obvious has been proven.

11. Allen's comment on Meehl, to the effect that some people respond well to "attention" and "love," thus representing probably the "placebo effect" or "spontaneous remission," coincides with my point 8 above. Consequently it *must* be important! Research along these lines also relates to the comment attributed to Meehl that the personal impact of the therapist is more important than his technique. I think this whole area is tremendously important.

12. The problem of how different therapists construe a patient's problem, after they have listened to him for a while, how they conceptualize his difficulties and what steps (however vague) they propose to overcome them also seems worth studying.

Response by Bergin

Reactions to your current thoughts of November 18:

1. I'm not sure that this is a correct analysis. It has been true in the past, but is less so now (e.g., Lovaas, Goldstein, etc.). Perhaps advances of the future will come from experimental therapy in which some virtues of practice and research coalesce.

2. Agreed; though I still believe experimental studies can tease out relatively unique variables which may be homogeneous. Of course, when applied in isolated or "teased-out" form, they may be less potent than when used in a complex context.

3. Yes.

4. Yes.

5. I think this is only true of *some* people and *some* symptoms.

6. Broad-gauged theories tend to obscure and to create narrowness in this field because the data-base is not matured. Data-bound mini-theories are OK.

7. Yes, *very* true. Cognitive variables are very powerful, and so far barely touched re: psychotherapy. Ellis has the right idea, but has never made anything systematic or defensible or substantive out of it.

8. I give this less priority than finding out which is more important for which patients. For a small subsample, nonspecific effects suffice.

9. P-T combinations could be diagnostically evaluated the same way as P characteristics. Why not?

10. As I said in Minneapolis, I don't think it's needed. We are beyond that now. Way beyond it.

11. Yes.

12. I don't know about this.

WORKING PAPER BY STRUPP

November 20, 1968

I am impressed with the variety of technical procedures used in psychoanalysis and the different kinds of learning that are mediated thereby; furthermore, the theoretical assumptions of psychoanalysis, particularly with regard to Freud's notions regarding instincts seem largely superfluous. As far as I can see, there is only a loose articulation of techniques to the theory. I shall attempt to list some different kinds of techniques:

1. What appears to be unique to psychoanalysis (in relation to other approaches) is the emphasis on primitive (infantile) fantasies which the therapist makes explicit (interprets) to the patient, but only when the patient is receptive, that is, when his emotions are mobilized, when he is aroused, desperate, and dependent on the therapist in the here-and-now. Examples: The patient believes that his anger can destroy others, as when he approaches a woman sexually or when he asserts himself. The patient believes that when he subordinates himself to male authority, he will be destroyed (homosexually assaulted). The patient may anticipate violent retaliation from a powerful male if he expresses anger, hostility.

2. A fairly simple kind of learning is mediated when the therapist does not scold, punish or reprimand the patient (as probably the parents have done, and as he does himself) when the patient "owns" feelings about which he experiences shame, guilt, and the like. The patient thus tests reality and gets relief. I don't think this kind of therapeutic learning goes very deep although in some cases the relief may be spectacular.

3. The patient sees that the therapist is not afraid of the things the patient dreads. Examples: He can talk about things the patient avoids and he can do so calmly. The therapist seems to be able to cope with situations that are anxiety-provoking to the patient, say, dealing with powerful (or seemingly powerful) women. In line with (1), the patient overestimates the size and power of other people as well as the consequences of their not loving him (seen as fatal). All of these things are "unrealistic."

4. The therapist forces the patient (through the submission of free-association) to trust him and the situation—this step is often a tough struggle against the patient's narcissism. He has to recognize the greater expertise and superiority of another and subordinate himself, which is often seen as a threat to his integrity (as he views it). One may speculate—here is an example of "bonus" reconstruction—that the patient needs to be omnipotent because as a child he found he couldn't trust important people and had to be independent and self-sufficient. This kind of extrapolation makes sense but

is totally unverifiable; this feeling of omnipotence may also be gratifying to the patient's intellect but this is not what produces the change or the pleasure or the gain.

5. The patient trusts the therapist sufficiently after a time so that he accepts unpleasant truths about himself, such as, greed, hostility, selfishness, ambition. The therapist does not retaliate but points these things out. It is done in a matter-of-fact way (one hopes) and while the patient suffers, he learns about his stimulus value, what he does to others (which he can recognize when he does it to the therapist), say, negativism, provocation. (Here seems to be an analogy to T or encounter groups which do the same thing but probably more crudely.) Implicit here is that all of us do things and operate on assumptions which we don't recognize (because they are too painful) or rationalize or reject (deny). Yet other people recognize them in us and react to them.

6. The therapist disregards feelings that are not in focus and concentrates on the patient's *here-and-now* experience, in relation to the therapist. This is regularly overlooked by critics of psychoanalysis. What goes on between the therapist and the patient *NOW* is what really matters. Thus, the interpersonal relation between therapist and patient is studied, explored, particularly the patient's unwitting (unconscious?) behavior. Repression may be a useful concept in the sense that implicit fantasies, strategies, and the like emerge only after a long time, and there seems to be a correlation between growing trust and more direct communication.

7. The patient often expresses his strivings and strategies symbolically. Here the therapist's familiarity with common primitive fantasies (for example, sado-masochistic ones) becomes crucial. This is an area that nonanalytic therapists simply don't appreciate. They take symptoms at face value and the patient's account as he verbalizes it becomes gospel truth. Psychoanalysis operates on the assumption that unless things are indeed different from the way the patient conceptualizes them (feelings about self and others, what they do to him, reality), therapy is not worthwhile. The therapist says in effect: There are other ways of looking at the world, but you can only learn them as you experience "the error of your ways." Here's where Ellis errs because he barges in and bombards the patient with some admittedly basic truths, but I don't see how they can make much sense unless the patient can relate them to something specific in his life.

8. The therapist capitalizes on the fact that the patient becomes dependent on him (and the excessive tendency of neurotics to do so is of course a large part of the problem).

A research problem here: Study the tendency of different *S*s to become dependent in a free-association situation or in a contrived situation over time and study other aspects of such *S*s. What kind of people are they? Types?

At the same time there is the paradox that while the patient seeks to become dependent, he also fights (denies) it. He may have fantasies of "castration" or fear infantile dependency because of what parents have done to him. The therapist encourages and teaches the patient to be comfortably dependent but he also extinguishes dependency by not giving the patient advice or guidance. Now, what is extremely clever in psychoanalysis (and one of Freud's great contributions) is the manner in which the dependency tendency (a part of transference) is used as a vehicle for mediating the other kinds of learning I have alluded to.

The question here arises: Does psychoanalytic therapy need to take as long as it does? Is it necessary to let fantasies and strategies emerge slowly? Can the process be hastened in ways other than interpreting the patient's "resistance," his avoidance maneuvers? Furthermore: If this is done, does it interfere with the patient's autonomy in the long run; does therapy become "suggestion"? A lot of this, it seems to me, is taken on faith, and has not been studied systematically. It is also hellishly difficult to do so.

The reason psychoanalytic therapy works so well is that the therapist remains shadowy and tries to stay out of the patient's maneuvers; he largely observes although willy-nilly he also participates. But, by being in the background, he highlights the patient's own contribution. Thus the therapeutic situation becomes a laboratory situation (approximately) in which the therapist observes what the patient does to him, about him, what he wants the therapist to do, how he wants the therapist to react, often in completely contradictory ways. For example, the patient may want to be independent and rejects anyone's advice and at the same time crave it. Much of this is a great deal more subtle than is recognized by nonanalytic therapists.

Personally, I think all of this can go far beyond what Frank has called the "nonspecific" (placebo) effects of all forms of therapy, and one should be able to show that, at least with certain patients, the kinds of changes achieved by this indirect procedure are far greater than if one merely exuded unconditional positive regard, reflected feelings, or desensitized the patient to a few specific situations. This should be demonstrable by a research project, but it hasn't been done. It is possible, of course, that I'm wrong, and warmth may enable some patients to make the kinds of "corrections" I have mentioned by themselves. But I doubt it. People don't seem to be that astute. We see here also that the patient learns by himself but the therapist helps him very considerably. In a sense it is teaching and learning, but it is these things in a very special sense. We have to assume here that the patient has certain "programs" (hypotheses, working assumptions) which have never been examined but which are unrealistic, cock-eyed, screwy, self-defeating, maladaptive. There may be various ways in which these programs can be changed. It may be possible, for example, to desensitize anxiety responses, but psychoanalytic therapy attempts to *demonstrate* to the patient what the programs are in a controlled laboratory situation (therapy) on the assumption that once he knows about them he can change them, if he wants to. (This is another way of saying that his discrimination is sharpened, his ego control is enhanced, he gains greater freedom over his impulses, id is replaced by ego.) Here lies a radical difference between psychoanalysis and other forms of therapy: In psychoanalysis the patient learns (within distinct limits) "what makes him tick" which in turn is supposed to help him change if he so desires, but some of the change really occurs simultaneously with the "insight"; in other forms of therapy, he is simply changed, or his response repertoire is changed. Actually, perhaps, psychoanalysis does both.

9. Throughout therapy the therapist provides a reasonable sample of a *good human relationship,* which the patient can learn to use as a model. The patient learns to cooperate, not to reject when he is not rejected, not to provoke when he is not provoked, abandon possessiveness, dominance, and exploitation. This interactive learning is probably limited because the patient-therapist relationship does not and cannot encompass all significant phases of human relationships; thus it may be a somewhat pale replica. The patient learns through interaction with the therapist but also through modeling after the therapist (who becomes a loved "object" and an "ideal").

Response by Bergin

Reactions to your thoughts on psychoanalytic techniques:

You are obviously comfortably at home in the world of technique and inference described therein. My respect and positive feelings toward you, thus, make it difficult to be critical or skeptical.

I can only say that this line of thought and method are a long way from where I live. It is probably true, as you suggest, that some of these methods have therapeutic value for some problems or cases; but I tend to think that where this is so, the methods are better developed within other approaches.

When the analysis is completed which you began in these pages, I think you will have isolated some relevant techniques which are no longer recognizable as being unique to the psychoanalytical tradition.

WORKING PAPER BY BERGIN

Further Vexations of the Spirit

The following is a mixture of ideas growing out of a meeting with Hans Strupp in Nashville on October 16th and meetings with Lazarus, Luborsky, Meehl, and others since then. This is a somewhat tortured attempt to come to a few very tentative and tender private conclusions. I give them no more weight than that of tentative intuitions as to where we have been, where we are, and where we may be going. The motivation for doing this is mostly personal. I like to formulate conclusions so that I have something explicit to work with, even though the ultimate conclusions may be quite different from the initial ones.

1. First of all, I can see that there are a number of possible projects which make very good sense, and I have the distinct feeling that while all of these projects may be of equal value scientifically, there are going to be distinct temperamental differences in the inclinations of different researchers to pursue these projects. This is probably no revelation to anybody else; but to me it is striking how enormously determining personal style is of the research topics, programs, and strategies selected. This personal, human aspect of the scientific enterprise is very vividly brought out by visiting different people in rapid succession. This is one of the important dimensions of the human factor Joe Matarazzo emphasized so strongly in our early meetings. This leads me to conclude that no matter how persuasive our evidence or how "right" our proposals for research strategy may be, if there are not a complementary set of personal motivations in researchers, our proposals will be pretty much useless. At least they will be relegated to the realm of stimuli for people's thinking rather than realistic maps for future research.

2. The second conclusion that I have come to pertains to design, and I believe it is one fully shared by Hans. This is that no one, including ourselves, is currently enthusiastic about an enormous, multivariate, comparative, collaborative research design. It seems to me we have come to a real crossroads on this one and that we have decided against it. Why is this so? One reason was given succinctly by Paul Meehl who pointed out that multivariate designs always yield weak statistical results; because there are so many variables operating that no one of them ordinarily can be shown to have a predominant effect. The importance of this point rests on the assumption that the psychotherapy research of the future should have a direct effect on the nature of practice. As Meehl points out, this is unlikely to happen unless the research strategy permits and even heightens the possibility of observing prominent consequences of specific interventions. Another reason for avoiding designs of this type is the overwhelming conceptual and technical problems involved in establishing appropriate measurements and controls. This field simply contains too much error in its measuring techniques; therefore, as the number of variables and measures thereof increase, the amount of error residual in the complex statistical calculations required becomes unsuitably large. As for controls, we are still at the stage where we do not know enough about the processes of change to institute adequate controls in the complex, total psychotherapy interaction. We can control more successfully under restricted conditions where we are attempting to study

certain specific effects of given interventions. As I stated before, this conclusion as well as the others, is tentative and subject to change; but at the moment all of the facts and my personal intuitive responses seem to support them.

3. The Bugaboo of Complexity. Each time we begin to discuss the possibility of increasing the precision of therapy research studies and, consequently, the precision of our specifications for which intervention creates which changes in which patients, we seem to get hung up on the dilemma created by the simplifications that are necessary in order to increase precision. The dilemma is that in order to treat complex problems effectively we seem to have to simplify in order to gain precision and power in our techniques; but when we simplify we seem not to do justice to the complexity of the phenomena in question.

We seem to vacillate around this dilemma a great deal and therefore find it very difficult to come up with an optimal research strategy. At this point, I think it is very important for us not to get hung-up on the complexity issue. It is an obstacle to progress. The best contributions have come from people who isolated dimensions, people such as Wolpe, Bandura, Rogers, Truax, Lovaas. While Freud called our attention dramatically to the whole schema of human experience, the fact that he did not isolate and dimensionalize may very well account for the weakness of the therapeutic methods which derive from his approach. As Hans mentioned in Nashville, it seems that all past major theorists have ignored complexity to some extent, and in doing this they may have increased the efficiency of their psychotherapeutic operations. Another illustration comes to mind from the field of intelligence testing. The IQ test is still one of psychology's proudest achievements, and it is an example of isolating dimensions which prove to be relevant to complex behavior.

One reason people seem to be so troubled by this dilemma is that they frequently seem to assume that changes in one dimension of a human being must produce changes in other dimensions, that is, that change takes place on a broad front and cannot be narrowed either in terms of the character of the interventions or in terms of the kinds of change looked for. I have come to the conclusion that this attitude may be very wrong. I have begun to view human psychology in terms of systems analogous to the biological systems in the human body. While it is true that our nervous system, circulatory system, endocrine system are interdependent, they also function somewhat independently. With regard to pathology, it is quite possible to exert certain controls on the remaining systems of the body while one operates on the nervous system. On the other hand, there are types of pathology which are of a multisystemic nature. For example, an automobile accident may cause damage to a number of systems simultaneously; but even in these cases where treatment proceeds on a broad front, usually rather specific interventions are applied to each system or subsystem.

When applying this concept to human psychology, we are essentially talking about dimensionalizing human personality, which is something that numerous people have been concerned with for decades; but I have the feeling that our experience in psychotherapy and psychotherapy research suggests the importance of moving more vigorously in this direction. Each time we talk about specifying relevant interventions for specific problems, we imply a conceptual systematizing of human psychology which has never been made explicit.

I have seen some of the old notions about various systems in the human psyche revived in recent years, and I have done this myself in one paper. I have the feeling that there are only a few broad systems in human functioning even though they may be broken down into more precise subsystems just as our biological systems are. I have the feeling that a good deal of thought and work need to be put into formulating a conceptualization along these lines; because I think an orienting theory which is closely tied to the data we have up to this point, if it is a really fertile theory, could help us become much more productive in this area. I tend to conceptualize the human psyche in terms of the following systems: a conditioned response or habit system, an emotion-motivation system, a cognition-values-self regulation system, and a performance-achievement system. Although this is a bit woolly, it helps me make a good deal of sense out of patients whom I see and it makes it easier for me to apply a number of different techniques to different problems in the same patient or to different patients. For example, some behavioral techniques are relevant to the habit system, traditional therapies are relevant to the emotion-motivation system, many techniques are relevant to the cognition-values system although none are really well-developed in relation to it (Ellis tries to do this), and possibly the vocational-educational psychologists have a leg up on the performance-achievement system. In any event, it seems to me that conceptualizations along this line must be developed as we attempt to increase specificity and enhance therapeutic potency.

4. The preceding ideas provide an important element in a rationale, which I find myself building, toward what I consider to be an optimal research strategy in this field at this time in its history. There are several additional elements which contribute to this growing conviction, they are:

a. The samples that we commonly use and the sampling statistics which we usually apply to them frequently seem to obscure realities rather than highlight them. I recently consulted with Rosedith Sitgreaves, a member of our psychology faculty, and currently secretary of the American Statistical Association. In reviewing the data which Sol Garfield and I had collected in our therapy project, she suggested that the statistics I had planned to apply would tend to obscure important processes. I had been planning to use typical correlations, means, standard deviations, t tests; but she dissuaded me from this by asserting that a series of individual curves might be highly appropriate, that small subsamples of homogeneous therapists and patients might be looked at descriptively in terms of which therapists seemed to be influencing which patients and in which way, that I might look at the differing kinds of change that seemed to be going on in different individual cases.

b. The contribution of behavioral methods, though these methods have their limitations, may well have been that they isolated phenomena, that they required therapists and theorists to put on blinders and thus to isolate out of the complexity of therapy one or two potent dimensions.

c. Now seems to be the time to dimensionalize and isolate, to find out what the building blocks are and how they operate, to determine what is potent and what is not, and then to put together these building blocks into systems of change which match the systems of human psychology and which match the complexity of a suffering person.

d. Systematically isolating single variables and manipulating "hell" out of them is, however, not enough. We must also examine the question of "pay-off" and thus justify our investment. This implies that variables isolated either from laboratory work or from careful manipulations of quasi-therapy interviews must then be experimented with clinically on live cases.

e. It is traditional in psychotherapy to apply our methods like buckshot and then we attribute change to whichever shot fits our predilections. This is equivalent to superstition.

f. The more involved I get the more convinced I become that the interview is out as a method of change.

g. I have also come to the conclusion that the day of the clinician's predominance in the development of new techniques is over. The new techniques are going to be more effective and they will not come from naturalistically studying on-going everyday practice.

h. The natural study of therapy in its complexity leaves a scientifically minded person with a real sense of being overwhelmed by the hundreds of variables over which he has no control. To conceptualize any kind of causality from such observations seems well nigh impossible. This does not, however, demean the contributions of people such as Carl Rogers who have indeed extracted important dimensions out of this natural process. My feeling at the moment though is that the traditional therapy processes have been pretty well milked dry.

i. I believe that characteristics of the patient are vital influencers of the course and kind of change which occurs; but I also think that usual methods of diagnosis or catergorizing or typing people are not adequate to the problem we have. I like the idea of experimenting with people and then classifying them in terms of how they respond to interventions rather than classifying them in any other way. I understand that this procedure is commonly used in drug research.

What all of this is leading up to for me is a kind of optimal strategy for teasing out the potent dimensions of change or change agents and then manipulating them with single cases. My idea is essentially to combine the virtues of carefully controlled work whether it occurs in the laboratory or in the experimental interview with the virtues of observing the effects of techniques with live cases. There are some illustrations of this already extant; although the paradigm which I have in mind is not adequately illustrated by them. They include work such as that by Lovaas in which he takes the dimensions isolated from the Skinnerian research laboratory and extrapolates them to the clinical situation by devising techniques based on them which he feels are relevant to a specific kind of pathology. He then employs a kind of repeated case design in which these interventions are applied to individuals one case at a time. However, the repeated case nature of the design permits observation of individual differences and also modifications of the technique itself as one proceeds to experiment with it across individuals. Another illustration might be Truax's study in which he experimentally manipulated congruence, empathy, and warmth in an interview. He was able to demonstrate direct consequences of these manipulations in the verbal behavior of the patient. Subsequently, attempts were made to either select therapists high in these qualities or to train individuals to become high in them before applying their technique to patients. Further illustrations include the work of Blocher, Strong and Schmidt who are developing experiments in therapist influence based on the communication and persuasion literature, and the suggestions of Goldstein, Heller, and Sechrest regarding potent dimensions of change.

Generally, I think that the important contribution is the isolation of dimensions that have power whether they come from the Skinnerian laboratory or from client centered therapy. The real key to success may be in taking the dimensions that are thus isolated and manipulating them in truly clinical trials. These applications to complex clinical cases may result in several different, but useful consequences. (*a*) It may be discovered that some modification of the particular change-inducing technique is required to make it effective with the particular case involved, or *type* of case involved. (*b*) It may be discovered that in addition to the technique employed, one or more additional techniques are required to effect change in the given problem or person. This is the building block notion, which assumes that it will be necessary in certain kinds of cases to gradually, by experimentation, build together the isolated elements of change into a complex process which to a reasonable degree matches the kind of pathology in the client. (*c*) It may be found that the particular technique is highly useful with a particular type of very specific problem. (*d*) It may be found that the application of several specific techniques in series rather than in a complex, simultaneous broad front approach will be more effective. (*e*) Certain questions may arise as a result of the experimental-clinical application or trial which will send us back to the laboratory or to the analogue study for refinements and then new applications to clinical cases. (*f*) We may find, if we persist, that there are certain people or certain kinds of problems which people have that we simply can't do much with, and we may learn to accept such limitations realistically by making it much clearer what we can do and what we can't

It seems to me that an approach like this permits a reasonable bridge to be built between laboratory and analogue studies and clinical practice. This approach could be, then, a way of effectively meeting the challenge by clinicians to make our research relevant to practice. The attractive thing about it to me is that the process can be a two-way one in which laboratory and clinic continuously influence each other in a mutual feed-back circuit.

Another methodology relevant to this paradigm is that of programming the therapist. That is, it may be possible to effectively experiment with patients by building a design into the naturalistic situation. The therapist who is so programmed may not necessarily be role-playing but he will be *systematic* in doing given things under specific conditions.

Another aspect of methodology relevant to this schema is the possibility of doing a multidimensional assessment or diagnosis in parallel with the organization of a multidimensional change methodology. Once the dimensions or processes of patient pathology are isolated which we wish to change or experiment with, then we may organize a multifactorial analogue study centered around this kind of patient and the dimensions of pathology and of change which we have theorized to be relevant. Then instead of a unidimensional analogue study, we mount a rather complicated analogue using a variety of interacting dimensions. Again, this cannot be too large or it suffers from the problem of weak results to which Meehl alluded so adeptly.

In thinking how a research program of the type described above might be approached by collaborative or coordinated efforts, I encounter a number of real difficulties. For the moment, let me set aside the problems and possibilities in that area and move on to a more likely possibility. This is the idea of organizing a psychotherapy research center which has many of the characteristics of the kind of research and development center which we find in some other fields, such as the recent ones organized for the purpose of educational research. A five story building for an R and D center is now in the advanced planning stages at Teachers College. It is one of a few in the country being funded by the Office of Education. Its purpose will be to focus entirely on research in learning and other processes relevant to education. Experimental classrooms are being constructed so that experiments with a variety of instructional methodologies can be conducted. Techniques are to be refined and evaluated and then tested on live classroom situations. Once a methodology is thus developed the center will have facilities for demonstration and dissemination of information to the educational profession in order to see that every opportunity is provided for full application of new discoveries to everyday practice. My thought in relation to psychotherapy is that we need a clinical sciences program or department coordinated with a clinical center of some kind. The clinical sciences faculty would be bridge-building types who would be devoted, as Goldstein et al. are, to either extracting relevant concepts and methodologies from the general psychology of change or developing such strategies themselves from relevant analogue or applied laboratory work. In addition there would be individuals who would creatively apply these methods to clinical practice, such as Lovaas does, and there may be still others who like to do both. In any event the coordinated program of research would probably most effectively be done in one large center which provides adequately for each of the necessary phases of research and technique development.

The next steps will, of course, include refining and testing ideas like the foregoing against the precise nature of what we know to date and also the nature of specific clinical cases to which this kind of strategy might be applied. In addition, much attention must be paid to the exact way in which the clinical trials will be objectified or quantified so that we know when we have tested the effects of an experimental technique and what consequences it has had. I suppose there is a certain prematurity about moving so far in one direction toward a research strategy so soon, and there may also be a certain narrowness involved in even believing there can be such a thing as an optimal strategy; but the fact is that this is where my thinking is at the moment and I find it helpful to make it explicit. In the long run, wherever my thinking may be led by continuing interactions with my creative collaborator and our brilliant consultants, I think this process will be productive.

While my predilections do not lean in the direction of studying therapy as it exists, I do find the study of experts design somewhat tantalizing, mainly because I really would like to see at least one major demonstration that experts really have a unique effect. I happen to believe that they do; although I think their effect may be largely due to personal impact rather than technique. If such a study were done, I would prefer to see experts of all types mixed into the design instead of trying to homogenize one or more groups and study their effects separately. With that parting shot, I await divinations from many directions.

WORKING PAPER BY STRUPP

November 25, 1968

1. We seem to become increasingly impressed with the importance of designing research that is *clinically meaningful,* that is, investigations which contain significant lessons to the practitioner and which have a reasonable chance of influencing the practice of psychotherapy. In part this trend seems to flow from the realization that previous research has had relatively little impact on therapeutic practice and that, somehow, we should be able to do better. One criterion for judging the potential value of any study is found in the question: Can the results foreseeably (or potentially) have an influence on therapeutic operations? This question has numerous implications, and among others it will automatically rule out large multifactorial studies which are bound to result in "weak" solutions. The clinician, for example, can do very little with statistical trends, say a correlation of .30 between some therapist and patient variable. We rapidly seem to reach a conclusion, arrived at independently and jointly, that large studies following standard statistical designs and involving group comparisons of one sort or another have very little promise of delivering anything of lasting substance. This conclusion is not new but we seem to subscribe to it with greater conviction than ever. Largely the problem is that in studies of the "naturally occurring" events in psychotherapy there are dozens (if not hundreds) of variables operating which are hopelessly interacting and confounded, and there is no hope of teasing out the influence of single variables. Even if one were successful, the contribution of any single variable (or a few variables) to the total outcome would still be very small. It seems to follow inexorably that the tremendous effort and expense in designing and carrying out such studies cannot be justified by the expectable returns. It seems to be easier to rule out the kinds of studies which are not likely to have important "pay off" than to design more promising investigations, but in delimiting the field we are more likely to arrive at the kind of focus we deem desirable.

2. Through research we should be able to clarify what kinds of changes a given form of psychotherapy can produce in what patients under specified conditions; conversely, it should lead to a better appreciation of what it cannot do. By "research" I mean not only experimental manipulation of some variable but also investigative efforts which will result in clearer specifications of conditions. The problem of diagnostic categories is a case in point. The existing nosological schemes, to put it charitably, are not very useful. If one were able to work "backwards," by studying which kinds of patients respond well (or poorly) to fairly specific kinds of therapeutic regimens and

to evolve groupings in terms of prognostic potential, we would be achieving a great deal. Just as we realistically appraise a person's educational potential, we should strive to evaluate his psychotherapeutic potential. We don't aspire to a graduate education for an individual whose I.Q. is 95, but it appears that psychotherapists have often undertaken the treatment of highly unpromising candidates (sometimes because they are affluent). Psychoanalysis obviously is not for everyone but it may be the treatment of choice for certain individuals. Similarly, desensitization is not likely to yield impressive results with individuals suffering from pervasive neurotic disturbances and whose emotional immaturity is considerable. Too many things are called "psychotherapy," which is partly the reason for the acrimonious debates between schools and the bad name the whole field has acquired in some quarters. The conceptual confusion has also supplied phoney ammunition to critics like Eysenck. What has been said about patients and techniques applies with equal force to outcomes. As long as we have no adequate ways of defining more stringently the kinds of changes a given form of psychotherapy produces, it is pointless to carry out comparative studies since we will never know what we are comparing. I am arguing then for some kind of conceptual "mopping up" operation which would be aimed at clarifying (1) patient, (2) therapist, (3) technique, and (4) outcome measures. It seems to me that such spadework, which shades into the areas of personality measurement and assessment, is bound to have salutary effects. I am also mindful of the enormous obstacles.

3. The effort at specification mentioned in the foregoing will inevitably result in a shrinking of grandiose claims for psychotherapy as a panacea but it will give psychotherapy a rightful and dignified place as *one* technique or a small set of techniques for combating some forms of maladaptive behavior in certain individuals. Thus both clinicians and theoreticians will become more keenly aware of the *limitations* of any therapeutic effort, as dictated by the patient's genetic make-up, possible irreversibilities of early traumatic experiences, I.Q., cultural factors, etc. I am reminded of a statement made by Colby (1951) in his *Primer for Psychotherapists,* to the effect that the psychotherapist must consider the raw material he is working with; the psychological make-up of some patients is more comparable to burlap than to silk and the kind of garment that can be fashioned is partly determined by the raw material.

I recently had the opportunity of listening to a case presentation by a young psychiatrist. He had been treating a young woman for some period of time in individual (psychoanalytic) psychotherapy, twice a week. Ostensibly the woman was functioning reasonably well except for (1) some marital difficulties and (2) the seemingly lasting effects of a turbulent youth which included persecution by the Nazis, deportation of the mother, and wanderings through France in frantic efforts to escape the oppressors. It was by no means clear *how* the therapist attempted to help the patient who had certain hysterical and seductive traits. Somehow the therapeutic experience was to "undo" the past, but could it be done? None of the participants at the case conference had any opinion on this subject except a senior psychiatrist who appeared fairly pessimistic (experienced therapists seem to be this way). What is the promise of such "open-ended" psychotherapy? What troubled me more was the fact that no one seemed to raise any question about goals or outcomes. Individual, analytically oriented psychotherapy simply seemed to be "the thing to do." I am not suggesting that this was a futile effort, but one should be clear *what* one is attempting to do and *how* one proposes to achieve it.

4. As another corollary of the preceding comments, it should be possible to clarify via research whether different forms of psychotherapy do in fact produce distinctive results or whether Frank's "nonspecific" (placebo) effects account for most of the variance in outcomes. Personally, I believe that if we had better measuring instruments we might be able to show that psychoanalysis produces changes that are qualitatively (and perhaps quantitatively) different from Wolpean therapy, and both may differ from client-centered therapy. A study in which the "therapeutic climate" (the relationship) is the sole or preponderant influence in one group, compared with another in which specifiable technical interventions are employed in addition, intrigues me as a possibility. I am strongly in agreement with Allen's current thinking on *intensive* designs, that is, the careful and meticulous study of single cases, combined with some experimental manipulations (which need not be terribly precise). This is in line with Chassan's proposals (whom we might consult fairly soon). Traditional experimental designs are not going to provide important answers.

5. We need to know a great deal more about the *mechanisms of psychological change,* which may be similar in ostensibly different forms of psychotherapy. This is one of my strong arguments for continuing to study individual psychotherapy since, as psychologists and basic scientists, we cannot rest content with the observation that a certain set of therapeutic operations seems to "work"; we want to learn about the underlying principles which will also enlighten us about range of applicability, conditions, limitations, and the like.

6. Here is where my ambivalence about *analogue studies* come in. Having invested a number of years in this type of research, I am still sympathetic to it. I am also impressed with the program advanced by Goldstein et al. and the fact that analogue studies are much more likely to yield clear-cut answers than naturalistic (in situ) research. The question, however, remains to what extent findings from analogue studies can be translated to the therapy situation, and whether they can become meaningful to the clinician. I am aware of arguments pro and con as well as pertinent examples from re-

search in medicine and the natural sciences. I am impressed with the importance of studying patients qua patients. A person who is (1) disturbed and (2) keenly desirous of gaining relief from his suffering (motivated) is a vastly different person from the college sophomore or graduate student participating in an experiment. The finding that "relief" may often be of the placebo variety does not seem to be a potent argument against this assertion. On the other hand, it seems to me that we are courting "weak solutions" from another standpoint if we concentrate on "well functioning" individuals. I also favor studying individuals whose disturbance is demonstrably chronic rather than acute. I would bet that in such persons the "placebo effect" would be significantly less spectacular.

7. I am becoming impressed with the necessity of involving astute clinicians in any research that may be planned. I have seen little evidence to revise my earlier opinion that numerous psychotherapy researchers are not very sophisticated clinicians (some of whom I continue to respect highly). The most productive research, I believe, will result if clinicians and researchers (who may or may not be the same persons) pool their efforts. The literature bears this out. It seems to me that the only things we have *really* learned in psychotherapy have come out of penetrating insights from clinical experience. Research has at times confirmed these insights but not enough has been done to exploit the *confirmatory* potential of research.

Einstein (1934) said:

> It seems that the human mind has first to construct forms independently before we can find them in things. Kepler's marvelous achievement is a particularly fine example of the truth that knowledge cannot spring from experience alone but only from the comparison of the inventions of the intellect with observed fact (p. 27).

8. With more specific reference to "Further Vexations of the Spirit," I find Allen's document a most admirable and penetrating analysis. Let me comment briefly on a few points, omitting large portions with which I find myself in full and wholehearted agreement:

a. Recognizing the personal motivations of the researcher, I wonder how realistic (albeit desirable) a psychotherapy research center will be. My question simply relates to whether it would be possible to gather a group of first-rate researchers and clinicians and have them work in *harmony*. In the fifties a committee that included Shakow, Hilgard, Kubie, and Blum drew up a somewhat similar proposal for the Ford Foundation, but nothing ever came of it. I don't know the exact reasons but have some vague notions. Nevertheless, the idea is splendid and should be pursued.

b. We are in full agreement on the multivariate design difficulties (2).

c. Concerning the complexity issue, I believe that Freud did isolate dimensions and sharply reduced complexity; however—and this strikes me as one of his great contributions—he faced complexity and did not ignore it. One of the principal troubles with the system is that available research techniques (that is, nonanalytic ones) are too primitive to help us confirm or disconfirm many of his assertions. The complexity issue is very much alive again, as shown by the work of the psycholinguists. I also find it fascinating that a man like Paul Meehl continues to be preoccupied with the problem.

I find the "systems" notion quite useful. Notice in this connection also the cognitive-emotional-motor division proposed by Al Ellis (1968) which we discussed in Nashville, and Ward's (1964) "spectrum" concept (see reprint). It may be quite feasible to dimensionalize therapeutic techniques along these lines, together with therapeutic outcomes. The problem of how a given therapeutic influence, say, an effort at cognitive restructuring, produces emotional reverberations is something we need to discuss further.

d. The strategy of teasing out potential dimensions of change or change agents and then manipulating them with single cases is well outlined and strikes a responsive chord. I consider it very promising. See also preceding comments.

e. I fully agree that in psychotherapy we usually apply techniques in analogy to a "shotgun" approach and attribute change to whatever happens to fit our predilections. This needs to change. A proposed study (alluded to earlier) of comparing warmth alone with warmth plus a given technique might help in this regard.

f. There must indeed be efforts to build bridges between laboratory and analogues and clinical practice.

g. I also continue to be intrigued by the "Study of Experts" design, perhaps in combination with the single case approach. For example, whatever may be said about the practice of orthodox psychoanalysis, it is quite systematic and attempts to minimize a variety of influences which are often left to vary freely in other forms of therapy. Few other therapists try to be as self-consciously aware of the potential effect of their interventions as the orthodox analysts. Heinz Hartmann, I understand, is a case in point. In this connection, it is worth keeping in mind that a good many top-flight therapists go about their business with a minimum of fanfare, and assiduously shun the limelight. Parenthetically, this also makes it difficult to enlist their help in research studies, but I am convinced we are in danger of falling victim to false generalizations if we judge the therapeutic enterprise solely by those who produce films, conduct demonstration interviews, or otherwise occupy the public arena. By the same token, some therapists may be mercifully obscure. I share Meehl's 20% competence estimate.

Finally, I observe in my comments and ruminations a certain reluctance to commit myself to an "optimum" design or study although I am developing a keener sense of what I consider "low yield" research and a predilection for some approaches we find ourselves discussing. I continue to be somewhat enamored with my idea for the anorexia nervosa study. All in all, we seem to be well on our way to becoming more specific about the kinds of things we need to become specific about.

References

Colby, K. M. 1951. *A primer for psychotherapists.* New York: Ronald Press.
Einstein, A. 1934. *Essays in science.* New York: Philosophical Library.
Ellis, A. 1968. What really causes psychotherapeutic change? *Voices* 4: 90–95.
Ward, C. H. 1964. Psychotherapy research: Dilemmas and directions. *Archives of General Psychiatry* 10: 596–662.

INTERVIEW: HOWARD F. HUNT AND BERNARD F. RIESS*

New York, December 2, 1968

Drs. Howard Hunt and Bernard Riess met with us in a joint session.

Riess described the operation of the Postgraduate Center, including its service, training, and research aspects. A few statistics illustrate the magnitude of what is unquestionably the largest outpatient clinic in the country. There are a total of 100 therapists. Of these about 55% are psychologists and the rest are psychiatrists or psychiatric social workers. Most are postdoctoral trainees and accumulate 1,400 patient hours per week (!), about 1200 of these in individual psychotherapy. Some 900 patients are admitted every year and they are seen for an average of 118 hours. All therapy is supervised, which is true even when the therapist is a staff member. Few patients terminate before having completed 50 hours although a number drop out after about 14 hours. The upper end of the skewed distribution extends to 300–400 hours, with about 10% of the patients reaching that level. Most patients are members of the middle class, with an average income of about $140 per week. Family therapy is on the increase and is growing at a faster rate than group therapy. The modal number of weekly interviews is about 1.7 and the range is from 1 to 4 hours per week. The Center is on the verge

* Dr. Hunt is Professor of Psychology at Columbia University and Chief of Psychiatric Research at the New York State Psychiatric Institute; Dr. Riess is Director of the Research Department of the Postgraduate Center for Mental Health.

of becoming involved in a sizable community mental health program which will involve services to lower class patients on a large scale. Despite some innovations, the Center remains committed to individual psychotherapy along psychoanalytic lines.

A center of this size obviously represents a huge resource of potential data, and the existence of a research department (headed by Riess) which has a number of projects under way exemplifies the Center's interest in this area. He cited a number of studies which are at various stages of completion at the center. He indicated that the replication of one outcome study which used change in patient income as a criterion indicated that patients improved their incomes significantly more than can be accounted for by natural rises in income. He also noted a study being done in Westchester County of sociological factors in the development of child psychopathology which indicates, for example, that a child who is in a home where the income is below the poverty line and where the father is absent is almost certain to become disturbed. On another topic, the Center is obtaining video tapes of initial interviews which could be compared with other types of diagnostic or assessment interviews, comparable to those done by British psychiatrists, using a highly structured approach such as that involved in Zubin's work. It would be feasible also to use brief videotape segments recorded at various stages of therapy for the purpose of assessing change in the patient's behavior, including interactions with the therapist. The potentialities and the flexibility of this medium as a vehicle for research are intriguing. There is also a fledgling study in the area of dance therapy. This is concurrent with the new interest in movement and touching. He told the story about a catatonic schizophrenic who had not spoken for years but who only bobbed his head up and down. One of the dance therapists noted that his head was moving with a musical rhythm and she began to tap dance to the same rhythm. The rapport thus established gradually resulted in the renewal of speech behavior in this patient.

The research department has ten staff members who also do therapy. Therapists and patients are willing to participate in research projects and research is fully accepted as part of the Center's operation. Thus it would seem possible to enlist the Center's cooperation in future investigative efforts provided both the research and clinical staff can see the relevance and become fully invested in the work. In past studies of therapy outcome conducted by the Center, the following measures have been used: (1) decrease of patient's visits to medical practitioners for nonpsychiatric reasons; (2) increase in income; (3) increments in planning for vocational advancement. Riess mentioned that the records of an outpatient clinic like the Postgraduate Center represent a large data pool which might lend itself to retrospective studies. Strupp observed that, on the basis of his experience, he found the completeness of such records wanting; as a matter of fact, at one clinic with which he had a close connection the recorded data were exceedingly shoddy.

Hunt introduced the important notion that we should look not only at the therapy situation but at the totality of people's lives. He recommended that we monitor their friends, parents, spouses, and in general focus on the patient's life outside of psychotherapy. In response to the question of how we might study the process of change in the life context, he suggested that a mobile team operating out of a store front may be the most effective agency; admittedly, this would require special training to make the observers effective. Howard emphasized the importance of extra-therapy experiences because we may find our most potent therapeutic influences by looking intensively in "nature" as it exists in society.

Confronted with the enormous methodological difficulties inherent in such efforts, he responded by saying that the sociologists have been quite adept at developing methods for studying people in their day-to-day activities. Strupp was troubled by the problem that many changes occurring in psychotherapy are not reflected in the person's gross behavior; instead they are reflected in subtle changes in their outlook, reactions to stressful situations, and better strategies of handling challenges encountered by all of us. Thus, while an increase in earning power may be a useful criterion—Riess reported that successful patients after 59 sessions increased their weekly salary by $12—it is obvious that other criteria must be used in addition.

There was some discussion of whether these natural therapeutic influences are powerful or weak and whether they are specific or nonspecific. It might appear from some of Jerry Frank's research and commentary that some portion of these natural effects are simply "placebo responses"; however, the general thrust of the discussion moved toward another conclusion with which we are in closer agreement. This was the view that nonspecific, spontaneous, and placebo effects are not only real but quite important, and we may enter into a valuable context for discovery if we focus on them with more vigor and precision.

Hunt commented, "You may think I've been influenced too much by Martin Orne, but I think Orne's got it right." That is, influences such as instructions, demands, and expectations are real and important and not artifactual. Some of the changes occurring due to such influences may occur very rapidly and may be major ones, at least in the subjective realm. Not that these effects are the only or the most important ones which may be studied or discovered by looking more intensively at natural change processes. The whole question of the natural history of neurosis and the natural history of positive personality change are at issue here, and have considerable appeal not only as a context for discovery but also as an avenue for establishing base lines which can serve as a type of control for psychotherapy outcome and process studies.

A related point by Hunt was that if many of these "natural" influences appear to be nonspecific or broad-gauged, then it will be important to tease out the relevant dimensions. He made the exceedingly cogent point that we have made little progress in isolating their respective ingredients. The so-called nonspecific effects are very much in need of specification and explanation. For example, warmth may be one of these but it is probably in fact a multidimensional process. It could be valuable to study the "anatomy" of warmth and to identify the specific behaviors that create in a perceiver the feeling that a person is being warm. Behaviors on the part of an influencer which create the feeling on the part of a perceiver of being understood could similarly be analyzed. Issues such as, "Can these behaviors be taught and learned?" would also be appropriate foci for inquiry.

Another related point was the fact that the personal impact of the therapist or other influencer is very important and usually occurs in a "total" relationship and is, therefore, nonspecific. The important research question is "What makes a person a powerful influencer?" The ingredients of this personal impact must be teased out. Hunt gave examples of animal researchers and dog trainers who simply don't have this personal touch and some of them get bitten quite often. The simple personal factors that may be involved seem like important things to look at.

Continuing along similar lines, Hunt argued that it seemed most relevant to him to study the live therapy process and the effects of therapists on a broad front rather than to focus upon experimental analogues or laboratory studies of basic change processes within the context of the general psychology of change. This was somewhat surprising to us, but he supported it by indicating a good deal of the research done in learning and social psychology as producing a lot of weak results loaded with artifacts.

These questions seem to touch on one of the crucial problems in psychotherapy, namely: What makes a therapist a powerful influencer? One of these ingredients undoubtedly is the patient's feeling that somehow he is "getting through" to the therapist. We need to explore what specific therapist behaviors are conducive to such an experience. It is difficult to conceive that laboratory studies can get at this problem in a very effective manner. This seems to be another argument for in situ studies.

In this connection, Frank's conclusions came in for some discussion. Frank seems to say that (1) psychotherapy produces improvement in persons who enter therapy when they are faced with a crisis and these changes are due to the "nonspecific effects" of psychotherapy; (2) severe limits are set to any kind of therapeutic improvement by constitutional factors. Riess disagreed with the assertion that the majority of their patients enter psychotherapy when they are in a crisis state; rather they seem to be faced with existential problems, vague malaise, and similar problems. Strupp's own experience with patients in an outpatient clinic supports this view. (Meehl also seems to feel that psychotherapy produces primarily *subjective* changes rather than modification in overt behavior.)

As the discussion progressed, Hunt expressed the view, for which there seems to be growing support, that learning principles are not in competition with the dynamic approach; rather they spell it out in detail. He would argue strongly for a clear empirical statement of what the effective therapy processes are and would not be happy with the return to "clinical lore." Allen expressed the view that there is no such thing as classical conditioning in behavior therapy; instead it is a multidimensional process.

Hunt does use learning conceptions, however, to tie together his views of the importance of studying the therapy process concurrently with a natural change process. He argues, for example, that most of the effects of psychotherapy and of behavior therapy are comparatively small and subtle. Where these influences gain their potency is by creating small changes that make a big difference in the environment. To illustrate, if a person is trying hard to help himself, or begins to change his attitude toward himself or towards significant figures in the environment, the reinforcing contingencies which exist in the community may alter drastically in relation to him specifically. He then may suddenly be the subject of powerful new reinforcing influences which are the real modifiers of major elements in his behavior. This is another way of saying a very important thing, namely that psychotherapy effects interact with situational effects to produce the final amount of change observed. He notes that the powerful change of reinforcements in the environment becomes especially relevant in work with children. In keeping with this argument, he has come to the conclusion that the most powerful variables are probably not in the psychotherapy process per se, that we are simply looking where the light is, but that we need to examine much more carefully the powerful variables which exist in the community. Aligning these influences with our purposes would be a straight function of producing specific behavioral or attitudinal modifications which would then become stimuli for new sets of reinforcements to be exercised upon the individual.

In a somewhat different context Hunt observed that we must squarely face the fact that a large number of therapists and patients in contemporary society devote significant amounts of energy to therapeutic work. Unless one is willing to assume that these people are grossly deluded (a rather unlikely assumption) it follows that, minimally, there is sufficient (intermittent?) reinforcement for the belief that therapy is worthwhile and that patients, by and large, are benefiting from it. Nevertheless, the process, as it is currently practiced, may not be terribly efficient. Education at all levels may not be terribly efficient either; people accept the fact that it takes long periods of time and that some students make slow or insignificant progress; yet no one is willing to throw it out the window. While Hunt did not put it in these terms, he rejected outright Eysenck's nihilistic assertions concerning traditional psychotherapy.

The idea of a possible research center for psychotherapy was criticized on the basis that such institutes often develop a form of "sclerosis." One way of overcoming the institutionalization syndrome might be to invite scientists to visit such a center for a maximum period of two or three years. Another way of combating the problem is to use the store front as the center of action, which will then permit a very flexible design to be implemented as needed.

We dwelled to some extent on the logistics of collaborative studies. Numerous reservations were expressed about the feasibility of such efforts. The perinatal study, sponsored by NIH, was cited as an example of a project in which many difficulties were encountered. In any such undertakings, provisions must be made for the autonomy of the collaborators. In this connection, we noted that we are not about to propose a large collabrative study of any kind.

Nevertheless, Hunt felt that there have to be collaborative efforts, even though they might involve only a very small number of centers. Otherwise research findings will be characterized by local and "charismatic" effects. Whatever collaborative efforts might be undertaken, they should be centered in a university.

Inevitably the discussion veered to the troublesome problems in diagnosis and nosology. Hunt discussed briefly a current study by Zubin in which initial interviews are rated by American and British judges. The question was raised whether structured interviews are more productive of diagnostic information than observations of a patient in some form of situational test. For example, one might study a patient's reaction to authority figures and deduce problems he might have in that area. Riess recounted that he has found an initial marathon interview lasting 4 hours useful in assessing prospective patients.

As was already observed in a follow-up study by Schjelderup in 1955, therapeutic changes take a long time to mature. Therefore, assessments immediately following the termination of therapy may not be nearly as adequate as appraisals at a later time. Intervening life events, of course, then present a problem because one cannot be sure whether any improvements that might be observed are attributable to the therapeutic experience.

Riess made the following additional relevant points:

1. He noted that he uses a kind of situational test with his patients as a diagnostic technique. He conducts a 4-hour interview in which he creates high levels of anxiety and tests the defensive structure of the patient.

2. He pointed out in response to the discussion of the relevance of social psychology to psychotherapy that most of the therapists he has talked with at the Postgraduate Center feel that the hypotheses in the Goldstein et al. (1966) book can fit psychodynamic therapy rather nicely. That is, formulations of the psychotherapeutic process in terms of general psychological principles are becoming increasingly acceptable to clinicians. This comment must be qualified, however, since Riess' respondents were predominantly psychologists.

3. Since a number of the therapists at the Postgraduate Center are quite willing to experiment with many techniques it would be quite feasible to interest them in studies involving the experimental manipulation of therapist behavior. This could be done by isolating a particular therapist behavior and then controlling the therapist's behavior in terms of certain specific criteria. Conceivably one could use a prompting device to keep the therapist's behavior on target.

4. He agrees very much with Hunt that studies of the live therapy process and outcomes are important and he found that most of his staff agreed with this. He advocated also the intensive study of single cases which we discussed at some length.

5. People at the Center are very open to collaboration and feel that it is quite feasible. He agreed with Hunt that there is a real question of how long people can sustain a high level of intensity of commitment to a particular project. He pointed out, as did Hunt, that individually people can be "marvelous" but when they are working corporately the effect on creativity can be deadly. This is due to the fact that procedures become ingrained and bureaucratic structures develop which make change and communication difficult. Before a project is initiated it would be important to establish that those participating have a genuine chunk of "the pie" and feel that it is partly their project. Furthermore, there would have to be agreement among them as to why they are interested in the specific problem under study.

6. He cited an example which resulted in the immediate application of a research finding (focused observation may be a better word). In this instance it was noted that a therapist was paying undue attention (in terms of comments, and the like) to the sickest members of a group, neglecting others. Thus he may have been reinforcing unwittingly the expression of "sick" feelings or behavior. When this was called to his attention, he was able to modify his therapeutic work.

Hunt made a number of valuable comments on methodology, which are summarized below:

1. The changes effected by therapeutic interventions are often subtle and subjective and we need measures that are specific to these kinds of change so that we know when they have occurred.

2. A useful technique for assessing changes in the quality of the patient's interpersonal interactions before and after therapy consists of a situational test involving role playing.

3. Since behavior seems to flow like water from a hose, it is necessary to formulate some hypothesis and on the basis of that hypothesis begin to unitize and score the "flow" of phenomena that is occurring. We then look for smooth fits during the process of testing these tentative hypotheses.

4. Many studies of psychotherapy look at the wrong thing and they search where the light is brightest not where treasures may be found. This is reminiscent of the anecdote concerning the drunk looking for his lost keys under the lamp post, not because he had lost them there but because that is where the light was. Hunt proposed that fruitful areas for investigation would be: (1) the patient's subjective feelings; (2) the totality of events in his life; (3) subtle changes that may defy ready measurement. For example, there seems to be evidence that many patients get a bit "looser" in the sense of being more relaxed in coping with problems in their lives. (In this connection, Strupp stressed the importance of the bias in the sample of therapists we study which everyone saw as a very serious and significant problem.)

5. Dyrud and Goldiamond are doing a behavioral analysis of psychoanalytic therapy. This sounds familiar, however, he suggests that there may be something new and important here.

6. We take too few measurements in psychotherapy research and therefore we do not have very good insight into the change process. Post-therapy tests in particular may be a bad place to measure change because covering up may already be occurring and there may be other "strange" effects at the time of termination. Some of the most important changes may occur rapidly and early in therapy.

7. Statistical averaging in typical therapy experiments tend to yield nonspecific effects, which is the reason that outcome studies in particular yield nonspecific effects. This kind of averaging washes out specific technical effects of different techniques and therapists and also creates the kind of problem Meehl referred to, namely that too many interactions prevent one from teasing out anything very dramatic. Furthermore, it may be inadvisable to look for dramatic effects of *single* variables. As long as we live and work with the complexity of human beings we may have to assume that a very complex, broad-gauged, change-induction process is occurring. Therefore, the search for the dramatic is folly and those who think they have found it (for example, in the process of desensitization) may really have a hold of something weaker than they think.

8. Another intriguing idea: Let's pull equivalent instances out of various cases which occur in therapy and study their effects, particularly on selected target problems. Riess noted that he has done this in cases of suicide threats,

that is, he observed what happened precisely before and after the threat was made and how the antecedents and consequents were related to characteristics of the therapist.

9. As an important innovation, therapists could signal the research team or some monitor when something important was happening in therapy, or had just happened, or when he expected that something important was about to happen. (Dr. Rosalea Schonbar subsequently mentioned another variation on this which would involve having the therapist push a button of some kind every time he felt something really important was happening during therapy. These signals could then be recorded along with video tape or other types of recordings and could easily be located for research purposes.)

10. Hunt argues strongly that it is important to sacrifice large numbers of subjects in order to study a few intensively, using particularly own-control designs. He feels that this would be a good way of teasing out powerful effects and we were rather inclined to agree with him. Parenthetically, the interest of practicing therapists in intensive single case studies is bound to be markedly greater than in any other approach.

11. Hunt expressed a preference for studying psychotherapy in different settings, such as "store front services." He felt that psychotherapy with Blacks, Puerto Ricans, poor whites, might be very different from therapy with the middle-class patients who have typically been studied in the past.

12. A final important point was that simulation of therapeutic techniques or influences may be a key to discovery.

Comments by Bergin. Following the meeting we discussed some specific questions about what might actually be done in the way of a study. It was determined that we really disagree on the value of studying psychotherapy as it is practiced. On the one hand Strupp, along with Riess and to a lesser extent Hunt, feels that there are important dimensions and processes occurring in therapy as it is practiced and it is worth the time and effort to extract them. My own feeling is that this is generally not correct although it may be true for a rather small and highly selected subsample of therapists who have very good success.

We did tend to agree fairly strongly on the value of a case-by-case experimental psychotherapy in which the case is studied longitudinally and in which specific therapists' interventions are programmed into the therapy itself. By this method specific interventions can be studied in one case in an own-control design and across cases in a comparative design. The advantage would be in coalescing the need for experimentation with the need for immediate relevance to practice.

We also strongly agreed that we need to emphasize the importance of subjective changes in people. This was probably unnecessary before the rise of behavioral therapies, but it now seems urgent that ways of measuring the profound subjective changes that take place in people be developed. Both we and our consultants noted a number of case illustrations of individuals we knew who had changed considerably in attitude and feelings about themselves and the world without changing their behavior markedly. This seems to us subtle but very significant because how a person feels about himself, what he is doing, and his life in the world is highly important. This does not mean that there exists no relationship between subjective experience and overt behavior, but it does suggest that they are not always corresponding and that overt behavior is not necessarily the most important criterion in every case.

We also agreed that childhood learning is very powerful and as a consequence the possibilities for change later in life may be limited. We cannot overlook the potency of maturational effects and other effects which may be difficult to reverse or to modify. This also makes us somewhat suspicious of dramatic changes or purported dramatic changes in chronic cases.

Comments by Strupp. One kind of study that currently fascinates me is a comparison between therapeutic dyads, one of which is characterized by "nonspecific techniques" (such as empathy, warmth, understanding, and respect), the other is treated by nonspecific techniques *plus* specific interventions (such as interpretations). If it were possible to achieve reasonable comparability between such dyads it would be possible to assess the relative effectiveness of specific techniques. "Orthodox" client-centered therapists seem to fit the first description reasonably well; analytically-oriented therapists seem to fall into the second category. The intensive study of such dyads (which seems to be very much in keeping with Allen's recent predilections) might be a productive way of shedding light on the problem.

I am increasingly convinced that we frequently get a biased sample of therapists in our studies and similar distortions are introduced if we accept films, demonstration interviews, and published writings as representative samples of therapy as it is practiced today. My point is that many therapists, including highly competent ones, shun the limelight and go about their work rather quietly. It would be of the utmost importance to enlist the help of such therapists in projected studies. This is in line with my strong conviction that we need to study what therapists do rather than what they say they do. There is nothing new in this statement but I feel it bears repeating from time to time.

Allen raised the question (which has occupied us for some time) whether the naturally occurring events in psychotherapy are powerful enough to be productively studied in situ. Clinicians tend to think so, partly because the transactions of therapy represent their "natural habitat" and the therapeutic situation is congenial to them; others have their doubts. Personally, I am ambivalent (I previously expatiated on the tremendous difference between bona fide patients and "subjects"). My reservations include (1) the seemingly hopeless complexity of interacting processes from which it is virtually impossible to tease out single variables or influences; (2) the slow pace of intrapsychic as well as behavioral changes; (3) serious problems of data collection over protracted periods of time, perhaps at different locations (not insuperable); (4) the resulting lack of comparability of therapeutic dyads; and numerous others. On the positive side, there is much to be said about studying therapy "like it is." Such studies also have a kind of face validity to clinicians, and findings resulting from such work may be more easily accepted by practitioners.

By monitoring behavior changes in the course of therapy (perhaps through videotape techniques) we may be able to plot *rates* of change, something which no one seems to have done. Periodic assessments by external observers may be helpful in such efforts.

It is difficult to summarize discussions of this sort but a number of trends are discernible. Indeed, they are reflected in the reporting itself. Perhaps the most important single point in this consultation was the expressed preference for our point 2a (in the set of Questions), that is, studies of the live therapy process and outcome, with emphasis upon the intensive study of single cases. Allen and I seem to concur that large-sample studies, based on traditional statistical designs, are bound to result in "weak effects," and while we are opposed to premature closure on any issue, we appear to develop a penchant for single case studies in which technical interventions are systematically varied or manipulated. (We probably differ on the precise nature of such studies, but it is too early to tell.) In keeping with this thinking we have scheduled an early visit with J.B. Chassan (early January), a statistician with clinical interests, noted for his interest in intensive designs. Clearly, the field must search for focus and specificity, as we have said so many times before. As a parting shot, it would be wise to abandon the umbrella term "psychotherapy" altogether since it comprises so many processes which are often incapable of comparison and since the term perpetuates the semantic confusion with which the field has been beset for so many years.

References

Goldstein, A. P., Heller, K. & Sechrest, L. B. 1966. *Psychotherapy and the psychology of behavior change.* New York: Wiley.

Schjelderup, H. 1955. Lasting effects of psychoanalytic treatment. *Psychiatry* 18: 109–33.

WORKING PAPER BY STRUPP

December 11, 1968

The following are a few disjointed remarks, in part a commentary on some points made in Allen's report of our discussion with Hunt and Riess as well as the article by Sanford and Krech (1968). Hopefully, they will eventually add up to something useful.

1. The question, What makes a person a powerful influencer?, strikes me as the crucial issue in psychotherapy research. While some persons undoubtedly have certain charismatic qualities, which may include warmth and empathy, I believe that these are preconditions which by no means exhaust the totality of the therapist's influence. In other words, in my judgment there are ways and means (techniques) which can be employed, intuitively or deliberately, to further the therapeutic enterprise. The future of psychotherapy as a science hinges on whether such techniques exist, whether they can be made explicit (that is, whether they are communicable and teachable), and whether the conditions under which they apply can be specified. The hope for teaching a neophyte technical skills seems to me infinitely greater than training him to become "warm." If it turned out that say 90% percent of the variance in therapeutic change were attributable to such nonspecific factors as being understood, "received," then psychotherapy would indeed be no more than "the purchase of friendship." Personally, I believe it *can* be (although often it is not) a great deal more. In this view analysts and behavior therapists concur, and I believe that therein lies the future of psychotherapy as a scientific discipline.

2. I continue to be troubled by the perpetual imprecisions in the use of the term "psychotherapy." As long as people persist in lumping a wide variety of processes with few common elements under one heading, the chance for clarifying the nature of the psychological influencing process remains slim. For example, 10–15 sessions of "brief psychotherapy" in the typical outpatient clinic (and the changes resulting from such transactions) *may* be (although admittedly we have not conclusively demonstrated that they are) vastly different from intensive psychotherapy over a period of 2–3 years. If one takes the former as a model for "psychotherapy," I tend to think that one becomes more impressed with the "nonspecific effects" than if one accepts the latter.

3. I strongly resonate to Allen's comment about the importance of *subjective* changes and his observation that "overt behavior is not necessarily the most important criterion in every case." If it is true, as I believe it is

(see empirical data reported by Strupp, Fox, & Lessler, 1969) that many people undergo changes in attitudes, feelings, and outlook without changing their behavior markedly, we must search for better and more precise measures of such changes. I contend that existing instruments do not permit us to do this very effectively, with the result that many important and real changes have continued to elude us. The trouble thus lies in part with the inadequacy of our assessment techniques, through which some of the really important phenomena vanish as through a sieve. At the very least, we need buckets!

4. The expectation that psychotherapy should rapidly produce spectacular or miraculous changes in a person's cognitions, emotions, or behavior strikes me as utterly fantastic and illusory. Such a belief can only result from a gross underestimation of the tenacity with which patterns of behavior are typically maintained. In many ways it is a good thing that a person's "character" is enduring and not subject to quick shifts, but this blessing can also be a curse when a therapist is dealing with deeply ingrained patterns that have been overlearned, repeated, and reinforced for many years. Since many of these patterns are rooted in childhood and the result of the individual's malleability and openness to influence at that time of life, it is hardly surprising that they are not easily "modified." I recall Paul Meehl's skepticism about ever changing a patient's "basic mistrust" of people or similar deeply held convictions. I assume here that *psychotherapy is concerned with changes in emotional or cognitive strategies, not with switching responses to a specific stimulus.* Considering the tremendous odds against which the psychotherapist is pitting his one or even four weekly sessions, should he be faulted if his successes are only modest? In saying this, I am not subscribing to the view that therapy is by definition interminable or that sooner or later something *may* change simply because therapy is continued, but I wish to underscore both the slowness of psychological change and the fact that many changes may be exceedingly subtle.

To cite a somewhat trivial analogy: I have for several years struggled to acquire a particular motor skill (piano playing) and have found progress excruciatingly slow (we need not consider here my musical talents or aptitude). My teacher does not get nearly as discouraged as I do at times because I suppose he is more realistic. My point is that the acquisition of a motor skill is probably child's play compared to the process of unlearning maladaptive techniques of relating to authority figures, members of the opposite sex, and others, and learning new strategies, all the more since there may be an enormous investment on the part of the patient to maintain the status quo. (Freud's concept of the "repetition compulsion" of course deals with this problem although it does not strike me as a very felicitious or heuristic term.)

Should the therapist or researcher quit? I think not, but I do think it is altogether fitting to continue the search for techniques which might help us do a more efficient job. We should also become more realistic.

5. The disagreement about the value of studying psychotherapy as it is practiced may be more apparent than real. I think we agree that in order to study psychotherapeutic phenomena one needs a therapeutic relationship. I continue to believe that the one-to-one relationship offers unique opportunities for studying at close range and in purest fashion the kinds of psychological processes we are interested in exploring. Indeed, I will go so far as to assert that there is no other situation which in principle lends itself so well to this purpose. Freud's concepts pertaining to the structure of the psychoanalytic situation and Sullivan's notions concerning participant observation point the way. Here is a relatively (though not perfectly) neutral observer who can "program" interventions without contaminating the field as usually occurs in such relationships as husband-wife, parent-child. At the same time, and most importantly, the therapist participates; that is, he is not an experimenter in the laboratory whose relationship to "S" is trivial. That's why I believe, as I said before, that analogues are of very limited value. If one wants to study the patient's interpersonal techniques for the purpose of helping him to change them, one must have an interpersonal situation in which to observe and "manipulate" them. Consequently, the therapeutic situation is itself an analogue, and a very unusual one. Just as the child learns about other people and their ways by accepting his parents as models of reality, the therapist provides conditions for corrective learning which we hope will generalize to other situations. That's of course "old hat," and we need to know more, as Goldstein et al. suggest about the extent and limits of generalizations from within therapy to extra-therapy situations.

Thus, I am all in favor of longitudinal studies of the therapeutic process, including certain programmed (experimental) interventions (whose characteristics we still need to explicate), with repeated measures taken at frequent intervals. Such a project would involve only a few dyads which however would be studied very intensively. (See my earlier suggestion for a warmth versus warmth-plus-technique study which may fit in here.) Finally, it is to be noted that some such design is a form of "action research" along the lines pioneered by Kurt Lewin some 25 years ago.

References

Sanford, N., & Krech, D. 1968. The activists' corner. *Journal of Social Issues* 24: 165–72.

Strupp, H. H., Fox, R. E., & Lessler, K. 1969. *Patients view their psychotherapy.* Baltimore: The Johns Hopkins Press.

INTERVIEW: THOMAS S. SZASZ*

Syracuse, December 17, 1968

We[12] spent two hours with Szasz on December 17. Most of the discussion took place over the luncheon table (which accounts for the absence of notes and my inability to reconstruct adequately the interchange). In retrospect, it was a most stimulating meeting and I only wish Szasz had afforded us the opportunity to talk with him at considerably greater length.

Szasz admittedly is no specialist in psychotherapy research nor did he have any particular recommendations about the kinds of investigations that might fruitfully be undertaken by researchers in the years to come. He did emphasize, however, the importance of studying what therapists are doing rather than what they say they are doing, a point which no one would seriously dispute. Beyond that, he called repeated attention to the need for studying the broader social context within which psychotherapy operates, the unstated assumptions governing the patient-therapist relationship (as elaborated superbly in *The Ethics of Psychoanalysis,* 1965, a book which I consider one of the most exciting contributions to what Szasz has called autonomous psychotherapy). Just as one achieves only a limited understanding of the institution of slavery by studying the social interaction between whites and Negroes in the Old South, one does not learn nearly enough about "psychotherapy" by studying the exchange of messages between the participants unless one supplements this work by analyzing the status relationships and the many implicit assumptions about the patient and therapist roles, the goals of "treatment" (which may vary between autonomy or social control), and the like. The views expressed by Szasz were very much in keeping with the "heresies" found in his published writings which sometimes overstate an issue but on the whole contain many important insights.

Much of the contemporary mental health terminology is "loaded" and one must guard against succumbing to the semantic quagmires that lurk everywhere. Szasz is working on a new book tracing the history of "mental disease" (long considered by him a myth) through the ages (see Szasz, 1970). The problem of involuntary treatment, particularly of patients committed to state hospitals, is a serious issue which has not received nearly the attention it deserves. Who besides the patient can (or should) decide what is in his "best interest"?

Szasz expressed his conviction that the ambitious theories propounded by Freud mainly served his own self-aggrandizement and are largely useless

* Dr. Szasz is Professor of Psychiatry at the Upstate Medical Center, Syracuse, New York.

12. Reported by Strupp.

today. However, he regards transference as a phenomenon (not merely a concept!) of lasting value, and perhaps Freud's greatest contribution. For the rest, Freud's greatest merit lay in the fact that he was an honest man who refused to accept the hypocrisy of his contemporaries (including Charcot and Breuer). He also was willing to *listen* to patients, something which up to then no one had been willing to do.

Following his writings, Szasz decried the medical and psychiatric domination of psychoanalysis, a situation he had termed elsewhere a "catastrophe" leading to the decline of a major development in the liberation of man's spirit. This trend, he feels, has gained momentum during the last 15–20 years so that psychoanalysis is becoming increasingly a "closed system." He pointed to the manifest hypocrisy that on the one hand the Standard Edition of Freud's writings is entitled "The Complete *Psychological* Works of Sigmund Freud," and on the other no psychologist can receive "full" *psychoanalytic* training in an "official" institute in this country.

There is a sharp contrast between the activities of the therapist whose "treatment" is designed to enhance the therapist's power and those of his confrère who wishes to help the patient achieve greater autonomy. In short, the power structure of the patient-therapist relationship must be scrutinized, and obviously it shows wide variations in terms of the therapist's personality which, in Szasz's opinion, is thoroughly intertwined with "techniques."

It was at times difficult to build a bridge between the context of Szasz's thinking and our approach. A greater rapprochement might have been achieved through more extensive discussion.

We found Szasz a fascinating man with a passion for truth!

References

Szasz, T. S. 1965. *The ethics of psychoanalysis.* New York: Basic Books.
———. 1970. *The manufacture of madness.* New York: Harper and Row.

INTERVIEW: ARNOLD P. GOLDSTEIN*

Syracuse, December 18, 1968

Psychotherapy and psychotherapy research, as far as Arnie is concerned, is still very much in the "Dark Ages" and we are not likely to see conclusive answers on most issues in this area in our lifetime. In keeping with our views, Arnie believes we need psychotherap*ies* which are adapted to specifiable conditions rather than a single model or technique. He also struck a re-

* Dr. Goldstein is Professor in the Department of Psychology, Syracuse University.

sponsive chord when he observed the difficulty of combining experimental rigor with clinical meaningfulness. Despite his own emphasis on analogue research—in the course of the day we were exposed to samples of some exciting studies Arnie and his students are currently carrying out—he is very much immersed in clinical activities himself and obviously gets significant "kicks" out of group therapy, sensitivity training, and the like. He seems to spend appreciable amounts of time with patients who are not usually considered well motivated for, or amenable to, psychotherapy.

Parenthetically, it is by now a regular occurrence that no consultant fits neatly the image we have of him through his writings and public utterances. In Arnie's case we were impressed by the breadth of his clinical interests which far outdistance and overshadow his research efforts and evidently provide powerful energy for his drive to understand the phenomena with which we are all concerned.

Goldstein suggested that there are three main types of variables which presently seem to have significance in the study of therapeutic change. These include: the therapeutic relationship, prominently defined by liking and interpersonal attraction; hope, expectancy, and influenceability; and technique.

The first and most important is the *therapeutic relationship*. The degree of liking and interpersonal attraction also impress him as necessary conditions in nearly all forms of treatment, and in some forms they are sufficient conditions for success. At present, he feels unable to differentiate these two sets of conditions. He agrees that a good many people suffer from "friendly deficiencies," along the lines described by William Schofield (1964). He regards his own research effort as directed at getting the therapist to *like* the kind of people we normally do not like. In this regard, he also sees community psychology as the "wave of the future" in that indigenous nonprofessional therapeutic agents employ a kind of therapy which places primary emphasis upon these relationship conditions (this of course is also the main thrust of client-centered theory and practice).

These conditions are frequently essential because they provide an opportunity to "hook" the patient which gives him motivation to work hard in the therapeutic process. The degree to which the therapist likes a patient may therefore provide important clues to the nature and outcome of the therapeutic transaction. (The deplorable lack of articulation between traditional diagnosis and therapeutic work was mentioned in this context.)

The second set of variables to which Goldstein attributes significance concerns *hope, expectancy,* and *influenceability* as a function of respect for the competence of the "sanctioned healer."

Strupp emphasized the importance of expectations and aims in a somewhat different way. He pointed out that it is necessary to specify the goals of therapy in advance and to place them in a reasonable context of reality.

He pointed out that in education we do not try to prepare people for graduate school if they are not capable of it, and therefore we need to develop in the therapeutic area a broad array of goals with regard to different problems and people. In addition, we need to establish specific methods for achieving these particular goals. The research question then becomes: "What kind of research will pay off most handsomely in terms of developing an array of methods which will permit us to achieve specific goals with specific patients?"

The third set of variables consists of *specific techniques,* such as relaxation. Arnie seemed convinced that techniques contribute little in and of themselves that is unique to the therapeutic process; rather, they accelerate or deepen the process that is already underway. He noted that the induction of relaxation may accelerate the therapy process but that it may not be any better than having a person lie on a couch, and the ultimate end point may not be different whether one or the other method is used. He also stated that "working through" by role-playing similarly accelerates therapeutic results. Again the absolute quantity of change may not be very different if other techniques are employed. Similarly, in the course of therapy, the behavior therapist as well as the analyst take on anxiety-reducing properties and their activities have many features in common.

Another interesting and provocative theme involved Goldstein's focus upon techniques for making the so-called untreatable person amenable to treatment, in other words training the patient in psychological mindedness or "hooking" patients to techniques which have some potency for effecting change. He reported to us brief excerpts from what he said was a total of 30 studies in this area. They consist primarily of specific manipulations for heightening the patient's attraction to the therapist, or on the other hand, explicitly increasing the psychological sophistication of the patient. He pointed out that many sessions of this pre-therapy treatment may be essential before one of the traditional forms of therapy can be initiated. He drew a time-line for us in which about the first quarter of the length consisted of conditioning the patient for therapy. About another 20 per cent of the period was therapeutic "manipulation," involving specific techniques to get the person moving. Said Arnie: "We must manipulate and influence with all the power that we have at our command during this early phase." These preliminary techniques are essentially his response to the observation that more than half of the patients who enter therapy don't last more than four to six sessions. Thus, as we observed jokingly, he is working on a "technology of seduction," which, according to Arnie, was once characterized by a critical psychiatrist as "infantilizing" the patient, obviously a cardinal sin. Throughout therapy, however, Arnie sees himself as a humanist who focuses upon increasing the patient's autonomy and maximizing his potential, in other words, helping him to steer his own ship in the real world.

Although the preceding implies that Goldstein's last phase of therapy employs essentially traditional techniques, he was quick to agree that we still need to search for new techniques. In this regard he is particularly interested in store fronts in ghettos and other forms of socially innovative change methods.

Arnie argued further that all forms of therapy are (or should be) aimed at increasing the patient's ability to make choices, to help him "steer his own ship," and to increase his *autonomy.* While this point is not novel—for example, it has been prominently stressed in the writings of Szasz—it is extremely important, partly because it provides a useful antidote to such persistent notions as "treatment" and "cure" which always carry the (erroneous) implication of somehow restoring the patient to a presumably healthy status quo ante. To achieve the over-all goal of greater autonomy it appears necessary to design adequate measures for assessing the patient's idiosyncratic needs, but at the same time it should be possible to isolate dimensions (probably a few salient ones will do) along which most patients find difficulties.

Arnie believes that there is a great need for developing new therapeutic approaches that are *patient-specific.* In this connection he reported some work he has been doing with prisoners whose "psychological mindedness" was rather low. It was noted that certain patients are completely unsuitable for individual psychotherapy; on the other hand, a group might provide valuable experience for interpersonal learning.

We all agreed that a multidimensional therapy is required and Goldstein emphasized the importance of group therapy as one element in this array of methods. He emphasized that group techniques can augment the transfer of learning outside of the therapeutic situation by permitting the opportunity for trial behaviors. In addition, the group can put considerable social pressure on a person to try new behaviors on the outside. Also there are various opportunities for interpersonal learning which are highly relevant for those who distort their interpersonal behavior and are not ordinarily receptive to social feedback. He noted that it is important not only to ask which therapy, but also *when.* He pointed out that some of his cases graduate from individual therapy to group therapy and then to a modified form of group therapy which meets by itself in alternate sessions. Thus, the point in time at which one employs a given method will be dictated by the status and direction of movement of the particular patient or his particular problem.

Bergin introduced the intensive, case-by-case, experimental type of clinical study which recently has occupied our attention as a means of developing new techniques. Arnie said, "I don't like it." He admitted that his reaction may partially be a function of a prejudice because this kind of investigation does not fit the statistical model of group comparisons in which we have been reared. Secondly, he considered it unlikely that the results of such studies would prove additive in the sense of lending themselves to generalizations even about particular types of individuals or specific target problems. He suggested that it may be appropriate to use a methodology like this but not as an exclusive strategy. He questioned whether it would be workable on anything but a very small scale, and suggested that while this approach may be important during initial stages, broader trials involving groups of subjects and therapists would be necessary. He also suggested that it is important not to restrict ourselves to one or two strategies. It is more important to find an effect via several methodologies and thus to demonstrate the effect of a given variable which might have greater power.

An extended discussion ensued about the feasibility of collaborative studies. Arnie's extensive experience with Lorr's group at the Veterans Administration provided rich material, including the enormous difficulties with which any such efforts are inevitably beset. Arnie's account amply corroborated the requirements for such undertakings which we had previously considered, such as: (1) strong common interests among the participating investigators; (2) willingness to subordinate personal interests to the group effort; (3) necessity for each participant to get important returns for his investment of time, effort, and energy (which need not be the same for all collaborators); (4) wholehearted commitment and—perhaps most important—(5) the personal integrity of each participant. Such a combination is exceedingly hard to achieve although it may not be impossible.

Arnie suggested that a few hypotheses might thus be tested in different settings, such as private practice, clinics, colleges, and the like. He thought the idea of different settings preferable to a central institution. He notes that people in different settings tend to get results in keeping with their own biases. Perhaps collaborative studies would get closer to scientific truth. Again, the goal would be to become more *client-specific* and determine where something works and where it doesn't. On the whole, Arnie seemed very favorably disposed to the general idea of collaborative research although he is fully aware of the obstacles which need to be overcome. If the obstacles could be overcome, such studies would contribute to "the larger good," have the potential of "removing blinders" (by studying a given problem in different settings), and possibly produce more than could be done through individual studies.

He believes that complexity is not necessarily a stumbling block to investigation and much of the so-called complexity is expendable for research purposes. By maximizing or minimizing particular therapeutic conditions we can learn not only about effects but also about interactions. Strupp likened this to manipulating systematically the rheostat on a sun lamp to observe the degree of tanning or other changes in the subject. In building "ideal therapies," Arnie feels, it is necessary to provide different *levels* of a variable, by which he specifically does not mean varying the *time* dimension, as has often been done by researchers in the past, perhaps because it is convenient to manipulate. Frank's study which provided different forms of therapy and compared outcomes comes closer. He also thinks that this kind of research which is characterized by successive approximations has promise for collaborative work.

Returning to the complexity issue, it seemed to us that even in a collaborative study it will be necessary to focus on a few important variables in several centers, variables which have a reasonable chance to account for a substantial portion of variance in outcome, perhaps 30%. In the course of the discussion we began to ask ourselves "30% of what?" What goals do we have in mind? How differentiated are they from person to person? Strupp restated in some detail the enormous problems involved in reducing the subjectivity and complexity of therapeutic phenomena to something that is scientifically manageable. This critical appraisal had a temporary depressing effect on us, and we all responded with various proposals for overcoming these obstacles.

1. Strupp suggested that we should first set goals that are realistic for therapeutic change. To this end, we must divest ourselves of unrealistic expectations that in ten hours we can change a human being. In medicine, we do not ordinarily expect to change a lifetime of pathology in a brief period, or necessarily at all.

Because of the rudimentary character of research in the area it is incumbent upon everyone to have relatively modest expectations of any study or series of studies. Just as the *furor sanandi* on the part of many therapists is a serious impediment, the zeal of certain investigators to solve a problem conclusively is similarly misplaced and out of keeping with reality.

2. It seemed that there may also be a relevant versus an irrelevant kind of complexity. It is important for us to formulate hypotheses regarding what types of complexity are relevant and which types we can safely ignore. In this regard, it may be possible to mount a program of research which covers a broad spectrum of pathologies by isolating relevant themes in each form of pathology and experiment with various interventions with each one. This is a return to the concept of doing an experimental psychotherapy in a repeated single case design. It would have the advantage of permitting isolation of one or two variables at a time and testing their effects. Thus, it would presumably be possible to build, bit by bit, new variables into these methods or interventions until we have a new technique. The research strategy, too, would be one of direct technique building.

3. Goldstein suggested that we look for change processes in the experimental literature, the clinical literature, and in "nature," meaning the social milieu. By thus tapping diverse processes and studying change across therapies and nontherapies we may have the greatest potential for finding payoff variables. Strupp suggested that in a sense psychotherapy may be a good ana-

logue. That is, we should look for change in nature and then use therapy as an analogue to nature, an artificial setting in which we experiment with natural change processes.

What is needed, in Arnie's view, is a *program* of research, which of necessity calls for a *long-term commitment* on the part of the participants. The starting point for such a program should *not* be psychotherapy-as-it-is-currently-practiced. We inferred that Arnie would assign low priority to research of the naturalistic process of psychotherapy.

Arnie distinguished the search for variables from the search for research strategies. With regard to the selection of variables, which need to be made patient-specific, we are not starting from "scratch"; as a matter of fact (and as our survey has shown), the literature provides some very promising leads. We might find patients of a given type, therapists of a given type, and patient-therapist interactions of a given type. Research then might take the form of "guided clinical observation." Strupp continued to be troubled by the difficulty of getting investigators subscribing to very different working assumptions to agree on any "type" of homogeneity, but perhaps it is not hopeless. A case in point would be agreement on a phobia seen as a form of behavior viewed in isolation versus a phobia regarded as the focal point of an underlying dynamic process.

Allen observed that in any science the phenomena can be reduced to manageable variables; even if the measures are crude, it is possible to "get hold of something."

At various points reference was made to *situational tests* for the purpose of assessing behavior and attitude change in which the patient's performance is studies in standardized situations. Arnie considers data obtained from parents, spouses, and others, as potentially promising. In view of his conviction that many therapeutic changes are highly subjective and by no means confined to overt behavior, Strupp had reservations about the extent to which such data can be useful. It must be considered, too, that a patient's "improvement," as seen by himself or his therapist, may be perceived as undesirable by his spouse whose domineering tendencies, for example, may have been thwarted.

How do the researcher's activities coincide with (or diverge from) those of the clinician? In a paper published in 1968, Arnie has cogently advocated the position that "the investigation and practice of psychotherapy are largely equivalent processes" (p. 15). Table 4.1 further documents Arnie's argument. This paper, clearly, has far-reaching implications for the problems we are exploring. Research in this area can make an important contribution, not through discoveries of new techniques or modifications of existing ones, but through more precise and systematic observations of the therapeutic process and its outcome. This statement does not preclude experimental variations of, say, a given technique variable (see the sun lamp analogy) or the

Table 4.1 Procedures and Course of Inference in Practice and Research

PROCEDURE	CLINICIANS	RESEARCHERS
1. Search for regularities	Within a patient	Across patients
2. Tentative prediction based on observed regularities	Within a patient	Across patients
3. Trial Intervention	Tentative interpretation or other planned therapist intervention	Pilot study
4. Initial test of prediction	Therapist's judgment of patient reaction to trail intervention	Analysis of pilot data
5. Decision regarding further potential of prediction	Based upon initial test of prediction	Based upon initial test of prediction
6. Revision and restatement of prediction	Based upon initial test of prediction	Based upon initial test of prediction
7. Standardization of data-gathering procedures	Free association, reflection of feeling, etc.	Selection of psychometric or other measurement devices
8. Manipulation of independent variable	Interpretation or other planned therapist intervention (Overlaps with step 7)	Manipulation of independent variable across patient sample
9. Measurement on dependent variable	Therapist's judgment of patient reaction to intervention	Scores on psychometric or other measurement devices
10. Decision regarding prediction	Based upon step 9	Based upon statistical analysis of step 9 and statistical confidence limits
11. Replication	"Working through" with same patient	With other patient samples
12. Generalization	To other aspects of the same patient's behavior and, at times, to other patients in his practice	To other patients in the universe sampled

We are not proposing that all therapies involve all steps indicated, nor in the exact sequence presented. Neither are we proposing that all research programs are either similarly inclusive or ordered. The steps and sequence represent more of a model or abstraction, most of whose steps find characteristic expression—in the general sequence presented—in both practice and research.

Manipulation is used here in its broadest sense and subsumes any planned, deliberate therapist activity which is purposefully employed for its intended effects on patient behavior. Thus, not only are interpretations, therapist role playing, and other overt therapist behaviors manipulation, but so are silence, restatement of content, simple acknowledgments, and other more passive therapist behaviors—when used in such a planned manner.

SOURCE: Goldstein, A. P. 1968. Psychotherapy research and psychotherapy practice: Independence or equivalence? In S. Lesse, ed., *An evaluation of the results of the psychotherapies*. Springfield, Illinois: Thomas, p. 13.

study of selected therapists who may naturally differ in terms of specifiable dimensions. For well-known reasons such comparative studies cannot be precise but they can provide approximations.

In the evening we become embroiled in an animated discussion centering around the topic of "the psychotherapy of the future." Parts of this, unfortunately, went unrecorded and it proved difficult to reconstruct the interchange.

Bergin expressed the view that the psychotherapy of the future will involve to a much lesser extent the traditional patient-therapist relationship, and he envisions "something mechanical" instead. He believes that a technology of behavior change without a relationship is possible. In his view, we need to decide what the patient "needs" and then dispense it systematically. This would entail the development of a sophisticated pairing process. The therapist, in the contemporary sense, might be the "supervisor" of the process rather than carrying it out himself, and greater emphasis would be placed on indigenous helpers. Commenting on a contrasting point of view advanced by Arnie (referring to the polarity of such contemporaneous orientations as behavior therapy and humanistic therapy), Bergin observed that in his judgment the self-actualization of normal (?) people cannot be regarded as falling within the province of psychotherapy. He also noted that "the learning approaches to psychotherapy are blossoming handsomely." While Arnie conceded that this might be an accurate "reading of the cards" and that his own research might be contributing to a mechanization of psychotherapy, he said he didn't like it.

Comments by Strupp. While not a perfectly faithful résumé of our interview, the report gives an inkling of the trend of our discussion. Personally, I believe that psychotherapy, at least in part, calls for the development of a technology, but I don't see how such a technology can be effectively applied without the context of an interpersonal relationship. It would take up too much space to develop my views, but basically I still adhere to the position I expressed some ten years ago that I regard the therapist's contribution as both personal and technical. It is of interest to note that Wolpe, as much as Freud, stresses the *technical* aspects of therapy, whereas Rogers and the existential-humanistic schools emphasize the *personal* ones. Personally, I regard the (ideal) therapist as a specialist in decoding implicit messages and strategies which emerge in the transference. In addition to his role as an expert in fouled-up human communications he provides the patient with a corrective emotional experience through his attitude of respect, tact, understanding, and other patterns which can serve the patient as a model. This has very little to do with "healing" (except in a metaphoric sense) but a great deal with teaching and learning.

One important purpose served by this (sometimes polemical) discussion was the extent to which it made explicit great variations among the participants in the basic assumptions about science, psychology, psychotherapy, and the nature of man. Such assumptions will inevitably permeate any collaborative research that might be undertaken, and they need to be dealt with in some effective manner if such projects are to bear fruit. Potentially, they are a source of difficulty which must be added to the more obvious ones which have been mentioned. But in the final analysis we are dealing here with the motivations and philosophical commitments of the researcher which are deeply rooted in his autobiography. At best, much patience, understanding, and reasonableness are needed to work through these differences. In principle, this feat should be possible; whether it can be accomplished in practice is a question which I can only raise.

Comments by Bergin. In addition to the foregoing thematic discussions, there were a number of incidental significant points which are listed below.

1. In light of the book which he has recently written, Goldstein appeared to be surprisingly humanistic and existentially oriented. He pointed out that he used to think that the personal impact of the therapist accounted for only a small percentage of patient change while technique accounted for most; but he now feels that the opposite is true. He also indicated that we are "still in the Dark Ages" in this field, a point with which we tended to agree.

2. He made the significant point that individuals like Leary, Rogers, Schutz, have left the university setting. Whatever other reasons led to their decision, they evidently felt that the important variables do not lie in analogue research, in the laboratory, or in the traditional clinical settings. Goldstein tends to think that our current measures of therapy outcome are questionable in light of the importance of variables like those on which these individuals focus.

Arnie views psychiatrists as the "prime change agents today" and enjoys talking to them and following their work. The university setting places an undue emphasis on the "publication game," often at the expense of creativity. Arnie himself confessed a keen personal interest in the kinds of therapeutic approaches currently grouped under the heading of "humanistic," although in his research he remains committed to the program outlined so well in the book by Goldstein, Heller, and Sechrest (1966).

3. There was a brief but very important discussion of the professional and social reward system that impinges upon our research efforts. It was agreed that people often live a kind of schizophrenic existence in the academic community. They frequently produce quite a bit of research in areas

that make grinding out research reasonably fast and easy, although they really prefer to be doing something else and in fact do as much as they can of this something in their spare time. Strupp agreed that there was a kind of duplicity in the academic subculture in which the powers that be pretend that academic faculty really want to do the kind of research they are doing and at the rate they do it. The faculty engage in the same kind of fakery. Because of this need to survive and advance oneself, there are real limitations to much of the research that is done and the journals tend to be filled with rather good counterfeits of true inquiry. We cannot let ourselves forget that these are significant issues as we proceed with our work.

4. Goldstein suggested an interesting idea for testing the effects of expectancies regarding the charisma of the therapist. He said why not name four people "Albert Ellis" and randomly assign patients to them who know of Ellis through his writings. We could then test the effect of expectations versus real charismatic influence by comparing results with these different people.

5. If we conduct experimental therapy it is very important to have objective observers watching what is being done.

6. Arnie reconfirmed his interest in contributing to a *broad psychology of behavior change.* As he put it: "I am interested in change processes. Period." Thus he is eager to look closely at all forms of the influencing process and resulting behavior changes.

7. It may be that we are 50 years too early in trying to build the ideal psychotherapy.

8. In implementing a research strategy, the important question is whether we want to homogenize cases or randomize cases. By collaborating, we can increase our *n* sufficiently to randomize if we want to. Although we argued that multifactorial designs yield weak results, Goldstein emphasized the importance of being able to study interactions. He pointed out that once interactions are discovered, even if they are weak, we can proceed to study individual differences in sequel experiments and that we may obtain through these interactions intuitive notions as to which people respond best under which conditions.

9. An interesting suggestion made by someone during the discussion was that if a variable is effective we should be able to show that different amounts of it have different effects. This of course implies a kind of mathematical sophistication and control over variables which it may be quite unrealistic to expect at this point.

10. It seems that there are enough variables occurring in behavioral change that we may need to work closely with experts in biology, sociology and mathematics in order to accomplish the most with the least waste.

11. It became entirely clear to us during this discussion that we must

propose a program of research and not one, two or three particular designs. At least in outline we must have in mind the characteristics of a series of studies leading toward particular goals. The importance of designing a *program* is a point which we must not lose sight of, for it is becoming increasingly evident that this is what is called for more than a single collaborative strategy at one point in time. Of course, we must also reckon with the limitations of our own prophetic powers in relation to the problems of forecasting what kind if a program or series of studies will yield the greatest payoffs with the best economy.

References

Goldstein, A. P. 1968. Psychotherapy research and psychotherapy practice: Independence or equivalence? In S. Lesse ed., *An evaluation of the results of the psychotherapies.* Springfield, Illinois: Thomas, pp. 5–17.

Goldstein, A. P., Heller, K., & Sechrest, L. B. 1966. *Psychotherapy and the psychology of behavior change.* New York: Wiley.

Schofield, W. 1964. *Psychotherapy: The purchase of friendship.* Englewood Cliffs, N.J.: Prentice-Hall.

INTERVIEW: GERALD C. DAVISON AND BERNARD WEITZMAN*

New York, January 3, 1969

The first part of the meeting[13] involved a discussion of Bernie's views concerning psychotherapy and psychotherapy research and his atttempts to develop new therapeutic techniques which merge analytical, client-centered, and behavioral methods. He indicated that he is presently "way beyond" his *Psychological Review* paper (1967) which first brought him to our attention. He emerged as a therapist with strong Jungian leanings (evidenced in part by a recent sabbatical at the Jung Institute at Zurich), very sympathetic to the ideas of Gene Gendlin, Fritz Perls, and Charlotte Selver, and interested in the methods of Joseph Wolpe.

The focus of the discussion was on patients who have anxiety symptoms. Weitzman goes along with Wolpe et al. in classifying a large spectrum of symptoms as essentially phobic responses. For example, he treats classical resistance and dream resistance as phobic responses by attempting a modified desensitization with the patient when such resistances appear.

* Dr. Davison is Associate Professor of Psychology at the State University of New York at Stony Brook; Dr. Weitzman is with the New School for Social Research.

13. These consultants were interviewed in a joint session.

He attempts to heighten a person's ability to discern organic experiences as a way of accelerating and deepening the effect of the desensitization process. In addition he feels that this procedure produces symbolic consequences that give a sense of meaning to the therapeutic process which is absent in routine desensitization. The importance of this meaning cannot be underestimated, according to Weitzman, because the sense of purpose and self-identity which emerges is the most critical element in his therapy.

Weitzman's procedure consists first of attending to bodily experience via what is called "sensory awareness experiments." This is an approach to sensory experience taught by Charlotte Selver. Essentially, it is designed to heighten the person's awareness of what he is currently experiencing, on both a somatic and feeling level. Allen characterized the approach as "the essence of subjectivism."

In one series of experiments, the patient might be asked to close his eyes and sequentially focus upon various parts of his body while the therapist asks him to attend to sensations such as movements, tensions, differences in pressure and temperature, and the like, which might arise from these parts of the body. It is essentially a way of inviting a person to become more conscious of his body and in this sense is similar to the relaxation induction procedure typically used by behavior therapists. One important difference is that instructions to relax are not explicitly given, rather just instructions to attend to certain portions of the body. This seems to induce relaxation as a by-product of focusing on sensations, as was noted by the three of us when we personally closed our eyes and responded to Weitzman's instructions. The difference between this and the more typical kind of relaxation is that it seems to be highly toned rather than the flaccid, sleepy kind of relaxation which is frequently induced during behavior therapy.

A more crucial consequence of the procedure is that when one simultaneously attends to felt somatic events and one's feelings images and ideas arise from the felt state. Monitoring these, one discovers something that "fits" and is "just right." Concomitantly, an associative network unfolds and a reorganization occurs. This process puts the person in touch with himself; it is an organismic experience and akin to the "aha" phenomenon of Gestalt psychology. This is important because it is the key to a kind of experiencing and symbolizing which forms the basis for therapeutic change. For example, the patient may be asked to visualize the highest item on an anxiety hierarchy (Weitzman always begins with the highest item in doing or conducting this procedure). While visualizing the scene, the patient is then instructed to focus on what is happening throughout his body. The theory is that as one does this he is focusing on his organic experiences in such a way that they give rise to new symbols. This means that body awareness becomes a source of imagery. If thoughts arise during this process the patient permits them to pass through but he is instructed not to start *thinking.*

In addition to the new experiences, symbols, or insights which occur, there appears to be a simultaneous desensitization of anxiety associated with the initial stimuli presented to the patient. Weitzman notes that he often has the patient proceed for a 15 minute period of silent focusing under relaxation. He claims that in several instances it has seemed that more change has occurred under silence than when the person talks about a specific feeling.

Apparently a key to this process is the ability of the patient to focus on the train of experience that is stimulated by the introduction of the hierarchy item.

In this connection, Weitzman noted the important influence of Gendlin's focusing paradigm which he felt held a great deal of promise. Gendlin's *Focusing Manual* (Gendlin et al., 1968) provides guidelines for content-free interviews, which Bernie favors. The capacity to focus, according to him, is an important prerequisite to successful psychotherapy. Reference was made to a study by Gendlin in which he compared two groups, one of which was instructed to verbalize their feelings continually, the other being asked to attend silently to their feelings. The silent group obtained a stronger desensitization effect. Weitzman and Gendlin seemed to feel initially that this focusing ability was a constant capacity that could not be changed. Gendlin argued that level of focusing ability was an excellent predictor of therapeutic outcome. Weitzman seems to agree with this but believes from his experience that he can train people to focus. The process of teaching this ability or refining it along with the other training techniques that take place seems to amount to a kind of "pre-therapy" therapy. This is reminiscent of Goldstein's work in that Arnie believes that a large percentage of patients need a substantial training period in order to become ready for the "higher" levels of therapy. Weitzman points out that if a person can be hooked into this focusing and sensory awareness procedure, he can then proceed to do a good deal of it himself. The idea is that this makes the person permeable to his own inner processes.

Bernie has encountered many patients who couldn't visualize or had a deficient capacity for "focusing" in Gendlin's sense. He has also dealt with "rejects" from other forms of therapy. He finds that by following this procedure even rejects and other poor risks can be made amenable to psychotherapy. Bernie considers the reclamation of poor therapy risks "the most exciting thing" he can think of in psychotherapy. Once the patient is put in closer touch with his own feelings he becomes his own therapist. Bernie also uses the focusing procedure as an introduction to ordinary face-to-face therapy. The emphasis rests on the patient's current experiencing: "How does it feel right now?" (Incidentally, this emphasis is also used by orthodox analysts for the purpose of studying transference feelings.) Bernie discusses with the patient only those feelings which arouse anxiety in the present context and, as indicated above, he begins with the *highest* item in an anxiety hierarchy.

Bernie believes that the ability to focus or "organismically experience" is autonomous and omnipresent but in many patients it is "clogged" or "blocked." This seems similar to Reich's notions of "character armor," which Bernie acknowledged to be the case. Inability to affirm reality and the self is "the problem of our time," according to Bernie. He tries to grasp the needs of the patient's inner life and helps him to create his personal mythology. The traditional dyadic group is a weak "self-confirmer"; a therapy group a stronger one; and society is the strongest. Thus encounter groups and the like have much to offer.

Weitzman has also done a good deal of classical desensitization with patients and found it quite successful. Bernie sometimes uses desensitization selectively early in therapy and then collects dreams. The purpose of the latter is to detect "objections from the unconscious." In practice he finds few. He asserted that he cannot think of a single anxiety situation which cannot be treated effectively with the desensitization procedure. In some instances the results are nothing short of "miraculous," a somewhat startling statement for a person who has been so involved in being analyzed and doing analysis. He gave some fairly dramatic illustrations of the effects of desensitization of phobic or anxiety responses. These were made more impressive by the fact that he used it as a last resort with patients who were just not getting better. Even though he and the patient in one instance were extremely skeptical about what they were doing they were amazed to find the patient's symptoms simply disappear. He says the experience was almost like magic. In fact, this is something that bothers him about typical desensitization. He feels that his own procedure adds a sense of meaning and personal control to the process of desensitization which makes patients feel a lot better about it and less inclined to feel that some kind of magic has been performed on them.

In the kind of therapy Bernie practices he hopes the patient will eventually do his own interpretation. In answer to a question raised by someone in the group Bernie stated that the focusing procedure by and large does not cause the patient to feel that "magic" is involved.

Weitzman notes that transference kinds of insight occur as a result of his procedure. Bergin has also noted a similar type of abreactive response to his modified desensitization procedure, and was inclined to agree that significant insights can *follow* from desensitization. Weitzman also noted that he has become quite a silent therapist. Interpretations are generated by the patient and seem to be more profound. The patient must do his own self-analysis and Bernie encourages him to do so.

Weitzman has seen one case of character disorder change under desensitization but it is the only one he has ever seen. He doubts that this procedure is very relevant for such people. He notes that with obsessionals he has had zero success and reports Wolpe mentioning the same finding.

He noted that in the ordinary desensitization process many patients have great difficulty holding the image that is presented in the hierarchy item. This is a crucial issue, as Davison pointed out. If patients are not literally holding to the image that is presented to them then the change process taking place cannot be literally anything like a conditioning process. Everyone seemed to agree on this point except Bergin. He believes that if one can induce a *process* in the patient by virtue of employing the hierarchy item as a stimulus, this makes the conditioning all the more effective. The point is that if the stimulus produces affective and symbolic experiences which tend to shift and proliferate as the person concentrates on them, then the counter-conditioning tends to be the totality of experiential elements surrounding the incident described by the hierarchy item. This should make desensitization more profound and more generalizable outside of the consulting room.

There was considerable debate over whether the image does shift or not. Davison does not believe that it does. Weitzman claims that it happens frequently in his clinical experience. This is a point of great import which could be studied experimentally in order to come to some conclusion about the nature of this mysterious process called "desensitization" which originally seemed to be so explicit and operationally defined. It looks as though the behaviorists have quickly found themselves, by necessity, totally immersed in the subjective experience of the patient.

Weitzman pointed out that with all of his cases he now induces relaxation via sensory awareness training, then trains the patient in focusing and then requires communication of the present felt experiences. He often initiates this from the very beginning of therapy. He then also responds to a certain extent with his own personal reactions. These include reactions and suggestions which are straightforward and concrete. He does not play the kinds of games which analysts do with the patient's content. He also does the desensitization face-to-face, focusing on one anxiety hierarchy at a time and beginning with the highest item. The latter is another crucial point. It appears from the work of Weitzman, Stampfl, and others that beginning with the item lowest in the anxiety hierarchy may not be crucial in the desensitization process. The one thing everyone seems to be agreed on is that there is a powerful process going on here, whatever it is.

Weitzman emphasized repeatedly the importance of meaning and a sense of community. He feels that the largest portion of the pathology which we see today arises from a lack of sense of confirmation of self and a lack of sense of community or identification with a group. He sees the Esalen Institute as a response to this but it is only a stop-gap. He therefore believes that some type of social change is needed which will create a greater sense of personal identification with the community and an opportunity for each person to repeatedly affirm his own identity. He believes that dyadic therapy provides an opportunity for this but that group and encounter therapy are even more relevant.

He believes that therapy and the community must be designed so as to create personal "myths." He is very hung up on this "meaning" and "selfhood" problem. He feels that anomie and alienation are the central sicknesses we live with. As long as these problems permeate society, the effects of individual therapy must be tenuous. Treatment then tends to be like going to a gas station to get fueled up for the next few days. To counter this he has wanted to use eight or nine patients from the same neighborhood in group therapy. He feels this might yield the highest sense of reality and self confirmation. He thinks this kind of thing could become the nucleus or source of a real sense of community.

The following suggestions were made by Weitzman as inquiries leading to potentially high pay-off:

1. Gendlin's focusing manual as a measure and prognostic indicator especially for the Rogerian kind of encounter. Will it predict outcome elsewhere?

2. Is Weitzman's training method effective in making good risks out of poor therapy risks?

3. Does capacity to carry experiencing forward differentiate good and bad therapy patients? When both the ability to focus on bodily experience and the ability to carry this experience forward into new symbolizations are high, positive outcome is a result. When both are low, outcome is negative.

4. Can people who are able to focus also communicate effectively?

5. Are focusing ability and empathic ability related? Are both necessary for therapeutic success? Study the patient-therapist interaction to find therapists who can engage in their own inner processes. These may be the good therapists. It is also possible that some therapists may be able to "focus" but they may not be able to communicate this understanding effectively to the patient.

6. What can we learn from encounter group research? Is this an important key to treating a large percentage of the kinds of problems we are facing today?

As the discussion progressed, research problems surrounding desensitization came under scrutiny. Jerry noted that Wolpe's descriptions of the process are not nearly specific enough and much work is needed to discover the mechanisms operating in desensitization because it does seem to be a useful procedure, even in its present rudimentary form. For instance, there may be a difference whether the patient who is afraid of cats imagines a kitten or a large cat, yet this is usually left out of the account. The problem of *generalization* thus appears to be a highly important area of investigation. This refers not only to desensitization but to any situation which is discussed, clarified, interpreted, or what-not in therapy. As Goldstein et al. have observed, we know next to nothing about how therapeutic learning is applied outside the consulting room. It is certainly conceivable that such translations can be expedited. Role playing in therapy perhaps comes closest to the real-life situation which, after all, is the ultimate proving ground.

Davison pointed out that he does not see the same phenomena during desensitization that Weitzman does. He believes that the visual image does "stick"; although he notes that he personally tends to use specific procedures for insuring that this happens. This may not be the case with other therapists. Davison points out that he writes out his items on cards, as opposed to Wolpe's rather vague items. For example, in treating a woman with a fear of cats, it turned out that she feared only big fat cats and not other kinds of cats. He has also discovered that it is important to specify the time of day, the social context, and the like, before an item is truly effective. He conceded, however, that in order to prove that a visualization can be held static for more than a few seconds, a careful experiment needs to be conducted. He indicated that if the stimulus cannot be held static, then this is embarrassing for behavioral therapy and theory. It would mean that there is a self-generated flow of images rather than a stimulus induced by therapist or experimenter. He would be willing to test this via subjective report, at least at the beginning. Jerry believes that analogue research has a "certain utility" and that there is a great need for studying process questions raised by a particular technique. He thinks we need no more new ideas with respect to technique and he is opposed to large-scale comparative studies (everybody seems to be) which he sees as unfeasible and even if feasible as not providing any penetrating results. We need to answer such questions as: What goes on in desensitization? What is "reflection of feeling" anyway? Is it a form of reinforcement as Truax implies? Does relaxation interfere with "holding" an image? Furthermore, he noted that human beings do not condition aversively. The exploration of cognitive variables in desensitization impresses him as another important research problem, on which he and Stuart Valins are currently making some inroads. Bergin stated that desensitization cannot be regarded as a specific denotative term; rather it is a broader process. Jerry feels that these questions can be profitably studied without going into the clinical setting.

It is crucial to arrive at better definitions of what different people mean by "psychotherapy." Bernie, for example, feels that psychotherapy is not "the business of symptom relief." He wants to help the patient get to know himself better and for this purpose engages him in a relationship. He feels he offers the patient "options" and defines himself as a participant. In this context he criticized the analysts for not squarely facing the problem of symptom improvement. Jerry disagreed with Bernie's definition of psychotherapy and seemed to feel that symptom improvement was indeed an important goal in itself. It could be that every therapist is basically doing desensitization but calls it by a different name.

The refinement of desensitization procedures and their broader applications was stressed repeatedly, especially in the area of psychosomatic medicine. For example, the technique might be employed very fruitfully with surgery patients suffering from preoperative anxiety which is a major killer. The technique also holds promise with patients suffering from such conditions as neurodermatitis in which repressed or suppressed anger demonstrably plays an important role. Weitzman noted the Schoenberg-Carr (1963) study at the Columbia Psychiatric Institute in which desensitization of fear of expressing anger yielded dramatic results in cases of neurodermatitis. He notes he has had a similar dramatic case. He also claims that he believes he can reduce and possibly remove many migraine headaches in five minutes using the sensory awareness approach. Quite a claim! Some forms of epileptic attacks, too, appear to have onsets triggered by phobias.

Jerry expressed himself in favor of laboratory studies of basic changes which derive from behavioral situations. He believes Gordon Paul's study (1966) was very good and timely when it was done. He now believes that we should work with greater precision in the laboratory, possibly not with patients. He is willing to ignore the complexity but is mindful of it. (In this connection, it is highly important to note the continued interest and immersion in clinical practice on the part of many researchers we have consulted. Clinical work keeps them both interested in, and attuned to, the "complexity bugaboo," besides providing other stimulations and benefits.) Research can help the therapist by informing him what we know about change processes and in this way research can influence clinical practice (?).

Bernie, on the other hand, regarded collaborative studies as "possible" and advocated the formation of small groups of researchers ("cells") who might work together on given problems. Thus a communicative network involving clinicians and researchers might come into being. He also mentioned the desirability of some kind of research and therapy institute to which visiting researchers might come.

Davison gave some further illustrations of the kinds of research he would like to see conducted:

1. He would like to see more research done with aversive conditioning. He would like to know what happens if one reverses the temporal relationship of the conditioned stimulus and the unconditioned stimulus. He points out that humans do not seem to condition aversively in the same way that animals do, and yet he is puzzled as to why aversive conditioning seems to take place in the clinical situation. He is presumably hinting at some symbolic process which makes the temporal relationship of CS and UCS insignificant.

2. He would like to see a comparison of a cognitive desensitization process with a behavioral desensitization process. He feels that it is very important to answer from a scientific viewpoint just how powerful cognitions are in desensitization. He feels that it is essential to conduct preliminary explo-

rations of this question in the laboratory. He notes that he believes the work of Nisbett at Yale, Schachter at Columbia, and Valins at Stony Brook will be among the most exciting of the next ten years because they focus on exactly this problem. He gave an illustration of Valins' work in which the patients were given false heart-rate feedback while watching snakes approach them. In a preliminary treatment the patients had observed their own heart rates increase while they were given shocks; but while they watched the snakes approach them their heart rates did not change. This seemed to result in rapid deconditioning. He also pointed out that Lazarus conducts a type of cognitive rehearsal in order to reduce responses to stress in life situations. In this connection he asked whether thought disorder (schizophrenia) might be made amenable to desensitization. He feels that a series of experiments on schizophrenia is of high priority. If any breakthrough on schizophrenia can be achieved via desensitization it would be a great contribution. (Brave New World!)

3. He believes that the primary question now is to answer what the mechanisms are. He feels the same with regard to empathy, a most important observation.

Davison offered the observation that one reason that the impact of research on practice has been poor is because training has been poor. If training included a proper connection between the research evidence and practice, there would be a more direct influence of research on practice. It seems that this moves the issue one step back, namely, why doesn't research have an effect on training?

Davison next responded to a number of questions in our "Questions for Consultants." He said he did not think it would pay off to study the live process of therapy as it is traditionally conducted. He thinks we should focus on basic change processes, through analogues, quasi-therapy situations and laboratory studies. We do not need more hypothesis-generation: "Let them arise from our experiments." In this connection, he believes that we can advance best by temporarily ignoring complexities and isolating and manipulating a few variables at a time.

Reiterating his skepticism regarding the possibilities of coordinated or collaborative research, he felt that we tend to disagree too much among ourselves and that people like to do things their own way, that is, to follow their own hunches.

In response to question 5a, he felt that it is impossible to design studies which do justice to the full complexity of therapy. He feels that it is not essential to do this. He does not feel that analogues can be substitutes for this complexity; rather they should permit us to zero-in on elements of that complexity. He responded positively to question 5c and 5d, that intensive single case studies with planned interventions can be quite fruitful.

He also feels that it is possible to observe the therapist and tell him what he is doing. We can then tell him what we know about change and let him devise techniques as he goes along with a case in all of its complexity.

With regard to optimal strategies, Weitzman feels that we need to focus on more than one strategy and do several things at the same time as opposed to Davison's focus on a few simplification strategies.

Comments by Bergin. In general, Weitzman seems to be creatively experimenting with a variety of methods. The possibility of efficiently coalescing some of the fruitful procedures of a variety of techniques is a most stimulating possibility, particularly if such a merging can heighten the efficiency and profundity of therapeutic effects. Personally, I tend to believe that it is Wolpe who has had the creative insight in this area. Many people, such as Weitzman and others, have followed Wolpe and attempted to improve on his method. I think these improvements may be real and may well accelerate our therapeutic effectiveness; but I think it must be recognized that the desensitization process as originally described by Wolpe is the essential ingredient. I am uncertain whether the particular procedures he is using are the key to the results. I am, however, convinced that we do have a hold of a powerful natural process here which has the potentiality of being refined into a potent technique once we know the actual mechanisms operating.

References

Gendlin, E. T., Beebe, J., III, Cassens, J., Klein, M., & Oberlander, M. 1968. Focusing ability in psychotherapy, personality, and creativity. In J. M. Shlien ed., *Research in psychotherapy*. vol. 3. Washington, D. C.: American Psychological Association, pp. 217–41.

Paul, G. L. 1966. *Effects of insight, desensitization, and attention placebo treatment of anxiety*. Stanford, California: Stanford University Press.

Schoenberg, B., & Carr, A. C. 1963. An investigation of criteria for brief psychotherapy of neurodermatitis. *Psychosomatic Medicine* 25: 253–63.

Weitzman, B. 1967. Behavior therapy and psychotherapy. *Psychological Review* 74: 300–317.

INTERVIEW: J. B. CHASSAN *

Union City, New Jersey, January 4, 1969

Introduction. We met with Jack Chassan on January 4, 1969 in Union City, New Jersey, and spent the morning together. By training a statistician,

* Dr. Chassan is Clinical Associate Professor of Statistics in Psychiatry at Cornell University Medical College.

Jack has made significant contributions to statistical designs involving the intensive study of individual cases. Jack and various collaborators have applied these "intensive designs" in drug and psychotherapy studies. His recent book, *Research Design in Clinical Psychology and Psychiatry* (1967), which departs significantly from standard designs in psychological research, has been received very well and holds a good deal of promise for research in psychotherapy. Strupp has known Jack since about 1955 and collaborated in a longitudinal study of three therapy patients who were rated by their therapists on some 30 variables following each hour. Several hundred hours were rated in each case. The study (Strupp, Chassan, and Ewing, 1966), an extension of an earlier investigation by Bellak and Smith (1956), appeared in Gottschalk and Auerbach (1966) and went largely unnoticed. Jack has long been interested in psychotherapy and psychoanalysis and has worked closely with psychiatrists and psychologists. In the recent past he has taken steps to become a therapist himself and is currently enrolled in a postgraduate training program in New York. These points are important for understanding Jack's position with respect to research in psychotherapy and they provide a context for his recommendations.

Interview. Essentially, Jack feels we need a careful naturalistic description of psychotherapy with refined analyses of what occurs in a variety of dyads; and, for some time to come, we must stay within the theoretical framework embraced by particular therapists rather than attempt to formulate general principles and specific operations for effecting change. Jack bases this conclusion on the belief that psychotherapy is at a very early stage of development; consequently, as a first step we must work toward more systematic observations and fuller descriptions of the process. He illustrated his point by comparing the status of the field to the history of astronomy as it developed over a period of two centuries from Tycho Brahe to Kepler to Newton. He argued that we are not in the Newtonian phase and likened the therapy researcher's efforts to the work of Tycho Brahe who spent countless hours on the rooftop of his house observing and recording celestial phenomena. Jack noted drily that everybody these days wants to make breakthrough discoveries in six weeks whereas Brahe spent many years in intensive observations. Does this mean, Strupp wondered, that we should spend two years watching videotapes of psychotherapy? Incidentally, what has happened to the videotaped therapy sessions of Bergman's at NIMH? The lack of information suggests that this work has not had much influence. Obviously, it is Jack's view that in psychotherapy research breakthroughs are not about to be achieved, either now or in a few decades.

In keeping with this position Jack regards psychotherapeutic phenomena as considerably more complex than anything in the natural sciences. Thus, if the psychotherapy researcher is intent upon imitating older and more developed sciences he is barking up the wrong tree and his efforts are foredoomed. This assessment should not be understood as an expression of hopelessness regarding the prospects of research in the area; it is simply realistic. (Strupp is convinced that the disillusionment with the achievements of psychotherapy research around 1960, to which Joe Matarazzo has frequently referred, was largely a function of totally unrealistic expectations on the part of researchers, critics, and granting agencies.)

Chassan suggested there are so many things going on in a therapeutic transaction that one cannot successfully do typical experimental or nomothetic studies at this time. One must study dyads and build from there. He suggested the paradigm of an inverted pyramid or cone, a concept that we have discussed in previous meetings. One would begin by studying the therapy process on a small scale but very intensively, and then proceed to develop a full embracing of the total, complex process. To illustrate this point, Jack noted that there is a lack of enchantment with research in neo-Freudian (as well as Freudian for that matter) therapy not because it is unfruitful or lacks potency but because we are not really describing accurately what is going on. The analytic literature is vague and unfair to the realities. Bergin suggested that we need to abstract and distill dimensions such as Rogers has done with client-centered therapy.

How can this be done? Jack's views may be summarized as follows:

We must start with descriptions that are systematic and superior to the usual case history. Let the therapist record his impressions and observations within each hour; let us note what particular therapeutic events have what particular consequences; let us study regularities as well as discontinuities; let us forget about traditional rating scales which attempt to capture "dimensions" of the therapeutic process; let us examine how long it takes to get from point X to point Y in the treatment of particular patients; let us make counts of the frequency with which particular events occur; let us observe changes in patients' verbalizations and other characteristics; forget about comparisons across theoretical boundaries; and above all, let us not attempt to prove whether one approach is better than another. With regard to the last point Jack feels that *behavior therapists, analysts, or any other therapists will not be impressed with such comparisons nor will they desist from practicing their preferred approach on the basis of research findings.* The fact that they find their respective techniques useful constitutes evidence that there is "something there" and in the end it will all come out "in the wash." Theories in any case have poor communicability and we must deal with events and data.

In short, Jack believes that efforts at *quantifying case histories,* however crudely this may be done, are bound to be rewarding and may lead to new discoveries. To do this, one has no choice but to stay within a given theoretical framework. His plea for *naturalistic* studies of the process was clear, as was his emphasis on the *intensive* study of single dyads. By contrast, we detected little enthusiasm either for analogue research or the kind of intensive-experimental type of study we have frequently talked about in the recent past. The latter resembles that of drug studies, which Jack considers vastly oversimplified. However, he seemed somewhat receptive to an approach in which the therapist might say: "The next time X occurs, I will do Y, and see what happens."

Jack feels that there is considerable substance to dynamic therapy and that it should be a prime object of the foregoing types of inquiry. We should study how transference, resistance, dream analysis and other techniques are tied together.

Within the investigative framework outlined by Jack one might test such fairly specific hypotheses as: What indications are there that psychotherapy will be successful; can one detect indications that therapy will terminate prematurely? (We were reminded of one of Meehl's hypotheses that every time a patient reports a dream involving fire the theme of the hour deals with ambition and shame surrounding it.)

In further discussing these views Chassan asserted that the previous kind of rating scales which have been applied to psychoanalysis are grossly deficient and that they don't fit what is happening. For example, rating an anxiety scale at the end of each session lacks meaning. Strupp pointed out that the scales are based on the wrong model and Chassan agreed heartily. He also pointed out that he is not concerned with the problem of objectivity versus subjectivity per se; this, he thinks, can be resolved although he did not say how. He did say that it is important to conceptualize the complexity of what is going on at one time and over time (in terms of delayed effects and sequential effects). This seems to him an area rich with possibilities because therapy has never been described in detail and therefore at the present time we cannot adequately compare the work of even two therapists.

Chassan suggested that we study therapy done by experts, especially those who work best with given kinds of patients. He gave as illustrations the work of Greenwald, who seems to work well with psychopaths, and Searles, who seems to be highly proficient with ambulatory schizophrenics.

Bergin observed that Rogers spent hundreds of hours listening to tapes, following which he developed his ten process scales. Perhaps there is no other way but to immerse oneself deeply in the process and to abstract from it regularities and consistencies much as Freud, Rogers, and others have done. What one focuses on is the product of one's vision, a hard commodity to come by for the average mortal; but out of this may come some kind of commonality. Individuals who have made significant contributions have succeeded in isolating and abstracting relationships among the phenomena. Bergin suggested that a key problem is indeed the lack of agreed-upon dimensions in psychotherapy and personality. We have had no Fahrenheit to build a scale for us yet.

Strupp suggested that the therapist reacts to a Gestalt in a very complex way. He pointed out that the psycholinguists suggest that Skinner and others have a simplistic, indeed, a wrong model for the complexity of human functioning. We then discussed the issue of isolating dimensions. Bergin compared Freud to Aristotle, arguing that they were both generalists who did not dimensionalize. He pointed out that the great advances in physics and biology came from dimensionalizing and then developing broad systems with commonality. For example, Galileo dimensionalized and then Newton systematized. Chassan and Strupp disagreed. They felt that Freud did isolate dimensions and did attempt to decipher complexity by reducing it to its lowest common denominator.

Jack made the observation (also one of Strupp's pet notions) that "the experiment" may be there (in psychotherapy) without our realizing it. The therapeutic situation, the therapist's relative objectivity and controlled participant observation in analyzing transference phenomena—these may indeed be the essential ingredients of the "psychotherapy laboratory." This experimental situation may be the most important and fruitful "analogue" for the study of interpersonal phenomena we have yet devised; the problem is how to mine the gold that is buried there.

With further reference to this type of study, Strupp argued that even if we proceed with descriptions, everyone seems to look at the phenomena differently. Chassan countered by claiming that people actually are practicing more similarly than it appears. For example, Freud treated phobias about the same way Wolpe does! Furthermore, Greenwald's active therapy technique is not very different from behavior therapy. Strupp then asked, how can we *describe* phenomena without theoretical predilections creeping in? The response was that Tycho Brahe did it. Of course, Tycho Brahe made the observations he did because he had certain ideas in mind ahead of time.

Strupp suggested that it might be possible to get people to agree on a way of conceptualizing therapy for research purposes. Chassan felt that this was impossible and that people needed to work within their own approach. He felt that it would be conceivable to select some homogeneous population, such as unmarried females over 30, and describe what happens to them in therapy. He agreed that control groups generally contributed little to an understanding of this kind of process. He also felt that trying to see which therapy is better is useless. It can't be done. Strupp then asked: "If we lived in the time of Mesmer and were studying his methods, what would we do?" Strupp and Chassan agreed that much of Mesmer's theory and certain parts of Freud's theory are "excess baggage"[14] and that we need to study what therapists do, not what they say they do.

14. Chassan clarifies this point as follows: "I feel somewhat uncomfortable about this 'excess baggage' statement. I don't know if we are actually talking about Freud's theory, or of some relatively minor points of the theory, or some of the ways in which

Jack brought out a variety of additional points which we note here more or less randomly.

He said he had been much impressed by a recent book by Robertiello et al. *The Analyst's Role,* (1963), in which confrontation, oneupmanship and role playing by the analyst were significantly portrayed. This surprised him at first but, as he pointed out, variations and deviations are the rule these days among analytic therapists.

He emphasized the importance of this new directiveness and activeness in psychotherapy. Waiting is rare, unless it is used to induce anxiety. He also pointed out the importance of encounter and other groups, and noted that all of these things must become grist for the research mill. He said that the earlier model of psychoanalysis is no longer recognizable due to the numerous active techniques now going on and he pointed out, interestingly, that psychologists seem to be in the forefront of most of these new techniques.

He also mentioned that the hippies have created a new set of problems for the clinician to which we must become as responsive as we are to the more typical problems that used to come to clinics. He characterizes these people as being "oral" types, that they often lack symptoms other than a certain kind of laziness and indifference to the world. He noted that in treating people like this it is important to nurture the development of a strong positive transference so that they can form some identification with the therapist and hopefully adopt some of his positive values. Parenthetically, he mentioned that he used a word association technique to overcome resistance with a young female patient of this type. For no apparent reason, she had an intense desire to go to Vermont. When he used the word "Vermont," he was able to bring out associations that brought forth her feelings regarding a boyfriend in Vermont and all that this implied.

There was also a despairing discussion of Chassan's work with drugs. He pointed out that clinicians simply can't predict responses to drugs very well: "We have more money and more opportunity and yet we are still not able to simplify enough to make specific predictions from specific interventions in the areas of drug research." Bergin raised the question of whether this meant we should focus on getting general large effects in groups and let this be our payoff, like drug companies do, and spend less time on individual differences or side effects. Chassan argued that we need billions of dollars, perhaps thousands of cases, the equivalent of what is being spent on the Vietnam war, in order to carry out a truly comprehensive program of research in psychotherapy.

---

the theory is applied in the course of psychoanalytic therapy. I would not want my own view to be misunderstood. I feel the main theoretical constructs are sound: the idea of the unconscious, the distinction between primary and secondary process, the mechanisms of defense, transference, resistance and psychodynamics in general are basic to the practice of psychotherapy, that is, to the practice of psychoanalytic psychotherapy."

Chassan offered an interesting idea, that psychotherapy needs its own model of science because it is so complex. It is more complex than biology and it involves values.

He also proposed the creation of an institute for psychotherapy research which might combine training, practice, and research. Such an institute might offer different forms of therapy which might be studied intensively by researchers over prolonged periods. Such an institute might also be a center for visiting scholars and researchers in the area. A similar idea had been proposed by other consultants, and indeed was discussed at some length in a report prepared in the early fifties by Hilgard, Gill & Shakow (1953) for the Ford Foundation, without visible results. The development of many new techniques in recent years and the quickening of the research pace places the idea in a new context and invites reexamination.

Comments by Strupp. Jack's general philosophy about therapy research brought us face-to-face with what Allen has aptly called "the bugaboo of complexity." While personally sympathetic to the naturalistic approach, I have long been troubled by such criticisms as the following: What about the selectivity of process notes? What about the therapist's theoretical biases? What about observer unreliability? How can we deal with the problem of achieving consenus on the complexity of interrelated events? How can we abstract even simple frequencies of particular occurrences from the mass of data? How can we compare one dyad with another? How do they add up? How can we generalize? What constitutes a particular event or phenomenon? What are the units? How can we delineate the boundaries of a phenomenon—when it starts and when it ends? How can we agree on concepts? How is it possible to make observations on which external observers will agree? True, as Jack says, we are always dealing with "the whole person" but that is a truism. We explored these criticisms in some depth but I was not reassured.

Finally, it impresses me that statisticians and specialists in experimental design whom one might expect to place the heaviest emphasis on rigor, quantification, and complex designs are the ones least likely to do so. Therein, I believe, lies a lesson.

Comments by Bergin. I severely questioned whether it is possible to build new techniques out of the natural study of therapy as it exists. It seemed to me that planned intervention and the application of the kind of intensive design which Chassan used in drug studies would be more appropriate. Thus, in order to meet the complexity of therapy, we use the therapy process as our model but we build experimental technique interventions into it. Chassan responded with an elaborate description of what goes on in psychotherapy which amounted to what I considered to be another description of "the bugaboo of complexity." Chassan responded to this by pointing out that dreams which his patients had presented had highly complicated meanings and were interpreted in a complicated way in a multidimensional transaction which had positive results.[15] On this basis, it appears necessary to describe what is happening before we start planning new interventions. My real question is whether there is enough of potency going on in such therapy to make the description worth the time.

It seemed to me at this point that we were again saying that we need some genius with great insight to tell us where the payoff will be. Can we say? Can we play God? Can we reconstruct in the psychological area the sequence of events that took place from Brahe to Kepler to Newton? It seems to me that in the history of therapy and psychology the only people who have made great contributions are those who have isolated and experimented with specific interventions. This was in a sense perhaps Freud's disservice to the field. He was a role model for doing all things at once, in mastering the complexity of life in one total system. This has caused others to try to do likewise and has perhaps retarded the discovery of specific mechanisms. Strupp and Chassan seemed to disagree that this was Freud's influence, although there was no resolution of the question as to whether the greatest contributions have come from those who isolated variables.

This session was probably the most persuasive of all in favor of doing naturalistic, intensive study of the complexity of therapy in order to extract the potent kinds of interventions and dimensions of behavior which produce the most change. While I personally believe that there is a great deal to be gained by naturalistic, educated observations, I seriously doubt that we are

15. Chassan comments: "Actually it seems to me that the order of complexity was not that great. Within the Freudian framework the dreams I had referred to, in the example I gave, all analysts (certainly all Freudian and I would say all neo-Freudian analysts as well) would have agreed were negative transferences from mother onto me as therapist. This was a rather clear tip-off to me in interpreting the transaction in the subsequent interview. It was very clear that the patient thought in entering the office that I would disapprove of her having had fun on a date the night before. In the preceding session, the transference dream was simply that I had yelled at her, told her to shape up, etc. This was very much in the style to which she had been accustomed in relation to her mother—a style which I had never used or even simulated in dealing with her. If she could see me in a dream, yelling at her like her mother, then she could also see me as her forbidding mother in relation to dates. The reason I bring this up is that the level of interpretation was not really deep. I did not interpret the transference, e.g., in terms of competition with mother for father or in any other particularly complex psychosexual developmental construct. What I am also saying is that there may be a lot more agreement on at least some level of interpretation *within* a broad theoretical framework than on some of the more esoteric types of interpretation."

looking in the right place when we look at psychotherapy as it is generally practiced. If naturalistic studies are to be done, I would prefer doing them on a small empirically selected group of highly proficient therapists. In addition I would want to enter into the community and watch for people who are changing and when we find them study them in great detail. This could be done on people who are changing positively and people who are changing negatively. We could look for what seems to be going on and perhaps thus discover in "nature" new dimensions of change. I agree with Hans that psychotherapy is more of an experiment, kind of a natural experiment, but not really "nature in the raw." I would prefer to see us come up with ideas as to what is effecting change and then use the therapy situation as an experiment to test our ideas about change. My own feeling is that most therapists are not very creative and they are not very industrious. I doubt that most of them are at their best most of the time. I also doubt that most of them are having much effect on very many people. I like Chassan's idea, that if we select experts we should select them in part in terms of people they work with best. Thus, we might select some people because they work very well with particular kinds of patients and we might then pair them with exactly these types of persons. I am glad we had a session like this where this point of view was so strongly advocated. Frankly, it did not change my mind very much about the relative virtues of therapy as it is generally practiced; but it did remind me that I do have a commitment to the power of natural observation. I think the crucial issue is where shall we observe and by what intuitions do we guide the selection?

Further Comments by Chassan. Since speaking with you, I have done a little more thinking about intensive-experimental studies, within the context of a given mode of therapy, in relation to intensive-naturalistic studies. I don't think a broad program of research in psychotherapy should necessarily favor one over the other. It would, for example, be ridiculous to impose a naturalistic approach to research upon an experimentally oriented behavior therapist. At possibly the other extreme it would seem to make little sense, at least at the outset, to expect a phenomenologically oriented existential analyst to look at what goes on between him and his patient in an experimental (consciously) manipulatory framework. More generally, however, I consider the naturalistic approach as basic for describing what does appear to happen within one and another context in sequences and over time. In this broad sense, the naturalistic approach to the study of process may also be regarded as preliminary to experimental studies, and suggesting directions for the latter.

Concerning the problem of objectivity and subjectivity, certainly part of the solution lies in consensual validation through the many audio-visual reproductive techniques now available. I would envisage, for example, a panel of expert therapists from a given theoretical persuasion viewing a sequence of psychotherapy sessions with the same patient in which the analyst conducting the therapy is one member of the panel; each member then describing what took place during each session and over the totality of sessions taken as a whole. Then, repeating this with other dyads in which each member of the panel, in turn, is the therapist treating one of his patients. This is, I realize, quite an order, especially if one thinks of applying this to all schools of psychotherapy, and with various classifications of dyads within each approach. The financial requirements for such a program would be astronomical to say nothing of the difficulty in making arrangements, some delicate interpersonal problems that might arise from time to time, and so forth. If this overall procedure would not lead directly to consensual validation, first between therapists of the same general theoretical orientation, and later perhaps across theories, it would at least promote reliable communication between the participants within the framework of the data thus made available. I don't know if all of this is absolutely necessary. It might be worth trying on a smaller scale, but again I would emphasize that in any single group study of this type one has to start out with people who at least speak the same language.

References

Bellak, L., & Smith, M. B. 1956. An experimental exploration of the psychoanalytic process. *Psychoanalytic Quarterly* 25: 385–414.

Chassan, J. B. 1967. *Research design in clinical psychology and psychiatry.* New York: Appleton-Century-Crofts.

Hilgard, E. R., Gill, M. M., & Shakow, D. 1953. *A planning proposal for research in emotional growth and mental health.* New York: Social Science Research Council.

Robertiello, R. C., Friedman, D. B., & Pollens, B. 1963. *The analyst's role.* New York: Citadel Press.

Strupp, H. H., Chassan, J. B., & Ewing, J. A. 1966. Toward the longitudinal study of the psychotherapeutic process. In L. A. Gottschalk & A. H. Auerbach eds., *Methods of research in psychotherapy.* New York: Appleton-Century-Crofts, pp. 361–400.

INTERVIEW: KENNETH MARK COLBY*

Palo Alto, January 15, 1969

Colby's views were most incisive and provocative. His opening statement was, *"I'm not so sure there should be any psychotherapy research."* As a

* Dr. Colby is Senior Research Associate in the Department of Computer Science, Stanford University.

corollary, he asked the question, "Why does NIMH care?" implying that the field is more or less worthless and questioning why a large funding agency should be concerned with it. He then stated that he felt none of the alternatives to psychotherapy research which we had posed in our review paper and in our list of Questions for Consultants were really fruitful. A good deal of time was spent in exploring the bases for these judgments.

In the first place, before we can get anywhere in this area we must have a way of classifying the phenomena with which we propose to deal. Ken pointed out that there are stages in inquiry and that it is difficult to do stage 3 until stage 1 is done. He felt strongly that the classification of disorders comes under the rubric of doing "first things first." In biology, classification in terms of morphological and physiological properties are of great help. In psychiatry, by contrast, we cannot classify behavior in this way nor can we get agreement on behavioral properties. Often this problem is resolved by personal loyalties to particular clinics, people, or schools of thought, or by appeals to authority, as occurs not infrequently when the senior member of a psychiatric team makes the final determination of how the behavior of a given patient shall be classified. He thought it was totally ludicrous that the American Psychiatric Association classification system was developed by voting.

A proper classification system is, however, presently impossible because the necessary bases for adequate descriptions have not been achieved in this area. We cannot expect to formulate viable, functional relationships until proper descriptions, classification, and measurement methods are developed. He declared: "I'd give a lot of money to a study of psychopathology and classification" but implied that he wouldn't give any money to a study of psychotherapy.

He elaborated on this problem at length, emphasizing that everyone runs away from the problem of classification because it is not as interesting or dramatic as studies of therapeutic intervention. He believes that psychoanalysis contributed to this avoidance syndrome because analysts do the same thing with every patient. Added to this must be the fact that the old classification systems were no good. Thus everyone repudiated them, together with any serious attempts at classification. Therefore, what we need is research in psychopathology, which in Ken's opinion may take 500 years to make significant progress. Existing systems of classification, like the Diagnostic Manual of the American Psychiatric Association, are hopeless. Psychiatrists, Ken feels, often confuse classification with the identification of a phenomenon. While the dynamic viewpoint in psychiatry no longer considers classification important, American psychoanalysis nevertheless has "swallowed" the APA Manual. This state of affairs was characterized by Ken as "absurd." Without being able to classify the phenomena in the domain we cannot hope to have "homogeneous" technical interventions. There is at present nothing approximating a homogeneous sample of "schizophrenics" or anything else. Until this problem is clarified, no significant progress may be expected.

For example, if an investigator wants to study fatty acids as a contributor to schizophrenia, he goes to a hospital and selects a hundred schizophrenics. The result is confusion because he has picked an extremely heterogenous population. Nothing of significance can be derived from studies like this because we must have homogenous entities and homogenous intervention in order to deduce anything of scientific value. This, of course, is quite consonant with the main theses of our own paper. Colby's point, however, was somewhat broader in that his argument was based on the idea that improved classification is an essential prerequisite to testing the effects of interventions on specific problems. We must be able to measure what is wrong because we cannot have adequate outcome measures unless we know what is wrong and can measure it. He pointed out that we cannot get agreement on the presence of particular properties of behavior and therefore we can't get agreement on the presence or absence of a given disorder. For example, delusions, anxiety, and depression are notoriously poor terms because they do not denote anything reliably.

Parenthetically, in commenting about Szasz' position, Ken noted that medicine no longer subscribes to the "medical model" of disease. At the same time, we must admit that "disorders" do exist and that people hurt when they seek therapeutic help. Paul Meehl, while keenly interested in problems of taxonomy, is doing it "the wrong way," according to Ken, because he accepts the classification scheme of the MMPI.

After this parenthetical but important discourse on the problem of classification and measurement, Colby launched into a further critique of the status of psychotherapy and psychotherapy research. Ken believes that there is no "standard scientific question" in the sense of "What specific therapeutic interventions produce specific changes in specific patients under specific conditions." One major reason is that psychotherapy is a technology, not a science. The former is characterized by goals, the latter by a subject matter. The problems are entirely different. Bergin considered this a dubious distinction since there seem to be substantial similarities in the processes of inquiry and discovery in both applied and basic science.

Ken pointed out that in the field in general and in our document in particular we have fostered a sense of urgency because patients are suffering and asking for help. He believes that this causes us to get the scientific enterprise out of its natural order, because we are not ready for questions of this type. This, he believes, is made quite obvious by the fact that there are so many unknown variables operating in the therapeutic process. Consequently we cannot study the process with any exactness and we cannot control variables that we don't understand and cannot measure.

He provided an interesting analogy by indicating that trying to answer questions about the therapeutic process was like flipping ping-pong balls out the window and asking a physicist to predict and explain their motion in terms of direction, velocity, etc. This, he said, a physicist would consider impossible because there are too many unknowns influencing the motions of the balls. Similarly, he indicated that the significance of studying a process like this was equivalent to asking a physicist to lie under a tree and attempt to describe the motion and movements of leaves as they fall from the tree. The scientific feasibility and the significance of the two are about equal, he claimed. In the same manner, we cannot study scientifically the therapy process which is a complicated mixture of powerful and poorly regulated unknown variables.

Again, first one needs to have phenomena before one can develop theories, and Ken for one believes that theories cannot be generated within the psychotherapy situation. One reason is that "clinicians don't know what the hell is going on." (The theme that the therapist is often "lost" was echoed also by Greenson and other consultants who qualify as expert therapists and it constitutes a remarkable contrast to the many treatises on psychotherapy from which the novice derives the expectation that the therapist is never, or only rarely, at loose ends.) He pointed out that when he was doing a good deal of clinical work he could give beautiful explanations of what was happening but he knew in his heart that he didn't really know what was happening. He said that when he was really honest with himself, he had to admit that he didn't know what he was doing. He pointed out that when you are getting money for doing something like this, you begin to feel like a quack. He also felt that most therapists recognize, as he did, that some of the people they are treating are getting worse. He indicated that one-to-one therapy did not pay off personally for him and it came to the point where he questioned the value of the activity and then got out. He indicated that when one begins to ask hard questions about therapy it is very difficult to formulate ways of obtaining answers while one is involved in the therapy process: "Patients have a tendency to grind you down and make it difficult to be objective." Furthermore: "It is hard to be scientific when you are doing therapy, particularly when you have one patient who is threatening to commit suicide, another who is going to leave his wife, etc. The therapy situation is not the best place for scientific inquiry or for theory building." Ken is uncertain whether Freud actually got his theories out of his therapy experiences. Colby, at any rate, feels he can generate better ideas via a computer science than via psychotherapy or anything close to it.

The mark of the creative scientist is that he selects only problems he can do something about. He does not rush in where angels fear to tread, and before he tackles a problem he "sniffs around" for a long time until he finds a "soft spot" which he can subject to exact analysis. Nothing of the sort can be done in psychotherapy, since more prior scientific work is needed before we can fruitfully study the art. Citing the situation of Pasteur and the wine makers, of which he is fond, Ken pointed out that (1) Pasteur happened to have a powerful theory which held that if you "boil hell" out of microorganisms, you kill them off, and (2) he identified the problem as one he could do something about. This combination paid off. Why? It paid off because Pasteur had reliable and known variables he could manipulate, such as heat. He simply elevated temperature up to a certain point in order to test his hypothesis and solved the problem in the art of wine making by killing microorganisms. In contrast, Ken pointed out, there are no precise inferences in our documents about what we are trying to explain. Not everything can be a problem at once, we must take one at a time. The art is enhanced only when we have greater scientific knowledge. Hospital records of pneumonia patients years ago were very thick because people collected everything in order to find out what was going on. But today, records of pneumonia patients are very thin because we know that much of the former jargon and description was quite irrelevant. Paradoxically, the more we know, the less we have to know. Scientific progress therefore yields synopsis or condensation, clarification, and precision.

We are not at this stage in psychology and psychotherapy. The difficulties we have in the art are unlikely to yield until we have more basic knowledge. "For example, when I was a young therapist, I had a case in which a guy slept all the time. The question was, what should I do with him? I tried to get help and wished there was a wise old man with 40 years of experience to whom I could go to get answers to questions like this. But there was no one like that. Now people come to me as though I were that kind of person, and I don't have the answers; I don't know what to do."

He gave some interesting analogies as arguments against doing psychotherapy research. He pointed out that if you study the natural therapy situation, you will never find out anything. He gave the graphic example of a Martian coming down to the earth to study the process and effects of medical practice by following a physician around and categorizing everything he does. Similarly, it would be impossible to discover the effects of surgery because it consists of a collection of heterogenous methods being applied to a similarly heterogenous set of problems. To study psychotherapy naturalistically by "following the therapist around" strikes Ken as equally useless. (See also Szasz's interview and his ideas about studying social and political variables governing human relationships.) If this reasoning is correct, it follows that it is a waste of money and manpower to support anyone doing the naturalistic study of psychotherapy, such as studying video tapes of the therapy process. He objects to projects such as those which Gill and others have worked on, in which they tape record psychoanalytic sessions and "shoot the bull" about what happened.

Colby feels that some of our problems in psychotherapy research derive directly from problems in the field of psychology at large. He pointed out that in psychology we tried to become respectable too soon by becoming methodological experts. By doing this we got the natural order of inquiry disrupted and made very slow progress. Ken noted the amusement often expressed by his friends in the natural sciences at the behavioral scientist's methodological preoccupations. Indeed, the behavioral scientist's expertise in methodology often exceeds that of his colleagues in the "hard" sciences by a considerable margin, which is of course no index to our progress. Indeed, Ken feels, there is nothing wrong with our methods; our trouble is that we cannot describe very well and our theories are highly inexact. The human sciences cannot "jump ahead of themselves"; they must solve basic problems first. He told an interesting anecdote about some psychologists at the Center for Advanced Study who were so zealous about methodology that the outstanding scientists in other fields were stunned by it. One of the most outstanding of them asked a question, "What is this methodology you are talking about all the time?" The psychologist can run circles around even physicists when it comes to methodological considerations; yet they are not nearly as fruitful in terms of discovery. What we need in psychology is more description and more theory building.

Ken feels there has been a sense of urgency in psychology which is also present in psychotherapy research, but which is less evident in other fields. He pointed out that in physics and biology people feel that they have their whole lives to work on problems, and there is less of a sense of urgency to solve a particular problem or to become respectable.

He indicated that it is important for us to step back and calm down, to realize that it may take 500 years to solve some of these problems. He pointed out that our biggest problem is a lack of understanding. We seem to have too many theories but really we have too few, if any, good theories.

It is important to recognize that just because a problem exists doesn't mean that it can be studied. High energy physics research is dying because there are no new ideas. Molecular biology is very hot because there are lots of ideas now. One of the important qualities of good scientists is that they believe in *gradualness* (see Morison, 1960) and that they have the patience to wait. Not infrequently it pays to wait until someone else does something. In order to be a productive scientist, one needs to have the feeling that he is doing something important; one gives ideas a chance to incubate. There are usually thousands of hypotheses and questions which come to mind or which are readily available, but the really fruitful scientist has a way of choosing only certain problems, the ones he believes to have payoff. There is no sense of urgency about picking the questions that have the greatest practical import or the greatest impressiveness; rather we should turn to questions that look answerable or exciting. He pointed out that rushing off and collecting data often makes us feel good and solves our puritan sense of guilt but this may be the worst thing that we can do. There are really only two motives in science; truth and intellectual satisfaction in playing this kind of boyish activity.

Bergin raised the question whether the behavior therapists might have found a "soft spot" in desensitization. Ken expressed the view that the process cannot be explained in S–R terms nor does he believe it has anything to do with "counterconditioning." Nevertheless, despite the vagueness of the process, there seems to be "something powerful" there. Ken made no claim to being thoroughly familiar with this literature but expressed skepticism about the results. He recognized that behavior therapy had generated much enthusiasm in recent years but characterized the therapies under this heading as "easy, untheoretical, and almost childlike." Part of the enthusiasm may be due to the fact that dynamic therapy has "a very poor record" as far as the treatment of phobias is concerned. He did agree very much, however, with the kind of research being done in the behavioral area such as isolating cognitive variables out of the desensitization process.

On the basis of the foregoing it will occasion no surprise that Ken found none of the designs sketched in our survey article particularly exciting. (This view was shared by most consultants, and we ourselves felt by this time that we were "beyond" these designs.) One of the major flaws Ken detected in most of this research related to the lack of standards for comparing individuals or groups. He strongly felt that much basic research is needed before anyone can tackle complex comparative studies. We need to know a lot more about language, about cognitive processes, and about thought. He pointed out that our illustration of Wolpe's case in our "Questions for Consultants" is full of inferences and evaluations. It is a good example, in his opinion, of the almost total imprecision in present clinical descriptions.

We discussed Ken's statement that the therapist needs help from the researcher to solve "acute difficulties in the art." The effective treatment of phobias is a technical problem; in contradistinction, the scientific problem relates to the crucial variables. Ken reiterated his views that (*a*) we don't have clear cases of what we are trying to explain; (*b*) not everything can be a problem in a science "all at once"; and (*c*) we do not know the nature of the relevant information.

Colby himself has shifted from the clinical setting to inquiries analogous to the clinical setting, and finally to inquiries which focus on basic processes such as those of thinking and cognizing. He is currently working on a project with 70 other people called "The Project on Artificial Intelligence." They are working in a large circular building with a rather sizeable computer set-up in the center. There are various sciences in different parts of this circular building such as aerospace and electronics. As a result of attempting to simulate via computer science the thought processes of human beings and by working in a setting with a number of physical and biological scientists, Colby has arrived at strong convictions concerning the process of scientific inquiry and feels that these ideas are very relevant to psychology. It should be noted that among his friends and colleagues are some very outstanding scientists in other fields including at least one Nobel Prize winner.

Ken would allot a high place to computer science in advancing research in the behavioral sciences, and indeed regards it as "our best hope." Work on "artificial intelligence," and the programming of beliefs, are in this category. (Despite my having read Colby's publications in this area and listened to explanations and examples I must confess that much of this still eludes me, nor does what I do understand infuse me with great optimism. H.S.)

We talked a good deal about belief systems and cognitive processes. Ken said there are some decidable questions in this area that ultimately will have relevance to personality modification. He gave the example of memory and thought. Is it stored and decoded like genetic information *à la* DNA and RNA? If we were able to discover an information-processing molecule, we could modify it. In this connection he dwelled on the great importance of being able to simulate belief systems via computers and possibly other ways. This methodology of simulating, he believes, should be applied more vigorously to the psychotherapy research enterprise. Simulating permits careful piece-by-piece inclusion of given variables and influences that can then be manipulated precisely, and effects and interactions can be studied.

There ensued a discussion of the idea that psychopathology is concerned with problems of essentially "nutty" beliefs, delusions, or false beliefs. Psychotherapy may thus be the business of changing people's beliefs, and the therapist is an expert in unscrambling neurotic beliefs. Ken felt work along these lines was indeed important, as was the study of linguistics as it is used to influence behavior. Ken observed that Chassan's chapter in Scher's book (*Theories of the Mind,* 1962) was one of the few significant examples recognizing the importance of this problem. The combination of cognitions and affects and their interaction was considered worth studying in terms of a dynamic model. Ken also referred us to Charles Peirce whose writings are interesting from an historical perspective. In this context we discussed the work of Festinger, Chassan, Abelson, Ellis, and Colby himself. He pointed out that belief structures are very complex and seem to move very quickly. They have cognitive and affective components and also an important information processing function which very rapidly assesses the probability of a given cognition or belief. For example, Ken asked: "If I said 'President Johnson committed suicide this morning,' your response would be almost immediate that this was highly unlikely. There was no thinking about it; it was an immediate and automatic response. Rapid responses like this are made accessible to study by computers. They are frequent in human functioning and are relevant to the attitude change process which goes on in psychotherapy."

Ken commented on a number of projects on which he is currently working, such as the simulation of belief systems and thought processes. He is working on a technique for inducing paranoia into this simulated belief system as a way of studying the formation of pathology. "Once this process is known, presumably it can be reversed, which in turn might reduce the paranoia." He has also developed a program for teaching mutes to speak and is experimenting with some children along these lines.

The history of his transition from psychoanalysis to computers is quite interesting. He pointed out that his book on *Energy and Structure in Psychoanalysis* (1955) was read by a computer expert who told him that his theory was logically impossible but that there were important elements in it. Colby agreed with his critic that a theory was no good unless it could be programmed or made precise enough to put into a computer. He then spent a year at the Center for Advanced Study learning about computers and making a transition. Once this had happened he began to simulate the therapy situation by programming a sick patient and also programming a therapists's response, which he called "the mad doctor." The more he became involved in these things the more he felt that the real answers were in the study of thought processes. Thus, he is now almost totally separated from, and even antagonistic towards, the clinical situation.[16] He believes he is working on basic processes that will eventually form the basis for a sophisticated technology. But he argues strongly that any attempt to build the technology at the moment is doomed to failure because we simply have not advanced far enough in our basic psychological knowledge.

Some sundry comments seem worth preserving:

Ken feels that students, particularly in psychiatry, are excluded from doing research and that the quality of potential scientists is decreasing. Of course, it is true that a research career in psychiatry has acquired high status and respectability in recent years.

Psychiatry currently is on the "biochemistry kick" which causes students to look in the "wetware" of the brain and the "juices of the body" for the answer to the problems in the behavioral realm. Medical training constitutes admirable preparation for this endeavor, if this is one's goal. He said there are also other "types" with mathematical and philosophical backgrounds who are going into research in psychiatry, people who are interested in information processing, some of whom are working with Colby.

16. Comment by Colby: "It's not correct to say I'm antagonistic to the clinical situation. As you can see from the enclosed reprints, I actively work at it. What I am opposed to is the belief that by studying the clinicians' operations in therapy we can learn what we most need to know."

For those of us who have entered middle age it is difficult to generate new ideas about psychotherapy because we are already too set in our theoretical biases. There is greater hope for the younger generation who are less encumbered, and significant contributions may perhaps come from people entirely outside the field.

Freud's original notion (ca. 1885) that hysterical patients were suffering from memories (reminiscences) was a valuable one. We now need to ask, Where is the information coded? How is it coded? The "talking therapist's" job may be summarized in this way: *What* to say; *how* to say it; and *when* to say it.

There was also a good deal of discussion about the corruption of the psychiatric profession, essentially by money and the prestige of being a "doctor." He spoke of the number of people he knew who were very bright and creative but who have succumbed to the temptations in this area and cheapened themselves by becoming "the doctor": "They are no longer the guys I knew; it's tragic." He pointed out that he thinks money is the new obscenity, that is, it is something no one will discuss.

Parenthetically, Ken said: "Nature is not organized the way universities are." "The boundaries of fields are breaking down," "We need to focus on discovery instead of on methods or boundaries such as those imposed by departments, etc." (Of course, one can see an autobiographical theme running through these and many of the foregoing comments.)

Comments by Strupp. I expressed the view that one of the therapist's important jobs is to make explicit the patient's implicit (often highly irrational, fantastic, and contradictory) beliefs which emerge only gradually in the transference situation and are "analyzed" in the context of the patient's emotional experience. Ken disagreed, asserting that many important beliefs which guide an individual's behavior as hypotheses or working assumptions about himself, others, and the world can be elicited from a patient fairly readily and do not require the transference situation. I remain unconvinced, for many reasons; however, this area impresses me as an exceedingly important one.

Ken obviously has thought long and hard about basic science problems in psychiatry and psychoanalysis. For one thing, he is imbued with a sense of the primitiveness of our knowledge in the area of psychotherapy, and he rejects as ill-founded the claims of many contemporary behaviorists who seem to feel that the development of a powerful technology for personality and behavior change is just around the corner. (Compare our interview with Bandura for a diametrically opposite view.) For another, while rejecting much of what passes for scientific work in the behavioral sciences today, he is a romantic in the sense of emphasizing the search for "great ideas." In his words: "In the final analysis no one knows where great ideas come from—

they are a gift from God. What this means for psychotherapy is that work may have to be done at another level, not within the psychotherapy situation."

Consequently, anyone approaching behavioral science with "Brave-New-World" ideas is bound to be rudely awakened by Ken's analysis of the current scene, which will cause him to take careful stock before he mounts grandiose projects. Ken's views are reasonably representative of a current trend in the behavioral sciences which seems to be gaining slow but steady momentum. We also had the feeling that Ken's view reflected a good many of the criticisms leveled at behavioral science by physical scientists and biologists with whom Ken hobnobs considerably. (Ken wondered where the term "Behavioral Science" ever came from. He said: "Why not call physics a behavioral science? After all, it deals with the behavior of atoms!") While we would strenously reject the imputation that we are suffering from the aforementioned grandiosity complex, we left Ken with very mixed feelings. The visit was tremendously stimulating and clearly one of the highlights of our journey.

Comments by Bergin. I found this meeting with Colby probably the most stimulating and provocative of all that we have had. This was for many reasons, but I think especially for the reason that Colby presented forcefully to us all of the arguments that are made against our type of work by scientists in biology and physics. Essentially, Colby was saying to us the critical things which other people, his colleagues in science, had been saying to him for several years. Apparently, they convinced him, and now he in turn is trying to convince us. I am not certain that his conclusions are correct; but I am reasonably certain that these scientists have asked very penetrating questions about what we are doing. Since they have been successful, it would pay for us to listen to them and perhaps to spend more time with people outside of our field as we proceed in this project. There are certain dangers involved in this, however. One of them is that many of the questions being asked are questions that are more appropriately addressed to basic scientific inquiry than to the kind of applied science we are interested in. Secondly, I think we have to recognize the fact that inquiry in complex human behavior may have to be qualitatively different from what goes on in other fields of science. This is a pregnant dilemma, and one which may not be resolved; but it is one to which we must address ourselves vigorously. Colby does not seem to think that a new philosophy of science is necessary for our field. He says that science is science. There are only a few things which characterize it and it is unimaginable that the basic procedures of science could be any different for psychology of personality than for physics. It may be true that we have greater complexity to deal with and less ability to control it, but the basic rules of evidence and inference remain the same. They are part of nature and as Colby seemed to imply, more or less immutable. This may be true, but the most bothersome fact of personality study is the fantastic domination of the whole scene by subjective experience. This experience must yield to scientific inquiry but it is wholly a different kettle of fish than physical phenomena. Of course, there may be analogous situations such as the need to use a cloud chamber for the study of atomic particles. The particles are usually never seen, but their effects are observed through this instrumentation. Perhaps a new instrumentation is our greatest need in the study of personality change, for if we could obtain the precision over subjective processes indirectly in the same manner that cloud chambers have obtained precision over unseen physical processes, we could be well on our way to a truly powerful methodology. In any event, questions and dilemmas such as these must be addressed with precision. The idea appeals to me very much of discussing issues like this with some outstanding scientists in other fields who have reputations for their humanism and interests in questions of behavior.

References

Chassan, J. B. 1962. Probability processes in psychoanalytic psychiatry. In J. Scher ed. *Theories of the mind.* New York: Free Press of Glencoe, pp. 598–618.

Colby, K. M. 1955. *Energy and structure in psychoanalysis.* New York: Ronald Press.

Morison, R. S. 1960. Gradualness, gradualness, gradualness (I. P. Pavlov). *American Psychologist* 15: 187–97.

INTERVIEW: ALBERT BANDURA

Palo Alto, January, 16, 1969

We met with Al Bandura on January 16 and spent most of the day with him. A sharper contrast between the views expressed by Ken Colby on the preceding day and those espoused by Al is hardly imaginable. Basically, Al seems to feel that we are much farther along in the behavioral sciences than Ken would concede. Whereas Ken believes that we have not even defined the phenomena in our domain and that considerable work at the descriptive level needs to be done, Al holds that experimental work on basic change

* Dr. Bandura is Professor of Psychology at Stanford University.

mechanisms is feasible, highly desirable and is already yielding informative results. Al presented his views in remarkably succinct and well organized fashion, a feat undoubtedly aided by the fact that he had recently completed a book on behavioral theory, research and therapy which promises to be a major contribution.

Bandura noted that experimental analogues (that is, research on quasi-therapy situations) are disappearing in the behavioral approach. He considered this method, as stated in our Question 2b, to be no longer optimal as a strategy. Instead, the behavioral model is being directly applied to patients in a systematic manner. Differences between the laboratory and the clinic are disappearing.

Bandura pointed out that there were three levels of research which can contribute to advancing knowledge of personality change.

1. The first level of study is concerned with basic change mechanisms. These need not be conducted with psychotherapy in mind, but they are very relevant in that they elucidate the mechanism through which changes are brought about. For example, counter-conditioning studies of humans and animals may yield parameters of the conditioning situation. To illustrate, the study of five extinction methods to remove avoidance responses in animals could provide the empirical foundations for applications.

2. Next, it is important to apply these principles under highly controlled conditions. The methods used in this case are not analogues but are similar to what will eventually be used in the clinical situation. The increment in control as compared with a clinical situation is introduced by applying the method to a restricted disorder. One might thus deal with a circumscribed problem, like a snake phobia, and design studies which form a graduated series. For example, one might contrast a social with an automated presentation of desensitization instructions, study differences in terms of whether *S* controls or does not control turning off the stimulus of an anxiety provoking situation. Al noted that there already are some 20 well-designed studies of this type in the literature. They are not applied to complex cases but to simpler ones which permit careful study of the mechanisms of change.

3. The third level, finally, consists of applications of the principles isolated at levels 1 and 2 to complex clinical situations. The purpose of research at this level is not to determine whether a given method is capable of producing changes (this is established at level 2), but to establish how proven methods can be extended and combined to produce optimal results. Optimization rather than verification is the major goal at the clinical level. This is much more difficult to do, and progress has been correspondingly slow. An example is provided by Marks and Gelder (1967) who applied counterconditioning procedures to transvestite behavior. Such studies call for intensive design. Presumably modification of the change methods

would result from these applications or at least more definitive statements could be made regarding to which syndromes or conditions the method is most applicable.

Al feels that by following the above three-stage approach we are building methods which will become increasingly effective as well as self-corrective, as occurs through clinical trials in medicine, where laboratory tests of efficacy precede clinical application. In this way, too, we are setting up conditions which make knowledge cumulative.

He pointed out that in all change studies we must differentiate between:

1. Conditions that produce change
2. Conditions that lead to transfer (generalization)
3. Conditions that maintain changes over time

He indicated that a technique may be powerful with regard to one or more of these but not the others. Powerful changes may be obscured by the fact that little transfer or endurance of change occurs; therefore, outcome studies may look bad because they have produced changes which do not last. In the latter case, the inducing procedure may be satisfactory but it needs to be supplemented with a transfer or maintenance program. We need to both measure such changes and develop methods to maintan the changes that have occurred.

In many studies of psychotherapy these distinctions have not been made. Goldstein, Heller, and Sechrest (1966), for example, state that we know next to nothing about how learning that occurs in the therapeutic situation is transferred and applied to real-life settings.[17] In terms of the psychoanalytic model, it is assumed that as the patient succeeds in clarifying his interpersonal transactions with the therapist, he can apply these learnings to extra-therapy situations. However, we do not know how this is done and to what extent such transfers are effective. Furthermore, the real-life situation may provide rewards, in which case the transfer would be facilitated, but they may also be adverse to the maintenance of therapeutically induced changes. Typically, the transfer problem is left to the patient's ingenuity, and he must proceed on a trial-and-error basis. This kind of "experimentation" of course may itself promote his sense of autonomy in that he begins to assume personal responsibility for his actions and their consequences. More likely, however, he will become discouraged by needless setbacks. Transfer and generalization should form part of the treatment plan rather than be left to fortuitous factors.

Considerable discussion centered around these main points; numerous examples and illustrations were provided; and difficulties were pointed out. On the whole, Al seems to feel that the road to progress, at least in principle, is

17. Comment by Bandura: "This is an extreme statement with which I would disagree."

reasonably clear and that substantive advances may be expected as research is pursued along these lines. In this connection, it may be noted that undoubtedly there is no "royal road" to the advancement of knowledge in this area and different investigators, in keeping with their temperamental and personal convictions, will proceed along different routes, thereby adding color to the tapestry of the scientific enterprise.

Al feels that one of the major contributions of behavior therapy has been the emphasis on specificity and the introduction of guided learning experiences, as opposed to the broader "corrective emotional experience" outlined by Alexander (1965).

In response to a question about the role of cognition in behaviorism, Bandura said: "What could be more cognitive than desensitization?" He then criticized Shoben and Murray regarding biotropism. He disagrees with their view that behavioral techniques are exceedingly mechanical and behavioristic. He pointed out that in desensitization even the anxiety is induced symbolically.

Al told a whimsical story in which he suggested that we desensitize a rat by asking him to tell us items that would be relevant for a sex anxiety hierarchy and then ask him to imagine these scenes after we had induced a muscle relaxation by verbal instructions and have him signal with his right paw whenever he experienced high anxiety in response to imagined scenes. The ridiculousness of this whole business highlights the point that behavior techniques involve a strong cognitive component. On the other hand, Bandura pointed out that there is very little coming out of cognitive psychology (that is, general psychology) which seems to be very potent in regard to behavioral change. He felt that behavior therapists have been manipulating cognitive variables more effectively than the cognitive psychologists themselves.

For example, Ayllon used cognition with his token economy (see Ayllon & Azrin, 1964). Verbal instructions are symbols that frequently yield great behavioral changes. For example: "You get a dessert if you use a fork," is a very powerful symbolic instruction. He also gave an illustration of Kaufman's work in operant conditioning. Kaufman showed that the reinforcement schedule in a person's head is often more powerful than the real one. If you use a real schedule and then tell the subject he is on a different one, he responds more to the fake one than to the real one. If we tell a person he is on a variable-interval schedule we get 260 responses per half hour if he thinks he's on a variable-ratio schedule, and 6 responses if he believes he's on a fixed-interval schedule.

Bandura also indicates that in regard to classical conditioning we can wipe out conditioned emotional responses with instructions, for example, that the subject will get no shock. But this kind of instruction doesn't affect phobic patients.

While Al's neo-behavioristic[18] position thus recognizes the importance of symbolic mediators, it raises the question of why cognitive variables are no more powerful under some conditions. Informing a subject that certain snakes are not dangerous or any other cognitive input clearly produces little change in a phobic's feelings and behavior. Contrariwise, how does it come about that even looking at the picture of a feared object arouses the person's anxiety? Al feels that self-arousal plays an important role in these situations, and obviously this must be mediated by strong beliefs which in turn trigger the emotional response. It is interesting, but perhaps not surprising, that even simple experiments in this area raise important questions about psychopathology. Al feels that the natural history of phobias (or other forms of psychopathology), as has been recommended by some, would be useful. For example, we know that many phobias in children are "outgrown" whereas others seem to receive reinforcement probably through the neurotic fears of parents and other models.

Al believes that in general cognitions and attitudes are probably powerful influencers on behavior when (*a*) behavior is in the person's repertoire and can be produced, (*b*) there is ambiguity with regard to what the consequences will be or where the payoff will be significant. On the other hand, it's less effective when a person is unable to perform the required behavior because of severe inhibitions or when it produces self-devaluative consequences. However, people who think expectations consistently produce significant personality changes are essentially saying that you can *con* people into lasting change. This does not mean, according to Al, that there is no attitudinal component in personality change; there is, but manipulating expectations does not seem to him to effect lasting change.

Bandura holds that behavioral therapy is a guided learning experience. The experiences are real, they are multidimensional (including cognitive and affective), and they provide new confrontations with the old threat experiences. There is a problem in causality involved here, however, which is hard to resolve. This is because a powerful therapeutic method could produce marked changes in attitudes, feelings, affect, and behavior but we have no way of assessing attitudinal and behavior changes simultaneously. For example, changes in the person's self-image might be consequent upon behavior changes; changes in self-concept might lead to behavior change, or attitude and behavior changes might occur simultaneousy. Because we can't measure all of these simultaneously it is difficult to arrive at a full description of causality. For example, if we measure behavior first it looks like it causes attitude change; whereas if we measure attitude change first it looks

18. Bandura noted that his is a *social learning* position, not a neo-behavioristic one. His comments on the term "neo-behaviorist" are as follows: "Since Behaviorists are mechanical salivators, I never had the heart to write to mother that I was a neo-behaviorist. Can you imagine a mother saying, 'My son, the Neo-behaviorist' "?

like it causes behavior change. Consistency theories argue that if you change one dimension of human experience there is a pressure or tendency for corresponding change to occur in other systems. Thus if we create a behavioral change there may be a consistency pressure which produces a concomitant attitude change. It is thus not so much that our technique has created the change in attitude but that by changing a behavior there is a corresponding change in attitude. Thus, the causality may not be from behavior to attitude, it could be just the opposite if the change induction technique modified an attitude first.

Bandura thinks that the problem here is that for the most part we have not bothered to measure many of the phenomena that are occurring during change. For example, Wahler studied a depressive child and changes in self-evaluation associated with changes in behavior (see Wahler & Pollio, 1968). He used operant conditioning to increase the boy's social responsiveness and then reversed the contingencies of reinforcement. The self-evaluations of this boy on the semantic differential changed and then reversed accordingly. Bandura, therefore, thinks that behavioral change is the most powerful and that it is the best basis for changing self-evaluation. When we produce behavioral competency we influence attitudes towards the self. Al nevertheless admits that it is very hard to separate cognitions, self-evaluations, and attitudes from behavioral change.

He gave an interesting illustration of the black militant movement to train children cognitively to accept the idea that "black is beautiful." Bandura considered this a weak approach and felt that it would have been more successful to produce specific behavioral changes in black children by making them feel that they are competent or "beautiful."[19]

At this point he referred to Festinger's review of literature on attitude change (1964). Festinger found that there was no consistent relationship between attitude and behavior although there were few studies that really focused on this in any adequate way. It also appeared from the literature that people needed behavioral support for attitude change, otherwise the attitude change did not seem to last. Bandura commented on some of his own work and that of his students. He has found correlations in the .50's and

19. Comments by Bandura: "My comment about the 'black is beautiful' approach is incompletely reported and therefore misleading. One may attempt to change people's self-evaluations by persuasive communications or by creating esteem-producing competencies. One can alter self-attitudes by persuasive efforts but the positive changes may not endure if the person repeatedly encounters failure experiences due to behavioral deficits. Therefore, enduring positive self-evaluations can be most effectively achieved by enhancing self-evaluation directly and by developing requisite competencies that realistically support positive self-attitudes. The 'black is beautiful' approach is likely to be most effective if combined with development of competencies. Rather than knocking the approach, I was specifying the conditions under which it is most likely to have enduring effects."

.70's between behavioral and attitude changes; however, he agrees that there may be partially correlated co-effects. The big question is, Does the powerful input yield behavioral change which in turn yields attitude change, or does a powerful input concomitantly yield behavioral and attitude changes?

Al made a strong pitch for "retiring brand names" of theoretical orientations in psychotherapy in favor of work on basic change mechanisms which operate to varying degrees in all the brands. With regard to modeling effects, it would be important to study how the basic mechanisms are applied in different forms of psychotherapy. What is being modeled? By whom? To what extent are the requisite conditions for modeling present? Strupp, for one, believes that modeling (identification) is a central mechanism in all forms of psychotherapy, including psychoanalysis, although it obviously does not encompass the totality of the therapist's influence. Approval-disapproval seems another highly important dimension cutting across theoretical positions, as is the "pattern of responsivity" by the therapist.

Parenthetically, we discussed the recent studies of snake phobics at Stanford. They found that 85% of their subjects had direct or frightening vicarious experiences with snakes. In 56% of the cases there seemed to be a parental modeling effect in that the parents were also afraid of snakes. Forty per cent appeared to actually have been traumatized by vicarious experience.

Bergin asked why some people don't become phobic even though they have had the same frightening experiences as others who have become phobic. Bandura pointed out that in their dog phobic studies kids who were phobic were more likely to have parents who were also phobic than did children who had no fear of animals. Bergin suggested that their parents might also be neurotic in a more general sense; therefore the children are essentially sensitized organisms who become phobic under stress. It could be that this is even a genetic phenomenon. There seemed to be no quarrel with this argument.

Strupp then pointed out that this made it even clearer that we need natural histories of these kinds of disorders. Bandura agreed emphatically that these would help. Strupp also pointed out that probably a high percentage of phobias are extinguished naturally, and gave an illustration of his own daughter's dog phobia which disappeared spontaneously. Bandura pointed out that there are many minor phobias that are overcome by informal influences equivalent to treatment. Severe phobias, however, require more carefully guided relearning experiences.

At this point we discussed the question of whether single case studies would be fruitful at stages 2 or 3 of Bandura's paradigm. He pointed out that the intrasubject replication design had been used by Skinnerians with considerable success. It gives us a chance to see whether a variable is controlling behavior by putting it in and taking it out. Also Marks and Gelder's (1967) study of a transvestite showed the specific influence of interventions on behavior, and a study in Vermont on hospital cases (Leitenberg et al., 1968) revealed the power of the single case design, particularly on a patient with a fear of knives. This study showed direct control over behavior by feedback of progress which was being manipulated. Strupp then raised the question of whether these changes are lasting. Bandura said the Skinnerians think that they can turn behavior on and off. This seems to be all right if we do not persist in influencing behavior too long; similarly, it is OK to artifically set up programs, but they are limited. To get transfer to everyday life we must shift contingencies to natural ones, like peer groups, and therefore shift the locus of support for the new behavior. We can also build in new social skills and competencies which permit participation in new behaviors which are enjoyable and which yield social and personal payoffs. We can build in autonomy and a self-reward system independent of social reinforcement. All of these must be actively promoted and we need to push for projects which will develop enduring and generalized change and not just the temporary kind which sometimes occur in these operant paradigms.

Bandura does not foresee any technical problems inhibiting collaborative studies; but there are problems of personality and values. For example, he pointed out that Lovaas, Bettelheim, and a group at Menninger's have all worked on speech in autistic children. The problem is getting them to use each other's measures but no one seems very interested in that. To cope with this problem, it may be necessary to fund different active centers. To do effective collaboration one needs a common interest and a large commitment to the project.

He suggested that a regular opportunity for communication provided in some funded way may be important. People who are doing "their own thing" might at least be talking to each other. Projects could perhaps be planned with some degree of cooperation or at least communication with others, and it may also be possible to agree on measures or to do the same study in two places. We would then be informed as to what is going on and could at least raise questions with each other. It may also be possible to exchange staff members for brief periods.

We discussed Jerry Frank's point that biochemistry may be the most powerful variable influencing behavior. Bandura said that, Delgado to the contrary,[20] there is research to show that physiological responses are a

20. Comments by Bandura: "In this context I was not disputing Delgado; on the contrary, I was citing findings of his research illustrating the limitations of neurophysiological explanations of social behavior. Numerous studies had been performed by other researchers showing that hypothalamic stimulation evokes stereotyped aggressive behavior in animals. Many researchers concluded from these findings that the answers to aggression reside in the hypothalamus. Delgado showed, however, that the explanation of aggression is furnished by social-learning factors rather than neurophysiological ones. Thalamic stimulation of a monkey who occupies a dominant role in the colony instigates him to attack subordinate male members but not females.

function of social learning. If Frank wishes to really push this why not apply it to education? "Does biochemistry dictate the content of the learning process in education? Isn't psychotherapy essentially a social learning process that is instigated, directed and sustained by environmental influences? Should education be considered in the medical domain because learning involves neurophysiological mechanisms? Will biochemistry ever provide us with reading pills, writing pills, and arithmetic pills, or should we develop more efficacious tutors?"

He responded to a question relating to the power of the therapist's personality by wondering whether the personality of a physician overrides the influence of his techniques. He does not think this overriding occurs and believes that if we have powerful techniques it will not happen in psychotherapy either. He does agree that something valuable may be obtained from naturalistic studies of the therapy process, but generally he thinks the variables thus extracted are weak. With regard to the problems of complexity, he takes this to mean simply that we have multiproblem disorders. We must break down the complexity and work on each specific problem: "There is no such thing as a global problem." Strupp mentioned that the client-centered people tend to do the opposite by treating the whole person. He also questioned whether the client-centered approach ever changed specific symptoms.

Al is not "worried" about problems of nosology (to which Ken Colby assigned a great deal of weight). His view is that if the therapeutic method is sufficiently powerful in terms of achieving the changes one sets out to produce, one needs not be overly concerned about "mixed" syndromes. The latter only become an important consideration when the interventions are on the weak side. Jerry Frank has voiced a similar opinion, which seems to flow from his conviction that all traditional psychotherapeutic methods produce weak results. This in turn leads him to advocate techniques (e.g., ether inhalation) which have been shown to bring about strong emotional arousal. It is well known of course that in psychoanalysis, interpretations are not considered effective unless they are made in in the context of emotions mobilized in the crucible of the transference situation. Freud himself made the observation that what the patient has experienced and learned in this context is most convincing and never forgotten.

By contrast, thalamic stimulation elicits cowing and submissive behavior in a monkey of low social rank. Even more impressive is evidence that electrical stimulation of the same cerebral mechanism can evoke differential amounts of aggression in the same animal as his social rank is modified by changing the membership of the colony. Thus, thalamic stimulation elicits submissiveness when he is not the dominant member of the group. What explanatory power does neurophysiology have with regard to the observed aggressive behavior? In this context, Delgado is not a foe as the interview report implies" (see Delgado 1964, 1965).

Comments by Strupp. In response to Bandura's emphasis on specificity, it appears that most therapists (with the notable exception of client-centered therapists) seem to address themselves to *specific* problems in therapy, regardless of how these "problems" are defined. They work on problems one at a time, disregarding or ignoring others which do not seem to be "in focus" at the moment (that is, no strong feelings accompany the patient's verbalizations). I believe this statement applies to behavior therapists as much as it does to psychoanalysts, although in the latter case the situation is often not as clearly defined. Personally, I believe that no one can deal with complexity *qua* complexity and that any problem situation in therapy must be reduced to manageable size.

In conclusion, Al's optimism about the future of research in the area is noteworthy and, as stated earlier, diametrically opposed to Colby's assessment of the situation. Whatever the merits of his approach (I consider them of considerable potential value), he has clear proposals about where the field should go from here and he has obviously given a great deal of critical thought to the problems.

Comments by Bergin. Hans raised a whole set of questions concerning the complexity of personality change and how Bandura felt about the bugaboo of complexity." Bandura responded with a good deal of optimism and claimed that we can measure what is going on and that we can observe the changes which are occurring. My own reaction was that I think the behavior therapists have "sniffed around" in the sense that Colby talked about and that they have found a weak spot in nature. They are now taking advantage of it and in my opinion their work can form the basis for future building of a full therapeutic system. It may well be that the behavioral approach in its research and therapeutic forms has begun to produce the basic building blocks for a truly complex and useful system that will eventually match the complexity of disturbed human beings.

Generally, I found this discussion very encouraging, particularly because it seemed evident to me that Bandura had addressed himself specifically to the kinds of issues that Colby so penetratingly presented. While it may be too narrow to assume that the behaviorists have begun to provide clear answers to these criticisms, I am at least for the time being quite encouraged by this approach. Some of the leading, most creative, people seem quite capable of a broad spectrum viewpoint and are not bound strictly to the ancient kind of behaviorism. Parenthetically, I might say here that in a sense I think Bandura's approach may be the best answer to Colby's critique. It would seem that Bandura and those whose work he is describing have pretty well met some of the scientific objections which Colby formulated, perhaps because Colby is historically connected with a psychoanalytic tradition which was less responsive than the behavioral tradition to the issues raised by these other scientists.

References

Alexander, F. 1965. The dynamics of psychotherapy in the light of learning theory. *International Journal of Psychiatry* 1: 189–97.

Ayllon, T. M., & Azrin, N. H. 1964. Reinforcement and instruction with mental patients. *Journal of Experimental Analysis of Behavior* 7: 327–31.

Delgado, J. M. R. 1964. Free behavior and brain stimulation. In C. C. Pfeiffer & J. R. Smythies eds., *International Review of Neurobiology*. vol. 6. New York: Academic Press.

———. 1965. Chronic radio-stimulation of the brain in monkey colonies. In *Excerpta Medica International Congress Series,* No. 87. Tokyo: Proceedings of the 23rd International Congress of Physiological Sciences.

Festinger, L. 1964. Behavioral support for opinion change. *Public Opinion Quarterly* 28: 404–17.

Goldstein, A. P., Heller, K., & Sechrest, L. B. 1966. *Psychotherapy and the psychology of behavior change*. New York: Wiley.

Leitenberg, H., Agras, W. S., Thompson, L. E., & Wright, D. E. 1968. Feedback in behavior modification: An experimental analysis in two phobic cases. *Journal of Applied Behavior Analysis* 1: 131–37.

Marks, I. M., & Gelder, M. G. 1967. Transvestism and fetishism: Clinical and psychological changes during faradic aversion. *British Journal of Psychiatry* 40: 261–72.

Wahler, R. G., & Pollio H. R. 1968. Behavior and insight: A case study in behavior therapy. *Journal of Experimental Research in Personality* 3: 45–56.

INTERVIEW: ROBERT S. WALLERSTEIN AND HAROLD SAMPSON*

San Francisco, January 17, 1969

Wallerstein initiated the discussion by pointing out that the field was chaotic for several reasons: (a) We were working in radically different frames of reference. (b) We perceive the whole field from different dimensions. (c) We use the same words with different meanings, and different words with the same meanings. He pointed out that the first psychotherapy research conference promised to help bridge this gap, but nothing really happened and the second and third conferences had little effect on this problem.

* Dr. Wallerstein is Chief of the Department of Psychiatry and Dr. Sampson is Director of Research, both at Mt. Zion Hospital in San Francisco.

He proceeded to state that the participants were exceedingly parochial, as exemplified by the fact that there was little overlap in the bibliographies accompanying each paper. Behavior therapy was not even represented at the 1958 conference. The schism between psychoanalysis, client-centered therapy, behavior therapy, and humanistic therapy (and other variants) is increasing and the field is fragmenting more than it is pulling together. Bob entertained the possibility that perhaps nothing can be done to change the parochialism at this time, and at most one might encourage people following a particular bent to pursue it. He based this pessimistic evaluation on the fact that we do not have common denominators upon which agreement exists. He therefore questions whether the field is ready to move in concert and sees little readiness for it. We asked whether he thought there was anything we could do to stimulate it. He felt it would be bucking a tendency toward schisms by trying to develop commonality or collaboration. Sampson also said that you cannot overcome the focus people are already fixed on. He pointed out that behavioral research will contribute something important and should be pursued; but he is convinced that studies involving "quick comparisons" won't work, and the same judgment was rendered concerning large-scale comparative studies. (On few points does there seem to be greater unanimity, regardless of the consultant's theoretical predilections.)

To illustrate the prevailing splits in point of view, Bob commented on what he considers to be ludicrous outcome criteria that are employed these days. In one study, a patient was described who suffered severe anxiety attacks the further she got away from home. The criterion of improvement was being able to drive ten miles away from home. When the patient was able to drive one mile alone without experiencing anxiety, does this mean the "cure" was $\frac{1}{10}$ complete?

Strupp cited the example of Bandura's work with modeling as an alternative to large comparative study. Why not study the mechanisms of change in this manner? Wallerstein suggested another alternative by pointing to the success of the Psychosomatic Society and its journal, the development of which were sparked by Flanders Dunbar's classic book, *Emotions and Bodily Changes* (1954). She started by cataloguing phenomena in a very fragmented field and wound up founding the *Journal of Psychosomatic Medicine*. She thus forced everyone to read and publish in the same place. This produced a remarkably nonparochial interest group, unfettered by professional rivalries and political considerations, which has managed to remain viable, active, and creative. Bob thought this group was well worth emulating by psychotherapy researchers and clinicians.

Bergin indicated that Miller's work and the work of other behaviorists demonstrated that they were not in a realm entirely different from that of Wallerstein in that conditioning processes involve symbols and cognition.

Sampson disagreed and said that he felt that there was a need for parochialism at this stage: Behaviorism will make its contributions and psychoanalysis will make its contributions. He became quite critical about psychoanalytic research, and provided a good statement of the reasons behind the deficiencies (see below). Bergin suggested that he still did not think it was necessary to fragment the field any longer by school affiliations, and suggested that perhaps the behavioral approach might be the foundation or provide the building blocks for a more complex system. He noted that behavior therapy has built on 30 to 40 years of experimental work and thought that this might form a solid basis for future developments.

Bob felt (and Strupp strongly agreed) that mechanisms like reward and punishment are fully operative also in psychoanalysis although they are not conceptualized as such. Wallerstein suggested that these are important dimensions in effecting change. He cited Gerald Patterson's work in using reward for modifying performances of children. He felt that this was a positive move and was pleased to see that Patterson (1971) saw the limitations as well as the assets of this approch.

Wallerstein then posed the question, "Where does psychoanalysis stand in regard to the basic mechanisms of change?" He said that the theory of therapy is not very well developed, and that the technique is essentially described by mechanisms operating in the preconscious and unconscious. He said that the basic mechanism is that interpretations make the unconscious conscious and that this is the substance of the whole theory of change.

Strupp pursued the topic by asking: "What are the 'mutative' operations in psychoanalysis?" "Interpretations" are probably not the answer. Strachey had made a beginning by raising this question at the Marienbad symposium but little progress has since been made. Rapaport observed that all we have in psychoanalysis is a "bunch of rules of thumb." Strupp noted that we can't study the effect of an interpretation because we can't isolate the damn thing. Sampson countered by saying he did not think this problem was insoluble and that we could do something significant about it. At this point Bergin intervened to suggest that Bandura's point was very important with regard to the three stages in change: (1) a technique may cause change to occur; (2) there may be new mechanisms or different ones that create generalization; and (3) there are additional mechanisms that make this change in generalization endure. Major changes can occur as a result of psychoanalytic interventions but they may not last. Strupp suggested that this was a very important point and should be followed up.

In discussing why psychoanalysts haven't done very much to advance the field, Sampson observed that they haven't gone beyond the descriptive state of the art. Systematic studies and theoretical formulations of change as well as the implementation of a verification process just have not been done. With regard to Bandura's three types of mechanisms of change, he said that in psychoanalysis one sees the patient over long periods of time and one has occasion to study how little people change, and how hard change is to come by. He pointed out that time-limited therapy with target symptoms is easier. In ten hours at Mount Zion patients seem to get a lot of symptom relief. Later, after they have gotten patients inducted into the therapy system, they see that their problems look different and they look worse than they did at the end of ten hours. This could mean that hidden problems emerge more clearly, that patients are really worse than they seemed at the beginning, or that long-term therapy makes them worse.

Strupp reiterated the importance of studying the mechanisms of change. Among other things, he called attention to the long periods in psychoanalysis in which nothing seems to be happening. He wondered out loud how powerful psychoanalysis is at those times. Of course, it is possible that in the process of working through the groundwork is laid for the more dramatic changes we observe now and then.

Sampson suggested that there are huge differences between behavior therory and psychoanalysis in terms of what is learned and how it is learned. He gave an example from a study at Mount Zion in which they are examining the covariation of changes in defenses and the emergence of new material. This is essentially a correlational study based on written process notes. The study is a collaborative study of Mt. Zion and the San Francisco Psychoanalytic Institute. It is an intensive *single case* study of a psychoanalysis in which reliable, objective measures of change are developed, and the purpose is to study contrasting hypotheses about how changes in defenses are associated with the emergence to consciousness of previously warded-off material. This is in fact a test of a mini-theory about defense-analysis. In one case, the patient's acquisition of control over the initially unconscious defense of undoing enabled him to experience formerly warded-off affects.

Unfortunately, this study is weakened by the fact that the measures are at a great distance from the raw phenomena; that is, they are based on inferences from clinical reports which in turn have been written retrospectively and already include numerous inferences.[21]

21. Comment by Wallerstein and Sampson: "It might be useful if your comment, 'Unfortunately, this study is weakened . . . ' is clearly attributed to Strupp or Bergin rather than to Sampson or Wallerstein, as the latter have given considerable thought to the nature of the data used [see their paper on "Issues in Research in the Psychoanalytic Process," 1971, in *The International Journal of Psycho-Analysis*], and would not conceptualize the limitations of process notes data in that way. It would be misleading, therefore, to represent the investigators as apologetic about this aspect of their method, when they in fact feel that no other choice of data would have done the job—which involved studying and measuring change taking place over the sweep of about a year of analysis."

Wallerstein then broke in with the question of how change really occurs. "How do we make the unconscious conscious? People learn through interpretation and by having made things explicit to them. A person learns how his mind functions, he understands something and he is aware, then he begins to learn that if he does things in one way it is more rewarding than in another way." He raised the question of whether this can be studied by psychoanalysis and behavior therapy and whether there is something in common between them here. Bergin suggested that it is not possible. Behavior therapy is training in behavior. Psychoanalysis is teaching a new belief system and helping the person to symbolize. It may well be that behaviorism produces changes in performance and that psychoanalysis could contribute something about how to symbolize change in order to insure greater generalization. Thus each might contribute to a different stage of the tripartite change process outlined by Bandura.

Sampson and Wallerstein suggested (and we agreed) that change is a very complicated process. Wallerstein gave the example of Caspar Milquetoast who might be taught *(à la* Albert Ellis) to be more assertive via suggestion and support. If he succeeds in being more assertive, he will become even more assertive in the future due to reinforcement for assertion. It is true then that he has changed and he has been rewarded for change, but *why* has he done it? He has done it with the support of the therapist and therefore he has developed a transference-submissiveness. Will it then be necessary, Sampson asked, for him to submit to a man in order to be more assertive? He suggested that one can get identical changes for different reasons via analytic therapy, and we need to examine the change process in all its complexity before we can be certain which change we prefer.

Strupp indicated that this is a prime example of the importance of using multiple criteria to evaluate outcome; but unfortunately people tend to part company here. He then raised the question of whether the therapy situation is actually the proper place for inquiry. Is it conducive to discovery? Will the payoff be here?

Wallerstein suggested that analogues are oversimplifications of nature and, while it is a matter of faith, prefers the clinical situation. "Can one demonstrate phenomena and verify them within this context at the same time?" Wallerstein argued that the clinical context has not been given a sufficient chance.

Sampson argued that this should not be an either-or question. Psychoanalysts have considered the matter in the way Wallerstein suggests, and they have rejected practically everything from the experimental laboratory except perhaps the Poetzl phenomenon. Sampson suggested, however, that we need both. We have to isolate variables even though they may be embedded in complexity. We can only deal with the complex by studying part relationships. He expects progress both ways. He stated that some people believe you have to stay with the complex completely; but he believes that this can ruin the field because you can never see the whole story all at once.

Wallerstein agreed that it is important to break things down and indicated that computer programming requires one to be very explicit and precise about what is going on. This is an important contribution. Strupp noted at this point that the behavior therapists have insisted on this, too, and seemed to be making a contribution by requiring precision in terminology and in the interventions being studied. He also indicated that changes that are lasting tend to be multidimensional. Conceivably, there are some techniques which produce only unidimensional change, but we don't know much about them. In general, psychotherapy works toward changes in attitudes, affect and behavior.

Wallerstein returned to a description of the psychoanalytical position by emphasizing that it is a motivational psychology. All behavior is seen as having purpose and meaning, and psychoanalysis uncovers hidden meanings and rewards. Bergin asked why we can't throw out theories like this and forget about them, and simply study mechanisms of change whether they are symbolic, affective, or cognitive. Sampson said it might be possible, but research can't be better than the ideas we have.

Strupp pointed out that in psychotherapy and in research it is important to recognize that as therapists or as researchers we strive to focus on *one* problem at a time; nevertheless, we must keep the context in mind. It is especially important for psychoanalytic therapists to isolate and try to influence what they think will yield results; indeed, there is good evidence to show that skilled therapists do this quite consistently.

Sampson and Wallerstein conceded that behavioral concepts do have power but they still do not believe that there has been enough mileage gained out of the main commitments in the traditional schools. In this connection, they talked about some of the problems which have prevented psychoanalysis from bearing fruit.

Why has psychoanalytic research made so little progress? This theme seemed to pervade much of Bob's and Sampson's thinking, and Bob called to our attention an excellent paper on this subject by George Engel (1968) followed by a collection of discussions, one of which was authored by Bob. This is a careful analysis of the social and political considerations which have deterred the progress of psychoanalysis as a science. The thrust of Engel's argument is that analysis did not grow out of an academic or experimental tradition; clinicians entering the field have not generally been interested in research; psychoanalysis has not "delivered the goods"; and clinical observation, while being an important prelude to research, is not and cannot be research. He places the blame largely on the character of psychoanalytic training in this country, the field's "splendid isolation" from the behavioral sciences, its antipathy to research, its undue emphasis on the training of practitioners, and its self-defeating exclusion of nonM.D. researchers. Bob's published discussion was strongly supportive of Engel's views and the most candid of the lot. It was revealing that Wallerstein and Sampson agreed with Engel's position that some radical revisions are called for in order to bring the psychoanalytic tradition fully within the scientific community. Sampson added that only recently has psychoanalysis begun to pay some attention to problems of verification. On the credit side, analysts have long had a healthy respect for the tremendous difficulties the therapist encounters in changing people.

Bergin then returned to the issue of trying to get away from schools by suggesting that perhaps we should adopt mini-theories and focus on specific mechanisms of change instead of searching for over-arching global theories. Wallerstein and Sampson agreed and said that they really were doing that, that they were following one strand at a time, but that each strand was derived from and related to a maxi-theory. Bergin said that he had no maxi-theory. Strupp said, "Yes, but we have to have some idea what we think will pay off." Sampson then suggested that a mini-theory should have at least some reference to a larger view, and that this can hasten our efforts at synthesis. Bergin reiterated his emphasis on the development of micro-theories, but it did not seem to strike a very responsive chord.

Regardless of the form of therapy, we must explain *what* is learned and *how* it is learned. In this universally recognized aim, naturalistic studies, in the view of these consultants, can play an important part. They seemed to urge the kind of research Chassan had advocated. Bob cited an example: Note changes in defenses as affects change and new material emerges. The specification of variables and other methodological problems are of course formidable in any such undertaking. Ultimately, one's research approach is a commitment of faith; there are no either-ors in this area; and the naturalistic approach has not been given a fair trial.

Wallerstein said that in the abstract he could see himself collaborating with others of different orientations, but realistically he is uncertain about this and feels that his personal priorities would go in other directions. Strupp noted that this was an important observation and noted that NIMH definitely gives research a direction, that their policies determine the kinds of projects that will be funded. Priorities are thus decided by NIMH, but we hope these priorities are inspired by an accurate reading of what the realities are in a given field.

Sampson suggested that the effect of what Strupp and Bergin are doing will be like the effect of interpretations on a patient in therapy. It will have a stimulating effect but will have variable effects on different persons. We are, in essence, raising important questions and forcing people to come to terms with them.

Wallerstein pointed out that he tended to agree with Kubie that research in psychotherapy won't get anywhere as long as those doing it have to make a living by doing clinical work and other things. What we really need is a center for the study of neurosis with a full time well-paid staff of clinical experts.

It is perhaps significant that throughout our discussion the Menninger Project, with which Bob has been prominently affiliated for a dozen years, received only passing mention, and Bob reported on the progress only after we specifically inquired about it. By this time there exists a sizable list of publications pertaining to this project and several monographs are still in progress. Bob admitted that he would not undertake a similar study today. Administrative problems, attrition of researchers, and other difficulties surrounding any major study, of which the Menninger Project is perhaps the most outstanding example, were explored in our conversation to some extent.

Wallerstein pointed out that he was the only survivor of the founding group but indicated that they held together longer than other large projects. He pointed out that all 42 cases have been completed including follow-ups. He noted that the project will be reported as a series of monographs by subgroups of two or three people doing each monograph. There will be no master project report. He mentioned one of the important articles by Helen Sargent et al. entitled "An Approach to the Quantitative Problems of Psychoanalytic Research" (1967). Other monographs will be (1) an analysis of the psychological tests before and after therapy, (2) a study on prediction in psychotherapy research which will appear as a *Psychological Issues Monograph,* Volume VI no. 1, (3) a paired comparisons project, (4) a multidimensional scalogram analysis applying facet theory to variables in the project *à la* Guttman and Lingoes, (5) a clinical summary (by Wallerstein) of what has been learned from the write-ups of the cases, and (6) a study of relevant situational variables.

Comments by Strupp and Bergin. In retrospect it appears that, while stimulating, this consultation, with the notable exception of the Engel paper, confirmed Engel's assertion that there is limited excitement to be found within the psychoanalytic framework, despite the fact that there is a storehouse of hypotheses in need of testing. The trouble seems to be that it is so difficult to formulate, design, and execute research problems relevant to psychoanalytic psychotherapy. This neither proves that it cannot be done nor that efforts should be abandoned. However, there is a strange discrepancy between Paul Meehl's recent dictum that psychoanalysis is by far the most exciting psychology around and the limitations of research in the area.

References

Dunbar, F. 1954. *Emotions and bodily changes.* New York: Columbia University Press.

Engel, G. 1968. Some obstacles to the development of research in psychoanalysis. *Journal of the American Psychoanalytic Association* 16: 195–204.

Patterson, G. R. 1971. Behavioral intervention procedures in the classroom and in the home. In A. E. Bergin & S. L. Garfield eds., *Handbook of psychotherapy and behavior change.* New York: Wiley, pp. 751–75.

Sargent, H. D., Coyne, L., Wallerstein, R. S., & Holtzman, W. H. 1967. An approach to the quantitative problems of psychoanalytic research. *Journal of Clinical Psychology* 23: 243–91.

Sargent, H. D., Horavitz, L., Wallerstein, R. S., & Appelbaum, A. 1969. Prediction in psychotherapy research. *Psychological Issues Monograph,* vol. VI, no. 1.

Wallerstein, R. S., & Sampson, H. 1971. Issues in research in the psychoanalytic process. *International Journal of Psychoanalysis.* 52: 11–50.

INTERVIEW: LOUIS BREGER AND HOWARD LEVENE*

San Francisco, January 17, 1969

Breger started off by saying that he disliked the "standard scientific question" which we posed. He said it implied the possibility of solving problems directly by research. Even if we could answer these questions, he doubted that such research would have much impact on practice. Thus, if we have outcome comparisons they are too threatening and people tend to sabotage them. For all of these reasons (and others), research is very difficult in this area. Instead, an important goal is to promote a more research-minded attitude among clinicians, epitomized by the injunction: "Let's examine the data." He then launched into a discussion of the sociology of knowledge and argued that the climate or atmosphere in the profession has to be changed before studies could have much impact. This was an important point (but one of which we were not personally convinced).

He expressed a preference for naturalistic research and considered many problems outlined in the book by Goldstein, Heller, and Sechrest (1966) as "irrelevant" to psychotherapy. However, like Goldstein, Lou has little enthusiasm for the various "schools" and feels they need to be superseded.

* Dr. Breger is Associate Professor of Psychology at the California Institute of Technology. Dr. Levene is affiliated with the Langley Porter Neuropsychiatric Institute, University of California.

He and Levene, together with Virginia Patterson, are currently doing a project in their own clinic. They have had a number of problems with this project and already realize that it is quite loose and may not yield definite results principally because they have attempted to study the clinical process as it proceeds in the clinic and to get clinicians to examine their work in a research context. Essentially, this is an outcome study in which an effort is made to study the results of brief therapy. They are assigning their residents and clinical psychology interns to one of five seminars and supervisory groups. These include behavior therapy, brief psychoanalytic therapy, group therapy, Jungian therapy, and more classical analytical therapy. The objective of this comparative study is to investigate the process and outcomes of therapy done by the trainees in these five different training groups. The groups meet over a one-year period during the trainees' stay at Langley Porter. The measures include patients' self-reports, therapists' reports, outcome evaluations, and follow-up (after 3 months). In addition, a content analysis of therapists' verbal communications is done.

In order to study the process, they are developing a new scoring system to rate therapist interventions. They want the content analysis system to cut across techniques. Generally, it is similar to many content analysis systems. It is clear, they claim, from listening to tapes that behavior therapists behave "differently." The point here is to forget about schools and simply study how people behave as therapists in the therapeutic situation.

One of the interesting features of this study is a so-called open intake, which dispenses with the traditional diagnostic conference and assigns patients promptly to one or the other group on a random basis. (See Breger's incisive paper in the *Journal of Counsulting and Clinical Psychology,* 1968, concerning the current status of diagnostic testing. The principal message is that psychodiagnostic testing and psychiatric diagnosis, in the traditional sense, are largely a waste of time because too often they have no bearing on decisions regarding treatment.)

Preliminary findings indicate that during the first six months drop-outs in analytic therapy are higher than in behavior therapy; during the second six-month period this difference disappeared. Patients tended to prefer behavior therapy, which evidently was more in keeping with their expectations of what "treatment" should be like since the patient role is closer to that in medicine. One important drawback of this study, readily admitted by Lou, is that the therapists are inexperienced trainees; more experienced therapists may be more successful in keeping patients in therapy regardless of theoretical orientation. Lou characterized the research as "sloppy" in the sense of inadequate controls, which are always difficult to achieve in a clinic setting, but also as "realistic" because it is done in a clinical setting. One of the important features of behavior therapy is the therapist's assertion (promise): "I can help you." This is in contrast to the analytic therapist's tentativeness.

Lou noted that we had paid insufficient attention to the role of free association in our survey paper. One of the essential ingredients of the analytic method is the therapist's steadfast refusal to engage in a neurotic relationship with the patient; instead, he insists on examining with the patient what he is unwittingly trying to do in therapy and with the therapist. Basically, no one welcomes such an examination unless he can become convinced that the unpleasantness and pain are outweighed by the immediate relief that follows. It is clear that a solid relationship must be established before transference problems can be analyzed.

Lou, like others, feels that no breakthroughs are about to occur in psychotherapy research. He also feels a need for translating analogue to clinical situations.

Comments by Strupp. Somewhere in this discussion I came back to the importance of focusing on the *evocation of affect,* the mobilization of strong emotions in therapy, which can lead to "catharsis" as well as to a reorganization of one's cognitions. I have elaborated on this problem elsewhere (1969, 1970) and won't repeat myself here. It strikes me that therapy is often ineffective because it does not succeed in getting the patient deeply involved emotionally, with the result that little experiential learning occurs.

Breger agreed strongly with this view, and asserted that in his experience "the most intense affects are likely to arise in therapy when troublesome aspects of the patient's personality are examined in the context of the *ongoing relationship* with the therapist."

Comments by Bergin. This meeting was relatively brief and therefore only sketchily describes the research program and viewpoints of the interviewees;[22] additional points issuing from it are of interest:

1. Levene argued that a phenomenological analysis of what is going on, sticking to the level of behavior, is important. This may yield less relevance for schools.

2. Breger pointed out that the main problem is the resistance of clinicians to research. (It seems to us this is not a problem for behavior therapy.)

3. They are limiting their goals to looking for small practical payoffs and do not have much hope for anything very significant or dramatic at this point.

22. For readers who may be interested in a fuller account of the research program, Drs. Levene, Breger, and Patterson have available a recent paper entitled: "A Training and Research Program in Brief Psychotherapy."

4. Levene pointed out that many of the younger residents are getting more mystical and that the Jungians are becoming very popular. He pointed out that some people are finding that residents in the United States are moving away from the body of clinical knowledge to "here and now" experience. They are looking for immediate emotional experiences, and fewer are enrolling in training at the analytic institutes.

References

Breger, L. 1968. Psychological testing: Treatment and research implications. *Journal of Consulting and Clinical Psychology* 32: 176–81.

Goldstein, A. P., Heller, K., & Sechrest, L. B. 1966. *Psychotherapy and the psychology of behavior change*. New York: Wiley.

Strupp, H. H. 1969. Toward a specification of teaching and learning in psychotherapy. *Archives of General Psychiatry* 21: 203–12.

———. 1970. Specific vs. non-specific factors in psychotherapy and the problem of control. *Archives of General Psychiatry* 23: 393–401.

INTERVIEW: RALPH R. GREENSON AND MILTON WEXLER*

Los Angeles, January 18, 1969

This consultation, held in the suite of two prominent Beverly Hills analysts, resulted in an animated and frank discussion of a number of important issues. Greenson is the author of a recent volume on psychoanalytic technique (1967; to be followed by a second volume) which holds promise of becoming the successor to Fenichel's (1945) classic and is much more readable and down-to-earth. Wexler, a psychologist who achieved prominence through his work with schizophrenics at the Menninger Foundation, shares offices with Greenson, and the two collaborate in research which, commendably, they carry on in their "spare time," with support from a small private foundation which they head.

One project to which Greenson and Wexler have been devoting considerable time and energy concerned the intensive study of unexpected failures in psychoanalysis. To this end they invited therapists of known competence to present in detail failure cases which initially had been accepted for therapy with a favorable prognosis.

* Dr. Greenson is Clinical Professor of Psychiatry at the UCLA School of Medicine. Dr. Wexler is a private practitioner in Los Angeles.

They have been collecting information on these cases for three years. Each case is presented in detail in three 3-hour sessions without comment to a group of four listeners (analysts). The group members, including the presenter, then independently write down what they think went wrong. This might include, for example, judgments about the patient's basic unsuitability for this type of therapy, errors in the technique or the conceptualization of pathology, reality factors, mismatching of patient and therapist. The group then devotes one session to communicating ideas to each other. Subsequently, they send the same written material to six more reviewers, and there is a new presentation and discussion of possible reasons for the therapeutic failure.

They found the procedure "terribly wearing" on the participants because it is cumbersome and they more recently turned to briefer presentations of failure cases. Apparently they have enlisted a rather select group of colleagues who are willing to do this kind of gruelling work, although each person is paid for the time he spends in the meetings. They admitted that a number of colleagues had turned them down. Some said they had no failures and others implied that all their cases were failures to some degree. It is important to note that all of the cases studied were seen for a period of years. So far, they have finished 5 cases. The patients they are studying include cases by prominent psychoanalysts. In addition, Greenson is working on a new project involving the exchange of case material with a Kleinian analyst. Greenson and his colleague each report on one neurotic patient and they tell one another what they think of the other's work. Greenson is also starting a similar exchange of views concerning the treatment of a schizophrenic patient by psychoanalysis.

These men are making a special effort to be honest about what is happening in therapy. They pointed out that there is a temptation to falsify reports, and in reviewing their own notes they have at times been shocked. For example, Greenson noted that things he thought were new at 6 months in a given case had actually occurred in the second session.

Bergin asked whether they had discovered anything new during their explorations. Greenson summarized his impressions: Patients often had been studied only superficially before they were accepted for analysis; mismatching was rare; the therapist's distortions of his recollections of what happens in therapy, even when he takes notes, are remarkable; therapists don't reflect nearly enough on what they are doing; there is tremendous variability in technique; and what therapists write is often different from what they do. Strupp had suspected the latter for a long time and advocated studying what therapists do rather than what they say they do. Furthermore, he asserted that there is only a tenuous relationship between technique and the theory purporting to account for it.

In general they said that it is important to study what is being done rather than what people say they are doing. They understand that their work may only lead to hypotheses, but they feel that it is essential to focus on what is really happening.

These men have concluded some interesting things from their experiences:

1. Interpretation alone is insufficient.
2. Analysis of transference alone is insufficient.
3. It is important to take account of the *real* relationship between the patient and the therapist instead of worshiping exclusively the phenomena of transference and interpretations. Analysts generally fail to have the proper perspective. Freud avoided focussing on the "real" relationship because he was afraid of acting-out by the analyst. Strupp, however, noted that Freud, albeit in footnotes and parenthetical statements, recognized the importance of the therapist as a mentor and model.
4. These apparently ideal psychoanalytical cases had "holes" in them, that is, the patients often turned out to have had psychotic dispositions. Poor diagnosis had assigned them to psychoanalysis.

Some additional things Greenson and Wexler had learned from this project and related observations: (1) It is very time consuming, expensive (to pay for travel and meeting time), and emotionally demanding. (2) Greenson felt his theories tended to be validated. (3) He has developed greater acceptance of some Kleinian views. He said that he had read all of their stuff before but had no real understanding of it until he began to exchange views at a clinical level. (4) They were surprised at the enormous variability in techniques. Some people, for example, tend to be very silent while others tend to give machine-gun like interpretations. Also, some therapists tend to cling ritualistically to their own theoretical framework and they do not really listen to the patient, especially if his talk does not fit their theory. (5) They found that even good therapists—perhaps especially good ones—keep on learning and that they do so mostly in the course of their therapeutic work. (6) Some therapists seem to modify their technical approach, even with the same patient, as therapy progresses. (7) As mentioned before, the real relationship between patient and therapist is also a crucial factor. Greenson has found that it is important to explain his techniques to the patient in advance. Thus he explains to the patient the process of free association and its rationale. He also states that he needs to work many hours with the patient to help him understand and to figure out how best to help the patient. In this connection, Greenson and Wexler stress the importance of developing a special relationship with patients who have marked ego weaknesses. They need to feel psychological contact with the therapist; otherwise they tend to get lost because their basic resources are too limited.

Greenson spent a fair amount of time elaborating on this view that the real relationship between patient and therapist is of the utmost importance, transcending interpretations and other efforts to analyze transference phenomena (Greenson & Wexler, 1969, 1970). In essence, unless there is a real relationship between the two participants, there is little possibility of effectively analyzing transference distortions. The therapist must make a determined effort to underscore *correct* perceptions on the part of the patient (in the sense of Sullivan's concept of consensual validation) and at times he must be ready to admit that he was wrong, angry, and the like. "If you want the patient to have sufficient trust in the situation so that he will regress, you have to show him that you are not God." Accordingly, Greenson spends a good deal of time at the beginning of therapy explaining the ground rules—the advantages of free association, the use of the couch, etc. The patient must be "prepared," and Greenson feels that the patient has a right to know the rules by which the game is palyed. (This is strongly reminiscent of Szasz's position, clearly stated in *The Ethics of Psychoanalysis,* 1965) It is interesting, too, that from a different theoretical position, Goldstein has been making the same point. All of these approaches are in sharp contrast to the traditional analytic position in which the situation is deliberately left vague and ambiguous, which supposedly permits a more effective analysis of transference phenomena.

Strupp suggested that this is an important problem for research. One might study, if only over a short period of time, the relative advantages of defining the situation more clearly, as opposed to leaving it ambiguous. One might find, for example, that one procedure permits the patient to get "into" therapy more expeditiously, is more facilitative of a good working relationship, leads to more productive interchanges, avoids sparring. There is some evidence, adduced by one of Bordin's students (Dibner, 1958) some years ago, that initial interviews in which the situation is left ambiguous are more conducive to heightening the patient's anxiety. In some cases, this may be desirable. At any rate, Greenson sets the stage by telling the patient early in therapy: "I need to know a great deal about you, and we've got to get to know each other." Since he is very direct and lacking in pompousness, he no doubt is quite successful in this. Again, if one wishes to analyze transference distortions, the patient must be placed in a position which permits him to differentiate clearly between reality and fantasy.

At this point Wexler indicated that it is not necessary to always treat the patient as though he is sick. Some of the patient's communications refer to realities. For example, the patient may say: "I feel you were angry yesterday." Under conditions like this it is sometimes necessary for the therapist to say "Yes, I was angry," and to make interpretations and explore the subject, but also to accept the reality that may be involved. The point of all this is to underline correct perceptions, attitudes and feelings, to reinforce them and to emphasize the necessity of consensual validation; otherwise we tend to leave the person in limbo, which is the more common therapeutic approach. Greenson points out that when he gives a speech on this subject, his colleagues sometimes respond by saying: "We have been doing this for years but have been reluctant to admit it." What price orthodoxy!

On the subject of future therapy studies, Greenson and Wexler suggested the importance of staying close to natural observation. They have found that when they read their notes even of a month earlier, they are often surprised by their selectivity. Bergin observed that Greenson is concerned with the problem of refining technique. Greenson stated that this was true and that he makes some effort to vary his technique. Both consultants noted that they had done this, for example with the Kleinian method regarding certain interpretations. The intervention, however, must seem plausible and fit the clinical context. Wexler pointed out that there may often be pure experiments in nature which occur accidentally. He related that when he was at Menninger's he found a female schizophrenic patient who spoke "word salad." He felt that he was failing in his therapy and decided she must be a totally incurable case. He then, under a research grant, used Rosen's technique whereupon the patient became wilder, more acutely disturbed, and finally sexually assaultive. At one point she made a violent assault and Wexler responded by meeting "force with force." This was followed by her first normal sentence, "Why did you have to do that?" He then realized that punishment and strictness by superego emphasis might work with her; he became like a priest to her (she had religious convictions). He told her sex and smoking were bad. Remarkably, each time he became strict with her, she became quite rational. One might say that he set up contingencies, defined limits, and controlled reward and punishment. Then he reverted to Rosen's technique and she got worse. The converse was also tried. He continued to emphasize control of her instincts. While the approach seemed naive, it worked. "There seem to be times when we really have to set limits hard, and if we don't we can send people right out of their skulls!"

Greenson also mentioned that one must intervene differently with different patients. For example, he does much more talking now, especially with sicker patients who seem to derive greater support when the therapist participates more actively. This is especially important when the person feels a sense of object loss. High frequency of talk by focussing the patient's attention seems to stem regression by maintaining object constancy. Strupp interjected that we need to define what *kind* of talking is done in therapy, to which Greenson agreed. They also mentioned the role of "object constancy" in coping with psychosis on a larger scale, that is, keeping the persons important to the psychotic in close contact with him. The practice in Holland of keeping patients in the community instead of sequestering them in state hospitals may thus account for a much smaller number of chronic cases than we see in the U. S. Social workers also go out and visit the patients and this again points up the effects of maintaining daily contacts or "object constancy."

Turning to problems of research, Strupp raised the question of whether it might be possible to isolate interventions from the therapy setting itself, and we both asked whether they thought it was feasible to extract variables from the clinical context. Greenson thought that in order to get a better understanding of the therapeutic process, "you need a highly experienced therapist who knows what he is doing or who has the potential of finding out what he is doing." This statement comes reasonably close to one of the projects we have outlined: studying the therapist's mental operations. Wexler pointed out that there were some kinds of experimentation that might be fruitful. For example, the Russians are using electrical pulsations to put people to sleep for 3 or 4 days by focussing these pulsations on the eyelids. Wexler raises the question of what we might be able to do if we could reach them during this period.

Bergin asked Wexler about his opinion concerning behavioral approaches in treating schizophrenics. Wexler thought some of it was "terrible." Greenson pointed out that he was appalled by what the operant conditioners are doing. Some of this reward and punishment reminds him of *1984*. In a similar vein Strupp asked him about reward and punishment or other behavioral variables in psychoanalysis. There did not seem to be much discussion of that point specifically although Wexler expressed the view that identification is an important process and it would be important if we could induce identification during therapy of schizophrenics so that we could create more profound changes. He emphasized, however, that we must always work within the whole context. There followed some discussion of modeling, spurred by a question raised by Strupp, in which Greenson suggested the possibility of the patient living in the therapist's home and the environment being a model for the patient. To observe what would happen to young patients under these conditions might be very instructive. In general, Greenson argued that conducting experiments like this required a highly experienced and a very aware person. Obviously, there is a wide range of methods available and the person employing them must have had previous experience with a wide spectrum of problems and patients.

Comments by Bergin. Greenson and Wexler are dedicated clinicians who are trying to do an intensive clinical, case by case analysis of what is going on in psychoanalysis. While there are real questions about the objectivity and quantifiability of what they are doing, it is probably as good an example as there is of a careful, laborious and emotionally taxing study of individual cases. In general, the scientific quality of this work seemed primitive. These investigators are just beginning to catch up with the rest of the field, and yet the intensity and apparent honesty with which they are going about it was quite impressive. One has the feeling that there are significant changes taking place in their ideas and that goals are emerging and progress is occurring. This is especially important for people who are involved in and identified with a more classical psychoanalytical tradition. This could have real reverberations if it influences the American Psychoanalytic Association to become freer and more open to scientific inquiry. This, combined with the paper by Engel and the comments by Wallerstein, etc., suggests that the times are changing.

Comments by Strupp. I was impressed by the fact that here are two analysts who are keenly interested in learning something new about the art they are practicing, and they are willing to devote a portion of their time to this goal. Their approach, obviously, is different from that of researchers in academia, and the time they devote to research (or, more accurately, focused inquiry) perhaps represents a greater sacrifice. Be that as it may, they are propelled by curiosity, skepticism, and dedication to their craft. They operate firmly, but perhaps too exclusively, from within the psychoanalytic framework, and it proved difficult to engage them in discussions about research proceeding outside that framework. Evidently, they did not see such work as relevant or they were not interested in it for other reasons. To them, research in psychotherapy largely means clinical observation, as it did to Freud, but they are willing and eager to pool resources with interested colleagues to examine what they are doing, study inconsistencies, regularities, and the like. It is a moot question, of course, whether it is possible in this way to isolate variables from the welter of observations, but perhaps it is possible to achieve refinements in this manner. Essentially they are engaged in the intensive study of single cases, and by studying unexpected failures they are looking for the unusual, the exceptional instances, an approach which has often led to progress. They represent the opposite pole of the laboratory researcher who attempts to isolate a process in an artificial situation. At the present state of knowledge, both approaches may be needed, and it would be foolhardy to predict which will be more fruitful in the long run. They have the freedom to look wherever their intuition tells them to: and they are not encumbered by pressures for "payoff." On the other hand, they have to find private funds to finance this luxury.

References

Dibner, A. S. 1958. Ambiguity and anxiety. *Journal of Abnormal and Social Psychology* 56: 165–74.
Fenichel, O. 1945. *The psychoanalytic theory of neuroses.* New York: W. W. Norton & Co.
Greenson, R. R. 1967. *The technique and practice of psychoanalysis.* New York: International Universities Press.
Greenson, R. R., & Wexler, M. 1969. The non-transference relationship in the psychoanalytic situation. *The International Journal of Psycho-Analysis* 50: 27–39.
———. 1970. Discussion of "The non-transference relationship in the psychoanalytic situation." *The International Journal of Psycho-Analysis* 51: 143–50.
Szasz, T. S. 1965. *The ethics of psychoanalysis: The theory and method of autonomous psychotherapy*. New York: Basic Books.

DISCUSSION: BERGIN AND STRUPP*

La Jolla, January 20, 1969

As always, we come back to a basic dichotomy which seems to thread its way through all of science: the dichotomy between the *tender* and *tough* minded approaches. We discussed the experimental-manipulative approach and the attempt to search for mechanisms of the influence process. On the other hand we discussed naturalistic approaches, the development of adequate descriptions of phenomena and the discovery of powerful processes occurring in nature. A critical issue was whether there is power in psychotherapy as it exists or whether there is not, regardless of which approach to inquiry we take. If we were to take a naturalistic approach, for example, it need not focus on psychotherapy but could focus on naturalistic change processes which occur in the social life of man.

I said that I felt it was important for us to repeatedly tell ourselves that we are at a point in history and that we must interpret the experience of the field and make that experience and its meaning more explicit just as a therapeutic interpretation tends to do. We also need to recognize that we are at a point of rapid change and development which is different from the history of the physical sciences. We cannot necessarily predict from one to the other.

Hans said that he was uncertain whether comparable time spans will be necessary for the evolution of physical science and psychological science. It would be presumptuous to assume that we know where we will be going or at what rate. The complexity is staggering in this field and this militates against rapid change. Psychology has generally tended to grossly underesti-

* This summary is by Bergin.

mate the complexity of man, for example Chomsky versus Skinner. Hans also mentioned the tendency of psychoanalysts to feel condescending toward experimentalists. They say that experimentalists deal in "kid stuff" with nothing very important.

I suggested that we may not necessarily be able to predict the future of the field but we may be able to point at what will pay off; for example, the predecessors of Einstein seemed to be pointing in the right directions.

Hans agreed but argued that there was a lot of knowledge around to be synthesized by Einstein. We need this too, but do we have it? We need to know more about the mechanisms of change before this kind of synthesizing will be possible.

Hans said that he was struck with what the man had said at church the day before, that his own father was the greatest man he ever knew. The achievement of independence and autonomy through obedience seems important. This seems to be a region in which religion and psychology overlap significantly. We have God the father and we have the biological father. The process by which a child internalizes teachings is important. Does imitation learning get anywhere close to this? These are basic mechanisms of change and development. In the absence of this internalization process you have anarchy, neurosis, anomie, and the lack of an internal guidance system. The problem is essentially one of how the son becomes the father. This is a crucial issue and relates to the complexity of therapy and of personality change and development in an important way.

I suggested that perhaps we may need more theoretical work now instead of rushing off and doing study X or study Y. Perhaps as Einstein did. He guided research by stating questions in a testable, explicit and fruitful manner and made some clear connections between events in nature. We also need theory regarding systems or variables in psychology like those in physics and biology. We need to undo the complexity and make it manageable.

Hans concurred and suggested that we need to focus on what we can do. The freaks of nature help us. They are natural experiments. However, psychotherapy is so complex that it is very difficult when we begin to talk to someone in a therapy hour to feel that we have any real control over the process or understanding of it. Actually, looking at the field quite broadly may be very important even though it may be very hard.

Hans then raised the question of what tends to get rewarded in the scientific community and raised the question as to why NIMH should expect payoffs. Could Mendel guarantee payoffs?

We both agreed again that identification and internalization bear upon a broad and complex process which affects all of life and involves many of the mechanisms which we have been discussing including reward and punishment, and the like.

I noted at this point the great power that exists in families.

Hans suggested that the founders of religion have gotten a hold of something powerful; but they were not too explicit and did not experiment. The person is closer to being cured when he develops faith in something. Perhaps we will enrich the religious literature, like Mowrer, after a while. But where do we go now?

I suggested that perhaps we do need to delve not only into the child development area but in other areas of psychology and fields outside of psychology. We must base the change processes of the future upon an intensive examination of what is known about the powerful processes in nature. We aren't experts in those areas but we do know psychotherapy and we know how to ask questions of others who are experts in these other areas. Perhaps through consultation with them we can systematize better and look for part-processes that are going on.

Hans suggested, however, that there are real limits in some of these areas, such as the attitude change literature. Is there really anything in these?

I suggested "yes" on the basis of my experience; however, there is a real need for clinical trials in these areas.

Hans suggested that there are limits to what can be done this way, although he was interested in Jerry Frank's suggestion that permeability to change might be heightened via drugs or via emotional arousal, such as in the case of religious experience.

I raised a question of whether we shouldn't state alternatives in February and consider some of the thoughts which we had just been discussing. We seemed to be moving toward stating, at least broadly, some preferences.

Hans suggested the importance of listing alternatives also and that we separately list what we personally prefer. It is perhaps important for us not to drop the ball at this point by simply making a report to the field which would end our work and leave others to pick up the ball.

I raised questions about how much instrumentation and measurement deficiencies limit anything we could propose at this point. I also wondered whether we couldn't study large individual differences in the capacity of people to be inducted into the therapeutic process. Perhaps it was Hans who suggested this and also the idea that in order to unscramble the confused beliefs of individuals it is necessary to establish a trusting relationship; therefore, complexity is automatically introduced into the change process.

Hans again raised the question of whether we do not need a new methodology or approach. Colby however says it is impossible, that there are only a few ways in which we can approach science. Perhaps we need to study the social context along natural lines. Psychotherapy is a contrived situation.

I suggested that the social context includes very powerful change agents. It is important to develop transfer from therapy situations by switching to these natural contingencies. We also need to bring cognitive processes into play here by developing self-reinforcing contingencies. Then generalization is automatic because the individual does it on his own.

INTERVIEW: CARL R. ROGERS*

La Jolla, January 21, 1969

Carl confided that he was not "taken" by the prospect of collaborative research, admitting that 15 years ago he would have considered it "great." Now he considers the "standard scientific question" (as stated in our list) obsolete and outdated. It tends to make therapy look more objective than it is or can be. We noted that we ourselves had come to feel that a number of our questions had already been superseded. On the whole, Carl feels "uncertain and confused" about the status of the field; he would prefer working with groups rather than single dyads, although he concurred with one of Strupp's biases that it is already hard enough to study what goes on between two persons. At any rate, he feels the yield of "orthodox" studies, many of which he had sired himself, is minute compared to the effort. Strupp reminded him of a comment he made to someone at the 1958 Conference on Research in Psychotherapy, to the effect that he had never learned much from controlled studies and that his insights had come from clinical work. He quoted Polanyi with approval: "Let's do away with 'Science' for 10–20 years and try to get some knowledge!" What is knowledge to Carl? "Something which is subjectively convincing to me; something I understand intuitively; it could be private but hopefully it can be corroborated by others." It may be private and not appreciated by *science.* He feels we get too much pseudo-truth through empirical research of the type conducted today. We are groping toward a new view of science in the human realm, a science that fits human experience and is not divorced from it, as is true of the "traditional" approach. He referred us to a recent book of his (Coulson & Rogers, 1968), which summarizes a symposium on this topic.

Contemporary philosophy of science has rejected the "traditional" approach, but there are no "prescriptions" available. Again, he referred to Polanyi's argument (1964) that even in the hard sciences a personal commitment to a personal view is always involved, even in the case of reading a dial. Rogers asserted that he thinks there is a general disaffection from the former philosophy of the behavioral sciences. We now know better what our *attitudes* toward inquiry should be like, but we know less about what the actual *content* of this approach should be. One possible direction is to take into account more effectively the subjective experience of both patients and therapists.

Strupp mentioned Paul Meehl's comment that many philosophers of science will not touch behavioral science any more. They say it is hopeless.

* Dr. Rogers is Resident Fellow at the Center for Studies of the Person, La Jolla, California.

Rogers responded by saying that knowledge is not advanced by facts but by scientists who have a view of what they think is worth following up. Science thus becomes a subjective interlocking community of workers. He pointed out that his two years of working at Cal Tech with some of their top theoretical physicists had taught him a great deal. They were not afraid of fantasy. Something they tended to dream up came close to explaining a lot. One fellow dreamed up a particle with the "damndest" characteristics and it required 250,000 photographs in a cloud chamber before they discovered the curve they were looking for. But this curve identified a new particle. (This seems similar to Colby's example of the scientists he works with.)

Rogers then emphasized the importance of *intuition,* that it is important to cut loose from pre-formed concepts and theories. "I'm not really a scientist," he said, "most of my research has been to confirm what I already *felt* to be true." Strupp then asked about his immersion in listening to tapes before writing the "necessary and sufficient conditions" paper. "Yes," he said, "that was the most scientific thing I ever did. But generally I never learned anything from research." He tended to feel that we are in a new field and no one knows a damn thing. What are the alternatives to traditional science? "Develop free spirits," the kind of individuals we find in the "hard" sciences. He added: "We really don't know a damn thing about how to find them."

He is very disillusioned and embittered by graduate education as it exists today, believing that it is completely antithetical to the above goals, that it reduces creativity rather than stimulates it. Nor is he sanguine about Government-supported research: "Anything significant will not be supported because of an undue emphasis on 'pay-off.' " Anything significantly new is unlikely to be supported by the government, the universities, or foundations. The most promising studies won't be supported by the National Institute of Mental Health. If a project is ridiculed, it puts them on the spot. Review bodies that sit in judgment sometimes seem to know too much regarding methodology and hardly a damned thing else. Strupp commented that they tend to prefer "sure things."

In what directions, then, does fruitful therapy research lie? Rogers suggested that the study of videotape records of the live therapy process might be the best strategy. More minute observations and elaborate records of the process of personal change, especially in single cases, will yield the most valuable hunches. The stress on causality, as exemplified by psychoanalysis, strikes Rogers as "sad." A field-theoretical approach may be more promising. Psychological causes will always be complete guesswork, which Rogers illustrated by referring to a statement by Thomas French, the Chicago psychoanalyst, that even the prediction of a rat's behavior is utterly impossible.

Bergin then asked about Carl's views on the possibility of breaking psychotherapy or behavior into part processes. Rogers suggested that we have to do it but that we need to avoid overdoing it. He gave illustrations of some mechanisms that might be studied, for example, (1) the immediate interpersonal experience, (2) the relationship with authority, (3) the concept of self. These may be separate and yet interact. Bergin said that he felt it was necessary to separate and isolate even these interpersonal processes, possibly in experiments on part processes, and then put them back together later as a form of psychotherapy. Rogers agreed that analogues may be valuable if we avoid overgeneralization to psychotherapy, especially if we are unsure about their applicability to treatment.

Somewhere along the line, Strupp referred to the Illinois (Shakow) project and NIMH (Bergman) project, both of which have resulted in extensive records of therapeutic interviews, but with which no one evidently has been able to do very much. The answer may lie in the fact that no one got inspirations from watching these films. We need to take a view of this natural material but we can't just describe everything; we have to start somewhere. The video tape or film record in and of itself is no good; one needs tentative hunches; and one must be able to hold hypotheses in abeyance. Few people can do this. Strupp recalled Sullivan's observation that most of us can entertain no more than a couple of hypotheses about a set of phenomena.

Real science holds hypotheses very tentatively and we must start somewhere with tentative hypotheses. Rogers feels that psychologists, however, tend to be more firm about their hypotheses. He then pointed out how he had met with a faculty group at Cal Tech and that one man hotly objected to hiring behavioral scientists. He then read Rogers and Dymond's (1954) book and also Rogers' Schizophrenia Research Design. The man then said, "My God, you people are in a field that *is* hard to study." He added: "You didn't leave enough room for alternative hypotheses—look at it this way and that way." The approach of yet another scientist seemed to be totally different from that of the psychologists. He was most interested in where the greatest mystery was. He was excited by hypnosis and things that were unexplained.

Strupp tried to elicit Rogers' position on the value of studying the one-to-one relationship as a source of knowledge. Carl stated that he is "conflicted." True, he has built his professional career on it, but he has lost enthusiasm. He feels changes occur more rapidly and more clearly in small, intensive groups. He noted that his process scale, which was developed on individual therapy, to his surprise worked quite well for groups also. Change does occur, and to some extent one can measure it. He noted that a thesis being done at Cal Western University showed positive change on the process scale in all 8 cases that were seen in a group. He noted interesting findings such as one woman who progressed up to a point where the therapist challenged her too much and then she regressed increasingly thereafter. Another man changed so fast that he scared himself and reverted back. It is important to conduct follow-up of the small group experience and to meet with people afterwards. He pointed out that the study of groups is more complex, but the changes that can occur on one weekend are exciting. This also avoids some of the problems involved with spontaneous change in control groups over long periods when you are studying individual therapy.

Bergin raised the question about the notion of an array of therapies to fit particular needs. Carl assented, calling attention to the importance of a careful matching between therapist and patient. For example, he feels that he is not very good with "constricted" people (faculty members, he thought, often fit this description). Some people can be changed through verbal experiences, others may benefit from a heightening of body awareness. He noted, however, that groups usually should include a broad spectrum of patients and that groups tend to be adept at individualizing approaches to different patients. He is thus not convinced of the desirability of homogenizing groups or group methods.

Bergin asked about the *who* of research and therapy. Rogers answered emphatically that it was essential to attract brilliant people to this field, ones with fertile minds. He told an anecdote about how he tried to attract a brilliant theoretical physicist into psychology. Strupp said he thought that this was very important, too, that we needed young men whose minds are not cluttered up with all the ideas and biases of the past. Rogers agreed further by saying that typical graduate training tends to be too narrow and it makes the trainee unfit for "real science." He noted that at Cal Tech the most productive events seemed to take place outside of the regular work. Most fields seem to do all they can to stifle creativity during work for degrees.

Like Colby, Carl believes that methodology is not our problem. We need to look for the most *mysterious* aspect of the field if we want to discover something new. One may have to be young to do this. After 32, a psysicist is "out." Colby, too, had said that we need young men with uncluttered minds who are unencumbered by our traditional biases. Most education, Carl feels, goes on outside of formal courses anyway, and each profession does its damndest to kill off new ventures in the field. His caveat: "Don't rush to conclusions!"

We then discussed what the two of us expect to do, what alternatives we are considering, whether we are going to engage in big projects, form centers, or what. Carl felt that by the time the studies in our paper were done, individual psychotherapy would have been given up for more effective procedures.

Where should we go from here? Carl feels we need better studies of the human relationship than have ever been done before; we need to study any situation that produces change, such as, parent-child relationships, and encounter groups. Study what goes through the patient's and the therapist's mind (for instance, play back three minutes of tape); in short, study the relationship in every conceivable way. It may be more fruitful to study therapeutic changes in people who are normal or not too sick (this was a lesson Carl learned from the Wisconsin schizophrenia project); study how trust unfolds gradually, and above all, try to *capture the subjective element!* (Here is a program for a lifetime of study!) "The variables we measure are usually damn remote from the change process." What we may need to do is to forget therapy and study broader issues that are widely relevant.

Rogers said it may be egotistical to reflect on the reasons his work has had such great impact on American psychology and many other fields, but he feels the reasons were that (1) he studied the human relationship in the widest sense and (2) he studied the process of change in a similarly broad sense. As an illustration of a change process outside of therapy, he gave the example of a marine drill sergeant who effects great changes in behavior. He stated that we need to look at other situations in nature where changes occur. He also feels that encounter groups in psychotherapy may yield knowledge of new change processes.

He noted that he would study troubled people or normals rather than the extremely disturbed, such as the schizophrenics, who seem not to change very much. He thinks that all positive relationships create change and that they should be studied in every way possible to gain knowledge of the details of the change processes that are occurring. For example, he would play back tapes and ask participants to tell what is going on in their minds.

Bergin responded by pointing out the importance of establishing a trusting relationship in order to get revelations of the kind of subjective material Rogers had just referred to. The relationship is thus a source of knowledge, particularly subjective knowledge, which we haven't pursued very systematically in our research. In other words, a methodology of the future may be to establish trust and then to inquire scientifically into the subjective realm.

Rogers agreed with this formulation and said it summarized well his view, that he had learned many things from the subjective world of people in psychotherapy because he had gotten hold of a process that is important across varied experiences. He said that in order to have our greatest impact we must forget psychotherapy and study the broader issue of change. He noted that in the case of the drill sergeant, trust is not a factor in change and that we must be aware of this type of situation as well as conditions under which trust is relevant. Bergin pointed out the example of a neurotic young man who had gone into the Air Force, responded to the reward-punishment system there, and became a very competent and effective officer. In the meantime, his self-image and interpersonal style also changed significantly. Rogers responded with the interpretation that many people thrive on a value system that envelops them, one that comes from outside of themselves.

The discussion then moved to a direct examination of how values are internalized and their relationship to therapeutic change. Strupp brought out the importance of the identification process and of obedience and submission in the service of ultimately developing autonomy and self-confidence. He cited Eric Hoffer's account (1958) of Moses' experience in this regard. Bergin pointed out that obedience often yields autonomy and that if one does not obey in the sense of learning to identify and internalize, the son never becomes a father.

Carl said that he previously didn't think much of the concept of modeling (as an identificatory process) but has changed his mind. However, he did not view this as a simple conformity process. With respect to child-rearing: "You have to adapt yourself to the feelings of others; it is not just a matter of discipline or learning to obey." In the therapeutic realm, if the therapist becomes a model, he tends most often to narrow the patient's alternatives and the person will have problems with autonomy. If the therapist is accepting, he tends to model the kind of acceptance the patient must learn to feel toward himself. Rogers then went on to disagree with much of what we had said about obedience in the service of autonomy. He stated that we must avoid this particular kind of identification process and use modeling in the way that he described.

Carl argued that we need a new model of man, which is contrary to what has been historically acceptable, and we need to be more explicit about it. This view eschews rigidity, dogma, and contempt for certain aspects of the self; it stresses such things as spontaneity and expressiveness, open communication, and a willingness to be "what I am." This model is summarized in Rogers' paper, "The Concept of the Fully Functioning Person" (1963). The people he would like to see develop within this model tend to be very different, and then he mentioned his objections to the prayers and what they symbolized at Nixon's inauguration. This view of man is not approved by organized religions. Parenthetically, right wing groups, from their particular vantage point, are correct in regarding sensitivity training as "dangerous" and their objections follow logically from their beliefs.

Can man be secure in espousing the "open self" and turning his back on a fixed belief system? Rogers doubts it. The "closed self" may have survival characteristics. For instance, a study of air crews which survived imprisonment in P.O.W. camps and a study of successful persons in pilot training showed that they tended to be religious and orthodox (in the traditional sense), secure in their families, and clung firmly to their values and beliefs; whereas the failures were more like his ideal model, people who were closer to their feelings, more flexible and open.

Psychotherapy, Strupp observed, is therefore basically *subversive* since it opposes what society stands for, a notion with which Carl agreed. This, of course, accounted for the hostility heaped on Freud when psychoanalysis attacked the hypocrisy of nineteenth-century Vienna. Szasz in his writings on autonomy reflects a similar theme. Rogers gave an example of his work at a school where he stated they didn't know what they were getting into. They didn't expect the consequences of the therapy that accrued. "We didn't try to deceive them but this kind of thing does happen."

We continued in the philosophical vein as Rogers said that he hoped man could learn to be secure in a process of change rather than just in something fixed. He pointed out that scientists tend to lack a strong faith in their theories and can give them up, but they have faith in the *process* of science. Can we have people like Rogers' ideal? He no longer sees this goal as just an end point of therapy, but as having broader social and philosophical implications.

Bergin asked about Carl's views on behavioral approaches to psychotherapy. He conceded the virtue of dealing with specific aspects of behavior, but also noted that behavioral therapy, in its emphasis on specific "chunks" of behavior it seeks to modify, actually comes closer to the medical model than most other forms of therapy (including client-centered therapy or psychoanalysis). In talking about behavior therapy, Carl remarked, "I become less of a scientist and more of a philosopher. The approach doesn't fit my philosophy. I am not interested in symptoms; I am interested in the *whole* person."

While he feels that people like Wolpe, Perls, Ellis and others have something valuable to offer, he still feels convinced of his own approach because it has had an influence on diverse fields and because people can pick it up, learn it, and make it part of their lives. Something like Perls' work is hard to learn. People are more impressed with him than they are with themselves. About the charismatic therapist: "When a patient leaves Fritz Perls, he probably feels Perls is a 'great guy' but he doesn't know how he touched the patient's 'inner spring.' I prefer for the patient to go away feeling: 'I can do a lot of things I formerly was incapable of doing.' Nor can Perls teach his technique to others." On the other hand, Rogers feels that others can learn his technique, even though they only know him through his writings. "Perhaps," he mused, "the approach is simpleminded enough to make this possible." (From some instances we have seen, some followers of Rogers are not such good Rogerians.)

We then discussed group approaches, and their merits and deficiencies. Rogers emphasized quite strongly his feeling that the intensive group experience was very powerful. He said that variations in groups were a function of values and goals. He pointed out that there is a broad spectrum of groups. For example, there are T groups or sensitivity groups, personal growth groups of the type which he conducts, the charismatic types of groups which Perls conducts, the fads and charlatans who are involved in some of the body movement and contact groups. He said it didn't seem to him that taking off your clothes necessarily removed inhibitions. He thinks the whole movement could be discredited if too many fads occurred. The valuable parts of the group movement may have to continue under other labels.

These groups, in Rogers' view, are different from group psychotherapy and people who come to group psychotherapy need help and are more disturbed. People who come to encounter groups are functioning in the normal range; they want change and development; the atmosphere creates a different climate; the focus is on the here and now, and the leader feels less responsibility to change the people. There are similarities, but encounter groups can't be called therapy. According to Rogers, it is very fruitful to work with groups whose members know each other. It is then possible for them to followup with each other, and also for him to followup with them more effectively. "Stranger" groups yield difficulties with followup and generalization.

Comments by Strupp. I wondered whether in Rogers' judgment therapists can be trained. He stressed the importance of *experiential learning* which in my translation means personal analysis[23] or a similar experience. Contrariwise, if one talks about a therapeutic technology, the cognitive elements are overemphasized.

Toward the end of the meeting Rogers expressed the opinion that universities exercise a constricting influence on innovation and open inquiry, and he confessed to "a sense of release" when he finally left the university setting. Of course, he admitted, one pays a high price.

Rogers' critical concern with the status of contemporary behavioral science, its methodology, and vicissitudes provides food for thought. For the rest, the report is a matter of *res ipsa loquitur*.

References

Coulson, W., & Rogers, C. R. 1968. *Man and the science of man.* Columbus, Ohio: Charles E. Merrill.

Hoffer, E. 1958. *The true believer.* New York: New American Library of World Literature.

Polanyi, M. 1964. *Personal knowledge: Towards a post-critical philosophy.* New York: Harper & Row.

Rogers, C. R. 1963. The concept of the fully functioning person. *Psychotherapy: Theory, Research, & Practice* 1: 17–26.

Rogers, C. R., & Dymond, R. F. 1954. *Psychotherapy and personality change.* Chicago: University of Chicago Press.

23. Comment by Rogers: "Oh, no. This *can* be very cognitive."

INTERVIEW: CHARLES B. TRUAX*

New York, February 7, 1969

Dr. Truax[24] began by suggesting that the study of the live psychotherapy process was the most valuable approach to research in personality change. He said that laboratory and analogue studies can be very misleading because there is too much pretense involved. The unreal aspects of such studies are the opposite of real therapy. For example, how can you simulate genuiness or warmth? In his own manipulative study in which he employed such variables, the client tended to make assumptions about the therapist's attitudes that simply were not correct. For example, when the therapist suddenly dropped his empathy level the patient seemed to think something was wrong; whereas, it was simply an experimental manipulation. He would like to believe that the findings of laboratory studies can be applied but generally they cannot. They are just about as irrelevant to psychotherapy as studies of learning are to classroom performance.

With regard to the question of whether we need better ideas or better research, Truax feels quite strongly that we have plenty of good ideas and, contrary to Colby's view, we need people to get out and test these ideas.

On the subject of complexity, Truax suggested that we ignore it and not do multifactorial studies. There are too many interactions which yield weak results and therefore they are inapplicable clinically. For clinical applications to occur, we must have powerful, obvious results. He said that essentially we are looking at the same kinds of problems that medicine does when it evaluates drug treatment.

At this point, I raised the question of whether we can really find powerful variables by studying live psychotherapy as it is presently practiced. Truax suggested that this is essential and that it is important to study heterogeneous samples of therapists and patients. He pointed out that most powerful dimensions apply across populations; this is the case even in eyelid conditioning. If we study homogeneous groups of therapists, it will be impossible to tell what effect they have unless the results can be contrasted with others who behave differently, or whose effects are different. In other words, if there is some powerful variable operating, we must observe variations in its intensity and this might be impossible if we homogenize therapist samples too much.

He reiterated that people need to get to work and stop trying to create job security by publishing a lot of "cruddy stuff." He indicated that he felt Ph.D.

* Dr. Truax is a Professor in the Department of Educational Psychology, University of Calgary, Alberta, Canada.

24. Interviewed by Allen Bergin in New York City.

candidates were the main producers of research in the field and that we needed to establish pools of data for their reference. He also noted that there were already vast opportunities for collecting research data. He gave the Veterans Administration system as an example of an enormous resource that could be used to develop a useful pool of data on psychotherapy.

At this point I mentioned Colby's view that we need better ideas and more fundamental research before we can even think about entering into the area of psychotherapy effectively. Truax strongly disagreed with Colby's view of the world of science. He said that it would be possible to construct the building in which we were meeting without physics, chemistry, or other sciences. He thinks we need quality controlled research with regard to applied work as opposed to basic studies of change. Basic studies, he asserted, are not relevant to changing people anyway. He also opposed Colby's view that basic research is more creative and demanding. He said he thought most experimental studies were merely technical routines and required very little creativity. He felt that applied research required a good deal more imagination and innovation. He said that he did not think that great scientists have followed fads and politics. In contrast to Colby, Truax believes that scientists who "sniff around" and look for weak spots in nature are the lazy and politically oriented types of scientists. He also said that he thought model building and theory construction were essentially unnecessary and that Colby was wrong about the importance of new ideas in this field. He said the crying need in this area is for more data, not for more ideas. As an illustration, he pointed out that there is very little good outcome research. He feels that this is a desperate need.

In spite of the fact that Truax feels we must study the live therapy process, he does agree that we must simplify in order to make progress. He says that this is the only way that science has progressed and one reason that psychoanalysis has not progressed is that it has done the opposite. It has tended to foster thinking in terms of complexity and has done little to simplify. Presumably what he means is that one must study the live therapy process, but extract from it what look like the potent dimensions, for example, empathy. He said at this point he did not think it was a problem to have different ideas or different theories for different parts of the data. These differences can be tolerated as we attempt to simplify.

At this point I asked about his views concerning the project on which Strupp and I were presently working. He said that he personally would not do such a project but he was glad that we were doing it. He believes that collaboration is a chance event and that it cannot be synthesized; most people are not very interested in collaboration. He also pointed out that he felt the young, new Ph.D.'s were the most creative individuals and that they were the ones most in need of collaboration. He felt that it might be fruitful for us to try to set up a project for a fresh group of Ph.D.'s. This might be done by getting a grant through the auspices of highly visible people and then turning it over to the younger ones. He feels that the highly visible people do not need collaboration because they can get grants, funds and staffs: "Most of them are burned out as researchers anyway." He thinks there is something enervating about not having to scratch hard, and this is the status of most of the visible people. He did feel that the Strupp-Bergin project was valuable in that it might change some of the attitudes of the National Institute of Mental Health.

At this point he made the following comments about NIMH:

1. He feels that their way of funding is counter productive. He feels that they should fund centers rather than individuals. We need a Max Planck Institute kind of approach.

2. Visible people should be able to nominate young people to receive a 3-year salary, plus $10,000–$15,000 per year. He feels that NIMH should do a lot of this because there are many places where there is little chance to do research, especially as an assistant professor.

3. Next he would like to see a national data bank in psychotherapy which could serve as a library and duplications resource. The material could be coded so that anyone could use it. He noted that this has been done in other fields, as in studies sponsored by the Atomic Energy Commission.

He said there currently are not any centers of research activity in psychotherapy. If a center was established he felt it would be important to avoid "hardening of the arteries." This could be accomplished by making it a center for advanced study with limits of tenure ranging between 3 and 5 years. It would also require a high ratio of young people, in other words, not very many chiefs. He suggested that places like Washington, D. C., or New York City were not appropriate places for such a center because there were too many distractions and meetings. He suggested as desirable locations, Palo Alto, Colorado, Florida, or Phoenix. He thinks that such a center should not only deal with psychotherapy but it should be a "center for advanced study in the social and rehabilitation sciences." He would probably not admit established people, that is, persons who had published more than 5 or 10 articles in the area of therapy research. Such people can usually get facilities and funds. He also feels that such a center should include people outside of the professional disciplines, such as Eric Hoffer.

In general, Truax feels that we have revered theorists and clinicians in psychotherapy and not researchers. He said that we need to reinforce research by rewarding it.

We then discussed problems relating to description, nosology, and classification—issues which are clearly essential to adequate therapy research. His response was "forget it." What we need is a functional analysis of the type that the *Psychiatric Status Schedule* gives us (Spitzer, Endicott, & Cohen, 1967). We need frequency counts of very concrete behaviors that are important, such as time out of hospital and marriage versus divorce. He believes very strongly that the utility of psychological tests is limited and that they are frequently used just for political reasons. For example, people often throw in such acceptable instruments as the MMPI and the Q-sort in order to make their grant applications look respectable.

We also discussed the question of single case studies. Truax is very enthusiastic about this approach. Such studies resemble small pilot studies, which should strongly be encouraged. Such studies are valuable, cheap, and can be done by anyone. He would encourage every therapist to do such studies on his own cases and he would build training in this kind of evaluation into every graduate program. He thought Lovaas' technique sounded great.

He thought that in general we should only play with robust variables in our inquiry. He thinks that they can often be found via case studies. This is essentially like screening in drug research. We try different things and then study those which seem likely to pay off. He thought relationship variables were very robust but they need refinement. For example, he believed there was no such thing as genuineness in psychotherapy. He said we really need to eliminate phoniness, and there is not much more to it. In this connection, he made an important point: He believes very strongly in using lay raters. If they can't detect the presence of a variable, it is unlikely to have an effect on clients in therapy; after all, raters see therapy from the same perspective that clients do. He also noted that if he were studying therapy with ghetto dwellers, he would use ghetto dwellers for judges.

Truax made a number of additional points: (1) Designs aren't terribly important. Control groups are not useful except in the very primitive stages of science. (2) There are too many theories and not enough research. (3) We should forget about schools. In science there shouldn't be such things because they are political groups. (4) The best hope for our field is converging evidence from various designs and sources, rather than any single strategy. (5) Breakthroughs are a certainty in this area. People are doing outcome research and looking at behavior instead of personality tests. The importance of a societal view cannot be underestimated. For example, since society spends a great deal of money on school counselors and the like there should be evidence that they have an effect on grades. Outcome criteria will be more and more socially oriented because of the great investment society is making in therapy and counseling. (6) Certain kinds of patient-therapist relationships make it impossible for desensitization to work at all. (7) Our model of research has been wrong. It hasn't been aimed at practice.

With regard to our question of whether psychological phenomena can be conceptualized in terms of semi-independent systems analogous to biological systems, Truax suggested that psychological phenomena are correlated but we need to act as if they aren't. Then, we can find examples of contradictions as we proceed.

He emphasized again the importance of heterogeneous samples: "We must have them because we are ignorant." David Grant used to say, "In the face of ignorance, randomize." Marks and Gelder couldn't have made the discoveries they did without heterogeneous samples. Also our prejudice against retrospective studies is bad. Marks and Gelder worked backwards.

We discussed the question of how to study the effects of interpretation in content analysis. Truax said that he thought initial inroads into this area could be made quite easily by simply counting the number of interpretations that people make, identifying high and low frequency interpreters, and then watching for short and long term effects.

He asserted that he did not think psychodynamic therapy was passé by a long shot. He does say that the psychoanalytical monolith is indeed passé; but there is a lot of conversation therapy and it is here to stay because most peoples' problems are very complex and idiosyncratic. He pointed out that he had no idea whether Goldstein's or Bandura's work was applicable in practice. He doubts that it can ever be replicated with interview therapy.

He expressed the hope that 20 years from now all practitioners would be nonprofessionals. We can probably train them better than professionals. He pointed out, for example, that at Columbia we select people for their academic credentials and cut out a huge number of people who might have excellent personality characteristics for becoming therapists. In this way we narrow the range of potential candidates for relationship therapy. If we select from nonprofessionals, we can perhaps select from among 40 million people and make our therapy much more potent. We can do on-the-job training better among nonprofessionals and can be more selective. We can select them out any time quality controls show they are not effective; whereas it is almost impossible to do this with regard to doctoral level people. He does believe there will be trainers, motivators, and consultants. In this connection, he pointed out the great need for courses on how to teach therapy, that is, how to be a good consultant.

Truax made the vigorous statement that he thought methodology and statistics had been a bad thing for psychotherapy research. He pointed out that he thought .05 or .01 levels were unimportant unless they were replicated under a variety of conditions. He said that he didn't think practitioners should attend to data like this because they were not powerful enough.

References

Spitzer, R. L., Endicott, J., & Cohen, G. 1967. *The psychiatric status schedule: Technique for evaluating social and role functioning and mental status.* New York: State Psychiatric Institute and Biometrics Research.

WORKING PAPER BY STRUPP

February 10, 1969

Current Status. During the first five months of the grant Allen and I have consulted with some 20 experts in different parts of the country, including most of the consultants mentioned in our grant application. While the starting date of the grant was September 1, 1968, we were not notified of its approval until about October 1. Thanks to a thorough planning meeting with Sein Tuma at NIMH in September and other preparations, we were able to move into high gear with virtually no delay. In addition to more formal meetings with consultants, Allen and I have spent considerable amounts of time in informal discussions—preceding and following consultations, in offices, motel rooms, airplanes, over the dinner table, via telephone, memos, and in other ways.

Everything has worked smoothly beyond my fondest hopes, and the collaboration has been extraordinarily productive and personally satisfying. I believe it is fair to say that we have learned a great deal from each other as well as from our consultants; and the total endeavor has been unbelievably stimulating, educational, and conducive to deepening our thinking not only about the status of psychotherapy research but about the enterprise of science in general. It is apparent from the summaries of our consultations that we personally have benefited immensely from the meetings, and we are grateful to NIMH and the Advisory Committee for this unique opportunity. For me (and I believe for Allen as well) the project has been a matter of "total involvement" despite other demands on our time. The generosity and eagerness of all consultants to share their ideas, biases, hopes, and uncertainties with us, often in remarkably frank and candid fashion, has been an inspiration.

Our consultants, in my judgment, have provided us with a reasonably representative picture of contemporary thinking in the area; they represent a wide band and perhaps the gamut of theoretical orientations, approaches to science, and research temperaments. I believe we are rapidly reaching a point on a negatively accelerating curve where additional consultations, particularly with experts in psychotherapy research proper, are adding relatively small increments in knowledge or insight. This is not to say that we should discontinue further consultations, but they should probably be even more selective and their number should be scaled down. In keeping with the foregoing, and perhaps more rapidly than we had expected, a number of trends seem to be emerging which transcend our earlier review article (currently on the verge of publication) and in some respects render it strangely obsolete. This is another way of expressing my feeling that our knowledge has deepened and that we have come to see the field in broader perspective. Furthermore, the experience of taking a closer look into "the workshop of science," as represented by some of the best minds, has given me a better view of the "forest," or so I like to think.

Emerging Trends. We have made a host of observations and gained numerous impressions, many of which are contained in our independently prepared summaries of the consultations. It seems too large a task to summarize them here nor does it seem called for (see sections on future plans). A few points, however, which impress me as salient, may be worth recording at this time. They are also indicative of my (our?) thinking, and point the way to the future. Much of what follows represents the outcome of an assessment of the situation conducted by Allen and myself in La Jolla, January 20, 1969.

1. No one (including Allen and I) is in favor of large-scale, multifactorial designs of the type outlined in our survey document. The reasons, which I shall forego detailing here, are most convincing.

2. There appear to emerge two poles along which various views may be ordered:

a. The first pole is represented by those who feel that the field is at a very early and primitive stage of development. They hold that copying older and better established sciences is useless and foolhardy; we must proceed gradually and slowly; we must clarify the phenomena in our demain, strive for better definitions, classifications, and essentially rely on *naturalistic observation.* Such observations may be guided by hypotheses, and they might encompass the study of psychological change processes in many areas other than psychotherapy.

b. The second pole is exemplified by those who feel that laboratory investigations of change processes are entirely feasible; they represent building blocks for a better technology and provide insights into the *mechanisms* of change.

The two poles can be characterized in many other ways. For example, *a* includes those who are not particularly sanguine about the future of behavioral science, subscribe to a humanistic view, oppose reductionism, prefer dealing with the whole person, and are firmly convinced that immediate breakthroughs are simply not in the cards. Adherents of *b* espouse behavioristic leanings, reject the "complexity" issue as a serious obstacle to the advancement of research and in general believe that we are farther along the path of scientific development than conceded by the first group.

3. A basic question arises whether it is possible to study basic mechanisms of psychological change in a meaningful way. At one extreme, laboratory experiments may be so far removed from real life that findings stand a poor chance of being translated to other settings; at the other extreme, real-

life situations are so complex and so confounded that it may be impossible to isolate variables, study interrelationships, and abstract principles. It may be possible, however, to combine the two approaches in some way, as for example through manipulation (even in an approximate way) of some influence variable(s) in a clinical or real-life setting.

4. Since progress in science depends on insights, ideas, reformulations, and genius rather than the accumulation of facts, it may be impossible to develop blueprints of where the field is going, might be going, or should be going. What may be needed more urgently than research in the contemporary sense (numerous people strongly believe that much of it is sterile, methodology-bound, and unimaginative) is work along *theoretical* or *conceptual* lines which might help to clarify issues in the field. We may have to look at "soft spots" that might yield to systematic inquiry, examine "mysterious" phenomena, and in general step back from the "busy-ness" of research. (The pressures of academia for "publications" and the apparatus of granting agencies are seen as antithetical to progress by some.)

5. Collaboration among researchers will be exceedingly hard to achieve, but it may not be impossible for a very small group of congenial people to work together on common problems. Large-scale collaborative studies, as already mentioned, are considered unfeasible, undesirable, and insufficiently productive. The creation of a small research center, largely unencumbered by administrative machinery, was greeted with some enthusiasm.

6. A distinction must be made between developing more effective therapeutic technologies and advancing the understanding of psychological change processes. The field, unfortunately, is inundated with therapeutic fads which seem to contribute little to science. If one wants to advance science, which is seen by many as the greatest need, one must resist the temptation of looking for quick "payoffs." However, the pressing social needs make such a distinction difficult.

In summary, it seems worth sketching (in quite unsystematic fashion) a few approaches, ideas, and conceptions.

People are generally disenchanted with:

1. Large, multifactorial studies of psychotherapy
2. Typical comparative outcome studies
3. Content analyses (largely unguided by hypotheses) of extensive film or video tape records of therapeutic interviews.

Varying amounts of enthusiasm, though often tempered by skepticism, were registered for:

1. Experimental analogues
2. Study of basic mechanisms of behavior change (whether or not they may be directly relevant to psychotherapy)

3. The therapist as an expert in human communications, particularly in unscrambling fouled-up beliefs and implicit assumptions about the self and others

4. Retirement of the brand names (therapy "schools")

5. Work on clarifying the *kinds* of changes one wishes to achieve through therapy and defining them more stringently (criterion problem). This area is still hopelessly confused.

6. Study of such problems as transfer of therapeutic learning to extra-therapy situations, including the kind, extent, and permanence of psychological change

7. Guided naturalistic observation

8. The nature of therapeutic learning, and the conditions for change, with emphasis on the problem of *identification*

9. Classification of relevant phenomena, including clarification of issues in the area of psychopathology

10. The study of phenomena usually grouped under the heading of *transference.* I hold a strong intuitive feeling (apparently not shared by others in this form, that this study is of crucial importance. Pertinent questions relate to the conditions under which these phenomena occur, their part in producing therapeutic change (see Point 3 above), and the like. I am also interested in the relationship between belief systems (which can be made explicit in the transference situation) and psychosomatic symptoms.

An Important Distinction. It is inevitable that in the course of our explorations we have been (and will be) influenced by our personal predilections, biases, career aspirations, and other factors which are partly hidden from us. Basically, it seems to me, we must make a distinction between our personal research and career plans and directions which other investigators in the field might pursue. In general, it may be presumed that NIMH is interested to a greater extent in the development of the field than our personal career plans, although they undoubtedly recognize that we are part of the field. In framing our recommendations it seems imperative to keep this distinction in mind.

Plans for the Summer, 1969. The question to which we must immediately address ourselves concerns our plans for activities during the coming summer. The following appears to me a reasonable approach.

1. Evaluate the results of our consultations, setting forth as concisely and as incisively as we can, promising directions for future research; describe alternative courses of actions, together with their respective advantages and disadvantages; summarize trends we have isolated from our discussions and our own thinking.

2. Make specific recommendations concerning promising courses of action, including projects and possible machinery for carrying them out.

3. Determine what we individually or jointly (or in collaboration with others) might want to do.

All of this might result in the preparation of a manuscript which might be published in book form, and serve as a guide to established researchers as well as aspiring graduate students. Such a book might be a very valuable outcome of our quest.

If we decide to pursue the above course it may be expected that the second year might be spent in completing the manuscript, occasional consultations with authorities (perhaps outside the immediate area of psychotherapy research); meetings with the Advisory Committee; and consultations with NIMH (Sein Tuna); possible spadework preparatory to any project(s) we might ourselves undertake; and efforts to induce others to take up recommendations we might advance.

An alternative to the above is to desist from drafting research proposals for psychotherapy research which we ourselves (or in collaboration with others) might undertake at this time or in the near future. Instead, we may want to engage in a broader and deeper exploration of cognate fields or explore basic science issues. In that event, we might want to lay the groundwork for such explorations during the second year, with the possible expectation that they might be pursued for another year or two.

WORKING PAPER BY BERGIN

February 18, 1969

At this point, I find myself debating between a need to accurately describe the position, views, and prognostications of the various individuals we have visited and attempting to draw conclusions from this experience which are filtered through my own biases and attitudes. I think at this point it is more relevant to try to arrive at some focus or some specific stimuli for discussion and for next steps. I find that I cannot really do justice to all of this complexity in the form of any kind of discourse, so I am listing below what I feel I can conclude up to this point.

1. First of all, it does not appear that a major collaborative approach is feasible at the present time. Of the 17 people we have talked with, only 6 are really interested in such efforts, and only 2 of these 6 have the resources for effectively engaging in a collaborative research program. It may still be possible to stimulate others to become involved in projects like some of the larger ones we proposed earlier; but there are enough obstacles to success that one must have real reservations about attempting any such thing. At the same time, it seems that small-scale collaboration may be feasible and economical. While the field is not secure enough for major efforts, it looks quite ripe for modest collaborative projects. As for the larger projects, there

is insufficient agreement, insufficient development of the field, and insufficient probability of significant contributions in proportion to investment of time, manpower, and funds. Smaller projects seem more feasible because individuals are already interested in working together on a modest level and there are several projects, or potential projects along these lines. In addition to these small clusters of interest, it seems possible to maintain and discard more readily the smaller programs of research as change inevitably takes place. Small foci of collaboration would, however, answer some of the problems which now occur because of poor sampling and poor comparability of measurement.

2. The kind of structure that might be most relevant for small-scale collaborative work is still open to question. There have been many suggestions regarding setting up some kind of a center and the frequency with which this topic is raised seems instructive in itself. The various views of such an enterprise have been described in our previous reports, and I will not repeat them here. I personally think considerable thought must be given to this question. At the present time my own inclination is to recommend that no new center as such be funded. Rather, I would prefer to see more ample funding of programmatic research in existing centers of inquiry. I would also be inclined to try to stimulate and be ready to fund small-scale collaborative efforts which look fruitful, or potentially fruitful. I do think, though, that this whole question of the structure of collaborative activity and the funding and stimulation must be the subject for a good deal more discussion. I do agree with those who have suggested that attracting outstanding people, particularly young people, to the area is of prime importance. We need to catch their imagination and provide motivation and conditions for helping them develop a commitment to and excitement about the field.

3. As I see it, the following strategies are the most timely and fruitful for moving the field ahead: (*a*) developing basic processes from the general psychology of change, including all areas of psychology, and naturalistic studies of change processes occurring "in nature"; (*b*) experiments in the mechanisms of personality change, for example, studies of the elements of desensitization; (*c*) clinical trials or demonstrations via single case replications. These would be demonstration projects by experts and innovators. It seems to me at this point that there is little to be gained by studying the usual psychotherapy processes as they exist. In this regard, I differ with a goodly number of people whom we have interviewed; but I must still confess to the presumptuous feeling that they are wrong.

4. As a corollary to the preceding thoughts, it seems to me that a more convincing measurement and manipulation of the subjective assumes a high order of priority. A real science of the subjective must be promoted and refined before we can expect to have a fully relevant therapeutic technology. While this area is gradually moving forward within the general psychology

of cognition and emotion, something more systematic and more relevant to the therapeutic issues needs to be stimulated. At this juncture, I have some temptation to assume that the behaviorists have made a substantial beginning in providing basic building blocks for us. While much of what they have isolated is quite simplified, it may be the kind of really substantial basis upon which the more complex and subjective can be effectively built. It may be a mistake to believe that we can get very far by entering this field of nature from the other end, namely, the more complex.

The experiences I have had recently have demonstrated to me that our problem in studying personality change is a problem of understanding the "nature" of human change. The fact that all nature is truly multidimensional must be recognized. If we take note of organic life, nonorganic phenomena, human bodies, plants, clouds, the ocean, and the soil, we see this complexity all around us. What science does is reduce this natural complexity to manageable proportions. We should note the precision that is achieved in works of engineering, in the development of drugs, and of surgery. These are all equivalent to having power over slices of nature but they never match the complexity of nature itself. This may be why I believe that psychotherapy must ultimately be an art just as medicine is ultimately an art. The practice, however, is refined by what we know and our purpose is to develop greater precision and applicability of what we know. A key thought here may be that we must learn to become more precise while remaining close to the practical problems of this field, instead of withdrawing from them or actually leaving the field itself, as some former researchers in the area have done. I think that parallel with the development of precision, it is essential to foster demonstration studies experimenting with live clinical cases. I would not, however, give much to a study of the typical therapeutic process. These case studies would have to demonstrate or test something new. We all need to admit that we need, simultaneously, people working from the simple to the complex and others working from the complex to the simple.

5. I have had an additional thought about the whole question of what we can learn from progress in other sciences. This is always a question that raises dilemmas for us; but perhaps we can learn and not be misguided by the styles that have proved fruitful in other areas. I still think we can learn something from the analogue situations which have been used in other fields. For example physics experiments were analogues of astronomical movements and yet in this case extrapolation from the simple to the complex worked beautifully. This success was based upon observation and description by astronomers plus extrapolation from simple analogue situations by physicists. Another thought in this connection is that it seems to me that the real scientist proves productive on the basis of the following: (*a*) He looks for something possible, something intriguing and mysterious perhaps.

(*b*) He bases his work on a lot of previous material that was lying around and which was the result of the hard work of many other people. (*c*) He avoids scientific rituals and codes of conduct. He pursues things on the basis of his own curiosity and ingenuity. (*d*) He works indefatigably.

6. It seems to me we need to see people in other disciplines who have tackled the problem of the articulation between scientific inquiry and the application to therapeutic process. These might be biologists or other people in the social and behavioral sciences. I personally think that the biological and medical field have a great deal to offer us in this regard. I was fascinated by an article I read recently on the subject of "biomedical engineering." This is a new field which is tying together the expertise of biologists, physicians and engineers to develop some of the most exciting new treatment techniques I have come across. It seems to me we need to think as imaginatively and as uninhibitedly as these people do. In other words, we need to think big not in terms of big projects but in terms of the great things that could be done if we really believed we could do it.

7. I often think that we need some new structures in this field that would help us move it along. Some of my thoughts include a new journal, a center for the study of change processes in the boadest sense of that term, and a much larger administrative context, such as a school of social, behavioral, and rehabilitation sciences. Such a structure would make possible all the supportive kinds of personnel, programs, and structures which would make major movements move forward more feasibly. Note the progress of medical research within certain structures as examples.

8. We do need studies which focus on the natural histories of disorders.

9. Sometimes I feel strongly the need for a new theory. Rogers says it will be a field theory, but I am not so sure. In any event, I am sometimes struck by the possibilities of brilliant thought in this field. We have our great examples from the physical sciences. The question is whether we have a potential like that in this domain as well. Is the field fertile enough to provide such a theory? I think so.

10. I was struck by the fact that Carl Rogers said, even though he has been immersed for a long time in psychotherapy, that he thought we would have our greatest impact as researchers if we forgot about psychotherapy and studied processes of change wherever they occur. He was even willing to present an example which involved a military situation as a personality change setting. This suggestion is hardly a comfortable one for a nondirectivist so I tend to take him seriously. Maybe there is a possibility for a systems theory of behavior and personality phenomena; but I must confess this is a subject in itself and I am not capable at the moment of being very incisive about it.

INTERVIEW: JOSEPH D. MATARAZZO*

New York, March 6, 1969

Joe saw the field of psychotherapy research as developing in three stages. In Stage I, from about 1947 to about 1957, therapy research reflected the emerging identities of the fields of psychology and psychiatry. These fields were attempting to form clearer academic and professional roles and their investment in psychotherapy and psychotherapy research was a reflection of this emerging status. Psychotherapy offered a much needed scientific identity to psychiatry in medical schools, and to clinical psychology in counseling centers and psychological clinics. The Rogers, Menninger, and other research groups also were searching for a research-based identity, and psychotherapy research provided one channel for alleviating anxiety surrounding this identity crisis.

During this same period, the well-publicized struggle ensued between psychology and psychiatry for relative position in the domain of therapy. Psychologists were attempting to make more credible the significance of psychotherapy and the role of the psychologist in it. (As an aside, Matarazzo mentioned that two of his medical school psychologist colleagues developed a very elaborate and carefully designed plan for psychotherapy research in the early 1950's. It reportedly was turned down by NIMH at that time because there were no psychiatrists involved. This was an indication of the status of psychologists at that time.)

The period of 1957-1965 (Stage II) saw a great upsurge of research, much of which focused on interaction problems. No longer were the politics and identity crises of the two major mental health professions as prominent, and because of its research base psychology began to assume the leadership role in psychotherapy research. The last stage (III) is represented by the Third Conference on Research in Psychotherapy which was a forum for the presentation of what may be the last papers on psychotherapy research as such. Broader research interests have begun to emerge, exemplified particularly by developments in the areas of general psychology, social psychology, behavior therapy, and psychopharmacology. The Conference thus was the "swan song" of interaction-process research, per se, which had preempted the scene for many years.

The number of people interested in process studies of psychotherapy has declined and their students are nowhere to be seen. Rogers, for example, did a heroic job, but abandoned it. Even though he was a gifted scientist as well as a sensitive clinician, the field wasn't amenable to this humanistic approach,

* Dr. Matarazzo is Professor of Medical Psychology at the University of Oregon Medical School.

which superficially represents an antithesis to research. The research by Joe's own group, by Auerbach, and by Howard and Orlinsky represents the efforts of investigators who, in Joe's judgment, have "refused to die." It was observed by us, however, that Marsden (1971) in a recent review of the literature on content analysis (prepared for the Bergin-Garfield project) had noted considerable growth in this area, which seemed to contradict Joe's observations; however, he may still be correct.

Joe implied that during this recent stage clinical psychology and the psychotherapy research area have grown up to the extent that the field is less obsessed with "proving" itself. Until 1964, we were overly concerned with design and methodology. This concern was a way of handling anxiety and defensiveness in medical settings and the problem of feeling inferior to the Division of Experimental Psychology type of colleague in universities. We tended to identify with the aggressor as a way of relieving our anxieties. Joe pointed out that he felt the more complicated designs originally espoused by beginning psychotherapy researchers were futile. He noted that people like Neal Miller and Harry Harlow (and we might add B. F. Skinner) don't have to do analyses of variance in order to show the effects of their research. There seems to be a negative correlation between the complexity of the research design and data analysis and the strength of the results.

Joe quoted a statement made to him independently in his early years by Walter Hunter, Edwin Boring, Bill Hunt, and Thurstone: "In order to be a good psychologist-scientist, once you have a good idea all you need in the way of instrumentation is paper, pencil, and the ability to add and divide." It is important to forget the questions and assumptions that are proposed in books which set forth all sorts of rules for analysis and design, and look at your data instead. "Look, count, observe, that's all you need at the present stage of psychological science and methodological sophistication." In a similar vein, Thurstone urged that the investigator look at his data. He told Joe: "Never mind such niceties as homogeneity of variance; substitute good sense and simple statistics." These views, which are echoed by an increasing number of critical thinkers today, are beginning to have a liberating influence on the field. It is becoming increasingly clear that complicated designs are unnecessary and indeed will retard progress of the field. What we need to do is to look for robust variables and for the rest employ "horse sense." Naturalistic observation may well be one of the prime avenues for research in the years to come. Carl Rogers' work was elegant because it was simple and brilliant. His contributions (in the Rogers and Dymond book, 1954) were very good because he limited the complexity in his chapters.

At this point Strupp suggested that we must set up the right conditions for the emergence of important contributions. We discussed the fact that science discovers by observation and also by confirmation; but most research (too much) is confirmatory in nature. Joe suggested that for his own work and, he suspected, for most serious scientists, the most powerful test of significance is a scientist's reputation after the research is once published. Joe said that statistics provide "the public apology for subjective insights." Statistical tests of significance provide merely support for the scientist's convictions which they serve to uphold. The subjective elements in a scientist's thinking are very important. Joe also noted the importance of not looking at any single study alone: One can tell more about a person's findings from the patterns of his research program than from his findings in a single study. The viability of an area of research or a research finding, according to a criterion proposed by Joe, is represented by the investigator's efforts to follow up on his work. If he does not follow it up in the sense of Thorndike's Law of Effect (Reward), one can safely assume that in his own judgment the study and its results, no matter how glamorously described, were not worth the trouble.

Strupp noted that many psychotherapy researchers who were active in the 1940's and 1950's are no longer "in business." Evidently, they felt that the rewards were not there, and they have turned to other pursuits. It seems that it would be important for us to make a list of psychotherapy researchers who have stayed with it as opposed to those who have left, presumably because there was nothing in it. Of course, it is not known how many investigators in other fields have similarly failed to persist.

Joe described how he gave up on the Rorschach as a criterion of therapy outcome in the 1950's. He then "grabbed" the Manifest Anxiety Scale as a measure of change because the early published results looked good. He later realized that it too was deficient and found that the more deeply involved he became in therapy research, the more he needed to study basic variables. This study seemed essential in order to move toward a payoff in the way of results. He thus parted company with the researchers of 1950–1955 who were planning to use many measures and many ratings of therapist behavior, even of the kind Truax now uses. Matarazzo decided that these measures were too "fickle" (including the TAT) and that the research was too much of a fishing expedition. He also did not want to devote 5 out of the 15 years of creative life he had in the field to one longitudinal study dependent upon a single set of then weak outcome variables (the Menninger Research Project).

He sees his 1955–1970 work on interview-interaction behavior as possibly much more rooted in basic principles of general psychology than in psychotherapy research. We then discussed some of the late paragraphs in Joe's annual review of psychotherapy (1965) which seemed to be of great importance, particularly in that there were some good predictions of what has actually happened in the field.

On another topic, Strupp pointed out the importance of the transference situation in psychoanalysis as a source of knowledge about change. It is a powerful influence situation and the analytic setting is an excellent laboratory for inquiry. Bergin's view was that maybe the transference situation is useful, that it develops a certain permeability to change, and that it is also a way of developing a knowledge of what might have happened in the family. It seems to be rather an inefficient approach, but could still be the only approach that can produce the kind of phenomena which Strupp is describing. Joe then suggested that he thought the transference relationship was not unique and that these phenomena appear in many of the human encounters we experience daily (thus, a more general law than Freud's transference may be operating). There is then no need to focus on the psychoanalytical situation, per se, to study this more general relationship. Strupp disagreed.

There seemed to be a consensus that the study of influence variables in a general sense was more fruitful than psychotherapy research proper. Goldstein, Heller and Sechrest, Allen, and Joe (in his 1965 Annual Review chapter) have been among the writers stressing this point.

There is some evidence that psychotherapy research is becoming less doctrinaire but there seem to be some camps within the behavior area forming clubs as exclusive as the psychoanalysts. At any rate, much of the "mystery" is going out of psychotherapy research and we stand less in awe of such phenomena as transference than we used to. Joe pointed out that psychotherapy research has enriched clinical psychology as well as psychology as a whole. Many of the studies and techniques being developed would have never occurred if it had not been for the fact that psychologists began to become professionals via clinical psychology. Joe then suggested that psychology is very different today than it was five years ago. It has gained self-confidence and lost its defensiveness. Joe also thought the "civil war" between the Division of Experimental Psychology and the Division of Clinical Psychology was over and that the pressure had been alleviated.

Hans pointed out that the Division 3 experimental psychologists' type of thinking had inordinately influenced NIMH granting practices. There needs to be a radical modification, he said, in the direction of supporting less rigid designs and supporting promising people. Joe added that the first NIMH research career awards went to major figures who in this way obtained research professorships. Thus the concept of stimulating young scientists to develop research careers in such new areas as psychotherapy almost fizzled.

Joe reiterated his view that interaction research in psychotherapy as such is passé and that it has become subordinated to behaviorally oriented research and more basic general psychological research.

Considerable discussion ensued about the work we (Strupp and Bergin) were doing under the current NIMH research grant.[25] Joe believes that we are in the position of Flexner in 1905 with regard to medical education and, like him, we are in a strategic position to give direction to the field. We could make suggestions which may have a far-reaching influence on research for the coming decades. Joe encouraged us to "kick the *Zeitgeist*" and to make our statements as forcefully as possible. We can also learn a lesson from the work of Alan Gregg (see Russell, 1968), whose influence on modern psychiatric education has been tremendous. Joe warmly seconded our idea to spend the second grant year in distilling the fruits of our labors, about which he was most complimentary. He feels we have been engaged in an intellectual odyssey and the question now becomes one of where to "push the *Zeitgeist*."

Joe felt it was also worth mentioning that currently there are no significant centers (including physical plants), such as the Menninger or University of Chicago centers, devoted to research in psychotherapy (or its more basic general principles) except for small groups of individuals who are pursuing their respective research efforts. In this connection, we explored the merits of (1) small scale collaboration; (2) increased funding of existing research groups; and (3) supporting the education of promising young scientists. We also discussed in some detail the idea of a center for research on influence processes of a more general nature and considered practicalities, such as possible locations and institutional affiliations. In order to round out our consultations, and particularly for the purpose of exploring the "center" idea, Joe recommended that we visit MacKinnon at the Institute of Personality Assessment and Research at Berkeley, the Research Center for Mental Health at the University of Michigan, and David Shakow at the NIMH Laboratories.

What is needed to make such a center a reality, among other things, is a university that is "ready" for it. In principle, if the idea is acceptable to NIMH, one could choose almost any place, and it would not be difficult to "sell the package" to an institution. Location in one of the less favored geographical areas of the country might be preferable to choosing one of the "major" universities. One could try to attract behavioral scientists of a wide variety of persuasions and orientations (for example, people interested in influence processes, memory, or child development) even if they make "strange bedfellows." Reference was made to the Mental Health Research Institute at the University of Michigan, the Rockefeller Institute, and the NIMH Psychology Laboratories which were created for comparable pur-

25. Since Matarazzo had been one of the "Founding Fathers" of the originating committee, recruited Strupp and Bergin to the project, and had actively participated in most phases of the current work, the meeting reported here diverges from the other visits and has a significantly greater *entre nous* flavor.

poses. Joe felt that the field was not ready for such centers previously, but it may be now.

Joe suggested we consult with Heinz Berendes concerning collaborative studies and his experience in coordinating NINDB's project on perinatal research. In the course of this work they coordinated the efforts of 15 medical centers along a basic design, but also allowed the 15 centers to go their own ways, and evidently the project was fairly successful. Two major reports have been published as well as a critique by Lilienfeld. They found some simple things like the nutrition of the mother and her smoking behavior to be highly related to child health. Robust variables came through in spite of various problems. Sometimes the simple variables show through even some of these multi-variable research designs.

One of the earlier efforts to create an institute, exemplified by Mark May's Institute for Human Relations at Yale, did not work very well. Hull's autobiography gives some indications of why the expected cross-fertilization did not occur. Such institutes require a charismatic leader who can effectively harness the personality resources of the members. Our forthcoming interview with Neal Miller, it was thought, might throw some further light on this problem (see the summary of this visit). To help us in our thinking about a similar center, Joe urged us to ask Miller such questions as: What did he like about Yale and the research institute there? Why did he stay? What happened to his ideas? Did he feel he had exhausted Hull's and his own S-R psychology? Is this how he came to want to get "inside the black box"? Joe believes that Miller's recent brilliant breakthrough shows the promise of a more *thorough* study of individuals achieved by teaming up mutually interested cardiologists, endocrinologists, biochemists, psychologists, and allowing the individual subject to serve as his own control.

In the course of our discussion we turned to the potential of research in psychosomatic medicine. There was a long discussion of psychosomatic theories, the potential of Miller's new work, the excitement pervading this area. We thought that this might be a place where people will cooperate in collaborative work. Joe considered psychosomatic research of the type found even in the skillful hands of Peter Knapp not very fruitful because the questions he and many others with dynamic persuasions ask are still "too esoteric for the level of sophistication and development of our fields"; he is looking for "universals" which Joe believes are not yet there. Franz Alexander's earlier "specificity" research also illustrates this point. (Incidentally, the first volume describing this work has finally been published, Alexander, French, & Pollock, 1968.) The stress which creates psychosomatic symptoms is nonspecific, contrary to some psychoanalytic theorizing. Joe observed that each of us has a "vulnerable" system and general stress could trigger off specific symptoms. However, the specificity comes in at the end organ; it is not "central." He thinks a psychoanalytically or psychodynamically oriented investigator could learn more about people's motivations by following them around 24 hours a day than by virtue of the esoteric interpretations of the symbolic "meaning" of symptoms made by these same dynamic therapists.

We asked him whether the field was ready for a major synthesizing or systematizing attempt. He did not feel that the field was ready for broad conceptualizations. He pointed out that William James' work along these lines was still as relevant now as it was in 1890. He noted that we are in a pre-scientific era and that psychotherapy research doesn't directly affect practice. It's an art. (Some people think it will never become a science or that we may have to wait another 500 years.) What the field needs is a few Darwins whose naturalistic observations might generate some brilliant insights. As far as clinical practice is concerned, there is good evidence to show that practitioners are influenced more by their personal experience, not by research findings provided by themselves or by others: "Even after 15 years few of my research findings affect my practice," Joe said. "Psychological science, per se, doesn't guide me one bit. I still read avidly but there is little direct practical help. My clinical experience is the only thing that has helped me in my practice to date. The same is in part true in the day-to-day practice of medicine. One develops a strategy and is no longer awed by the bewildering array of one's patients. We need to train our therapists in the style that a skilled craftsman does." Joe does think we have had some great breakthroughs and that we have had some geniuses in psychology. He would argue that Thorndike or Binet (earlier) and Miller and Harlow (currently) are psychology's Galileos, or at least rank with Copernicus vis-à-vis the relative development of psychology.

On a related subject, Joe observed that the structure of matter was a problem of interest to scientists before the time of Christ, but that it took the technology of the twentieth century to make effective analysis of it possible. We need some Darwins in psychology like Freud. *Darwin probably couldn't have made his discoveries in the research laboratory. We need to stop using paper and pencil tests and watch a few good therapists. Science is egocentric, narrow, committed, and the scientist doesn't necessarily read the literature.* He came back to the idea that we cannot study psychotherapy alone, but we must look at change processes more broadly.

Joe pointed out that many of the great discoveries have been accidental and cannot be planned. Some people break their backs to come up with a discovery and somebody else finds it by accident. He mentioned the example of Skinner who said that when the dispenser broke and he found the extinction curve, he found himself in league with Pavlov. This was a serendipitous discovery. He thinks the work of Neal Miller was also probably a happy accident, as was (admittedly) Harlow's.

From our discussion, the following miscellaneous points seemed worth preserving:

Joe called attention to the importance of naturalistic studies and gave as an example a case study of his own pertaining to the thoughts of an obsessive patient. He believes that anxiety is frequently triggered by specific thoughts and he had the patient note when certain thoughts arose. He stated that his practice is mostly pragmatic and not complex. Until recently few of our textbooks on psychotherapy actually described our real practices.

Joe formulated another interesting research problem which has numerous implications. The basic question to be explored here is: Since study after study has revealed that sizeable percentages of patients quit after the first interview, why do the others come back for a second interview? Strupp agreed that this research question could yield rich returns. Joe underscored his point by urging investigators to pursue any question such as this last which intrigues *them* and not to pursue esoteric questions. The latter have been posed by textbook writers who write about but do not practice psychotherapy. They cannot truly fathom the simplicity of the two-person interaction called psychotherapy.

Somewhere along the way the point was made that environmental (experimental) factors in the genesis of neurotic disorders have been vastly overstressed, but the pendulum is now swinging in the opposite direction, as exemplified by research on genetic and biological factors.

As noted earlier, Joe felt we are no longer awed by psychotherapy. He gave illustrations of how many colleges, junior colleges and high schools are training college students, volunteers, and aides to become mental health counselors on a one-to-one basis with severely disturbed patients with heartwarming levels of success (return to community living).

With respect to changes in theoretical orientation, it appears that most of the dynamic clinicians of the 1950's are becoming existentialists and most of today's younger clinicians are becoming behavior therapists. The clinical psychology of even five or ten years ago no longer exists!

Joe was pessimistic about Bergin's suggestion that there might be a lot of data around that could be conceptualized differently and more effectively. He cited the book by Berelson and Steiner (1964) as an example of the futility of efforts to "distill" general principles.

Joe did not think major complicated collaborative studies were appropriate at the present time; but the small collaborative efforts might well be. He also supported the idea of funding existing groups in a more programmatic way and providing more ample funds for young people to give them free time for inquiry.

With respect to the format of the book Joe urged us to write, he referred us to Lee Cronbach's 1955 ONR report forming part of a series dealing with the status of psychology in Europe. At that time, a number of prominent American psychologists visited different countries for the Office of Naval Research and summarized their observations and impressions. We might also obtain from Neal Miller a view of psychology in Russia (Miller et al., 1962). He might also have some personal memoranda on the subject.

Comments by Strupp. The discussion touched on many points relative to the status of psychological science in general and research in psychotherapy in particular. It was agreed that the next step is to explore the situation with Sein Tuma and to get a reading of NIMH's needs and wishes. Likely alternatives are: (1) a center of the kind described above; or (2) a "loose federation" of researchers (see notes on the meeting with Neal Miller which spell out the plan, as I visualize it at present). On the whole, I see considerably greater merit in Plan 2.

References

Alexander, F., French, T. M., & Pollock, G. H. eds. 1968. *Psychosomatic specificity: Experimental study and results.* Chicago: University of Chicago Press.

Berelson, B., & Steiner, G. A. 1964. *Human behavior: An inventory of scientific findings.* New York: Harcourt, Brace, & World.

Marsden, G. 1971. Content-analysis studies of psychotherapy: 1954 through 1968. In A. E. Bergin & S. L. Garfield, eds., *Handbook of psychotherapy and behavior change: An empirical analysis.* New York: Wiley, pp. 345–407.

Matarazzo, J. D. 1965. Psychotherapeutic processes. In P. R. Farnsworth ed. *Annual review of psychology. vol. 16.* Palo Alto: Annual Reviews, pp. 181–224.

Miller, N. E., Pfaffman, D., & Schlosberg, H. 1962. Aspects of psychology and psychophysiology in the USSR. In R. A. Bauer, ed., *Some views on Soviet psychology.* Washington, D.C.: American Psychological Association, pp. 189–252.

Rogers, C. R., & Dymond, R. F. 1954. *Psychotherapy and personality change.* Chicago: University of Chicago Press.

Russell, J. M. 1968. The Alan Gregg Memorial Lecture—A letter to Alan Gregg. *Journal of Medical Education* 43: 1135–42.

INTERVIEW: NEAL E. MILLER*

New York, March 7, 1969

We met with Dr. Miller at lunch, at his suggestion, and devoted about two hours to the topics discussed below.

* Dr. Miller is a Professor at The Rockefeller University, New York.

In response to Bergin's statement that psychotherapy as it is practiced today is not a very powerful technique, Miller said (somewhat to our surprise) that it may be undesirable to give up prematurely on outcome studies of traditional therapy. On the contrary, he thought that comparative studies, whether they are evaluative or designed to follow the process naturalistically, might be quite worthwhile. Cases would have to be selected carefully but useful information might accrue from comparing different techniques, such as analytically oriented therapy, behavior therapy, and group therapy. He felt that group therapy especially needed to be evaluated and that he would probably use as a control some type of religious group or a group with similar characteristics. This was an interesting idea suggesting an overlap between religious-like groups and phenomena that occur in group psychotherapy.

Miller felt that some people perhaps do not want to evaluate or collaborate in psychotherapy research because they are afraid to face the realities of the effects or noneffects of psychotherapy. He likened this to the fear of evaluating the Rorschach in the 1940's. He feels that it is essential to do evaluation or outcome studies in order to show whether there are any robust variables in the therapy process.

Therapeutic interventions in such a study should be made as carefully as possible, so that one could observe the results. Interestingly, Miller did not seem to be nearly as concerned about neatness of design or precision of measurement as many researchers in the area. Here and elsewhere, he emerged as anything but a purist, emphasizing that the "discovery phase" of science (which is the phase of current therapy research) should not be constrained by methodological perfectionism. This comes later during the "confirmatory phase" of an inquiry.

Miller expressed a number of cautions relevant to evaluation studies. Obviously there is a great difference between a patient who is motivated to improve as opposed to one who is getting something out of his symptoms. Then, too, there may be aspects of the environment which can have a powerful influence on therapeutic consequences. For example, we may begin to obtain a significant effect by means of a technique on some fellow, and then the guy's wife may leave him and ruin the effect. We must be very conscious of and take into account variables of this kind.

Contrary to what might be expected from a learning theorist, he did not voice any hostility or rejection of the psychoanalytic approach to therapy. In fact, he felt that Freud had made astute observations and that his ideas still had a good deal to offer. Somewhere along the way he quipped: "Psychoanalysis may make the patient feel better, and behavior therapy may make the relatives feel better."

To our surprise, he did not give a great deal of support to the behavioral therapies. He felt that, while they look promising, they were still in a primitive, developmental stage. He said that if someone close to him were in difficulty, he would probably send the person to a good psychoanalytically oriented therapist or possibly to a broad spectrum behavior therapist who is not too strictly behavioral.

We were of course interested in hearing Miller talk about his own research; and his recent article in *Science* (1969), which already has had considerable impact on the field, provided a convenient springboard. We were also interested in his views concerning the implications of his approach for psychosomatic research, an area he touched on briefly in his article. In this connection, he stressed the importance of focusing on measurable symptoms which can be attacked by different techniques, thus leading to objective measures of change. In elaborating on his conditioning techniques, he stated that the objective is no different from psychoanalysis which attempts to bring symptoms and behavior patterns under control of the executive ego. Interestingly, he said, "We are trying to take the behavior of this organ (heart) out of the control of the id and put it under the control of the ego."

In any case, it is important to zero in on an important disabling symptom, such as tachycardia, and to assess the effects of divergent techniques. As long as there is neural control, Miller hypothesizes, we can effect changes in a symptom through conditioning techniques. Why particularly treat patients suffering from cardiac symptoms? Miller's principal reason seemed to be that objective measurement is possible. In the process of producing therapeutic changes, Miller is not particularly interested in antecedents, that is, the question of how the symptom originally came into being. Unsophisticated patients may be particularly good subjects in this regard.

Strupp was reminded of one of Freud's early accounts of a peasant girl whom he freed of hysterical symptoms in the course of a few sessions during a summer vacation. The reward employed by Miller consists of telling the patient that he is getting better as he acquires greater control. One requirement is that patients are selected properly in the sense that they are seriously disabled and strongly motivated to seek change. The question one needs to ask is: Can we produce effects? If so, we need to evaluate them in various ways, including their permanence.

Miller related the case history of one tachycardia patient whom he treated successfully by conditioning techniques. Again, Miller seemed quite satisfied to work with single cases, at least in the early phases. In so doing, he is following his hunches and obviously making valuable observations which can be incorporated into larger, systematic studies. There is an important lesson here. Miller subscribes to the paradigm that a symptom has been learned, and the task of the therapist-experimenter is to help the patient unlearn it.

In the case study of changing heart rate, Miller and coworkers used a "beep" which begins to sound when the interval after the last systole exceeds a criterion time and it continues to sound until the next systole. The "beep" is controlled by apparatus attached to the patient, and the subject is instructed that the longer the "beep" continues the better he is becoming. Miller has been able to significantly reduce the heart rate of one patient in this way. He is developing a technique using a case-by-case replication, which is similar to the style Lovaas has used and which we have discussed many times.

He felt that in work like this it is necessary to agree on a criterion established in advance. This might be a change in the person's autonomic profile, as described by John Lacey. Unless we can agree upon some specific criterion ahead of time, it is very difficult to come to any conclusions about the effects of any particular techniques.

In studying the effects of conditioning on definable symptoms we are of course addressing ourselves to limited objectives, but we may learn more about the mechanisms of change in this way. In addition to cardiac symptoms, Miller expressed an interest in studying such conditions as high blood pressure and persistent muscle aches. He thought that some of the common psychosomatic conditions, like peptic ulcer and bronchial asthma, might be a bit too complex, but the problems may not be insuperable.

Strupp trotted out his example of anorexia nervosa as a condition for studying the effects of divergent therapeutic approaches. In some sense this fits with Miller's notion of zeroing in on an important symptom and objectively measuring it so that we can tell when the person has lost it, which in turn tends to solve the criterion problem. Miller seemed to agree that anorexia nervosa might be a useful problem to attack.

He suggested however that we might make more progress by studying children instead of adults. They are more manageable, more accessible, and the payoff is greater. He noted the importance of experiments on enuresis because here is a problem that makes a difference. Certainly it is more significant than a snake phobia. He also suggested studying college students because they are readily available, they can be followed up, and their environment can be studied. (The biases resulting from psychologists' preoccupation with college students may be a serious problem, however.)

It is interesting that he made a number of simple suggestions like this that show the importance of a pragmatic approach to research. Clearly, we cannot solve everything at once; we must tackle things that can be done, do them well, and move forward from there. If we make significant inroads on a small problem, this may make it easier to solve the next larger problem.

We then discussed the problem of complexity, and Miller tended to agree that it is important to break nature into manageable pieces. He used the nice analogy of slicing through natural planes of cleavage so that we get crystals instead of mush. In spite of the importance he places on refinement and isolation of variables for breaking down of nature, he also feels there is still value in studying the psychotherapeutic process per se.

One of the tasks we had set ourselves was to explore with Miller his notions concerning the merits of a research center. As we brought the discussion around to this topic, he spoke quite freely about the difficulties encountered at the Yale Institute for Human Relations prior to World War II. Despite strenuous efforts, there proved to be little interaction among the institute members. Each man had his own department affiliation and the institute was largely a paper organization. He mentioned some of the great people who were housed in the same building in order to cross-fertilize fields, such as Gesell, Sapir, Hull, and Yerkes. Unfortunately (for the Institute), each man kept doing his own thing even though occasionally they had dinners and discussions. Since the plan was not working, they decided to get some younger people who might be more willing to work together. These younger people included such individuals as Miller, Dollard, Sears, Mowrer and others who became well known. They chose theoretical problems that cut across fields and worked on them together quite productively. The book *Frustration and Aggression* (Dollard et al., 1939) is a good illustration. Thus, collaboration improved for a while, but then World War II intervened and the participants went their separate ways, never to reassemble. The fact that the Institute's grant support was discontinued by Griswold, the new President of Yale, of course, contributed to this. Miller quoted him to the effect that "institutes stifle creativity," and the idea of "the lonely scholar" may have much greater viability and promise.

However, there were other problems inherent in the Institute. For example, people often scrambled to leave in order to obtain tenured jobs in regular university departments. This could also be a problem in any future institute unless involvement were sufficiently sustained and long enough so people would not have to struggle for status and security. One of us observed, "Nothing helps so much as a significant pot of money." If we were to stimulate the formation of a loose federation of centers, as opposed to one center, it would certainly still be necessary to have a pipeline to funds so that people would not have to worry continually where their next dollar is coming from. Miller feels that funds and space are more important than having some charismatic leader. Furthermore, if one could find a problem that might be attacked jointly by a group of investigators, the center idea might be worth thinking about, but we sensed no great enthusiasm. (The sharp cutback in research funds occurring in the year following our visit has cast a long shadow on any such scheme.)

Comments by Strupp. Personally, I am becoming increasingly enamored of the "loose federation" concept, which impresses me as having only advantages and no drawbacks. Essentially the plan would work as follows: Invite a small number of productive researchers, say 6 to 10, to form a network for the purpose of exchanging ideas, plans, research results. The group members would meet two or three times a year for several days, critique each other's work, assess current status and future plans, and some members might pool resources in colaborative or coordinated studies if they are so disposed. If not, they can pursue their own research projects as they are doing already. If one or the other member wishes to withdraw, he can do so at any time; by the same token, new members can be added. One of the group members might assume the responsibility for coordinating the exchange of information, arrange meetings, and the like. In any case—and I see this as a great virtue—the coordinating office has no executive control over the activities of any participant. In order to attract a cadre of bright young minds, there might be one- or two-year fellowships which would permit young scholars to spend a period of time at one or more centers. The selection of group members would present no formidable problems. Ideally, they would work on projects relevant to the general problem of personality and behavior change, broadly construed, and they would do so from different vantage points and theoretical assumptions. In other respects, too, they might be "strange bedfellows." Thus, cross-fertilization hopefully would occur, but there is no *requirement* for a consensus or master plan. The absence of administrative controls and the fact that the group members do not work under one roof will prevent rivalries and other interpersonal problems that are almost certain to be encountered in a center which would bring people together in one place to work on a common task. Furthermore, under the proposed arrangement, there is no need for a "charismatic leader." Finally, the "loose federation" could be created at minimal expense, although there might be some increased funding of individual projects, provisions for fellowship stipends, and monies for periodic meetings. If the idea does not work, no great investment has been lost, and a new group could be constituted if this were deemed advisable.

On the whole, I feel Miller's research approach has considerable implications for psychotherapy research, and I am particularly excited about its potential for research in the psychosomatic area. Much of this, I feel, remains to be spelled out. Many people believe that Miller may be the first psychologist to win a Nobel prize. I would not be at all surprised.

References

Dollard, J. A., Miller, N. E., Doob, L. W., Mowrer, O. H., & Sears, R.R. 1939. *Frustration and aggression*. New Haven: Yale University Press.

Lacey, J. I. 1956. The evaluation of autonomic responses: Toward a general solution. *Annals of the New York Academy of Science* 67: 123–64.

Miller, N. E. 1969. Learning of visceral and glandular responses. *Science* 163: 434–45.

COMMENTS ON STRATEGY AND TACTICS OF RESEARCH: NEAL E. MILLER

Perhaps some of the interviewers' surprise at my apparent tolerance for lack of extreme rigor comes from the fact that there are two phases of research: that of discovery and that of proof. Usually, I only publish the results of the final, or proof, phase.

During the discovery or exploratory phase, I am interested in finding a phenomenon, gaining some understanding of the most significant conditions that affect it, and manipulating those conditions to maximize the phenomenon and minimize the "noise" that obscures it. During this phase I am quite free-wheeling and intuitive—follow hunches, vary procedures, try out wild ideas, and take short-cuts. During it, I usually am not interested in elaborate controls; in fact, I have learned to my sorrow that one can waste a lot of time on designing and executing elaborate controls for something that is not there.

After I believe that I have discovered a phenomenon and understand something about it comes the next phase of convincingly and rigorously proving this to myself and to the rest of the scientific community. The more thoroughly one has performed the exploratory work of maximizing and refining the phenomenon and the better one understands the relevant variables, including interfering factors, the easier it is to design an efficient, neat, convincing experiment. During this phase it is essential to use the controls that demonstrate that the phenomenon really is what one thinks it is.

Whereas during the discovery and exploratory phase one is interested in gathering information efficiently for oneself, during the proof stage one is interested in communicating it efficiently to others. This latter phase of the work should be designed with such communication in mind; frequently, additional effort and ingenuity on design and execution will save considerable time in the statistical analysis and the exposition of the research. During this phase, the tempting short-cut often proves to be a disaster by greatly complicating the exposition, weakening the conviction, and ruining the esthetic elegance of the experiment.

My research on whether or not rats paralyzed by curare can instrumentally learn glandular and visceral responses has progressed from the discovery to the proof stage, which is summarized in Miller (1969). Research on whether or not such learning can have therapeutic value for noncurarized patients who are suffering from symptoms mediated by the autonomic nervous system is still very much in the discovery phase. We are still trying to find ways to train noncurarized people to learn as well as do curarized rats (Miller et al., 1970).

To clarify another point covered in the interview, I completely agree that at present psychotherapy is far too uncertain and effortful a technique, so that with it our resources fall vastly short of the enormous social need for better mental health. Under these conditions, we need to encourage research to discover (and eventually to prove the usefulness of) radically new methods and new combinations of methods for the prevention and the treatment of mental disease (Miller, 1964, 1968). Thus, I welcome the contributions of behavior therapists and of other innovators. And, to express a possibly prejudiced opinion, I believe that as the behavior therapists move into more difficult cases and find that it is important to discover and countercondition the "real" underlying phobia, a process which often can be like peeling off the layers of an onion, and as the psychoanalysts are forced to stress ego mechanisms, working through, and the fact that patients get well in real life, they both may be converging toward an improved version of the kind of formulation that John Dollard and I put forward in *Personality and Psychotherapy* (1950). Incidentally, if I were revising that book, I would emphasize much more strongly counterconditioning, specific psychotherapeutic training in social skills, and the possible roles of special groups or clubs in social and emotional education.

To return to the main theme, I am strongly in favor of as much freedom as is compatible with the welfare of the patient in diverse attempts to discover improved therapeutic techniques. But, before a discovery is widely applied, it should pass through the phase of rigorous proof. In this connection, I believe that some points that I have made before (Miller, 1967) are still valid in their general application to behavioral science, including psychotherapy:

> Many of those who are used to dealing with the older, physical sciences have learned that it pays to invest time and money in basic research as well as in the sometimes lengthy program of practical development and field-testing often necessary to transform advances in pure knowledge into practical engineering achievements. In spite of all the practical and theoretical knowledge in the automobile industry, no one of the large manufacturers ever considers putting out a radically new model without extensive road tests of a prototype model. And even after such tests there may be a few bugs that have to be ironed out after use by masses of customers. Similarly, one can never be certain that a new social program actually will be a cure or that it will not have unexpected undesirable side effects. To start such a program without some plan for evaluating it is just as inefficient as it would be to start mass production on a radically new automobile without any road tests.

It is understandable, but ironic, that it is just with the new sciences, such as those dealing with behavior, that the would-be users often are so impatient for quick results of practical value that they will not support the long program of developmental research and field-testing that often is especially needed in just these cases. Thus, there has been a tendency for the results of behavioral science either to be applied too soon or to be discarded as impractical and not applied at all. Furthermore, in this situation, not enough of the best and most tough-minded behavioral scientists have been willing to try to help with the practical applications which would almost certainly repay them by calling their attention to new and significant variables that would enrich their pure-science activities. Similarly, we do not train our students in the special attitudes and skills that are needed for the successful application of science. Fortunately, these situations are improving.

I am quite aware of the difficulties of conducting research to evaluate psychotherapy and of the design considerations so admirably summarized by Fiske et al. (1970). But one should not rush into spending many millions of dollars on applications of therapeutic techniques, such as the recent expansion of community health centers, without first spending whatever is necessary, which certainly will be a considerable but yet much smaller sum, to evaluate a pilot project. Exactly the same goes for any other new therapeutic technique, including that of visceral learning, the human applications of which I hope may pass from the phase of discovery to that of proof.

References

Dollard, J., & Miller, N. E. 1950. *Personality and psychotherapy*. New York: McGraw-Hill.

Fiske, D. W., Hunt, H. F., Luborsky, L., Orne, M. T., Parloff, M. B., Reiser, M. F., & Tuma, A. H. 1970. Planning of research on effectiveness of psychotherapy. *Archives of General Psychiatry*. 22: 22–32.

Miller, N. E. 1964. Some implications of modern behavior theory for personality change and psychotherapy. In D. Byrne and P. Worchel, eds., *Personality change*. New York: Wiley, pp. 149–75.

———. 1967. Some contributions of behavioral science. In E. and E. Hutchings, eds., *Scientific progress and human values*. New York: American Elsevier, pp. 109–20.

———. 1968. Chairman's closing remarks. In R. Porter, ed., *The role of learning in psychotherapy*. London: Churchill, pp. 329–33.

———. 1969. Learning of visceral and glandural responses. *Science* 163: 434–45.

Miller, N. E., DiCara, L. V., Solomon, H., Weiss, J. M., & Dworkin, B. 1970. Learned modifications of autonomic functions: A review and some new data. *Supplement I to Circulation Research* 26 & 27: I–3 to I–11.

March 20, 1969

Dear Allen:

I am enclosing a somewhat lengthy quotation from Perry London's *Modes and Morals of Psychotherapy,* (1964) which impresses me as a remarkably articulate statement concerning the essence of the psychotherapeutic influence. To me, this is the most important scientific problem in the whole enterprise; needless to say, it has enormous implications for other branches of psychology as well. Ostensibly, London addresses himself to commonalities and differences in the approaches of Wolpe and Stampfl, both of which he regards as inferior to Mowrer's views. Be that as it may, what I find remarkable about the exposition is that, despite his strong anti-psychoanalytic bias, he does a superb job of describing what I regard as the bedrock of analytic therapy. Unfortunately, this is often misunderstood, a situation which is fostered by a lot of theoretical excess baggage and garbage. It may take a long time, but I am convinced that sooner or later someone will undertake the mammoth job of sifting the wheat from the chaff and recast the theory in more up-to-date terms.

Getting back to the quotation, I would put the matter as follows: To have maximum psychological impact, the therapist must create a condition in which the patient experiences sufficient trust in the security of the situation, specifically, in the therapist as a person, so that he will permit himself—there is nothing voluntary about this on the patient's part, it "happens"—to experience vividly and in the here-and-now a considerable charge of painful affect, such as anxiety, anger, and grief. In keeping with the transference hypothesis, I would add that these feelings are at least in part directed toward the therapist, or to put it somewhat differently, the person in relation to whom the feelings were originally experienced, merges with the person of the therapist. In any case, the feelings are strong and undeniably real. In this context, the affect is partly abreacted, but, what is more therapeutic, the possibility now exists for effecting a reorganization of beliefs, attitudes, etc. In short, experiential learning occurs, part of which entails cognitive corrections.

I do not mean to suggest that this is the beginning and end-all of psychotherapy, but what I have attempted to describe is a culmination point (there usually need to be numerous ones for extensive change to occur) of a process in which the patient becomes increasingly open and amenable to influence, that is, his defenses are gradually being eroded. In a sense I am returning here to Freud and Breuer's notion of the "strangulated affect" as a potent factor in all manner of symptoms, including psychosomatic ones, but I am allowing for the possibility that along the path of learning to trust another person, the patient also learns to tolerate frustration, to model himself after the therapist, to examine flagrant contradictions in his expectations and demands, and he begins to acquire greater faith in the strength of his own personality resources.

The trouble with all of this is that it takes a long time, and the process is anything but leisurely. Another problem is that the above culmination points are difficult to reach. Some people, as you know, are attempting to short cut the process by hypnosis, pharmacological agents, etc., and I take it that Jerry Frank's current work with ether as a means of producing "arousal" is predicated on similar assumptions. It may well be possible to modify certain symptoms in this way, and perhaps such modification may produce wider ramifications in the patient's feelings and behavior. This remains to be seen.

It is also apparent that I am talking about certain kinds of neurotic problems, and omitting many others. For example, some patterns of behavior (for example, characterological problems) may not be the consequences of "traumas" but may have been learned in entirely different ways. This underscores from a somewhat different perspective a point we have made repeatedly, namely that the term "psychotherapy" covers altogether too much territory and that we must begin to think more clearly about particular "problems" and techniques for dealing with them. I see the creation of trust as a necessary but not sufficient condition for major therapeutic change. Perhaps this is a problem one could begin to research, at least in a limited way. For example, one might attempt to combine Miller's conditioning procedures with a "relationship" of the kind I have sketched.

I am not sure about the comprehensibility of these ruminations, but anyway. . . .

Best regards,
Hans

A COGNITIVE THEORY OF ACTION THERAPY: PERRY LONDON

Wolpe and Stampfl, you will recall, both propose true learning theories of psychoneurosis and psychotherapy, and both claim very great effectiveness for their practical applications of them. The singular difference in their

* Dr. London is Professor of Psychology and Psychiatry at the University of Southern California.

presentations is that Wolpe says he is "desensitizing" people to anxiety by a technique that avoids *anxiety* insofar as possible, while Stampfl says that he is producing "extinction of anxiety responses" by *eliciting* it as much as possible. Even more remarkable is the great similarity in what they both describe as their essential therapeutic procedure: *They create as vivid a mental image as they possibly can of all the different things that arouse anxiety in their patients.* Wolpe says that the preliminary procedure of relaxation produces a response state which is incompatible with anxiety, so that patients unlearn anxiety responses, in effect by counterconditioning. Stampfl claims that he reproduces anxiety without reinforcing it, and it therefore reduces by simple extinction.

Neither considers, however, that a third possibility may exist, in which both counterconditioning and extinction responses are facilitated: The repeated elicitation of vivid imagery produces a discrimination set such that the patient increasingly learns to distinguish between the imaginative, cognitive, affective aspects of experience, and the sensory and overt muscular aspects. The very process of repeatedly inspiring imagination, in other words, may dispose the patient to discriminate between imaginary and "real"—between mental and physical experiences—more readily than any other means. Anxiety is reduced as he develops increasing ability to tolerate the imagery, which both Wolpe and Stampfl agree is necessary, and the ability to tolerate the imagery is progressively increased in turn as the patient makes an ever-finer discrimination between the impulsive, motivational, cognitive aspects of experience, and the sensory muscular ones. The closer the imagery comes to representing "real" experience of the most complete sort without being followed by the actual experience it stimulates, the more the patient's expectation of disastrous action, with its disastrous consequences, is reduced. By this means, he learns increasingly that the most intense thoughts, feelings, and motives do not impel him helplessly to perform those concrete acts whose punishment would realistically produce intense pain. Thus the patient learns control, so to speak; the differentiation process, as it becomes more efficient with repetition, creates a new response alternative to anxiety in the face of provoking stimulation; it might be labeled mediation. By this process, it becomes increasingly possible to think over the stimulus instead of automatically trying to escape it. Since by definition the threatening stimulus really is harmless, its discrimination becomes increasingly easy and unimportant at the same time, so that its stimulus value gradually decreases beneath the threshold of observation.

The principle of discrimination is hardly new to students of learning, and it is also thoroughly applicable to cats and rats. In this sense, its use does little violence to either Stampfl or Wolpe. But the variant I have termed *cogni-*

tive discrimination has two functions in this paradigm that limit it more specifically to people:

1. It explains why speech on the therapist's part can be sufficient to arouse imagery that has no innate connection with the purely auditory aspects of the stimulus.

2. It suggests that the only critical issue in the stimulus input is its capacity to elicit imagery, not its success at either producing or avoiding anxiety. In that event, neither Wolpe's verbal brinkmanship nor Stampfl's verbal brutality count as much towards success as the skill they both have in vivid description, and perhaps the luck they have in patients whose imaginations can be so aroused.

The speculation above illustrates how the cognitive behavior of man can be incorporated into anxiety models of neurosis and therapy such as those some Action therapists use. But it may be even more to the point to observe that the anxiety model is itself a very limited one which fails to account for the wide variety of human anguish which cannot very well be represented as a mere extension of the reaction of a caged animal to an electrified floor. The anxiety model fails to countenance the fantastic capacity of humans to remember long past experiences and to plan distant future ones, attenuating reinforcements and maintaining stable behaviors at such length that no present stimulus-response theory of learning suffices to explain very refined and sustained adult behavior.

The Need for Meaningful Action. If a single generalization is in order in this connection, it might be this: The more complex the problem behavior in question, the less any pure Action model of psychotherapy seems applicable to its solution. Perhaps the failure of such models ultimately results, not from the inability of the therapist to identify mechanisms of action for the achievement of goals, but from the fact that, for complex issues, he is unable to specify very fruitful goals. When he does the latter, moreover, it may be argued that he only does so by establishing or supporting a meaning system to which the patient can refer his acts.

It may be demonstrated without doubt that a psychotherapy does not require a system of meaning in order to function within some limits and with some demonstrable effects. But in view of the history of the enterprise, as well as of the logic of the continuity of human experience from misery to other states, it is hard to see how it can avoid any implications of meaning. Granted that people come to therapy seeking comfort, not knowledge, and that they are entitled to surcease of pain without the inevitable imposition of self-consciousness, it still seems likely that they will finally seek the latter, once healed, if for no other reason than that, at their best, men tend to see themselves as creatures of purpose.

If this is true, then pure Action therapies may be challenged even when represented at their best, not for being unable to accomplish their goals, but for an excess of modesty that limits them to all to demonstrable empiricisms. Ultimately, they beg all ultimate questions, which are necessarily questions of meaning.

But Insight therapies, whose only coin of worth is the facilitation of meaning, have not succeeded well enough in the prior, if less important, task of easing personal suffering, to take title to offer the profundities they claim to have. And it is possible that they could not, in their most common current forms, in any case effect some satisfactorily permanent amelioration in people's lives. For their referent, by and large, is the individual himself, and the chances are good that most people cannot find their lives meaningful except in some context of experience which is greater than themselves. For most people, the most likely context would be a social one.

The significance of socialization has certainly not been overlooked by students of psychotherapy; relatively early in the development of this field Adler and Sullivan were very concerned with it. More recently, and more broadly, Fromm, whose orientation derives from an Insight system, and Skinner, the purest Actionist, posit the necessity for sane societies of rather similar kinds, the one finding it truly meaningful, the other truly functional, both finding it of greatest value for the development of man. But in all these cases, the social interest is either academic and peripheral, from the therapeutic point of view, because it offers no counsel of value for individual therapists or patients, or it is ineffective, for it offers only insight, from which significant actions may or may not result. Neither speaking of "sick societies" nor of the need of individuals to have "real relationships" tells a man much that he can use to meaningfully relate his own life to a social order or the individuals who people it.

A comprehensive psychotherapy of the kind implied by this argument would be one that uses both insight and action to attack complex psychological problems. But insight, within this system, would no longer focus so much on motives as on those behaviors, present and historical, that produced disorder by violating one's relationship with the functional context that lends meaning to one's life. And its primary purpose, once achieved, would be to steer the development of a new action system, one which channels the individual's behavior in ways intended to restore his functioning within that context. And the context, the referent that makes the action system meaningful, would be neither the painful symptom, nor the wounded selfhood that may lie beneath it, but something external to the individual. For most such therapies, a social system, real or hypothesized, must provide that context.

INTERVIEW: HENRY B. LINFORD*

New York, March 21, 1969

I[26] met with Professor Linford (formerly President of the Electrochemical Society) in the hope that I might learn something more about the process of bringing basic science to bear on problems of application. In this instance, I was interested in the possibility of learning something about how knowledge in chemistry has been used to develop a technology in chemical engineering.

I had sent Professor Linford our usual set of materials, including a copy of the Strupp-Bergin Monograph. His immediate reactions were most interesting and I suspect typical of the attitudes of many physical scientists. He pointed out the following with regard to the problems we are facing:

1. The basic problem we face is a problem with our basic science of psychology. Essentially, he feels that psychology is at the present time too primitive to yield an effective applied science or technology.

2. He bases his position on the assumption that the influence of the observer or the experimenter is too predominant in the observations being made in psychology in general. Too much judgment is involved, and the reliability of measurement is too low to expect effective results in application.

3. He pointed out the usual simple, basic rules of science which he feels are not adequately fulfilled at the present time in psychology. These include such matters as having systems of objective measurement, applying numbers systematically to these measurements, and replication and experimental manipulation of variables.

In general, he was quite skeptical of the scientific status of psychology and entertained some doubt that it could ever become a science in the sense of the physical sciences. He seemed very sympathetic with regard to the problems we face, but he wondered whether it would ever be possible to solve them.

He gave some illustrations from the history of chemistry and chemical engineering which were of interest. He pointed out that at first there were people like Boyle (17th Century) and Faraday (19th Century), who were primarily experimental laboratory "types." They might be likened to our experimental psychologists or behaviorists. Later, the "process" types came along. These individuals were essentially interested in developing industrial applications from basic knowledge in chemistry. In many instances they were motivated by an interest in commerce and in making a profit. He mentioned the development of a soda process by LeBlanc, the aluminum form-

* Professor Linford is a Professor in the Department of Chemical Engineering, Columbia University.

26. Interview and report by Bergin.

ing process which was developed simultaneously in France and the U.S., the artificial graphite process which was developed by Atcheson, and the work of Herbert Dow who essentially began the chemical industry. He mentioned that these people were Edisonian types who had some knowledge of the basic experimental work but who were essentially inventors, pragmatists, or perhaps artists. Despite their lack of laboratory expertise, they were quite successful. In our discussion we likened these people and the processes they developed to the Freudians and the other clinically oriented psychotherapists.

It was only in the present century that chemical engineering became a reality and emerged as an explicit attempt to develop a functional and scientific connection between laboratory work and application. He likened the development of chemical engineering (as an applied science) to what Strupp, I and others are attempting to do in trying to base psychotherapy on a solid scientific substratum.

This was an interesting set of analogies, and I suspect there may be some real truth in them. It does seem that we are attempting to build an applied science instead of simply producing clinical "inventions." Linford's question as to whether we are historically ready for this is obviously a sobering one.

He made some interesting observations, such as the fact that there are still many very significant chemical processes which make a lot of money for people but which are poorly understood by chemists. They essentially don't know what is going on. This statement was at least modestly encouraging.

We then discussed some of the research problems that arise in chemical engineering. He mentioned the fact that a zinc plant had been built in Illinois a number of years ago and that certain problems had occurred with it. This new facility was prepared to start producing a certain amount each day [as in psychotherapy, we want effects] but when they pushed the buttons and observed the processes for a day nothing had happened. There was no zinc forming even though everything looked right. The chemical engineers were then brought in to examine the situation. They had to do so-called "wet" analyses because there was no such thing as spectrographic analysis at that time. After considerable analysis, they found a tiny bit of germanium in the ore which was being used to produce the zinc. They had to increase the amount of iron in the ore in order to take out the germanium. The amount of this contaminating material that was present amounted to one-tenth of one per cent of the main body of ore. So, even though the method of analysis was crude by modern standards, it was still possible to detect the presence of such a tiny amount of substance. When they proceeded to modify the ore, they got the results they sought.

It seems that there are certain lessons in this experience. For example, the mere capacity to detect a small amount of a contaminating variable was very important; and it is a capacity which we simply do not have in our field at the present time. Even among the chemical engineers, there were many who at that time didn't know anything about germanium. It was only those who were really up on the latest who knew what was happening.

We also talked about the problem of scaling and how the Fahrenheit, Centigrade, and Kelvin scales were developed. Linford noted that there was indeed crudeness in the initial estimates of heat. Fahrenheit apparently classed a large sample of phenomena under the rubric of "heat." He used the freezing of water as a low point and the temperature of the body as another standard point and then later on the boiling of water as another standard. He was then able to gradually develop a carefully calibrated scale which responded to variations in physical phenomena which were scientifically important. It seems that our problems are similar and yet we often do not seem to know even what class of phenomena to start dimensionalizing. It is instructive, though, to see how pragmatic and inventive physical scientists have been. It is also of interest how their advances were almost always based on someone getting a bright idea that a particular variable was robust or powerful in nature. Thus, fluctuations in heat seem to have significant effects in varying directions depending upon the level of heat. Perhaps we can learn something from this in any attempts we might make to select variables as promising ones for inquiry.

In general, this conversation was quite interesting even though it yielded a certain amount of discouragement. The discouragement was only to a slight degree created by the very fundamental criticisms Linford leveled at the whole field of psychology, but more as a result of the degree to which physical scientists (if Linford is representative) do not understand or perhaps sympathize with the struggles of psychology.

I must note, however, his pleasure at noting our sincere attempt to evaluate current therapeutic methods. He feels this evaluation is very important and is quite concerned about the fact that the evidence of the effectiveness of psychotherapy is so limited. He noted that medicine is still an art and that psychotherapy probably always will be too but that we can develop a more effective art or skill on the basis of a more substantial empirical background. He noted that he thought NIMH was doing a very significant thing in having us conduct our present project. He said this was most unusual in the history of science and that it was a marvelous opportunity. He suggested that it is a very important thing for this field to do at the present time and he wished us well in giving the *Zeitgeist* a good kick!

INTERVIEW: PETER H. KNAPP

Boston, May 15, 1969

As was true of virtually all previous consultations, we were accorded a cordial welcome by this research group, with whom we spent the morning of

* Dr. Knapp is Professor of Psychiatry at the Boston University School of Medicine.

May 15.[27] In addition to Dr. Knapp, our principal consultant, we had the opportunity to meet Dr. Louis Vachon (who works closely with Knapp on the asthma research project), Dr. Martin A. Jacobs and Dr. Douglas McNair.

Knapp told us that basically he is not a psychotherapy researcher although his research is certainly relevant to investigative work in this area, and he has been continually interested in it. His major goal is to develop a comprehensive theory of emotion and affect, and he regards his asthma research studies as a means toward this end. In essence, the focus of his research rests on the study of the vicissitudes of bronchial asthma in relation to psychological material with emphasis on monitoring autonomic activity.

Somewhere in the course of our discussion I asked how he happened to single out bronchial asthma as his major research topic. (I realize of course that choices of this kind are frequently determined by highly personal considerations, not necessarily by "scientific" ones, and, like all human activity, they are "overdetermined.") Knapp replied that in his judgment bronchial asthma provides him with an important "anchoring focus." At the same time, his research has taught him that this psychosomatic condition (like all phenomena in this domain) is considerably more complex than was originally realized; however, in addition to its psychological aspects the topic is "exciting" from the standpoints of pulmonary physiology, the functioning of the autonomic nervous system, and immunology.

One of the fascinating paradoxes that exists in this area concerns the function of adrenalin in asthmatic attacks. While there is no simple relationship between the occurrence of an asthmatic attack and anxiety in individuals who have this particular predisposition, anxiety is correlated with hyperactivity of the adrenal glands; however, it is also known that the administration of adrenalin is one of the most effective ways of terminating an asthma attack. Consequently, the asthma sufferer should "cure himself" if the original hypothesis were correct. This, however, is not the case. Therefore, it has become necessary to search for other explanations.

It is now being realized that the relationship between asthma and anxiety is much more complicated than had previously been assumed. While anxiety involves an increase in adrenalin secretion, inhibition of some kind must also occur, and the well-known fight-flight mechanism somehow must become inhibited or paralyzed. This may occur in other psychosomatic diseases as well. In the asthma patient the direct expression of anger and aggression is "turned off." Through psychoanalytic study of such patients it has become evident that they are passive and that they have strong longings for closeness with a mother figure, separation from whom they dread. The expression of destructive aggression is felt to result in such a separation. For these reasons they are terrified of their aggressive impulses, which they have

27. Résumé by Strupp.

learned at an early stage in life to inhibit. In addition, of course, there must be a biological vulnerability (as shown by the correlation between asthma, atopic excema, allergies, including hayfever, and other conditions). It is interesting, too, that stress, both of a psychological and physiological nature, may induce an asthma attack in individuals so predisposed, but it is virtually impossible to produce an attack in individuals lacking this predisposition, no matter what the nature of the stress may be.

From the psychological side, it appears that the earlier formulations by psychosomatic researchers concerning the personality structure of the typical asthma patient are basically sound, and I take it that Knapp sees no possibility of producing any radical personality change in such patients short of psychoanalysis. (I failed to inquire about his views concerning the possibility of basic change even under the condition of intensive psychotherapy over a period of years although I must assume that Knapp is somewhat optimistic about the prognosis.) On the physiological side, various new hypotheses concerning autonomic functioning have emerged during the last few years. (Since Allen and I claimed anything but expert knowledge in this area but expressed an interest in learning more about it, Knapp and Vachon gave us a somewhat extended lecture. This material is spelled out and referenced in several of their forthcoming papers, from which the following is adapted.)

Several years ago Ahlquist formulated the existence of so-called alpha and beta adrenergic receptors as two differing functional efferent sites of autonomic response, and interest has evolved in the possible role of these receptors in bronchial asthma. This formulation suggests that the two components within the sympathetic nervous system may be in ways opposed to each other. Specifically, the beta adrenergic receptors have bronchodilator activity. Szentivanyi has proposed that the key feature in asthma is dysfunction of the adrenergic receptors in the lung. According to this investigator, asthma is not primarily an "immunologic disease" but rather is based upon an abnormality of sympathetic nervous function, which then leads to "a unique pattern of bronchial hyperreactivity to a broad spectrum of immunologic, psychic, infectious, chemical and physical stimuli."

To account more adequately for some of the clinical aspects of asthma, Mathé has advanced an alternative hypothesis about sympathetic nervous dysfunction in the disorder. He assigns a key role to impaired mobilization of epinephrine, and has found some experimental evidence to support his view. Mathé speculates that there may be some kind of "reversal" of centrally organized emergency responses, a notion which Knapp considers consonant with clinical evidence. He cited a state of "frozen anxiety" he observed in one of his patients.

A more extensive technical discussion and review of the research evidence is found in Knapp's recent paper, "The Asthmatic and his Environment," of which he gave us a preprint. Knapp summarizes this work in the following propositions:

Centrally organized neurophysiologic processes—subserving riddance, blocking out and conserving—are able to reinforce and complement local allergic-inflammatory processes to produce the bronchiolar obstruction of asthma (the nature of the linkage between the brain and lung remains obscure). Along with activation of these incorporative and eliminative mechanisms (purging) there is reciprocal inhibition (curbing) of "flight-fight" mechanisms in asthma; (thus there is not only parasympathetic nervous activation but relative insufficiency of the beta-adrenergic system, though its nature and scope are still undetermined). The total complex of biologic processes in asthma is subject to modification by experience (learning) and can come under a large measure of control by the social environment (which in the human is mediated by public and private symbolic systems).

We spent a fair amount of time discussing relationships between Knapp's research and the investigations of Neal Miller, concerned with bringing autonomic functions under voluntary control. (Knapp was not familiar with Peter Lang's work, which has a similar focus.) Knapp is very interested in this line of investigation, and asserts that, while the mechanisms are obscure, learned effects of the kind described by Miller might play a crucial role in illness. He quoted with approval Miller's statement: "The fact that glandular and visceral responses can be instrumentally learned opens up many new theoretical possibilities for the reinforcement of psychosomatic symptoms." Miller had suggested the use of hypnosis with human subjects (analogous to curare in animals), and there may be a valuable suggestion for further work in Knapp's advocacy of sleep studies. The fact that asthma attacks are often a nocturnal occurrence, after the patient has been asleep for several hours, may hold promise in this regard.

As Miller pointed out, it is essential in this kind of work to devise instrumentation which permits continuous monitoring of the particular autonomic response under investigative scrutiny. In the case of heart rate, this is relatively simple; in the case of bronchial asthma, the problem has been rather difficult. Knapp and Vachon have employed the whole body plethysmograph and a recently developed device called a "magnetometer" which permits continuous monitoring of respiration. Some preliminary results comparing tracings with speech samples obtained during therapeutic hours have recently been published by this group. In an earlier series of studies, Knapp and his associates had interview material judged by external observers who were asked to rate whether the material was conducive to an asthma attack or not. While they did better than chance, such studies imply a simple relationship between the patient's affective state during the therapeutic hour and the occurrence of asthma, a fallacy of which Knapp is of course aware. In any case, Knapp regards rapid feedback of autonomic functioning in therapy as "promising."

Immediate feedback has also been employed in other studies by playing back, through video tape techniques, segments of therapeutic hours, and the

April 1969 issue of the *Journal of Nervous and Mental Disease* is devoted to this topic. In general, Knapp feels that audio playback has been disappointing, perhaps partly because of the complexity of the events in therapy. Furthermore, playback may interfere with the therapeutic process. An important question revolves around the issue of whether the patient or the therapist has control over the feedback. Knapp thinks that it may be preferable for the patient to exercise the option. In this connection, Allen referred to one of Bandura's studies in which the subject controlled the playback of a feared situation.

Knapp and his associates, Mushatt and Nemetz, are firmly committed to the use of psychoanalytic sessions as a research instrument, particularly with reference to the study of transference phenomena and the patient's defensive operations. He thinks (and I agree) that we have no really good conceptual scheme for defenses, and Anna Freud's formulations, which still serve as the major frame of reference, are almost "prehistory." Measures of affect, Knapp believes, are not nearly as important as measures of defenses, and we must learn to differentiate between "competent" and "maladaptive" defenses. Asthma may be viewed as a "defensive failure."

We talked about Jerry Frank's current interest in the study of affect and arousal, and Knapp reminded us of Grinker's earlier work with narcosynthesis during World War II. I gathered that he was not overly impressed with the therapeutic effectiveness of these procedures. Kubie and Margolin have also written on the subject of drugs and their effect on defenses.

Knapp emerged as a "liberal" in his views on the contemporary status of psychoanalysis. For example, he mentioned a recent conference he attended dealing with smoking behavior. He found that, while the various theories expressed by the participants were far apart, there seemed to be greater openness and willingness to listen to the other fellow's viewpoint. With respect to psychotherapy, Knapp emphasized the overall framework of an interpersonal relationship, and he fully acknowledged the importance of such factors as trust, confidence, and the patient's expectancies. (These, too, may play a crucial role in work on autonomic monitoring and feedback, which need to be explored.) Clearly, therapy is a social learning process of major proportions. It is becoming increasingly clear that it does not take place through the verbal messages as such, but it is embedded in the process of "working through" (that "awkward teutonic phrase"), by which Freud essentially referred to social learning albeit not in a very explicit way. In therapy, however, the feedback is so random that any effort to make it more precise should be welcomed. In a searching paper ("Image, Symbol, and Person"), Knapp states: "I believe, along with Erikson, that a more sophisticated psychology of personal relationships is emerging, more firmly tying the individual to the milieu around him. If this view is correct, there should also emerge a more broadly integrated social psychology." Knapp considers metapsychology largely a "pseudotheory," which is in need of radical revision. As it stands, it is largely divorced from clinical and empirical data. Finally, a distinction should be made between institutional psychoanalysis and what analysts do. Knapp readily admits that there is a vast hiatus between codified statements on theory and technique and actual practice.

Experimentation in this area, as in others, is certainly a crying need, and efforts to make symptoms "a concrete bit of behavior" appear to be a promising goal. Knapp wondered however at which point in therapy it may be desirable to focus on structured activity. The use of single-case studies as a fruitful source of hypotheses is certainly well exemplified by the work of Knapp and associates. "The good scientist," Knapp stated, "focuses on a problem but keeps his mind open to the broader context." I cannot think of a better credo.

In a recent paper Knapp (1967) explored what he calls the "riddance-disgust-satiety constellation," linking it to autonomic activity. I was particularly interested in his observations concerning blushing, which is governed by the parasympathetic branch of the autonomic nervous system, and according to Knapp, the only physiological aspect of shame about which there is a certain amount of information. Knapp asserts that "It is unclear whether blushing results from direct vasodilatory impulses or from reduction of vasoconstrictor tone, or from both effects; but in any event it represents a shift of forces toward parasympathetic dominance" (p. 529). "In the case of asthma," he speculates elsewhere, "there is accentuation of dysphoric, incorporative and eliminative processes—having to do with 'blocking out and washing away' [a phrase coined by Harold Wolff]—and inhibition of active 'fight-flight' responses" (Knapp, 1969b, p. 404). I have a strong hunch that we might learn a good deal from studying (1) the kind of learning that can be effected along the lines sketched by Miller, and (2) the socio-cultural context in which particular autonomic responses are originally acquired. The latter undoubtedly will be a good deal more difficult than the former. With further reference to (1), it seems to me that the interpersonal context in which such therapeutic learning proceeds should receive further attention as it might hold important clues for the specification of the conditions under which it is effective or ineffective. In this connection, I feel that emphasis on transference phenomena, that is, the patient-experimenter (therapist) relationship in a broad sense, is crucially important. The conceptualizations of Knapp and associates, more than their experimental findings, impress me as among the most sophisticated I have encountered.

In the course of our consultation Martin Jacobs gave a brief presentation describing his recent Ego Strength Rating Scale. This instrument consists of a number of scales which can be completed by multiple observers, such as the patient, family members, and therapists. The ESS was designed primarily to measure personality change as a result of psychotherapy, and consists of the following dimensions: obsessiveness, impulsiveness, social intrusiveness, social isolation, defiance, helplessness, guardedness, vulnerability, grandiosity, worthlessness, and five summary ratings of ego strength. Each subscale is bipolar; for example, the "impulse control" poles are "obsessiveness" and "impetuousness." The scales have good face validity, and in a recent study were reported to differentiate reliably between normals and psychiatric patients.

The scale has been applied in a ward setting (psychoanalytic orientation) where acute patients are treated, and seems to differentiate patients who are doing well from patients who are doing poorly. Standard diagnostic categories were not prognostic of differences in outcome, but the Ego Strength Scale was. They facetiously broke their groups down into three types: "the mad," "the sad," and "the bad." They confirmed a finding that patients who are impulsive and defensive and turning outward did not improve. The impulse control measure is a good differentiator of these two groups and of outcome by itself. Depressive patients are more often like those who got better, but a depressive diagnosis alone did not differentiate. Of those who turn outward, no more than 60% improved, while of those who turned inward 80–90% improved. They also developed a measure of "understanding," which could be relevant for process studies.

Altogether, the ESS appears to be a significant improvement over the Barron Scale, derived from the MMPI, which has been criticized on the grounds that it measures little more than defensiveness. (See: Jacobs, Pugatch, & Spilken, 1968.)

References

Group for Advancement of Psychiatry (GAP) Committee Report. 1970. Knapp, P. H. (Chrmn.), Brosin, H. W., Meyer, E., Offenkrantz, W. C., Robbins, L. L., Scheflen, A. E., Shands, H., Tower, L. E., & Luborsky, L. *Psychotherapy and the dual research tradition.* American Psychiatric Ass.

Heim, E., Knapp. P. H., Vachon, L., Globus, G. G., & Nemetz, S. J. 1968. Emotion, breathing and speech. *Journal of Psychosomatic Research* 12: 261–74.

Jacobs, M. A., Muller, J. J., Eisman, H. D., Knitzer, J., & Spilken, A. 1967. The assessment of change in distress level and styles of adaptation as a function of psychotherapy. *Journal of Nervous and Mental Disease* 145: 392–404.

Jacobs, M. A., Pugatch, D., & Spilken, A. 1968. Ego strength and ego weakness. *Journal of Nervous and Mental Disease* 147: 297–307.

Knapp, P. H. 1967. Purging and curbing: An inquiry into disgust, satiety and shame. *Journal of Nervous and Mental Disease* 144:514–34.

———. 1969a. The asthmatic and his environment. *Journal of Nervous and Mental Disease,* 149:133–51.
———. 1969b. Image, symbol, & person. *Archives of General Psychiatry* 21: 392–406.
Knapp, P. H., Mushatt, C., & Nemetz, S. J. 1969. Rating Manual: Boston University Psychosomatic Asthma Study.
———. 1970. The context of reported asthma during psychoanalysis. *Psychosomatic Medicine* 32:167–88.

Supplement by Bergin. Knapp noted the need to identify a symptom which can be fed immediately into an apparatus and then get very rapid feedback of information to the patient and to the therapist. Asthma and other somatic symptoms presumably provide such a possibility. This advance in technology makes it possible to more clearly identify the symptomatic process as it fluctuates in the context of a variety of psychological stimuli. He pointed out that the psychoanalytic interview is too chaotic a morass to do this effectively, and not enough feedback goes on.

He noted, however, that he is conducting two research psychoanalyses at the present time in which he is watching shifts in the psychotherapy material along with changes in somatic responses. He carries a few patients himself for this purpose on a regular basis. He believes that psychotherapy involves a feedback process; but he believes that it is important to break feedback down in some systematic way.

Knapp is inclined to believe that it is still fruitful to study the psychophysiology of the psychoanalytic session. He pointed out that transference focuses upon powerful emotions and heightens physiological responses. This focus perhaps reveals the defensive process as it occurs. Would it be possible, then, to see with our own eyes how defenses seal over emotions and close off what was formerly exposed? We need, in this context, to reconceptualize the defensive processes. Anna Freud's conception is out-dated. We need to classify, describe and quantify defensive successes versus defensive failures. He noted also that he believes the affect which pours out without control when defenses are broken down is the therapeutic thing in therapy!

Strupp observed that part of the therapist's job is to find pockets of affect and mobilize this affect. Knapp agreed, but said that psychoanalytic papers have addressed this only sketchily. Psychoanalysis got entangled in pseudotheory instead of staying with the clinical phenomena.

Strupp noted in this connection that he thought the *Studies on Hysteria* were very important and that they focussed on a technology of change and on the power of affect in the process of change. Then, metapsychology took over and the significance of the early attempts to do something specific about patients' problems was lost. Reference was made to Grinker's work on narcosynthesis, and to Jerome Frank's work using ether to produce an emotionally labile stage in the patient. Knapp pointed out that many patients go to sleep under these conditions or are "turned off." We must do something about these defenses and these procedures do not seem to do that something. At this point he mentioned a reference we should read, Kubie and Margolin (1945).

It was noted that psychotherapy is very complex but people look at it differently. Wolpe sees what he wants to see in it and he sees it more simply than other people. Hans suggested that in spite of this, in various areas people are becoming more open to different views. Knapp agreed and referred to his experience in a recent "smoking conference." He noted that a number of behavioral therapists were there and a good deal of agreement occurred among different people on the phenomena and techniques for intervention, but the theories were still very disparate. One important result of that meeting was the conclusion that it is important to give people quick feedback on the consequences of their behavior. For example, if one could give rapid feedback to the smoker on the effects of smoking on his physiology, this might have a powerful effect.

Hans drew attention to the importance of Edward Murray and Leonard Jacobson's chapter in the Bergin-Garfield *Handbook* (1971) which points out rather well the elements that are common to the various psychotherapies. While Murray uses a social learning model, he seems able to embrace most of psychotherapy within it. Knapp feels that social learning occurs by continuous feedback and interaction. The cognitive message of an interpretation is not what the patient experiences. The patient learns gradually over time, by repetition of this message. The meaning that a patient attributes to the therapist's intervention is vital. The cognitive elements in desensitization are a case in point.

Knapp referred to an article by himself and Mathé which recently appeared in the *New England Journal of Medicine* (Mathé & Knapp, 1969). They subjected asthmatic and normal subjects to stress stimuli and found that the asthmatics showed an extraordinarily flat response on physiological measures and subjective experience of anxiety. The normals showed a rise in free fatty acids and a rise in epinephrine. The asthmatics' angry responses somehow were "turned off" and it appears that primitive aggressive impulses immobilize and terrify them. Normals tend to have an angry, aggressive response.

There followed some discussion about a form of treatment by which one might modify these responses directly instead of using a traditional psychotherapeutic procedure. In this connection, Strupp noted that Neal Miller was less concerned with dynamics and more with symptomatic control.

Knapp said that he agrees with Miller, especially since 3 to 5 years of analysis may still not achieve positive results. He also noted that patients of this type who are stimulated to express aggression seem to show improvement.

Strupp pointed out that cognitive variables are important here, too. The assumptive world of the patient is vital. Can we more directly modify these cognitions as well? Jacobs believed this would apply to secrets which the patient harbors but not to unconscious material. Knapp intervened at this point and indicated that psychoanalysis is a kind of waiting game. The question is at what points we can introduce structure and directly try to modify symptoms without destroying the therapeutic process. Moreover, it appears that the therapist's attitude and orientation are important. For example, the patient's perception of the therapist's sustained struggle against the patient's problems regardless of how difficult they may be necessarily has a powerful effect upon the patient. This determination to succeed is important and is placed in opposition to ritualistic bargains and agreements to failure to which patient and therapist sometimes implicitly agree in order to avoid confronting the real problems.

There was a further discussion of the work by Peter Lang, Neal Miller, Joe Kamiya, and Mulholland in modifying autonomic responses by conditioning. Knapp was especially impressed by the fact that Miller had been able to influence the volume of renal clearance by reinforcement methods; he considered this truly extraordinary.

In these approaches it is important to have a good symptom on which to focus and give feedback. For example, it might be possible to give continuous feedback on blood pressure, but traditional measures are weak because they do not provide immediate information. To illustrate, we can take perhaps one or two blood pressure readings per minute which only permits us to provide one or two reinforcements for every 70 heartbeats. This is a poor procedure.

There was some discussion of the nature of psychosomatic disturbances in general. It was considered that they may indeed be conditioned responses and may originate as classically conditioned behaviors. Operant conditioning may then take over and the symptom may acquire meanings and reinforcement values, thus creating many psychological sequels. Furthermore, there may be an inherited abnormal vulnerability in psychosomatic patients which sets the stage for accidental conditioned responses. Some people who are asthmatics at age 7 or 8 seem to have symptoms which disappear in many cases; but the child is always biologically different, and demonstrably so. It is important to recognize that biological bases tend to sensitize pathways which yield strong individual differences in behavior and symptoms. Vachon observed that sensitivity to drugs and other influences in humans varies by a factor of 10 (!).

Additional Miscellaneous Points. In relation to methodology, Vachon pointed out that it is now possible to put a magnet on the front and back of an asthmatic patient and the fluctuations in the magnetic field will give an excellent reading on a continuous basis of the tidal volume in the lungs. There are many other ingenious measuring methods evolving from this work which are impressive and inspiring.

Knapp, Vachon and others are working on the problem of gaining greater control over airwave resistance in asthmatic patients. They hope to do this by providing immediate feedback to the patient of the amount of air volume in the lungs. The person breathes into a complex apparatus which provides immediate visual feedback. They then plan to use natural fluctuations in breathing volume as an opportunity to reinforce a higher breathing rate. This may yield some kind of voluntary influence over what ordinarily might be considered an involuntary response.

There was an interesting discussion of the use of plasma free fatty acid as a measure of adrenergic activity. The problem with using this measure is that there are eleven other things that influence fatty acids besides the secretions of the adrenal medulla. All of these obviously must be controlled before one can use this measure. (What implications this might have for psychological measurement!)

Knapp said it might be important to study the relationsip of breathing to speech behavior. He raised the question of whether the "breath group" is a natural unit of speech. If it is, we may succeed in developing a natural way of quantifying speech and thus get a mechanical, automatic monitor of speech, a very difficult problem at the present time.

Finally, there was discussion of Delgado's use of implanted radio transmitting instruments, and the possibility of measuring the effects of adrenergic action by such means. It is now possible to use sensors by swallowing them and measuring acidity, motility, instrinsic pressure of the stomach, and the like. The possibility of implanting a "couple" on blood vessels also seems to be a possibility.

In general the work of this group was impressive; they seem to be focussing on important problems and are developing an increasingly powerful technology for bringing them under control.

References

Kubie, L. S., & Margolin, S. 1945. The therapeutic role of drugs in the process of repression, dissociation, and synthesis. *Psychosomatic Medicine* 7: 147–51.

Mathé, A. A., & Knapp, P. H. 1969. Decreased plasma free fatty acids and urinary epinephrine in bronchial asthma. *New England Journal of Medicine* 281:234–38.

Murray, E. J., & Jacobson, L. I. 1971. The nature of learning in traditional and behavioral psychotherapy. In A. E. Bergin & S. L. Garfield, eds., *Handbook of psychotherapy and behavior change: An empirical analysis.* New York: Wiley, pp. 709–747.

INTERVIEW: JOHN M. SHLIEN*

Cambridge, May 15, 1969

We spent the afternoon of May 15 with John,[28] discussing the progress of our own work and listening to his ideas concerning possible areas of growth and development in the psychotherapy field. We began by presenting a brief overview of our experience on the project to date, and indicated a number of difficulties with large-scale collaborative efforts. John readily assented to our decision not to mount a major, multifactorial, complicated design at this time. He pointed out that there are many problems with the scientific status of the field, and that if things had been going well we wouldn't be looking at ourselves in the way that Linford and Colby had also done. It is unusual for a study to be devoted to an examination of one's own field of inquiry.

John saw considerable merit in our proposal to write a book as the best way of sharing our experiences with others. As other consultants have pointed out, we are in a unique position of taking a look at progress in the field. He added that, as scientists and as individuals, we tend to look more self-consciously at ourselves when things don't go too well.

We talked at some length about the broader issues to which we addressed ourselves in visits with various consultants and dwelled on the small impact research in psychotherapy has had on practice. John pointed out that not only do people use different variables, instruments, and subject populations, which detract from comparability of research findings, but sometimes two investigators looking at the same data interpret the results in opposite directions. As an illustration he referred to the fact that Truax and van der Veen, in the same research group, went over the same data and came to different conclusions.

John raised the question of whether we are talking about knowledge or opinion in psychotherapy research. He pointed out that perhaps we are studying the sociology of knowledge in our field and this may be as important as anything we can do. Our casual approach to this as opposed to a planned experimental design focussed on the sociology of knowledge may be a much more important and effective approach. If we used a carefully ob-

* Dr. Shlien is a Professor in the Graduate School of Education of Harvard University.

28. Shlien, like Matarazzo, was a member of the originating committee.

jectified study of the sociology of knowledge we might find out less. For example, there are the self-revelations people permit themselves under the informal conditions of an interview. We all seriously doubted whether statements of this type would ordinarily get into textbooks.

We considered the question of why people codify views of a field instead of telling it "like it is." In this context Allen related an observation by Arnold Lazarus, made to us around 1:00 A.M. after many hours of discussion. We had asked Arnold to what factors he attributed his effectiveness as a therapist, to which he responded: "Well, I really don't know what I do that helps people; I suppose it's just the fact that I'm a sympathetic listener and am interested in their problems." John agreed with our continuing interest in studying "mechanisms" of psychological change. He noted that this is indeed the "ultimate goal" and the point at which "science begins to take place."

On the topic of transference phenomena, John noted that this is an "obfuscation," a fiction invented and maintained to protect the therapist from the consequences of his own behavior. He concurred that interpersonal processes should be studied but not under the rubric of transference, even if such phenomena can be demonstrated and replicated. Often there is no original experience to transfer. Warmth, for example, may feel good because it's "wired-in" and not because the person experienced it this way in childhood. Although a behavior pattern observed in the present may have its roots in the past, this realization does not help us very much in dealing with it: "A lemon may taste sour regardless of antecedent experiences with a lemon's sour taste." (Strupp largely disagrees but it would take too much space to document his views.)

John felt strongly that we need to scrutinize the person of the therapist, recognizing that in the past the therapist has typically not lent himself to this kind of examination. For one thing, it is certain that the therapist is not the representative of a "technique." In this connection, John described a project in which he proposes to use children between the ages of 7 and 12 as therapists. His notion is that one child's sensitive understanding of another can be of great therapeutic value. He believes that children are the most therapeutic element in our culture, and that their directness, honesty, and openness unfortunately are lost as a result of the interpersonal phoniness pervading our culture, to which they become exposed and to which they fall victims.

John described one-to-one interviews conducted by children where one is distressed and the other listens. He noted that these interviews are very impressive and that the children manifest a good deal of sensitive understanding; he plans to film this material. He feels that the effects of children are similar to emotional returns from growing flowers or working in one's garden; therefore, he thinks there are no psychological cripples among gardeners. Perhaps one of the most important things we can do for mental health in the community is to encourage everyone to have a garden. For instance, he thinks that anyone tending a plant and watching it grow would never commit suicide.

He then described a personal experience he had years ago in Chicago in a supermarket. He accidentally smashed a jar of applesauce, and his daughter who was small then took his hand and said, "Don't be scared, Daddy." He tended to withdraw his hand and said, "Don't be silly, I'm not afraid." She had sensed his underlying fear or dread, and then he had denied it. He realized he was training her to deny emotion and deceive herself. This illustration shows how psychological energies are caught up in a system of deceptions. Conversely, honesty releases emotion and produces help from others. Strupp remarked that Freud, too, was concerned with this kind of phoniness in the Viennese culture of his time.

John elaborated on the phenomenon of phoniness, contrasting it with honesty which most forms of psychotherapy try to engender. He asked how we can figure out the "mechanisms" of phoniness. In any case, he reiterated his conviction that the person of the therapist should be thoroughly investigated. This emphasis is shared by many specialists in the area, including Strupp who has struggled with research on this topic for the last 15 years.

We then talked briefly about community mental health and John stated: "I really don't think community mental health has much of a future. It is okay at the level of changing pathological social institutions, but we must not equate clinical psychology with social action. The latter involves politics, economics, and sociology. Community psychology essentially proposes that half of the world talk to the other half. It is okay to do this but there is some doubt that the aims of social action are the same as those of clinical psychology."

As the interview progressed, he made a very interesting assertion, namely that we do not talk very much about the self-regenerative powers of a person. Surgeons know about this but we don't. We talk of procedures and therapeutic influence, but what about the power for self-change? We then got on to the topic of desensitization, wondering whether one could desensitize oneself without the interpersonal influence of a therapist, and thus in a sense be self-regenerating. John believes that auto-desensitization is real. The relationship is not necessary and conditioning without the therapist is possible. To support his view he referred to studies by Kahn and Baker and by Lang. Certainly in these studies the personal influence is minimal, although as the incisive chapter by Murray and Jacobson for the Bergin-Garfield *Handbook* (1971) attests, it is ubiquitous even when it *appears* to be a negligible factor.

We turned to the question of how much influence the therapist has or should have. John noted that some forms of psychotherapy are democratic and others are not, at least in the view of some people. He feels he has come to an important conclusion about democracy: "Democracy does not mean who has the vote, but democracy means due process! Thus, in our social system, we are protected more by due process than by our right to vote." We then spoke of the relevance of this concept to psychotherapy and Hans mentioned Szasz's "autonomous psychotherapy."

Eventually we found ourselves immersed in a wide-ranging discussion of society and of the role of young people in it. In general, John does not seem to be very optimistic about the present generation, including those who function as psychotherapists. John thinks that many therapists are inadequate people, that they are motivated by a morbid curiosity and that they continue to work out their own "hang-ups" in therapy with their clients. Unfortunately, we have "no quality control" to determine what constitutes a competent therapist and the competence of the same person may vary greatly from client to client. In Rogers' terminology, many therapists are not "fully functioning persons." John has greater faith in the new generation and considers our children considerably more healthy psychologically than we are. If this is so, they might perform much more adequately as therapists. By the same token, they would present to patients a finer image than the therapists of the past, an image less power seeking and less greedy for monetary returns. John summarized this point by saying: "We need to preserve the field for those who have had a better growth experience than the members of our generation." We may need another try at psychotherapy with a new group of therapists.

In this connection, Hans said that if someone does bad surgery on an appendix, he is likely to get kicked off the hospital staff; but there is no good way to check up on the effects of the psychotherapist. Hans quoted Colby's comment to the effect that in order to make progress in science it is necessary to be young and not biased by traditional knowledge and theories. John tended to agree with this and pointed out that "many therapists transcend themselves as therapists, but most of them are still inadequate human beings." He said that he felt that in the sexual realm students today are finding out for themselves what the students of the preceding generation found out by exploring the lives of their patients. Students today are less power seeking, less concerned with money and status. "In a few years we will have people doing therapy who don't have so many inhibitions."

Allen raised the question concerning John's views on client-centered therapy. He noted that its virtues will undoubtedly be absorbed by other forms of psychotherapy and some of its less valuable idiosyncrasies will drop out. John remarked that one can hardly teach new students client-centered therapy and its major tenets because the students already know them, and what formerly were secrets of interpersonal dissimulation are no longer secrets to the younger people. The good aspects of the client-centered view have thus been absorbed into the youth subculture.

John thought that greater efforts should be made to research the therapist and the patient as a unit, which would give us a chance to elucidate the vicissitudes of matching and mismatching. A successful "case" is one in which both participants grow; a failure, on the other hand, is a situation in which both participants experience defeat and regression. John thinks there is much more mutuality in psychotherapy than had traditionally been acknowledged, and we would do well to focus on the client's experience in understanding the therapist and his skills. One of the valuable things in group psychotherapy is the individual patient's experience that he is not unique, and that others have similar problems which perhaps they can handle with greater competency than he does. Similarly, in individual psychotherapy, the patient must be given the opportunity to learn something significant about the therapist's competence as a person, an opportunity which is only rarely realized. In this context John expressed the opinion that therapists recover from their neuroses through their therapeutic activities. Their therapeutic work gives them strength and helps them overcome their own weakness. The client should have a similar experience.

In this context, John saw a good deal of merit in the intensive case studies of the type we have been writing about, particularly if the investigator is able to keep in mind the broader social context.

John wanted to call our attention to numerous other points which had been stimulated by our summaries and other communications, but time was running short and so he promised to write us about them at greater length. A few topics only briefly mentioned included:

1. The psychology of secrecy. John thought this was an important problem. The process of sharing secrets, thereby depriving them and the person harboring them of power and dread was certainly implicit in Freud's work, and has recently been given prominent expression in the writings of Sidney Jourard on self-disclosure.

2. Accept cases for therapy which are considered to have poor prognosis and try to subvert the prediction and study what happens.

3. Send sophisticated patients through different forms of psychotherapy. This procedure might result in accounts like those of a group of sophisticated psychologists who underwent psychoanalysis in the late 1930's (Boring et al., 1953). (Strupp's view of this particular publication is that the authors either did not have a genuine therapeutic experience or their published reports are so "edited" that the essence of the experience got lost. They approached psychoanalysis as an intellectual exercise or as scientists who desired to approach a phenomenon "objectively." Perhaps they were also ashamed to admit that the experience had been therapeutic.)

4. The function of sleep as a factor conducive to mental health should receive greater attention. John referred to sleep as a largely neglected human need and to deep rest as something that is highly prized by the organism.

5. Another important problem is the study of the personalities of legislators. He feels that "most legislation is *by* neurotics *for* neurotics." He feels that much of the sickness of our society is due to the fact that a proper psychological influence has not been exercised in the realm of legislation and civil government.

Some of the comments on youth, democracy, and government here and elsewhere perhaps arose because Harvard's first major student riot had recently occurred.

References

Boring, E. G., ed. 1953. *Psychoanalysis as seen by analyzed psychologists: A symposium.* Washington, D. C.: American Psychological Association.

Murray, E. J., & Jacobson, L. I. 1971. The nature of learning in traditional and behavioral psychotherapy. In A. E. Bergin & S. L. Garfield, eds., *Handbook of psychotherapy and behavior change: An empirical analysis.* New York: Wiley, pp. 709–47.

INTERVIEW: DAVID BAKAN*

Toronto, May 16, 1969

We spent the better part of May 16 in a consultation with Dave, in the pleasant surroundings of a brand new, sumptuously furnished behavioral science building.

The first part of our discussion was devoted to a detailed consideration of a recent article by Dave (1969b) which draws parallels between unrest on university campuses and unrest within the field of psychology. The fundamental problem in psychology today, according to Dave, is the problem of *alienation* which pervades contemporary conceptualizations in psychology and represents its mainstream. Dave believes that the enterprise of psychology is "politically quite serious" and deplores the fact that the literature dealing with the psychology of learning (conservatively estimated at 50,000-100,000 journal articles) has had little payoff; for example, it has had virtually no impact on education, and yet experimental work in learning is the primary model for research in the whole field of psychology. Dave listed the following six characteristics inherent in experimentation in the area of learning but also elsewhere (these are spelled out in greater detail in the aforementioned article):

1. Statistics and rigorous design represent the prevailing ideology of American psychology. This approach embodies alienation, and psychother-

* Dr. Bakan is Professor of Psychology at York University, Toronto, Ontario, Canada.

apy is supposed to be opposed to alienation. Not only does research in learning systematically eliminate or repress the most significant qualities of human experience; it is also slavishly committed to statistical tests of significance. This is bad because the test of significance is wrong technically, yet researchers in learning are in love with it. The marriage of these two is perhaps a sign of the corruption of both.

Bakan argued passionately that there is something very wrong with the application of statistics to psychology. Statistics has become an ideology which is being imposed upon students. When students rebel, it is often the computer that is the first thing to be burned up. It is the symbol of alienation. (We noted that Paul Meehl and David Lykken have discussed this issue in similar terms.) Dave, of course, is not against statistics per se but he sees our present day "methodolatry" as a great evil.

2. The problem of *kinship* is ignored by American psychologists. The writings of a man like Erik Erikson are diametrically opposed to the academic tradition, and his book, *Childhood and Society* (1963), is one of the few significant contributions which takes the cultural context fully into account. The book is a better introduction to language, learning, and culture than most of the research-based treatments and yet it is ignored by experimentalists. The influence of kinships upon learning and development are very powerful. Leaving them out of psychology makes it more difficult for learning research to have an influence upon education.

3. The emphasis on physiology and psychophysiological research ignores the social-cultural context of man's existence and views the organism as "all inside the skin."

4. Again, in the study of language the cultural context is frequently left out of account.

5. Prediction and control, the shibboleths by which the modern scientist lives, represent a power fantasy of the *Brave New World* variety. Dave contrasted psychoanalysis (not as it is practiced today but as it was viewed by Freud) with the contemporary psychologist's effort at predicting and controlling behavior. The goal of psychoanalysis was liberation and autonomy —not the production of automatons. For these reasons too, Dave expressed himself as "suspicious" of behavior therapy as it has pre-empted the scene today.

Strupp was struck by the remarkable similarity between Dave's views on this last subject and Thomas Szasz's on thinking about "autonomous psychotherapy" as set forth in the book, *The Ethics of Psychoanalysis* (1965) which Strupp strongly recommended to Dave.

Strupp observed that behavioral therapy attempts to break down the full man into manageable pieces. It then proceeds to take specific interpersonal situations, and helps a person feel a sense of mastery and control over them; thus, in a sense it may also provide for autonomy and freedom of the individual. Bakan presented a number of ideas partly countering these notions. He first referred to Durkheim who taught that when you begin to atomize society, you create alienation and frequently produce suicide. The behavioral-learning approach is both "atomizing" and alienating.

6. The typical psychological experiment is a ritual of alienation, and the development of a therapeutic technology is a similar step in the direction of alienation.

Pursuing the topic of alienation as the fundamental problem of modern man, Dave discussed the nature of disease. He cited Selye (1950), who argues that in nearly all diseases, physiological and psychological, a subsystem existing within a total system goes out of control. The patient who develops a compulsion exemplifies the point. The cure consists of getting the subsystem back into the larger system, or, in psychoanalytic language, to develop greater ego control. Stated otherwise, the goal is to get the individual back into the group from which he had become estranged. Dave argued that individuals may be viewed as being composed of and representing subsystems within society. It is necessary to keep these three domains closely articulated. A breakdown in society often results in a breakdown in the subsystems of the individual and perhaps vice versa. Durkheim has expressed similar ideas. The task of psychotherapy, at least according to psychoanalytic doctrine, is to bring subsystems which are running wild and "go by themselves" back under the executive control of the ego. The transference paradigm permits the patient to develop trust in the therapist; he becomes "united" with another person and in this way overcomes his alienation.

Based on the foregoing logic, Bakan went on to argue that alienation is a fundamental disease. He supported this by referring to the notion that some form of separation or estrangement is a primary psychological trigger for many psychological and physical diseases. Psychotherapy is an attempt to win people back into a system. He presented an example with which Bergin readily empathized, namely the fact that in New York City everybody is working for himself, thus all the subsystems are out of control.

There is a paradox in the fact that growth means differentiation and differentiation means separation of subsystems. While differentiation is the goal of human development, it breeds alienation at the same time. The problem lies in finding a viable balance between growth (differentiation) and group membership. Dave used the development of cancer, for example, as an instance of differentiation and of subsystems getting out of control. In the same vein, death is inevitable because of the organism's growth and differentiation; ultimately the organism becomes so differentiated that survival is no longer possible. Dave has elaborated on this topic in his recent books *The Duality of Human Existence* and *Disease, Pain, and Sacrifice.*

In expatiating on the problem of disease, Dave remarked that disease means separation in our society. The impersonal character of modern hospitals testifies to this observation. Many people die of bereavement, and it is well-known that the death rate among mourners is high. In Spitz's terminology, all diseases are a form of marasmus. Selye noted that when a person is threatened, he gets sick. His defenses kill him because they are out of control. Thus, it may be said that a person dies because of his own psychological or physiological defense mechanisms which have gone out of kilter.

Some dominant trends in the field of psychology tend to be "cancerous" or diseased in the foregoing sense. A technological kind of psychotherapy leads toward alienation and separation of the subsystem from the larger system. As already stated, the general style of psychological experiments is a "ritual of alienation." Students, Dave claims, want a more humanistic approach.

By contrast, Dave regards the ideology of psychoanalysis as "the only decent one"; that is, it is a view of the world which deals with the problem of alienation. Medical people, unfortunately, misused psychoanalysis and made it a main source of alienation; but this need not be the case. Strupp interposed the thought that Freud himself deliberately depersonalized psychological phenomena since he wanted to develop a technology. Bakan countered by saying: "I don't think Freud was a good analyst." He was a profoundly alienated man and may not have been a good therapist; however, his idea was good. He gave a license to listen. The magic of understanding, of I-am-with-you, was a vital contribution to society. In essence, Bakan argued, "psychotherapy is love"; it is "community." Freud recognized, as had no one before him, that the magic of understanding heals. Resistance may be viewed as a state of alienation, and overcoming resistance represents a process of restoring the individual to group membership.

Strupp remarked that the major world religions have long recognized that we must get the alienated person back into the fold. Bakan replied that we must have the security of belonging to the group and freedom at the same time. This paradox is least troublesome when the individual is a microcosm of the group. For example, the Israeli army was so effective because every soldier was in a sense also a general.

Dave is deeply pessimistic about psychology in an alienated society, and in keeping with his previous statements, he sees contemporary psychology as a faithful reflection of the prevailing ideology: "We have a rotten psychology because we have a rotten society." Psychology lives off of the society and reflects it.

There followed an extended discussion of how to make a science out of psychotherapy. With respect to research grants, Dave stated: "If a project deals with technology, it gets supported; if it is devoted to humanistic concerns, it get disapproved." Dave feels that money is plentifully available for technological research (for example, of brain physiology) but not for humanistic endeavors. This is also true of academic departments. The technological types are rewarded; and most real humanists are outside of academia. It was the same in Freud's time. He was outside of the system. Dave stated emphatically that real psychology is not "scientific psychology." What we call scientific psychology today is a fake. It is representative of the technological ideology of our day and is therefore political. He noted that we (Strupp and Bergin) have been put in an embarrassing position because in a sense we are employed by the technologists but our real mission is to see whether we can get the genuine psychotherapists and psychologists together and to encourage their being supported as opposed to those who continue to promote alienation in society via psychology and its techniques.

The discussion then turned to the consideration of training in clinical psychology as it is administered today. Strupp cited John Shlien's view that most psychotherapists are inadequate individuals and Bakan responded that this situation exists because there is no good training. Dave stated categorically (he made the same statement in his *Ontario Psychologist* article) that there are today no adequate training facilities for psychotherapists and that no "decent" clinical psychology program exists in North America. Clinical training, such as it is, is "snuck in" and devalued in comparison to training in technology.

Training must be done by people who are more humanistically oriented and who are willing to share of themselves and their knowledge. NCGEP (National Council on Graduate Education in Psychology) is on the right track. We need a school which will really train students but we can't get money to support such a project because all of the money goes to technological institutions. Strupp argued that this may be fine but there are many second-rate people who might attach themselves to such a humanistically oriented program. Bakan felt strongly that there are plenty of second-rate people in physiology and experimental psychology and that we should not kid ourselves that they are any different. He said: "The *Journal of Experimental Psychology* types study the mindless organism; whereas they are the mindless men."

We engaged in some speculations about what it might mean to "kick the *Zeitgeist*" in psychotherapy research, and what the world might look like in 50–100 years. Dave pointed out that we need more resources in the field of psychotherapy and psychotherapy research. We have too many problems and not enough money; whereas other fields have lots of money and lots of resources. Practically all of the psychotherapy research in the world is a part-time activity. No one is supported full-time to engage in this form of research; so how can we hope to overcome the problems? Strupp raised the question of how ripe the field is for a vigorous kick, for strong forward motion in some new directions. Bakan felt that if we are to do this we must do it in relation to society at large. We must project a society of the future because psychology reflects the state of society. We must be willing to consider a form of therapy research that is more consistent with the true needs of man than what is being done at the present time.

Dave reiterated his viewpoint that psychology is peculiarly responsive to societal needs and he feels that psychology should do something about them. Psychoanalysis accompanied the radicalism of the period 1910–1915. Marxists and psychoanalysts joined hands, and subsequent writers like Fromm and Marcuse reflect the same closeness between psychology and political ideology. Psychoanalysis grew up in bohemian circles whereas behaviorism spread in the academic situation. We must ask ourselves, Dave said, whether modern man's needs can be satisfied by a technological approach or whether we need changes in the structure of our society.

The goal of psychology should be self- and mutual-understanding, and our work should hold out the possibility of people understanding each other. The fundamental problem of modern psychology, as Dave sees it, concerns arrangements between human beings. We need a new psychology, a psychology of human understanding and mutuality. We need to know the nature of the psyche. If focusing effectively upon this domain does not work, then the world is doomed.

A *verstehende* psychology offers greater promise in this regard than Skinner's technological approach which tries to deal with human problems by means of "tricks." Said Dave: "My major quarrel with Skinner is that he tries to do everything with tricks." It is a technological approach, an engineering approach, and it is not the thing for psychological problems. It is true that technology and engineering have contributed greatly to mankind; but the two major problems (overwork and malnutrition) to which they were addressed have been basically solved, and we must move on to the more human problems, the social problems that are so urgent at the present time.

We next discussed how students reflect the status of society and the field. Quoting Ginsberg, Dave made the distinction between the "straights" and the "broads." The "straights" are students who prepare for a professional career, and they constitute no problem. The "broads," on the other hand are the revolutionaries, and they exemplify the unrest on our campuses. They will go into either politics or education. The world of the future depends on politics and education, and unfortunately neither is informed by psychology. We need a psychology that serves politics and education. Psychoanalysis at one time provided an answer, but regrettably, it fell victim to the establishment, and it needs to be rescued from the money-making guilds. It has fallen into the politics of the medical profession. Psychoanalysis has had a tremendous influence on literature and the arts, and more can be learned from the "underground" literature today than from psychology textbooks.

Dave believes that the revolution of the "broads" is taking place and that the "technicians" are losing power. Schools are instruments of social ideology and policy; therefore, they must change under this pressure.

It is an undeniable fact that new students want to engage in some form of psychotherapy; yet, because there is not a single "honest" clinical psychology training program in the country, the student is forced to learn the skills by himself. Dave also feels that there is no "real" research in psychotherapy, only "varieties of fakery." From a historical prospective, Dave thinks that the last 50 years will become known as the "Dark Ages" of psychology, most of the blame being attributable to the teachings of behaviorism. "We have had a psychophobic psychology," Dave believes. We need to return to a psychology which openly recognizes the tripartite aspects of man's functioning, namely thinking, willing, and feeling. In this context, Dave called our attention to L. Farber's, *The Ways of the Will.* The few revolutionaries that exist in American psychology are working alone and part-time.

A worthwhile psychology, Dave feels, must concern itself with meaningful problems. For example: Let us study such problems as the psychology of terror. Let's study what the "hells of the world" look like, as revealed through such things as myths and religions. He pointed out that he could use a million dollars to make such a study, but it would be impossible for him to get a grant of any kind to do what he really wants to do. For example, he would like to have conducted an initial three-year study in the library on "hells" in the world's history. We could probably learn more about the nature of terror this way than through any use of experimental or control groups. NIMH would never support such an approach. Strupp wondered whether such a study would be acceptable as a Ph.D. dissertation, and Bakan indicated he would supervise one, but that academic departments are as negative toward this kind of inquiry as is NIMH.

Dave said, "Let us also study the psychology of 'being thrown out' of organizations, clubs, universities, etc. Let us study the reactions of parents who have lost a child through illness. Such research could well be empirical, which should be taken literally as 'informed by experience,' although it would certainly not be experimental. There has been an unfortunate equation in American psychology between empiricism and controlled experimentation, with the result that the two terms have become almost synonymous." He added: "Let's be empirical! Let's get data! Let thought be informed by data. But let's not get hung up on methodological issues."

By Dave's reckoning, Machiavelli was a real psychologist,[29] and the

29. Comments by Bakan: "Don't let Machiavelli stand alone. Gives the wrong impression because Machiavelli is both a good psychologist and has a manipulative orientation. I was alluding only to the first characteristic and not the second. I usually like to say 'Machiavelli and Jesus were real psychologists.' I, of course, do not remember exactly what I said, but would appreciate it if you were to modify it to 'Machiavelli and Jesus were real psychologists.' "

psychological literature between 1910 and 1913 was "beautiful." Behaviorism gave it the death knell. (Dave has a fascinating article on behaviorism in American psychology in the *Journal of the History of the Behavioral Sciences,* 1966b).

He pointed out that there are a variety of fake psychologies. The market is full of them, and the academic system reinforces this fakery. Students often prefer it because they can get a Ph.D. by running two groups of rats instead of producing a truly intellectual dissertation.

With reference to our questionnaire to consultants, Dave had a number of suggestions and comments:

1. He recommended that we study the larger social context, as had been advocated by Freud and, more eloquently, by Fromm. Any psychotherapy that doesn't take society into account can't be very good, and this holds true for therapists also. This is why Freud was forced to study "civilization and its discontents" and why Fromm studied the larger society. Generally this means that the education of clinical psychologists is inadequate.

2. Following Freud, he argued that having self-understanding is equivalent to having freedom. We need to test this statement, however, by examining what is good in psychoanalysis, at least in its theory. Psychoanalysis does not necessarily try to modify, but to understand. Nothing about the patient is "changed" or "modified" by an "expert." The latter-day expert-client model unhappily mirrors the view of the dominator versus the dominated.

3. With reference to the advancement of science: If we recognize that we are ignorant about many subjects and the nature of scientific development in psychology, we must not presume to know the nature of our ignorance or the directions we must pursue to overcome it. To Wittgenstein's "Whereof one cannot speak, thereof one must be silent," Dave added: "Whereof one does not know, thereof one cannot prescribe." Dave highly recommended Selye's book, *From Dream to Discovery* (1964), in which the epigram occurs: "Science is an art, not a science." Said Dave: "You cannot compensate for stupidity by neatness of design," as is frequently attempted by American psychologists. Dave regards reductionism as another disease of our time.

4. Dave emphasized that the major discoverers in psychotherapy did not distinguish between practice and research. Maybe this is essential in this field and it thus sets it apart from other fields.

5. It is impossible to write a research proposal if the applicant does not know (or presume to know) the answers. There are no surprises in research as it is practiced today, and we must come to a point where science can be an adventure again. Careful designs inhibit discovery. They almost presume that you know ahead of time what you are going to discover. A well-known technique of grantsmanship is to write up a proposal which largely describes one's most recent study. This technique permits one to use grant money to

pursue one's personal inclinations until he discovers something, rather than following a pre-set design.

6. Returning to one of the earlier points, Dave asserted that replicability of findings is essentially impossible. The null condition rarely exists in nature, and it is a silly thing to test. To get statistical significance, Dave advises his students, all one needs to do is to add more cases, and any result will become statistically significant. "The superego of contemporary behavioral science is a fake!"

7. What horses, then, should we bet on? Dave's answer was twofold: (*a*) Pursue a humanistic approach to psychology and spend money on that; (*b*) underwrite professorial chairs to "nonmethodological" people. However, he emphasized that we should not expect results too quickly from such moves. He pointed out that the government really controls education in the United States and perhaps it can underwrite chairs in humanistic psychology. For example, it is ridiculous that Carl Rogers does not have a huge salary and unlimited resources to educate students. Unfortunately, it is impossible to do anything new in the universities because they are dedicated to a technological ideology. As a result, we may expect the students to tear down the universities.

8. The ignorance of clinicians with regard to statistics tends to perpetuate statistics as an academic requirement and as a dominant influence in the field. As Riesman said: "People are easily intimidated by their ignorance." Thus, if clinicians really knew much about statistics they would quite happily reject it.

On a related topic, Dave said that there is a powerful taboo in American culture against intruding upon another person's privacy. Yet, how can one have a meaningful psychotherapy without such intrusions? American psychology, primarily through behaviorism, has arrived at a pseudo-solution to the problem, by declaring a person's inner life "off limits." By this reasoning, psychoanalysis is truly an "insult" to the American ideal of inviolable privacy, which Dave sees as deeply rooted in the Protestant ethic of our society. We live by the credo that a person's privacy must be guaranteed, and the Constitution is very explicit on this subject. For this reason, too, psychoanalysis in this country has flourished only in the large metropolitan areas, where the patient's visits to the therapist remain largely unnoticed. (Strupp recalled distinct difficulties which therapy patients encountered in a small university community where everybody knew about everybody else's business, and where patients and therapists were frequently thrown together at cocktail parties, on the job, and in other situations). The recent upsurge of encounter groups, sensitivity groups, T-groups, marathon therapy in the nude exemplifies the pervasive need for intimacy, which in these settings significantly occurs typically among strangers and with the explicit recognition that it is temporary. Dave's harsh dictum is that in a sense American culture does not really want a genuine science of psychology. As a way out, we have created the *Psychological Experiment* which provides powerful protection against any real encounter between psychologist and "subject." Organized psychology thus blocks progress and stands in the way of the masses of people who really want a psychotherapeutic experience and who need therapists.

Comments by Strupp. In his book, *On Method,* Dave contributed a series of essays which are aimed at a reconstruction of psychological investigation. To a large extent, our conversation with Dave proceeded along similar lines. In diagnosing the ills of contemporary psychological investigation, Dave is probably right on a good many points and dead right on a few. Like Thomas Szasz he views psychological research in a broad socio-cultural context, and he regards our research efforts as fraught with political and ideological implications. It is apparent that Dave levels a serious indictment at the bulk of psychological research as practiced today and reported in our journals. There is no question but that his views must be taken seriously. Particularly in an area like psychotherapy which is deeply concerned with such issues as freedom versus control, where the values of the therapist and the patient powerfully interact, where we have to decide whether we wish to "modify" behavior or help the patient achieve "growth" and "autonomy," we are forced to take the broader context into account and be aware of its meaning. That is, we cannot ignore ethical and moral issues while we are bent on the development of an efficient technology. The technology modern man has acquired in dealing with nuclear energy, for example, can of course be used for destructive as well as constructive ends. The scientist qua scientist may say that the moral issues are separate and distinct from the investigative enterprise although as a private citizen he must be seriously concerned about the uses to which his work is put. In psychotherapy, it seems to me, the situation is considerably more complex, and it may prove difficult to make neat distinctions between "pure" and "applied" science. It can be shown that every utterance and every intervention by the therapist conveys his values, convictions, and beliefs and, whether he likes it or not, he communicates something to the patient about his views of man's place in the world. As Dave says, psychology (and particularly psychotherapy, concerned as it is with education in a broad sense) is "politically serious." It must also be realized that our conceptions of the investigative enterprise, the kinds of problems we select, the goals we attempt to reach, and the methods we employ toward these ends are deeply rooted in our ideology. While we may not be able to cope very adequately with these issues, we can at least try to be keenly aware of them and their implications. What we can ill afford is to ignore their existence.

I am not sure whether the discussion provided much enlightenment about *where* to look for advances, *what* problems we might tackle, and what *methods* we might employ to decrease our ignorance. Perhaps it is true, as Dave asserts, that there are no "prescriptions" in areas where we are ignorant, but at the same time I think our peregrinations have given us some glimpses of "soft spots" which might lead to advances. That is, we may not be completely in the dark although there is the dangerous temptation to look under the lamp post for the lost keys because there is more light there. Dave's recommendation to select *meaningful* psychological problems for empirical study, instead of letting the inquiry be determined by available methodology whose primary purpose is to achieve scientific respectability by aping the physical sciences, is undoubtedly sound; and he gave a few examples of such research. I find considerable wisdom in his statement: "Whereas knowledge may have practicality as its ultimate objective, it has been found that we sometimes do better, both practically and theoretically, if we temporarily forsake the practical objective" (*On Method*, p. 102). As far as research in psychotherapy is concerned, I take this dictum as confirmation of my belief that as scientists (as distinct from practitioners and private citizens) we should be less concerned with the development of "quick-and-dirty" technologies—there are already plenty of those around—and more with the systematic study of "basic" problems of psychological change, which I for one prefer not to equate with efforts at "behavior modification."

Comments by Bergin. In general this session was a jolting critique of rather basic fundamentals which are woven into the fabric of psychology as it currently exists. It may be a bit over-done and extreme in the sense that what was attacked is certainly not all there is to psychology as it currently exists; however, it is clear that academic-experimental psychology continues to be pretty much in the driver's seat. I am also doubtful that behaviorism has had such an influence upon clinical psychology and upon society. As a person oriented toward a partially technical therapy, I have found it difficult to get a hearing in what is essentially a predominantly psychoanalytically oriented field. I see clinical psychology as predominantly psychoanalytical. In addition, I believe that American culture has been much more influenced by psychoanalysis than by the behavioral movement; and I would attribute more of the problems of society to this influence than to the influence of a psycho-technology. I do, however, find myself greatly in agreement with many of the views regarding the primitiveness of many traditional, experimental and statistical approaches to the study of human complexity and experience. I think Bakan is adding a strong and persuasive voice to the movement to radically modify the criteria for what is fruitful research or perhaps to remove criteria altogether. In general, it was a rather provocative and unsettling session.

References

Bakan, D. 1966a. *The duality of human existence: An essay on psychology and religion*. Chicago: Rand McNally.

———. 1966b. The influence of phrenology on American psychology. *Journal of the History of the Behavioral Sciences* 2: 200–20.

———. 1968. *Disease, pain, and sacrifice: Toward a psychology of suffering*. Chicago: University of Chicago Press.

———. 1969a. The psychology of student unrest. *The Ontario Psychologist* 1: 14–24.

———. 1969b. *On Method*. San Francisco: Jossey-Bass.

Erikson, E. 1963. *Childhood and society*. 2nd ed. New York: W. W. Norton.

Farber, L. H. 1966. *The ways of the will: Essays toward a psychology and psychopathology of will*. New York: Basic Books.

Selye, H. 1950. *The physiology and pathology of exposure to stress*. Montreal: Acta.

———. 1964. *From dream to discovery: On being a scientist*. New York: McGraw-Hill.

Szasz, T. S. 1965. *The ethics of psychoanalysis: The theory and method of autonomous psychotherapy*. New York: Basic Books.

INTERVIEW: MARVIN A. SMITH*

New York, June 5, 1969

I[30] took advantage of an opportunity to interview Dr. Marvin Smith, while he was in the New York area. He is a biochemistry professor and is one of the brilliant young researchers in this field. He was in the area to participate in the Cold Spring Harbor[31] Symposium on Quantitative Biology, an international symposium on the topic "The Mechanism of Protein Synthesis." Such international meetings focussed on a specialized issue are relatively common in the biological and physical sciences and have a facilitating effect upon the field analogous to what we are hoping to accomplish through our planning study toward collaboration in psychotherapy research.

* Dr. Smith is Chairman of the Graduate Section of Biochemistry at Brigham Young University.

30. Résumé by Bergin.

31. The Cold Spring Harbor Laboratory is directed by James Watson of Nobel Prize and *The Double Helix* fame.

This conference on protein biosynthesis was attended by virologists, cell biologists, biochemists, physiologists, bacteriologists, and others. The field of protein synthesis has yielded many of the Nobel Prizes in medicine and physiology in recent years. Dr. Smith has participated actively in this field of research as a Postdoctoral Fellow under Dr. Severo Ochoa, who won one of these Nobel Prizes for his work. Dr. Smith recently left Ochoa's group at the New York University Medical Center to accept a position at Brigham Young University.

I devoted considerable time to reviewing with Dr. Smith the problems of research in psychology and particularly in psychotherapy. We raised a number of questions regarding parallels between problems in the biological and the psychological sciences, and in applications thereof. After having oriented him to our field, we decided to proceed by having him trace the history of work in his area and then try to draw parallels to our problems where appropriate.

A fascinating line of inquiry and discovery has taken place in this field, and Marvin suggested that if we wish more detail in the general history of certain areas of Medical Science we should contact Dr. Isidor Greenwald at the New York University School of Medicine. For a brief and accurate portrayal of the mechanism of protein synthesis itself, he suggests that we obtain at a modest fee a copy of the film "DNA—A Key To All Life" which has been published by *Life* magazine. The history, as he sees it, proceeded pretty much as follows:

1. It was first noticed that various single-celled bacteria of basically the same species vary in morphology. For example, the bacterium pneumococcus appears in a variety of strains. One, for example, has a rough coat and another has a smooth appearance. Here was the first point of discovery, namely, the observation of individual differences in otherwise similar organisms. The question of what produces these individual differences" led to the second stage.

2. It was found by experimentation in relation to this problem that if one takes the cell sap from inside the rough strain and adds it to a growing culture of a smooth group, the product will yield offspring with a rough-coated morphology. Many investigations were possible at this level, for example, which strains produce results like this and which do not, in which kind of bacteria does it occur in and in which doesn't it? These questions are obviously very similar to ones that we ask about human personality. The study of individual differences is one of our major fields, but it will soon become obvious that we are pretty much stuck at that level whereas the molecular biologists have moved way beyond it. On the basis of this line of inquiry, they began to raise questions about the molecular basis of genes and chromosomes. Apparently the nature of the genetic material was being modified

chemically in some way within these cells when grown in the presence of certain other cell saps. This led to the third stage of inquiry.

3. The question at this point was: "What is it in the cell sap that causes these consequences?" What are the ingredients or agents? It seems to me that there are certainly similarities in the way this question has been asked and the way in which we are asking what the ingredients or agents are in the changes that occur in specific individuals during psychotherapy and also the reasons for individual responses to interventions. Of course, this is a very loose analogy, and the application of molecular biology to psychotherapy is certainly conceptually limited. It is however stimulating in many ways.

It has become possible to systematically extract components from the cell sap and then to put them back into the system one at a time in order to see which parts cause which transformations. It seems to me again that there are analogies here to our desire to extract or isolate elements out of the psychotherapy process and then systematically manipulate them and combine them until we have caused the kinds of transformation which we desire, or even discover new transformations. On the basis of a series of research studies along the foregoing lines, the hypothesis was drawn that nucleic acids are the main factors determining genetic characteristics of cells. This hypothesis provided a crucial and brilliant breakthrough in that it formed a bridge between classical (Mendelian) or morphological genetics and molecular genetics. Thus, instead of talking about genes, we begin talking about nucleic acids.

4. Next came a surge of experiments testing the relationship of nucleic acids to modification in progeny. It thus became possible to attack the problem of chemical transformation in cells via these highly refined and isolated agents as opposed to studying the entire cell sap itself. We now have the cell broken down considerably: We have excluded its nucleus and most of its sap or cell body in order to study a highly refined minute process. It was determined from this series of studies that the nucleic acids in fact do control the genetic process. The next question was: "How do nucleic acids do it?"

5. The molecular biologists then ushered in the most exciting research on genetics since the time of Mendel. It is of great interest to note what the status of the field was at the time that this latest advance began to occur. It was noted by Dr. Smith that protein chemistry was already a highly developed field and that it was known that all enzymes were proteins and that cells differed in terms of what enzymes were present in which cells. It is important to recognize that there was a lot of material available for synthesizing and coordinating efforts toward discovering the precise mechanics of the genetic chemistry of the cell.

Parenthetically, I believe that it is important for us to try to educate people in our own field in regard to the history of science and how it has proceeded. I think we must continue to emphasize the importance of the development of measurements, of techniques, and of the general body of knowledge before we are ready to mount a sophisticated technology. It should also be noted here with a touch of humility that this exciting work on protein synthesis and cell biology has been taking place in organisms which are extremely simplified representations of life. Nearly all of the work has been done on one-celled bacteria. The question for us psychologists is whether we can isolate such a small piece of psychological nature and manipulate it until we know the mechanics of what is going on; that is, "what is the potential for a micro-psychology?"

In general it appears that the biochemists have been able to isolate the protein manufacturing part of the cell and have been able to study this under a whole series of varied conditions. It is fascinating that one process is isolable out of this complex system; however, it has not been possible to make this isolated system really work as efficiently as a natural system. Regardless of the extent that these variables have been varied, biochemists have not managed to find a system that could closely mimic comparable *in vivo* protein synthesis. (I wonder if there are lessons here for psychology. Namely, that some systems may be isolable even though they may not function exactly as they do in a natural context. Simply isolating the mechanisms may give us a handle on the natural process without necessarily yielding the ability to precisely replicate it.) Smith pointed out that even though the isolated manufacturing process is different from a natural one it has been possible to relate the two rather well. The main thrust of the laboratory work in this field has been motivated by a desire to isolate small segments of the complex processes going on in cells, and in some cases it has been possible to isolate rather "pure" elements from these already isolated processes. For example, some enzymes have been isolated and crystallized from extracts which have been drawn from cells. The key is to then add back various isolated elements in order to produce a particular desired result as is being done today in the field of protein synthesis.

The foregoing is a good demonstration of the value of reducing a complex process to a highly refined system and then adding elements back in until we are able to produce a small but significant real process synthetically. Perhaps synthetically is not the right word. We have gained control over a natural process so that we can produce natural consequences by synthetically manipulating certain variables. This type of procedure has worked successfully in the synthesizing of carbohydrates and lipids also.

A number of Nobel Prizes have been won in this area by people who have essentially succeeded in breaking down the mechanics of these small within-cell manufacturing processes. For example, Severo Ochoa with whom Dr. Smith worked, got his prize for isolating polynucleotide-phosphorylase, an enzyme which catalyzes the synthesis of polynucleotides, that is, RNA-like material. This was isolated from A. vinelandii which is a single celled bacterium. It was then possible to use this enzyme in order to synthesize or produce RNA. It was this sequence of discoveries or of obtaining control over tiny processes within the cell for which Ochoa won his Nobel Prize.

Parenthetically, it is of great interest to note some of the characteristics of the research related to the foregoing discovery. For example, the sequence of basic units in RNA determines the sequence of amino acids in proteins, which sequence gives proteins their biological activity. The biological activity of proteins, of course, determines to a great extent the ultimate nature of the organism itself. Thus, nucleic acids are one of the keys to the entire life of the organism and to its method of passing on its hereditary characteristics. These types of studies have also revealed a fascinating set of regulatory processes that take place in cells. For example, there are very sensitive control mechanisms for determining the level of blood sugar. These mechanisms turn on and off the conversion of glucose or sugar to glycogen, which is the stored form of sugar, and vice versa. The manner in which these processes operate is truly amazing, and it is especially interesting that it has been possible to isolate them from a complex context and learn to understand them and begin to have some control over them in spite of the fact that the entire context is not fully understood.

Another Nobel Prize was won by Arthur Kornberg who isolated DNA (Deoxyribonucleic Acid) polymerase which is an enzyme that catalyzes the synthesis of DNA. He was then able to use this enzyme in the synthesis of DNA-like material. In the process of these researches it was discovered that DNA is the controlling mechanism in the production of proteins and in the passing on of hereditary materials. RNA is the agent of DNA and follows the instructions of the master life code which is contained in the DNA molecules. Khorana was then later able to synthesize DNA using a combination of chemical and enzymatic methods and he also won a Nobel Prize.

The foregoing background helps to provide some context for the discussions that ensued as we tried to relate this type of work to the problems which exist in psychology.

Smith pointed out that every time that he started to think of psychology and what it dealt with he had a feeling that it was like electricity; it's not something you can see. He said that it was very difficult for him to visualize how one would go about studying something he could not see (though he said that we don't see DNA but we have other methods of showing its presence). He asked whether human psychology or the psychology of a personality is a "thing." He said that he could clearly visualize an atom or a cell, but when we talked about psychology he tended to think of things like "love." It bothered him that he could not put psychological phenomena into packages and see them clearly. I then attempted to give a number of illustrations of how psychology operates around observable events; although they frequently are based on or arise from nonobservables. I argued that there may not be a difference, in principle, between this type of work and the type of work that occurs in biological and physical sciences where many unobservables are inferred from what can be observed. Nevertheless, we did not discount completely the notion that psychology may ultimately be different from other sciences.

I then switched the topic to the question of whether Smith could imagine the idea of psychological systems parallel to biological systems, and I also raised the question of basic units in psychology and whether there might be any which parallel the kinds of basic units we see in biology (the cell) and in physics (the atom). Smith then talked of a variety of biological phenomena and noted that some seemed to involve basic units and others did not seem to. For example, he asked "what is the basic unit of the circulatory system?" He doubted that there was one. He also pointed out that some other systems or organs do have basic units; for example, the liver is composed of liver cells. These cells are repeating units which form a system called the liver. Similarly, the blood is a system built of blood cells. Similarly, nucleotides are units of nucleic acids. In each of these instances it is impossible to break the unit down further without violating the nature of the system. Thus, these are repeating units that cannot be broken down further so long as we are talking about the particular system named.

Smith then pointed out that there do not seem to be repeating units in the circulatory system; but rather it is a thing in itself composed of parts that may have repeating units within them. For example, the heart is a component of the circulatory system.

Smith also noted that the various types of tissue which exist within the body can be broken down into their basic units which are the cells, like liver cells, or skin cells, or muscle cells; but if you break down the cell further into its components you have sliced nature to a point where you have changed it significantly and it no longer has the same identity that it previously had. Thus, you may extract out the nucleus or the cytoplasm but you do not have then a smaller unit of skin tissue for example. You have changed the nature of the thing and you simply can't add them together to reproduce the larger part anymore. Of course, it is still valuable to break cells down into their parts, but it is interesting and perhaps instructive to us as psychologists to realize that there may be certain kinds of processes or certain kinds of elements within psychological processes that cannot be broken down further without drastically altering the nature of the thing being studied.

It was a fascinating thought for me to consider that in conducting psychotherapy research we may wish to define or classify certain systems or processes in the personality of an individual and separate them from each other. We then might wish to break down a particular system into its component parts and see if we can't discover some basic units operating in these processes. These basic units might then be ultimately broken down even into smaller mechanisms. Obviously this has happened not only in biology but also in physics when we break or split the atom. When we do this we destroy the nature of the element or substance originally put into the experimental situation and we come out with at least two new elements plus released energy.

Obviously, the search for appropriate units has been a continuing and frustrating one for psychology as it has ranged from the "Reflex Arc" to "quanta" of anxiety in personality inventories. Nevertheless, the successes of other fields continue to inspire hope that this search still has meaning.

In relation to the problem posed by the naturalists or the clinicians as to doing violence to the process when we break things down in their elements too much, it is fascinating that the cell biologists frequently argue with the biochemists and microbiologists because they say that these people break the cell down into its parts and isolate them and thus are dealing with artifacts because they have separated elements from their context. This, they argue, yields differences in the nature of the isolated parts. This is the old argument that when you study certain things you change them simply by observing them or manipulating them and they are no longer the same thing that exists in nature. The nice response to this which Smith uses, and which I think is a good one for us too, is that once things are isolated we can start putting them back together systematically until we obtain the kind of result we want. Then we have our cake and eat it too. We are able to control the process precisely and yet we have put it back into a relatively natural context.

We then talked about the question of whether psychology should depend more upon the mature sciences and derive inspiration and ideas from them or whether this might unduly bias us and thus be a disservice to our field. It may be that we need fresh approaches that are special to our own field. Smith thought we needed both, those that are completely divorced from the thinking of other fields and those that are not. He pointed out that theoretical chemists and theoretical physicists are devoted to the mathematical analysis of atomic phenomena independent of other fields but physics and chemistry teach their own brand of quantum mechanics. Both are playing the same game, but with different sets of rules. This example seems instructive in that it may be that differing approaches to the very same phenomena may yield different but significant results. Thus, there is no one way to play the game. I had the strong feeling at this point in the interview that it was important not to follow too many guidelines. It is important to simply follow the basic rules of scientific evidence and to forget about "codes" for inquiry. At this point I asked myself the question of whether it is possible to come up with an entirely new strategy of inquiry by facing *our* phenomena head on, a strategy that will be especially appropriate to very complex systems not occurring in any other field.

Smith suggested that he felt that the complex always grows out of the simplified; but he would not swear to this as far as psychology is concerned. I then pointed out that I was somewhat suspicious of some of the medical and biological progress that has been achieved with rather simple manipulations because I think they pretend to have single effects unrelated to their contexts whereas such isolated interventions too often have undesirable side effects. Smith said, "yes, but it was necessary to break things down first and then gradually put them back together." I tend to agree that it is necessary to break down the complex in order to make nature manageable and then try to reproduce nature by putting things back together into a more complex system.

We got on to the question again of whether psychology was unique. Smith pointed out that it was possible to take the basic elements of knowledge in biology or in physics or astronomy and to make predictions which were stunningly accurate. He noted that it had been possible to predict the place where a new galaxy should appear and did. The same has been true in the discovery of new physical elements on the earth which were predictable from gaps in the periodic table. He also noted that once you have discovered a new thing like an element you can subject it to all kinds of tests and experimental manipulations to gain an understanding of its nature and control over it; but this seems very difficult to do in psychology.

Smith also raised a question of whether psychology is not trying to apply very *simple rules* to very complex systems. He said that he believed we would progress much better by sticking to the simple elements of these complex systems and stop trying to apply some of the simple rules of inquiry and of science to these very complicated systems. It is not impossible to embrace complex systems within the basic simple rules of science.

I had an association at this point that *fear* is a big hang-up of people in the area of psychotherapy research. They are essentially really afraid to meet the phonemena head on, try to manipulate them, and break them down. I referred to this fear once before as the "bug-a-boo of complexity." I suspect psychology may ultimately prove to be as complicated as the chemical mechanics that take place within a single cell; but I tend to believe that psychology has not progressed because we have not learned to reduce psychology down to simpler systems that are manageable and understandable, and it is not just a gimmick or a trick to do this. It seems to be in the nature of things that simple and tiny processes underlie the complex in every region of nature. It is fantastic, for example, to consider the fact that there is enough energy in one glass of water to power an ocean liner across the ocean and back numerous times. This knowledge, however, would not have been obtained without breaking elements down into their sub-atomic structures. The control we now have over the kind of energy that exists within a glass of water is truly phenomenal. Perhaps it is simply fantasy to imagine that some day we might have a parallel kind of knowledge in the field of psychology and of therapeutic change, a kind of micropsychology. It may be questionable whether psychological processes can be broken down into tiny parts, and it may also be questionable whether these parts, if they do exist, have the kind of highly specific operation which occurs in the biological and physical world.

We discussed briefly the *who* of research and Smith pointed out that he had noted many biological scientists make derogatory remarks about psychologists. He said that in general they seem to be a different breed and there were further questions of the kind that Linford had raised earlier as to whether psychologists are really scientists anyway and whether it will ever be possible to have a science of psychology. Certainly, we do not seem to have the same proportion of remarkably ingenious experimenters that some of these other fields do. The *who* of research, as Colby has suggested, may thus be more important than ever.

I personally tend to think that psychology is different than other sciences in some ways and not in others. It is essentially different in content but not particularly in method. I think we must stick with the basic rules of evidence, but we must use them in relation to a special kind of content. This leads me to believe that we need a *science* of self-report. I tend to think that this is quite a crucial line of inquiry and development that will ultimately prove to be a necessary prerequisite for fully achieving an effective technology of personality change.

In general, I found this lengthy session with Smith quite interesting and quite stimulating. It provided me a number of concrete handles or hooks on which to place a variety of ideas about the nature of the phenomena with which we may be dealing.

For anyone who is interested, there is a very well done and very understandable account of the nature of cell biology, including a pictorial analysis of the functioning of DNA and RNA within the cell in the *World Book Encyclopedia* under the subject "cell."

INTERVIEW: PETER J. LANG*

Madison, June 18, 1969

Peter classifies his current research under three major headings: (1) Research on fear and methods for reducing its pathological forms; (2) auto-

* Dr. Lang is a Professor in the Department of Psychology, University of Wisconsin.

nomic control; and (3) studies of orienting behavior and its physiological correlates, including simple processing and reaction time.

We initiated our discussion by referring to his work with DAD, Device for Automated Desensitization. He pointed out that DAD is an attempt to simplify and simulate some of the processes which occur in psychotherapy. He noted that people in society want certain things in the way of a therapy which DAD won't provide; however, there are other agencies or other parts of psychology which will fulfill their needs. Lang felt that DAD is "just a place to start," and perhaps the approach is "oversimplified." Nevertheless, it seems to hold promise for the future.

Bergin gave a brief account of his recent interview with a microbiologist, whose approach to research may provide a valuable model for research in the psychotherapy area as well. By breaking down the cell and simulating processes in the cell, this researcher was able to produce "movement." He raised the question of whether this approach to research does violence to the processes one is interested in studying. Lang answered in the affirmative but added that in this way it is possible to achieve rigorous control.

Life, Pete observed, is interactive and not segmented. For the purpose of studying psychological processes, the human observer (clinician) is "great" but he is also subject to various biases and limitations which may constitute a serious interference with the advancement of knowledge. To aid man's limited powers of observation, the digital computer might resolve some of the problems. For one thing, it is very flexible; for another, it has enormous storage capacity, both of which seem to render it an ideal research instrument whose potentialities Lang is beginning to explore.

With respect to psychotherapy, Lang noted, we need to find out what it can do effectively and what it cannot do. This search may lead to schisms in the field but this is the price we may have to pay for advancing knowledge. His convictions are predicated on a sense of optimism concerning the potentialities of behavioral control. He believes that the behaviorists are in a very exciting phase of their work. He stated: "We are starting to get hold of things. We are getting on to some hot variables and the potentials for behavioral control are great. We can do some shaking and a lot of things start to rattle."

He also described himself as being "close" to research in physiology, and referred to what he considered highly important work in the areas of brain mapping, brain stimulation, research on the limbic system and the reticular formation. At present, Pete feels, this work is tangential to psychology, but within 15 years it should have considerable influence on psychological research. Pete added that he is currently doing a lot of work on imagery and its psychophysiological implications.

Strupp noted that psychotherapy research in the past has been too narrowly conceived, as has psychotherapy itself. It does not focus on mechanisms which are specific to itself, but rather depends upon and merges into processes that range from the physiological to the social. The time of highly specialized psychotherapy research focusing upon an esoteric process is rapidly fading.

Lang agreed and pointed out that he felt it was necessary for students to be familiar with the broad range of phenomena that are relevant to personality change. Among the important topics which students should know about, he included a knowledge of the digital computer and how to use it effectively for therapy and for research, a knowledge of physiological processes, interpersonal sensitivity, and bio-electric measurement. He states that he is asking an enormous amount of his students in these areas and it is hard to find people who can stretch this far. He feels, however, that the growing technology in the domain of behavior change requires that a sophisticated practitioner or researcher in the area be familiar with these and other domains.

In Pete's view there is an area of great importance developing which focuses on the concept of organizing a flexible, programmable environment as a method of therapeutic intervention. He noted the possibility of complex computerized programs with multiple branches and feedback loops for controlling such a programmed environment. He then introduced a personal note referring to this training in a traditional psychoanalytically oriented program. He recalled that during his graduate training there was discussion of a local therapist who used environmental manipulation as a way of modifying a patient's behavior. Everyone, including himself, considered this ludicrous. He pointed out how dramatically this has changed and how our once narrow repertoire of therapeutic strategies has been broadened. Today innovative efforts are no longer greeted with disdain, at least not by the scientific community. Behavioral therapy has changed this and it is exciting because it has brought clinical psychology back to its basic scientific roots. (A raised eyebrow by Strupp.) The clinician is encouraged to base his methods on the results of experimentation, rather than intuition. Lang, of course, does not adopt the position that the basic scientific roots of clinical psychology consist of learning theory alone.

We then launched into a discussion of the place of therapy research in the domain of science. Lang placed strong emphasis on the importance of basic psychology within a natural science orientation. The focus on objectivism and standard scientific procedures, including the use of mathematics, is essential. He pointed out that such an orientation is self-correcting and that it is the only one that has ever spawned a useful technology. Of course, he conceives of psychotherapy as a technology. While Lang is willing to entertain and accept a form of practical eclecticism in therapeutic technique, he is unwilling to accept theoretical eclecticism.

Lang holds that theories with different basic postulates cannot be usefully integrated. Any theory of man must start from a set of primary metaphysical assumptions. For example, an existentialist assumes that there are two kinds of being: the human, thinking entity and brute nature. Thus, psychology for the existentialist is automatically the study of human consciousness and the primary method is introspection. According to Lang, a natural scientist makes other metaphysical assumptions (which are no more "true" than those of the existentialist). The scientist assumes that there is only a material world, which can be shown to follow mathematical laws. Only measurable events can be part of the scientists' domain, although he accepts unprovable rules such as the "law of parsimony" as a guide to his theorizing. In effect, he takes on faith the proposition that the simple is "good." Neither the scientist nor the existentialist can lay claim to absolute truth. Lang prefers the scientific approach in trying to solve practical problems of mental health, because it is the only philosophy that has generated practical technological by-products. In any event, he holds that there is no value achieved and great confusion generated when we try to mix thought systems which have conflictng basic assumptions. Philosophies are like games with rules. You cannot play one game by the rules appropriate to another. If you place your queen's pawn four spaces forward on a single move, it is no longer chess.

He feels that too much of psychotherapy and psychotherapy research continues to be dominated by a nineteenth-century philosophy and manner of thought, including that of Freud. He pointed out that such concepts as will, intent, and other phenomenological views were not generated from quantitative data. We must approach the therapeutic problem from a scientific and technological point of view. If the subject says "I am afraid," our problem is to influence his behavior in such a way that we modulate his verbal system so that "I am not afraid" comes out. We might also want to help him to approach previously avoided objects or events, and to do this without undue sympathetic arousal. This essentially places the subject within an objective frame of reference.

As an aside, Peter remarked, "I am supposed to be a good therapist because I write about therapy." Then, returning to the main topic, he noted: "If I operate on the patient's behavioral output, I try to stay out of the 'phenomenal system.' It is very hard to be 'objective' and not to get hung up in the patient's phenomenology. Our cultural background encourages us to see the patient through our own (often misleading) introspective experience. The problem in therapy is often not how to be empathic, but *how not to empathize.*"

Bergin raised a question concerning Pete's views about recent developments in behavior modification. Lang registered certain reservations but thought that the approach had brought clinical psychology back to empirical data. He thought this was "great," but he showed little enthusiasm for what appears to be the emergence of yet another "school."

We discussed at some length Lang's recent case history in the *Journal of Abnormal Psychology* (1969) concerned with aversive conditioning of a 9-month old baby who was suffering from severe vomiting every time he ingested food. The approach followed by Lang consisted of carefully monitoring the vomiting reflex and administering electric shock whenever it occurred. Vomiting stopped within a week, and follow-up study showed that the child had maintained his improvement. He pointed out that continuing follow-ups show that the child has continued to eat regularly, to gain in weight, and to manifest no adverse side effects. This is a rather dramatic demonstration of the superiority of the behavioral approach over the traditional approach when the chips are down.

When Pete was called in to examine this difficult case, the personnel in attendance tended to use a phenomenological or experiential frame of reference in treating the child. They had theories, such as the notion that the child was angry at its mother and attempted to get back at her by vomiting food which the mother fed it. Lang feels that his approach succeeded because he was able to get out of introspective life. The important thing was to eliminate the pathological behavior. "Dynamic theory," he said, "gives you a good feeling of mastery and understanding, but it has no real technology of behavior change."

Lang pointed out that he analyzed the child's behavior in terms of measurables, even though he recognized that dynamically there was much going on, including the whole set of psychodynamic conditions which theoretically are associated with anorexia.

Psychodynamic interpretations can of course be made of interactions in any family. However, when applied *post hoc,* they can be made to explain anything.

Lang thinks that the emphasis on psychological testing that developed during World War II and the premature professionalization that grew out of the need to treat the large veteran population caused clinical psychology to become separated from general psychology. He sees this separation as very unfortunate because in the 1920's and 1930's clinical psychology was tied to experiments in pathology and to the general psychology of change. However, everybody abandoned this approach for a premature professionalization and the apparent success of psychoanalysis. In Lang's view, clinical psychologists should have maintained their scientific identity. Unfortunately, they often did not. Thus, the years 1941–58 saw a slowing in the development of clinical psychology as a science. The 1940's and 1950's witnessed a division between clinical and scientific psychology, which benefited neither.

To further illustrate the philosophical problems that dominate the therapy field, Lang pointed out that he thought it was a mistake to try to build phenomenological experiences into a scientific framework. The temptation to generate theories in clinical psychology through "phenomenal attribution" is terribly compelling, but phenomenology is not a suitable vehicle for advancing our science. He gave as an example the attempt by Dollard and Miller to encompass the psychoanalytic concept of anxiety within a scientific frame of reference. He considers this to be an impossibility. He feels that fruitful theory comes out of the relationship between things we measure, not by the attribution of our inner experiences to the behavior of the subject. To illustrate, one might anthropomorphize why physical bodies fall to the earth and argue phenomenologically that it is because they love the earth. This would then become a theory of love supposedly accounting for the fact that bodies fall to the earth. On the other hand, physics has succeeded by studying the relationships between objective *things.*

Unfortunately, in psychology almost all of our systems have started with the private experiences of the experimenter, or at least they have come to significantly influence his attitudes and his procedures. It is more important to start with verbal behavior, or other overt behaviors such as approach and avoidance which are observable and measurable and less subject to anthropomorphizing. As one changes behavior, one changes a person's phenomenology. This position is hard to communicate to sensitive therapists, and even harder for them to accept. Pete noted: "You can't do it if you practice therapy eight hours a day." However, if science is to advance, we must make the clinical investigator a "hard head." In short, *theories may not be isomorphic with phenomenology.*

Strupp pointed out that this kind of objectivity is hard to come by in our field; and, indeed, it may be impossible. At any rate, the difficulty has yielded rather complex and fuzzy theories.

Bergin pointed out that he felt that the field of psychotherapeutic technology was currently where medicine was in 1850. There were few effective drugs, some were downright harmful, and the pharmacological action of most was unknown. Lang seemed to agree with this point, which helps to place our work in historical perspective and suggests that we should not expect too much of ourselves.

Strupp contrasted the *technological* approach to psychotherapy research with the *phenomenological* one and characterized them as poles of a dimension along which practice and investigative efforts might be ordered. By this scheme, Lang would be at one pole of a bipolar dimension. He wondered whether it might be possible to combine the phenomenological and the behavioristic or objective approaches. Bergin, in turn, raised the question of whether it is possible to objectify the subjective. Strupp referred to the work of Peter Knapp and Neal Miller, noting that Miller feels that we must attend to the broader context while focusing on specific things.

Lang felt that this approach was not correct and appeared slightly offended by the implication that his approach was oversimplified. He noted that complexity is as much a variable in science as it is in phenomenology, and that this point does *not* differentiate these viewpoints. We should not abandon the scientific method just because problems become difficult. The basic principles of science are the same whether we are dealing at a complex or a simple level although the rates at which we move differ. Lang believes that his approach is the scientific one. He pointed out that we deal with complexity to some extent by using computers. In fact, the possibilities of machine analysis in some ways greatly exceed the power of the human observer to handle multivariable situations.

These queries stimulated Pete to further delineate his position. He observed that it is painful and "not human" to be a basic scientist. We get easily confused and fall prey to anthropomorphizing our science. We have to be most careful of our constructs and avoid the phenomenological "trap." The clinician and the basic scientist necessarily "wear different hats" and it is difficult for all of us to separate these positions. In some sense it is easier to work on basic physiological mechanisms than it is to work on problems in psychotherapy, and a number of researchers have taken "flight from therapy." Nevertheless, despite the difficulties attending the role of the basic scientist, it remains a worthwhile goal.

Lang went on to qualify his preceding statements by noting that when we move into the realm of actually helping people we must be guided by ethical philosophies which have little to do with science. Science can only provide tools for behavior change; it cannot tell us how they can be best used to help man.

He then raised some ethical issues by pointing out that he feels we will be able to change society by changing the knowledge or enhancing the knowledge of how to modify behavior. He believes we will soon develop "dangerous" knowledge that can affect society greatly in a negative way if it is not controlled. If the new techniques derived from this knowledge are properly utilized, they can be highly beneficial.

Strupp stated that the study of behavior change is replete with value assumptions and that it cannot be otherwise. We discussed and generally agreed with this notion.

Strupp proceeded to point out that, according to some people, Polanyi, for example, we can only learn about personality change via empathy or "indwelling." These same people argue that this type of process is the peculiarity of human nature and is opposed to the depersonalizing technological approach which Lang advocates. They say that his type of approach amounts to depriving ourselves of the ability to really understand what's going on.

Lang, of course, strongly disagreed, and in his rebuttal made reference to his own professional development. He pointed out that he stumbled into psychology by accident. He started out as an artist and was studying in

France. He returned to the U. S. and got a degree in Romance languages with a minor in philosophy and did some work in psychology. His interest in psychology at that point, however, was that of a dilletante. He underscored that his original temperamental commitment as well as his current one is to humanistic activity; however, he believes it is increasingly important to use science to achieve humanistic goals. He argued that our basic assumptions will determine the consequences of our research and the results we get. He stated: "I know you can't move ahead within a phenomenological framework." He does not deny the importance of beliefs, values, ethics, or religion. These are real, but we must divest ourselves of the tendency to project our own inner experience upon the phenomena we try to study. He feels that thought systems are tools and that a person should be able to pick them up and put them down depending upon the job at hand. When acting as scientist, he tries to put down all of the subjective philosophical beliefs that are somewhere in his psyche.

Bergin raised the question of objectifying the subjective by inferring inner processes from external responses in the sense that physicists have worked for a long time by inference in relation to the study of atoms. Lang responded by saying that he feels this is an appropriate approach. Perhaps, if we can objectify the subjective, we will find, ultimately, that Freud was "really right." By analogy, Democritus proposed that atoms existed before the time of Socrates. However, it remained for modern physics to develop control over empirical realities about which Democritus had only speculated. Freud may some day hold a similar historical position. We are gradually getting control over phenomena to which he had called attention. Eventually we may find an isomorphism between intuition and scientific knowledge. He pointed out parenthetically that physiologists tend to be much more subject to fuzzy thinking than behavioral psychologists. He said they sometimes express concern over the locus of consciousness and try to pin it down somewhere in the brain; this is OK for them because in their *actions* they behave like scientists. It is much more important for us psychologists to watch out for this because we have such a strong inclination to anthropomorphize and to become easily confused by our phenomena. *We* must watch our metaphysics.

Lang stated that self-discipline is required to study psychotherapy in this manner. He pointed out that he often has a strong impulse to leave the study of psychotherapy because it is so difficult and because he wants to avoid making the mistakes noted above. It is much easier to do a study of the electrophysiology of the orienting response. He reiterated that it is painful and possibly even inhuman to have to discipline oneself and force oneself to keep the two strong needs separated, that is, the need to anthropomorphize or to project one's own inner feelings upon psychological phenomena and the need to be strictly scientific. (Parenthetically, Bergin noted that this problem is often intensified for psychologists because they do not have a strongly developed belief system. For this reason, all of their natural religious tendencies tend to get projected into their scientific work and it is thus difficult for them to maintain objectivity.)

Strupp introduced a discussion of Neal Miller's recent work in conditioning autonomic responses. Lang was very interested in this area and has done a great deal of work in it himself. We therefore discussed it at some length. He pointed out that Lisina in Russia (see Razran's articles) used an arm plethysomograph and had her subjects watch a polygraph record of their own vasoconstriction and vasodilation. She shocked the subjects for certain responses and was able to reverse the normal physiological response in humans by this conditioning procedure. This and other evidence flies in the face of Hilgard and Marquis' assertion that it is impossible to operantly condition autonomic responses.

Lang indicated that he and his group started their experiments in 1962. They were stimulated by a student of R.C. Davis (University of Indiana) named Shearn, who published an article in *Science*. The experiments involved avoidance conditioning of human heart rate in which the subjects were trained to accelerate their hearts using exteroceptive feedback by which they could hear their own hearts. They pursued the kind of work pioneered by Shearn and were able to manipulate heart rate to a certain extent by getting subjects to keep tones up to a level of heart rate. The tone was used as a reinforcer and subjects were not given specific instructions on "how to drive your own heart." Results tended to be equivocal and Lang observed "some funny effects." He was concerned with the problem of stabilization, and found that subjects who were correctly informed were able to stabilize their heart rates.

They independently confirmed Lisina's findings, although the subject's task was somewhat different since he was required to stabilize the heart rate and to reduce its variability around a central or median point. They tried to take labile subjects and make them stabile with regard to their own heart rates. They were able to achieve this goal by transmitting the heart rate impulses through a meter and onto a visual display. A light shifted from left to right, swinging as a function of the rate of the heartbeats. A narrow band in the center of the visual display was the target for the subject. He was to attempt to push his own heart rate into that center area. He also pointed out some similar work by Kimmel with GSR in response to odors. He provided pleasant and unpleasant odors and was able to affect the skin conductance. This work is reviewed in two recent articles (Katkin & Murray, 1968; Crider, Schwartz & Shnidman, 1969).

Lang then went on to describe some rather complex experiments his group has carried out at Wisconsin which extend this work on influencing heart rate. Because of the complexity of the design we did not go into too many details and Pete promised to send us reprints (Lang, Sroufe, & Hastings, 1967). However, he described one experiment in which an attempt was made to reduce the standard deviation of the *S*'s heart rate. Subjects who received direct feedback on their own heart rates were able to drastically reduce this variability. Other subjects who were tracking a meter display based on someone else's heartbeat and who were not given instructions to reduce variability nevertheless were able to reduce variability slightly over time. A third group was asked to simply track their own heart rates and their variability actually increased. A fourth group was asked to reduce variability but given incorrect information and their variability increased. All four of these groups were significantly different. On obtaining subjective reports as to what the subjects were experiencing or saying to themselves during the experiment, they all had different answers which makes it appear that each had an idiosyncratic response to the experimental conditions; however, these idiosyncratic self-reference statements may be associated with some physiological constants.

A fortuitous finding that emerged from the foregoing study was the observation that people can get locked into a vicious cycle. For example, if a person feels anxious his heart may begin to beat faster and the heart rate feedback increases his anxiety which in turn increases his heart rate. It has been found that this type of vicious cycle can be reversed experimentally. This finding appears to be a dramatic one. Bergin stressed the importance of students in psychology knowing something about these areas and obtaining a strong scientific base for their practice much as medical students must learn the scientific basis of medical practice. Lang responded by stating that in theory this was correct; but he added that medical students are just as resistant as clinical psychology students to lectures by Ph.D.s. They often question the relevance of this type of research to helping people.

Lang proceeded to describe an experiment by one of his students, Alan Sroufe. He was able to get subjects to stabilize their respiration and cope with a heart-rate learning task at the same time. He was able to show that change in respiration was not necessarily related to or causative of a heart rate change. Thus, he corroborated Miller's findings obtained with curarized rats.

Strupp was particularly interested in the implications of some of this work for research in the psychosomatic area. Lang agreed with Miller that we are dealing with an "open question." He cited some research by Bernard Engel, who has conditioned some patients suffering from cardiac arrhythmias, and the work of Forster with epileptics. Clinically, it would be useful to focus on striate muscles in conditioning work. Bergin agreed that this was potentially a very fruitful area for research. Lang also noted that he had been stimulated in various ways by Lacey's work.

Some of Lang's previous work has provided feedback to subjects by means of meter displays. Currently, he is beginning to use the computer to provide feedback through an oscilloscope.

Commenting on his work dealing with visualization in desensitization, Pete remarked that "psychotherapy by machine" is "sexy"; in a more serious vein, on-line computer feedback may provide "a handle" on visualization. Bergin noted that poor visualizers may be "suppressors." In this context, Lang regretted that we are largely indifferent to biological dissimilarities in subjects.

We talked at some length about organizational aspects of Lang's research. His group consists of a number of students (perhaps 6–8) who work closely with Lang and are in a sense collaborators. Pete has no keen desire to engage in collaborative research with investigators elsewhere. He stated: "There is no need for me to collaborate with guys who have the same skills I have; however, there is so much to know in this work, that collaboration with people who have special technical skills or abilities (e.g. computer programming, medicine, bio-engineering) has become increasingly important." He added that, rather than collaborative or coordinated research, we need more independent replications. On this subject, Bergin made the observation that the desire for collaboration seems to be inversely related to the satisfaction of the feeling of worthwhileness an investigator has in what he is doing. Strupp agreed.

Bergin also raised the question of the potential value inherent in naturalistic studies of change. Pete believes that naturalistic observation is a "very preliminary method," that it is "an idea book" rather than a "blueprint," and that the investigator's biases are a formidable obstacle to distilling useful knowledge in this way.

The several subjects we discussed during lunch are itemized below:

1. We discussed various ways of computerizing experiments and Lang pointed out that he felt most laboratories will have systems for computerizing experimental procedures in the future. This will eliminate many of the sets and expectations and personal variations introduced by human error. We also discussed at this point the view of Murray and Jacobson that there are many sets and attitudes which are independent of the experimental procedure which must either be measured or controlled.

2. Lang discussed at some length the problem of hooking up too many machines in a serial fashion in order to conduct an experiment or record responses in an experiment. He noted that an investigator of his acquaintance had set up a highly instrumented physiological psychology laboratory. Unfortunately, when it was finished it was totally unusable because too many machines were linked together. The problem was that each machine had a small amount of error involved in its measurements, thus when the machines

were hooked together serially the errors multiplied rather than added; thus, he had a system whose ultimate measurements amounted to almost perfect uncertainty!

3. Lang talked about three systems of responses or behaviors in people which he termed the verbal, the autonomic, and the behavioral. He pointed out that conditioning or shaping may be more effective if it is specific to the system under study. Fear, for example, doesn't develop all of a piece. People who are habitual behavioral avoiders may not give verbal material that is consistent with this behavior. There are probably interactions among the systems which are poorly understood at this time.

Comments by Strupp. Lang obviously has an exciting program of research under way and he is a scientist who has tremendous confidence and conviction that his approach is one of the promising roads, if not the royal road, to progress in the area. There can be no doubt that his enthusiasm is infectious and that students respond to it in kind. He has a keen sense of direction, and, as far as he is concerned, the steady progress of the scientific enterprise is assured. This attitude represents a marked contrast to the skepticism espoused by such people as Colby, Rogers, and Bakan (whose views are of course by no means homogeneous).

While I firmly believe that the future of psychotherapy is that of technology, I tend to think that Lang espouses too narrow a view of the phenomena with which the psychotherapist and the researcher in psychotherapy ultimately (and perhaps consistently) needs to deal. It should be possible, it seems to me, to combine the technological approach of Miller and Lang with clinical data and observations in a broader sense, and I must reject Lang's wholesale dismissal of anything but behavioral data. I don't think it will do to regard man as a stimulus-response machine without considering mediational processes, such as the symbolic meaning of symptoms.

On the other hand, I believe there is a good deal of merit in regarding subjective data (such as a patient's feeling state) as epiphenomenal and to operate on the forces which give rise to the subjective experience. As a matter of fact, I continue to be impressed by the fact that the enlightened psychoanalyst, perhaps implicitly, subscribes precisely to this position when he operates upon the patient's defenses against painful affects, and he takes account of the *complex symbolic meanings* which, at least in part, determine a person's behavior. It must also be remembered that, particularly in his early work, Freud was firmly committed to the development of a therapeutic technology to deal with specific problems he encountered in his patients. This trend unfortunately has become obscured.

I am becoming increasingly convinced that one fruitful way for advancing knowledge in this area is the single-case approach, in which clinical observations (carefully described and recorded) serve as the base line against which the effects of specific experimental interventions, introduced at carefully selected times, can be measured. In this way it would be possible to take advantage of clinical data as they emerge in the course of therapy and to augment (hopefully) therapeutic effectiveness through planful experimental interventions whose effects, at least in an approximate way, might then be studied.

For example, I have thought of the possibility of studying bronchial asthma in this way. In general terms, one would proceed along clinical lines, and in the course of the treatment explore the contingencies which determine asthmatic attacks (for example, by learning about situational determinants, psychophysiological monitoring, and the like). Then, at appropriate times (to be determined by the investigative team, of which the therapist is a part), it may be possible to bring specific technology to bear upon modification of the symptom, which in turn might have considerable implications for the progress of therapy. While this sketch is crude, I conceive of the possibility of refining it. It seems to me that the implications of such an approach for the purpose of developing a more focused therapeutic technology and gaining a better understanding of the process of symptom modification might be considerable.

References

Crider, A., Schwartz, G. E., & Shnidman, S. 1969. On the criteria for instrumental autonomic conditioning: A reply to Katkin and Murray. *Psychological Bulletin* 71: 455–61.

Katkin, E. S., & Murray, E. N. 1968. Instrumental conditioning of autonomically mediated behavior: Theoretical and methodological issues. *Psychological Bulletin* 70: 52–68.

Lang, P. J., & Melamed, B. G. 1969. Case report: Avoidance conditioning therapy of an infant with chronic ruminative vomiting. *Journal of Abnormal Psychology* 74: 1–8.

Lang, P. J., Sroufe, L. A., & Hastings, J. E. 1967. Effects of feedback and instructional set on the control of cardiac variability. *Journal of Experimental Psychology* 75: 425–31.

Razran, G. 1961. The observable unconscious and inferable conscious in current Soviet psychophysiology: Interoceptive conditioning, semantic conditioning, and the orienting reflex. *Psychological Review* 68: 81–147.

Routtenberg, A. 1968. The two-arousal hypothesis: Reticular formation and limbic system. *Psychological Review* 75: 51–80.

Shearn, D. W. 1961. Does the heart learn? *Psychological Bulletin* 58: 452–58.

———. 1962. Operant conditioning of heart rate. *Science* 137: 530–31.

DISCUSSION OF CASE STUDY APPROACH

Chicago, June 20, 1969

We discussed case studies as contexts for planning interventions and studying their effects.[32] It was surprising that the entire group of 6 people who were involved in the lengthy discussion seemed to agree readily that single case studies would be an extremely fruitful approach to research in therapy. It seems clear enough that an objectified or quantified single case approach which involves replication across cases has the advantages of objectivity and of direct and immediate relevance to practice. These advantages lend an appealing aspect to this approach, which turned us on quite a bit. There were, however, a number of differences of opinion as to how the approach might best be implemented. We discussed several approaches, including (1) the traditional clinical case history, (2) the objective or quantitative case history, (3) planned intervention in single cases, and (4) ideographic generalization, (which amounts to focusing on some subsystem within the person and generalizing to the larger psychological system which is his personality).

I focused on the notion which Strupp and I had discussed, that the importance of the case study approach is that it permits technique building. This is made possible by experimenting with a planned procedure with a specifically identified symptom or problem. It should be quantified, however, and thus combines points 2 and 3. For example, I described a case of female homosexuality which I had treated. I began the case with a course of straight empathic type therapy which established a certain degree of progress, but found it necessary to add desensitization of fear toward male figures as a second stage in the process.

A third stage was necessary which combined an empathic and desensitization process, a procedure reported recently in a book on behavior modification techniques (Bergin, 1969). Finally, role playing and operant techniques for increasing the patient's repertoire of heterosexual behavior were added. This sequence of procedures achieved successful results.

The single case approach thus provides the advantage of permitting continuous experimentation across the history of the case until a combination of procedures is arrived at which seems to work. Once this is achieved, then

32. A psychotherapy research conference sponsored by Division 29 of the American Psychological Association in June of 1969 overlapped with our other activities and provided, among other things, a forum for me to discuss some of our ideas about the case study approach. I am particularly indebted to Kenneth Howard, who was present at the conference, for helping me clarify many thoughts in this and related domains of research. Résumé by Bergin.

the same sequence can be applied to a second case which is as similar as possible to the original.

In addition, it would be possible to isolate out parts of this sequence and apply them homogeneously to single cases in order to determine whether the same effects could be achieved by one or some other combination or order of the procedures used in the original study.

There are many modifications of this procedure, which is based in part on the operant paradigm used by reinforcement therapists. This approach, however, has the advantage of assuming that the process of change is multidimensional and will require a number of techniques employed in some specific sequence. Thus, an operant procedure might be applied to a specific symptom until it reached the limit of its effects, and then other procedures would be employed to move the case forward to a predetermined criterion of change. The important point is that one approaches the case or problem with the conscious intent of *technique building* within an objective framework in the live (but preplanned) clinical process.

Another approach to case inquiry is described by Chassan (1967). His paradigm is somewhat more applicable to drugs; but it is also adaptable to psychotherapy. To illustrate, if we take patient type A, we might wish to apply two procedures to him in a particular order such as X, Y, X, X, Y. It would then be possible to statistically determine the particular effects of X or Y or the combination thereof, following Chassan's procedures. We might then take case A^1 which differs in some specific way from case A and see whether a similar combination of interventions has the same or a different effect. We might, for example, simply have the cases identical except that one is a chronic schizophrenic and the other is an acute schizophrenic. There are difficulties in applying this paradigm but it is not beyond testing.

There was some discussion interjected with regard to the question of whether single factor research will be as fruitful as research which focuses upon a pattern of intervention and change. This question was considered by some to be essentially analogous to the conflict between a behavioral and a gestalt approach to psychology and to change. This issue is certainly important to consider; however, I argued that we cannot make progress without simplifying even though ultimately we may not want to reduce everything to single factors.

The difference between the case study approach, as we have discussed it, and Chassan's is illustrated in Figure 4.1. I noted that there is nothing unique to this approach. It is simply a way to emphasize the importance of a systematic, planned series of interventions with regard to specific syndromes, that these interventions should be programmed, and that the process should be carefully recorded and quantified so that the specific procedures which effect change may be isolated and their effects identified. We

CHASSAN DESIGN

A X- - -Y- - -X- - -X- - -Y- - -→ Define A as 30 yr. old chronic schizophrenic

A^1 X- - -Y- - -X- - -X- - -Y- - -→ Define A^1 as 30 yr. old acute schizophrenic

Determine that X is effective agent with A; then test on A^1.

BERGIN DESIGN

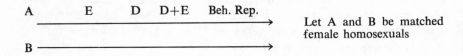

A E D D+E Beh. Rep. ——→ Let A and B be matched female homosexuals

B ——→

Develop an effective technique via experimentation with A. Then replicate on B, or switch order on B, C, etc.

E = empathy
D = desensitization
D+E = empathy and desensitization combined
Beh. Rep. = increasing the behavioral repertoire

Figure 4.1. Two Objective, Experimental Case Study Approaches

discussed one problem with this approach which is quite important to take into consideration. That is, when one intervention is introduced, it changes the context in which the second or later intervention is introduced. This can be handled by alternating the order in which the procedures are introduced; but it does complicate matters and requires an increasing number of cases depending upon the number of different interventions one wishes to cumulatively apply to a given problem.

We then discussed the role of the case study within the general context of the study of change. I presented a paradigm for inquiry in the field of psychotherapy research, which arose from the Strupp and Bergin project, in which we give the case experiment a prominent role but in which we saw it as only one part of a series of types of inquiry that necessarily must be conducted and which interact with each other. The process of inquiry and of development of techniques is illustrated in Figure 5.1, (p. 433). This paradigm seemed well received and I felt reinforced in my convictions about it.

References

Bergin, A. E. 1969. A technique for improving desensitization via warmth, empathy, and emotional reexperiencing of hierarchy events. In R. D. Rubin & C. M. Franks eds. *Advances in behavior therapy,* 1968. New York. Academic Press, pp. 114–130.

Chassan, J. B. 1967. *Research design in clinical psychology and psychiatry.* New York: Appleton-Century-Crofts.

June 30, 1969

Dear Allen:

Your notes on our visits with Shlien, Knapp, and Bakan have arrived, and as usual I enjoyed reading them.

Before I forget I want to comment briefly on your observation that you find clinical psychology a predominantly psychoanalytically oriented field, and that you personally have found it difficult to get a hearing for your views of a "partially technical therapy."

Not long ago, at a conference in Chicago, I had occasion to discuss this problem with Joe Wolpe, who expressed very similar views. For example, he noted that it was virtually impossible to introduce behavior therapy into psychiatric residency programs.

I find these observations very interesting because I see them very much at variance with my own perceptions. I think Wolpe is probably right with respect to psychiatry, but as far as psychology is concerned, I see the field dominated by behavioristic theories, and I believe American psychology has always had a strong ambivalance about psychoanalytic teachings. I recognize that following World War II clinical psychology embraced psychoanalytic concepts for a time, but the period was short. In this connection, too, I remember an obituary on David Rapaport which made the point that he never was really accepted by American psychology (nor was he fully accepted by the psychoanalysts, largely because he was a PhD).

How can we account for this discrepancy? I think a good part of the answer lies in geographical factors and what goes with them. In New York City and other metropolitan areas (like Los Angeles, Philadelphia, Washington, D. C. and a few other cities) psychoanalysis has had a tremendous influence and psychology departments located in these cities reflect it. (You may remember my comment about Kadushin's book[33] whose applicability

33. C. Kadushin, *Why people go to psychiatrists* (New York: Aldine • Atherton, 1968).

seems largely restricted to New York City). However, if you consider the views propounded in psychology departments at other universities (in the midwest, south, etc.), there is no question but that you get a very different picture. I could name many universities where psychoanalytic doctrine is regarded with deep distrust and largely rejected by both faculty and students.

We must also consider that our respective perceptions may well be influenced by our personal predilections but I don't think that is the whole story. Rather I tend to think there is a fair degree of veridicality in our observations. The problem also has other important sociological implications, some of which Bakan touched on (e.g., the problem of greater privacy in the urban centers).

By the way, I still subscribe to the view that psychoanalytic psychotherapy, at least as Freud conceived of it, is definitely aimed in the direction of a *technology*. I believe it is important to point this out.

As ever,
Hans

FURTHER WORKING PAPERS BY STRUPP

September 29, 1969

I continue to be interested in some variant of the project we discussed under the heading of "therapy as practiced by experts." That is, I believe it is possible to design research which would add to our knowledge concerning the kinds of therapeutic changes that may be expected under *optimum* conditions. The research I envisage would entail (1) clarification of the kinds of patients who benefit from a particular form of psychotherapy; (2) clarification of the kinds of therapeutic changes achieved in such individuals that is, elucidation of the criterion problem) and (3) further insight into the therapeutic strategies employed by skillful therapists in reaching these goals. The following ideas (based in part on empirical research) impress me as pertinent:

1. In my judgment, by far the greatest proportion of the variance in therapeutic outcomes is accounted for by patient variables. Thus, it follows that an important problem in psychotherapy research and practice is that of *selection.* In this connection, intelligence measurement provides an important parallel. While I. Q. is certainly not an infallible predictor of school or college success, it is a very powerful index. Notice, too, that we take it for granted that good teaching (analogous to a good patient-therapist relationship, and more importantly, therapeutic skills) may enhance the student's success, but we do not seem to be overly concerned about student-teacher *complementarity*. I would be the first to admit that some patients work bet-

ter with certain therapists and vice versa, but—within certain limits—the problem of matching patient and therapist does not strike me as a crucial one. (This statement needs to be qualified.)

2. There continues to exist widespread confusion about the kinds of changes produced in certain people under certain therapeutic regimes, and the term "psychotherapy" is so broad as to defy specification. As we have said many times before, we must become clearer about the kinds of changes we are attempting to achieve, the routes by which they are to be achieved, the assessment of changes, and the kinds of people in whom we want to produce certain changes. Thus it seems to me a worthwhile objective to clear the ground by a demonstration study which might lay a good deal of the confusion to rest.

3. Garfield (1971) in his review of client variables, echoes the charge made previously by others that "the best therapeutic results have been obtained with those clients who are the least disturbed, or who, as some have said, are in the least need of treatment" (p. 294). And further: "we must not find ourselves in the position of devoting most of our professional resources to working with those who may be in least need if our help" (p. 294). While the literature clearly shows that some candidates for psychotherapy are markedly better risks than others, I think it is unwarranted to conclude that the majority of these poeple were not seriously disturbed or that it was wasteful to expend therapeutic efforts on them. "Disturbance" is certainly a relative term, and, as I see it, the argument makes as much sense as the statement that patients suffering from disease X are less entitled to treatment than patients suffering from disease Y because (*a*) a larger number of people suffer from disease Y, (*b*) fewer physicians are interested in disease Y and the people suffering from it, and (*c*) disease Y is a more serious disease. As far as emotional problems are concerned, one might be willing to say on economic grounds that a person who is anxious, depressed, and inhibited but who is able to earn a living is less seriously disturbed than a person who cannot hold a job and is intermittently hospitalized, but I wonder whether such comparisons are very meaningful. There can be no doubt that there are large numbers of people who need psychotherapeutic help but are not getting it, but this is a different issue. Garfield, it seems to me, confounds scientific issues with social considerations.

It could be argued that psychotherapy as it has evolved over the years makes definite demands, such as youth, intelligence, and motivation, on the patients who are to benefit from it and that, realizing these requirements, therapists have selected patients on the basis of these (and other ill-defined) criteria but that, by and large, the selection has been reasonably good. If it could be improved, then we might be in a better position to assign people to the kinds of therapy from which they are most likely to benefit. In this way, we might sharply curtail the radius of applicability of certain forms of therapy, which might also point up the need for developing new techniques for those who do not fit the criteria, but we might also significantly increase the likelihood of success for those who have been selected.

Again, the I. Q. analogy seems pertinent. We can safely predict that a student with an I. Q. of less than 120 will experience difficulty in completing college. We accept this fact and select students accordingly. However, we do not conclude that too much attention has been lavished on higher education. Instead, we say that candidates who show less aptitude should receive other kinds of education.

It is possible that we may learn as much (or even more) about the process of therapeutic change (the science issue) from new forms of therapy with patients who do not fit the traditional model, but personally I doubt it. Certainly, the one does not exclude the other, and much depends on the investigator's preference. There is no question that we can change behavior by all manner of techniques, from coercion to subtle persuasion, and we are dealing not only with the problem of effectiveness and efficiency but also appropriateness (to the client and the circumstances), humanitarian considerations, the client's wishes and expectations, etc.

In short, we need *specificity* on a larger scale, and research must be tailored to take this into account. For this reason I believe that large correlational studies in which patient, treatment, and outcome variables are studied in muddied fashion will not provide the answer. What will then?

4. I foresee several possibilities (although the details need to be spelled out):

a. One might select a problem, for example, depression or obsessions, and ask therapists employing divergent techniques to treat a very small number of clients of their choice. One might study outcomes in considerable detail and depth, for example, through assessments by a panel of experts of divergent orientations. Initial assessments might be made in similar fashion. Goals would have to be specified. Records of such therapists (such as sound recordings) might be helpful, but I have no longer any great faith in minute analyses of content. I believe it is the broad strategies that matter and the *quality* of the patient-therapist relationship as it evolves.

b. One might carry out a retrospective study of clients who have been treated by therapists of divergent persuasions who employ very different techniques and assess the kinds and quality of changes. (Such a study might begin to illuminate the criterion problem.)

c. One might ask therapists, perhaps as part of the study described under (a) to become maximally explicit about their selection criteria and determine similarities and differences between therapists participating in the study. It is conceivable that "good candidates" are regarded as "promising" across the board.

References

Garfield, S. L. 1971. Research on client variables in psychotherapy. In A. E. Bergin and S. L. Garfield, eds., *Handbook of psychotherapy and behavior change: An empirical analysis.* New York: Wiley, pp. 271–98.

October 5, 1969

In the course of a recent discussion concerning the work of Polanyi and R. C. Cantor, Dr. Richard Blanton (a Vanderbilt colleague) said students find it difficult to grasp the idea that a machine cannot be explained by studying the metal and its physical make-up; instead you have to understand the design, the purpose, the function which cannot be isolated by studying the parts. These comments emerged from a dialogue concerning placebo effects in therapy, the experimenter-subject relationship in many psychological experiments (Rosenthal's, 1966, experimenter effects) and a recent paper by D. Schultz (1969), dealing with the subject of distortions that creep into our science through such things as deception and use of college students as subjects who know they are being deceived. Often it is best to ask people what they interpret the situation to mean and what they are supposed to do in it. Dick talked about the constraints of the situation.

My own associations concerning cognitive factors in psychotherapy turned to psychosomatic problems and primitive constructions antedating language development in the child which form part of his belief system. The latter, in turn, governs his relationships with other people and the manner in which beliefs influence physiological functioning as well. I understood Dick to say: The body follows its physiological functions and superimposed on these (in psychosomatic conditions) are the person's primitive assumptions about his relations to others. These assumptions might result, for example, in holding in one's body contents (bowels, air), in warding off the evil influences of others by shutting oneself off, or in seeing one's own fantasies as dangerous and destructive. Lack of spontaneity results and further holding in, preserving one's precious possessions, fighting off intruders who want to deprive one of one's treasures, and similar actions.

How can one modify these assumptions short of a prolonged relationship in which they are gradually exposed, eroded, and corrected? Of course, massive assaults on the physiology are possible[34] and one may be able to produce "modifications" without tracing back the route by which the original patterns originated or dealing with the patterns themselves. A hammer

34. W. H. Auden wrily observed that torture "works" too in changing people.

can serve to break a structure and one might be able to reassemble it in other ways if it can be molded and is not set too much, but a gradual erosion of defenses attempts something different, namely to soften up the structure and recast it. The new organization or gestalt then produces changes in these basic patterns.

We know patients overgeneralize. For example, they believe that *all* people are dangerous and they have one (stereotyped) way of dealing with people, based on early experiences which may have been insulting, destructive, vicious, and injurious. The new relationship with a therapist, upon which the old patterns are imposed, makes it possible to point out that discrimination is possible. As the broad generalizations are undercut, the patient can begin to discriminate and he achieves greater flexibility in doing so. "Improvements" in psychosomatic symptoms and new ways of relating to others result. It should be stressed that these beliefs are *primitive* and operate at unconscious levels; that is, they are not recognized by the patient. Specific examples have to be adduced that make profound sense to the patient and drive home a point. Thus, one needs to relate one's operations closely to the patient's personal world. To be sure, there are only a few basic patterns which everyone uses, but the idosyncrasies which people develop are innumerable. Therefore, one cannot present general principles and expect the patient to be able to grasp the implications and ramifications. They must make sense to him in the context of his own living. In this sense, too, the therapist is a decoder of scrambled messages, communications, and beliefs. He also exerts influence through his nonjudgmental attitudes, presumed expertise (which however is demonstrated as he "makes sense" to the patient), his patience, and the support he provides.

I continue to be preoccupied with the problem of the *nonspecific* effect in therapy and *specific* technical operations. Can one separate these experimentally? From the above it is amply clear to me that laboratory situations or other analogues cannot take one very far because the patient does not believe they are "real." On the other hand, a person *wanting* help and change because he is distressed is something entirely different. *How can one contrive experimental situations in which one can tease out the utility of specific operations from the nonspecific ones?* I am impressed with Shapiro's (1971) emphasis on the therapist's belief in the utility of his methods. This belief constitutes a powerful influence. Thus, the effects of therapy can not be accepted at face value in proving anything about the effectiveness of the method itself. It is my personal observation that all great therapists I have known have a profound faith in the utility of their therapeutic operations, to the point of fanaticism. Analytic training, at least in part, is designed to remove the ambivalence and the doubts in the trainee. Once he becomes a "true believer" he is considered to be a first-rate therapist.

The heart-rate studies in normal subjects are too contrived. However, it may be possible to study the make-up of those people who can participate in these experiments effectively and those who cannot. For example, the presence of anxiety, the degree to which S believes that the experiment is somehow going to "help" him may make a great difference. Contrast this with the usual instructions in which S has no personal investment. Why should he please E? What is in it for him? Thus it appears to me that if one were able to meet somehow a *need* in S, one would do a lot better and the studies would be a great deal more meaningful. I would also hypothesize that if S is somehow in a meaningful personal relationship with E, the results might be much more impressive. As it is, we are operating very much at the surface in these experiments. There is no meaning, no investment, no pay off in being able to change some aspect of one's autonomic functioning. If the context were more meaningful, then S might see some purpose in slowing down his heart, regulating his breathing, or what have you. He might do it then to please E but on a deeper level (for the sake of pleasing E *and* getting something valuable personally for himself). In such studies, too, one might try to study the response of positive placebo reactors or negative ones or nonreactors (as assessed independently). For example, a positive reactor may be better able to control his heart and other autonomic functions (say EEG) as well; a negative one may generally do poorly, but again much may depend on the *meaning* of the whole enterprise to S.

How can one make some real inroads on the problem of modifying the belief structure which govern patient's interpresonal behavior as well as his autonomic processes? One of the dilemmas, as I have mentioned, is that *efficiency* of change is not necessarily the most useful index. Different kinds of "appeal" may apply to different patients. Certain people may respond well to interpretations because this kind of intellectual appeal is meaningful to them; others may react better to manipulations via drugs or desensitization in which they are told specifically what to do and this makes sense to them.

October 6, 1969

What seems to be needed for a meaningful study of autonomic control in relation to the specific versus nonspecific effects of psychotherapy and changes in structure of beliefs:

1. An autonomic function that is somehow involved in the patient's psychological functioning, for example, a psychosomatic symptom. It does not seem to be particularly interesting per se to demonstrate that heart rate can be altered in normal subjects.

2. The autonomic function must be capable of being monitored, at least in some crude quantitative way.

3. The experimental task must make sense to the patient on a personal level; that is, he should not be required to engage in some activity, like slowing down his heart rate, for some purpose he does not understand, to please the experimenter. In order for this requirement to be fulfilled it is probably necessary to structure the situation in terms of a therapeutic intent. The subject must feel that his cooperation in some way is going to "help" him.

4. The foregoing implies that there has to be some meaningful relationship between subject and experimenter (patient and therapist).

5. Somehow we must learn something about the manner in which the symptom functions, the *purpose* it serves in the subject's adaptation. I question whether such knowledge can be acquired without engaging the subject or patient in some kind of therapeutic relationship.

Here we might have a testable hypothesis: Is symptom modification more effective if the foregoing conditions are met than when the structure of the situation is purely experimental?

References

Rosenthal, R. 1966. *Experimenter effects in behavioral research.* New York: Appleton-Century-Crofts.

Schultz, D. P. 1969. The human subject in psychological research. *Psychological Bulletin* 72: 214–28.

Shapiro, A. K. 1971. Placebo effects in medicine, psychotherapy, and psychoanalysis. In A. E. Bergin and S. L. Garfield, eds., *Handbook of psychotherapy and behavior change: An empirical analysis.* New York: Wiley, pp. 439–73.

October 13, 1969

Specific versus Nonspecific Factors in Psychotherapy. In contemporary conceptions of psychotherapy, the psychotherapeutic influence (that is, the force impinging on the patient) is usually divided into two broad components, conveniently labeled (1) specific and (2) nonspecific factors. Grouped under (1) is that part of the influence which is hypothesized as being due to the method (techniques and procedures), exemplified by such things as interpretations, reflections of feeling, desensitization. A method can be described, communicated, and taught; usually it is supported by a theory or rationale which is designed to explain its modus operandi and its effectiveness. Although a method can be practiced with varying degrees of skills and is always influenced and modified by personality characteristics of the person using it, it nevertheless has an existence apart from the practitioner.

Category (2) includes a broad group of variables, such as the therapist's belief in the efficacy of his methods, his ability to inspire hope and trust and alleviate guilt, and his charismatic qualities. The operation of both sets of variables is of course circumscribed by attributes inherent in the patient or the situation, which may potentiate or impede their effectiveness.

It is important to note that the development of psychotherapy as a scientific discipline has placed great emphasis on category (1), whereas category (2) has been treated, at least until fairly recently, with a certain amount of disdain. Freud, for example, sought strenuously to differentiate psychoanalytic technique from "suggestion," which obviously he viewed as a nefarious and ephemeral force. The thrust of behavior therapy, too, has stressed techniques, although in the recent past some attention has been paid to "relationship" factors.

The nonspecific (or "common") factors in psychotherapy have been slow in gaining recognition, partly because they are often exceedingly elusive and difficult to define, partly because they form part of man's everyday repertoire for influencing others (see Scriven, 1964) and are thus seen as unscientific. Frank (1961) incisively explored the parallels between such things as psychotherapy, religious conversion, and faith healing; and his book stands as a major contribution to the elucidation of the nature of the psychotherapeutic influence. Extensive research on the placebo effect (documented recently by Shapiro, 1971) likewise calls forceful attention to the phenomena in this domain. A point deserving particular mention is that placebo effects are produced not only by the therapist's charismatic qualities but also by his *belief in the efficacy of the methods* he employs. In this respect, the psychoanalyst's unshakable conviction in the soundness of his method may form an important part of its efficacy and worthwhileness. The same may apply, *mutatis mutandis,* to any psychotherapist. If the patient is appropriately impressed or responsive, there occurs a self-fulfilling prophecy in which the method is continually validated by the observed success. By this reasoning, almost any method, as long as it has sufficient plausibility to the patient and is espoused with sufficient conviction by the therapist, may be effective. This is one important reason for the difficulty encountered in separating specific from nonspecific effects.

Rather than considering variables in category (1) as "scientific" (or potentially scientific) and variables in category (2) as "unscientific" ("effects merely due to suggestion"), it seems more appropriate to consider both as central to the nature of the psychotherapeutic influence. Frank and others have seriously questioned whether much specific variance is "left over" once the nonspecific effects are properly accounted for, and the waxing and waning of treatment methods in medicine as well as psychotherapy supplies powerful support for this position. In any event, the effectiveness of a given method cannot readily be used as a criterion for validating its underlying theoretical assumptions.

The conclusion to be drawn from the foregoing considerations is that the nonspecific factors in psychotherapy must receive increasing attention from researchers in our effort to analyze the nature of the therapeutic influence, which I regard as a task of the first magnitude.

In this connection, we may speculate that the therapist's conviction about the usefulness of his method(s), coupled with the patient's perception of the therapeutic intent which fills a highly personal need for him, is a more potent factor than the method itself. That is, from the patient's standpoint, the therapist's operations must make sense. This feeling is augmented when the patient experiences relief, which he may well attribute to the method. Acceptance, respect, nonjudgment, lack of censure, common in all forms of psychotherapy, seem to provide base line conditions, over which specific technical operations may not be able to improve in any spectacular way. I believe Shapiro is correct in calling attention to the salutary effects attendant upon guilt reduction which is facilitated by all forms of psychotherapy. In many cases this factor in itself may help the patient to mobilize latent strength in *mastering* troublesome interpersonal problems, although there are undoubtedly other forces at work. Parenthetically, behavior therapy may be highly effective with certain patients precisely for the reason that the therapeutic method *bypasses* highly personal matters instead of forcing the patient to "come clean" and face unpleasant truths about himself. Furthermore, since the method spells out a program in highly specific fashion, it enables the patient to gain a "handle" on his problem, as he sees it, which formulation the therapist accepts at face value. Thus, the method "makes sense" to the patient. Similarly, to highly intelligent patients, psychoanalytic interpretations, for other reasons, may "make sense" and become embraced by them. With such patients, the danger of intellectualizing as a defense against revealing deeply personal matters is frequently noted.

Therapeutic intent and patient's motivation. Several studies have recently called attention to the importance of the variable of therapeutic intent and demonstrated that operations by a therapist which are espoused as therapeutic and experienced by the subject as such have a greater chance of producing therapeutic effects than operations whose therapeutic significance is either nonexistent or obscure to the subject. In one study (Paul, 1969) subjects were told that training in relaxation and related techniques would help them to deal with a variety of anxiety-provoking situations. Here, it may be presumed that the subjects experienced the intent as therapeutic (as opposed to experimental) and that the technique appealed to them on a personal level.

The patient's *motivation* to seek and accept help appears to be the counterpart of therapeutic intent. A person who is cognizant of a personal problem for which he engages the services of a professional helper is obviously in a very different situation from a subject who is *selected* for a psychological experiment. It appears that the chance of demonstrating therapeutic effects are *greater* in a situation in which there is congruence between the patient's needs and the therapist's intent than when these conditions are not met. In the latter case, obtained findings may well be artifacts or at best difficult to interpret.

The foregoing points are particularly important in studies pertaining to autonomic control, which are typically presented to the subject as a laboratory task. He is usually not informed *what* the experimenter expects him to do or *why* he is expected to do it. For example, it may be presumed that instructions to regulate his heart rate make little sense to the subject nor does he see any benefits that may accrue to him. To be sure, the task may present some form of challenge, in which case it might be comparable to an athletic feat. More commonly perhaps S is a college sophomore who is meeting a course requirement and who is not profoundly interested in E's intent. At any rate, the subject's motivation in these experiments apparently has not been dealt with; instead, the focus has rested on the demonstration of a phenomenon. On the other hand, a patient suffering from a cardiac arrhythmia may approach the task of controlling his heart rate with a very different set. My point is that before the kind of "therapeutic learning" outlined by Miller (1969) can become reality it will be necessary to map out the parameters of the experimental (or more correctly, therapeutic) task in much greater detail. One important objective of research may be to examine, in the course of several studies, differences in individuals' ability to achieve autonomic control depending upon whether the task has therapeutic relevance to the subject as compared with the more common situation in which it has little relevance. In addition it seems appropriate to study more generally the *meaning* of the experiment to the subject as a function of the manner in which the task is structured by the experimenter and the nature of hypotheses the subject adopts on the basis of the instructions.

Receptivity to Therapeutic Influence. There is a sizable literature (see Garfield, 1971) pertaining to characteristics of clients which render them suitable or unsuitable candidates for psychotherapy. Within the range of the typical middle (or upper middle) class patient, there apparently is no evidence that a patient is more suitable for one form of psychotherapy than for another. Despite certain differences I have alluded to (namely, that some patients may be more attracted to one form of psychotherapy than to some other variant), it is more likely that suitability for psychotherapy is a more general disposition consisting of such qualities as motivation, intelligence, youth, a certain psychological mindedness, "relatability," a fair amount of "ego strength," relatively minor incapacitation. It may be hypothesized that certain patients are more responsive to the nonspecific factors inherent in all forms of psychotherapy than others and that clinicians for some time have been able to assess intuitively this suitability or amenability. As stated elsewhere, the efficacy of all forms of psychotherapy could be markedly improved if it were possible to refine the selection criteria for prospective patients. (While the term "positive placebo reactor," is probably unfortunate, because of the negative connotations in the word "placebo," it seems likely that the "good patient" to a considerable extent coincides with the positive placebo reactor. I also suspect that the "good" patient is one who is judged to be better able to form a good therapeutic relationship, that is, he has considerable transference potential.) Furthermore, all forms of psychotherapy are aimed at helping the patient gain more adequate control over internal events, variously defined as ego mastery, control, and coping. The achievement of control over internal events is also central to the growing body of research in the area of autonomic control, which, at least in the course of laboratory studies, has demonstrated that some individuals (as yet undefined) are markedly superior in achieving control over, for example, their heart rate than others. Accordingly, it is hypothesized that there are common core elements characterizing (1) the good prospect for psychotherapy; (2) a person's tendency to react positively to placebos (that is, the nonspecific effects of psychotherapy), and (3) his ability to achieve control over autonomic events. On the basis of the foregoing considerations it is proposed to map out in greater detail and specificity salient characteristics of the "good" psychotherapy patient, with special emphasis on the ability to achieve control over autonomic phenomena. (Such persons, too, are hypothesized to possess marked transference potential in the sense of being significantly susceptible to the nonspecific factors in psychotherapy.)

In the following are listed several thumbnail sketches of possible projects along the lines indicated above, any one of which would have to be developed in much greater detail. The listing is merely intended to serve as a basis for discussion.

1. In studying the therapeutic applications of phenomena in the area of autonomic control, it appears highly important to develop a task that is personally *meaningful* to S. For patients with cardiac irregularities, the control of heart rate would be such a task. For patients in whom hyperventilation is a central symptom, the control of breathing may be of therapeutic benefit. In these and other instances it may be possible to give the patient a measure of control over anxiety by enabling him to achieve cognitive (?) control over autonomic responses (heart rate, breathing, and the like). Autonomic control, conceivably, could be combined with desensitization in clinical populations for the purpose of bringing about a reduction in anxiety. Autonomic control could become a highly meaningful task for a wide variety of persons. (I believe the behavior therapists' emphasis on the treatment of phobias has been of considerable heuristic value, partly because phobias

represent a problem the scientist can do something about.) Thus, the meaningful task would also allow the introduction of therapeutic intent, as sketched above.

2. Working with clinical populations, such as, applicants for outpatient psychotherapy, one might begin to explore in greater detail the concomitants of the "good patient" syndrome as they might be related to aptitude for control of autonomic phenomena, such as heart rate, EEG, reactivity to the type of falsified feedback pioneered by Valins. It may be that there is a general factor operating here, perhaps amenability or receptivity to the nonspecific effects of psychotherapy. (Evidently, this factor is not closely related to hypnotic suggestibility, but I do not believe that the available evidence is convincing.)

3. In the typical autonomic control studies reported to date, little attention has been paid to individual differences. Major emphasis has been placed on the phenomena per se. From the existent literature it appears that marked individual differences exist; these may be of considerable importance as far as the exploration of individuals' responsiveness to nonspecific factors in psychotherapy is concerned. Likewise, the *meaning* of the experimental task to S has not been adequately explored. In some instances Ss were asked, following the experiment, what they thought they were being asked to do. Even those who were able to perform effectively were often in error about the hypotheses and what they were actually doing.

4. The study of phenomena in the area of autonomic control, particularly to the extent that it can be linked to personally meaningful tasks, appears to have considerable potential for exploration of therapist (experimenter) variables which mediate the nonspecific effects of psychotherapy. One reason for this assertion is that in the autonomic area we have reasonably precise response measures. It may then be entirely feasible to study in greater depth the effects of therapists' attitudes toward the patient, belief in the efficacy of the method, ability to inspire trust, hope, and other elements. In no area of scientific or professional work are the "experimenter effects" which Rosenthal has documented in a host of laboratory studies more ubiquitous and of more pervasive importance than in the psychotherapeutic situation, and they may constitute a large segment of the "nonspecific factors" in psychotherapy.

References

Frank, J. D. 1961. *Persuasion and healing: A comparative study of psychotherapy*. Baltimore: Johns Hopkins Press.

Garfield, S. L. 1971. Research on client variables in psychotherapy. In A. E. Bergin & S. L. Garfield, eds., *Handbook of psychotherapy and behavior change: An empirical analysis*. New York: Wiley, pp. 271–98.

Miller, N. E. 1969. Learning of visceral and glandular responses. *Science* 163: 434–45.
Paul, G. L. 1969. Physiological effects of relaxation training and hypnotic suggestion. *Journal of Abnormal Psychology* 74: 425–37.
Scriven, M. 1964. Views of human nature. In T. W. Wann, ed., *Behaviorism and phenomenology*. Chicago: University of Chicago Press.
Shapiro, A. K. 1971. Placebo effects in medicine, psychotherapy, and psychoanalysis. In A. E. Bergin & S. L. Garfield, eds., *Handbook of Psychotherapy and behavior change: An empirical analysis.* New York: Wiley, pp. 439–73.

Research Institute Proposal by Strupp

February 10, 1970

The purpose of this paper is to outline a plan for a research institute devoted to the broad problems of personality and behavior change. The proposal is supported by the following working assumptions:

1. Problems surrounding personality and behavior change as a function of planful psychological interventions administered with therapeutic intent represent a highly important area of scientific inquiry. In addition to its intrinsic importance, research on these problems has considerable implications for related areas as well, areas such as education, developmental psychology, and cognitive psychology. In discussing the need for relevance of a science, Weinberg (1970) states: "The scientific merit of a field of science is to be measured by the degree to which it illuminates and contributes to the neighboring fields in which it is imbedded" (p. 142). By this criterion, research in psychotherapy has at least the potential of being highly relevant.

2. While psychotherapy by definition focuses on the amelioration of human maladaptive behavior and thus is an applied endeavor, concerted effort must be made to advance basic knowledge in this area. To be sure, the dividing line between "basic" and "applied" research is always fluid, but the distinction serves to emphasize that applied work in psychotherapy has insufficiently benefited from the work of "basic" research; similarly, numerous innovative therapeutic approaches developed by clinicians have not adequately been scrutinized by basic research. A major goal in this area is to build stronger bridges between clinicians and researchers, between applied and basic knowledge, between theory and practice.

The need for systematic efforts to foster *basic* research in psychotherapy cannot be emphasized too strongly, particularly in view of the proliferation of new techniques in the area. Just as large technological laboratories support basic science research which undergirds their predominantly applied mission, so basic research must be fostered on basic psychological processes in psychotherapy. Weinberg (1970) states the issue succinctly:

> In such institutions (such as Oak Ridge or General Electric or Bell Laboratories) basic science is conducted not primarily for the breakthroughs that will lead to new technologies; these occur anywhere and are not confined to the laboratory. Rather, basic science, even very basic science, must be conducted there (aside from the kind that is obviously directly relevant) because basic science sets the tone and standard for all the rest. . . . Basic scientists keep their technological colleagues honest. They are the eyes through which the institution keeps in touch with the rest of the world of science . . . (p. 144).

Admittedly, there are no comparable psychological laboratories, and the analogy is deficient in other respects; however, it serves to make the point that clinical-applied work in psychotherapy is currently advancing at a much more rapid pace than basic research. The latter kind of research must be encouraged for the reasons stated by Weinberg.

3. Related to the last point is the need to foster improved communication and cooperation among researchers (as well as clinicians) subscribing to divergent theoretical views, to coordinate their respective research efforts, to enable researchers and clinicians to profit from their respective insights, and to work toward the development of a common set of concepts and principles to account for psychotherapeutic change.

Implicit in this statement is the view that psychotherapeutic change is mediated by psychological principles, most of which may be subsumed under the heading of common or "nonspecific" elements (Frank 1961) or "placebo effects" (Shapiro, 1971). These mechanisms are probably operative in all forms of psychotherapy, and they may vastly overshadow the so-called specific effects, that is, changes attributable to definable technical operations. Examples of nonspecific effects include: on the patient's side, faith, trust, and hope, and, on the therapist's side, activities designed to produce (and perceived as achieving) goals such as respect, tolerance, guilt reduction, understanding, attention, interest, support, and impulse control. Specific technical operations are exemplified by interetations, reflections of feeling, and systematic desensitization or counterconditioning, among others. Regardless of whether psychotherapeutic change is encompassed by "specific" or "nonspecific" factors, in either event the mechanisms are in need of explication, definition, and specification. While conceptualized in divergent terms by diferent "schools" of psychotherapy, it may be anticipated that eventually *a common set of concepts and principles* will emerge to account for seemingly diverse processes. If this assumption is correct, the time may be ripe to work more systematically toward the achievement of the stated objective.

4. While large-scale coordinated or collaborative investigations have been judged unfeasible at the present stage of knowledge (see chapter 5), modest efforts along these lines may be quite promising. To realize an approximation of the preceding objectives, it appears essential to achieve not only a greater rapprochement between researchers and clinicians but also to *train* a small cadre of individuals who are equally conversant with clinical practice and research, and who fully respect the goals of scientific inquiry as well as the complexities of the complex socio-cultural context.

5. It is apparent that scientific advances cannot be legislated and cannot be produced synthetically. However, it may be worth a try to see whether modest advances can be achieved by creating a favorable intellectual climate within which research, clinical work, and theorizing can flourish. What can be done at the present stage of knowledge is to create conditions which may make it possible (1) for fertile minds to develop their own ideas, research projects, theoretical notions, and to test new techniques; and (2) to attract a small group of young people who can acquire the requisite skills in this context, which in turn may stimulate their own productivity. If successful, this would be no mean achievement.

Proposal for a Research Institute. To implement the objectives outlined in the preceding section, it is proposed to create a research institute for the study of psychotherapeutic change. While details obviously remain to be worked out, the following general specifications are envisioned:

1. The institute is conceptualized as a combination of research center, clinical facility, and advanced training center. Essentially, it is a center for advanced study in which researchers, clinicians, and other scientists pool their respective skills and at the same time pursue their respective chosen endeavors. Collaboration is encouraged but not demanded, and each staff member is at liberty to follow his own plans, intuitions, and hunches.

2. The professional staff of the institute will consist of approximately 10–12 persons who, as demonstrated by their productivity, are firmly committed to the advancement of knowledge in the area of psychotherapeutic change. There will be a balance of "basic" scientists, "applied" clinical workers, as well as others (for example, people in the social and biological sciences) whose contributions may enhance the research perspectives.

3. In addition to the "permanent" staff, the institute will provide for visiting investigators and clinicians as well as postdoctoral students (1–2 years).

4. The institute will be affiliated with a major university in a favorable geographical location. While close to behavioral science departments, the institute will be independent and largely autonomous. Regular institute staff, however, should have appropriate faculty appointments. The institute must have full access to all university facilities, including clinical centers.

5. While the institute is broadly committed to the advancement of knowledge in the area of psychotherapeutic change, institute members are encouraged to pursue their own ideas, research projects, and theories. The institute is viewed as a loose federation of investigators, clinicians, and related scientists who, it is hoped, will benefit from each other's efforts through informal meetings, seminars, clinical discussions, and the like.

6. Responsibility for administering the institute will rest with a director assisted by an executive committee composed of staff members and/or an external advisory group. While obviously of crucial importance, the creation of an appropriate structure must await decisions concerning the proposal's general acceptability.

If the proposal is deemed worthwhile, a planning period of 1–2 years is probably necessary to implement it.

References

Frank, J. D. 1961. *Persuasion and healing: A comparative study of psychotherapy*. Baltimore: Johns Hopkins Press.

Shapiro, A. K. 1971. Placebo effects in medicine, psychotherapy, and psychoanalysis. In A. E. Bergin & S. L. Garfield, eds., *Handbook of psychotherapy and behavior change: An empirical analysis*. New York: Wiley, pp. 439–73.

Weinberg, A. M. 1970. In defense of science. *Science* 167: 141–45.

FIVE

New directions in psychotherapy research: A summary statement

Following the period of interviewing and formulating tentative positions, we embarked upon a brief, intensive attempt to draw some specific conclusions. These were written in the fall of 1969 and published originally in the summer of 1970. We have reproduced them below in the form of brief assertions about the major issues with which we began our study.

Conclusions Regarding Collaborative Studies

1. Based on a large number of convergent considerations, we have reluctantly reached the conclusion that large-scale, multifactorial studies of the kind sketched by other investigators and ourselves are not feasible at the present time or in the immediate future. On balance, we believe that the expectable returns, in terms of research findings that might contribute to the accretion of knowledge as well as practical applications of such findings, do not justify the very considerable investment of manpower and financial support which such studies would inevitably entail. In stating this decision, we are not saying that such studies are in principle futile or that all efforts at collaboration on large-scale ventures should be abandoned; however, we are asserting that the *likelihood* of success at the present time impresses us as

Reprinted by permission from A. E. Bergin and H. H. Strupp, New directions in psychotherapy research. *Journal of Abnormal Psychology* 76 (1970): 13–76.

low or at least incommensurate with the required expenditures in terms of effort, manpower, and funds. Major reasons supporting this judgment include:

a. Because of the complex interactions among patient, therapist, technique, and socio-environmental variables, it will prove extraordinarily difficult to isolate the effects of one or a limited number of variables, with the result that large-scale multifactorial studies are almost certain to lead to "weak" results. As a corollary, the necessary experimental controls which would be required to counteract these tendencies are virtually impossible to achieve at the present time, a problem which is aggravated if studies are carried out in different locations, by therapists of diverse theoretical orientations whose techniques (even within a given "school") are bound to be heterogeneous, and on patient samples whose homogeneity may be questionable.

b. Because the preceding weaknesses of large-scale studies will not be remediable in the near future, it is predictable that such studies will have minimal effect on prevailing practices and they are not likely to sway clinicians from their personal beliefs.

c. There are virtually no research centers which would be willing or able to observe meticulously the requirements called for by large-scale efforts.

d. With few exceptions, we found insufficient motivation and commitment on the part of leading researchers and clinicians to design and execute such studies.

e. The implementation of large-scale studies necessitates the creation of complex administrative machinery which would be costly to inaugurate and maintain. In view of the foregoing factors, it seems unlikely that a central coordinating agency, even if it had broad executive powers, would be able to effectively implement the necessarily stringent design, and bring to a successful conclusion the elaborate data collection and analysis.

f. Large-scale studies would at best serve as demonstrations that one set of techniques seems to be preferable to another set of techniques under broadly defined conditions but they are not likely to shed much light on specific mechanisms of psychological change, specific techniques that might be necessary to produce such changes in patients of a certain "type," and the nature of therapeutic change. Stated otherwise, we believe that such studies will add only insignificant amounts to existing scientific knowledge.

g. In view of the current state of knowledge and technology in the area, it is considered more desirable to encourage research developments along lines other than large-scale collaborative studies, such as systematic research on basic mechanisms, naturalistic observations of psychological change, and intensive study of single cases.

The foregoing conclusion will be more fully documented at a later time. At this point, it is important to note, however, that we approached the issue of collaborative research with a positive bias and came away with a much less optimistic conclusion.

2. While collaboration on a large scale does not appear propitious at this time, more efforts at coordination should be encouraged. For one thing, it is considered essential to improve communication, exchange of research ideas, plans, and research findings among productive investigators, and to stimulate collaboration on smaller-scale projects. We have begun to explore several possibilities and shall devote further effort toward this objective. Under such arrangements, investigators might begin to apply common measures in their respective studies, pool research data, and design coordinated studies which would directly further their research programs. A few attempts in this direction have already occurred, but more are needed. For our own part, we expect to devote a portion of our own fuιure effort to the furtherance of this kind of small-scale collaboration.

Conclusions Regarding Other Directions of Therapy Research

While our primary goal was to determine the feasibility of large collaborative efforts, a corollary objective was to explore theoretical issues, research, strategies, therapeutic techniques, and relevant variables in order to determine whether selective research emphases might possibly accelerate advances in the field. Some of our salient conclusions are presented below. Again, because of space limitations, they are presented without documentation; however, we believe that each assertion is adequately defended elsewhere in this volume.

3. We have become convinced that further study of the therapeutic process and evaluations of outcomes resulting from traditional therapeutic practice offer little hope for significant scientific advance. While such studies may further expand our understanding of the therapeutic process and lead to refinements of traditional procedures, the potential yield resulting from pursuing other pathways appears incomparably greater. One exception would be to study the performance of unusual therapists. In this case, one might, through naturalistic study, succeed in extracting from their performance principles or strategies that make their therapeutic operations unusually effective. Even here, however, the inquiry may be expected to lead rapidly to formulation of new techniques on the basis of the principles so extracted.

The foregoing conclusion is of course a relative judgment. No doubt, further inquiry into psychotherapy as it is ordinarily practiced will continue to bear fruit, particularly if such studies are systematic and increasingly responsive to the special problems in the area. However, at present there is no "normal science" in Kuhn's (1962) sense in psychotherapy; therefore, research in the area is not likely to lead to a questioning of a "paradigm," and even less to a "revolution." In general, no field of scientific inquiry can probably be advanced by synthetic efforts, and lines of advance are impossible to predict. Nevertheless, we venture the prognostication that in psychotherapy, advances will not come from dissection of the therapeutic process as it generally occurs, no matter how precise or sophisticated such studies become. Instead, new departures appear called for. As we see it, this means a movement away from the gross, complex, and relatively nonspecific traditional therapeutic operations. Stated positively, we must achieve greater specificity and, concomitantly, greater power in the sense of making therapeutic operations and strategies count therapeutically. Efforts in this direction would also make technique more adequately teachable and learnable.

4. While there is limited promise in the naturalistic study of the therapeutic process, there does seem to be a significant source of hypotheses and methods in the observation of spontaneous change processes which occur in the natural course of life events. It seems likely that a careful study of "the psychotherapy of everyday life" will yield valuable results. Accordingly, at the present stage of knowledge it may be valuable to study in greater depth "experiments of nature." Many examples in other sciences (e.g., the discovery of Vitamin C) underscore the merit of this approach. It has frequently been pointed out that the study of complex psychological processes requires approaches that are radically different from those employed in the physical and biological sciences, but the implications of this proposition still remain to be taken seriously. We have in mind studies that might deal with documentation of conditions under which personality changes occur "naturally," a "natural history of the neuroses," and similar investigations. Such work may also lead to new ideas regarding methods which will more effectively and more straightforwardly produce desired personality change.

Note: Up to this point, and again in conclusions 15 through 21, the authors generally concur; however, on several specific points our emphases and interpretations differ. For this reason, conclusions 5 through 14 were written independently and the author of each is identified. While we agreed on the major recommendation concerning the potential value of the intensive study of individual cases embodying experimental interventions (Bergin's conclusion 9 and Strupp's conclusion 14), the reasoning underlying this recommendation is partly based on divergent theoretical biases and interpretations of the current status of the field; therefore, we considered it advisable to present our respective formulations of that issue separately also.

5. (Bergin) The influence of behavioristic therapies has become an important phenomenon of the 1960s and cannot be overlooked in stating conclusions about the status of the field. The new techniques, case study methodologies, research evaluations, and general style of inquiry and innovation

which have been implemented by this group have stimulated considerable optimism and controversy. The number of new journals, research studies, and young people opting for this approach is impressive; however, all innovations are subject to a kind of fadism and behavior therapy is clearly no exception. There are exaggerated claims and a certain zealousness or tendency to rigidify ideas and techniques; but in spite of these signs, which are held in common with most innovations, there appears to be more substance to this movement than is typical of fads.

While the behavioristic theories which presumably underlie this approach are difficult to justify and defend, there have been other conceptual contributions coming forth which are worth noting. The first of these is the notion of specificity. Not that human behavior or the human psyche is a collection of specific mechanical connections of the kind found in an automobile engine, but it is assumed that there are identifiable mechanisms which have reasonably homogeneous effects and which can be manipulated with a greater degree of specificity than has been historically associated with the practice of psychotherapy.

This manner of thinking, though it is spawned by a weak and probably irrelevant theory, is a most significant contribution in that it has dramatically brought the therapeutic domain within a much more clearly objective frame of reference. Thus, while we may object to some of the exaggerated claims and theoretical weaknesses associated with this point of view, we must acknowledge the power of its methodological contribution and its conceptual tools. These conceptual tools have to do with notions of simplifying nature and making it manageable.

Thus, the field may well owe the behaviorists a very real debt, but it is probably not the one which they would most like to be remembered for. Their demonstration that it is possible to focus on specific mechanisms within a highly complex context is a signal contribution. Surely the mechanisms and theories of the future will look far different from the picture thus far painted by arch-behaviorists, but the process by which we arrive at these new conceptions will have been facilitated and shaped to a great extent by the focused, penetrating work of these particular innovators.

6. (Bergin) It is most interesting that the behavioral approach, in bringing about a focus on the mechanics of change, has elicited a new interest in cognitive processes. This is evident: In Bandura's (1969) emphasis on cognitive mediation processes even though he still argues for a basically neo-behavioral viewpoint, in the work of those doing cognitive desensitization (Davison & Valins, 1969; Marcia, Rubin, & Efran, 1969; Valins & Ray, 1967), in the use of conceptual and symbolic processes by the groups who are conducting instrumental conditioning of autonomic responses (Miller, 1969; Lang, Sroufe, & Hastings, 1967) and in the increasing evidence of

cognitive mediation or control of classical conditioning processes in human subjects (Murray & Jacobson, 1971).

While this domain has only begun to be exploited and has hardly been conceptualized with rigor, it is further evidence of the notion that the behavioral style of inquiry can bear fruit with regard to discovering the mechanisms of change, even though these mechanisms may bear little relation to behavioral theory.

Thus, we may be on the threshold of discoveries within the realm of cognitive processes which will permit understanding and control over powerful change mechanisms. The intimations drawn thus far from preliminary experimentation are impressive. The fact that a man's heart rate can be modified by focussing his own symbolic processes upon his bodily activity is an accidental by-product of conditioning studies which is intriguing. If this work is expanded and adequately replicated, we may be able to grasp the mechanics of personality and behavior change as it flows from conceptual reorganization. Thus, the behaviorists would have unintentionally provided new knowledge of a dominant process in traditional therapies, a process which had long been considered of fundamental importance in personality reconstruction. If that happens, it will be further proof that progress in complex domains is achieved by a zealous devotion to objectivity and by a willingness to simplify and experiment rather than simply sit back and watch the complex process flow naturally.

7. (Bergin) Further evidence of the virtue of simplification and specificity is gained by observing the contributions which the client-centered group have made in extracting, measuring, and testing the effects of supposedly single variables like empathy or warmth. Even though it is now clear that these variables are more complex than originally appeared, the study of them has made a rich contribution to the therapeutic research literature and the results have stimulated a renewed focus on relationship factors in the therapeutic enterprise. It seems unlikely that this knowledge would have developed if the researchers involved had not specified some particular influences and then studied them assiduously while at the same time ignoring much of the surrounding context and complexity. Indeed, some of the authors have made this point quite clear in referring to the fact that variables such as warmth and empathy account for only a minority of the variance in outcome. At the same time these procedures seem to be powerful and their potency has been brought out by isolating them from their context to an extent (Truax & Carkhuff, 1967).

While research in psychoanalysis and related interventions seems not to have produced a great deal in the way of empirical validity or technique innovation, this does not mean that the practice of these procedures is to be ignored. Clearly, many of the same processes which operate here must also operate in other therapies and it is conceivable that powerful processes will yet be extracted and manipulated in a more experimental way from within this framework.

8. (Bergin) The fruitfulness of attempts to simplify, isolate, extract, and manipulate new variables from the context of practice is not the only way to approach the study of the mechanisms of change. The potentialities for applying evidence from diverse areas of psychological research seems considerable. The recent efforts by the Goldstein group at Syracuse University (Goldstein & Simonson, 1971) provide one example from a social psychological frame of reference. It seems equally likely that the study of cognitive processes, of human development, of motivation and emotion, etc., will prove equally fruitful in their yield of ideas, methods of inquiry, and new technologies.

A general conclusion may be drawn from the foregoing points, namely, that we are in a phase of our history in which we are moving rapidly away from the gross, placebo-laden, general doctor-patient relationship influence in therapy. We are moving more rapidly toward an understanding of the mechanisms of change and toward a more explicit technology of behavior and personality modification based upon the substantive evidential base of the behavioral sciences. It seems that these efforts should be encouraged. They underline the importance of a departure from traditional procedures while at the same time not indulging in a premature commitment to fads. A commitment to the study of the mechanisms of change, their experimental refinement, and their practical elaboration will probably bear greater fruit than other potential approaches.

It is important to note here that the strategy of simplification need not and should not ignore the complexity of personality functioning and change. However, it is unlikely that the complex gestalt of behavior change in the clinic will ever be fully understood and placed under our control unless we first break it down into its part processes. Once this is achieved, we may then put the parts back together again, as building blocks, in order to match the degree of complexity required for practical purposes. This concept is discussed and illustrated in the next section.

9. (Bergin) As for a general paradigm of inquiry, the *individual experimental case study* and the *experimental analogue* approach appear to be the primary strategies which will move us forward in our understanding of the mechanisms of change at this point. Other strategies, such as the possible derivations from general psychology, the potential leads from the naturalistic study of "spontaneous" and traditional therapeutic change, and from field trials on large groups of cases will all be fruitful and they are all necessarily interrelated. However, the cycle of interrelationship which exists among these styles of inquiry will probably be put in motion more effectively at this time in history by a greater focus on the two processes just

mentioned. Obviously, such a focus will have to be more a matter of emphasis than a matter of exclusion for it would be impossible to concentrate on them totally exclusively, for scientific fertility is bred by the natural interaction of this diverse range of approaches.

The details of the foregoing system of inquiry using the analogue and case study approaches as foci need substantial elaboration and discussion. While this will be one of the prime objectives of a later document, a further description of this schema is referred to in Figure 5.1.

It may be observed there that ideas about change mechanisms are likely to derive either from clinical phenomena or from behavioral science research. They may then be subjected to testing, experimentation, and refine-

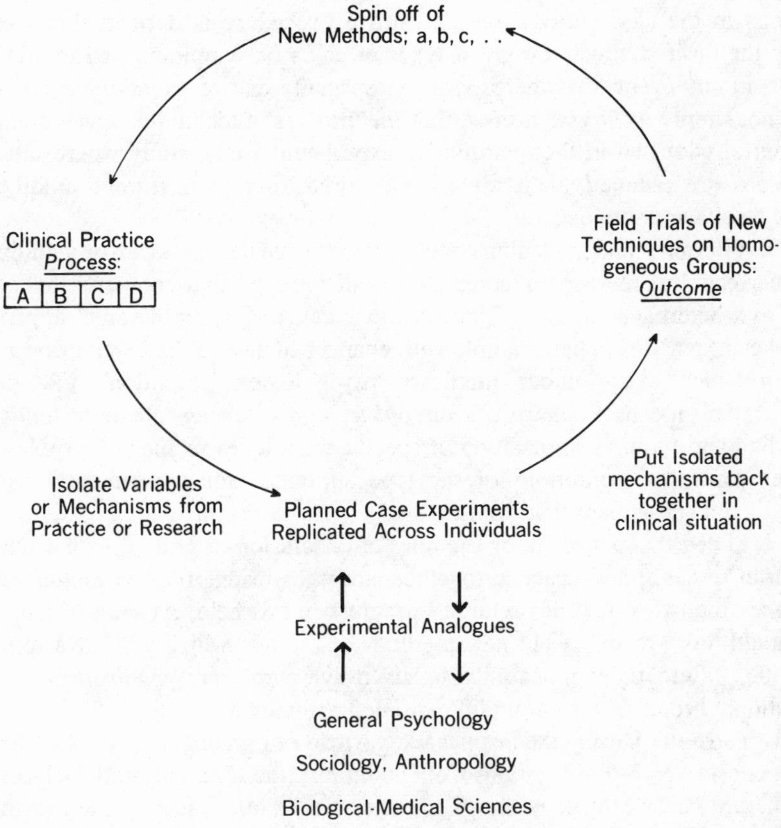

Figure 5.1. The Process of Therapy Technique Development and Refinement. Lower half of diagram illustrates process of isolating, testing, and manipulating change mechanisms; upper half illustrates extrapolation from research programs to clinical practice.

ment by means of analogue studies and single case experiments. For example, if empathic responding were the variable in question, its nature might be clarified by traditional laboratory-type empathy studies and then variations in "live" empathy might be programmed into a case study in order to observe its specific clinical effects as Truax and Carkhuff have done (1965). Once the morphology of this therapeutic agent and its effects on given symptoms are defined by means of quantitative case studies, then field trials on larger samples of homogeneous cases could be conducted to demonstrate its clinical usefulness. After clinical validity was established, the procedure could be incorporated into the repertoire of clinical practices.

On the other hand, single case experiments could reveal that the procedure is ineffective or needs modification or amalgamation with other procedures. This might stimulate further analogue research or immediate modifications in the case study situation until a procedure is derived that does have the desired effects on given types of cases or symptoms. It should be clear, in any event, that the process is especially one of *technique building* and not simply *technique testing,* that this process of technique development is centrally located in the quantitative experimental case study where interventions are planned, their effects monitored, and their format modified until results are obtained.

10. (Bergin) The preceding conclusions provide a clear basis for avoiding further classical therapy outcome studies of the type that compare changes due to a heterogeneous set of interventions called "psychotherapy" applied to a heterogeneous patient sample with changes in an equally diverse control group which exists under unknown psychological conditions (Bergin, 1971). This means a departure from *old-technique* testing to *new-technique* building and requires application of specific techniques to specific problems under controlled conditions of the type stipulated for experimental case studies and subsequent field trials.

It is hoped that action along the lines of conclusions 9 and 10 would tend to mold research and practice together, and thus bridge the traditional gap between the two which has retarded progress in this field. At the same time it should more readily yield new methods of therapy which will have more specific, differential applicability to given symptoms and syndromes than traditional broad spectrum, undifferentiated techniques.

11. (Strupp) During the last decade the field of psychotherapy has undergone considerable proliferation. Concomitantly, the classical model of psychotherapy, exemplified by the psychoanalytic situation, has receded to the background and largely lost its appeal to therapists and patients. Originally conceptualized as a form of medical treatment, the meaning of the term psychotherapy has become increasingly fuzzy and more than ever defies precise definition. Diverse human interactions, from individual psychotherapy to encounter groups, from aversive conditioning in the laboratory to token economies in mental hospitals, are subsumed under the heading of psychotherapy

or under the new rubric, behavior modification. To characterize the field as chaotic is hardly an exaggeration.

Particularly noteworthy in this respect is the emergence of a wide diversity of new techniques and therapeutic modalities, most of which may be viewed as a response to modern man's insistent clamor for self-awareness, interpersonal intimacy, surcease from alienation and the constraints of a "sick" society. New treatment methods in this area, it may be observed, do not arise from the efforts of researchers or as a result of experimentation in the laboratory; instead, they emerge in response to social needs which are met by the ingenuity or inventiveness of charismatic therapists whose individual temperament and philosophy of life are thoroughly intertwined with the therapeutic approach they espouse. The "system" or "theory of psychotherapy" propounded by them is inevitably a belated attempt to conceptualize what they have found to be of pragmatic value. Obviously, this is not to deny that theories of psychotherapy contain important psychological principles although often, because of divergent conceptualizations, they are impossible to compare. It follows that: (1) New techniques in psychotherapy, unlike new drugs, are not developed in the laboratory, tested, and then applied, but typically they are "invented" and applied long before they are tested; (2) psychotherapeutic techniques are very loosely articulated to theories of psychotherapy, which largely precludes the testing of any theoretical formulation per se; (3) the researcher in psychotherapy, in comparison to the innovative clinician, has been relatively uninfluential as far as developments in the field are concerned; (4) the field of psychotherapy is at an extremely rudimentary stage of development, and it seems safe to predict that neither research nor clinical ingenuity are about to produce a dazzling technology for psychotherapeutic change (measured against what therapists have been able to accomplish in the past). This is not to assert that the field can afford to rest content with its achievements or that progress is impossible; however, it seems only realistic to recognize the formidable difficulties confronting both clinicians and researchers in this murky field.

I conclude that the field as a whole is currently beset with innumerable fads, considerable conceptual unclarity, muddy theories, and grossly unwarranted claims for the effectiveness of simplistic techniques. All of these factors have conspired to impede progress and to retard dispassionate examination of basic scientific issues. There exists at present a dire need for separating the wheat from the chaff, for taking full advantage of earlier insights which in terms of their sophistication often surpass contemporary formulations, and for discarding obsolete theoretical notions which have questionable relevance to empirical data. Withal, a serious return to empirical data is imperative.

12. (Strupp) While the preceding conclusion has emphasized the arena of clinical practice, it is equally important to acknowledge the substantial growth of research in psychotherapy since the late 1950s, supported by a

new wave of enthusiasm. The preponderance of this work has been inspired by behaviorally oriented researchers and, to a lesser extent by client-centered investigators, whereas psychoanalytically oriented workers have all but abdicated serious research interest.[1] It seems premature to assess the lasting value or promise of these endeavors, a fair segment of which must certainly be characterized as crude; however, there can be no doubt that the work has had the inestimable merit of providing a renewed *focus on empirical data* which had become all but lost in sterile discussions about the relative merits of theoretical propositions. Furthermore, there is an increasing recognition that *psychotherapy* (in the sense in which I propose to use the term) *consists of a set of specifiable technical operations to reach specifiable objectives.* If this assumption is granted, it follows that we must work toward the specification of problems we seek to solve as psychotherapists, the goals we aim to achieve, and the procedures we employ to reach these objectives. Thus, if psychotherapy in an important sense is a technology, we must concede that a set of technical operations can be more or less effective in reaching a particular goal. While psychotherapy is likely to remain a practical art for a long time, the task of the researcher is to document, with increasing precision, the conditions under which a therapeutic strategy or a set of techniques forming part of that strategy is relatively effective or ineffective. Accordingly, he must succeed in defining "the problem" (that is, the patient state to be modified), the kinds of personality and behavior changes to be achieved, and the procedures to be employed in reaching them. In short, the therapist and the researcher must become increasingly *explicit about the operations of psychotherapy and the nature of the therapist's influence.* Existing knowledge, while undoubtedly embodying important psychological principles, is altogether too general, broad-gauged, and imprecise. I conclude that future research in this area must firmly rest on empirical data; it must tend toward increasing explicitness and specificity; and it must seek to isolate psychological principles embedded in, and often obscured by, divergent theoretical formulations.

13. (Strupp) There has been insufficient clarity about the role of the researcher in psychotherapy and the kinds of contributions he may reasonably be expected to make. The fact is that to date research has exerted little influ-

1. Luborsky comments: "This is overstated! I think there's been a shift to more serious research interest on the part of some psychoanalytically oriented workers. As you yourself point out in the discussion with me and Art, the *Zeitgeist* is conducive to the research of the Psychoanalytic Research Group of the Institute of the Pennsylvania Hospital. Also for example, the huge work of Hartvig Dahl and Merton Gill in constructing psychoanalytic dictionaries for computer analysis of psychoanalytic sessions at the Research Center for Mental Health, and the project of Bob Wallerstein at Mt. Zion. Contrary to some people's expectations, the Menninger project has just been written up in final form with some interesting findings—not to mention our own work here at the University of Pennsylvania.

ence on clinical practice, and the clinical work of therapists has generally not been informed, much less altered, by empirical research results. It is possible that the researcher's insistence on empirical evidence and intersubjective verification has subtly modified the attitudes at least of the younger therapists toward the subject matter, but that influence appears to be rather intangible. An incisive examination of this issue would far exceed the scope of this paper, but—perhaps somewhat cavalierly—it may be concluded that the researcher has not provided the clinician with insights or useful information which he can employ in his daily work. However, there may be an important lesson from scores of studies that almost any set of procedures in the context of a benign human relationship, presented to, or viewed by, the patient as having therapeutic value will result in psychological or behavior change describable as therapeutic. At times, such changes produced by nonspecific techniques may be quite impressive and rival in significance those attributed to planful technical interventions. As a corollary, it may be noted that the theoretical formulations invoked by the therapist to explain the effects of his work may grossly lack parsimony and be deficient on other grounds.

Despite certain appearances to the contrary, research in psychotherapy, as it has evolved since approximately 1940, has failed to provide incisive answers to important issues, such as the problem of outcome, the relative effectiveness of different techniques, etc. While a form of cultural lag may in part be responsible, the prevailing investigative model may not be the proper one to use. For example, the clinician has no way of utilizing statistical trends based on mean differences between samples of broadly defined patient groups; he cannot be guided by findings that certain diffuse techniques *in general* tend to lead to certain patient responses under poorly defined conditions; etc. (This view is expanded in conclusion 18.)

As Colby has pointed out, not everything can be a problem for the scientist at the same time, and for fruitful results to occur it is of crucial importance to ask questions which permit relatively unequivocal answers. In psychotherapy research, it appears, we have not yet reached great sophistication in asking the "right" questions.

14. (Strupp) The field urgently needs greater collaboration of a different sort. We need improved communication between clinicians and researchers, and between researchers of divergent theoretical orientations. I believe Scriven (1964) is correct in asserting that progress in psychology is hampered not by a lack of knowledge but rather by a surfeit of commonsense knowledge shared by all individuals (e.g., the effects of reward or punishment on behavior). Since the time of Freud, largely as a function of his contributions which remain close to empirical observations, therapists have acquired a vast fund of knowledge, exemplified by man's ingenious tendencies to hide painful truths from himself, to disguise to himself and others, primi-

tive and self-defeating beliefs which profoundly influence the manner in which he construes himself and others, the profound but hitherto unrecognized effects of early traumatic experiences which have been "stored" in memory, etc. The therapist, above all, is an expert in decoding scrambled human communications which the patient continually sends to himself and others. This fund of knowledge is impressive, but it is largely ignored by researchers and others who restrict their focus to observable behavior. Thus, it is a strange phenomenon that the importance of "cognitive factors" is currently being rediscovered. The point is that clinicians and therapists build as yet insufficiently on each other's work, and because of theoretical or temperamental blinders they reject data which colleagues in other camps have to offer.

It is likewise important to record that the fund of clinical knowledge to which I have referred, poorly formulated as much of it is, has been acquired not through the study of mean differences between samples but through painstaking study of individual cases, by a process of "listening," which is closely akin to Polanyi's (1966) concept of indwelling. Man's capacity for discerning patterns, organization and structure of beliefs, etc. in another person is infinitely greater than that of any man-made machine or rating instrument, and while the researcher can undoubtedly provide great help in systematizing and objectifying clinical observations, he hamstrings himself if he *substitutes* crude measuring devices for clinical insights instead of *articulating* his observations to the subtle functioning of the sensitive clinician. A wedding of clinical observation and research operations has yet to occur. From everything that has been said it follows that significant increments in knowledge, at least within the therapeutic framework, is likely to come from the intensive study of individual cases in which disciplined observation is complemented by, and takes account of, the complex interaction of variables, a task which cannot be accomplished by statistical manipulations, although certain statistical techniques may be helpful in other respects.

It is conceivable that significant advances in the area will not come from within the traditional clinical framework, since it will prove extraordinarily difficult to disentangle the clinical complexities. It is also questionable whether "part processes" can be productively simulated in the laboratory or in quasi-therapeutic situations. Thus, it appears that new insights may come either from basic research in the disparate areas, or, stated less esoterically, through a combination of clinical and experimental methods within the clinical context. In the latter kind of investigation it may be possible to introduce, at selected points in time, specific experimental interventions whose effects, albeit in a relatively gross way, may then be assessed. This approach is reminiscent of the work of all clinical innovators, from Freud to Alexander to the behavior therapists, in which experimentation with relatively specific techniques occurs within the clinical situation. The current research on therapeutic learning through conditioning of autonomic responses (as pioneered by Neal Miller) may be an important area for significant advances.

There is no question that greater specificity and a return to empirical data are absolutely essential, but it seems unlikely that the therapeutic process can effectively be broken down into "parts" which can be studied in isolation (e.g., the research on "empathy"), and then be "reassembled." The scientist, as Colby observes, must first isolate a problem he can do something about, and he must then test its limits. The identification of important problems is solely a function of his ingenuity and intuition, and no prescriptions can be given.

As part of this effort, we need to achieve greater clarity concerning the principles of psychological change at work in all forms of psychotherapy, and to articulate them to relatively specific therapeutic operations. Comparable to the researcher, the therapist must learn to recognize problems he can do something about and to employ better strategies to reach a particular goal. With varying degrees of emphasis, all forms of psychotherapy employ a limited number of psychological principles, but the theoretical formulations in which they are couched typically obfuscate these commonalities. The task of reformulating these principles in terms which do greater justice to the phenomena in need of explanation remains an important assignment for the future.

15. The foregoing set of conclusions embody of course certain guidelines for the kinds of research directions we consider promising, investigations we ourselves might undertake or which we, as individual researchers, would find congenial. It would seem presumptuous, however, to make categorical assertions about the potential promise of research proposed or currently being carried forward by other investigators. No one can forecast future developments in as poorly developed a scientific discipline as psychotherapy, and, as indicated previously, significant increments in knowledge may come from quite unsuspected sources. For this reason, too, it appears unwise, at the present state of knowledge, to propose complex research programs or to recommend the creation of research centers or institutes which might undertake concerted research efforts to "solve" specific problems in the area. Since we cannot identify the nature of the problems currently capable of solution and for other reasons, it appears best to leave the initiative for creative work with individual investigators who may succeed in bringing new ingenuity to bear on the field. However, we feel that the time for discerning a new Gestalt in the multifarious concepts and bits of evidence may not be too far off. Intuitively, we feel that future research will build on and produce a closer integration between experimental and clinical approaches.

16. The foregoing conclusions clearly imply certain negative recommendations, that is, classes of investigations which we consider to be of limited promise at the present time or in the foreseeable future. This list promi-

nently includes large-scale collaborative studies, naturalistic studies of psychotherapy as it is usually practiced (see Conclusion 3), traditional outcome studies, comparative outcome studies pitting broadgauged therapeutic techniques against each other, and studies attempting to evaluate the respective merits of divergent theoretical orientations. Our emphasis on studies dealing with the mechanisms of psychological change regardless of which particular "school" has laid proprietary claims to them suggests the desirability of "retiring brand names" (Bandura's description) which at present continue to befog major issues in the field.

17. We also wish to note the great importance of wedding the study of change more closely to biological disciplines. The recent successes in conditioning visceral responses, and the advances in behavioral genetics are only two of several strands of evidence which have convinced us that research in therapy will be more fruitful when coordinated more closely with that of specialists in biological areas. We witness today a renewed emphasis on a holistic view of man which is beginning to take seriously the interaction between psychological variables and biological variables. Thus, increasing collaboration between psychologists and biologists should certainly be welcomed. We would like to see a center, for example, where the mechanisms of change were focused upon by various experts in the psychological, medical, and biological aspects of psychosomatic problems.

18. Among researchers as well as statisticians, there is a growing disaffection from traditional experimental designs and statistical procedures which are held inappropriate to the subject matter under study. This judgment applies with particular force to research in the area of therapeutic change and our emphasis on the value of experimental case studies underscores this point. We strongly agree that most of the standard experimental designs and statistical procedures have exerted, and are continuing to exert, a constricting effect on fruitful inquiry, and they serve to perpetuate an unwarranted overemphasis on methodology. More accurately, the exaggerated importance accorded experimental and statistical dicta cannot be blamed on the techniques proper—after all, they are merely tools—but their veneration mirrors a prevailing philosophy among behavioral scientists which subordinates problems to methodology. The insidious effects of this trend are tellingly illustrated by the typical graduate student who is often more interested in the details of a factorial design than in the problem he sets out to study; worse, the selection of a problem is dictated by the experimental design. Needless to say, the student's approach faithfully reflects the convictions and teachings of his mentors. With respect to inquiry in the area of psychotherapy, the kinds of effects we need to demonstrate at this point in time should be significant enough so that they are readily observable by inspection. If this cannot be done, no fixation upon statistical and mathematic niceties will generate fruitful insights, which obviously can come only from the research-

er's understanding of the subject matter and the descriptive data under scrutiny.

This conclusion may be perceived as a rather broad and unwarranted repudiation of hard-won methods of rigor; but we are gratified to note the increasing concurrence in this viewpoint by knowledgeable statisticians (Tukey, 1969; Bakan, 1969).[2]

19. There is a renewed appreciation that internal, intrapsychic, or experimental processes, whether they be of a feeling or of a cognitive nature, have considerable power to influence bodily processes, behavior, and the general state of the organism. Since these processes are obviously private and unobservable directly, their study will require development of a sophisticated technology for studying private experience. Massive denials of the problem since the time of J. B. Watson have not obviated its importance, and, more than ever, it is with us demanding recognition. The revival of interest in cognitive processes is exemplified by recent studies of conditioning which have shown that verbal reports of various kinds are absolutely critical for an understanding of the processes under study. While the behaviorists have traditionally eschewed efforts to conceptualize or *objectify* inner experiences, there is no question that this task can no longer be avoided. To be sure, this is a major technical problem, to which scores of psychologists and therapists have made notable contributions (e.g., in the heyday of the dynamic theories) but which has not been blessed by impressive breakthroughs. Although we have no concrete recommendations, it will be absolutely necessary to take full account of intrapsychic processes as we seek to imbue the study of psychotherapeutic change with greater specificity, objectivity, and precision. This could be an exciting and productive area of future inquiry beckoning the imaginative researcher.

20. We are impressed with the impoverished character of the major theories in the area. Running the gamut from psychoanalysis to behaviorism, we fail to see fertile theories emerging. While the global theorizing which has dominated the field of personality has become largely defunct, more appropriate mini-theories centered around specific clusters of data have not emerged. We view the need for new theories as a vital one. Crucial concepts, such as "repression," "defense," "cognitive mediation," "conditioned response," and "experiencing" all need major overhauling or replacement. We view this as a prime task for advancing the field.

21. We have been deeply impressed with the personal human aspect of the scientific enterprise which became particularly vivid as a result of visiting a number of people in rapid succession. Largely because of this human

2. We do not by this argument deny the significance of the distinctive contributions by psychologists to research on behavior, especially in basic fields, but the unique sophistication of psychologists in experimental design has led to compromises with crucial clinical issues, which implies that a new style of clinical research must emerge.

element we came to realize the virtual impossibility of artificially stimulating particular lines of investigation short of massive (and probably futile) external inducements. It is clear that proposals for programmatic inquiry, besides being contingent upon a certain maturity of the field of inquiry, must match to a significant extent the basic motivations and personal styles of researchers. Collaboration of any kind must emerge from these personal bases and cannot be superimposed upon them. This is a vital lesson learned at great expense by the designers of some previous collaborative efforts in other areas. It appears that crucial ingredients for successful collaboration include a confluence of intellectual interests, mutual need, and social rapport among collaborators which can neither be dictated nor deliberately "arranged." Any attempt to mount collaborative efforts must consider these variables to be as central as the scientific ones, regardless of the difficulties they pose.

Numerous additional points could be made but perhaps these highlights will suffice to indicate the direction of our current thinking and provide interested colleagues with a general picture of our basic conclusions. This project has been a most illuminating experience for us and we hope our digest adequately conveys to the reader the important shifts in direction we believe are now needed in this field.

References

Bakan, D. 1969. *On method*. San Francisco: Jossey-Bass.

Bandura, A. 1969. *Principles of behavior modification*. New York: Holt, Rinehart and Winston.

Bergin, A. E. 1971. The evaluation of therapeutic outcomes. In A. E. Bergin & S. L. Garfield, eds., *Handbook of psychotherapy and behavior change: An empirical analysis*. New York: Wiley, pp. 217–70.

Bergin, A. E., & Strupp, H. H. 1969. The last word (?) on psychotherapy research: A reply. *International Journal of Psychiatry* 7: 160–68.

Davison, G. C., & Valins, S. 1969. Maintenance of self-attributed and drug-attributed behavior change. *Journal of Personality and Social Psychology* 11: 25–33.

Goldstein, A. P., & Simonson, N. R. 1971. Social psychological approaches to psychotherapy research. In A. E. Bergin & S. L. Garfield, eds., *Handbook of psychotherapy and behavior change: An empirical analysis.* New York: Wiley., pp. 154–95.

Kuhn, T. S. 1962. *The Structure of Scientific Revolutions.* Chicago: University of Chicago Press.

Lang, P. J., Sroufe, L. A., & Hastings, J. E. 1967. Effects of feedback and instructional set on the control of cardiac-rate variability. *Journal of Experimental Psychology* 75: 425–31.

Marcia, J. E., Rubin, B. M., & Efran, J. S. 1969. Systematic desensitization: Expectancy change or counterconditioning? *Journal of Abnormal Psychology* 74: 382–87.

Miller, N. E. 1969. Learning of visceral and glandular responses. *Science* 163: 434–45.

Murray, E. J., & Jacobson, L. I. 1971. The nature of learning in traditional and behavioral psychotherapy. In A. E. Bergin & S. L. Garfield, eds., *Handbook of psychotherapy and behavior change: An empirical analysis*. New York: Wiley. pp. 709–47.

Polanyi, M. 1966. *The tacit dimension*. New York: Doubleday.

Scriven, M. 1964. Views of human nature. In T. W. Wann, ed., *Behaviorism and phenomenology*. Chicago: University of Chicago Press.

Strupp, H. H., & Bergin, A. E. 1969a. Some empirical and conceptual bases for coordinated research in psychotherapy: A critical review of issues, trends, and evidence. *International Journal of Psychiatry* 7:18–90.

———. 1969b. *Research in individual psychotherapy: A bibliography*. Washington, D.C.: National Institute of Mental Health.

Truax, C. B., & Carkhuff, R. R. 1965. The experimental manipulation of therapeutic conditions. *Journal of Consulting Psychology* 29: 119–24.

———. 1967. *Toward effective counseling and psychotherapy*. Chicago: Aldine • Atherton.

Tukey, J. W. 1969. Analyzing data: Sanctification or detective work? *American Psychologist* 24: 83–91.

Valins, S., & Ray, A. 1967. Effects of cognitive desensitization on avoidance behavior. *Journal of Personality and Social Psychology* 7: 345–50.

Some Reactions to "New Directions" by Consultants

Our interviewees were invited to respond to our conclusions and several replied as follows:

COMMENT BY ALBERT BANDURA

If many of your interviewees dwelled on the shortcoming of psychotherapeutic approaches, I would add the following general recommendation to the section on Reactions and Critique:

Progress in psychotherapy can be best advanced by observing the wisdom contained in a Chinese fortune cookie: "What psychology needs is fewer critics and more good models."

Cordially,
Albert Bandura
Ancient Chinese Scholar
President, Roadrunner
Cookie Factory

COMMENT BY GERALD C. DAVISON

I could not be more pleased and in agreement with most of your conclusions, expecially one of the principal ones, namely, that any kind of large-scale centralized research effort would be fruitless. You and Hans have presented scholarly and insightful arguments as to why this couldn't possibly work, and it must be seen as especially to your credit that you came to this conclusion after having undertaken your project with the opposite possibility in mind.

As you caution the reader, many sweeping assertions are made which you promise to back up before long. I must admit that I found myself a little frustrated at times in not knowing exactly what you were basing certain conclusions on, e.g., the "crudity" of certain theories. Part of my curiosity stems from considering many of the pronouncements of my own behavioral colleagues as rather exaggerated, so I suppose I'm keen to see if you and Hans agree here and there.

One specific point: near the end you criticize "the behaviorists" for ignoring intrapsychic processes. I'm sure that the validity of your remark depends importantly on whom you consider a behaviorist. Was Tolman? Hull? Or do you restrict the term to Watson? But if so, can you consider people like Wolpe and Eysenck behaviorists? The issue is one of mediating processes and I hope that in your extended report you grapple with this. It is really terribly important and contributes, I believe, to much misunderstanding.

COMMENT BY HAROLD SAMPSON AND ROBERT S. WALLERSTEIN

We should like to comment briefly on directions for psychotherapy research as viewed from our particular psychoanalytic perspective and our recent research experiences.

Psychoanalysis, behavior therapy, client-centered therapy, and other theoretical positions propose *radically* different paradigms (in Kuhn's sense) about human nature, about what ails the patient, about the processes by which he gets better or worse, and about what constitutes improvement. Distaste for "schools" or "brand names" should not cause us to blur the actual incommensurability of these paradigms. Observations or measures which are of great interest within one system are often enough irrelevant or meaningless in another, and this incommensurability will not be resolved readily by pooled data or multiple measures. From this perspective about the field, we see our task as to pursue specific issues about how change takes place by careful empirical research informed by the particular sets of paradigms we believe are most relevant. In our view, psychoanalysis does have "normal science" paradigms about human nature, the patient's psychopathology, processes of therapeutic change, and what constitutes improvement. These paradigms have not ordinarily been explicit enough, or linked in a simple enough way to observations, to permit close, rigorous empirical study; and it is in this direction that psychoanalytic psychotherapy research must proceed. People with greater faith in other paradigms should of course pursue investigations based on those paradigms. It would be unwise for the field as a whole to deplore, or to attempt to prematurely overcome, this type of "parochialism," in which dedicated investigators, working within paradigms they have found meaningful in accounting for some classes of empirical phenomena, engage in systematic empirical studies to clarify or test important hypotheses.

Psychoanalysis has only recently begun to go beyond the informal case study method of making observations, and developing and testing hypotheses. The case study method has demonstrated great power in the development and refinement of psychoanalytic theory; but it has been less adequate as a method for verifying hypotheses in a rigorous manner, or resolving differences between qualified investigators. In general, it has been difficult for psychoanalysis to combine great rigor in research methods with the complexity of its explanatory concepts; and "objective" research has of course tended to sacrifice theoretical complexity and clinical relevance for apparent rigor. Psychoanalysis has therefore not participated as fully as other theoretical orientations in contemporary objective research on therapeutic processes—to the detriment, we believe, of this research area as well as of psychoanalysis.

We would not underestimate the difficulties of conducting rigorous research on the psychoanalytic process (see Wallerstein & Sampson, "Issues in Research in the Psychoanalytic Process," in *Intl. J. of Psychoanalysis,* 1971, 52:11–50) but we believe that such research, combining rigor with complexity, is possible. Here, our view approaches that of Bergin and especially of Strupp. We see the need for studying specific mechanisms or part-processes, albeit within a highly complex context; and concur in the need to explicate "mini-theories" to account for particular sequences of observations, or aspects of complex treatment situations. In accord with this view, we would now go beyond the original Menninger Foundation Psychotherapy Research Project toward more *focussed* studies of *particular* hypotheses about change. Two examples from our current work may be described briefly:

1. Mt. Zion Hospital, in collaboration with the San Francisco Psychoanalytic Institute, is conducting a study in which *alternative hypotheses* about the relationship between changes in a defense and the emergence to con-

sciousness of the mental contents initially warded-off by the defense have been made explicit. Intensive single case studies using objective measures provide a test of the correspondence between hypotheses and observations, allowing an empirical choice between (or correction of) different models of defense-analysis. Here, mini-theories are articulated and checked against observations.

2. Another collaborative study between Mt. Zion and the San Francisco Psychoanalytic Institute is currently being planned in which a class of patients will be treated by two differing psychoanalytic approaches in order to study, and provisionally test, an hypothesis about why this class of patients ordinarily achieve only limited improvement in psychoanalysis. The hypothesis is derived from findings of the Psychotherapy Research Project of the Menninger Foundation, and the projected study is thus a more focussed sequel to the original investigation.

These kinds of focussed research on the psychoanalytic process are just getting underway. We believe that studies of this kind, which attempt to combine theoretical complexity, clinical relevance, and a commitment to empiricism and objectivity, are the only way in which certain powerful psychoanalytic paradigms about therapeutic processes, not encompassed within other theories, can be explored and can contribute to our (eventually) common scientific understanding.

SIX

Epilogue

The substance of our mission, its history, purpose, and yield, have been reported in the pages of this volume. As is customary for committees or task forces, we have presented a set of conclusions and recommendations; we have also taken pains to sketch the broader context of our effort. Thus, we have in a sense asked the reader to accompany us on our journey and to share our involvement in the tantalizingly difficult but fascinating problems we have struggled with. As travelers returning from a journey, we have tried to give a faithful account of the places we have visited, the people we have met, and the impressions we have formed. Since many colleagues are familiar with the terrain, many points will strike a familiar note. However, there were also many personal, idiosyncratic impressions some of which are difficult to communicate and others which discretion prompts us to omit. Still, a few personal observations may appropriately be made at this point.

The strongest impression I carried away from my work with Allen Bergin was that of a tremendously enriching experience, a kind of postgraduate education for which a stroke of good fortune had singled me out, an opportunity that comes one's way perhaps once in a lifetime. I remain grateful to Joe Matarazzo, our mutual friend, for bringing us together and to the National Institute of Mental Health, notably in the person of Dr. A. Hussain Tuma, for initiating the effort and paving the way. Many other friends and colleagues whose help is acknowledged elsewhere spurred us on and gave generously of themselves. Such debts are not uncommonly incurred by authors and investigators, and they are usually acknowledged in this manner. What was remarkable about our work was the singular atmosphere of freedom surrounding it. No one suggested, intimated, or even vaguely hinted at views, evaluations, or recommendations that might be desirable or expedient. Thus, our initially more sanguine attitude about the feasibility of large-scale collaborative studies elicited the same degree of respect and acceptance as the final, more skeptical, conclusions (presented by us with much greater conviction). Hence, whatever partiality and tendentiousness may have marred our work cannot be blamed on anyone else.

On the subject of biases, we have striven hard to be honest with ourselves and with each other. In the first phase of our work (the review of the literature) we attempted to resolve certain theoretical differences by presenting an amalgamated view a solution which one of our discussants characterized as an "uneven meld," but we subsequently realized that it might be preferable not to force a reconciliation where fundamental divergences existed. So, in some instances we presented our respective views, leaving the final judgment to the reader.

Having long been partial to the psychoanalytic approach, I was forced by the nature of our task to take a close and hard look at competing viewpoints reflected by the mass of research publications they had generated in recent years. I was challenged by the literature, my collaborator, and our consultants to critically examine my position. As a result, I have come to take a firmer stand on the side of empirical data and concomitantly have become more critical of *all* prominent theoretical formulations. In the end I concluded that the insights of Freud, particularly as set forth in his early papers on psychotherapy, remain unsurpassed in depth and scope; they still contain a wealth of hypotheses beckoning the ingenious investigator. While Freud pointed the way, he did not enunciate immutable truths, a point still insufficiently appreciated. Despite a certain amount of lip service to what should be a commonplace, many clinical techniques and practices in the psychoanalytic tradition persist, with relatively few clinicians questioning them or seriously considering alternatives. The younger generation of psychotherapy researchers, represented preponderantly by psychologists with strong behavioral leanings, deserves a great deal of credit for rejecting orthodoxy and for its eagerness to experiment with new techniques. While the emergence of a new orthodoxy threatens from this quarter, it is undeniable that a fresh breeze now pervades psychotherapy research and that the field has been infused with a new vitality.

However, whether one subscribes to psychoanalytic or behavioral teachings, much remains to be learned about the nature of the psychotherapeutic influence and the problem of personality and behavior change. Although significant inroads have been made, there are strong indications that we are still very much in the Dark Ages. One of the greatest obstacles to progress in this area, as I see it, is the fairly prevalent illusion that we know more than we do, which may have the unfortunate consequence of stifling open inquiry with the concomitant tendency to hide from ourselves the nature and extent of our ignorance. Part of this syndrome is the credo that advances in this area will largely come from improvements in technology.

In this connection, I must touch on one of the thorny problems which recurrently crop up in this volume: What is psychotherapy? What does it try to accomplish? The kinds of questions the researcher may formulate and try to answer clearly depend to a large extent upon his conceptualizations of the problem and the results he is looking for. The spectrum extends from modification of a narrow segment of behavior to reorganization of a person's life style, values, beliefs, and *Weltanschauung*. What kinds of changes are we concerned with? By what criteria do we evaluate changes as desirable or undesirable, healthy or unhealthy, good or evil? We have passed the time when neurosis was seen as a medical problem, to be treated like a focal infection. But we have yet to define stringently the psychotherapist's role and the radius of his activities. While sharing important qualities with the teacher, parent, priest, healer, sage, and behavior technician, none of these terms fully describes what he actually *does*. I submit that we cannot evaluate the fruits of a man's labors until we have clarified what we expect him to accomplish and the rules by which we expect him to play the game. Many theoretical conflicts in the area, the confusion of patients, and the skepticism of the general public concerning the "effectiveness" of psychotherapy are traceable to these unclarities. The social role of the psychotherapist is in great need of specification.

In my opinion, psychotherapy is something of a cross between a technology for planful change of a person's attitudes, beliefs, feelings, and behavior and an educational process which, unlike any other, brings man face to face with his inner conflicts and contradictions, his strivings for self-realization and autonomy, and the complex facets of his being which for complex reasons he hides from himself. Unless we resign ourselves to a purely intuitive approach, the goal of achieving this self-confrontation and insuring an orderly process of growth requires a technology; thus, we may characterize psychotherapy as a personalized technology.

Since psychotherapy is uniquely focused on man's humanity and what it means to be human, it is exquisitely relevant to man's place in the world and the concerns of our time. In the words of one of our consultants, it is "politically sensitive." Such concepts are a far cry from the antiquated view of psychotherapy as a form of medical treatment for a "nervous disease."

I remain in conflict on the central subject of our quest—how significant scientific advances can be brought about. I feel very strongly that at the present time one or a series of large-scale comparative studies are not the answer, but I am far less certain about positive steps. I vacillate between the relative advantages of the *clinical method,* to which the field owes so much, *experimental studies in situ, analogue research,* or some combination of these. Irrespective of what anyone may prescribe, the field will follow its autochthonous development, and advances may come from quite unsuspected sources. While starting with a fairly narrowly defined mission, our attention was forcefully drawn to these broader philosophical problems of the evolution of a science.

I hope the volume communicates something about the excitement of the field and our own involvement in the important issues. In the short span of a generation, psychotherapy research has come a long way. Its growing pains are still abundant, and future directions are difficult to discern. But it is certain that we are not tilling the soil in a dull, esoteric area; on the contrary, psychotherapy research is very much in the mainstream of psychological science.

Hans H. Strupp

Each time I take a retrospective view of our work, I discover myself dwelling upon the personal aspects of our collaboration and the psychological nature of science itself. It has become clearer to me than ever before how much inquiry is influenced by personality. Certainly, it must have been a sensitivity to this fact by the originating committee, whom Hans has so rightly and appropriately applauded already, to ask the two of us to collaborate on this project. Not knowing each other before, except for a brief symposium encounter, we found ourselves frequently remarking with surprise at how fruitful and enriching our joint venture had become despite the fact that we were asked to work together because our views of theory and practice were divergent.

These personal matters would not justify a description here if they concerned only the development of a strong friendship, important as that is. Rather, the impact of friendship upon intellectual commitments and style of inquiry justifies a special reference. Hans' psychoanalytic training and orientation are well known. My own history, first as a graduate student with Bandura and later as a postdoctoral student of Rogers, has lead me to adopt a paradoxical mixture of behavioral and client-centered convictions which were not exactly favorable to psychoanalysis. Working together intensively for more than three years forced us frequently to consider our differences. As our respect for each other grew this became more imperative. The dissonance created in us by constantly exchanging divergent viewpoints was intensified by a mutually perceived credibility and a growing personal relationship. Actually, much of this dissonance was never resolved and probably never will be, but in an atmosphere of mutual regard and trust we were able to consider and toy with interpretations of facts and designs for inquiry with which we were unfamiliar or toward which we had little sympathy. In so doing, I believe we empathically received each other's communications and gradually developed the ability to enter into the other's perceptual world.

As this happened, attitude change occurred. I doubt that Hans ever came to have a truly high regard for behavioral thinking and I know that my skepticism about psychoanalytic concepts persists; however, affective and cognitive changes did occur in relation to these views. We did not reduce dissonance by compromise, as it might seem. Instead we were able simply to look at the phenomena the other person was talking about in a new way, not accepting the other person's theory but rather looking at and experiencing the facts more fully. It is as though the gold we hoped to mine in the literature and among our consultants, we ultimately found in ourselves. We discovered domains of experience and perception that our viewpoints previously kept us from processing in any complete sense through our organisms. I believe that this was made possible by the sincerity and trust we developed during the project. It convinces me more than ever that in psychology the most powerful instrument of observation is the person and that the accuracy of the person's observations are a direct function of the interpersonal conditions prevailing in the situation. It reminds me of one of Carl Rogers' favorite sayings: "That which is most personal is most general". This experience of "opening perception" to old and familiar phenomena by itself made the entire period of collaboration worthwhile.

What did I learn as a result that I didn't know or feel convinced of before? Of the several insights thus engendered, one of the most important to me was that I found that there are some psychoanalytic therapists who get results. Some of them are doing something that makes a difference under certain conditions. I asked myself repeatedly whether this was simply the impact of a therapeutic personal relationship or the charisma of a few gifted people which is common to all therapies. I concluded not. It is that but much more. It is the ability to somehow modify the connections between cognitions and affects which control behavior. I came to realize that only a few people do this well but that it is an integral feature of an effective change process for many neurotic disorders. Even more important was the observation that this is essentially the same process that governs the systematic desensitization procedure. Recent evidence on the role of cognitive factors in desensitization, discussions with Hans and our consultants, and experiences in my own practice have convinced me that the dominant processes in desensitization and traditional therapy are essentially the same. In each case, an attempt is being made to break the cognition-affect bonds that control behavior. In a phobia, for example, the multiple presentations of hierarchy items are the equivalent of dozens of persuasive communications repeatedly asserting that the feared stimulus is harmless, that the client will be supported by the therapist in his approach to them, and that his fears are actually groundless and neurotic. This rational or cognitive therapy is, however, supplemented by the suppression of the fearful affect usually bonded to the neurotic cognitions. This suppression is achieved via relaxation or other methods. As the phobic's "crazy" beliefs begin to modify and are forcibly disconnected from their old affective base, the cognition-affect bond is broken and the person's behavior is freed from the automatic control of formerly fear-provoking stimuli. Thus, desensitizers are manipulating roughly the same variables as are traditional therapists. Certainly, there is nothing behavioristic about desensitization except perhaps the goal of changing a target behavior. The entire procedure is cognitive and affective from start to finish: from the imagination of hierarchy scenes to the symbolic monitoring of one's state of relaxation.

I now view the main difference between the two approaches to therapy to be one of specificity and simplicity. The desensitization approach takes the global confusion of affects and thoughts in fearful behavior and breaks it down into manageable proportions which can be overcome one piece at a time. The variables managed are the same as always, but an advantage is gained by reducing the complexity of a phobia into simpler parts that can be attacked one at a time.

I have therefore gained a greater insight into what traditional therapists have been driving at and a more accurate appraisal of what behavior therapists have added; although the foregoing is only a minute portion of the full story that needs to be written. In any event, I have found it by now completely impossible to accept any of the theoretical positions currently popular. They seem to be weak, superfluous and irrelevant. Indeed, I have come away from this experience with the conclusion that our greatest need is for new theories, perhaps mini-theories centered around limited domains of the therapeutic process. Surely, the global theories that absorb the minds of therapists and fill the pages of countless books require replacement by views that will better coordinate the facts now so abundant and confusing in the field.

A second important learning experience for me was the realization that traditional experimental designs and inferential statistics have little relevance to the study of clinical problems in the currently primitive state of therapeutic technologies. Most of the methodological sophistication I learned as a graduate student and postdoctoral fellow and which is constantly reinforced by the criteria of major journal editors is too precise, too demanding of controls, too far advanced for most studies of clinical intervention. I am convinced by experience that our conclusion in this book favoring the experimental case study, the intensive analysis of a limited range of phenomena, is correct and appropriate for the field in its present stage of evolution. Most of our studies of clinical phenomena suffer from weak results dictated by overly heterogeneous samples, a divergent aggregate of interventions, and measurements too imprecise to keep the margin of error in our definitions of syndromes and of change within reasonable limits. I have come to agree with many of our consultants and with many practicing clinicians that we need more description, more simple counting of frequencies of occurrence, more observation of the natural course of interventions as they occur clinically or according to planned intervention.

Some readers will find my "new" learnings hardly new; but as an experimentally-empirically oriented clinician this has required some rather profound reorienting. Not that I now endorse speculative clinical theorizing without quantification or verification, but rather that I feel liberalized in my attitude toward the phenomena and that I have an attitude of experimentation, curiousity and openness toward observing human nature independently of any special methodology or theory, a feeling that makes me feel refreshed, inspired, and perhaps liberated! I no longer feel frightened as I once did that by making some methodological slip I am fatally obscuring the nature of things. On the contrary, it is as though my past concerns with methodological finesse and theoretical precision have themselves diluted my personal contact with the phenomena of life that matter most in building a powerful science of man.

The foregoing illustrate well what I believe to be the type of learnings that have mattered most to me during this project and which I think will ultimately matter most to the field. They are a small but hopefully useful sample. In retrospect then, my deepest learnings have arisen from a base of personal change promoted by personal relationships. I have thus found my perceptions of phenomena, my style of inquiry, and my beliefs about psychotherapy changing in profound ways. I therefore believe that I have learned more about human nature and the nature of science by observing myself and my esteemed colleague through the course of this project than in any other way. I have come away feeling fortunate that at an early age I have learned that the quest for truth proceeds best when unfettered by dicta, that observation is controlled by personal conditions, that intuition is a common base for discovery and that, ultimately, true science is art.

Allen E. Bergin

Name Index

Subject Index